RAYMOND DANILOFF
Purdue University

GORDON SCHUCKERS
*Louisiana State University
Medical Center*

LAWRENCE FETH
Purdue University

THE PHYSIOLOGY OF SPEECH AND HEARING

AN INTRODUCTION

Prentice-Hall, Inc., Englewood Cliffs, New Jersey 07632

Library of Congress Cataloging in Publication Data

DANILOFF, RAYMOND.
   The physiology of speech and hearing.

   Bibliography: p. 435
   Includes index.
   1. Speech – Physiological aspects.   2. Sensory-motor
integration.   3. Hearing.   4. Oral communication.
I. Schuckers, Gordon, joint author.   II. Feth, Lawrence,
joint author.   III. Title.   [DNLM: 1. Speech –
Physiology.   2. Hearing – Physiology.   WV501 D186p]
QP306.D36 1980   612'.78   79-12256
ISBN   0-13-674747-7

Printed in the United States of America
10 9 8 7 6 5 4 3 2 1

Editorial/production supervision by Colette Conboy
Interior design by Linda Conway
Cover design by Linda Conway
Manufacturing buyer: Harry P. Baisley

PRENTICE-HALL INTERNATIONAL, INC., *London*
PRENTICE-HALL OF AUSTRALIA PTY, LIMITED, *Sydney*
PRENTICE-HALL OF CANADA, LTD., *Toronto*
PRENTICE-HALL OF INDIA PRIVATE LIMITED, *New Delhi*
PRENTICE-HALL OF JAPAN, INC., *Tokyo*
PRENTICE-HALL OF SOUTHEAST ASIA PTE. LTD., *Singapore*
WHITEHALL BOOKS LIMITED, *Wellington, New Zealand*

CONTENTS

PREFACE

The anatomy of the vocal tract has been known for centuries, but until recently there was little interest in the physiology of human speech and hearing. Now there is an explosive growth in knowledge: advances in technology have given us sophisticated new research instruments; new knowledge and new techniques in psychology, linguistics, and engineering have been applied to the study of speech and hearing mechanisms; and social concern for improved verbal communication has motivated researchers to greater efforts.

The human speech and hearing mechanisms comprise a system of interrelated parts that function jointly in a complex way. Before a speech pathologist can work with an abnormality, he or she must have a thorough knowledge of normal structure and function of the vocal tract. The therapist must know how the normal vocal tract looks and works before he or she can determine what is wrong and begin to repair the dysfunction. The student of speech physiology must spend hours studying normal speech and hearing mechanisms, as well as the body of theory that has accumulated in the field. In a way, the speech pathologist must be like a combination of an auto mechanic and automotive engineer. When diagnosing and repairing defective cars, the mechanic bases his work on the practical knowledge of the normal structure and functioning of the various systems. When designing an automobile, the engineer utilizes theoretical knowledge of the various systems and subsystems and how they are inter-related, as well as how they should function. Speech pathologists need both kinds of knowledge. They must have theoretical knowledge of the anatomical and physiologi-cal subsystems of speech and hearing, and their interrelationships. They must also have practical knowledge of diagnosing and correcting system defects. But, unlike the mechanic and the automotive engineer, speech pathologists deal primarily with com-munication behaviors; they do not ``replace'' or redesign defective parts of the speech and hearing systems. They can help an individual to relearn, adapt, rehearse, and automatize new or compensatory behaviors.

This book was designed as an introduction to the physiology of speech and hearing for beginning students. Following the principle that understanding of the system must precede understanding and treatment of defects or malfunctions, we have presented the "normal" before the "abnormal." Anatomical information is included to provide a basis for the discussion of physiology, and short descriptions of various pathologies follow the appropriate section on normal physiology. We have used the most current research throughout so the beginner can get a clear idea of the current state of our knowledge. Because every book must be selective, this one also reflects our biases and experience. We have pooled our own teaching experiences to give the beginning student a thorough grounding in the aspects of speech and hearing physiology we have found to be important in the training of speech pathologists.

This book is designed to be a basic text for introductory courses in speech and hearing physiology or speech and hearing sciences. When supplemented with additional anatomical material, it can well serve as a text for an introductory course in the anatomy and physiology of speech and hearing mechanisms. Instructors in psychology, speech, nursing, linguistics, and phonetics may find this text useful as a secondary reference, suitable for illustrating problems of speech and hearing physiology that may relate to the broader concerns of their courses.

Noam Chomsky has said that language mirrors the functioning of the human mind. It is logically impossible for the mind ever to comprehend itself completely. Because speech is an integral part of language, mirroring the mind, we may never achieve an adequate description of speech and its underlying mechanisms. But perhaps the thrill is in the chase, and perhaps not in capturing the fox. With this in mind, we dedicate this book to the students who patiently endured our attempts to teach them the physiology and pathology of speech and hearing.

ACKNOWL EDGMENTS

Text writing is a part of teaching. We were inspired to our efforts by the example set by our teachers, whom we wish to acknowledge: O. Ray Bontrager, Robert Bilger, Thomas Shriner, David M. Green, Lambert McCloskey. We wish to thank our students for reading and criticizing early versions of the text, Honor O'Malley in particular. Our illustrators, Vladimir Bektesh and Kathy Shuster, and Bobby Bowers, typist of a horrendous first draft of this work, are to be thanked as well. Jan Abel is especially thanked for her patient and insightful typing and correction of later drafts of the text.

Without the encouragement and moral support of our wives, Rita and Elly, this work might never have been finished. We also wish to thank David Aiken for the solitude of his Indiana farmhouse where writing began in earnest. Finally, we wish to acknowledge the hundreds of students of anatomy and physiology whose discontent with existing texts motivated this endeavor. We hope that it lives up to their expectations.

OVERVIEW

1

language and evolution / the unique structure of the human vocal tract
the act of communication / the development of spoken language
the importance of the auditory system
the vocal tract as an acoustic system / suggested readings

All forms of life, from bacteria to humans, communicate with one another. All use a signaling system to transmit information from one creature to another. Communication generally facilitates the social and personal survival of the communicating organisms. Examples of communication systems include birds' cries, wolves' howls, the chemical odors of ants, and the facial grimaces of chimpanzees.

As the phylogenetic scale is ascended from simpler to more complex life forms, from bacteria to mollusk to fish, to reptile to mammal to human, communications systems become increasingly complex. This elaboration reaches its peak in the primate species, and in humans in particular. We have developed the most complex of all communication systems—*language*. Language can be expressed (or encoded) in terms of writing, sign language, Morse code, etc., and—most important—speech. Humans can express (encode) language in almost any physical medium. They utilize many sensory systems to receive, and nearly every muscular system of the body, from eyelid to toe, to express language. Perhaps more than any other behavior, language differentiates humans from other creatures. As Buckminster Fuller put it: "... when in due course, man invented words and music, he altered the sound scape and the sound scape altered man."

Alfred Korzybski, the general semanticist, eloquently stated the importance of language to humans when he noted that language permits us to be "time-binders." That is, language permits us to record and transmit the accumulated experience and wisdom of the past to present and future generations; it permits discussion of the future of the world. No other creature has ever demonstrated the ability to time-bind, to record and transmit a record of experience in such a manner.

2

language and evolution

Language is primarily (most efficiently, easily, and directly) encoded as *speech*. It is the form of encoded language used by the vast majority of children during the process of language acquisition. In addition, humans appear to have evolved a vocal tract uniquely adapted for the production of speech sounds for spoken language. This new viewpoint, advanced by Lieberman (1975), replaces an earlier idea that the vocal tract was only one of several systems for encoding language and that its form and function were in no way especially adapted for speech production.

Human speech can be described in a simplified way as a stream of acoustic vibrations created by the flow of air through the vocal tract. The vocal tract is a series of connected cavities, a tubelike structure whose walls are formed by various articulatory organs. When the column of air inside the vocal tract is excited by a source of vibration, these acoustic vibrations travel through the tract and are emitted from the speaker's lips and/or nose (see Figure 1.1). Evolution-

figure 1.1

A schematic view of an adult vocal tract. Notice the column of air extending from the glottis to the lip or to the nares, if the soft palate is lowered. Shown below is a schematic view of the vocal tract as an acoustic tube.

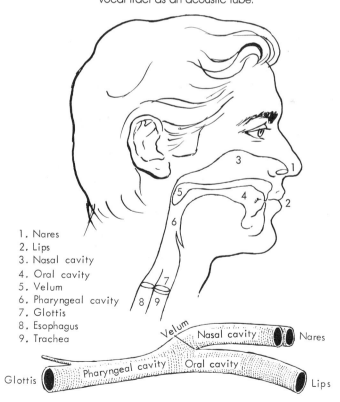

1. Nares
2. Lips
3. Nasal cavity
4. Oral cavity
5. Velum
6. Pharyngeal cavity
7. Glottis
8. Esophagus
9. Trachea

ary theory (Lieberman, 1975) suggests that the vocal tract evolved into its present form via the processes of selection. Evolutionary selection operates in such a way that those creatures best adapted for life in their environment survive long enough to reproduce themselves successfully, begetting young whose survival rates are also high. Thus, the heritable body structures and behaviors that promote survival are passed on to the animal's offspring. For example, fruit flies raised on a salty diet generally die except for a few whose metabolic systems, because of genetic variation, can cope with the stress of excess salt. The salt-resistant individuals tend to reproduce "salt-resistant" offspring, and thus are successful competitors in the salty environment.

Mutations of genetic material caused by environmental influences such as radiation, chemicals, or heat result in an ever-changing gene pool within a species of animals. Most mutations of genetic material are neutral or even harmful to survival, but occasionally changes in the environment tend to favor the animal whose mutations or unique genetic combination have conferred upon it certain physical or behavioral characteristics. That animal's survival is enhanced, and generally so are the chances of its offspring, since they tend to inherit the favorable bodily traits.

How does this relate to the structure of the vocal tract? First, body structures important to the survival of an animal tend to be strongly heritable—they vary little among members of a species from generation to generation. Birds are rarely born without wings or fish without gills—such variations would create havoc in air and water. Second, aspects of body structure not essential to survival tend to vary more freely among members of a species—for example, the color of a horse's coat or the length of a man's foot. If a physical characteristic is not important to survival, then the pressure of evolutionary selection does not result in extinction of variations associated with that characteristic.

the unique structure of the human vocal tract

Examination of the anatomy of the vocal tract reveals that differences in vocal tract shape (morphology) among humans are small and relatively insignificant the world over. This suggests that in the past strong pressure of evolutionary selection resulted in highly similar human vocal tracts. Certain peculiarities in the shape and functioning of the vocal tract may have had great evolutionary importance to have been selected so strongly.

Lieberman and his colleagues (1975), for example, have compared the vocal tracts of the primate species—those of modern adult humans, apes, monkeys, newborn humans, and human fossil species such as the Neanderthals and Cro-Magnons. Data derived from anatomical measurements of the shape of the various vocal tracts were used as input for a computer model, from which the researchers were able to predict the possible range of vowel-like sounds primates could produce. The predicted sound patterns and anatomical data revealed that the vocal tracts of modern humans and fossil Cro-Magnons were

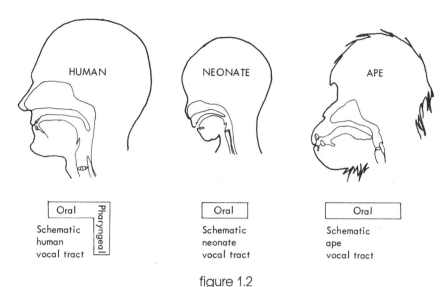

figure 1.2

The vocal tracts of an adult human, a newborn human, and an ape. Pictured above are their schematized one- and two-tube vocal tracts.

uniquely different from those of apes, monkeys, newborn humans, and Neanderthals (see Figure 1.2). The adult human's vocal tract is a deep, two-tube system consisting of a horizontally directed oral cavity joined at nearly right angles to a large and more or less vertical pharyngeal cavity. Because of the separation between the velum and the epiglottal cartilage, food and air must pass through a single common passageway. As a result, humans can choke to death on food and drink, a phenomenon rare in animals. Also, the right angle bend in the human vocal tract offers increased resistance to airflow during strenuous breathing. During running and heavy work, for example, significant energy is lost forcing air past the kink in the vocal tract. This phenomenon is also rare in animals, who neither share the shape of the human vocal tract, nor the human predisposition to work.

Several factors account for the adult humans' relatively large and deep two-tube vocal tract as compared to the infant's and ape's shallow, single-tube tract. First, the adult larynx is low in the neck, at about the level of cervical vertebra 4 or 5, whereas the larynx of the ape is higher, so that there is literally *no* pharyngeal tube. Second, because of the domelike vault of the adult humans' maxillary and palatine bones, the oral cavity is deep (see Figure 1.2). The ape's maxillary arch is relatively long, stout, and flat, resulting in a shallow oral cavity. In addition, the adult human's tongue is short, thick, and extraordinarily mobile; a flexible blade and tip enable humans to produce dozens of differing shapes and positions. The ape's tongue is thinner, less flexible, and not so easily maneuvered to alter vocal tract shape.

The adult human's large, deep, two-tube resonating system contrasts strongly with the shallow one-tube system of apes and newborns. Furthermore, by moving the tongue, an adult human can far more easily, smoothly, and swiftly create constrictions and changes in the shape of the vocal tract at differing places, creating vocal tract tubes of varying length. Were the ape to articulate sounds, his shallow single-tube system and tongue could not produce the multitube vocal tract shapes characteristic of humans. This ability to create a multitube resonating system therefore strongly differentiates the human vocal tract from those of other primates.

THE QUANTAL VOWELS   Movements of the tongue, jaw, and lips cause changes in vocal tract shape. Each change in shape results in the formation of a new and different double-tube acoustic resonator. Each different resonator system (vocal tract shape) will resonate at different frequencies, thus producing different sounds. Figure 1.3 shows that constrictions of the vocal tract

figure 1.3

Tongue positions for articulation of the quantal vowels. Also shown is a plot of the point of greatest constriction of the tongue, horizontally and vertically, for these three vowels.

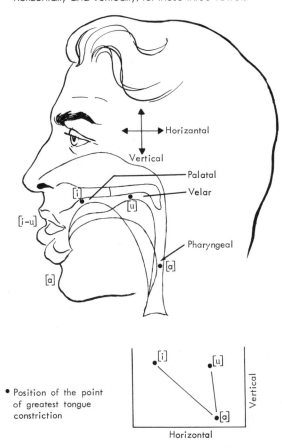

• Position of the point of greatest tongue constriction

at palatal, velar, and pharyngeal locations produce vocal tract shapes appropriate for the vowel sounds [i], [u], and [a], respectively. Stevens (1972) has demonstrated that these vowels are unique in several ways. First, they are present (or were historically) in the sound patterns of the vast majority of human languages. Second, these vowels represent extreme positions of the tongue, with tight constrictions in each of three widely separate regions of the vocal tract: palatal, velar, and pharyngeal. Third, Lieberman demonstrated that apes, most fossil hominids, and newborn infants cannot make these three "extreme" vowels because they do not have a two-tube resonating system. In itself that might not be extraordinary, but Stevens indicates that [i, a, u] are special or *quantal* in nature. They can be produced only if the vocal tract is tightly constricted in such a way as to form two tubes. For [i], the oral cavity is tightly constricted and the pharyngeal cavity is expanded. For [a], the opposite holds: The oral cavity is fully expanded and the pharyngeal tube is tightly constricted. For [u], the oral cavity is slightly more expanded than the pharyngeal cavity, with a tight constriction between the two tubes. For all three vowels, there are sharp changes in vocal tract size near the midpoint of the vocal tract. It is this midpoint discontinuity in the two-tube vocal tract of humans that permits quantal vowel sounds to be produced.

Stevens' calculations indicate that a speaker can be relatively *imprecise* in positioning the tongue and jaw for these three vowels. That is, sloppy articulation still produces reasonably good acoustic approximations of these three vowels. Other vowel sounds demand more careful articulation. The resistance of [i, a, u] to precise articulation (they can be spoken sloppily, yet be understood), means that they are stable speech signals. In addition, the three vowels are useful to the listener in identifying the sex and age of the person speaking them. Children have very short vocal tracts, women have vocal tracts of intermediate lengths, and men have relatively long vocal tracts. For a given vowel sound, the characteristic vowel resonance frequencies increase as the vocal tract becomes shorter in length. Thus, if a man, woman, and child spoke the vowel [æ] as in *had,* the resonance frequencies of their vocal tracts might be:

		MALE	FEMALE	CHILD
RESONANCE	1	650	850	1000 Hz
FREQUENCY	2	1700	2000	2300 Hz
IN Hz	3	2400	2800	3300 Hz

Notice in Figure 1.4 that the vocal tracts are different in absolute size and shape; the female and child vocal tract differ mostly in overall size (length), but the relative shape of all three is nearly the same.

A listener must learn to recognize that the vowel sounds produced by these three different vocal tracts are the "same" insofar as they are to be identified as [æ]. The listener somehow "calibrates" these differing vocal tract lengths by shifting his or her perceptual image of the resonance frequencies of the male, female, and child vowel sounds so that they match each other. In this way,

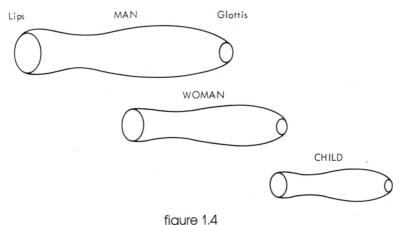

figure 1.4

Idealized vocal tract shapes for a man, woman, and child
during phonation of the vowel [æ].

sounds that differ only because of sex-age related differences in vocal tract size
can be recognized as the "same" vowel. Research suggests that when listeners
are allowed to hear two or three of the quantal vowels, they can easily perform
the needed calibration and recognize the *same* vowel sounds when produced by
vocal tracts of differing lengths.

Lieberman speculates that the unique shape of the human vocal tract was
important for primitive people's speech communication in the following ways:
Social beings like humans needed effective communication systems. Using the
vocal tract allowed the speaker to communicate without using the hands and
feet, thus freeing them for work, use of tools, hunting, and so on. The speech
signal can be transmitted over long distances, around corners, beyond obstacles, at night, and when the face and body of the speaker cannot be seen. Visual communication would fail in darkness, when there were obstacles to line of
sight, or too much distance. Efficient communication systems must be rapid
and powerful enough to carry over long distances. The means of communication must be easily learned and manipulated by all members of the human
group, whether young or old, ill or well, female or male.

Quantal vowel sounds are satisfactory for communication in many ways.
First, they are acoustically powerful and can carry hundreds of yards in the
open air. Second, since only a quasi-human vocal tract can produce them, hearing them would indicate a human signal, rather than that of prey or predator.
Third, rapid, efficient speech production involves the swift articulation of
streams of syllables. Since each syllable generally contains a vocalic (vowel-
like) nucleus, [i, u, a] could serve as the basis for an efficient, syllable-based
speech production code. Because [i, u, a] are quantal in nature, most members
of a human group could produce these sounds sufficiently accurately to be recognized, despite sloppy articulation. And because it is known that many con-

sonant sounds are identified by the accompanying vowel, the differences in identical vowels caused by differences in vocal tract length could be calibrated. That is, both sex and age of the speaker could be identified so that the consonant sounds could be more easily identified. Efficient verbal communication also demands that speech sounds be distinctive and not easily confused with one another. The quantal vowels fulfill this requirement because their resonance frequency patterns are quite different and not easily confused, even under adverse conditions.

Several important conclusions can be drawn from these data and speculations on evolution. First, it would appear that selection resulted in a human vocal tract unique in form and function for the production of highly distinctive speech sounds. Thus, evolutionary processes led humans to use the vocal tract and the speech it produces as the prime, earliest, and major means of expressing language. In an evolutionary sense, spoken language is our prime mode of communication. The crucial importance of the shape and function of the vocal tract to the efficient production of speech supports the notion that the structure of human language reflects a strong dependence on the vocal tract. That is, the existence and use of a specially adapted vocal tract to express language had a profound effect on the nature of the linguistic code.

For many years this close relationship between the structure of language and the vocal tract was unacknowledged. Some theorists held that other encoding systems, such as writing or sign language, might have served just as well to express language. We now understand that the mental and cognitive strategies which underlie language in humans may have been specially adapted for the generation of *spoken* language. And this probably means that the unique sound-generating properties of the vocal tract are utilized in a maximally efficient manner.

the act of communication

The act of communication involves the transfer of information from one creature to another—in our case, from human speaker to human listener. If communication is successful, the listener can successfully repeat the message or perform some action to demonstrate understanding. Every speaker is also, said Wendell Johnson, "his own most enchanted listener." The speaker hears his own voice, and feels himself talking with sensory receptors inside his vocal tract. Figure 1.5 shows the speech communication process in schematic form. Meaningful information stored in the brain of the speaker is communicated to the listener. The speaker uses knowledge of the structure of his native language and employs an elaborate set of grammatical rules (see Chapter 3) to produce a string of morphemes (a morpheme is the smallest meaningful unit of speech) set in proper order and in proper shape. For example, if the speaker wishes to communicate "my friends ate some apples some time ago," he or she would

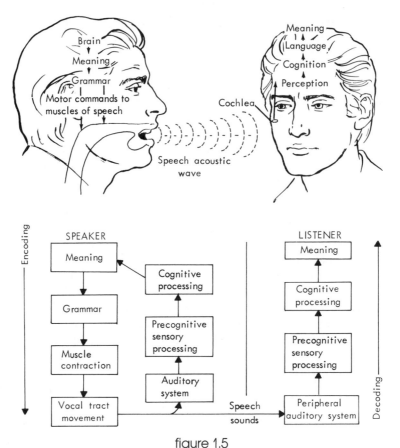

figure 1.5

A schematic illustration of the act of communication.

encode the message into the form "They ate some apples." Such a message is governed by the following rules:

1. The morphemes must have the right order: "Apples some ate they" is incorrect.

2. The morphemes must have the right phonetic shape: "Day aid sam apples" is incorrect. The morphemes must have the correct sounds within them.

3. The morphemes must be properly inflected (reflect proper time, plurality, sex, possession differences, and so on): "They eat some apples" is incorrect because the form of the verb "eat" implies that they are eating the apples right now, whereas they ate them in the past.

4. The morphemes must show appropriate agreement: "They ate an apples" is incorrect because the noun "apples" is plural (more than one) and the modifier "an" indicates only one apple.

Linguists speculate that the speaker's use of grammatical rules results in the creation of a sentence-sized string of morphemes. The rules of phonology are then used to give the morphemes in the sentence the proper sound pattern. For example, the morpheme "apple" is converted to

$$/\text{apple} + \text{plural} / \rightarrow / \text{ apple } + \text{ z } / \rightarrow \text{ "apples" } [\text{æp}^\text{h}\text{łz}]$$

a pluralized form such that the plural marker is indicated as a [z] sound, and the [p] sound segment is marked as the aspirated form [p$^\text{h}$], to be spoken with a burst of air as the lips open. The output of the phonological rule system ultimately results in a sentence which has a phonetic specification, or shape, that can be converted into neural commands that are sent to the muscles of speech. The muscular movements of the speech organs cause the vocal tract to adopt a particular shape, cause the buildup of airflow and pressure in the vocal tract, and result in acoustic vibrations that are heard as "speech" sounds. The process of converting meaning into audible sound is called *encoding*. Information represented in the brain as electro-chemical activity is converted into an acoustic vibration. *This conversion of meaning to sound is the core of the speech act.*

The smoothly changing stream of speech sounds travels through the air to strike the listener's eardrum, causing a mechanical vibration of the bones of the middle ear. This vibration transfers energy from the eardrum to the fluids of the inner ear. The inner ear vibrations excite the hair cells of the cochlea, which in turn excite the 8th auditory nerve. A smoothly changing stream of nerve impulses ascends the auditory pathways through the brainstem, the midbrain, and on up to the cortex of the brain.

The listener does not deal directly with the acoustic sound wave, but with the neurological representation of it aroused within the brain. If a sufficient pattern of activity is aroused in the brain, the listener then applies his or her knowledge of language to analyze, synthesize, and eventually "recognize" the intended meaning of the message. The entire sequence of events is called *decoding:* (1) passage of sound from the speaker to the listener's outer, middle, and inner ear; (2) conversion of the acoustic stimulus to ascending patterns of nerve discharge; (3) cognitive analysis of the meaning of the message. The conversion of speech sound into electrochemical brain activity and resulting recognition of the meaning of the message is the *speech decoding process*. Note that the decoding process is the inverse of the encoding process. Encoding of an idea yields an output of speech sounds that decoding then reprocesses to recover the meaning of the message. The meaning itself never leaves the speaker's or listener's heads, but is symbolized by the speech sounds. Speech is the elaborate way in which we use ordered patterns of human sounds to *represent* our thoughts.

The encoding process is quite complex. The units of language, be they sounds, words, or phrases, are not produced as neat, serially ordered sets or units. Rather, close examination of the sounds of speech reveals a complex tapestry of quickly and smoothly changing patterns of integrated, overlapping sounds that vary in systematic and nonsystematic ways. *The systematic variations of speech sounds are predictable and reflect (a) the structure of language, and (b) the physiological operations of the encoding process.* Nonsystematic variations are associated with unique, idiosyncratic mental and physical variations peculiar to the speaker—sex, age, fatigue, and so on.

It is the task of the phonetician to discover and account for all the predictable variations in the speech signal. Phoneticians do this on at least three levels. The first, called *articulatory phonetics,* is the physiological description of speech production. The domain of articulatory phonetics is the encoding process up to but not including the speech acoustic wave. Thus, studies of articulator shape, positions, and movements, muscle contraction patterns, air pressures and flows, and the neurological activity responsible for activating the muscles of speech production are all within the realm of articulatory phonetics. *Acoustic phonetics,* a second level of description, is the analysis of the speech signal at the acoustic level. Acoustic phoneticians study the speech acoustic wave in order that the relevant time and spectral acoustic cues present in the speech wave can be identified and accounted for. *Perceptual phonetics* is a study of listeners' reactions to the speech signal. At this level, the phonetician seeks to determine the listeners' linguistic reactions to the speech signal—how sounds, syllables, and words are labeled, identified, and discriminated, and how listeners' reactions change as the speech signal is manipulated. In this book we will focus on articulatory phonetics, but acoustical and perceptual phonetic data will be included to account for certain physiological phenomena.

the development of spoken language

As a prelude to our discussion of the physiology of speech, a brief overview of some of the physiological and behavioral requirements for speech production is necessary.

Language is an instrument of thought that allows us to bind time and to see part-whole relationships. It permits us to *internalize* the structure, order, and relationships we observe in the world about us. In order that language develop smoothly, certain cognitive processes must be relatively well developed, among them attention, memory, and the ability to fashion mental models and other ways of representing the world.

The vast majority of human beings acquire language in its spoken form. After the acquisition of language in the form of speech, it can then be generalized with relative ease into other forms, such as writing. During the relatively short period of infancy and early childhood, humans rapidly acquire the rules and codes of their native language. The ease and swiftness with which the child learns languages at this age has led some observers to call babies "learning machines." Such an observation, however, suggests that a machine is capable of learning. Clearly, such observers know even less about machines than they do babies. When cognitive processes are present and functional, children can sort, categorize, and store attributes of the world and their interactions with it; they form schematic representations of reality using both language and nonlanguage symbols. The child's environment is crucial to normal language development. There are recorded cases of "feral" or wild children who were raised with little or no human interaction, and with almost no language stimulation. When discovered, these children were extremely retarded socially and linguistically. A normal human family and community environment is therefore crucial to adequate language development.

The course of language development involves the following stages: At birth, infants vocalize reflexively. They wail, cry, or coo as hunger, discomfort, or pain trigger whole-body reflexive behaviors, among which *cry-vocalization* is only one. With increasing neurological, physiological, and social maturation, they gain greater control over their speech apparatus, and nonreflexive (voluntary) babbling behavior appears. The sound patterns of babbling, although different from adult speech sounds, reflect a well-patterned, highly organized form of sound production. Babbling reflects infants' increasing control of their muscles and curiosity about sounds and the way the vocal tract works during interaction with themselves and the family. Somewhat later, children master the production of many of the syllables of the language and produce them repetitively. Still later, they can creatively imitate many of the words and short utterances spoken by parents, friends, and family. By the age of four to six, children have mastered almost the entire sound pattern of their language as well as many of the grammatical rules needed to produce meaningful, well-formed sentences.

The process of speech acquisition reflects increasing control over the movements of the vocal tract. At the same time that control over voluntary muscle movements is growing, children are developing the auditory-perceptual system so that they are increasingly able to process the complex speech signals they and those around them produce. This development of the auditory-perceptual system includes increasing powers of identification, discrimination, association, and sound memory. The net result of the joint motor-sensory development is that children can delay between hearing a speech signal and formulating an output of verbalization in response to it. During that crucial delay, they can decode the speech heard and use their knowledge of language to encode a response as speech. Once in full voluntary control of their language responses, children can categorize, catalogue, and generalize both speech they have heard and events they have experienced by use of their language system.

The development of language, then, involves maturation of both sensory and motor systems, ongoing development of certain cognitive behaviors, and the learning of the social responses necessary for language interaction with family and playmates. Indeed, language acquisition is one of the most difficult and critical challenges that a human child faces. Acquisition of the verbal form of language, even if only quasi-normal, is eloquent testimony to the integrity of the child's sensory, motor, cognitive, and social behaviors.

the importance of the auditory system

A description of verbal communication would be incomplete without a discussion of the contribution of hearing. To begin with, there would have been no evolutionary incentive for any animal to make communicative sounds unless there were some way to hear them. Most linguists believe that the developing child encounters and learns the rules of his or her native language by hearing both his or her own speech and that of others. Recent evidence suggests that the sound-producing and auditory systems of many animals are uniquely specialized for each other. For example, bullfrogs show unusual ability to detect and discriminate the mating cries of their fellows; moths are specialized for detection of the sounds produced by the bats that eat them. Apparently, evolution has selected the communication systems of animals so that their auditory systems are adapted for the detection of sounds produced by their own, predators', or prey's sound-generating systems.

Investigators who believe that the human auditory system is specialized for recognition of human speech have examined the auditory reactions of infants to human speech. They believe that infants' ability to discriminate among speech sounds in an adult fashion long before they have any language is proof of hereditary specialization for speech perception. Recent research reveals that chinchillas and monkeys can make identifications and discriminations of human speech sounds in much the same way that the human infant does. Because these animals have neither a human vocal tract nor language, it would appear that the mammalian brain possesses neural mechanisms sufficiently developed to process speechlike signals. We may assume that in the course of human evolution such speech-processing mechanisms were refined and perfected to a high degree.

Whatever the degree to which the auditory system is specialized for speech-feature detection, there is agreement that the loss of hearing at or near birth has a disastrous effect on the development of normal spoken language. The hearing-impaired infant who cannot adequately hear speech signals is deprived of the opportunity to experience much of spoken language. The hearing loss prevents the child from hearing his or her own speech and that of adults. He or she thus hears very little speech upon which to base linguistic hypotheses that can be tested with his or her own sound-production apparatus. Nor can such a child evaluate the success of his or her own speech production via hearing. A hearing loss almost guarantees that the child will have a drastically altered and impoverished speech and language output. Such children generally develop a substitute encoding system based on sign language.

Speakers who suffer profound hearing loss after childhood generally display a slurring of sounds, a general imprecision of articulation that most severely affects consonants, especially those characterized by high-frequency sounds, such as [s, tʃ, ʃ]. Studies of speech in the presence of noise powerful enough to block the auditory sensation of one's own voice show only small effects on speech production. Because the ear can be damaged by long-term exposure to such intense noise, these studies cannot test the effects of prolonged auditory interference. Other research involving the creation of an artificial time delay between the production of a sound and when the speaker hears it reveals that for delays of about $\frac{1}{4}$ of a second, there is a profound disruption of speech: The speaker appears to stutter, makes false starts, shows hesitations, makes syllable repetitions, and so on. For both children and adults, the auditory system is an integral, crucial link in the speech production process.

the vocal tract as an acoustic system

To emphasize the importance of the physiological systems of the vocal tract, we need to look briefly at its acoustics here (Chapters 4 and 7, of course, contain detailed discussions).

The vocal tract contains a column or tube of air extending from the superior surface of the vocal folds to the lips (and nares if the velopharyngeal port is open; see Figure 1.1). The walls of the vocal tract are composed of both fixed and movable structures, many of which are "articulators." Movements of the speech articulators alter the *shape* of the vocal tract, which can be defined as its physical dimensions—the overall length and the cross-sectional area at every point along its length. Any change in length or cross-sectional area is a change in vocal tract shape. And each unique shape of the vocal tract produces a uniquely shaped air column.

The physics of the vibration of vocal tract air columns is the same as that of many musical instruments. Organ pipes, woodwinds, and brass instruments such as trumpets, for example, contain air columns that are set into vibration by successive bursts of compressed air injected at the mouthpiece or reed. The vocal tract can therefore be thought of as a musical instrument, an acoustic tube containing a column of air that is excited into vibration by bursts of compressed air. For purposes of discussion, let us choose the simplest vocal tract shape: a right-circular column of air contained within the vocal tract tube, closed at the glottal end by the vocal folds and open at the lips (see Figure 1.6). At the closed end is a small hole (glottis) through which bursts of air can be injected.

As bursts of air enter the tube at one end, they shock the column of air into vibration, and the acoustic vibrations travel back and forth along the length of the tube, reflecting from the closed and open ends. Depending on the length (L), of the tube, a very large pressure builds up in the tube at certain select "resonant frequencies" of vibration. For the tube open at one end, the resonant frequencies can be predicted if the length of the tube is known:

$$F_n = \frac{NC}{4L}$$

where $F_n = n^{th}$ resonance frequency
$\quad\quad C =$ speed of sound in air
$\quad\quad L =$ length of tube
$\quad\quad N =$ odd integers (1, 3, 5, etc.)

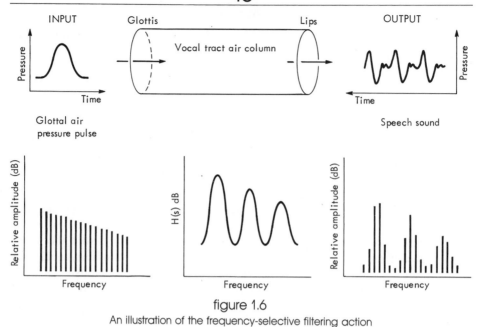

figure 1.6

An illustration of the frequency-selective filtering action
of the vocal tract.

The tube has infinitely many resonant frequencies, each one higher than the next; that is, if the incoming airbursts were to excite the tube into vibration at each of these resonant frequencies, then the resulting sound wave emitted from the tube would have concentrations of energy at each of the resonant frequencies. The human ear is sensitive to the location of the resonant frequencies, and the "phonetic" quality of the resulting sound depends on the location of the first four or five resonant frequencies of the vibrating air column.

When a speaker articulates different speech sounds, he or she uniquely alters the shape (cross-sectional area or length) of the vocal tract for each different sound. This in turn causes the resonance frequencies to shift to a new position for each sound. With each unique vocal tract shape, there is a unique set of resonance frequencies. In theory, each change in vocal tract shape results in a new set of resonance frequencies and hence a perceptibly different sound. One might say that the speaker plays upon his or her instrument (the vocal tract) by altering its shape, by constricting it at various places along its length and causing resonance frequencies to shift. Figure 1.7 shows this graphically. For a 17 cm right-circular vocal tract shape with *no* constrictions, the resonance frequencies are evenly spaced at odd multiples (3f, 5f, 7f) of the first resonance frequency [see (G) in Figure 1.7]. If the vocal tract is constricted near the hard palate (A), the oral tube is short in length and small in cross-sectional area. R_1 shifts to a low frequency of 250 Hz, and resonances R_2 and R_3, to high-frequency positions. Constriction of the vocal tract near the soft palate and at the lips simultaneously (B) yields a low-frequency position for resonance frequencies R_1 and R_2. Constriction of the vocal tract in the pharyngeal region (C) yields resonance frequencies R_1 and R_2 in close proximity near 1000 Hz.

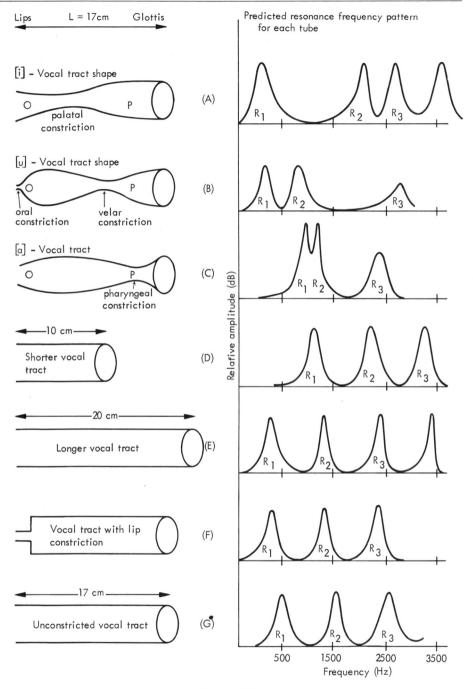

Lips   L = 17cm   Glottis

Predicted resonance frequency pattern for each tube

[i] – Vocal tract shape (A)
O   P
palatal constriction

[u] – Vocal tract shape (B)
O   P
oral constriction   velar constriction

[a] – Vocal tract (C)
O   P
pharyngeal constriction

—10 cm—
Shorter vocal tract (D)

—20 cm—
Longer vocal tract (E)

Vocal tract with lip constriction (F)

—17 cm—
Unconstricted vocal tract (G)

Relative amplitude (dB)

500   1500   2500   3500
Frequency (Hz)

figure 1.7

Resonance frequency patterns for vocal tracts of differing length, or constricted at differing places along the tract. All resonance patterns should be compared to that for (G₁), which is the resonance pattern for an unconstricted vocal tract.

Lengthening the tract to 20 cm (E) yields a lowered set of resonance frequencies for all vowels, while shortening it to 10 cm (D) yields a raised set of resonance frequencies for all vowels. Constricting the vocal tract at the lips (F) causes resonances R_1 and R_2, especially, to shift to lower frequencies.

The picture of the vocal tract which emerges is that of an acoustic tube with a varying pattern of resonance frequencies. As the vocal tract tube is constricted—that is, as its shape is altered by articulatory movements—the resonance frequency pattern shifts, and resonances R_1, R_2, and R_3, especially, move about in predictable ways. The speaker, as he or she articulates, manipulates the tube resonance pattern (and thus the perceptual quality of the emergent sound) by changing the shape of the vocal tract. Whereas a trombonist alters horn shape by increasing or decreasing the *length* of the horn, we alter tube resonance by constricting the cross-sectional shape of the vocal tract at differing points.

The behavior of the vocal tract can also be shown by using systems analysis. Figure 1.8, for example, shows a schematic diagram of the entire speech production system. An overall picture of the operation of the vocal tract during speech production includes the following elements:

1. *Power supply* (airstream mechanism): The power source for speech is generally compressed air. The compressed air causes the vocal folds to buzz, and is used to create noises such as pops and hisses as well.

2. *A buzzer* (phonation mechanism): The potential energy of the power supply's compressed air is converted into acoustic vibrations by the actions of the larynx. The larynx is a compressed, airdriven buzzer that modulates the airstream being driven out of the lungs into a series of energizing airburst pressure pulses. Other sources of phonatory vibration are noises—hisses or explosions caused by the rapid flow of compressed air through a constriction in the vocal tract.

3. *A resonating system* (articulatory mechanism): Once the vibration, whether noise or buzz, has been created by a phonation source, it is selectively filtered by its passage through the vocal tract tube. Each vocal tract shape has a different set of resonance frequencies—that is, a different filter function. The net result of the filtering function of the vocal tract is that the emerging speech soundwave shows greatest concentrations of energy near the resonance frequencies of the vocal tract. The listener, sensitive to the concentrations of energy in the spectrum of the emerging speech sound, generally perceives a differing quality for the sound as the position of the resonance frequencies changes.

It is this process of systems and subsystems generating sound via the use of air bursts or noises, and the frequency-selective filtering action of the resonating vocal tract tube on these sounds, that we will examine closely in succeeding chapters. The highly interrelated functions of such systems and subsystems are best described as being synergetic or synergistic in nature. Although the word *synergy* has not been frequently applied to the study of physiological systems, its conceptualization is particularly applicable to our study of speech and communication. Synergy, by definition, refers to the corre-

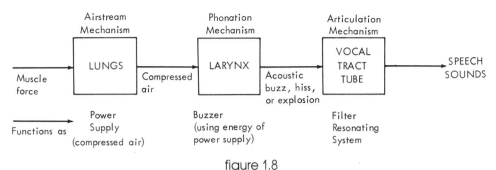

figure 1.8

A diagram of the three neuromuscular systems of the speech
production process.

lation or concurrence of action between different organs in health or disease, or
between different chemicals or drugs. More importantly, it implies a *relativity
of function* or integration of the various behaviors of nature. As such, synergy
refers to the *behavior of a system unpredicted by the behavior of its components or any subassembly of its components.* Thus, in viewing the production of speech and the total act of communication we become immediately
aware that in order to understand or predict the function of the overall system,
it is necessary to view neurophysiological, linguistic, respiratory, phonatory, articulatory, and auditory systems as being synergetically related. At certain
points, we will discuss the effects of organic and behavioral pathology on vocal
tract behavior so that the reader can grasp how knowledge of normal functioning permits a clear understanding of abnormal, pathological functioning. We
will close with an examination of the auditory system, since this is the mechanism by which speech is ultimately decoded.

SUGGESTED READINGS

DENES, P., and E. PINSON. *The Speech Chain.* Bell Telephone Laboratories, 1963. A
simple and readable and by now classic introduction to the process of speech encoding and decoding, including a brief treatment of physiology, acoustics, and psychoacoustics.

KORZYBSKI, A. E. *The Manhood of Humanity.* New York: E. P. Dutton, 1950. In this
treatise, the author identified clearly those aspects of our behavior that characterize
us as "human". Among these are language and our use of this behavior to bind
time.

LENNEBERG, E. H. *Biological Foundations of Language.* New York: Wiley, 1967. A
classic description of the language acquisition process in children along with evi-

dence and speculation concerning humans' innate, biologically determined predisposition to learn or acquire speech and language.

LIEBERMAN, P. C. *On the Origins of Language: An Introduction to the Evolution of Human Speech.* New York: Macmillan, 1975. A major new treatise that reviews the literature and sets forth the author's experiments and hypotheses concerning the evolution of the human vocal tract and speech. An important contribution to linguistic science.

STEVENS, K. N. "Quantal Nature of Speech." In E. E. David, Jr., and P. B. Denes (eds.), *Human Communication: A Unified View.* New York: McGraw-Hill, 1972. The theoretical article which first set forth the notion that speech is "quantal" in nature, and that much of this "quantal" nature is attributable to the unique shape and functions of the human vocal tract.

BASIC NEUROSCIENCE

2

the nervous system / structure of the nervous system: neuroanatomy
functions of the nervous system: neurophysiology / suggested readings

The term *neuroscience* refers to the study of nervous systems. Such studies may fall within one or more of the traditional areas of the biological sciences. Thus, the study of the structure of an organism is called *anatomy,* the study of the biological functions of the organism is called *physiology,* and the study of the behavior of organisms is called *psychology.* When an investigator in one of these disciplines focuses on the nervous system, we may find the work is described as neuroanatomy, neurophysiology, or even neuropsychology. In this chapter, we will introduce the basic concepts and terminology of neuroanatomy and neurophysiology. Our attention will be focused on the human nervous system, and we will emphasize those parts of the system that are essential to verbal communication.

the nervous system

The telephone company refers to itself as the Bell System. A mathematically inclined gambler may invent a "system" for winning at blackjack or roulette. Computer experts talk about systems programs and systems analysis. A system is generally defined as a set of objects having attributes (or properties) subject to relationships between the objects and between their attributes. That is, a system exhibits *organization.* When used in reference to the study of living organisms, the word "system" is further restricted in its usage.

All living organisms, and those that were alive at one time, are made up of a material called protoplasm. No one has yet solved the mystery of what gives protoplasm its unique property of life. When subjected to physical and chemical analyses, protoplasm is found to be composed of ordinary elements such as oxygen, carbon, hydrogen, and nitrogen. These ordinary elements are organized into units called *molecules.* Biological molecules are often larger and more complex than molecules of nonliving materials. They are sometimes called macromolecules because they are so much larger than the molecules of air, water, or minerals. Further organization of protoplasm is found in the living cell. All living things are built up of almost countless numbers of cells. Many cells are too small to be seen by the unaided eye, but one does turn up in our daily lives. The chicken egg is a single living cell, and its construction is typical of that of most living cells.

Every cell is surrounded by a protective covering known as the *cell membrane*. Inside the cell membrane is a substance known as *cytoplasm,* which makes up the bulk of the cell material. If we use our example of the chicken egg, just inside the eggshell is a cell membrane. The albumin (egg white) is the cytoplasm. Cytoplasm contains water, metabolic material, and a number of microscopic structures called organelles, that keep the cell alive and healthy. The cell nucleus is also found within the cytoplasm. The nucleus contains the materials that make it possible for the living cell to reproduce itself. You may think of the egg yolk as the nucleus.

Living cells are further organized into groups known as *tissues.* These are classified as, for example, connective tissue, muscle tissue, or nerve tissue. Each type is specialized for some function. Muscle tissue is specialized for contraction; nerve tissue is specialized for the generation and conduction of electrochemical impulses. Tissues collected together to perform a single function form *organs* such as the lung, heart, and liver. For example, the lung is an organ composed of epithelium, connective tissue, nervous tissue, and muscle tissue that works to exchange oxygen for carbon dioxide in the bloodstream.

Collections of organs organized for special functions are known as body *systems*. The heart, the blood, and the blood vessels make up the circulatory system. The brain, spinal cord, and peripheral nerves make up the nervous system. Organs or tissues may be classified into more than one system if they serve more than one function. Because the blood vessels, a principal component of the circulatory system, also conduct the hormones secreted by various glands throughout the body, they may be classified as part of the endocrine system as well.

A body system may be further subdivided. The nervous system is composed of sensory, motor, and autonomic systems. Sensory systems such as the auditory or the visual system carry information to the brain and spinal cord. Motor systems conduct the commands of the brain to the muscles. The autonomic systems regulate vegetative functions.

structure of the nervous system: neuroanatomy

Before we can appreciate the role of the nervous system in coordinating all bodily functions, we must have some knowledge of its structure. This is like preparing a map of the nervous system. The prerequisite to map making is, of

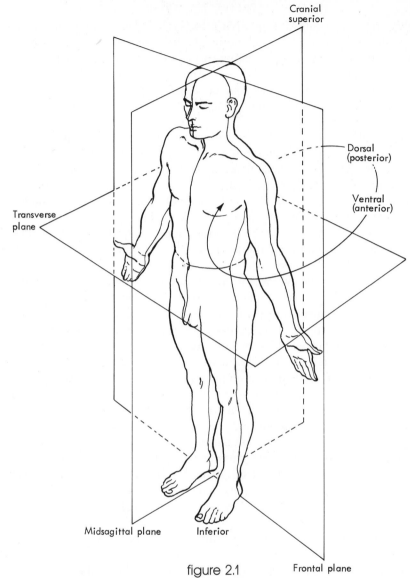

figure 2.1

The anatomical position in humans. The three major mutually
perpendicular planes are indicated. Reprinted by permission from
R.L. Memmler and D.L. Wood, *The Human Body in Health
and Disease,* 4th ed. © 1977, J.B. Lippincott Company.

course, laying out the coordinates in a standardized fashion so that any potential user will not be confused by a new system of directions. In mapping the
earth's surface, we use north, south, east, and west as the major directions. A
similar standardized set of directions is used in anatomical maps.

First, the body is put into the anatomical position shown in Figure 2.1,
standing upright with palms turned toward the front. In four-legged animals the
anatomical position is similar, but of course the animal is standing on four legs.

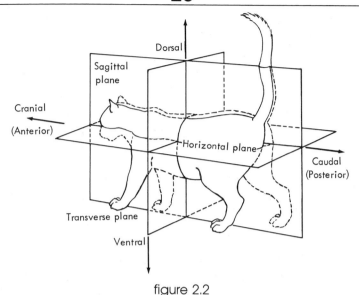

figure 2.2

The anatomical position in four-legged animals. The three
major mutually perpendicular planes are indicated.

The difference between the human and the four-legged anatomical position has led to some confusion about the terminology. In both human and four-legged animals, six major directions are indicated in Figures 2.1 and 2.2. These directions may be given independently of particular structures or they may be given in relation to major structures, such as toward the head or the tail. For independent directions, imagine that the animal is enclosed in a six-sided cubicle or room. The ceiling lies above the animal and is said to be superior to it. The floor is in the opposite direction, inferior to the animal. The wall in front of the animal lies in the anterior direction. Behind the animal, we find the posterior direction. The remaining directions are to the left and the right of the animal. Anatomical references given in relation to major structures of the animal use terms such as these: Toward the head of the animal is the cranial or rostral direction; toward the opposite end, the tail in four-legged creatures, is the caudal direction. Toward the animal's back is the dorsal direction (like the dorsal fin on a shark or sailfish). Toward the belly, and opposite to the dorsal direction, is the ventral direction.

Confusion often arises because a reference to the cranial direction in the four-legged creature is the same as a reference to the anterior direction. In the human, the cranial direction corresponds with the superior direction. Likewise, the dorsal direction is superior to the ventral in four-legged animals, posterior to the ventral in humans. Further, relative directions are given as medial (toward the middle) or lateral (toward the side). There are also references to proximal or distal structures. Proximal refers to the direction toward the attachment of a body structure, distal refers to the opposite direction. Thus, your fingertip is at the distal end of your finger, and your shoulder is at the proximal end of your arm.

To help in establishing these standardized directions, anatomists have defined three mutually perpendicular planes. We can imagine the body in anatomical position being divided by these planes (see Figures 2.1 and 2.2). The sagittal plane divides the body into left and right halves. It would pass through the very center of the spinal cord, navel, and other midline structures. Slices of the body parallel to the sagittal plane are called parasagittal sections. The frontal plane divides the body into anterior (or ventral) and posterior (or dorsal) halves. It would pass through the ears, shoulders, and hips of a human. In four-legged animals, the ventral-dorsal division would be accomplished by a transverse or horizontal plane. In humans, the transverse plane, parallel to the floor and ceiling, divides the body into superior (upper) and inferior (lower) halves. These standardized anatomical planes and directions are much more obvious when we are describing parts of the whole body, but they are also used to describe the components of each part as well.

When we describe the nervous system, we also group structures. Thus we have the *central nervous system (CNS)* and the *peripheral nervous system (PNS)*. The CNS is made up of the brain and the spinal cord. The PNS is made up of cranial nerves and spinal nerves. Spinal nerves extend from the spinal cord throughout the body. Cranial nerves extend from the brainstem, which joins the brain with the spinal cord. Cranial nerves are, with a few exceptions, confined to the head and neck regions. Many of the peripheral nerves function to direct information to the CNS. Such nerves are generally called *sensory (afferent)* nerves. The information may originate either from outside the body, or from muscles, organs, or glands within the body. Those fibers carrying neural commands from the CNS to muscles, organs, or glands are generally called *motor (efferent)* nerves. The commands may result in conscious, voluntary actions or unconscious, involuntary actions. Many of the unconscious, almost automatic, functions of the body are controlled by the autonomic nervous system, which is composed of portions of both the CNS and the PNS. It is itself divided into sympathetic and parasympathetic subsystems. Most organs receive nerve fibers from both subsystems, and usually their actions are antagonistic—that is, one system may work to activate an organ, and the other to shut it down. When systems work together like this, they are said to exhibit synergistic action.

THE SINGLE NEURAL CELL   The nervous system is made up of two kinds of basic cells. The majority, called *glial* cells, are supporting cells that hold the nervous system together. They probably constitute 80 to 90 percent of the total number of cells of the nervous system. The remaining cells are called *neurons* and are found in a variety of sizes and shapes. The smallest neurons, deep within the CNS, are microscopic in size. Millions of them are packed within one cubic centimeter of cortical material. On the other hand, some motor neurons extend from the spinal cord to the distal ends of the extremities (arms and legs).

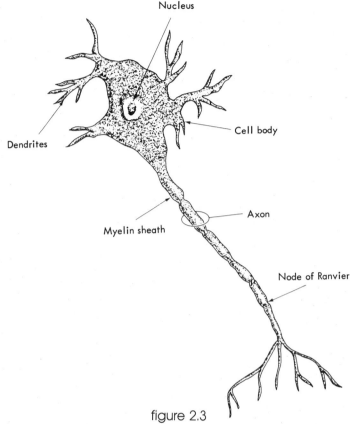

Nucleus

Cell body

Dendrites

Myelin sheath

Axon

Node of Ranvier

figure 2.3

A schematic representation of a typical motor neuron.
Reprinted by permission from F. D. Minifie, T. J. Hixon, and
F. Williams, eds., *Normal Aspects of Speech,
Hearing and Language.* © 1973, Prentice-Hall, Inc.

The common components of every neuron are shown in Figure 2.3. Each has a dendritic zone, a cell body, and an axon. The dendritic zone is the region of the neuron that receives input from other neurons or sensory receptor cells. In many neurons, a number of treelike branches extend from the cell body. These extensions, or *dendrites,* and the surface of most of the cell body make up the dendritic zone. The cell body of a neuron carries out the usual functions required of any living cell, but nerve cells do not reproduce themselves. They are quite sensitive to damage and often do not regenerate after an injury.

Neurons have one fiber that carries information away from the cell body, the *axon.* The entire neuron (cell body, dendrites, and axon) is enclosed by the cell membrane. In addition, the axon may have one or two special coverings. All PNS axons have a Schwann cell covering; oligodendroglial cells surround CNS axons. The axons of many neurons are also enclosed in a *myelin sheath.*

Basic Neuroscience

Such fibers are said to be myelinated. In fresh neural material, the myelin appears to be white, while the remaining material appears to be gray in color. Thus, "gray matter" usually refers to clusters of cell bodies; "white matter," to myelinated axons in large fiber tracts and peripheral nerves. Myelin is found in conjunction with *Schwann cells,* which play an important role in the regeneration of damaged PNS axons. Schwann cells are wrapped around an axon a number of times, with a layer of myelin in each fold. The myelin layers tend to insulate axon fibers from one another and generally to speed up the conduction of neural impulses. Breaks between individual Schwann cells appear along the axon as *nodes of Ranvier.* It is thought that the neural impulse may jump from node to node as it travels along myelinated fibers.

A neuron has only one axon, but the axon may have branches, or collaterals, which supply endings to different cells. Near the distal end of the axon, there are generally bushlike projections called *telodendria.* Each fiber has specialized terminal endings that contain a chemical transmitter substance. Each terminal ending is very close to the dendritic zone of another neuron or to the receptive surface of a muscle fiber. This arrangement is called a *synaptic junction,* or *synapse.* There is no continuity of neural material at the junction, but a very tiny space (about 200 Angstroms) called the *synaptic cleft.* Chemical transmitter substances must cross the synapse if the next neuron is to be stimulated. If the connection is between a motor neuron ending and muscle fiber, generally the final common motor neuron and the muscle fibers it supplies are called a *motor unit,* and the neuromuscular junction is called a *motor endplate.*

To distinguish the direction of information flow in the nervous system, we use two terms. Information flowing toward a cell body, or larger neural center, is said to be *afferent.* Information flowing away from that cell body or center is *efferent.* (The similarity in sound and spelling of these two terms has caused more confusion among beginning students of neurophysiology than all the other terms combined.)

Within the CNS and PNS, the cell bodies and axons of a number of neurons are often grouped together. Within the CNS, a group of cell bodies is called a *nucleus* (plural *nuclei*). In the periphery, a clump of cell bodies is called a *ganglion.* Axons bundled together in the periphery are called *nerves.* Bundles of nerve fibers in the CNS are generally called *tracts.* Occasionally the term *plexus* is used to describe a collection of cell bodies and fibers in the periphery. Thus, the solar plexus is in the center of the chest region.

NEUROANATOMY OF THE
CENTRAL NERVOUS SYSTEM   The CNS is composed of the brain and the spinal cord. The spinal cord occupies the spinal canal, which extends vertically through the center of the vertebral column. The vertebral column is divided into cervical, thoracic, lumbar, sacral, and coccygeal segments, and sections of the spinal cord are often named according to the division they occupy.

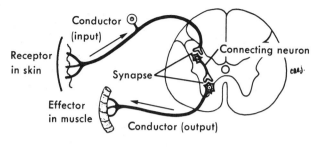

figure 2.4
A schematic representation of a simple spinal cord reflex arc.
Reprinted by permission from J. Minckler, *Introduction to Neuroscience*, © 1972, The C. V. Mosby Company.

Between each pair of vertebrae, the spinal cord sends out on the left and right sides 31 pairs of spinal nerves. Each spinal nerve is divided into a ventral root and a dorsal root.

The Spinal Cord Reflex Arc   Figure 2.4 illustrates a spinal cord *reflex arc,* the simplest connection of sensory and motor functions in the body. Afferent information travels to the spinal cord from a sensory receptor cell, perhaps a heat sensor in the fingertip. The information that the fingers are in danger of being burned is carried into the spinal cord along the dorsal root of the spinal nerve. Notice in Figure 2.4 that the cell body for the sensory fiber is in the dorsal root ganglion, just lateral to the vertebral column. The impulses enter the spinal cord where there is a connection between the terminal ending of the sensory fiber and the dendritic zone of a CNS neuron. The central neuron, which is called an *interneuron,* makes a synaptic connection with one or more efferent neurons. The cell bodies for these motor neurons lie within the spinal cord. The axons of the motor neurons leave the spinal cord by the ventral root. Eventually they form motor nerves which are supplied to the skeletal muscles that, we hope, will remove the endangered fingers from the heat.

The action just described does not require conscious intervention. Reflex actions in the nervous system often have protective functions that ensure the survival of the organism. By not requiring conscious intervention, the action is much more efficient than one mediated from higher levels of the CNS. In fact, the action is so fast that we become aware of the pain of a burn after the reflex has taken place. Of course, many more connections are involved in most actions of the body. For voluntary actions, sensory input is also necessary. Sensory receptors are located throughout the voluntary muscles, ligaments, and tendons. Changes in length or tension of muscles are relayed to the CNS, and

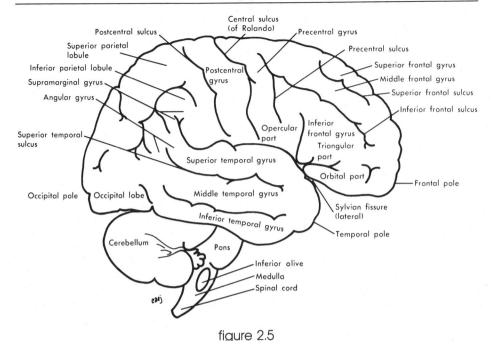

figure 2.5

Diagram of the lateral view of the brain. Reprinted by permission from J. Minckler, *Introduction to Neuroscience.* © 1972 by The C. V. Mosby Company.

such sensory input is used by the CNS to control the movements of the muscles. This control information is usually called *sensory feedback,* because a sample of the output is returned to the controlling system to aid in effecting the action.

The Brain

Above the spinal cord, within the cranial cavity of the skull, is the brain itself (Figure 2.5). The spinal cord continues into the cranial cavity as the *medulla oblongata.* Above the medulla is a region known as the *pons,* and above the pons we find the *midbrain.* The medulla, pons, and midbrain form the *brainstem.*

Sitting atop the brainstem and surrounding much of the midbrain is the *cerebrum,* the large, wrinkled mass often called "the brain" in nontechnical writing. The cerebrum is divided into left and right hemispheres. Posterior to the cerebral hemispheres and superior to the brainstem (that's behind and above for those of you who have yet to master the anatomical directions) is the *cerebellum,* which also has left and right hemispheres and appears to have a wrinkled surface. The wrinkled surfaces of both the cerebrum and the cerebellum are called "*cortex.*" However, these wrinkled surfaces look different from one another to the observer, and their functions are very different from each other as well. The word "cortex" is derived from a Latin word meaning "bark." Early anatomists thought that these surfaces looked like the outer covering of a tree. The wrinkled appearance is caused by the folding of the surface. (Folding permits much more surface area to be contained in a restricted volume.) The ridges in the folded surface are called *convolutions* or *gyri* (singular *gyrus*); the valleys between them are called *fissures* or *sulci* (singular *sulcus*). Three major fissures are indicated in Figure 2.5. The longitudinal sulcus along the midsaggital plane divides the cerebrum into left and right hemispheres. The central sulcus (also sometimes called the Sylvian fissure) is located approximately in the major frontal plane. The lateral sulcus runs diagonally, then horizontally along the outer or lateral surface of the cerebrum.

Each cerebral hemisphere is divided into four major lobes. Most anterior is the frontal lobe, which extends back to the central fissure. Next, as we move from anterior to posterior, comes the parietal lobe. At the base of the cerebrum just superior to the cerebellum is the occipital lobe. The temporal lobe is divided from the frontal lobe by the lateral fissure. It is misleading to attribute unique functions to the various lobes of the cerebrum. Their names were derived from those of the overlying skull bones, so that they are anatomically but not necessarily functionally distinct. A given function such as speech communication may require action from several cerebral centers. We will focus on the temporal lobes, which contribute a great deal to speech and hearing.

Inside the cerebrum are four fluid-filled spaces known as *ventricles*. There is one inside each cerebral hemisphere, and two along the midline that extend downward into the brainstem. The fluid that fills the spaces inside both the cranial and spinal cavities is called *cerebrospinal fluid (CSF)*.

Deep inside the cerebrum, at the very top of the brainstem, is the *diencephalon*. The remainder of the cerebrum above and lateral to the diencephalon is called the *telencephalon*. Sometimes these areas are called the old and the new brain, respectively. The diencephalon contains the *thalamus* for the relay of input to the cerebral cortex. It also contains the centers for regulation of unconscious control of essential functions in the *hypothalamus*.

Twelve pairs of peripheral nerves are supplied to the head and neck region from the brainstem. These cranial nerves are functionally equivalent to the spinal nerves that serve the remainder of the body. The functions of the head and neck (and upper torso in the case of the vagus nerve) are even more specialized than those in the body proper. Since speech production and audition are mediated predominately by head and neck structures, it is essential to know the anatomy and physiology of the cranial nerve supply. Figure 2.6 shows a view of the cerebrum and brainstem with the paired cranial nerves clearly labeled. Often the nerves are given Roman numeral designations beginning with the most anterior pair, the olfactory nerve (I) and proceeding posteriorly toward the spinal cord to the hypoglossal nerve (XII). Table 2.1 summarizes the information about the cranial nerves essential to the study of speech and hearing physiology.

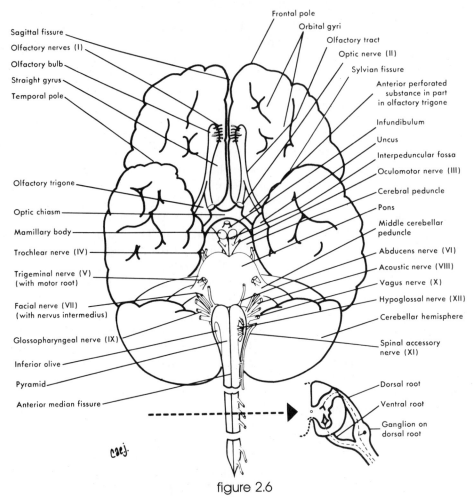

Frontal pole
Orbital gyri
Olfactory tract
Optic nerve (II)
Sylvian fissure
Anterior perforated substance in part in olfactory trigone
Infundibulum
Uncus
Interpeduncular fossa
Oculomotor nerve (III)
Cerebral peduncle
Pons
Middle cerebellar peduncle
Abducens nerve (VI)
Acoustic nerve (VIII)
Vagus nerve (X)
Hypoglossal nerve (XII)
Cerebellar hemisphere
Spinal accessory nerve (XI)
Dorsal root
Ventral root
Ganglion on dorsal root

Sagittal fissure
Olfactory nerves (I)
Olfactory bulb
Straight gyrus
Temporal pole
Olfactory trigone
Optic chiasm
Mamillary body
Trochlear nerve (IV)
Trigeminal nerve (V) (with motor root)
Facial nerve (VII) (with nervus intermedius)
Glossopharyngeal nerve (IX)
Inferior olive
Pyramid
Anterior median fissure

figure 2.6

A schematic representation of the ventral surface of the human brain. Reprinted by permission from J. Minckler, *Introduction to Neuroscience.* © 1972 by The C. V. Mosby Company.

We have, so far, defined the coordinates of the anatomical mapping system and introduced the major structural components of the nervous system. This brief discussion of neuroanatomy is essential to the understanding of neurophysiology—the functions of the nervous system.

functions of the nervous system: neurophysiology

An entire text would not be large enough to present all that is known about the functions of the nervous system. For our purposes, we have been very selective in our choice of topics for discussion. Here we will first consider the ac-

table 2.1
cranial nerves

NUMBER	NAME	TYPE	FUNCTION
I	Olfactory	Sensory	Sense of smell
II	Optic	Sensory	Vision
III	Oculomotor	Motor	Eye movements and focusing
IV	Trochlear	Motor	Eye movements
V	Trigeminal	Both motor and sensory	Motor: muscles to raise and lower mandible, raise soft palate Sensory: skin of face in general, upper and lower jaw, teeth, mucous membrane of nose and upper pharynx
VI	Abducens	Motor	Eye movements
VII	Facial	Both motor and sensory	Motor: muscles of facial expression (including lips) Sensory: sense of taste for anterior two-thirds of tongue, sensation from mucous membrane of pharynx
VIII	Acoustic	Sensory	Cochlear branch: sense of hearing; vestibular branch: sense of body position and movement
IX	Glossopharyngeal	Both motor and sensory	Motor: one muscle of pharynx Sensory: sense of taste from posterior third of tongue, sensation from mouth (mucous membrane)
X	Vagus	Both motor and sensory	Motor: nonstriated muscle in lungs, muscles of larynx Sensory: mucous membrane of larynx and lungs
XI	Accessory	Motor	Lowers soft palate (also helps raise soft palate)
XII	Hypoglossal	Motor	Controls all intrinsic muscles and many extrinsic tongue muscles (therefore responsible for almost *all* movement of the tongue)

tion of a typical single neuron in receiving a neural impulse and delivering it to a subsequent neuron in the chain. Then we will discuss the input (sensory) and output (motor) neurons, and finally we will try to indicate the coordination of sensory and motor systems in speech-related activities.

THE SINGLE NEURON   Figure 2.7 shows three types of neurons, each of which exhibits three main zones: the dendritic, the conducting, and the transmitting. These neurons are classified according to the number of fibers (or poles) projecting from the cell body. Note that in the unipolar and bipolar cells, it would be incorrect to say that the axon conducts information *away from* the cell body. A fiber may be classified as an axon by the way in which it conducts information, but *not* by the direction in which that information flows. The "typical" neuron, if there is one, is the multipolar neuron reproduced in Figure 2.3. This type is most commonly found within the CNS. It receives stimulation from other neurons, and also transmits impulses to other neurons. The bipolar neuron, which is rather rare, is found in the auditory system.

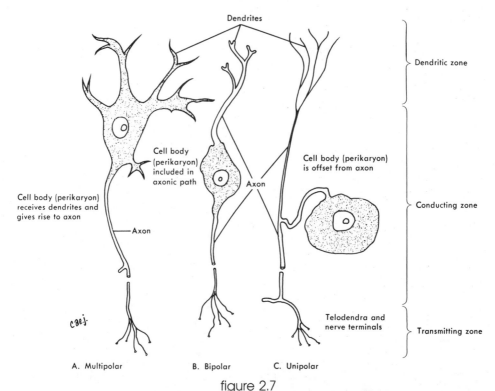

Dendrites

Dendritic zone

Cell body (perikaryon) included in axonic path

Cell body (perikaryon) is offset from axon

Axon

Cell body (perikaryon) receives dendrites and gives rise to axon

Axon

Conducting zone

Telodendra and nerve terminals

Transmitting zone

caej·

A. Multipolar   B. Bipolar   C. Unipolar

figure 2.7

Schematic representations of three types of neurons. Reprinted by permission from J. Minckler, *Introduction to Neuroscience*. © 1972 by The C. V. Mosby Company.

Information is carried through the neuron by two different electrochemical conduction mechanisms. At the dendritic end of the neuron, a chemical transmitter substance released from the preceding neuron reacts with the cell membrane. If we base our reference at the synapse, then the dendritic membrane is a postsynaptic membrane. Within the dendrite, the transmitter substance generates a postsynaptic (electrical) potential. Chemical action leads to a small localized electrical voltage change. These postsynaptic potentials can be of two types: excitatory postsynaptic potentials (EPSP) or inhibitory postsynaptic potentials (IPSP).

Let us first consider the action of an EPSP alone. All living cells maintain a small difference of potential across the cell membrane. If we measured the voltage between the cytoplasm inside the cell and the fluid surrounding the outside, we would find that the inside of the cell is electrically more negative than its outside surface. The voltage (or electrical potential) is very small—perhaps about 70 millivolts (that is, 70/1000 volt; a single dry cell for a flashlight is 1.5 volts). We say that such cells are *polarized*.

The neuron, like other living cells, maintains this small potential difference. Unlike other living cells, the neuron can, under the proper conditions, alter its polarization for a brief period of time. The EPSP represents a change in the polarization of the cell localized to the dendritic zone. The chemical transmitter that leads to an EPSP produces a state of *depolarization* inside the cell. When the cell is depolarized, the size of the normal potential is reduced toward zero. The depolarization that begins at the synaptic site travels through the dendritic zone by ionic conduction, also called *diffusion*. The strength of the stimulus determines the strength of the depolarization. Thus, the EPSP is said to be graded, or proportional to the stimulus strength. If the stimulus is strong, the EPSP is strong; if the stimulus is weak, then the EPSP is faint. Weak EPSPs have little effect on the neuron.

One region within the neuron can be affected by EPSPs of sufficient strength. That region is called the spike generator or initial segment of the axon. It is thought to be at the proximal end of the axon in multipolar neurons and is sometimes labeled the *axon hillock*. The spike generator has a limit to the amount of depolarization that it can withstand. If that limit, known as the *threshold,* is exceeded, then the spike generator is set into an irreversible reaction. The result of the irreversible reaction is the generation and transmission of a neural spike along the axon of the fiber.

The neural spike that travels the length of the axon is also an electrochemical response in the neuron, but it is very different from the graded postsynaptic potentials. These decay over time and distance from their source, whereas the axonal spike is produced by a regeneration process. That is, a self-sustaining action literally creates a "new" spike with the current one. The neural spike is named for its shape on a plot of the electrical potential within the cell. Figure 2.8 shows a typical axonal spike. Notice that once the depolarizing EPSP has reached threshold, the generation of the spike is automatic. For a given neuron, the spikes are identical in size and shape. Unlike the EPSP, the neural spike is

figure 2.8

An illustration of the electrical activity at the axon hillock which leads to the generation of a neural impulse.

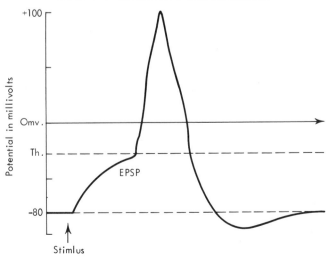

not a graded potential. It has been called an all-or-none response because once triggered, the full spike occurs. Otherwise, there is no response.

The speed with which the neural spike travels the axon depends on the size of the axon, not the strength of the stimulus. Fibers with large diameters conduct neural impulses faster than thin ones, and the presence of a myelin sheath also helps to speed up conduction. The rate, number of spikes per second, however, does depend on stimulus strength.

The action of some synaptic connections is not excitatory; at such connections, the release of the transmitter substance leads to greater polarization of the cell, or *hyperpolarization*. The inside of the cell is made even more electrically negative than the outside. These connections are said to be inhibitory synapses because they counteract the excitatory action of other synapses. The wave of hyperpolarization generated at inhibitory synapses is called an inhibitory postsynaptic potential (IPSP). Within the cytoplasm, the EPSPs and IPSPs add algebraically. Under normal conditions, a number of synapses may be active at one time. Some synapses are excitatory, others are inhibitory. The effect at the spike generator depends upon the *net* potential. If there is an excitatory action strong enough to exceed the threshold, then a spike will be generated and transmitted along the axon. If inhibitory synapses are active, then the cell may not generate a spike. In order to generate a spike in the face of inhibitory action, the excitatory stimulus must be strong enough to counteract the IPSP and still exceed threshold.

The summation of postsynaptic potentials may occur in two ways. We have discussed the summation of excitatory and inhibitory potentials from different synapses. These synapses are located at different places on the dendritic surface, and such summation is commonly called *spatial summation*. The activity at different locations in space is summed at any given time. Notice that in Figure 2.8 the postsynaptic potentials persist for a brief period of time. If the stimulating fiber is firing rapidly, then the postsynaptic potentials may be summed in time. Thus, although one impulse delivered to a synapse may be too weak to trigger a response, a series of pulses in rapid succession could generate an EPSP of sufficient strength to trigger it. This action is often called *temporal summation*. Both spatial and temporal summation act within the cell to determine the net postsynaptic potential. Thus, the possibilities for the control of information flow, even at a single neuron, are enormous.

CONDUCTION OF THE
NEURAL IMPULSE

The electrical activity within the dendritic zone and cell body of a neuron is said to be *graded*. The strength of the postsynaptic potential depends on the strength of the stimulation delivered to the neuron. The electrical activity that travels the axon from the spike generator to its terminal endings is very different from the graded postsynaptic potentials that trigger the neural impulse. The neural impulse travels the length of the axon without loss of size or shape. It is said to follow an "all-or-none" law, since the result of triggering an impulse is always the full measure of the response.

Here we cannot give a detailed description of the electrochemical processes that underlie the conduction of the nerve impulse, but several references listed at the end of the chapter do give sufficient details to satisfy the beginning student. We will simply indicate the major points in the so-called sodium pump explanation of neural impulse conduction.

The electrical difference of potential between the cytoplasm inside a cell and the fluid surrounding it is due to an imbalance of ions. Ions are atoms with either less than their normal complement of orbital electrons (a net positive charge—positive ions), or a surplus of orbital electrons (a net negative charge—negative ions). Normally, an atom contains the same number of protons (positively charged particles) and electrons (negatively charged particles), and has no net electrical charge. The atoms of many elements are arranged in such a way that they either gain or lose an electron rather easily. Such atoms become ions. The outer ring of electrons around an atomic nucleus is most stable when it contains eight electrons. Thus, atoms of elements such as chlorine (Cl), which contains seven outer electrons, often attract an extra electron. The result is a chloride ion having one surplus negative charge. The ion is shown symbolically as Cl^-. Atoms of elements having one or two electrons in the outermost orbit and eight in the next outermost orbit often lose those outer electrons rather easily. Atoms of potassium (K) and sodium (Na) each have one outermost orbital electron. When the outer electron is lost, such an atom becomes a positively charged ion—K^+ or Na^+, respectively.

The cell membrane is said to be semi-permeable because it allows some ions to pass freely through its structure, but blocks the passage of others. Inside the neuron, the concentration of potassium ions (K^+) is found to be 20 to 50 times higher than the concentration in the extracellular fluid in which it is bathed. A high concentration of negatively charged biological ions helps to neutralize the positive charge due to K^+ ions. Thus, the electrically negative potential difference between the inside and outside of the neuron (the resting potential) is due to the surplus of negatively charged macromolecules within the cytoplasm.

Outside the cell, the fluid has a high concentration of sodium (Na^+) and chloride (Cl^-) ions. (The crystalline form of sodium chloride is common table salt, NaCl. Dissolved in water, the atoms separate into ions and move about the fluid independently.) The cell membrane acts to keep K^+ ions inside the cell and Na^+ ions outside the cell. If Na^+ ions were injected into the neuron, the cell would exchange Na^+ for K^+ by moving those ions through the membrane to return to its previous state. The normal negative electrical charge of the cytoplasm with reference to the extracellular fluid is due to the ability of the cell membrane to maintain the imbalance of ionic concentrations. The active mechanism that ejects Na^+ ions from the cell is commonly called the *sodium pump*. In a resting—that is, unstimulated—state, the cell expends energy

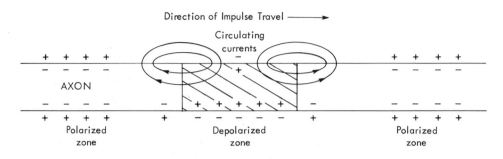

Direction of Impulse Travel ⟶

figure 2.9

A schematic representation of the regenerative process
by which the all or none impulse travels along an axon.
Reprinted by permission from B. Katz, *Nerve, Muscle and Synapse.*
© 1966, McGraw-Hill Book Company.

simply to maintain this imbalance. The electrophysiological evidence of that work is the resting electrical potential that is recorded from every living cell.

Neurons differ from other cells because the sodium pump action can be temporarily interrupted. In fact, when the neuron encounters a sufficiently strong stimulus, the sodium pump temporarily reverses its action. Na^+ ions rush into the cell. The resting potential changes from a small negative voltage (approximately $^-70$ millivolts) to a small positive voltage (perhaps $^+50$ millivolts); it does not simply collapse to zero (see Figure 2.8). The temporary reversal of the resting potential is thought to be due to a brief change in membrane permeability. Almost as soon as the disturbance begins, two internal mechanisms act. The sodium pump begins to eject Na^+ ions, bringing the potential back toward the resting levels. More important, however, is the effect of the electrochemical activity at one place on the axon upon adjacent regions, as shown in Figure 2.9. The flow of ions through the cell membrane sets up local circulating electrical currents. These local currents pass through neighboring segments of the axon that had remained at rest and activate them. The wave of electrochemical activity, once initiated, passes through the length of the axon in this self-sustaining or regenerative way. The neural spike does not decay or lose its shape as it travels the axon; it constantly triggers a new impulse in an adjacent segment.

When the neural impulse reaches the terminal ending, it activates the mechanism that releases the transmitter substance into the synaptic space between the terminal ending and the dendritic zone of the next neuron. Each terminal ending has many tiny *vesicles* that contain the transmitter substance. The arrival of a neural impulse apparently causes one or more of the vesicles to release the transmitter substance into the synaptic space.

Throughout this section we have referred to transmitter substances without specifically naming one. This is because although most motor neurons release acetylcholine (ACh), several other agents have been identified. Some neuro-physiologists think that inhibitory synaptic connections may contain a different transmitter substance. Others suggest that the transmitting agent may be the same, but the inhibitory postsynaptic membrane differs from the excitatory one. It is clear that we still have much to learn about the interactions of neurons.

SENSORY SYSTEMS   Information reaches the central nervous system through the sensory nerves and pathways. The first in this chain of cells is specialized for *irritability*. That is, the cell responds to stimulus energy presented to its receptive area. Different sensory systems employ different receptor cells. In some, the receptor cell is a neuron with a dendritic zone adapted to the reception of heat, light, or mechanical energy. In hearing and in some of the skin senses, this first cell does not look like a neuron at all. For example, the sensory receptor cells in the cochlea (inner ear) are specially adapted to respond to the mechanical bending of the hairlike structures at their tops.

Each sensory system or *modality* employs receptor cells specially adapted for response to a given form of energy (see Chapter 4 for a discussion of energy). The energy may be in the form of light (vision), sound (hearing), heat (temperature sense in the skin), or mechanical deformation (tactile senses). The energy that stimulates the receptor cell may come from some distance away from the organism. The visual, hearing, and vibratory senses, for example, may respond to energy sources far removed from the body. Some sensory systems respond when external energy (a gentle touch or heat) is applied directly to the body surface. Much of our sensory input comes from muscles, joints, tendons, and organs deep within our bodies, and it is processed below conscious levels.

When stimulus energy is applied to a sensory receptor cell, that cell may respond by releasing a transmitter substance at a synaptic junction with the primary neuron. We say *may,* because sometimes stimulus energy does not activate the sensory system. The receptor cell may still be recovering from a previous stimulus, or it may be prevented from responding by other units. Such action is called inhibition. Often a sensory receptor will not only actively stimulate its primary CNS neuron, but also inhibit nearby sensory cells. Such lateral inhibitory action has been well documented in the visual and cutaneous senses, but its existence is still hotly debated with respect to hearing.

A sensory nerve fiber may be connected to more than one receptor cell. The entire array of receptor cells and their fibers might be called a sensory unit. If we take into account the surrounding receptor cells that may be inhibited by an active sensory unit, then we define the *receptive field* of a sensory unit. Generally, a receptive field is composed of an excitatory central region surrounded by inhibitory areas. The inhibitory regions are thought to improve the contrast between activated (or excited) sensory units and nearby units that are inactive.

Sensory input to the CNS passes through several nuclei before reaching the cortex. In each nucleus there is the probability that the sensory information is processed before being passed to the next center. Thus, many of the consequences of sensory inputs are mediated below the cortical level. The spinal column reflex discussed above is a simple example. Perhaps it is fortunate that much of the activity of the body is under automatic control—otherwise, the more absent-minded among us might "forget to breathe" and die of asphyxiation.

MOTOR SYSTEMS   Body movements are carried out by coordinated contractions of muscles. In particular, the movements required for breathing, phonation, and articulation are effected by muscle contractions. Commands from the CNS are delivered to the muscles via the motor pathways within the brain and spinal cord and through the peripheral motor nerves. Muscle tissue is made up of thousands of individual muscle fibers. These fibers may vary in size and shape, but they possess the common property of *contractability*. That is, when a muscle fiber is properly stimulated, it shortens in length. In order for a whole muscle to contract, a large number of its fibers must be stimulated in the correct temporal pattern. The stimulus for muscle fiber contraction is a chemical transmitter substance released from the terminal endings of the final motor neuron.

A large-diameter myelinated nerve fiber (called an alpha fiber or α fiber) may be connected to a number of muscle fibers. This array of one neuron and its muscle fibers is commonly called a *motor unit*. When the neuron is active— that is, conducting an impulse—all its muscle fibers contract. To produce smooth, coordinated movements, the contractions of whole muscles must be smooth and graded. To accomplish that end, the number of active motor units may vary over time. Thus, a large number of small, twitching contractions is evened out into a gradual, controlled movement.

At the junction between the final motor neuron and the muscle fiber, known as the *motor endplate,* a complex electrochemical process leads to the contraction of a muscle fiber. When a neural impulse reaches the endplate, a transmitter substance is released. Release of the transmitter substance leads to the generation of an *action potential* that spreads along the muscle fiber. This action potential is similar to the postsynaptic potential produced in the dendrite of a neuron. The spreading of the muscle action potential eventually leads to the contraction of the muscle fiber. The number of muscle fibers served by one motor neuron varies from a number perhaps as small as 10 to as many as 2,000 or more. This number is commonly called the *innervation ratio*. It is generally true that muscles required to make very fine, delicate movements have low innervation ratios (that is, each neuron serves a small number of muscle fibers). Large skeletal muscles have much higher innervation ratios. The smallest innervation ratios in the human body are found in the muscles concerned with articulation and in those of the fingers, thumb, and eyes.

The neuromuscular system we have described so far is highly oversimplified. No muscle in the body is controlled in an "open-loop" fashion; a much more complex sensory-motor control system is required for even the most gross movement or gesture. Most skeletal (voluntary) muscle is found to contain groups of richly innervated fibers called *muscle spindles.* These fibers are called *intrafusal* to distinguish them from the main, or *extrafusal,* fibers.

The nerve supply to the muscle spindle is very complex. There are probably two separate motor supplies as well as two separate sensory supplies for each spindle. As we learn more about the structure of the spindle and the nature of its nerve supply, the proposed functions become more complex. When first discovered, the muscle spindle was thought to be necessary for muscle regeneration. After its sensory innervation was established, the muscle spindle was found to act as a stretch receptor. Thus, when an antagonistic muscle contracts, the spindle reports the application of force to its muscle to the CNS. The CNS can then cause just enough contraction in the muscle to smooth the movement. Later studies of the muscle spindle have shown the existence of a motor nerve supply to the muscle fibers within the spindle. Many of these nerve fibers are of smaller diameter than the large α fibers which supply the extrafusal fibers and are called *gamma efferents* (γ fibers). Neural impulses delivered to the intrafusal fibers in the muscle spindles can cause contractions of the whole muscle. Contractions of the fibers in the spindle activate the sensory receptors within the spindle. Stimulation of these receptors then leads to activation of the α fibers to the extrafusal fibers.

It is now generally thought that a complex feedback loop controls the contraction of skeletal muscles. Even in a very crude muscle action, such as the spinal reflex discussed earlier, there is probably a complex interaction of the reflex arc with the afferent and efferent neural supply to muscle spindles. Muscle tension is maintained through the afferent supply of the spindle (stretch) receptor in a reflex connection with the α motor neurons supplying the extrafusal muscle fibers. A change in muscle tension or length can be brought about in a number of ways. If an outside force attempts to stretch the muscle, the stretch receptors in the muscle spindle will signal the CNS. The CNS will increase the impulses delivered to the muscle via α neurons and thus oppose the outside force. Voluntary contraction can also occur, either by direct command to the α motor neurons, or by commands to the γ efferent motor neurons supplied to the muscle spindle. Contraction of the intrafusal muscle fibers in turn activates the stretch receptors and effects a muscle contraction.

COORDINATION OF SENSORY AND MOTOR ACTION

The coordination of sensory and motor action is much more complicated than the simple picture of muscle contraction we have just given. There is now evidence that some muscle spindles are supplied with collaterals of the large α motor neuron axons which innervate extrafusal muscle fibers. Some of the efferent innervation to the muscle spindle apparently alters the sensitivity of the sensory receptors rather than causing contractions of intrafusal fibers.

This interaction of sensory and motor systems is the rule throughout the nervous system. Central control of sensory input is easy to demonstrate. The pupillary reflex is a clear example. Take a friend into a darkened room. After a short while, your friend will be able to see rather well in the dim light because the pupil changes size in response to the amount of light striking the retina. In the darkened room, the pupil dilates (opens) to a large diameter in order to "collect" as much light as possible. When the eye is exposed to bright light, the pupil becomes constricted to reduce the amount of light reaching the retina. Stimulus input level to the sensory system is thus regulated by motor commands to the ciliary muscles of the pupil.

As we shall see in the chapters that follow, there is continuous interplay between sensory and motor systems in the production of speech. One that is easily demonstrated is called the Lombard effect. It happens that we, as speakers, monitor our own speech output (we all know someone who seems to produce speech *only* for his or her own listening pleasure). Auditory monitoring of speech is necessary for proper production, as the speech of a deaf person reveals.

The Lombard effect demonstrates the role of auditory feedback in the control of speech output level. If a person is asked to read aloud from a book or magazine, he or she will produce speech at an intensity that his or her nervous system judges as sufficient to be heard. If the speaker is asked to wear earphones and external noise audible only to that person is introduced, when the external noise is increased in intensity, the speaker will raise his or her voice to overcome the background noise. An audience not hearing the noise in the headphones can be greatly amused by the increases and decreases in the talker's speech level.

It is the opposite of the Lombard effect that causes a talker suffering from a conductive hearing loss to talk too softly in a noisy environment. This person's auditory system does not receive the background noise, but it does receive the self-generated speech by bone conduction. Thus, the speech level is inadequate to overcome the background noise. These examples show how sensory input is actively involved in the regulation of motor output. In subsequent chapters, we will look at this interconnection in detail.

This brief discussion of the anatomy and physiology of the nervous system has introduced the concepts and terminology necessary for a better understanding of speech production processes and the functions of the auditory system. More detailed explanations of nervous system activities and muscle physiology will be given where needed in later chapters. The reader interested in further study is also directed to the suggested readings that follow.

SUGGESTED READINGS

BRODAL, A. *Neurological Anatomy in Relation to Clinical Medicine,* 2nd ed. New York: Oxford University Press, 1969. An excellent treatment of the human nervous system. Although it is written for the advanced student, the discussions of pathologies affecting speech and the auditory and vestibular systems will be of value to the speech pathologist and audiologist.

KATZ, B. *Nerve, Muscle and Synapse.* New York: McGraw-Hill, 1966. This small paperback contains an excellent treatment of the microscopic aspects of nervous system functions. The level of the mathematical treatment may be beyond the beginning student.

MEMMLER, R. L., and D. L. WOOD. *The Human Body in Health and Disease,* 4th ed. Philadelphia: Lippincott, 1977. This introductory anatomy and physiology text contains excellent chapters on the nervous system, sensory systems, and muscles.

MINCKLER, J. *Introduction to Neuroscience.* St. Louis: C.V. Mosby, 1972. The illustrations of actual nervous system tissues are an outstanding feature. It is a more detailed text and assumes a basic science background.

TYLER, T. J. *A Primer of Psychobiology—Brain and Behavior.* San Francisco: Freeman, 1975. This text contains a very good discussion of brain functions and how they relate to observable behavior.

LANGUAGE

3

As students of physiology, we study speech at the neurophysiological, acoustic, respiratory, phonatory, articulatory, and perceptual levels. Consequently, it is important to know how these different levels of speech are regulated. The control mechanism that organizes and regulates the combined operation of the overall speech systems is language. Since our primary concern is the study of physiology, our review of language will be like an introduction survey rather than a comprehensive discussion. All the descriptions and examples will be simplifications of an extremely complex system. We will look first at how language is organized, then at the ways in which we describe its structure, and conclude with an outline of its interrelationships.

the organization of language

Language can be compared to the musical score of a symphony. The written score charts the rhythm, harmony, and intensity patterns of the orchestra as written by the composer. In addition, the score specifies which members of the orchestra will play and when. The written score is interpreted by a conductor, who adds his or her own variations. Similarly, as language users, we are constrained by certain linguistic rules. However, each speaker is also a conductor, and he or she determines what, how, and when the linguistic orchestra will play. To gain a clearer understanding of the interrelationships among the various levels of linguistic activity that lead to speech, it is particularly important to understand the concept of synergy.

In Chapter 1, synergy is referred to as the behavior of a whole system that is not predicted by the behavior of its component parts or any subassembly of components. If we look at the physiological-anatomical components of the speech mechanism, for example—the lungs, the vocal folds, the multichamber resonance system (vocal tract), the mobile valve (tongue), the teeth, the vermillion cushions (lips), the multichannel auditory monitoring system (ears)—we would never predict that these parts working together could produce speech. It is only through study of the integrated synergetic behavior of the vocal tract components, and anditory system as governed by neurophysiological processing, that we can understand the phenomenon of speech.

The speech production system is best seen as a hierarchy of components. The concept of hierarchy, like that of synergy, is crucial to a better understanding of components and subassembly relationships and integrations. Koestler (1967) provided the following discussion of hierarchical order:

> The first universal characteristic of hierarchies is the relativity, and indeed ambiguity, of the terms "part" and "whole" when applied to any of the sub-assemblies. Again it is the very obviousness of this feature which makes us overlook its implications. A "part," as we generally use the word, means something fragmentary and incomplete, which by itself would have no legitimate existence. On the other hand, a "whole" is considered as something complete in itself which needs no further explanation. But "wholes" and "parts" in this absolute sense just do not exist anywhere, either in the domain of living organisms or the intermediary structures on a series of levels in an ascending order of complexity; sub-wholes which display, according to the way you look at them, some of the characteristics commonly attributed to parts. We have seen the impossibility of the task of chopping up speech into elementary atoms or units, either on the phonetic or syntactic level. Phonemes, words, phrases, are wholes in their own right, but parts of a larger unit: so are cells, tissues, organs; families, clans, tribes. The members of the hierarchy, like the Roman god Janus, all have two faces looking in opposite directions: the face turned toward the subordinate levels is that of a self-contained whole; the face turned toward the apex, that of a dependent part. One is the face of the master, the other the face of the servant. This "Janus effect" is a fundamental characteristic of sub-wholes in all types of hierarchies. (Koestler, 1967, pp. 47–48)

The language component of speech represents the "brain-mind" map, which looks both forward and backward within the hierarchical process that leads to the production of speech. Similarly, as one component of the speech hierarchy, language itself is also a hierarchical framework.

Language consists of three interrelated components: (1) content, (2) structure, and (3) function. As Figure 3.1 shows, *content* refers to so-called nonverbal ideas or cognitions; our observations-integrations-generalizations of environmental or mental events. It represents those things about which we wish to talk and think. *Structure* refers to the organization of utterances, the way in which sounds, syllables, words, phrases, and sentences are ordered and structured so that they can represent the content of speech. Structure (or grammar) provides a way in which to talk about something. It includes the organization-description of sound patterns (phonology), word construction (morphology), reference-meaning (semantics), and word-phrase-sentence relationships (syntax). Structure is the crucial link between content (cognition) and the final component of language, *function* (our reasons for talking). There is an awe-inspiring list of reasons for talking, but in general, we talk in order to communicate information and to manipulate others and determine our own behavior.

Once again our example of a musical score is helpful. The composer of the score and the speaker have "ideas" (content) about something they want to communicate. They are motivated to convey information via speech or music (function). Both have several available alternatives from which a selection can

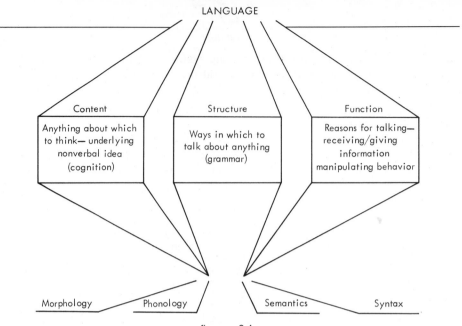

figure 3.1

The hierarchical order of language.

be made to structure their ideas into a composition. Musical ideas may be structured according to a specified form—a sonata, symphony, fantasie, fugue, and so on. The composer must also further delineate intent by choosing certain instruments. The choice of instruments or sounds and their combinations (phonology and morphology) then enable the composer to express intended meaning (semantics) through carefully phrased musical passages (syntax). Obviously, the meaning the composer intends to convey is inextricably linked to sound combinations and phrasing. If, for instance, the composer's or speaker's idea includes a message intended to tell someone to refrain from talking, they may choose one or more available alternatives. Either the musical or verbal message can then be structured to form the signals "please be quiet," "shut up," or "knock it off." Such an example is necessarily oversimplified, but it does serve to illustrate a comparison between two forms of communication.

Language should be viewed not only as the medium by which we communicate, but also as the final determinant of the ways in which we choose to adapt to an ever-changing environment. The significance of the language we use on ourselves, as well as on others, is illustrated in this statement: "You can't make me angry without my permission." We, as language users, hold ultimate responsibility for the degree to which we act and react to language. Clearly, we have choices in its use and abuse.

As stated earlier, *structure* is the subcomponent of language that serves as the crucial link between content and function. Suppose, for instance, you have been given the task of tape-recording an explanation of how to ride a bicycle. You mention mounting procedures, grasping handlebars, initiation of pedaling, balance, adjustment to objects in space, and so on. In the end, you realize that a descriptive analysis of bicycling is nearly impossible. Descriptions of language structure are similar to behavioral events that have the properties of "it's difficult to explain, but easy to demonstrate." The processes involved in speaking occur so effortlessly that we pay little attention to how it is accomplished. In other words, as speakers of a language we possess "knowledge" of the linguistic rules of that language, but often we cannot state these rules. We can, however, differentiate between grammatical and ungrammatical utterances. In the same way, certain kinds of observations and analyses can give us a clearer understanding of what is involved in the study of language.

phonology

The sound pattern of a given language is fundamental to its structure. As we will see in Chapter 8, it is unrealistic to specify a sound pattern as a set of idealized sound segments at the physiological-production level; it is convenient, however, to consider segments to be ideal, and to make such specifications invariant units at an abstract phonological level. These highly idealized abstract patterns are called *phonemes*. A phoneme may be defined operationally as representing the sound segment which, when changed by the substitution of another sound segment, changes the meaning and sound shape of a word. For example, if the initial segment in the word stem -il is fil, bil, til, sil, wil, dil, kil, and so on, we notice that the substitution of each different phoneme causes a change in meaning as well as sound shape. Ideally, to qualify as a phoneme, a sound segment must be capable of appearing anywhere within a word in contrast with other phonemic segments. For example, consider [p] and [k]. Then contrast [pɪl/kil], [tapɪŋ/takɪŋ], and [lip/lik]. Thus, a phoneme is a class of sounds that are perceived by listeners as equivalent. But what do we mean by "a class of sounds"?

Suppose, for example, we choose the phoneme [p] and place it in the word frames "speech," "peach," and "cheap." Note, as you say each word aloud, that there are minor variations in the way [p] is produced. If you hold your hand in front of your lips as you produce each word, you will notice that production of [p] in "peach" results in a noticeable burst of air compared to its production in "cheap" and "speech." The burst of air and hiss accompanying the quick release of a stop consonant is called *aspiration* and is symbolized by a small raised *h*. Thus, the occurrence of aspirated stops is written in this way: [pʰ, tʰ, kʰ]. In this example, the [p] in "cheap" differs from the others because it is usually unexploded or unreleased. In addition, the [p] in "speech" involves lip movement to constrict, stop, and release. As a result, it differs from the aspirated [pʰ] and the unreleased [p-]. The class members or *allophones* of the phoneme are marked with brackets [pʰ], while phonemes are marked with slashes /p/. In so doing, we clearly differentiate between the phonological, which represents an ideal for a class of equivalent sounds at the phonetic level, and an allophone or sound segment which represents a variant of the ideal at the phonetic-production level.

We can further extend the general class of allophones belonging to /p/ by comparing the word frames "spook," "pool," and "soup," to "speak," "peak," "seep." As you say the first set of three, notice that your lips are rounded, while in the latter three the lips are spread. In each of these examples, variations in the production of [p] occurred as a result of certain characteristics or features of the surrounding sounds as well as the location of [p] within the word. Since the English language has no pairs of words which differ in meaning because of the features of rounding, spreading, releasing, aspirating, or unreleasing of /p/, all these variations are grouped as members of a class of sounds that are equivalent and representative of phoneme /p/.

Contrasting classes of sounds, or phonemes, are abstractions. That is, they represent a composite series of nearly simultaneous events. For example, when we write the series of phonemes /lʌv/ (at an idealized level), or [lʌv] (at the production level), we are simply representing a series of events with a set of symbols. When we utter the word "love," we become immediately aware of:

> **1.** The segment [l] involves elevation/contact of the apical region of the tongue to the alveolar ridge, vibration of the vocal folds, and lateral emission of the sound stream around the sides of the tongue.
>
> **2.** The segment [ʌ] involves a low-mid tongue constriction within the oral cavity and vocal fold vibration.
>
> **3.** The segment [v] involves mandibular elevation that lifts the lower lip until it contacts the upper frontal incisors, vocal fold vibration, and a secondary sound source resulting from air hissing between the lip and the teeth.

These physiological specifications illustrate the manner in which sound characteristics become identified as features. Feature systems have been designed in an effort to more elaborately describe the universal characteristic of spoken languages.

PHONETIC FEATURES   Each unique phoneme consists of a mutually exclusive set of abstract, idealized features. However, at the physiological and acoustic levels of description, sound segments are variable.

Featural descriptions of phonemes are important, but controversies exist as to which features are most appropriate. This can be best exemplified by the abstraction "bravery." At the level of actual human performance, the abstract mental concept of bravery may translate into:

> **1.** Rescuing a drowning child
> **2.** Refusing to cry or moan in the face of pain
> **3.** Attacking an enemy in the face of certain death
> **4.** Telling the truth at the price of personal ruin

Thus, you can see that even though a phoneme must exist mentally as a real unit of mind-brain activity, when the time comes to convert the mental image into muscular action, the phoneme can appear in many differing forms. But the forms are sufficiently similar to be called members of the "same" phoneme class. Let us look at one of the accepted current feature systems. Table 3.1 illustrates those abstract features that specify the phonetic characteristics of

table 3.1
phonetic features

FEATURE	DESCRIPTION
CONSONANTAL	A speech sound is consonantal if it is produced with a constriction along the center line of the oral cavity. Only the vowels and the glides (/w/, /h/, and /y/) are nonconsonantal.
VOCALIC	Vocalic sounds are those which have a largely unobstructed vocal tract. The liquids /l/ and /r/, which are consonantal, see also vocalic. This is true because while there is a central obstruction for the liquids, there is a large unobstructed area to either side of the tongue. Although there is no central obstruction for glides, the most narrow area in the vocal tract during the production is not large enough to qualify them as vocalic. The glides, therefore, are nonvocalic.
ANTERIOR	A sound is anterior if the point of articulation is as far front in the oral cavity as the alveolar ridge. Thus, all the labial and dental sounds are anterior, while sounds produced farther back are nonanterior.
CORONAL	A sound is coronal if its articulation involves the front (or corona) of the tongue. A sound is noncoronal if another part of the tongue is used (such as in /k/) or if the tongue is not involved in the production of the sound at all (such as in /p/).
CONTINUANT	A sound is noncontinuant if it is produced with a complete obstruction in the oral cavity. Only the nasals, stops and affricates are noncontinuant. (The nasals are considered to be noncontinuant because while there is an opening in the nasal cavity, the oral cavity is completely obstructed.)
STRIDENT	A strident sound is produced by an obstruction in the oral cavity which forces the air through a relatively long, narrow constriction. As the air rushes out of the opening of this constriction, its turbulence serves as a primary noise source. This turbulent air is then directed against a sound obstruction which causes a secondary noise source.
VOICE	Voiced sounds are those in which phonation (vibration of the vocal folds in the larynx) takes place as the sound is articulated.
LATERAL	A lateral sound is one which involves a contact between the corona of the tongue and some point on the roof of the mouth, along with a simultaneous lowering of the sides of the tongue. In English, /l/ is the only lateral sound, and this feature differentiates it from /r/, the only other liquid, which is nonlateral.
NASAL	Nasals are characterized by a lowering of the velum, which opens the nasal cavity for sound resonation.
HIGH	High vowels are those which involve the highest tongue position, and thus the narrowest constriction in the oral cavity. /u/ and /i/ are the only high vowels; all others are nonhigh.
LOW	Low vowels are those which involve the lowest tongue position, /æ/, /a/, and /ɔ/. All other vowels are nonlow. Note how the so-called middle vowels are classed in this system; /e/ and /o/ are nonlow and nonhigh.
BACK	The traditional back-front distinction is accounted for by the back/nonback distinction. Thus, /u/, /o/, and /ɔ/ are classed as back, while /i/, /æ/, and /e/ are nonback.
ROUND	As in traditional classifications, the rounding of the lips is a feature for vowel differentiation. Thus, /u/, /o/, and /ɔ/, are round. Others are nonround.

Source: Language by C. E. Cairns and F. Williams in *Normal Aspects of Speech, Hearing, and Language*, edited by Minifie, Hixon, and Williams, 1973, p. 424. Reprinted by permission of Prentice-Hall, Inc., Englewood Cliffs, N.J.

English. A description of phonemes according to their specified features follows in Table 3.2.

Notice in Table 3.2 that the presence of a given feature for any phoneme is indicated by the (±) mark. Such an indication should alert us to the fact that, as an all or none system, feature designation at the phonetic level is both over-simplified and highly idealized, since it does not allow for the substantial variation we see at the physiological or acoustic level. This is both a strength and a weakness. It should serve to alert us to the fact that at an abstract mental level, it is probably quite necessary to avoid highly detailed specifications of features at a level which governs or oversees sound production. For example, when the general in command of an army issues an order to advance, he issues only a blanket order. The troops who actually advance translate the command into movements that carry them up and down hills and across valleys. If the general's orders had to be so specific that they would tell each soldier where to put one foot and then the next, it might take forever to move an army even a few miles. Such overspecification is self-defeating, and the same is true for the phoneme. Many of the variations seen at the output level can be accounted for by simple low-level processes, so that the phoneme can be kept abstract and described as simple all/none (±) features. That such an assumption may be valid is illustrated by MacNeilage (1970) in his discussion of the motor control of the serial ordering of speech:

> Each phoneme, by definition, requires a unique constellation of articulator positions. Therefore, the sum of the mechanical demands in achieving a second phoneme positioning will necessarily vary with the identity of the preceding phoneme. It thus appears likely that some aspect of the motor control of the 44 phonemes of English will vary depending on which of the approximately 20 possible phonemes precedes or follows it. This gives a total of approximately 17,000 motor patterns, without considering stress effects, speaking rate effects, and segmental effects which stretch across one or more phonemes.

If we were forced to take into consideration all the possible featural variations that result from contextual sound influences, our feature system would be overwhelmingly complex. Our language guidance system is probably governed by simple, all/none, idealized features bundled into phonemes. The neuro-muscular processes of speech production introduce a multitude of variations into the phoneme-feature commands, so that at the articulatory level, the allophones of a phoneme are highly variable.

PHYSIOLOGICAL FEATURES

Place   The physiological features of spoken language are of particular interest and importance to the study of both normal and disordered sound patterns. Figure 3.2 illustrates the principal anatomical cavities and components involved during sound production. Figure 3.3 illustrates those *places* where a constriction may be made to produce a given sound. In varying combinations, the components illustrated in Figure 3.2 alter the vocal tract shape in such a way as to either stop or modulate the airflow

table 3.2
distinctive features of English phonemes

	l	r	n	m	ŋ	z	s	ð	θ	t	v	f	b	p	ž	š	ĵ	č	c	g	k	u	a	o	i	æ	e	w	y	h
consonantal	+	+	+	+	+	+	+	+	+	+	+	+	+	+	+	+	+	+	+	+	+	−	−	−	−	−	−	−	−	−
vocalic	+	+	−	−	−	−	−	−	−	−	−	−	−	−	−	−	−	−	−	−	−	+	+	+	+	+	+	−	−	−
nasal	−	−	+	+	+	−	−	−	−	−	−	−	−	−						−	−									
lateral	+	−																												
anterior	+	−	+	+		+	+	+	+	+	+	+	+	+	−	−	−	−	+											
coronal	+	+	+	−		+	+	+	+	+	−	−	−	−	+	+	+	+	+											
continuant	+	+	−	−	−	+	+	+	+	−	+	+	−	−	+	+	−	−	−	−	−									
strident						+	+	−	−	−	+	+	−	−	+	+	+	+	+	−										
voice	+	+	+	+	+	+	−	+	−	−	+	−	+	−	+	−	+	−	−	+	−	+	+	+	+	+	+	+	+	−
back																				+	+	+	+	+	−	−	−	+	−	−
high																				+	+	+	−	−	+	−	−	+	+	−
low																						−	+	−	−	+	−			
round																						+	−	+	−	−	−	+	−	−

Consonants

/l/	ill	/θ/	thigh
/r/	rill	/d/	drill
/n/	nil	/t/	till
/m/	mill	/v/	ville
/ŋ/	tang	/f/	fill
/z/	zeal	/b/	bill
/s/	sill	/p/	pill
/ð/	thy	/ž,ʒ/⁴	rouge

/š,ʃ/	shall
/ĵ,dʒ/	Jill
/č,tʃ/	chill
/g/	gill
/k/	kill

Vowels and glides²

/u/	boot	/w/	will
/a/	saw	/y/	yet
/a/	cot	/h/	hoe
/o/	boat		
/i/	beet		
/æ/	bat		
/e/	bait		

¹ Alternative symbols are given.

² The simplified system portrayed here is meant to illustrate the application of the feature concept to vowels in general rather than a complete description of the vowel system of English. English also contains a distinction between tense and lax vowels as in "bait" [bet] and "bet" [bɛt]. Moreover, there are several different phonetically occurring vowels, such as the vowels in the words "cut" [kʌt], "bird" [bɜd], "sofa" [sofə]. Students who wish to see the feature system applied in detail should consult Chomsky and Halle, *The Sound Pattern of English*, 1968.

Source: Language by C. E. Cairns and F. Williams in *Normal Aspects of Speech, Hearing, and Language*, edited by Minifie, Hixon, and Williams, 1973, p. 426. Reprinted by permission of Prentice Hall, Inc. Englewood Cliffs, N.J.

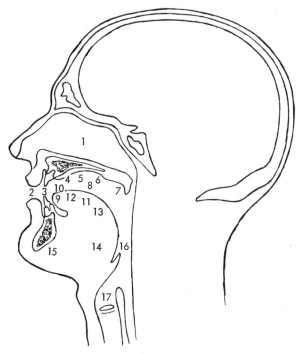

1. Nasal cavity
2. Lips
3. Teeth
4. Alveolar ridge
5. Hard palate
6. Velum

7. Uvula
8. Oral cavity
9. Tongue tip
10. Tongue apex
11. Tongue blade
12. Tongue front

13. Tongue dorsum
14. Tongue root
15. Mandible
16. Pharyngeal cavity
17. Vocal folds

figure 3.2

Cross-section of vocal tube, illustrating the principal
anatomical cavities and components.

and/or create a constriction where a second sound source is generated. Examples of sound segments that illustrate the place features of articulation noted in Figure 3.3 include the following:

bilabial	[p]	putting
labiodental	[f]	French
interdental	[θ]	things
alveolar	[t]	to
postalveolar	[r]	rest
palatal	[ʃ]	she
velar	[k]	kept
glottal	[ʔ]	latin

Manner   *Manner* refers to the degree of constriction that occurs within the vocal tract during sound production. We may identify six conditions within three categories to describe such constrictions:

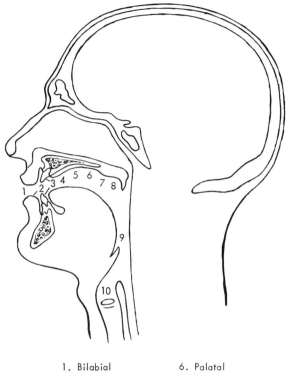

1. Bilabial	6. Palatal
2. Labiodental	7. Velar
3. Interdental-dental	8. Uvular
4. Alveolar	9. Pharyngeal
5. Post alveolar	10. Glottal

figure 3.3

Cross-section of vocal tube, illustrating places of articulation.

(1) *obstruents:* complete stoppage of airflow (stop), restricted airflow (fricative), and complete stoppage followed immediately by restricted flow of air (affricate); (2) *approximants:* relatively unimpeded air flow: nasals, central liquids, laterals, and glides; (3) *vowels:* unimpeded (except at the larynx) airflow. The following words contain sound segments that characterize six of the consonant manner features.

	stop	[p]	play
Obstruent	fricative	[s]	some
	affricate	[tʃ]	Tchaikovsky
Approximant	liquid	[l]	loudly
	liquid	[r]	ray
	glide	[w]	with
	glide	[j]	your
	nasal	[n]	new
	nasal	[m]	machine

Nasality   The nasal sounds of English, /m, n, ŋ/, are produced by completely occluding the oral cavity at three places of articulation (bilabial, alveolar, velar). Simultaneous lowering of the velum results in the coupling of a nasal cavity, which functions as an additional resonance chamber. Since the lowering of the velum results in the addition of a secondary resonant chamber during the production of nasals, sound segments (particularly vowels) that occur in combination with them also become somewhat nasalized. Notice, for instance, the difference between the vowels [æ] and [æ̃] in the words "hat" and "ham." We will look at effects such as these in more detail in Chapter 8.

Voicing   The final feature that serves to differentiate or specify speech sounds is *voicing*. Voicing, by the very nature of its name, refers to the presence of vocal fold vibration during sound production. Nonvoicing refers to the absence of vocal fold vibration. In the case of stop consonants, voicing is often determined by the voice onset time, that time period between the release of the stop constriction and the onset of glottal vibration. Thus, for many of the sounds of English which are produced at the same place and in the same manner, presence or absence of voicing will result in two mutually exclusive classes of sound. Figure 3.4 presents the composite classificatory matrix of English consonants using a system of physiologically based features.

figure 3.4

Classification of English consonants.

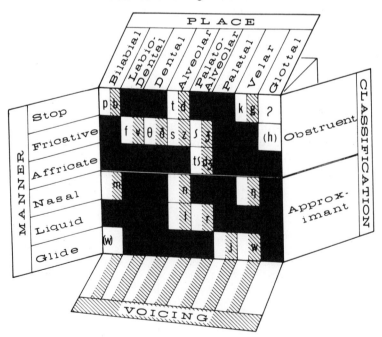

morphology

Traditionally the morpheme is not only the smallest unit of grammatical analysis, but also the indivisible or smallest unit of meaning. The concepts underlying the unit referred to as a morpheme can be viewed from several perspectives. For instance, in speech the morpheme can be studied as a physical unit based upon its phonetic shape (the number, identity, and order of the sounds in a word). In addition, it conveys meaning and is crucial to the organization of larger semantic and grammatical units. For example, let us analyze the sentence "The eight girls listened to the man." Obviously, the morphemes "the," "eight," "to," and "man" are meaningful, minimal, syntactically relevant units. "Girls" and "listened" each consist of two units. If we take the [z] (plural morpheme) away from "girls," we have the meaningful and distinct unit "girl." Thus the [z] conveys a singular/plural distinction. Finally, if the "ed" is removed from "listened," tense is changed from past to present. Therefore we conclude the words "girls" and "listened" are composed of four morphemes, [girl + z] and [listen + ed].

These examples typify the manner in which morphemic units have been identified. As we shall see, however, the complexities of our language are such that the oversimplification of examples such as these tend to lead us in a circular path. Let us return for a moment to our earlier example. Notice, for instance, that although the word "the" was counted only once, it occurred twice as the same morpheme. Notice also that the phonetic shape of pronunciation of "the" preceding "eight" differs from the pronunciation of "the" preceding "man." Nevertheless, we consider both as being derived from or identified as the same morpheme. We do so because in English when "the" precedes a word beginning with a vowel, it is produced as /ɪ/ as opposed to /ə/. To account for such variation, we assume that each of the two occurrences are allomorphs of the morpheme [the].

A similar example involves the occurrence of [s] signaling plurality. In this instance, the [s] morpheme of the English language has three distinct phonetic shapes: [s] as in "facts," [z] as in "holes," and [əz] as in "noses." In each case "s" signals plurality, but phonetic differences occur as a result of the sounds they follow. When "s" follows [p, t, k, f, θ], then [s] occurs. When "s" follows [b, d, g, v, ɚ, m, n, ŋ, r, l], then [z] occurs. And when "s" follows [s, z, tʃ, ʃ, ʒ, dʒ], then [əz] occurs. Each of the three variants is considered to be an *allomorph* of the morpheme [s]. To account for such differences, we say that morphemic variants (or allomorphs) occur as a result of phonological conditioning. But even this explanation is an oversimplification.

Our language provides numerous exceptions to explanations such as that of phonological conditioning. If we return, for instance, to the example of noun + plural, we are faced with the problem of providing explanations for irregular forms. Instances such as "facts" [fæks], "holes" [hoʊlz], and "noses" [noʊzəz], are readily explained. However, a singular "goose" [gus] alerts us to the fact that the plural "geese" [gis] occurs without addition of an allomorph. Unless, of course, we consider "geese" to be an allomorph of "goose." Similar examples include "tooth-teeth," "mouse-mice," "child-children," "woman-women," and "man-men." Such examples should indicate to the reader the complexity of the concept of morpheme.

The problems encountered in attempting to account for morphemes as minimal units of grammatical analysis are not unexpected. If we recall our earlier discussion of parts and wholes, we realize that within the hierarchy of language structure, the morpheme looks both forward and backward. Like the phoneme, which looks forward to the sound segment and feature and backward to the morpheme, the morpheme looks forward to the phoneme and backward to semantics and syntax. The interrelationship of the phoneme and morpheme is such that phonemes (or bundles of features) vary according to the context of certain morphemes. Such variations include the production differences in the morpheme "atom" and "atom + ic"; "electric" and "electric + ity"; or "photo," "photo + graph," or "photo + graphy." Similarly, certain morphemes vary as a result of the particular phonological contexts in which they occur. Within linguistic theory this interrelationship is called morphophonology or morphophonemics, and specified units are called morphophonemes. At the same time, morphophonemes in combination form larger units called morphotactics. We have ascended the hierarchy of language structure from phonology to morphology, have loosely determined their interdependence, and must now consider their relationships with semantics and syntax.

semantics

The semantic subcomponent of language structure is the knowledge speakers and listeners must have in order to create and understand meaningful messages. All too frequently, semantics is simply and rather glibly referred to as the "science of meaning." The major weakness of much that has been written about semantics concerns the static, rather magic quality of a supposed meaning which is assumed to be contained in the word itself. By this time it should be evident that the words we speak are ultimately produced as a varying stream of speech sounds. To our knowledge, there are no physiological features directly associated with meaning. To assume that "meaning" exists anywhere except in the brain-mind of the speaker or listener borders on witchcraft. Depending upon the ways in which we "talk" to ourselves and others, we can always decide to say a little more about anything. This, of course, immediately opens the possibility of saying or thinking a little more about what we have just said or thought. The so-called meaning we associate with language must then be thought of as a highly generalized relationship between our adaptation to the environment and our ability to code, store, and associate past experience to present and anticipated events. Thus, semantics is that subcomponent of language structure which is most directly associated with content or cognition. The *expression* of our ideas simply cannot be separated from the *kinds* of ideas we have to express. As thinkers and speakers, we tend to behave in predictable ways based upon past experience and behavior.

Kelly (1955) wrote that "a person's processes are psychologically channelized by the ways in which he anticipates events." Further, we "anticipate events by construing their replications." What Kelly points out is that, following storage of our experience with the environment, we employ a pattern or construct of experience as we encounter present or anticipate future events. This in no way implies that such events will be the same; in fact, they never are. As pointed out by Bontrager (1962), "It is a common habit of all of us that when unfolding events do not fit our expectations, we blame the events." In other words, when there is not a one-to-one correspondence between what we expect to happen and what happens, either in a classroom or a kitchen, we tend to blame the teacher or the cook rather than our expectations. Such behavior clearly indicates that "convicts and convictions are similar in that each involve a locked-up person." One of the best examples of differences between expectations and events is related to a story that came from the European underground during the Nazi era.

> In a railroad compartment an American grandmother with her young and attractive granddaughter, a Romanian officer, and a Nazi officer were the only occupants. The train was passing through a dark tunnel, and all that was heard was a loud kiss and a vigorous slap. After the train had emerged from the tunnel, nobody spoke, but the grandmother was saying to herself, "What a fine girl I have raised. She will take care of herself." The granddaughter was saying to herself, "Well, grandmother is old enough not to mind a little kiss. Besides, the fellows are nice. I am surprised what a hard wallop grandmother has." The Nazi officer was meditating, "How clever those Romanians are! They steal a kiss and have the other fellow slapped." The Romanian officer was chuckling to himself, "How smart I am! I kissed my own hand and slapped the Nazi." (Korzybski, 1950)

Such an example clearly illustrates that meaning is in the eye of the beholder, and that each of us constructs meaning according to his or her preconceptions.

What must be understood in any explanation of semantics or meaning is that, as a process and a system, it is dynamic in nature. Unless a person suffers from premature hardening of the categories, no two events should ever be construed as being identical. This concept was brilliantly discussed by Bontrager (1962), when he wrote:

> First of all, the human nervous system is the most intricately complex structure known. This structure performs, to use Herrick's terminology, analytic and integrative functions. The analyzers respond to a fantastic array of energy changes in the surrounding environment, thus giving us the basis for differential activation that is unmatched in the organic world. For example, tactile receptors contact to over 1500 contacts per second. The ear is capable of differentiating vibrations with a range of about 9 octaves, or 30 to 20,000 vibrations per second. The eye is sensitive to vibrations ranging from 4×10^{14} to 8×10^{14} per second. The eye alone contains more than 100 million photoreceptors. This means that the eye can exist in $2^{100,000,000}$ states. The human cortex contains in the neighborhood of 10,000 million nerve cells. The number of different circuits possible from such a collection of cells staggers the imagination. It exceeds the total number of atoms in the visible, sidereal universe. This means that we have a structure that permits us to react differentially in a dynamic environment with its endless succession of complexities. There is no rigid connection between an event and the behavior that follows. The analytic structure means we can detect differences and respond differentially. It means we can exercise choice. (p. 16)

The fact that our nervous systems are constantly being subjected to an unimaginable number of energy changes in the environment perhaps necessitates a subsystem which can selectively store and relate or disregard sensory input. Thus far, attempts to account for such a subsystem by linguists, psychologists, and psycholinguists have resulted in relatively divergent and unsatisfactory theories. Keeping in mind the vast complexity of both the human nervous system and the environment in which we live should, however, alert us to an appreciation of those who choose to ask new and difficult questions. The coding and organization of experience for later recall or generalization to other experience involves the most intricate subsystem of language structure.

MEANING AND REFERENCE   The so-called meanings for many words may frequently be associated with a particular object or refer to some aspect of the environment. The object or environmental aspect to which a word refers is called its *referent*. For example, "blue" refers to a range of colors, "rabbit" to a category of animals, "car" to a class of vehicles, and "Boeing 747" to a particular type of airplane. In each case, the object or aspect of the environment serves as a referent to the word. At one time, a theory called the referential theory was quite popular. Certainly it is not difficult to understand why. If we put our imagination to work, we could assume, almost by intuition, that words and their meanings might be learned by hearing the word "blue" spoken while seeing a particular bluish object; "rabbit" spoken while seeing a particular long-eared, fuzzy tailed quadruped; "car" spoken in reference to the vehicle in the driveway; and "Boeing 747" spoken while looking at a particular type of airplane.

The referential theory was consistent with similar theories in education and psychology. However, the theory has several weaknesses. For instance, the Chicago El may serve as the same referent for the morning train and the evening train. If we connect the two, it becomes obvious that they have different meanings. That is, *The morning train* and *the evening train* are both the Chicago El. In a similar manner, the same word can have different referents. Words such as "he," "she," "it," "they," "I" may be used interchangeably within the same group and often at the same time while the referent is changing constantly. That is, as we talk to each other, "you" and "I" are the same person. Finally, many words have no referents or have referents which are idealized abstractions. In the latter case are such words as "atom," "neutron," "electron," "power," "electricity," "wind"; in the former, such words as "a," "an," "the," "and," "either," "also," and "etc." While we may be able to verbalize differences between each word, there are simply no direct referents.

SEMANTIC CLASSIFICATION   The statement that meaning exists only in the brain-mind of the speaker/listener is of particular importance to a clearer understanding of semantics. As we have briefly seen, there are inherent difficulties in a referential theory. In addition to those previously mentioned, the same object or event can be referred to with numerous labels. For instance, the optical prosthesis that enables people to see things with clearer definition can be referred to as glasses, eyeglasses, spectacles, goggles, cheaters, and bifocals. Similarly, a particular label can refer to numerous objects or events. Glasses can refer to binoculars, shades (sunglasses), or drinking vessels. Thus, labels for objects or events tend to be classificatory in nature. The word "blue" may refer to a class of objects or events that reflect only the blues of the color spectrum, the "downs" of a psychological spectrum, or the musical arrangement of a sound spectrum. Something as concrete as a "quarter" may refer to a class of objects or events that include twenty-five cents, two bits, a coin, money, bread, or a bicentennial quarter. However, it may also refer to a time division of a football game, a fiscal report, a journal publication, or a prime section of beef. In each example, the labels are related to special classifications of objects or events. These classifications or codifications of reality represent human attempts to organize interactions with the environment. The meanings of what I say and what you hear exist only as references to our classifications or codifications of reality.

COMPREHENSION: MEANING
AND WORD RELATIONSHIPS
The comprehension of speech/language references or labels involves numerous factors. In a way, label relationships are similar to phoneme relationships; they are not simply strung together like beads on a string. Aside from certain rule-governed constraints that will be discussed later, certain relationships are significant for semantic classifications. Among these are antonymy, synonymy, inclusion, and reciprocity.

Antonymy refers to words that represent unlike or opposite categories. Word pairs such as "tall-short," "laugh-cry," and "right-wrong" are examples of antonymic pairs. *Synonymy* is the opposite of antonymy and refers to words which represent similar classifications. Word pairs such as "stone-rock," "woods-forest," and "road-highway" are examples of synonymic pairs. Concepts involving antonymy and synonymy are of particular interest in the development of feature theory. For instance, although we say that antonymic pairs represent opposite categories, a closer look reveals that this may not be the case. For instance, the pair "tall-short" shares the common feature of height; "laugh-cry," the feature of emotion; "right-wrong," the feature of correctness. In this sense, antonymic pairs are not quite as unlike as we may have thought.

Likewise, synonymic pairs are not as similar as we might wish to think. But then, why should they be? There are so many different things about which to talk it would seem a waste of time to maintain several words to identify the same category. Thus, while we can clearly see similarities in our earlier examples, we must also admit that although "stone" and "rock" are similar, being "stoned" or "rocked" refer to quite different events. We might attend a rock concert, build a rock garden, or collect rocks but not stones.

The final two factors, inclusion and reciprocity are of particular interest and importance to the speech and language pathologist. *Inclusion* refers to words such as "hammer," "screwdriver," "square," and "wrench," which also represent or are included in the category tool. "Lime," "lemon," "orange" include the categories fruit and citrus and the feature roundness. Words such as "child," "adolescent," and "adult" include the category human and such features as upright, armed, legged, and talking. *Reciprocity* refers to word pairs such as "borrow" and "loan" or "sent" and "received." Although such pairs are somewhat antonymic, they differ in that they can occur reciprocally. For example, the sentences "Brent will borrow Jeff's mini-bike" and "Jeff will lend Brent his mini-bike" describe the same event. Similarly, the same event is described in "Rita sent Mary a letter" and "Mary received a letter from Rita." In addition to vocabulary development, the complexities involved in such factors as inclusion and reciprocity enable the language learner to more successfully adapt to the environment. To name or label represents only a storage-retrieval function. However, inclusion and reciprocity involve generalization from concepts such as similarity-difference to those underlying mathematics. It is, for instance, only a few steps from "A table, chair, sofa, and desk are furniture," to "This and this (addition) are also this."

COMPREHENSION-MEANING AND WORD-SENTENCE RELATIONSHIPS

From our discussion of comprehension-meaning and word relationships, it is apparent that the meaning assigned to a word is dependent upon the words of the sentence in which it occurs. Since many of the words of English may refer to several classifications (meanings), we regard them as being ambiguous. Such ambiguity permits varying degrees of flexibility with regard to the word's occurrence within a sentence. As a result, the number of alternatives to which the sentence may refer is reduced. In other words, if we assume the ambiguity of several words within the same sentence, we realize that as they are combined, their individual sets of features correspond in such a way as to reduce ambiguity resulting from their combination. For example, if we construct a sentence such as "A tall oak bush sat near the rippling river," we notice several semantic inconsistencies, or violations of semantic restrictions. That is to say, the combinations of words representing classifications of events violate our experience. First, "oak" and "bush" are not permissible. "Tree," while permissible, might be redundant. Is "a tall oak" anything other than a tree? If not, then saying "a tall oak tree" is like saying "a widow woman." Similarly, while bushes may sit, trees must stand. Furthermore, "rippling" and "river" are less than compatible, since rippling in this sense implies shallowness; a feature rarely associated with river. Thus, if "river" is used, then "rippling" should be replaced. If "rippling" is used, then "river" should be replaced. We would probably agree that the sentence "A tall oak stood near the rippling brook" is most compatible with our life/language experience. Another example which illustrates an additional dimension of semantic complexity occurs in sentences such as "Jeff hit Brent and then Rita hit him." As you read the sentence aloud, note that if you stress the word "Rita," the intended meaning differs from the same sentence within which "him" is stressed.

The latter example raises additional questions regarding the reduction of ambiguity resulting from various word combinations. We assume, for instance, that ambiguity regarding the word "rat" has been reduced or eliminated when we include it in the sentence "The white rat was trained by the psychologist." If, however, we ask manufacturers and government inspectors of rat food and rat food containers, printers of rat food containers, and transporters of rat food about this sentence, they will discuss it in terms of everything from profit margin, chemical/additive analysis, and container strength, to Teamster contracts. Each, we must agree, is a valid aspect of reality related to the nonambiguity of "rat." Just as real are the tuitions, stipends, or so-called salaries paid to or by students who either feed and tend the rats or observe their training. To the psychology chairperson, the rat represents expense — housing, maintenance, air conditioning, care, and so on. To the psychologist, the nonambiguous rat represents challenge, recognition, appreciation, publication, and promotion. Interestingly enough all, save the rat, respond nonambiguously to its socioeconomic contribution.

SEMANTIC FEATURES   In an effort to account for reduction of ambiguity, it is most convenient to regard the classifications of experience (words) using a feature matrix like that which we applied to phonology. Classifications of experience represent combinations of subunits or elements. Simply stated, the semantic feature theory suggests that word meaning consists of a set of semantic features and selection restrictions. A *semantic feature* is a segmented aspect of experience classification as related to others which in combination are represented by a word. According to a feature theory, each word represents a composite set of features based upon selected aspects of environment and behavior.

At least two additional approaches to semantics extend feature analysis to include structure and relational information. One approach argues that although a set of features may identify a particular classification, it may inadequately distinguish between polar extremes represented within the class. The word "car," for example, might include the features vehicle, four-wheeled, combustion engine, passenger, noncommercial. While such a feature set may appropriately identify the car classification, it does not delineate distinctions among the features, or the degree of difference between cars. If we are asked to visualize and describe a car, we will most likely select one with which we are familiar. Moreover, if we are asked to rate "ideal car-ness," compacts and sports models would rank higher than station wagons and used Buicks, Chryslers, and Lincolns. Similar preferences apply to a wide range of classifications. As a result, it has been suggested that words and their corresponding classifications should also be analyzed according to descriptions based on central or core values and features.

Another approach to a semantic feature system implies that classification of an event or item must include information relating to features and concepts as well as feature descriptions and central value concepts. To illustrate such an approach, let us consider the following example. The word "linebacker" is a classification that might include the features human (sometimes questionable), male, athlete, football, defense, secondary. On the other side of the field,

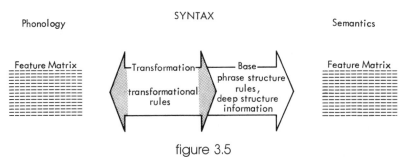

figure 3.5

Relationship of syntax to semantics and phonology.

"cheerleader" is a classification that might include human, athlete, gymnastics, vocal. As is obvious, certain features appear in each set and indicate commonality. However, as a result of feature set specifications, certain selection restrictions constrain possible combination of words. When, for instance, we utter the sentences "The linebacker stopped the cheerleader for no gain" and "The linebacker kissed the cheerleader," we immediately realize the vast amount of relational information necessary for an understanding of athletic events.

syntax

During our discussion of language we progressed from sound segments through meaning. We are now at a point within our hierarchy where it is necessary to discuss how the various subcomponents of structure may be interconnected. The subcomponent of structure that serves to combine phonology and semantics is syntax. Interestingly enough, by definition, the word *syntax* has as its derivation F ∠ syntaxe ∠ syntaxis ∠ GK syntassein ∠ join together + *tassein* − arrange.

As illustrated in Figure 3.5, the syntactic subcomponent may be regarded as consisting of a base subassembly and a transformational subassembly. The base is similar to what is referred to in linguistics as *phrase structure,* and its function is to provide the underlying bases of sentences. The bases provide deep structure information that is subsequently resolved in two ways: One involves conversion to phonologically constrained sentence frames by way of the transformational subassembly of syntax and phonology; the other involves specification and assignment of meaning via the base subassembly of syntax and semantics.

THE BASE SUBASSEMBLY:
PHRASE STRUCTURE RULES   Syntactic structure may be considered to involve combinations of morphemes, or constituents that compose phrase structure. Phrase structures, in turn, are referred to as constituents which compose sentence structure. As a simplified example, we will choose a sentence that has two phrase constituents, a noun phrase (NP) and a verb phrase (VP):

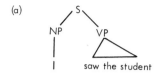

Such a sample is representative of major constituents of the highest-level syntactic analysis. Sentences may also be further reduced to smaller constituents; for example, the verb phrase can consist of a verb followed by a noun phrase or of a copula followed by an adjective.

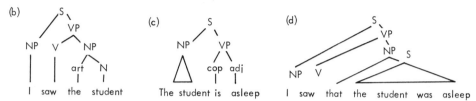

In sentence (b), the noun phrase could also be reduced to an article followed by a noun, or, as in sentence (d), by *that* followed by a clause or embedded sentence. Having just reviewed four combinations of phrase structure, we can now state the examples in the form of the following descriptions or rules:

(1)   S   NP $+$ VP   (a)

(2)   VP $\rightarrow \begin{bmatrix} \text{V} & +\text{NP} \\ \text{cop} & +\text{adj} \end{bmatrix}$ (b, c)

(3)   NP $\rightarrow \begin{bmatrix} \text{art} & +\text{N} \\ \text{That} & +\text{S} \end{bmatrix}$ (d)

In these rules, S refers to the *sentence* and the arrow indicates *rewrite as*. The brackets in rules 2 and 3 indicate a choice between those constituents which may be rewritten. In rule 2 the VP can be rewritten as a verb followed by an NP or as a copula followed by an adjective. In rule 3 we have the option of rewriting the NP as an article followed by a noun or as "that" followed by a sentence or clause. Such rules are descriptions of the constituent structures of a set of sentences. Figure 3.6 illustrates their application to four examples. Constituents are any word or set of words included within a single labeled intersection (node).

In sentence (a), "the student," "passed the test," and "the test" represent the constituents NP, VP, and NP, respectively. Note that in each instance the constituents may be traced to the nodes in the diagram. In sentence (a) there are two levels of constituent division. The highest is NP and VP (the student + passed the test), followed by V and NP (passed + the test).

Using the rules, we can generate an infinite number of sentences. Notice that within the NP constituent outlined in rule 3, it is permissible to generate

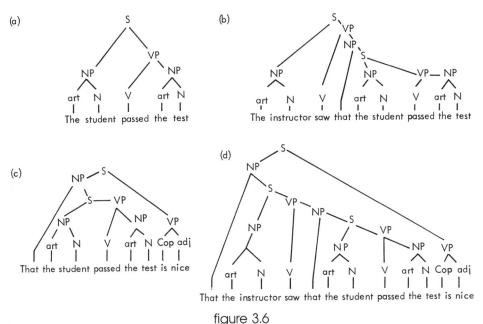

figure 3.6

Phrase marker derivations from rules 1, 2, 3.

an additional sentence or clause, which in turn contains another NP which might contain another S, and so on. Sentences (b), (c) and (d) outline examples of embedding sentences and clauses within the main sentence and illustrate that although the process can be repeated, the sentences become increasingly unwieldy.

TRANSFORMATION SUBASSEMBLY:
TRANSFORMATIONAL RULES   The second subassembly of syntax is called *transformation.* As illustrated in Figure 3.5, this subassembly, including transformational rules or descriptions and phonological rules, or descriptions, ultimately specifies the preparation of surface structure and pronounceable sentence strings. Compared to phrase structure, elements of some constituents of surface structure are not adjacent to one another. Such *discontinuous constituents,* as they are called, are described via reference to transformational rules which are different from the rules of phrase structure. For instance, if we compare the sentences in Figure 3.7 with reference to their verb phrase construction, we might revise the earlier NP rule 3 to form rule 4.

In addition to the rule 3 options, rule 4 describes the NP constituent contained within the VP as consisting optionally of the particle "to" followed by the VP "study the textbook." Rule 5, however, describes the NP constituent of (b) in a much different manner. Obviously, the NP of (b) is similar to that of (a), since it contains the VP "study the textbook" and the additional morpheme "ing." Difficulty arises, however, in determining where the major constituent break within the NP occurs. Unlike sentence (a), where the break occurred between "to" and "study the textbook," the morpheme "ing" is included within

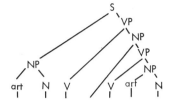
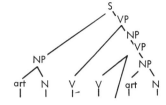

The student loves to study the textbook   The student loves studying the textbook

$$(a) = (1,2) \& (4) \; NP \longrightarrow \begin{bmatrix} art + N \\ that + S \\ to + VP \end{bmatrix}$$

$$(b) = (1,2) \& (5) \; NP \longrightarrow \begin{bmatrix} art + N \\ that + S \\ \begin{bmatrix} to \\ ing + VP \end{bmatrix} \end{bmatrix}$$

figure 3.7

Phrase markers from rules 4 and 5.

the VP, so it cannot be described in a manner similar to that of (a). Once again, although it is obvious that the NP of (b) should be described as consisting of the two constituents "ing" plus "study the textbook," there appears to be no way of doing so. The problem of discontinuant constituents, as mentioned earlier, makes transformational rules necessary.

The generation of transformational rules implies that rules such as those described above should be viewed as basic to a theory which describes the principles of sentence construction. Rules 1 through 4 describe dynamic processes which allow the regeneration of sentences (a), (b), (c), (d) in Figure 3.6 and sentence (a) of Figure 3.7 via the indicated phrase markers. Finally, we would replace rule 4 with rule 5.

Such a revised set of rules would enable us to generate each of the previously illustrated sentences, in addition to the phrase marker for sentence (a) in Figure 3.8. However, sentence (a) indicates a need to state an additional rule to resolve the structure of sentence (a) with that illustrated in sentence (b). The following rule would describe "ing" as occurring after or to the right of the verb "study."

(6)   Transpose: ing + V to V + ing

figure 3.8

Phrase markers including discontinuous constituents.

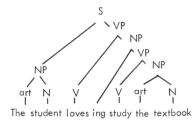
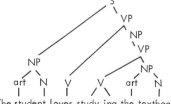

The student loves ing study the textbook   The student loves study ing the textbook

As a result, application of rule 6 to the phrase marker in (a) produces the phrase marker illustrated in sentence (b) of Figure 3.8. Such a description is characteristic of many examples of transformational rules. Obviously, numbers of such rules are necessary to account for the wide spectrum of syntactic variants that occur in our language.

As a result of rule 6 it becomes possible to describe the NP constituent that occurs as the VP object in sentence (b) of Figure 3.8. As illustrated, it includes the VP constituent "study the textbook" plus "ing," where "ing" and the VP make up an NP constituent. However, it is impossible to complete this derivation without referring to sentence (a) prior to an application of rule 6. Thus, to provide a description of the constituent structure of sentence (a), we employ an abstract phrase marker resulting from the structure of an actual sentence occurring via application of rule (6)

Our major objective in the preceding review was to show that rule derivations must involve more than lists of sentence descriptions. Examples, as illustrated in rules 1 through 4, represent statements of processes underlying sentence generation. Additional examples illustrated a distinction between surface and deep structure. Sentence (a) of Figure 3.8 is an example of deep structure, whereas sentence (b) is an example of surface structure. Finally, application of descriptions such as rule 6 enable the conversion or transformation of deep structure phrase markers to those of surface structure. The important difference between rule 6 and rules 1 through 5 is that the latter are phrase structure rules which generate phrase markers beginning with the S. Rules such as 6 are *transformation* rules. Their role is to provide descriptions that transform phrase markers rather than generate them. Thus, phrase markers are generated by phrase structure rules and phrase marker rules are transformed by transformational rules.

conclusion

In this chapter, we have provided a brief and simplified outline of the *structure* of language. This discussion, although highly simplified, reflects current linguistic theory.

THE FUNCTION OF LANGUAGE   Language is that process involved in the transfer of ideas or information between human beings (Figure 3.9). When we speak, we talk about something: sports, business, the weather, a lecture, gossip. Such subjects constitute the content of language. When we communicate, we communicate content for a reason: to preach, to teach, to persuade, to excite, to inhibit, to display our knowledge (or lack of it). Whatever the reason, we refer to that component of language as its *function*. The rules and processes that determine the ways in which ideas are converted to sentence-sized utterances are called *encoding*. As students of speech and language we are concerned with the structure of encoding—not the encoding itself, but the underlying ways in which ideas are converted into sentences. Figures 3.9 and 3.10 provide schematic diagrams which illustrate the various components of language as they appear to relate to each

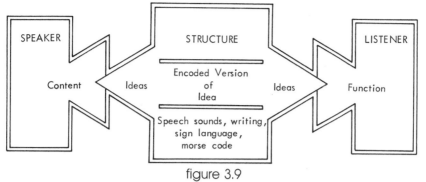

figure 3.9

A schematic illustration of the relationships between
the content, structure, and function of a language.

figure 3.10

A schematic illustration of the components
of language which operate between inception
of an idea and production of speech sound.

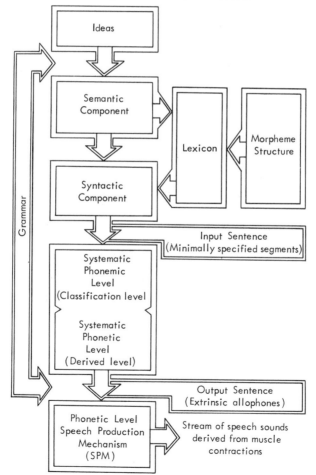

other in a hierarchical structure. We will return to these diagrams as we review and summarize the nature of structure.

Following Chomsky, we can divide the task of determining the structure of language into two smaller, more manageable factors.

> **1.** *Competence:* What a speaker knows (or needs to know) about encoding/decoding language. Such competence would provide a structural description of all possible grammatical sentences in a given language.
>
> **2.** *Performance:* How the speaker/listener actually uses this knowledge in general and on any occasion when he or she encodes (speaks, writes) or decodes (listens, reads) language or observes behavior.

Competence is at present a focus of study among linguists. We may compare competence to the blueprints needed to construct an engine, building, highway, or table. Performance, which varies day to day and moment to moment, is the way in which the blueprint is actually used or read in completing the intended task. Competence refers to an idealized system; performance to a realized one. Competence refers to a prototype or an invariant system; performance, to a phenomenon or a variant process.

The data on which linguistic theory is built are of two kinds, both empirical in a sense:

> **1.** *Intuitive* or *abstract data* derived from the native speaker's reactions to samples of language. This is used to provide data for semantics, syntax, and phonology.
>
> **2.** *Nonabstract data,* experimentally derived by examining the speech and listening behavior of speakers and listeners and from a close acoustic analysis of speech. These data are used primarily in studying the structure of and relationship between phonology and phonetics.

The modeling of encoding-decoding processes involved in language is facilitated by subdividing structure into the levels illustrated in Figures 3.9 and 3.10.

> **1.** Semantics: Analysis of meaning in a logical sense.
>
> **2.** Syntax: The ordering of words in sentence/utterance frames.
>
> **3.** Phonology: The idealized sound patterns of sentences.
>
> **4.** Phonetics: The eventual realization (production) of sound patterns as muscle movements and acoustic vibrations.

Semantics   Semantics involves the knowledge of complex ideas and their analysis into a logical system suitable for direct encoding. The rules of semantics are, in a sense, dominated by the form of complex ideas and by the syntactic possibilities in subsequent stages of encoding.

Syntax   Syntax refers to rules governing the encoding of ideas from the semantic level into the arrangement of words in a sentence. The system must be generative (rule-governed) and cannot consist of memorized extraction of complete sentences, since the number of sentences in a language is potentially infinite. Such rules operate on single sentences in addition to classes (families) of sentences. All but the final stages of syntactic encoding are in terms of abstract syntactic categories—that is, the classes of morphemes (noun, noun phrase, verb, verb phrase, article, determiner).

Lexicon   The dictionary entries of all morphemes is the lexicon. Entries are in the form of feature matrices. Each morpheme consists of phonological, semantic, syntactic, and rule matrices.

The syntactic component, after lexical insertion has replaced the "abstract" syntactic categories, has as its output a well-formed string of morphemes. Each morpheme in the sentence consists of a phonologically distinctive feature matrix that indicates the potential sound shape of the sentence. This represents the systematic phonemic level of representation of the sentence.

Phonology   Phonology refers to a linearly ordered set of rules characterizing knowledge of transformations to be applied to potential sound shape for two purposes:

1. Adding of language-specific variations of phonemic segments which are semantically unmotivated (for example, semantically motivated [l] in English is converted to [l] or [ł] as idiosyncratic, but never meaningless, variants).
2. Transformations dictated by later phonetic possibilities or nonpossibilities.

The input to the phonological component is the systematic phonemic level. Potential sound shapes are minimally specified; that is, they are only well enough specified to maintain distinction between morphemes. At the output level, or the systematic phonetic level of sentence representation, all linguistically relevant variations are added. Such information then permits automatic operation of the phonetic (sound system) component.

MORPHEME STRUCTURE
CONDITIONS   The subcomponent meta rules or conditions governing the structure of morphemes consist of two parts:

1. Segment structure conditions: These concern the hierarchical feature structure of simple segments.
2. Sequence structure conditions: These concern permitted and nonpermitted sequences of segments within the morpheme.

PHONETICS   This is the rule-governed process whereby the output of the phonological component, a sentence fully specified with all information needed to create a speakable sentence, is converted to the neural commands to muscles needed to make the sounds of speech. The phonetic system processes have knowledge of the neurophysiological and acoustic characteristics of speech. The phonetic component (speech production mechanism) within linguistics, to be compatible with other components, must also be abstract and concerned with knowledge or competence.

SUGGESTED READINGS

BATES, E. *Language Thought and Culture*. New York: Academic Press, 1976. An excellent presentation of the integration of language within the context of social and cognitive interactions.

BLOOM, L. (ed.). *Readings in Language Development*. New York: Wiley, 1978. A collection of readings by scientific and clinical leaders in the field dealing with both normal and disordered language development.

DALE, P. *Language Development: Structure and Function*. New York: Holt, Rinehart and Winston, 1976. A concise and well-written introductory review of the components and processes involved in language acquisition.

DONALDSON, M. *Children's Minds*. Glasgow: William Collins Sons, 1978. A truly outstanding, sensitive, and well-written book dealing with a child's early confrontations with language and learning.

FULLER, B. *Ideas and Integrities*. New York: Macmillan, 1963. Buckminister Fuller must be considered to be among very few twentieth century geniuses. His work is central to the concept of synergy and this volume represents an intimate and personal reflection of his life and thought.

INGRAM, D. *Phonological Disability in Children*. London: Edward Arnold, 1976. A synthesis of linguistic theory as related to a systematic design for analysis of disordered phonology.

KATZ, V., and P. POSTAL. *An Integrated Theory of Linguistic Descriptions*. Cambridge, Mass.: MIT Press, 1964. An early classic designed to integrate generative phonology, syntax and semantics.

KOESTLER, A. *The Ghost in the Machine*. New York: Macmillan, 1967. A brillant thesis on the nature of human behavior as related to brain/mind creativity and pathology.

LADEFOGED, P. *A Course in Phonetics*. New York: Harcourt Brace Jovanovich, 1975. An excellent introduction to linguistic aspects of phonology and phonetics.

MOERK, E. *Pragmatic and Semantic Aspects of Early Language Development*. Baltimore: University Park Press, 1977. An exceptional text in psycholinguistics that includes areas such as biological bases, perceptual, motor and cognition as related to language.

ACOUSTICS

THE
SCIENCE
OF SOUND

4

sound as energy / simple harmonic motion
how sound travels: the elastic medium / resonance / filters
measuring and describing sounds / suggested readings

The link between a speaker and a listener is predominately an acoustical pathway. That is, the speaker's thoughts are encoded into patterns of neural impulses in the brain, and then encoded again into coordinated movements of muscles. These thoughts enter the outside world as complex, microscopic vibrations of the molecules of air surrounding the speaker. They fan out in all directions to be detected and decoded by any listener with the ability and the inclination to do so. The production of those molecular vibrations which we call sound, their transmission to the listener, and the preliminary stages of the listener's detection process obey the laws of physics. If we wish to understand how speech sounds are produced by the speaker and processed by the listener, we must become familiar with the physical laws governing the behavior of sound waves. The study of the science of sound is called acoustics, and it is one of the oldest branches of physics.

At one time, most textbooks in audiology, sensory psychology, and acoustics began their discussion of hearing by posing the philosophical question, "If a tree falls in the forest and there is no one around to hear, was there a sound?" One might as well have asked, "If the tree falls in the forest and the lumberjack is stone deaf, was there a sound?" This is because sound is commonly defined as anything that can be heard. The definition has led to terminology such as ultrasonic vibrations (higher than audible frequency) and subsonic vibrations. Unfortunately, *sonic* can also be used to refer to the speed at which sound waves travel, so we have terms such as supersonic flight (speeds faster than sound waves travel in air). We are dissatisfied with the definition of sound as anything that can be heard. Those vibrations at frequencies too high or too low to be heard obey the same physical laws as do the vibrations we are able to hear. Since the ability to hear a given wave in the air may vary from individual to individual and from species to species, the operational definition of sound as "that which is heard" is not precise.

sound as energy

If we adopt an empirical point of view, then we may say that sound is a form of energy, like heat, light, electricity, and mechanical motion. Now that we have defined sound as a form of energy, we may ask, "But what is energy?" and perhaps, "What does energy have to do with the way in which humans communicate with one another?" Let us first expend some energy on the second question. Energy has everything to do with communication. It is impossible to convey information without transmitting energy from one place to another. A signalman on a ship sends coded messages to another ship using an Aldis lamp, or a Boy Scout with a pair of semaphore flags signals to another on a distant hill. Both use light to convey information. Radio and TV communications depend upon the transmission of electromagnetic radiation. The telephone and telegraph utilize the flow of electricity in wires. Even those who believe in ESP often speak of "psychic" energy.

FUNDAMENTAL QUANTITIES   To understand the definition of sound as energy we must return to some basic concepts from physics. In the study of physics, or more specifically in the branch of physics known as mechanics, everything can be specified in terms of three fundamental quantities: length, mass, and time. For each, a set of units of measure has been defined. Two systems of measurement are widely used today: the metric system and the English system. Actually, there are two versions of the metric system (cgs and MKS units), one much older than the other, but their relationship is easily specified. Conversion from either version of the metric system to the English system is not as simple because a number of conversion constants must either be remembered or readily available.

Let us begin with the metric measuring system, which specifies length, mass, and time as fundamental quantities. If we define length and time by indicating how they are measured, then we have operational definitions. *Length* is the quantity which is a measure of extent in space, or simply, distance. It is difficult to define *time* without saying that it is that quantity we measure in seconds, minutes, or hours. Any physical event that recurs on a regular basis can be used to mark off equal intervals of time. Thus, the period required for one complete revolution of the earth is identified as one day.

The concept of *mass* is probably less well understood by the nonphysicist, perhaps because this quantity is not a fundamental unit in the English system that Americans use in everyday transactions. We may most simply define *mass* as the quantity of matter. That is, two objects are equal in mass if they contain the same amount of matter. Mass is often confused with *weight,* which is a measure of a special kind of force (gravitational force). Most of us are comfortable with the everyday concept of body weight. We will define force later, but we can quickly illustrate the difference between mass and weight with some examples. When an astronaut is on the surface of the moon, his or her weight is about one-sixth that recorded on the earth's surface. This is because the pull of

table 4.1
standard prefixes for metric units

PREFIX	SYMBOL	MULTIPLE	
Giga	G	10^9	(1,000,000,000)
Mega	M	10^6	(1,000,000)
Kilo	k	10^3	(1,000)
Deci	d	10^{-1}	(0.1)
Centi	c	10^{-2}	(0.01)
Milli	m	10^{-3}	(0.001)
Micro	μ	10^{-6}	(0.000,001)
Nano	n	10^{-9}	(0.000,000,001)
Pico	p	10^{-12}	(0.000,000,000,001)

earth's gravity is about six times stronger than that of the moon. The astronaut has lost weight in going to the moon, but not mass. He or she will contain as much mass returning to earth as he or she did before departure. Confusion between mass and weight arises because the gravitational force between two bodies is proportional to the masses of the two bodies. More massive (and usually larger) bodies exert greater gravitational force than do less massive (usually smaller) bodies. Thus, here on earth, a person with more mass will always weigh more than another with less mass. The astronaut weighs less on the moon not because his or her mass is smaller, but because the moon has less mass than the earth. Perhaps one day the confusion will be eliminated when we abandon our earthbound concept of weight in favor of the concept of mass.

Given the fundamental quantities of length, mass, and time, we can specify units of measure for each. The two versions of the metric system differ in this assignment. Since acoustics is one of the oldest branches of physics, many of its important quantities were defined in the older cgs system. The letters stand for centimeter, gram, and second, which are, respectively, the fundamental units of length, mass, and time. Recently, there has been a move toward a newer version of the metric system, the MKS system. MKS stands for meter, kilogram, and second. Both systems are used in acoustics, and the student in speech and hearing science must become familiar with both. Conversions from one system to the other are always done with multipliers which are whole number powers of ten. Thus, 1 meter is equal to 100 centimeters. A standard set of prefixes that specify the exponent of ten are given in Table 4.1. The English system is sometimes called the fps system—foot, pound, and seconds. The pound is not the English unit of mass; rather, it is the unit of gravitational force. Some common conversion factors for expressing English units in the metric system are given in Table 4.2.

table 4.2
conversion of common
English units to metric units

MULTIPLY	BY	TO OBTAIN
inches	2.54	centimeters
feet	0.305	meters
miles	1.609	kilometers
pounds	0.454	kilograms
ounces	28.35	grams

DERIVED QUANTITIES   We began this discussion because we wanted an answer to the question, "What is energy?" To achieve that goal, we must introduce several derived quantities and their units of measurement. Derived quantities are those quantities which can be expressed as products or quotients of fundamental quantities.

Displacement, for example, is the change in spatial position of an object. To measure displacement, we must first determine the distance between the initial position (starting point) and the final position of the object. Then, using the initial position as a reference, we must specify the direction in which the final position lies. A displacement may be to the left or to the right, up or down, or at some angle to these perpendicular (right-angle) directions. Other systems of direction may be used as well. For example, on a map the major directions are north, south, east, and west. When we combine both distance and direction, we may specify the displacement required to get from one point in space to another. As a practical example, an uncountable number of points may lie on a circle at a distance of 180 miles from Indianapolis, Indiana, but only Chicago, Illinois, is 180 miles north-northwest of Indianapolis. A complete specification of displacement must always include both distance and direction.

When an object travels from one point to another, we may simply note that it has undergone a displacement. If we are also concerned with the time that has elapsed while the object was moving, then we must determine the object's *velocity,* the displacement per unit of time. Velocity can have units of meters per second or cm per second (or even miles per hour or furlongs per fortnight). To specify velocity completely, we must include direction. If direction is not given, then we can only compute speed, which is distance per unit of time. A moving object undergoes a change of velocity when either speed or direction is changed. Even if an object such as a racing car moves in a closed circular path at a constant speed, it is still undergoing a change in velocity because its direction of travel is constantly changing — that is, it is not moving in a straight line.

Just as we define a change in displacement over time as velocity, we define the rate of change of velocity as *acceleration*. Its units are given as meters per second per second or centimeters per second per second. (In everyday usage, we might have miles per hour per second.) To specify completely the acceleration of an object, we must include its direction. Frequently, the direction of acceleration is not the same as the direction of displacement or velocity. If a moving object is losing velocity, its acceleration will be in the direction opposite that of the velocity. That is, we may think of a decrease in velocity as an acceleration in the opposite direction. A common example is that of an object following a circular path at a constant rotational speed. Because the direction of its velocity is always changing even though the magnitude (speed) is not, the object undergoes an acceleration at right angles to the direction of velocity. This acceleration gives rise to the familiar centrifugal force that keeps the water in a bucket when we swing it in an arc over our heads.

We are now prepared to offer a more formal definition of force. *Force* is defined from Newton's second law of classical physics as the product of mass times acceleration. Newton was apparently the first to realize that a given mass could be accelerated only if an outside force was applied to it. He further found that the acceleration was directly proportional to the applied force, and inversely proportional to the mass being accelerated. That is, for a given mass, the acceleration will be greater with the application of a larger force. You alone may not be able to move your stalled automobile fast enough to get it started when the battery is dead, but with the help of several friends, and thus greater force, it is possible. On the other hand, if a given force is available, it will impart greater acceleration to an object with less mass. If you can't afford a new battery, it is better to own a sports car than a four-door sedan. In equation form, this relationship is

$$a = F/m$$

The equation can be manipulated to give

$$F = ma$$

that is, force is proportional to mass times acceleration.

Newton also identified a property of matter that we call *inertia*. He found that a body in motion at a constant velocity would continue to move with that velocity unless an unbalanced (outside) force acted upon it. The unbalanced force would cause an acceleration in proportion to the mass of the object. Thus, the inertia of a body is proportional to its mass, so much so that often the terms mass and inertia are used interchangeably. The units of force are derived directly from Newton's equation. Thus, in the MKS system, the unit of force is

$$1 \text{ kg} \times 1 \text{ m/s}^2 = 1 \text{ Nt}$$
$$\text{mass} \times \text{acceleration} = \text{force}$$

The MKS unit of force is the *Newton* (abbreviated Nt). In the cgs system, the unit of force is the *dyne*. One dyne is equal to 1 gm times 1 cm/s². Since 1 kg

= 1000 gm (or 10^3 gm), and 1 meter = 10^2 cm, we can see that

$$1 \text{ Nt} = 10^5 \text{ dyne}$$

In discussing the generation and transmission of sound waves, we are often not directly concerned with the forces exerted by one air molecule upon another because these forces are too small to measure. However, there are usually a very large number of infinitesimally small forces acting on some given surface. What we look at is the sum of these tiny forces over the area of interest, and the quantity we then measure is *pressure,* the total force applied to a surface divided by its area. In cgs units, pressure would be given in dyne/cm². In the MKS system, the unit of pressure has been given the name Pascal (Pa).

$$1 \text{ Pa} = 1 \text{ Nt/m}^2$$

In our discussions, we will be interested primarily in the pressure exerted on a given surface, perhaps the eardrum or the surface of a microphone, due to the vibratory motion of air particles conducting a sound wave. We will call this special quantity *sound pressure.*

ENERGY: POTENTIAL AND KINETIC   We are now in a position to offer a definition of energy. Formally, *energy* is a measure of ability to do work. So if we define work, we can define energy. Formally, *work* is defined as the product of an applied force to an object times the distance that object is moved by the force. More simply, work equals force times distance. Thus, 1 cgs unit of work, the *erg,* is equal to 1 dyne times 1 centimeter. In the MKS system the unit is named the *Joule,* and

$$1 \text{ Joule} = 1 \text{ Nt} \times 1 \text{ m}$$

The units of work and the units of energy are equivalent. Thus, the MKS unit of energy is the Joule; the cgs unit of energy is the erg. It may help to remember the relationship between work and energy if one keeps in mind that there is a present tense–future tense relationship between them. If you are applying force and moving an object, you are doing work; if you simply have the ability but not the inclination to do work, you have energy.

Because energy is a measure of ability to do work, every time work is performed, energy is transferred from one place to another and possibly from one form to another. A dry cell battery converts chemical energy into electrical energy; an electric motor converts electrical energy into mechanical energy. In both examples, work is done in the process. The energy is not "used up," it simply changes form. In fact, if we consider only nonnuclear physics, then energy is neither created nor destroyed in any process. This rule, called the law of conservation of energy, is very useful in studying the behavior of mechanical devices because it requires us always to account for the total energy in a system. If we have an unexplained gain or loss of energy in our analysis of the operation of some system, then we have not fully documented its behavior. We will have to invoke the conservation of energy rule in our analysis of sound transmission in air.

We use energy, or more properly, we change it from one form to another, in accomplishing all sorts of mechanical, electrical, or chemical work. Often our interest lies in the rate at which the energy is used. The rate at which energy flows, in Joules per second, for example, is properly called *power*. In the MKS system, the unit of power is the watt. Here, 1 watt = 1 Joule/sec. In the English system, the unit is the horsepower, and 1 hp = 550 ft-lb/sec. Although gasoline engines are still rated in horsepower, most other power measures are given in terms of watts. Electrical appliances, for example, are rated in watts. You may use a 100-watt lightbulb to illuminate this page as you read, or a 1500-watt blower to dry your hair. Those ratings indicate that the devices will use, respectively, 100 Joules/sec or 1500 Joules/sec when they are in operation. Unless you inhabit a cave, you must pay for the use of electrical energy delivered to your home by a utility company. We usually say we are paying for electrical power, but that statement is incorrect. If we check the billing statement, we will find we are paying for the kilowatt-hours used. Since power is determined by energy divided by the time of use, multiplying kilowatts by time gets us back to energy.

We have one final observation to make on the concept of energy. Energy in most of its forms can be stored. The flashlight battery and the stretched spring are examples of devices in which energy can be stored. In mechanical systems, the stored energy is called *potential energy (PE);* the energy associated with movement is called *kinetic energy (KE)*. Thus, a ball poised at the top of a steep incline, as shown in Figure 4.1, contains an amount of potential energy that was delivered to it in the process of lifting it to the top of the incline. If the ball is released, its potential energy is converted to kinetic energy. The kinetic energy is proportional to the mass of the ball times the square of the velocity. In an equation

$$KE = 1/2 \ mv^2$$

At the bottom of the incline, all the potential energy has been converted into kinetic energy, except for that lost to friction. Since the incline is U shaped,

figure 4.1

An illustration of the exchange of potential energy
for kinetic energy in a ball rolling down an incline.

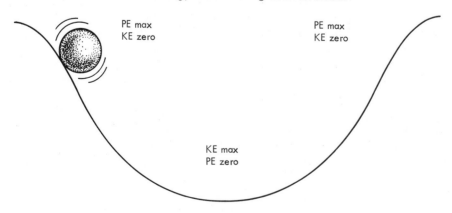

PE max
KE zero

PE max
KE zero

KE max
PE zero

the ball would continue beyond the valley and begin to travel up the opposite side. As it did, its kinetic energy would be converted back into potential energy, until the ball came to rest briefly near the top of the opposite side. At that point, the process would continue in the opposite direction, with the conversion going from potential energy to kinetic energy and back to potential energy again. The process could continue forever if there were no energy losses due to friction. Unfortunately, no matter how carefully we construct the system, there are always some losses to friction. In the incline example, on each pass the ball would reach a slightly lower point up the incline because some of its kinetic energy was converted into heat (another form of energy) in overcoming the friction, or resistance, of the incline. Although the motion of the ball on the incline may continue for several passes or cycles, eventually all the initial potential energy is dissipated by the friction and the motion comes to a halt.

OPPOSITION
TO ENERGY FLOW: IMPEDANCE

The U shaped incline of Figure 4.1 illustrates the principles underlying much more complicated processes. In order to have repetitive, or periodic, action energy must be changed from potential to kinetic and back again. In all real systems, the process is somewhat like trying to slosh water back and forth from one tumbler to another. No matter how carefully it is done, there is always some spillage with each pass. Eventually all the water is down the drain or on the floor, and the tumblers are empty. Every real system, whether mechanical, electrical, or acoustical, has an inherent opposition to the flow of energy. This inherent opposition to the flow of energy can be used to characterize the properties of the system. In general, if we determine the ratio of the applied force to the resulting flow, we may define the input impedance of the system. A system exhibiting high impedance would permit relatively little flow, whereas a low-impedance system would permit a greater flow for the same applied force.

Opposition to the flow of energy takes several forms that can be combined to define a quantity called impedance. An understanding of this concept is important because the impedance of any given system summarizes that system's performance in response to well-defined input signals. When we determine the impedance of the normal human middle ear, we condense a potentially complex response to sound-wave inputs into a few numbers or graphs. Middle ears with certain clearly defined pathological conditions exhibit impedance functions that differ demonstrably from the normal. Thus, a number of instruments for determining the impedance of the middle ear have been developed, and impedance audiometry is an active and useful diagnostic procedure in audiology (see Chapter 9).

The action of any sound-conducting medium, whether it be air, water, or the middle ear structures, can be characterized by its impedance. The impedance of any conducting medium has two distinct components: an energy-dissipating component and an energy-storage component. The energy-dissipating component, called *resistance,* offers real opposition to the flow of energy, usually by converting the energy into another form which is not useful in the system. The energy-storage component of impedance, which is called *reactance,* requires the capacity for energy storage in two different forms. To illustrate, recall the example of the ball on the incline of Figure 4.1. At the top of the incline, mechanical energy was stored in the ball because of its elevation above the valley. All the energy was in potential form because at that instant the ball was not moving. After rolling down the incline, the ball reaches its maximum velocity at the lowest point in the valley, and except for frictional losses, all the potential energy that was available at the top of the incline is now contained in the ball in kinetic form. As the ball rolls down one side of the incline and then up the opposite side, mechanical energy is changed from potential to kinetic and back to potential form again. This exchange of energy from PE to KE and back again is essential for the continuation of the motion of the ball, and ideally no energy is lost in the process. In the real world, however, energy losses do occur, and they are characterized by the resistance of the system.

Both resistance (energy loss) and reactance (energy storage) of a conducting medium depend upon the physical properties of that medium. In our example from Figure 4.1, these properties are the mass of the ball and the height of the incline. A second simple example will illustrate the resistive and reactive properties of sound-conducting media. Figure 4.2 (a) shows a simple mechanical system composed of a spring and a ball. We know that because of its inertia, the ball will neither begin to move nor alter its velocity unless an outside force is brought to bear upon it. The spring in this case represents the elastic restoring forces found within any sound-conducting medium. We know that the spring will oppose being stretched by exerting a force which tends to shorten it; it will oppose being compressed by a force tending to lengthen it. If the spring is either stretched or compressed and then held in position, energy can be stored in it for use at a later time. Thus, the spring in this example replaces gravitational pull in the ball and incline example. The opposition, or re-

figure 4.2

(a) Spring and ball model of the simplest system
to execute simple harmonic motion.
(b) Ball displaced downward and released.

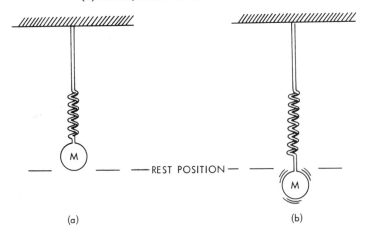

(a)   (b)

storing force, exerted by the spring is proportional to the distance the spring is stretched or compressed times a spring constant that depends upon its physical characteristics. In an equation, $F = -kx$. The spring constant (k) is large for a very stiff spring, and small for a compliant spring. Again, kinetic energy can be stored in the moving ball in proportion to its mass times velocity squared.

If we displace the ball downward as in Figure 4.2 (b), and release it, a repetitive or cyclic motion will occur. Energy flows from stretched spring to moving ball, to compressed spring and back to the moving ball, as the motion continues. Although a source must initially supply the energy being exchanged by the spring and moving ball, no energy is lost in the process except that used to overcome the friction in the system. The pattern of motion of the ball in this example is a very special one in the study of acoustics. It depends completely upon the cyclic exchange of energy between the spring and the moving ball, which in turn depends upon only two physical parameters, the spring constant (k) and the mass of the ball. This pattern of motion is called *simple harmonic motion (SHM)*, or sinusoidal oscillation.

simple harmonic motion

Many of the quantities that describe mechanical or acoustical systems change in value with the passage of time. A graphic record which shows that variation in time is called a *waveform*. If we make a recording of the motion of the ball in Figure 4.2, perhaps by taking high-speed photographs, that recording is a displacement waveform. Almost any quantity displayed as a function of time can properly be called a waveform. If we are able to record the velocity of the ball in Figure 4.2, we can display its velocity waveform. Likewise, we might display acceleration or force waveforms.

PERIODIC WAVEFORMS   The displacement waveform exhibited by the moving ball is an example of simple harmonic motion. This waveform has a very special shape and some very interesting and important properties. The waveform of simple harmonic motion most often called a *sinusoidal waveform*, or simply a *sine wave*, is shown in Figure 4.3 (a). The sinusoidal waveform is first of all *periodic*: it repeats itself exactly in equal intervals of time. That interval is equal to the *period* of the waveform; its units are units of time. The course of the waveform from any given point to the next occurrence of that point (A to A', for example, in Figure 4.3) is called a *cycle* of the waveform.

It is often useful to characterize simple harmonic motion as an endless succession of identical sinusoidal cycles. If we do, then the motion may be specified completely simply by stating that it is a sinusoidal waveform, and giving the values of three of its parameters [see Figure 4.3 (b)]. We have already discussed one of them, the period, briefly. The period (T) of a sinusoidal waveform is that interval of time over which the waveform repeats itself. Many other nonsinusoidal waveforms may be periodic—that is, they may repeat identically in a given interval of time. When dealing with a sinusoid, we often are interested in the number of complete cycles (of the wave motion) that occur in a

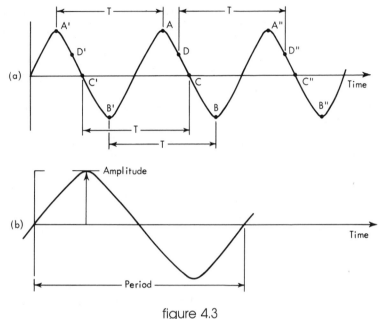

figure 4.3

An example of the sinusoidal waveform and two of
the three parameters necessary to specify it.

one-second interval of time. That is, rather than asking how long one cycle lasts, we may ask how many cycles occur in one second. The number of cycles in one second is called the *frequency* (*f*) of the sinusoidal waveform, and it is related to the period by the equation $f = 1/T$. Here, T is the period in seconds. The units of frequency are one divided by seconds, and they have been given the name *Hertz (Hz)*. Thus, when we refer to a 1000 Hz pure tone, we are indicating a sinusoidal waveform with a period of 1 millisecond (msec). In one second of time, the waveform would undergo 1000 complete cycles.

The second parameter required to specify the sinusoidal waveform is its *amplitude*. There is some ambiguity in the usage of this term. Some authors mean the instantaneous point-to-point value of the waveform when they write "amplitude." Others mean the maximum of the waveform, as indicated in Figure 4.3 (b). We will choose the latter usage, with the understanding that if we are interested in the point-to-point values, we will use the phrase "instantaneous amplitude." Most often in specifying the waveform, it is wise to denote the quantity being described. Thus, we can refer to an amplitude of displacement or to an amplitude of sound pressure, often shortened to displacement amplitude or sound pressure amplitude.

The third parameter necessary to completely specify a sinusoidal waveform is its *phase*. The definition of this parameter is sometimes a bit more difficult to understand. The sinusoidal waveform is related to uniform circular motion, which is motion described by a point on a circle undergoing rotation at constant velocity. For example, we might mark one point on the rim of the turntable of our stereo system. The turntable moves at a constant velocity of 33 $\frac{1}{3}$ or 45 rpm (rotations per minute), and the marker would be performing uniform circular motion. If, as in Figure 4.4 (a), we hold a flashlight at a level even with the surface of the turntable, then the shadow of the marker will execute a curious back-and-forth linear motion on a screen placed behind the turntable. Its velocity along the line is *not* constant. Rather, the marker moves with maximum velocity as it crosses the midpoint, but slows to zero just before reversing direction. If the screen were moving vertically at constant velocity, and if it were able to record the pathway traced out by the shadow of the marker, then that pathway would be a sinusoidal waveform. Therefore, we say that a sinusoidal waveform may be characterized as the linear projection of a point undergoing uniform circular motion.

figure 4.4
(a) An illustration of the projection of uniform circular motion onto a surface to produce a sinusoidal waveform.
(b) Relationship between the major phase points on a circle and on a sinusoidal waveform.

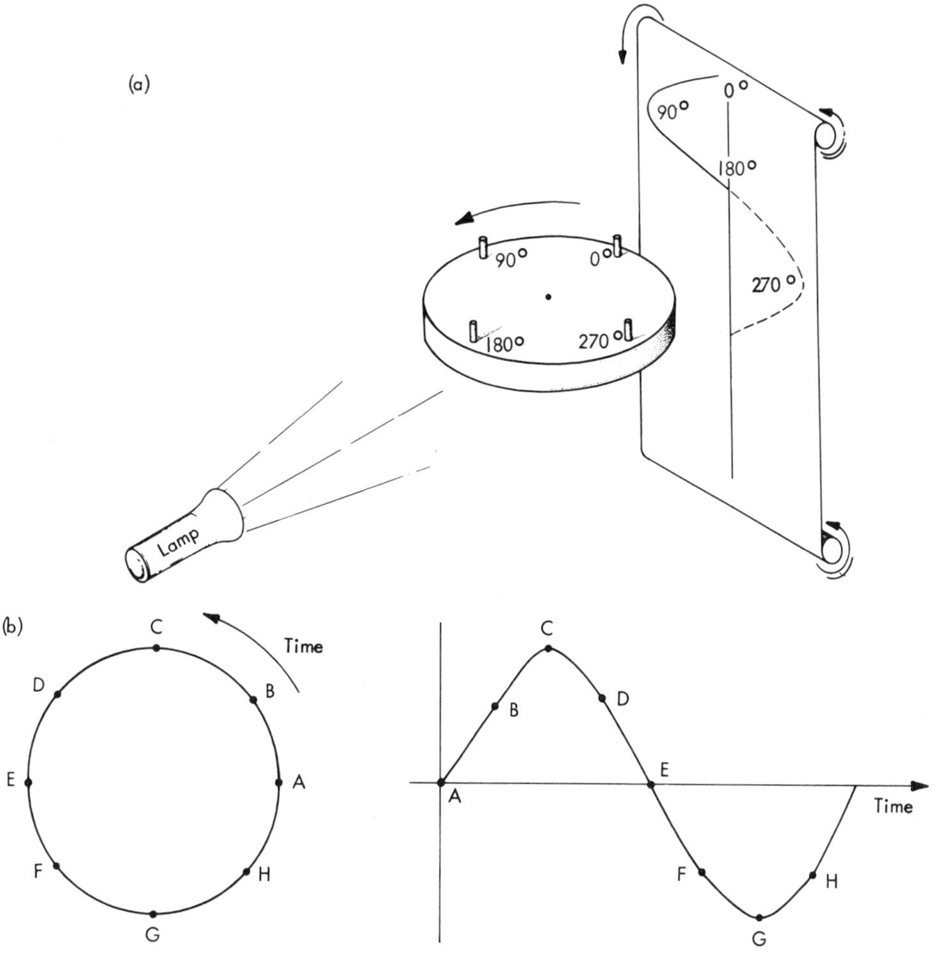

A circle may be divided into 360 degrees. Thus, instead of reporting rotational velocity in rpm, we may report the number of degrees moved per second. Thus, 45 rpm is 45 r/min × 1/60 min/sec, or $\frac{3}{4}$ rotation per second. Then, $\frac{3}{4}$ rotation per second would be $\frac{3}{4}$ × 360° = 270°/ sec. That is, the turntable moves through an angle equal to $\frac{3}{4}$ of a circle (270°) every second. Since sinusoidal motion is the linear projection of uniform circular motion, we may label every point on the sine wave with the corresponding point around the circle. Thus, in Figure 4.4 (b), the points for 0°, 45°, 90°, 180°, and 270° have been marked on both the rotating circle and its associated sinusoid. We may begin our sinusoidal waveform at any point, and to indicate that starting point we specify its starting phase. Thus, in Figure 4.5, there are sinewaves begin-

figure 4.5

Examples of sinusoidal waveforms differing only in their starting phase. Amplitude and frequency are the same for each waveform.

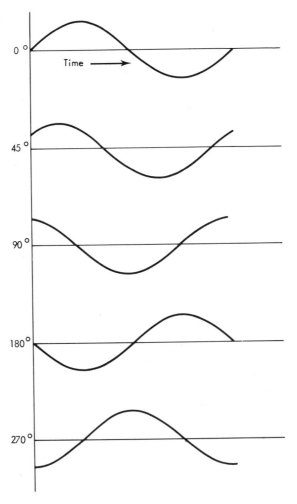

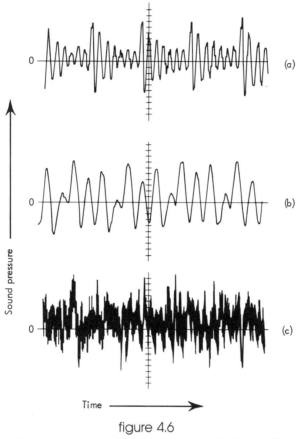

figure 4.6

Three complex periodic waveforms recorded for "real"
sounds: (a) human voice saying [a]; (b) middle C
played on the piano; (c) the sound of an electric motor.

ning at 0°, 45°, 90°, 180°, and 270°. The amplitude and frequency for each waveform are the same; only the starting phase is different.

We have discussed simple harmonic motion in some detail because an understanding of it is essential to our understanding of complex waveforms. It happens that many speech, musical, or other environmental sounds may be represented quite accurately as complex periodic waveforms. We learn a great deal about the production or perception of such signals when we first analyze them into a collection of simple sinusoidal waveforms. Figure 4.6 gives some examples of complex periodic waveforms that represent everyday sounds. Note that each waveform repeats itself identically in an interval of time (T), its period.

What is not obvious from the waveforms of Figure 4.6 is the fact that each may be analyzed into a unique collection of sinusoids. The collection of sinusoids can always be recombined to reproduce the complex waveform exactly. Mathematically, this process is called Fourier analysis, after the French mathematician who first described the procedure. In practice, we most often resort to

Acoustics: The Science of Sound

special laboratory instruments to perform the analysis of real waveforms. These instruments are called wave analyzers or spectrum analyzers. Although the techniques for the mathematical analysis of an arbitrary complex periodic waveform are well beyond the scope of this text, several fundamental rules are essential to our understanding of speech production or auditory perception. As indicated in Figure 4.6, every complex periodic waveform has a definite period, T. It is always true that the lowest possible frequency in the collection of sinusoids which represent that complex waveform is uniquely related to the period. This lowest possible frequency is often called the *fundamental frequency* and given the symbol f_0. If we determine the period of the complex waveform, then its fundamental frequency is given by $f_0 = 1/T$ Hz. Furthermore, the frequencies of all other sinusoids in the collection that make up the complex waveform are simply related to f_0. These frequencies are said to be *harmonics* of the fundamental frequency, and are always whole-number multiples of f_0. Thus, the period of a complex periodic waveform determines all the frequencies allowed in the collection of sinusoids into which it can be analyzed. The difficulty, of course, lies in determining the amplitudes and starting phases of each of the sinusoids at frequencies f_0, $2f_0$, $3f_0$, and so on. Laboratory determination of the phase of each harmonic component in a sound wave has often been ignored, partly because of a long-standing belief that the ear is insensitive to the phase of such harmonics, and also partly because the measurement has been difficult to make. But recent advances in computerized processing of sound waves have made amplitude and phase measurement a relatively simple process.

Figure 4.7 illustrates a complex periodic waveform and some of the sinusoids into which it can be analyzed. If we carefully measure the height of each sinusoid at some instant of time, for example t_0, it will be found that the sum of

figure 4.7

An illustration of the analysis of a complex periodic waveform (a triangular waveform) into its sinusoidal components. The amplitude of each component projected onto the amplitude-frequency plane produces a line spectrum.

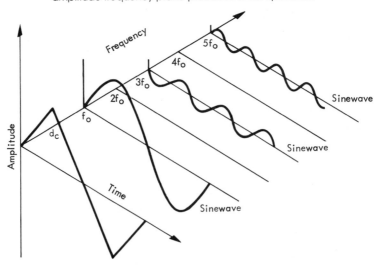

Acoustics: The Science of Sound

these values is equal to the height of the complex waveform at time t_0. (One must, of course, always remember that negative values must be subtracted from the sum where appropriate.)

Rather than a display of each sinusoid at every frequency of interest, as in Figure 4.7, we usually use a shorthand representation called the *spectrum*. The spectrum for any waveform is a graphic representation of the analysis of that waveform into its sinusoidal components. If we plot the amplitude of each sinusoidal component of the complex waveform as a vertical line at the appropriate frequency, we obtain the *amplitude spectrum* of the complex waveform. The amplitude spectrum for our complex waveform is shown in Figure 4.7 (b). In order to describe completely the complex waveform, we must also give the starting phase of each sinusoidal component. That display, when given, is called the *phase spectrum* of the complex waveform. Just as the graph of a quantity as a function of time is properly called a waveform, a graph of that quantity as a function of frequency may be called a spectrum. Thus, we may have not only an amplitude or phase spectrum, but also a power spectrum or an energy spectrum.

NONPERIODIC WAVEFORMS   We may generalize from the line spectra in Figure 4.7 to continuous spectra associated with nonperiodic signals (Figure 4.8). For complex periodic waveforms, we asserted that the lowest possible frequency in the spectrum is the fundamental frequency and that all other frequencies are whole-number multiples of the fundamental frequency. Thus, the spacing between the lines of the spectrum will be equal to the value of f_0. Consider what would happen to this spacing between the lines as the period of the complex waveform grew longer. As the period T increases, its reciprocal $(1/T)$, the fundamental frequency f_0, becomes smaller and the spacing between the lines of the spectrum also decreases. If we ignore some mathematical niceties, we can intuitively see what would happen if the period extended to a very long time: the fundamental frequency and the line spacing would approach

figure 4.8

An example of a continuous spectra.

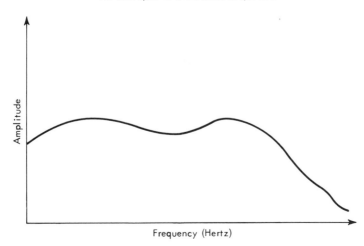

zero. The discrete line-spectrum representation would become a continuous one. Rather than drawing the entire line segment, we simply indicate its top, and the result is a continuous smooth curve that represents the spectrum of nonperiodic signals.

There are basically two types of nonperiodic signals, and both are important in our understanding of speech communications. The first type is a continuous one of long duration that never repeats because its value is determined by a random process. Many signals that we call noise are of this type, although random signals are also evident in both speech and music. The fricative consonants [s], [ʃ], [f], and [θ] are each characterized by a continuous random waveform. When viewed on an oscilloscope, they never seem to repeat. A spectral analysis of such continuous random waveforms would show a function that contains energy at all frequencies, unlike the line spectra of periodic waveforms. If the spectrum is flat (if there is equal energy at all frequencies), then we say that the random signal is a *white noise*. This term was chosen to be analogous to white light, which is a mixture of electromagnetic (light) vibrations at many frequencies. Each frequency of vibration for a light wave arouses a different sensation of color in the eye. White light contains all colors at equal energy; white noise contains all audible frequencies at equal energy. A curious derivative of this analogy is the pink noise often used in testing amplifiers, hearing aids, and other communications devices. The waveform of pink noise is a continuous random one, but low frequencies are more prominent in the spectrum. This signal is called pink noise because a similar emphasis of the low frequencies in light would give a pink color.

The second type of nonperiodic signal is one that lasts but a brief period of time. Typically, such signals are called *transients*. Although transients also are often classified as noise — think of sonic booms or gun shots, for example — they are equally important in the production and perception of speech and music. Stop consonants such as [p, t, k] are best represented as transient signals. Since transients are not extended in time, their spectral representation is somewhat different from that for continuous signals. Continuous signals are represented by power spectra or by amplitude and phase spectra; transient signals yield energy-density spectra. (The concept is the same, but the mathematical details differ.) The spectra for transient signals are continuous functions of frequency, as are the spectra for random signals. But although the spectrum for a continuous waveform may be restricted to a narrow range of frequencies (for example, narrow-band noise), the spectrum for a transient always extends over the whole range of frequencies. Thus, transients are said to be broad-band signals.

how sound travels: the elastic medium

Now that we have discussed vibratory motion in general, it is time to consider the question of how sound energy travels from one place to another. In any communications system, we must have a message sender, or source, and a receiver. When the message is to be sent by sound waves, there must be a third, very important part of the system: the *elastic medium,* which must possess restoring forces. Any elastic medium — air, water, metal — may serve as a sound conductor.

Let us consider the behavior of an ideal gas as a model of an elastic medium. An ideal gas is one having the same simple behavior at all possible values of temperature and pressure. Real gases approximate this behavior if their temperature is not too low or their pressure is not too high. A given number of molecules of an ideal gas will completely fill any container because of the elastic restoring forces among the gas molecules. These forces of electrical, magnetic, and gravitational attraction serve to keep the average distance between adjacent molecules the same throughout the entire volume of the container. The spacing remains the same, on the average, although the molecules are moving about on random pathways, crashing into one another and into the walls of the container. The force of these molecular collisions, averaged over a surface area, is the gas pressure. For a given enclosed volume of gas, we may increase the kinetic energy of each molecule by increasing the temperature. With increased kinetic energy, each molecule moves more rapidly (with higher velocity) and engages in more collisions. Thus, if the volume remains unchanged, the pressure of the gas increases with increased temperature. We can look at sound propagation through an ideal gas from either a microscopic or a macroscopic point of view. That is, we could focus on the behavior of one gas molecule as it participates in the transmission of a sound wave (microscopic), or we might consider the action of a large number of molecules and report only their average behavior (macroscopic). Useful insights can be gained from each approach, and we will take each in turn.

Let us first describe the motion of a single molecule of our ideal gas. The model we will adopt is a familiar one. The mass of the molecule we assume can be concentrated at a point; the elastic restoring forces are represented by a spring. If anything acts to move the molecule to greater than average separation from its neighbors, the restoring force will act, as a stretched spring would act, to return the molecule to its average or equilibrium position. Likewise, if external forces were to push the molecule closer to its neighbor than the average position, the restoring forces would work in the opposite direction, as a compressed spring would, to return it again to its position of equilibrium. If we ignore for the moment the fact that all the gas molecules are in random motion, then we may depict single ideal gas molecules as we have in Figure 4.9 (a). Each molecule is a microscopic-spring-mass system. Each is capable of the exchange of potential and kinetic energy and the resultant sinusoidal motion we described above. If a molecule of ideal gas could act in isolation, then its motion would be just that simple. However, it is unrealistic to assume that each molecule acts in isolation; molecules are tied together by their mutual restoring forces. A better approximation of their behavior can be gained from a representation such as that in Figure 4.9 (b). Here every molecule is "tied" to its neighbor by elastic restoring forces. If an outside agent, represented by the surface of the loudspeaker cone in the figure, acts to crowd the first layer of molecules, then the restoring forces will react by moving the molecules away from the

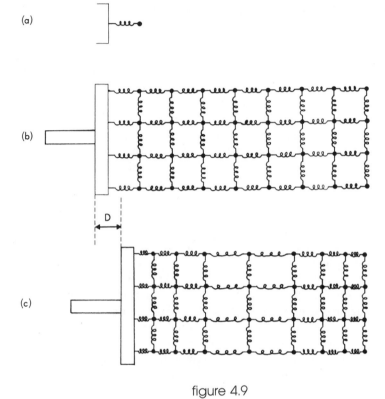

figure 4.9

An illustration of the restoring forces that act on particles of air:
(a) one air particle in isolation; (b) air particles adjacent to a
stationary loudspeaker cone; (c) a soundwave being transmitted
through the air particles by the moving loudspeaker cone.

loudspeaker cone but closer to their neighbors. This encroachment is opposed by still other restoring forces which act to push the first layer of molecules back toward the loudspeaker cone and the second layer toward the third. In this manner, the initial disturbance of equilibrium introduced at one place is transmitted from molecule to molecule. The action is similar to that seen in a long freight train that is just beginning to move away from the station. As each box car is jerked into motion, it passes the insult to the next one in line.

Because each gas molecule has mass, and consequently inertia, it cannot be set into motion instantaneously. Thus, there is a constant rate of travel of the disturbance through the gas. Also, because of the inertia of each mass, the molecules do not come to rest in an instant, but tend to keep moving, over-shooting the equilibrium position. One brief disturbance of the gas molecules would continue to reverberate throughout its volume, if it were not for the frictional losses present in every real gas. If we were able to observe one mole-cule responding to an impulsive disturbance, we would see a decaying sinusoi-dal pattern of motion centered about its equilibrium position. The molecules themselves do not move far from their rest positions but the "disturbance" will travel to the limits of the enclosure. The transmission of the "disturbance" represents the transfer of energy from molecule to molecule through the coupling provided by the mutual restoring forces.

Now let us consider the pattern of molecular motion when the source in Figure 4.9 (b) moves in simple harmonic motion. We will ignore the brief transient response associated with the initiation of movement and observe the action for one cycle of the driving source. If the source (for example, a loudspeaker cone) is moving to the right, as in Figure 4.9 (c), toward the enclosed gas, then those molecules closest to the surface of the cone will be temporarily squeezed together. In that region we might say that the gas is compressed— that is, the pressure is slightly higher than average because the molecules have been crowded a little closer together. Because the molecules are closer together, they undergo more collisions and the air pressure increases. The slight compression at the surface of the cone will be transmitted to the adjacent molecules, just as the transient disturbance was, by the action of the restoring forces. The compression will begin to move away from the cone. As this is happening, the cone, undergoing sinusoidal motion, will have reached the limit of its movement to the right and will begin to move away from the volume of gas. As the cone moves away, the molecules rearrange themselves to fill the newly available space, creating a local decompression or *rarefaction*. Again, the neighboring molecules act to restore equilibrium, and in the process the rarefaction travels away from the driving piston. All the while, the compression generated half a cycle earlier is still traveling away from the source at a uniform speed determined by the physical state of the gas.

As the loudspeaker cone reverses again and begins to create another local compression, we should visualize the entire sinusoidal motion pattern of the cone distributed through a portion of the gas and traveling at a constant velocity away from the source. One cycle of the cone's motion has been transferred to the vibratory action of the gas molecules. If we know the rate at which the disturbance moves away from the loudspeaker cone and we determine the period of the sinusoidal motion, then we can calculate the distance that a given point on the waveform will travel before another just like it is generated by the source. This distance is called the *wavelength* of the traveling sound wave and is given the symbol λ. In an equation

$$\lambda = cT \text{ meters}$$

Here c = speed of sound propagation and T = period. Recall that the relationship between the period of a sinusoidal oscillation and its frequency was given by $f = 1/T$. Then we can rearrange this equation so that $T = 1/f$. Substituting $1/f$ for T in the equation above, we find that

$$\lambda = c/f \text{ meters}$$

For a traveling sound wave, the wavelength, λ, is the distance in space spanned by one cycle of the motion. Similarly, for any sinusoidal motion, traveling wave, or vibratory pattern, the period is the time spanned by one cycle.

The picture of molecular action we have presented is highly oversimplified in several respects. First, we have ignored the constant random motion that all gas molecules exhibit. Our description would be more appropriate for molecules held in a rigid crystal structure than for freely moving liquid or gas molecules. A second oversimplification concerns the dimensions of the model. We discussed the propagation of a disturbance through a gas as though the gas were two-dimensional and the disturbance acted in only one direction. All real situations must consider sound propagation throughout a three-dimensional medium. Only in special cases will it be possible to approximate the three-dimensional case by a two-dimensional one. In general, in a three-dimensional medium, the sound wave propagates in all directions from the vibrating source. Ideally, as in Figure 4.10, nothing is present to interfere with the progress of the wavefronts. Since all points on the front travel at the same speed, the disturbance may be visualized as a large, ever-expanding sphere. The disturbance, and hence the sound energy, continue to form the surface of a large sphere. If the total energy in the sound wave is fixed, it will be spread over an expanding surface area as it moves away from the source.

We almost never measure the total sound energy or total sound power produced by a vibrating source in a three-dimensional medium. Instead, we determine the sound power distributed over a given surface area—the surface of a microphone, for example. Power divided by surface area is given the name *intensity*. Intensity is probably the most often used—and misused—parameter of a sound waveform. To be strictly correct, we must consider the sound energy per unit of time, or sound power, flowing through an imaginary window of standard dimensions. Thus, the intensity is given in units of watts/m^2 or watts/cm^2. If the window size remains fixed at one square centimeter (or one square meter), then the intensity of any sound wave measured at this window in a three-

figure 4.10

An illustration of the concentric spheres of compression and rarefaction surrounding a sound source in a free sound field.

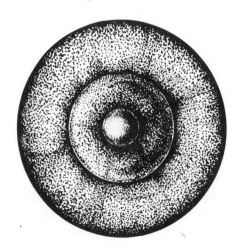

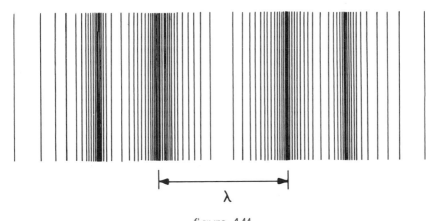

figure 4.11
A representation of a plane progressive sound wave.

dimensional medium will naturally decrease as the distance from the source increases. Remember that the total power over the surface of the sphere is constant. As the distance from the source, the radius (*r*) of the sphere, is increased, the surface area increases in proportion to the square of the radius. (In an equation, the surface area of a sphere is given by area $= 4\pi r^2$.) Since the intensity is the power distributed over a fixed area, say one square centimeter, the intensity will decrease at a fourfold rate every time the distance from the source is doubled.

Suppose we first determine the intensity at a given radius, say 1 meter from the source. At 2 meters from the source, the intensity will decrease to $\frac{1}{4}$ of the intensity at 1 meter. This is because *r* changed from 1 to 2 meters. In the equation we must square the radius to calculate surface area, so the area of the sphere at 2 meters is four times larger than the area at 1 meter. (The fourfold increase comes from the r^2 term, not the 4 in $4\pi r^2$.) The general form of this relationship is called the *inverse square law:* The intensity of a sound wave decreases in inverse proportion with the square of the distance from the source.

When the receiver, be it microphone or eardrum, is far away from the sound source, the surface of the sphere seems to be flat. (The surface of the earth, a sphere, seems flat because we are over 7000 miles from its center.) When the surface is apparently flat, we can approximate the spherical wavefronts by flat (or plane) wavefronts. We say, then, that these wavefronts are approximately plane, progressive (traveling) wavefronts (see Figure 4.11). The intensity of a true plane, progressive wavefront does not decrease with distance from its source, since there is no spherical expansion. If we observe a spherical wavefront at a reasonable distance from its source, traveling over a distance much shorter than the distance to the source (the radius), then we may safely ignore the inverse-square law.

It is important to discuss one final detail of sound-wave propagation. The direction in which the sound wave travels is the same as the direction in which the microscopic vibrations of individual molecules occur. This mode of vibratory motion is called *longitudinal* propagation. We must be careful to distinguish longitudinal waves from the more easily visualized *transverse* vibrations. Ripples on a still pond disturbed by a single pebble (see Figure 4.6) represent transverse vibrational motion. There, the water molecules bounce up and down in the vertical direction, while the disturbance moves along the horizontal surface of the pond. Plucked or bowed strings, vibrating reeds, and drumheads exhibit transverse motion, but sound waves in air travel by longitudinal propagation.

resonance

The simple spring-ball system illustrated in Figure 4.2 exhibits a behavior known as *resonance*. Resonance is a term that has popular, musical, and scientific meanings which are related, but not equivalent to one another. Thus, we could indicate that two like-minded people were in agreement on an issue by saying that they exhibited "resonance." Their thoughts were "in tune." The popular usage thus derives from the idea of resonance in music. Musicians may describe pleasing musical tones as being resonant. Also, in music we encounter the notion of sympathetic resonance, an object beginning to vibrate in synchrony with another vibrating body. Examples are the sounding board beneath the strings of a piano or the little wooden boxes on which tuning forks are often mounted. The resonator, or sounding board, usually has a much larger surface than the vibrating body (or driver). When the resonator vibrates, more air molecules are set into motion and we hear a louder sound. Some would say that the original sound is amplified by the resonator. Technically, however, that is incorrect; the sounding board simply makes possible a better acoustical impedance match between the vibrating body and the air surrounding it. As another example, there is a principle in electrical circuitry called the maximum power transfer theorem. Briefly, this theorem states that to deliver the greatest amount of power into a circuit, the source and receiver should be matched in impedance. Obviously, when the impedances are matched, there are no reflections at the interface between the source and the receiver. All the available power is delivered into the receiver. In our example, the source of sound power is the piano string or tuning fork, and the receiver is the air surrounding the source. The sounding board effects a better impedance match between the vibrating source and the air, and more sound power is delivered into the air. We have belabored this "impedance matching" concept here because we will need this principle when we discuss the delivery of speech sounds from the mouth to the air surrounding the speaker, and also when we discuss the function of the middle ear.

The scientific use of the term resonance carries the same connotation as the popular and the musical ones, but the definition is more carefully stated. In discussing impedance, we indicated that it is made up of an energy-dissipating part (resistance) and an energy storage part (reactance). We said further that the reactance component was made up of mass reactance (inertia) and compliant reactance (stiffness). These two components of reactance always oppose one another in their action. Thus, when the mass reactance is storing energy, the compliant reactance is giving it up. The magnitude (size) of the reactance depends upon both the physical properties of the system and the frequency of the vibratory motion to which it is subjected. (Think of rocking a car slowly versus trying to shake it 20 times per second.) The magnitude of mass reactance grows with increased frequency. The magnitude of compliant reactance diminishes with increasing frequency. At most vibratory frequencies, then, the magnitudes of mass and compliant reactance will be unequal. However, at one or more frequencies, the two magnitudes will be exactly equal. Since they act in opposition, when mass reactance equals compliant reactance in magnitude, their effects cancel one another. At that point, we say the vibrating system has achieved resonance. Since the net reactance is zero at the resonance frequency, the total system impedance is determined by the resistive component alone. Thus, the magnitude of the total vibrating system impedance is at a minimum. Since impedance represents opposition to energy flow, more energy will flow through the system at the resonance frequency than at any other frequency, and the vibrating system will be most efficient at conducting energy. This greater energy-conducting efficiency at resonance can be a useful feature in a mechanical or acoustical system.

DETERMINING
RESONANCE FREQUENCY   It is easy to determine the resonance frequency of a simple mechanical or acoustical system. Let us return to the simple spring and ball example of Figure 4.2. When this system is disturbed by stretching the spring, some energy is added to the whole system. When the ball is released, it begins to execute a sinusoidal motion as energy is exchanged between the spring and the moving ball. The frequency of that sinusoidal motion is sometimes called the *natural frequency* of the system. The system can be forced to vibrate at any arbitrary frequency, but if set into motion and left alone, it will vibrate at its natural frequency. This frequency is sometimes called the frequency of the free response. It is also the resonance frequency. To illustrate, let us assume that we can attach a driving motor to our simple spring and ball system. For a given driving force, we measure the movement of the ball. If we vary the frequency of the driving force, we will see a variation in the resulting movement. At some frequencies, there will be very little movement of the ball; at others, the displacement may become quite large. All these observations must be made with the driving force kept at the same magnitude for each frequency. If we made a graph of the size of the response as a function of the frequency of the driver, we would plot the *transfer function* of the system. A transfer function (see Figure 4.12) shows the relative efficiency of our system for a wide range of frequencies. We will always find that the system is most efficient at its natural, or resonance, frequency.

The resistance in the system also influences the resonance curve. Since the reactances cancel each other out, the magnitude of the impedance will be equal to that of the resistance at the resonance frequency. If the resistance is large,

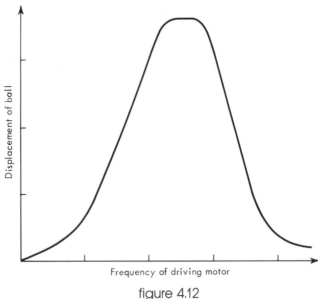

figure 4.12
A hypothetical transfer function.

then canceling the reactances will not produce a large change in the magnitude of the total impedance. If the resistance is much smaller than the reactances, there will be a large change in the magnitude of the impedance as the frequency approaches the resonance frequency. The sharpness and width of the resonance curve is thus determined by the resistance in the system. Low resistance leads to a sharp resonance; high resistance yields a less pronounced resonance curve. Some typical curves are shown in Figure 4.13.

The resistance in a tuned or resonant system is sometimes called *damping*. The term is apt, if we consider the waveform of the free vibration. A resonant system with very little resistance will continue to vibrate for some time after being released from an initial displacement. On each cycle of the motion, the resistance will turn a small fraction of the available energy into heat. Eventually the oscillations decay to zero, as the energy is turned into a nonrecoverable form. If the resistance, or damping, in a resonant system is high, then the vibrations will decay to zero very quickly, as Figure 4.13 (b) shows. If vibration is undesirable, then the addition of resistance will help to subdue it. Shock absorbers on an automobile act to reduce the bouncing effect produced when bumps in the road excite the spring and mass system in the suspension. Typical waveforms for highly and lightly damped resonators are shown in Figure 4.13.

filters

Systems more complicated than our simple ball and spring may have more than one resonance frequency. Because various combinations of mass and compliant reactance cancel at different frequencies, the transfer function may exhibit nu-

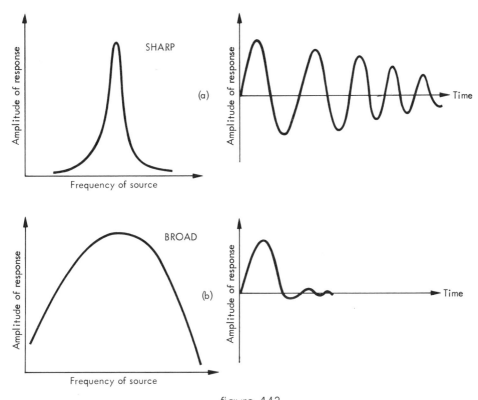

figure 4.13

Sharp and broad resonance curves and the decaying
sinusoidal waveform that would be produced by each resonator.

merous peaks and valleys. One primary use of resonance is in the building of
frequency-selective *filters*. In the chapters that follow, the vocal tract is often
called a variable acoustical filter, and the mechanical response of the ear is
compared to that of a collection of narrowband filters. We therefore need to
understand the fundamental behavior of a filter.

Those of you who make coffee by pouring hot water through a paper cone
filled with ground coffee beans probably call the paper cone a filter. You may
have used a similar filter in a chemistry lab. The little roll of fibrous material
on the end of a cigarette is also called a filter. Filters are found in furnaces and
air conditioners, in automobile engines, and in many other places. The underlying principle is the same. A filter sorts things into well-defined categories. It
allows liquid (the coffee) to pass through, but not solids (the coffee grounds),
for example. Or, air may pass through, but not particles of dust and dirt. These
are all mechanical filters that sort objects according to size. It is also possible to
build mechanical, acoustical, or electrical filters that sort vibrations according
to frequency. These filters work just like the mechanical ones. Vibrations at
some frequencies pass through the filters; others are rejected or greatly reduced
(attenuated) as they pass through. When a vibration is attenuated, its amplitude

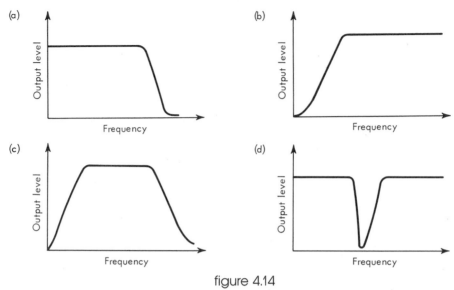

figure 4.14

Typical filter functions showing: (a) a low-pass filter; (b) a
high-pass filter; (c) a bandpass filter; (d) a band-rejection filter.

is reduced without other alterations or distortions of the waveform. Such filters are classified according to the frequency region (or band) they transmit without attenuation. Figure 4.14 shows some typical filter transfer functions. The low-pass filter transmits vibrations without attenuation at frequencies from 0 Hz to an upper limit called the cutoff frequency. Beyond the cutoff frequency, the vibration will be attenuated. As the frequency is increased beyond the cutoff, the degree of attenuation is increased. Usually the rate of attenuation is given in decibels of attenuation per octave of frequency.

The other transfer functions shown in Figure 4.14 are the high-pass, bandpass, and band-reject filters. The high-pass filter attenuates vibrations with frequencies from 0 Hz up to the cutoff frequency. The bandpass filter attenuates vibrations with frequencies below a lower cutoff and above an upper cutoff, passing only those falling into the band of frequencies between the two. Our simple spring and ball system is an example of a bandpass filter. Finally, the band-reject filter passes all signals except those within a selected frequency region. More complex filters can be represented as combinations of two or more of the simple filters. A relatively simple acoustical system can therefore have a complicated filter transfer function. Figure 4.15 shows a simple circular tube. If the tube is sealed at one end and open to the air at the other, soundwaves traveling in the air inside the tube undergo a series of reflections. It is perhaps easy to see that soundwaves would bounce off the sealed end of the tube because of its high impedance. However, reflections also occur at the open end of the tube because the air outside the tube has a lower impedance than the air inside.

At every vibratory frequency, the soundwave traveling in the tube interacts with its reflections or echoes. At some points along the length of the tube they

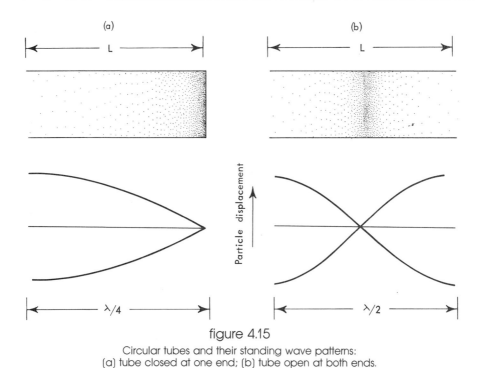

figure 4.15
Circular tubes and their standing wave patterns:
(a) tube closed at one end; (b) tube open at both ends.

may reinforce one another to produce an increase in sound intensity; at other places there will be cancellations that reduce the intensity. Because the soundwave and its echoes are moving along the tube, the interactions at a given location vary from reinforcement to cancellation and back to the reinforcement again. At some very special frequencies, the length of the tube is just right so that the reflected wave is always in phase with the incident wave, or exactly 180° out of phase with the incident wave. When this happens, the original soundwave and its echoes interact to produce *standing waves* (see Figure 4.16). Standing waves do not appear to travel within the tube. A point of cancellation, called a *node,* remains at the same location for a given standing wave frequency. Likewise, a point of maximum reinforcement, or *antinode,* does not travel along the tube. But the component waves are traveling. Do not be confused; it is the *sum* of the traveling components that seems to stand still. If you have ever watched a guitar or piano string vibrate, you have seen a transverse standing wave. The string vibrates rapidly, but there appear to be places along its length that do not move. These are the nodes. At other points, midway between the nodes, the displacement of the string is at a maximum. These are the antinodes. Nodes and antinodes always alternate, so that the pattern is node, antinode, and so on.

A similar type of standing wave is possible in the air enclosed in the circular tube in Figure 4.15. Nodes and antinodes are arranged in an alternating sequence. Here a node denotes a point where air molecules are not in motion in

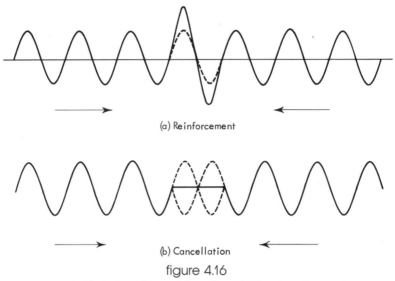

(a) Reinforcement

(b) Cancellation

figure 4.16

An illustration of wave interactions: (a) Two traveling
waves meet in phase to produce a reinforcement.
(b) Two out-of-phase traveling waves produce cancellation.

response to the sound energy. Air molecules at the solid surface of the closed
end cannot vibrate freely. When a standing wave is established, there is always
a node at the closed end of the tube. At an antinode, the air particles vibrate
with maximum displacement. The open end of the tube allows the maximum of
air molecule displacement, so the open end must always have an antinode.
Given a circular tube closed at one end, as in Figure 4.15, we may guess the
standing wave patterns that can be set up inside. The simplest pattern would
have one node and one antinode. There must be a node at the closed end. If
we then put the antinode at the open end, we will find that the standing wave
pattern is exactly one quarter of a full traveling waveform. Thus, a second
wave could establish this standing wave pattern if its wavelength were four
times the length of the tube. This line of thinking is given in a simple equation
for the first resonance frequency of the circular tube. The equation for the relationship between the frequency of a traveling wave and its wavelength is $f =
c/\lambda$. Our reasoning tells us that $\lambda = 4L$. Thus, the resonance frequency is $F_R =
c/4L$. Suppose that the tube in Figure 4.14 is 17 cm long. Then, if we use the
accepted value of $c = 34000$ cm/sec, we can find the value of F_R by simple division.

$$F_R = 34000/(4 \times 17) = 500 \text{ Hz}$$

For this simple tube, 500 Hz is not the only resonance frequency. If we continue to add nodes and antinodes to the pattern established in Figure 4.15, we
will find that every odd-numbered multiple of the first resonance frequency (1,
3, 5, 7 and so on) yields another resonance peak in the transfer function. Three

additional patterns are illustrated in Figure 4.17. In the transfer function, there are peaks at 500 Hz, 1500 Hz, 2500 Hz, and so on. At the even multiples of the first resonance frequency, reflections are at their worst for establishing a strong standing wave pattern. Thus, these frequencies (1000 Hz, 2000 Hz, 3000 Hz and so on) are in the valleys between the peaks in the transfer function. The final transfer function for the straight tube, closed at one end, is a compound one that can be approximated by a series of simple resonators. Each resonator is tuned to a resonance frequency in the transfer function. (We have discussed this simple acoustical filter in such detail because it is the model on which all acoustical models of speech production are based.)

If the acoustical tube is open to the air at both ends or closed at both ends, then a different transfer function is obtained. Again, we may guess the simplest standing wave pattern. If we choose to study the tube open at both ends, we must have antinodes at both ends, and a node midway between the antinodes. The result is a one-half wavelength representation of the standing wave. Thus, for a tube open at both ends, the longest wavelength that will produce a standing wave is $\lambda = 2L$. We again assume a 17 cm tube and use the equation for calculating frequency from the wavelength. Then $F_R = c/2L$, and $F_R = 34000/2(17) = 1000$ Hz. Notice that the first resonance frequency for the tube

figure 4.17

Family of standing wave patterns for $n = 3, 5,$ and 7
in a tube closed at one end.

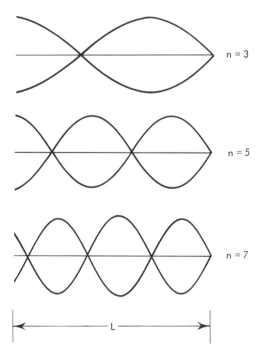

open at both ends is twice the frequency for the same tube with one end closed. You can test this assertion by obtaining a cardboard tube used to roll paper towels. Purse your lips and make a buzzing noise into the tube. Listen for a musical pitch in the buzz. Move the tube away from your mouth and again buzz. There should be an increase in the pitch of the buzz.

The circular tube open (or closed) at both ends also has a transfer function made up of peaks and valleys. The peaks occur at every whole number multiple (1, 2, 3, 4, 5 and so on) of F_R. The valleys are at frequencies midway between the peaks. This simple circular tube sometimes serves as a model in speech production. The human ear canal is also normally thought to be a tube closed at one end, although when a hearing-aid earmold is inserted into the canal, it acts more like a tube closed at both ends.

The two simple acoustical structures we have just discussed have rather complicated filter transfer functions. Changing the shape of the tube, perhaps by adding a small constriction along its course, would seem to complicate matters further. Surprisingly, however, the changes introduced by constricting the tube at various places simply move the peaks in the transfer function to different frequencies in an orderly way. But if the basic circular tube is tapered in diameter, or if a series of holes is drilled along its length, then more complications arise. These changes are just like those introduced when a wind instrument is produced for music. There are some advantages to our thinking of the vocal tract as the first, and still the most versatile, wind instrument.

The acoustical analog of the simple spring and ball mechanical system is known as a *Helmholtz resonator*. A typical Helmholtz resonator is shown in Figure 4.18. The bulb at the bottom contains a volume of air that can be compressed and expanded, but not moved out of the resonator. The neck is an air-filled tube. The air inside this tube moves as a single slug, having only mass.

figure 4.18

A Helmholtz acoustical resonator.

Thus, the volume, *V*, represents the spring, and the tube, *M*, represents the mass in this resonator. The system, which appears to be more complicated than our simple acoustical tubes, has only one resonance frequency. It depends on the volume of air in the base, and the mass of air in the neck of the resonator. Helmholtz resonators are often used in combination to make more complicated acoustical filters that eliminate unwanted sounds. An automobile muffler is an example of such an acoustical filter.

measuring and describing sounds

Throughout this chapter we have referred to a soundwave as a disturbance traveling through an elastic medium. In order to describe and quantify the sound wave, we must determine the effects of the disturbance on the medium through which it travels. We can no more measure the soundwave than we can see the wind. We see the effects of wind—trees swaying, smoke and dust swirling about—but never the wind itself.

In describing the propagation of a soundwave through a gaseous medium, we referred to the displacement of individual gas molecules and to the generation of local regions of excess pressure. Several additional properties of the medium vary as a soundwave passes through. In addition to the displacement of a gas molecule, we could specify the velocity or acceleration of a single molecule. Because there are brief local variations in pressure above and below the resting or ambient pressure, there are also local variations in the density (mass per unit of volume), and even in the temperature of the medium, which could be used to indicate the passage of a soundwave.

Before a soundwave passes through in a gaseous medium, the molecules are moving along random pathways, colliding with each other and with the surface of the enclosure and any object within the medium. On the average, however, the gas is at rest. That is, considered as a whole volume, it is not being displaced. Thus, we would say that the average molecular displacement is zero. If displacement is at zero for more than a brief instant, then molecular velocity and acceleration also must be, on the average, at zero. It is the convention in acoustics to refer to particles rather than to molecules or atoms of a gas. Thus, in a medium not transmitting a soundwave, the particle displacement, particle velocity, and particle acceleration due to sound are each equal to zero.

In our description of sound propagation, we noted that local variations above and below the ambient or resting pressure were the result of the alternating crowding (compression) and uncrowding (rarefaction) of molecules. Of course, the ambient pressure is due to the almost countless number of collisions of molecules with the walls of the container. Since one factor in determining the pressure is the number of molecules in a given volume, crowding them closer together will increase the pressure, while spacing them farther apart will reduce the pressure. The passage of a soundwave through a medium creates alternating local changes in the pressure which are often called the *sound pressure wave.*

table 4.3
various units of sound pressure

ABSOLUTE UNITS	RELATIVE UNITS
MKS units: 1 Pascal = 1 Newton/m² MKS→CGS 1 Pascal = 10 dyne/cm² CGS units: 1 dyne/cm² = 1 microbar (μb) CGS→MKS 1 dyne/cm² = 0.1 Pascal	0 dB SPL = 0.0002 bar = 0.0002 dyne/cm² = 20 μNt/m² = 20 μPa 1 Pa = 94 dB SPL 1 dyne/cm² = 74 dB SPL

Just as our description of sound generation and transmission in an elastic medium may take either a microscopic or a macroscopic viewpoint, our measurements too may have either basis. In the microscopic sense, we would define particle displacement, particle velocity, particle acceleration, and sound pressure at some given point. Specifically, *particle displacement* is the movement of one gas particle, in a stated direction, caused solely by the passage of the sound energy through the medium. If we could observe one single particle in a gas and then obtain its particle displacement, we would have to subtract the movements of the whole body of gas from the movement of the one particle. We would then have the displacement due to the sound energy alone. It is not yet possible to observe and measure one single gas molecule, but we can define and measure such microscopic quantities indirectly. *Particle velocity* is that portion of the velocity of a single gas molecule that is due to the passage of sound energy. Likewise, *particle acceleration* is excess acceleration due solely to the passage of sound energy. *Sound pressure at a point,* is the instantaneous change in pressure at a single point within the medium due to the sound wave. It reflects the very small variation in pressure about the much larger ambient pressure. In the following discussions, we will be most concerned with particle velocity and sound pressure at a point. The units of particle velocity are meters/sec (MKS) or cm/sec (cgs). The units of sound pressure have changed over the past several years, so that we can find references to sound pressure in microbars, dynes/cm², Nt/m², or Pascals. Table 4.3 gives the relationships among these units.

Let us switch now to the macroscopic viewpoint. In the macroscopic view, we consider a standardized volume of the medium and report the average displacement, velocity, or acceleration of the particles within that volume due to the soundwave. Often, it is mathematically useful to consider that these average values represent the motion of a hypothetical three-dimensional cube of the medium. Textbooks on acoustics treat displacement, velocity, or acceleration of a small volume of the medium. These quantities are, respectively, volume displacement, volume velocity, and volume acceleration. Our concern will be with volume velocity, usually given the symbol U and reported in either m³/sec (MKS) or cm³/sec (cgs). In any sound-conducting medium, there is a relationship between particle and volume velocity. If we consider that volume velocity represents the particle velocity of the molecules flowing through a standard area, S, then we may obtain volume velocity, U, by multiplying the particle velocity, u, by the area, S. In an equation

$$U = S \times u$$

Likewise, sound pressure is averaged over the same surface area, rather than being specified at one point in the medium.

In an earlier section we indicated that the opposition to the flow of sound energy through an elastic medium is called the acoustic impedance of that medium. We are now able to define acoustic impedance more precisely. For any given medium, the acoustic impedance is the ratio of applied sound pressure to the velocity produced. If we use microscopic terms, then we define the *specific acoustic impedance*, Z_s, as (sound pressure at a point)/(particle velocity). In an equation, $Z_s = p/u$. The units are (dyne/cm²)/(cm/sec), which are called *rayls*. In a free, plane progressive wave, the specific acoustic impedance is called the *characteristic impedance*, Z_c, of the medium. The characteristic impedance of a medium is also equal to the product of the ambient density of the medium, ρ_0, times the speed of propagation of soundwaves in that medium, c. Thus, in an equation

$$Z_c = \rho_0 \ (g/cm^3) \times c \ (cm/sec) \ rayls$$

In considering macroscopic quantities, the impedance is simply called *acoustic impedance*, Z_A. Acoustic impedance is given as the sound pressure, p, divided by the volume velocity, U. In an equation

$$Z_A = p/U$$

The units are (dyne/cm²)/(cm³/sec), which are called *acoustic ohms*. If MKS units are used, then we have $Z_A = (Nt/m^2)/(m^3/sec)$ in MKS acoustic ohms. An MKS acoustic ohm is 10^5 cgs acoustic ohms.

Since most of our measurements are made in air at approximately standard pressure and temperature, we are rarely concerned with calculating acoustic impedances. The characteristic impedance of air is usually built into measuring instruments as a calibration constant. When we wish to describe a sound waveform, we use a calibrated microphone to convert the sound energy into an electrical form. Standard instruments for making electrical measurements can then be used to determine the parameters that describe the soundwave. Let us assume that the soundwave we want to describe is a sinusoid. Recall that three parameters are sufficient to describe completely any sinusoidal waveform. Thus, we may describe the soundwave by measuring its amplitude, frequency (or period), and starting phase.

In many cases, we do not consider the phase of a sinusoidal sound pressure waveform delivered to one ear to be a necessary descriptor, because the normal listener is relatively insensitive to phase. That is, a change in the starting phase of a sinusoid delivered to one ear does not alter the listener's perception of the sound. Two-eared listening is another story. Using both ears, normal listeners are very sensitive to differences in phase between the sinusoids delivered to each ear. In any case, if starting phase is of interest, we most often use an oscilloscope to display the waveform and to determine its phase. The frequency or period of a sinusoidal sound waveform is also measured directly from the electrical signal delivered by the microphone, after any amplification that might be necessary. The instrument used is a specialized counter/timer. That instrument either determines the number of cycles of input waveform per unit of time (the frequency), or measures the time required for one cycle (the period).

The measurement of the amplitude of a sound waveform presents special problems. First, we must decide which amplitude to measure. We might wish to know the sound pressure amplitude, but it would be equally valid to try to measure the particle velocity amplitude, volume velocity amplitude, or displacement and acceleration amplitudes. Most often, we measure sound pressure amplitude. The reason for this choice is simple. A pressure-sensitive microphone converts sound energy into an electrical waveform with voltage proportional to the sound pressure. Thus, if we measure the voltage from a carefully constructed and calibrated microphone, we can determine the sound pressure of a given sound waveform. Unfortunately, we rarely use the sound pressure measurement directly. The quantitative attribute of sound intensity is loudness. That is, when we sense that there is "more sound," we report that the sound is louder. The loudness of sound is most directly related to the sound power or intensity. The intensity of a soundwave can be determined by multiplying the sound pressure, p, times the volume velocity, U. In an equation, we write $I = pU$ watts/cm^2 (or watts/m^2 MKS). There is also a relationship between sound pressure and volume velocity in the impedance equation $Z_A = p/U$. We may rearrange this equation to get $U = p/Z_A$. Now we may substitute this for U in the intensity equation $I = p(p/Z_A)$ or $I = p^2/Z_A$. Thus, sound intensity can be calculated by first measuring sound pressure.

In practice it is difficult to measure sound intensity directly, but relatively easy to measure sound pressure. Sound pressure is measured by an instrument known as a sound level meter. This instrument is made up of a high-quality sound-pressure-sensitive microphone, some electronic circuitry, and an indicating device, usually a meter. The pressure-sensitive microphone acts to convert the sound pressure at its surface into an electrical voltage. The electronic circuitry may be considered a special type of analog computer, since it produces an output for the meter that is proportional to the root mean square (RMS) value of the sound pressure. The RMS value of the amplitude of a waveform is obtained by taking the square root of the average (mean) of the squared values of the waveform. The average is taken for one cycle of a periodic waveform, and hence its RMS value is a constant. For a sinusoidal waveform, the RMS value is always equal to 0.707 times the amplitude. RMS values are used because they can be related to power or intensity by a simple multiplicative constant. The meter could be calibrated to indicate sound pressure directly in either dyne/cm² or Nt/m². Most often, however, the sound-level meter contains some additional circuitry which in effect multiplies the voltage analog of sound pressure by itself (a squaring circuit), then divides by a factor proportional to the acoustical impedance of air, Z_A. The meter indication is thus proportional to intensity, although the quantity actually measured is sound pressure. The electronic circuitry has implemented the equation $I = p^2/Z_A$.

A further complication is introduced because a logarithmic transformation of the intensity is conventionally used. This logarithmic transformation is the basis of the decibel scale, which is a relative rather than an absolute measure of intensity. In almost all our work with sound intensity, we seek relative measurements not absolute ones. We ask, "How much poorer than normal is the threshold of the patient with a hearing loss?" Or, "How much louder than the average is the stressed syllable?" Let us consider a simple example to illustrate the utility of relative measurements. Suppose that you and a friend decide to lose some weight for health, fun, and profit. Your friend tips the scales at an even 200 lb (only 90.7 kg). You are a petite 120 lb (54.4 kg). It would be unfair to base the bet (remember the profit part) on the absolute number of pounds lost. A 10 lb loss to your heavy friend would be only a 5 percent reduction in body weight. A 10 lb loss for a 120 lb person is an 8 $\frac{1}{3}$ percent reduction. Since you are starting at different weights, it is only fair to compare relative weight losses. Thus, if you lose 10 lb from 120 lbs, your friend should lose 16 $\frac{2}{3}$ lb to keep up with you.

When we wish to compare one sound intensity with another, we almost always use a relative measure. The *decibel scale* was devised in order to facilitate relative measures of sound intensity and to make measurements comparable from one clinic or laboratory to another. The decibel scale provides a standard normative intensity to which measured intensities may be referred. The normative intensity is often called the reference intensity. In addition to providing a widely accepted reference for all relative intensity measurements, the decibel scale also provides a common set of units.

Further incentive for the relative measurement of sound intensity is found when we examine the range of absolute intensities covered by sounds in our daily lives. If we were to measure the intensity of a sound just detectable by the listener and then measure the most intense sound that the same listener could tolerate, the second number would be about 10^{12} times larger than the first (10^{12} represents 1,000,000,000,000). The range of numbers that describe the absolute intensities to which our auditory systems respond is thus very

table 4.4
typical sound pressure levels for everyday sounds

SOUND PRESSURE		SOUND PRESSURE LEVEL[b]	ENVIRONMENTAL CONDITION
(μb)	(N/m² or Pa)		
0.0002	0.000020	0	Threshold of hearing
0.00063	0.000063	10	Rustle of leaves
0.002	0.0002	20	Broadcasting studio
0.0063	0.00063	30	Bedroom at night
0.02	0.002	40	Library
0.063	0.0063	50	Quiet office
0.2	0.02	60	Conversational speech (at 1 m)
0.63	0.063	70	Average radio
1.0[a]	0.1	74	Light traffic noise
2.0	0.2	80	Typical factory
6.3	0.63	90	Subway train
20	2.0	100	Symphony orchestra (fortissimo)
63	6.3	110	Rock band
200	20.0	120	Aircraft takeoff
2000	200.0	140	Threshold of pain

[a] $1\mu b = 1$ dyne/cm² $= 74$ dB is a common reference pressure for instrument calibration. It is also a reference pressure for measurements in underwater acoustics.
[b] Reference is $2 \times 10^{-4} \mu b = 2 \times 10^{-5}$ N/M² $= 2 \times 10^{-6}$ Pa.

Source: F. A. White, *Our Acoustic Environment.* © 1975, John Wiley & Sons, Inc. Reprinted by permission.

large. Table 4.4 illustrates a set of typical numbers spanning this range. In absolute terms, they are difficult to handle. By writing the numbers in scientific notation, we reduce the bookkeeping problems tremendously. The use of scientific notation is the first step toward a relative measurement. If we agree to use 10 as the base, then every number can be expressed as an exponent of 10. Thus, 10^2 can be expressed as 2 relative units; 10^9 as 9 relative units, and so forth. The relative unit in this system has the name *Bel* (after Alexander Graham Bell). Thus, a measurement of 10^2 is 2 Bels.

In actual practice, the intensity that serves as a reference is 10^{-16} watts/cm². That is, 0.000,000,000,000,000,1 watt/cm². All sound intensity measurements made in air are expressed in relation to that accepted reference quantity. The standard symbols are I_0 or I_{ref}. Any measurement of sound intensity, I_1, can be expressed as a ratio relative to the reference. Thus, we would calculate I_1/I_0. If we express this ratio in scientific notation and use only the exponent of 10, then the measurement is in Bels.

It will be rare indeed when the ratio of intensities is expressed simply as a power of 10. More often, there will be some multiplier out in front of the 10. Thus, 20 is 2×10 and 2000 is 2×10^3. Mathematically, it is possible to express

Acoustics: The Science of Sound

any number as a power of 10 if we allow fractional (or decimal) exponents. Thus, 200 is $10^{2.301}$. These fractional exponents are tabulated so that there is never a need to work them out. The table is called a table of common logarithms. Thus, a logarithm is simply an exponent of the number 10. In an equation, we calculate the relative intensity of a sound in Bels by the formula

$$\text{Bels} = \log_{10}(I_1/I_0)$$

But the Bel is too gross for many of the measurements required in acoustics. Thus, the more common unit is the *decibel (dB)*. The prefix *deci* means $\frac{1}{10}$; thus, 1 Bel equals 10 decibels. In the formula, we have

$$\text{Number of decibels} = 10 \log_{10}(I_1/I_0)$$

Relative intensity has no absolute units, and the decibel is often taken as a unit of intensity. To distinguish absolute from relative measurements, we use the term *level*. If we measure absolute intensity in watts/cm², we report the intensity. If, however, we express an intensity in relative terms, we report an *intensity level* (IL) in decibels. If the reference is not the standard one, then it must also be given—for example, 13 dB re: 1 milliwatt/cm².

The reader must be especially wary of the term *sound pressure level (SPL)*. We said above that often sound pressure is measured instead of intensity. The sound pressure is transformed by the measuring instrument so that the meter indication is proportional to relative intensity. The term sound pressure level has evolved from the realization that the sound level meter actually responds to the sound pressure at the surface of its microphone, but the electronic circuitry has been designed to indicate intensity level. It must be kept in mind that sound pressure level and intensity level are always synonymous and always numerically equal. To state this in equation form, begin with the two equations

(1)
$$I_1 = p^2/Z_A$$

(2)
$$IL = 10 \log_{10}(I_1/I_0)$$

We may substitute equation (1) into equation (2) twice for both I_1 and I_0. Then

(3)
$$IL = 10 \log \frac{p_1^2/Z_A}{p_0^2/Z_A}$$

Since Z_A is the same in both numerator and denominator, it can be canceled out. Thus, we arrive at

(4)
$$IL = 10 \log(p_1^2/p_0^2)$$

This is the same as $IL = 10 \log(p_1/p_0)^2$ which is equal to $IL = 2 \times 10 \log(p_1/p_0)$, and

(5)
$$IL = 20 \log(p_1/p_0)$$

Thus, we have $IL = SPL$ always. A number of texts provide greater detail concerning the use of decibel notation in practical problems, and some are listed at the end of this chapter.

In this chapter we have introduced the basic concepts of acoustics. We have attempted to show the reader the relationship between the transmission of information and the transmission of energy. The chapters to follow will discuss the production of speech and the function of the auditory system in terms of the generation and transformation of energy forms. The concepts of impedance, resonance, and filtering will be used again and again to describe the actions of the larynx, vocal tract, or cochlea. Our final concern in this chapter has been the measurement of sound. It is unlikely that our knowledge of acoustics would be of value if we were unable to quantify them.

SUGGESTED READINGS

EARGLE, J. *Sound Recording.* New York: Van Nostrand Reinhold, 1976. An excellent treatment of acoustical principles for those working in the sound recording industry. Easily understood by the nontechnical reader.

KINSLER, L. E., and A. R. FREY. *Fundamentals of Acoustics,* 3rd ed. New York: Wiley, 1962. This text is the standard reference for advanced students in acoustics. A knowledge of calculus is essential to understanding most of the material.

SHIVE, J. R. *Similarities in Wave Behavior.* Bell Telephone Laboratories. Baltimore: Waverly Press, 1961. An excellent introduction to wave motion for the nontechnical student.

WHITE, F. A. *Our Acoustic Environment.* New York: Wiley, 1975. This text presents an up to date discussion of applications of basic acoustics. It is written for engineering students, but much of the discussion will be of value to the nonengineer.

THE RESPIRATORY SYSTEM

5

A POWER SUPPLY

the movement of gases / the process of breathing
respiratory muscles: movements of the thoracic skeleton and diaphragm
breathing for speech / the relationship of respiratory pathology to speech
suggested readings

Human speech sounds are generally produced with outwardly flowing (egressive) air. However, sound can also be produced by inward flow (ingression) of air into the vocal tract. For example, when a mother scolds her child by saying "tsk, tsk, tsk," she makes the clicks by using her tongue to draw air into the vocal tract. We are all familiar with the loud sounds associated with vigorous kissing. These sounds are caused by the ingressive flow of air created by the puckering and quick release of the lips. Another example of sounds produced during ingressive airflow are those which occur during the act of crying. It is of particular interest to note that crying sounds, associated with sadness, are typified by ingressive airflow, and laughing, associated with happiness, is typified by egressive airflow. The compression or rarefaction of air is necessary for producing egressive or ingressive airflow; the compressed or rarefied air is the source of power for sound production. To visualize the power of compressed air to create sound, use your lips to create the three general classes of speech sounds. First, close your lips, then blow them open with a *pop*. This is an *explosive* (plosive) sound. Next, blow air through partially closed lips as if you were cooling a cup of hot coffee. This is a *friction* (fricative) sound. Now buzz your lips as if you were imitating the sound of a motor or expressing disbelief; place your hand near your lips and feel the air flowing outward. A clear understanding of this flow is based upon knowledge of the physical principles governing the flow of air. Therefore, we will begin our discussion of breathing and the respiratory system with an examination of these principles.

the movement of gases

We breathe to maintain life; only secondarily do we breathe to speak. Breathing for life is of paramount importance.

Our bodies need a supply of energy; without it, muscles weaken, cellular activities cease, and we die. Our energy supply comes from foodstuffs that release their energy as they are burned or oxidized inside our bodies. We can "burn" things in many gases, but oxygen is the preferred agent. Air is about 21 percent oxygen, and our food consists primarily of hydrocarbons. Hydrocarbons and oxygen combine so that

$$2\,(C_6H_{14}) + 18\,O_2 \rightarrow 12\,CO_2 \uparrow + 14\,H_2O + \text{energy} \left\{ \begin{array}{l} \text{heat} \\ \text{light} \\ \text{energy-rich} \\ \text{molecules} \end{array} \right\}$$

hydrocarbon + oxygen → waste products + released energy
(carbon dioxide,
water)

Oxidation of our food is not as violent as wood burning in a fireplace; rather, the food is burned inside our cells cooly and cleanly by using enzymes. Enzymes are complex molecules that promote and assist chemical reactions, one of which is oxidation.

On the average, the typical human being consumes 21 lb of dry food, 61 lb of water, and 60 lb of air containing about 6 lb of oxygen per week. The respiratory system serves to bring in a fresh supply of oxygen during inhalation, and to carry away excess CO_2 during exhalation. The air we inhale is about 21 percent O_2 and 0 percent CO_2; the air we exhale is about 17 percent O_2 and 4 percent CO_2; that is, it is O_2 depleted and CO_2 rich. A complex exchange process of oxygen absorption and CO_2 release occurs in our lungs. A buildup of excess CO_2 in the bloodstream during exercise tends to make the blood acidic, which is life-threatening. Our body is provided with detectors that monitor CO_2 levels in the bloodstream. As CO_2 levels increase, signals are relayed to the brainstem which cause us to automatically increase the depth and frequency of respiration to overcome the oxygen deficit. During quiet, noneventful breathing, we *respire* (inhale and exhale) about 12 times per minute, although newborns may breathe as fast as 40 times per minute and a yogi as slowly as 2 to 3 times per minute. While we do this, our bodies are exchanging gases according to certain physical laws. Let us look first at the units of measurement in which the operation of these laws is expressed.

UNITS OF MEASUREMENT   Air is a mixture of gases, and the laws governing the motion or flow of gases are similar to those for the flow of fluids. Our understanding of airflow will begin with a review of the units of measurement needed to describe certain physical properties of gases. As you will recall from Chapter 4, the fundamental units of physical description are mass *(M)*, length *(L)*, and time *(T)*. These basic units can, in turn, be combined to define other dimensions of physical description, such as motion, force, or energy. For example,

$$\text{velocity (v)} = \frac{d}{t} \left(\frac{\text{distance}}{\text{time}} \right) = \frac{m}{\text{sec}}, \frac{\text{ft}}{\text{sec}}$$

$$\text{force (f)} = \text{mass} \times \text{acceleration} = M \cdot A$$

The unit of force, the Newton, is defined as:

$$1 \text{ Newton} = 1 \text{ kg} \times 1 \text{ m/sec/sec} = \frac{1 \text{ kg} \cdot \text{m}}{\text{sec}^2}$$

When a force acts through a distance, work is done and energy is expended. For example, if my car runs out of gas and I am energetic enough to push it toward a gas station with 550 lb of force over a distance of 100 feet, I have theoretically expended this much energy:

$$\text{energy} = \text{force} \times \text{distance}$$
$$= 550 \text{ lb} \times 100 \text{ feet}$$
$$= 55000 \text{ ft-lb}$$

The metric unit of energy, the Joule, represents 1 Newton of force applied through 1 meter of distance:

$$1 \text{ Joule} = 1 \text{ Newton} \times 1 \text{ meter}$$
$$1 \text{ Joule} = 1 \text{ Nt} \cdot \text{m}$$

Energy must be expended when a gas is compressed above the ambient or surrounding pressure or decompressed (rarefied) below it. The rate at which energy is expended may be slow or rapid. The great explosive force of dynamite results from the instantaneous release of the energy in the nitroglycerine. Energy release is slower when wood burns. If the wood is only decaying, it may be years before the energy is released. Thus, *power* is the rate of expenditure (release) of energy:

$$\text{power} = \text{energy/time}$$

The unit of power is the watt:

$$1 \text{ watt} = 1 \text{ Joule/sec}$$

If we examine any physical system, the total energy remains constant over time unless energy enters or escapes the system. Let's look now at gas pressure and how it is measured.

GAS PRESSURE   The air we breathe and use for talking is a mixture of gases, and each gas has a different molecular structure. A cubic meter of air contains billions of gas particles and has a density only about .0129 Nt/M³. A cubic kilometer of air at sea level, however, weighs almost 13 million Newtons. The earth is bathed in an ocean of gas particles. Air is held in place around the earth by the force of gravity. Atmospheric air pressure and density are greatest at sea level. The force a column of air about 400 kilometers high (which is about the effective height of the atmosphere) exerts on a square meter of surface at sea level is 1.013×10^5 Nt/m², or about 14.7 lb/in.². Pressure, as you recall, is defined as:

$$\text{pressure (P)} = \frac{\text{force}}{\text{area}} = \frac{\text{Newtons}}{\text{m}^2}, \frac{\text{dynes}}{\text{cm}^2}, \frac{\text{lbs}}{\text{in.}^2}$$

Consider the following example: 10 lb of force applied to an area of $\frac{1}{4}$ sq ft yields a pressure of 10 lb/$\frac{1}{4}$ ft^2 = 40 lb/ft^2. This is about the pressure exerted by slamming your open hand down on a table. Suppose that instead of your hand you used 10 lb of force to stick a knife into the table. The total area of the knife tip is .00001 ft^2. The pressure exerted by the knife tip is $^{10}/_{.00001}$ = 1,000,000 lb/ft^2, a very high pressure. This high pressure allows the knife to cut or to penetrate the table. The difference between a pat on the back and a stab in the back is the area of the instrument to which the force is applied: a knife's point versus a hand's width and length. Thus, pressure can be increased by increasing force *or* by decreasing area. The knife, as a tool, is a pressure amplifier that operates by slicing area to a bare minimum.

What does it mean to say that a gas "has pressure"? Within a container of gas, individual particles move in all directions, colliding with one another and the walls of the container. During collision with the walls of the container, the force of impact between the particles and the wall is transmitted to the wall. Imagine, if you will, billions of collisions per second occurring between gas particles and the walls of a container. Gas pressure is the sum total of the forces of collision of gas particles distributed over the area of the container's walls. When a container of gas is compressed to half its original volume, pressure doubles because there are twice as many particles per unit volume and hence twice as many collisions per unit area. Furthermore, the velocity of the gas particles increases as temperature increases. The faster-moving the particle, the greater the momentum at impact and the higher the resulting pressure. Thus, if temperature increases or volume decreases, the pressure of a volume of gas rises.

Measuring Pressure

The force exerted by air against a square inch of earth at sea level, 1.013×10^5 Nt/m^2 (14.7 lb/in.^{2}), is called 1 *atmosphere* of pressure. Suppose that the surface area of a body was about 3000 in.^{2}; then the total force pushing inward upon it is 14.7 lb/in.$^2 \times$ 3000 in.^{2} = 43,100 lb! But the pressure inside the body exactly counterbalances that outside, and the body is not crushed.

Early scientists measured atmospheric pressure by measuring the push (downward force) of the atmosphere on columns of fluid. A tall tube was first filled with liquid and sealed. Then the bottom of the tube was opened, as shown in Figure 5.1. The fluid began to fall in the tube under the accelerating force of gravity, until the atmospheric pressure at the surface of the fluid reservoir matched the downward pressure exerted by the fluid column. When the two pressures are equal, the fluid column has a height *h*. The fluid in the pipe exerts a pressure:

$$P_{fluid} = P_F = \rho g h$$

where h = height of fluid column
ρ = density of fluid
g = acceleration of gravity

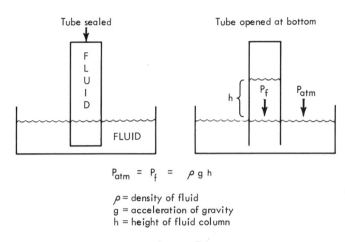

$$P_{atm} = P_f = \rho g h$$

ρ = density of fluid
g = acceleration of gravity
h = height of fluid column

figure 5.1

An example of how to measure the pressure of
the atmosphere by using a column of fluid.

Thus, atmospheric pressure is equal to the pressure exerted by the column of fluid:

$$P_A = P_F = \rho gh$$

Above the fluid column is a vacuum, which is needed so that the atmosphere is not pushing the fluid column downward, but only the weight of the fluid itself. It was found that 1 atmosphere of pressure counterbalanced a 32-foot column of water (384 inches) or 760 mm of mercury, each fluid of different density being supported at a different height. Pressure can therefore be expressed in terms of the height of a column of fluid which that pressure will support. It can be measured with a variety of devices, one of which is called a manometer. Figure 5.2 shows a man blowing into a manometer. The man builds up a pressure in his mouth, P_m. The total pressure in the man's mouth is $P_m + P_{atm}$; the pressure exerted at the other end of the tube is $P_F + P_{atm}$. P_{atm} cancels, and $P_m = P_F = \rho gh$.

$$P_m = \rho gh$$

where h = height measured in cm
ρ = 1.00 (for water)
g = 980 cm/sec/sec

If the man develops a pressure of 4900 dynes, his breath will support a column of water 5 cm high. How much excess pressure (above ambient or atmospheric) do we develop in the lungs for speech? Rarely more than 30 cm H_2O, and usually only 5 to 12 cm H_2O. Contrast these small lung pressures with atmospheric pressure, which is about 975.36 cm H_2O!

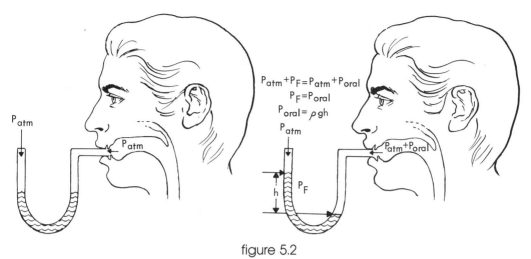

figure 5.2

An illustration of the use of a water manometer to measure
the pressure developed by blowing into the manometer
P_{atm} = pressure of the atmosphere, P_{oral} = pressure in the
mouth, P_F = pressure fluid, h = height of fluid, P_p = ρgh.

Boyles Law: Pressure and Volume   If we treat a volume of gas as a closed
system (not in contact with the outside world), we can easily understand the
discoveries of the British physicist Sir Thomas Boyle, who examined the relationship between the pressure and volume of a fixed amount of gas.

First, it is important to understand that given a container of "ideal" gas
with volume V, we can estimate the energy content of the gas volume if we
know the gas pressure, P. That is, the energy of the volume of ideal gas is the
product of its pressure times the volume:

$$E = P \times V$$

$$\text{energy (force} \times \text{distance)} = \text{pressure} \left(\frac{\text{force}}{\text{area}} \right) \times \text{volume (distance}^3)$$

$$\text{energy (force} \times \text{distance)} = \frac{\text{force}}{\text{dist}^2} \cdot \text{distance}^3 = \text{force} \times \text{distance}$$

$$\text{energy (force} \times \text{distance)} = \text{force} \times \text{distance}$$

The law of conservation of energy (and mass) states that the total energy (and
mass) in a closed system is constant over time. Stated simply, energy can neither be created or destroyed beyond what is already present in the system.

Boyle experimented with fixed amounts of gases inside airtight containers
by applying pressure and observing changes in volume. He conducted his work
at constant temperature to avoid temperature-related pressure fluctuations.
Boyle discovered that: Given a volume of gas (V_1) at pressure (P_1), a shift in
pressure to (P_2) causes the gas volume to change to V_2. Boyle demonstrated

that the product of pressure and volume was constant for a given mass of gas such that:

$$P_1V_1 = P_2V_2 \quad \text{or} \quad \frac{P_1}{P_2} = \frac{V_2}{V_1}$$

But, since energy $= P \times V$, energy$_1$ = energy$_2$. Thus, any increase in pressure causes a proportionate reduction in the volume of a gas. This must be the case: any change in the volume of a gas *must* be associated with a change in gas pressure such that the energy content of the gas is unchanged (conserved). Thus, if a 10 m³ volume of air at 20 Nt/m² pressure were decompressed to a 5 Nt/m² pressure, the volume would increase to

$$P_1 \times V_1 = P_2 \times V_2$$

$$20 \text{ Nt/m}^2 \times 10 \text{ m}^3 = 5 \text{ Nt/m}^2 \times V_2$$

$$V_2 = 40 \text{ m}^3$$

To increase the pressure of any gas, we need only compress it (make the volume smaller). To lower gas pressure, we need only increase the volume of the container.

THE FLOW OF GASES   Humans breathe by forcing gas to flow first outward (expiration) and then inward (inspiration). We do this by rhythmically increasing and decreasing the pressure in our lungs, P_{lung}, above and then below atmospheric (P_{atm}) pressure.*

What happens if a body of gas experiences two different pressures? Simply this: gas flows from the region of high pressure toward the region of low pressure. Anyone who has watched weather reports on TV suspects that wind travels (is forced) from high-pressure (highs) toward low-pressure regions (lows). Let's examine why this happens. Suppose two gas volumes are at different pressures; then let the two pressures in Figure 5.3 be such that pressure A is greater than pressure B. If so

$$P_A > P_B$$

since

$$P_B = \frac{\text{force B}}{\text{unit area}}, \quad P_A = \frac{\text{force A}}{\text{unit area}}$$

then

$$\frac{\text{force A}}{\text{area}} > \frac{\text{force B}}{\text{area}}$$

and

$$\text{force A} > \text{force B}$$

*Lung pressure, P_{lung} or P_L is also called alveolar pressure, P_{alm} since the lung is composed of air sacs called alveoli.

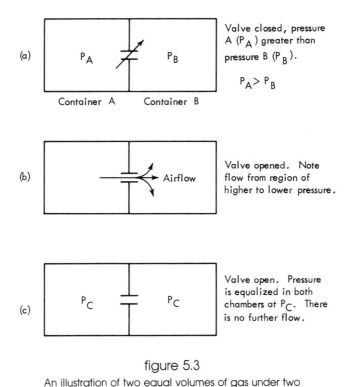

(a) P_A　P_B

Container A　Container B

Valve closed, pressure A (P_A) greater than pressure B (P_B).

$$P_A > P_B$$

(b) Airflow

Valve opened. Note flow from region of higher to lower pressure.

(c) P_C　P_C

Valve open. Pressure is equalized in both chambers at P_C. There is no further flow.

figure 5.3

An illustration of two equal volumes of gas under two differing pressures. In [a] the valve connecting them is closed. In [b] the valve is opened and air flows, and in [c] pressure is equalized, and no further flow occurs.

Thus, there is a net (unbalanced) force, ΔF, pushing from chamber A toward chamber B:

$$\Delta F = F_A - F_B$$

Newton's laws indicate that an unbalanced force acting on any body (solid, liquid, or gas) will cause an acceleration. When the valve connecting the chambers shown in Figure 5.3 is opened, the excess force in the region of higher pressure accelerates gas particles away from container A toward container B. Stated simply, a *wind* will blow from A to B until pressure is equalized, $F_A = F_B$; $\Delta F = 0$. When pressure is equalized, there is no accelerating force and there is no further flow of gas. Thus, if we wish to pump gas from point A to point B, we need only increase pressure P_A so that it is greater than P_B; gas will then flow until pressure is equalized at the two points. For example, if you select a pressure of 30 lb/in.² to inflate a car tire, air will flow from the pump into the empty tire until both pump and tire register 30 lb/in.² pressure. We also function as air pumps during respiration. Let us look now at how we breathe.

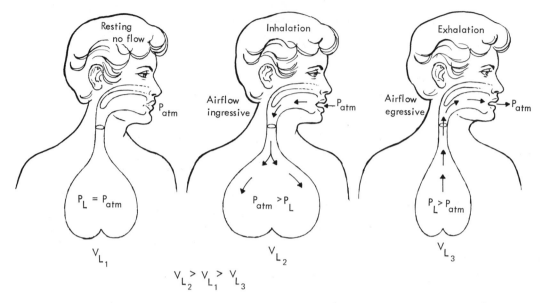

figure 5.4

Pressure and volume relationships in the respiratory
system during inhalation and exhalation.
P_{atm} = atmospheric pressure; V_L = volume of lungs.

the process of breathing

When we wish to inhale, we make our body (and lungs) bigger, and air flows
inward. To exhale, we make our body smaller in volume, and air flows out.
That is, we utilize the principles of Boyle's law. To convince yourself of this,
the next time you engage in the hopefully frequent experience of taking a bath,
fill the tub so that it covers your chest. Then, brace yourself under water and
inhale. As you inhale the water level in the tub will rise as the increased size of
your thorax forces water outward and upward. Be sure you hold yourself under
water, or the increased volume of your lungs will only cause you to float on the
water. Inside the thoracic cavity, which functions as an air container, the following manipulation of pressure and volume occurs: as volume increases ($V \uparrow$),
pressure must decrease ($P \downarrow$) in order that $PV = K$ (a constant amount of energy). As the volume of the thorax increases, pressure falls below atmospheric
in the lungs; if lung volume decreases, pressure in the lung, P_L, rises above atmospheric. Figure 5.4 displays the pressure/volume relations that occur during
inhalation.

Thus, we breathe by manipulating the size of the thorax. As thoracic volume ($V \uparrow$) increases, P_L decreases below atmospheric pressure, and air is
forced inward until lung pressure equals atmospheric. The thorax is then de-

flated, lung pressure rises above atmospheric, and air rushes outward until $P_L = P_{atm}$ once again.

To illustrate, suppose that 2 liters of air are under 6 Nt/m^2 of pressure. If the volume of the container is doubled from 2 to 4 liters, pressure will fall to half the original value:

$$P_1 V_1 = P_2 V_2$$

$$6 \cdot 2 = P_2 \cdot 4$$

$$3 \ Nt/m^2 = P_2$$

THE ANATOMICAL
FRAMEWORK FOR BREATHING   To understand the movements needed for breathing, we need to understand the anatomical structure of the thorax and abdomen. Figure 5.5 presents a frontal view of the body and shows two major body cavities, the thoracic and abdominal. These cavities are separated by the diaphragm, a dome-shaped muscular partition set between them. Within the air-tight thorax lie the lungs, heart, and various respiratory airways. The lungs, to-

figure 5.5

A frontal section of the body illustrating the thoracic and abdominal cavities. Reprinted by permission from F. D. Minifie, T. J. Hixon, and F. Williams, eds., *Normal Aspects of Speech, Hearing, and Language.* © 1973 by Prentice-Hall, Inc.

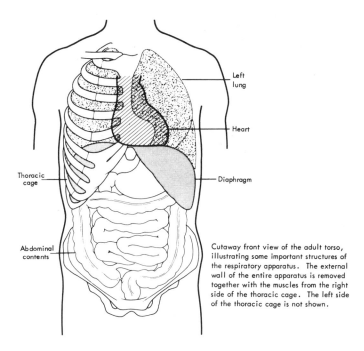

Left lung

Heart

Thoracic cage

Diaphragm

Abdominal contents

Cutaway front view of the adult torso, illustrating some important structures of the respiratory apparatus. The external wall of the entire apparatus is removed together with the muscles from the right side of the thoracic cage. The left side of the thoracic cage is not shown.

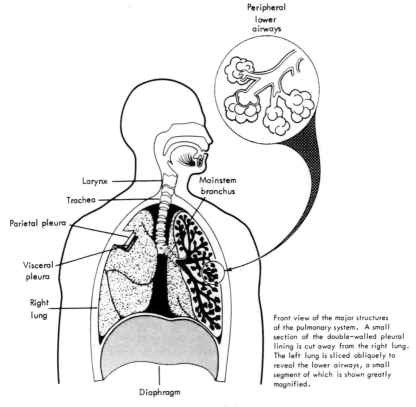

Peripheral
lower
airways

Larynx

Trachea

Parietal pleura

Visceral
pleura

Right
lung

Mainstem
bronchus

Diaphragm

Front view of the major structures
of the pulmonary system. A small
section of the double-walled pleural
lining is cut away from the right lung.
The left lung is sliced obliquely to
reveal the lower airways, a small
segment of which is shown greatly
magnified.

figure 5.6

A schematic view of the respiratory system. Reprinted by
permission from F. D. Minifie, T. J. Hixon, and F. Williams, eds.,
Normal Aspects of Speech, Hearing, and Language.
© 1973 by Prentice-Hall, Inc.

gether with the airways leading to them, are called the respiratory system (see
Figure 5.6).

The Thorax   The thorax or chest (see Figure 5.7) is
a large, rounded container, almost barrel-shaped. Its walls can be divided into
back (posterior), side (lateral), front (anterior), top (superior), and bottom
(inferior) margins.

The posterior thoracic margin is formed by the spinal column, an interconnected pillar of 34 vertebral bones subdivided into groups according to position or function. The top 7 vertebrae, C_1 to C_7, are the cervical or neck vertebrae. The skull rides atop cervical vertebrae one (C_1), the so-called Atlas.
Beneath the cervical vertebrae are the 12 thoracic vertebrae, T_1 to T_{12}, of the
upper back. Attached to each thoracic vertebra is a pair of ribs. Beneath the

thoracic vertebrae are the 5 lumbar vertebrae L_1 to L_5, then the 5 sacral verte-brae, S_1 to S_5, of the lower back, followed by the 5 rudimentary coccygeal ver-tebrae, C_1 to C_5. The 12 thoracic vertebrae form the posterior margin of the thorax.

The lateral thoracic walls are formed by the 12 pairs of ribs. Each rib of a pair is a roughly semi-circular bone, one for each half of the thorax. The ribs arch outward and downward from the vertebrae toward the sides, and rise from their low point at the angle of the rib toward the costal cartilages, which in turn are attached to the sternum. The sternum (breast bone) forms the anterior mar-gin of the thorax. The ribs are arranged so that ribs 1 to 5 attach (articulate) to separate costal cartilages, ribs 6 to 10 share a complex, common costal carti-lage attachment, and ribs 11 and 12 have no anterior attachment.

The superior margin of the thorax consists of the clavicles and scapulae. The clavicles (collar bones) are two long bones that span the distance between the top of the sternum and the scapulae (shoulder blades), a pair of triangular shaped bones attached to the upper back wall (ribs) of the thorax.

figure 5.7

The skeletal structure of the thorax shown in frontal and
posterior views. Reprinted by permission from F. D. Minifie,
T. J. Hixon, and F. Williams, eds., *Normal Aspects of Speech,
Hearing, and Language.* © 1973 by Prentice-Hall, Inc.

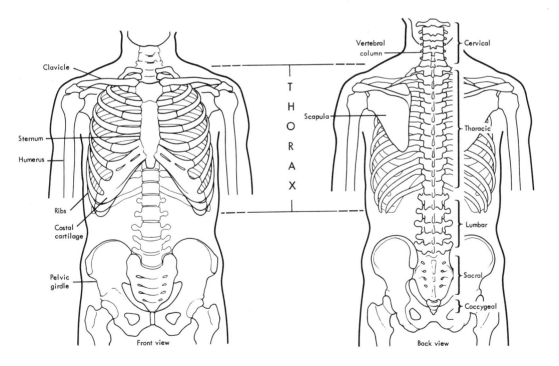

The Abdomen   The abdominal cavity has the lumbar, sacral, and coccygeal vertebrae as its posterior margin. The two coxal bones jointly form the cup-shaped pelvic girdle in which the abdominal organs rest. Anteriorly and laterally, the abdominal walls are primarily muscular.

THE PULMONIC SYSTEM   The pulmonary system consists of the lungs and the airways that connect them with the outer air. The pulmonary system can be compared with an inverted tree in terms of structure (see Figure 5.8). The vocal folds of the larynx divide the airways into upper and lower portions and act as a valve that controls air flow. The oral, nasal, laryngeal, and pharyngeal cavities collectively make up the upper airways. The lower airway begins at the trachea, a flexible tube composed of about 20 interconnected, C-shaped rings of *cartilage*. The opening in the rings faces posteriorly, where the muscular wall filling the opening also forms part of the esophageal wall.

The trachea divides into left and right main-stem bronchii, which in turn branch into lobar bronchii, and so on through about 20 generations of branching. At the end of the airways, bronchioles connect with alveolar sacs that contain the alveoli, tiny chambers within which CO_2/O_2 exchange occurs. The interior membraneous lining of each alveolum is richly supplied with enzymes that promote the passage of oxygen into the tiny arterioles lining its walls, and the escape of CO_2 from the blood vessels into the airways.

Lung tissue has a spongy, porous consistency and is highly compliant in nature. The inner surface of the thorax is lined with a thin, airtight parietal pleural membrane, and each lung in turn is wrapped individually in a pleural membrane termed the visceral pleurae. Between the two pleural membranes is a thin layer of fluid. Both pleural membranes tend to absorb gases within the fluid as well as the fluid itself; this absorption causes the occurrence of a large, negative pressure within the fluid. The intra-pleural fluid always has an internal pressure which is negative, averaging about −10mm Hg. This negative pressure links (sucks) together the visceral and parietal pleurae, and hence, holds the lung to the thoracic wall. Thus, there is a hydrostatic linkage between lung and thoracic wall. The smoothness of the pleural surfaces and the inter-membrane layer of pleural fluid provide low-friction surfaces against which lung and thorax may move during the expansions and contractions of thoracic volume which occur during breathing. Thus, the negative fluid pressure of the intra-pleural fluid layer compels the lungs to follow the movements of the thoracic walls.

THE ELASTIC PROPERTIES
OF THE THORAX AND LUNGS   As we breathe, the walls of the thoracic cavity must rhythmically expand (inflate, move outward), and then contract (deflate, move inward) so that the resulting variations in lung pressure will cause inward and outward airflow. The thoracic cavity is held together by a complex set of ligaments and tissues, and is encased in muscular walls. Ligaments, tendons, and muscles are elastic tissues. In addition, as the muscles of

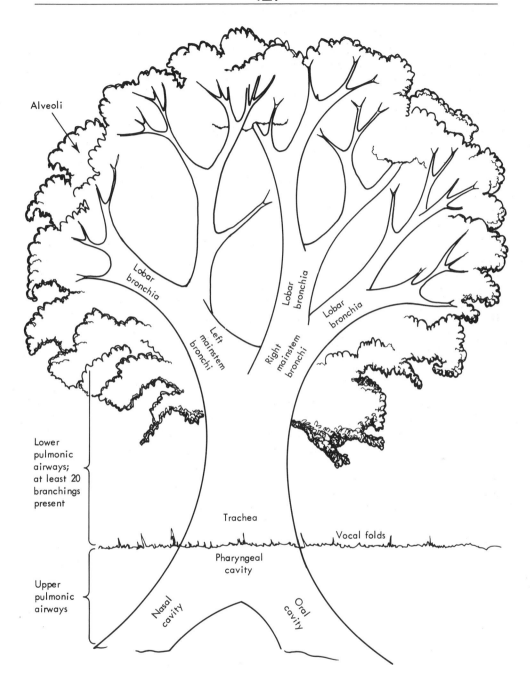

figure 5.8

A schematic drawing of the pulmonic system, shown upside-down to better illustrate the treelike structure of the system.

the thorax contract, their inherent elasticity changes as well. Moving the highly elastic thoracic walls and lungs in and out demands the use of muscular energy; that is, to breathe, our muscles must do work.

Elasticity is that property of matter by which it resists stretching, compression, twisting or any other distortion of resting shape or volume. The elastic body of material resists by offering a counterforce, which causes the body to spring back to its original shape or volume when the distorting force is removed. Suppose you squeeze a rubber ball, forcing it into a different (distorted) size. The more you attempt to compress it to smaller sizes, the more the ball resists with a counter-force. When you release the ball, it springs back into its original shape. Conversely, if the hollow ball is forced to expand into a larger than usual size by being blown up, it exerts a counter force which tends to make it smaller. The combined thoracic cavity–lung system is highly elastic, and has considerable mass and mechanical resistance. In fact, the pulmonary system has a substantial mechanical impedance (see Chapter 4). Any attempt to move the lung-thorax system toward a volume which is either greater or less than resting thoracic volume demands the use of considerable muscular force to overcome the mechanical impedance of the thoracic system.

If the thorax of a freshly killed animal is opened, air penetrates and destroys the pleural linkage, and the lungs separate from the thoracic walls and collapse. The lungs are observed to shrink to a smaller, resting size, and the thorax, relieved of the tug of the lung, expands to a larger size (see Figure 5.9). Even when the muscles of the thorax are at rest, the lungs and thorax are in a state of dynamic equilibrium, the outward expansion of the thoracic wall counterbalanced exactly by the inward contraction of the lung. The tendency for a body to spring back toward its original shape is called *recoil*, and the elastic restoring forces that force the body back into original shape are the *elastic (recoil) forces*.

figure 5.9

A diagram displaying the difference in size (volume) of the resting lungs, thorax, and combined lung-thorax system. Note that when lung and thorax are coupled, neither is at resting size.

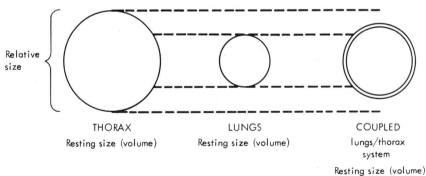

Relative size

THORAX	LUNGS	COUPLED
Resting size (volume)	Resting size (volume)	lungs/thorax system
		Resting size (volume)

Expansion of the thorax, then, results in increased lung volume, causing P_{lung} to fall below P_{atm}, resulting in inward airflow. Deflation of the thorax decreases lung volume, raises P_{lung} above P_{atm}, and causes egressive, outward air flow. The size of the highly elastic thorax can be shifted from resting volume *only if muscular energy is used to overcome the elastic recoil forces of the system.* A simple analogy can explain this statement. Suppose a marble were inside a cup with gently curving sides. The marble comes to rest at the lowest point of the cup. To move the marble up the side of the cup, I must push it with the muscular force of my finger. Once it is up on one side and then released, gravity will pull it down toward the center. Similarly, the respiratory system lung-thorax unit rests at the *resting expiratory level (REL),* the thoracic volume achieved when no respiratory muscles are active. To expand the thorax above or deflate it below REL demands use of respiratory muscle force. However, once expanded above or deflated below REL, elastic recoil forces will tug the lung-thorax unit back to REL.

THORACIC ABDOMINAL
MOVEMENTS DURING RESPIRATION   Figure 5.10 presents a simplified view of the thorax and abdomen as they move through a cycle of respiration. During inhalation, muscles tug the walls of the thorax outward and upward to increase its lateral dimensions. The diaphragm muscle can be contracted so that it moves downward, pushing the organs of the abdomen against the relaxed abdominal wall, which bulges outward. This movement increases the vertical dimensions of the thorax.

During exhalation, movements almost the opposite of those for inhalation occur. The elastic recoil forces of the expanded thorax and the thoracic muscles of exhalation tug the thoracic walls downward and inward while the active inward contractions of the muscles of the abdominal wall push the viscera and relaxed diaphragm back up into the thorax, thus reducing thoracic volume. The abdominal muscles are a functional part of the respiratory system. The intestinal contents (viscera) function as if they were an incompressible fluid, coupling the diaphragm to the abdominal walls. There is a synergy (cooperative function) between the abdominal muscles and the thoracic muscles of exhalation, with each contributing to reduction of thoracic volume.

FORCES INVOLVED IN RESPIRATION   The movements of the walls of the thoracic cavity toward expansion or contraction in volume are caused by unbalanced forces of two kinds: muscular forces (F_M) and elastic recoil forces (F_R). Both kinds of force may increase or decrease the volume of the thorax. Let us look first at the elastic recoil forces.

The resting size (volume) of the thorax (when all muscles are relaxed) occurs at the resting expiratory level. In most people this involves a lung inflation of nearly 37 percent of vital capacity. At REL, the inward lung recoil counterbalances the outward recoil of the thorax walls. As stated previously, recoil is

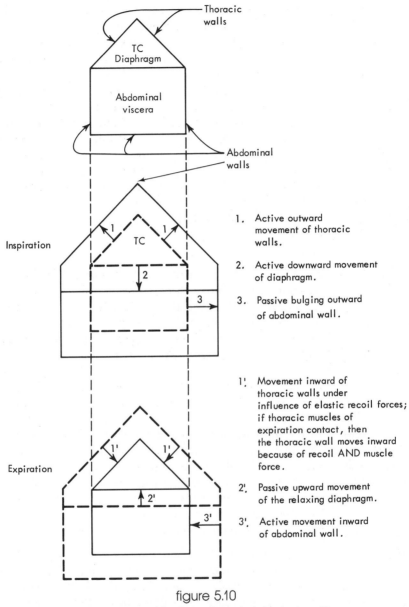

Thoracic walls

TC
Diaphragm

Abdominal viscera

Abdominal walls

Inspiration

TC

1. Active outward movement of thoracic walls.

2. Active downward movement of diaphragm.

3. Passive bulging outward of abdominal wall.

Expiration

1'. Movement inward of thoracic walls under influence of elastic recoil forces; if thoracic muscles of expiration contact, then the thoracic wall moves inward because of recoil AND muscle force.

2'. Passive upward movement of the relaxing diaphragm.

3'. Active movement inward of abdominal wall.

figure 5.10

A schematic view of the thoracic and abdominal cavities as they move through a cycle of respiration. A movement is said to be active when a muscle contraction causes the movement.

the elastic restoring force which a stretched/compressed body will exert in attempting to regain resting size. A body compressed to a smaller size exerts recoil force outward as it *expands* to resting position, see Figure 5.11. A body expanded to greater than rest size will exert a recoil force inward as it collapses (recoils) toward resting position. You can achieve REL with your lung-

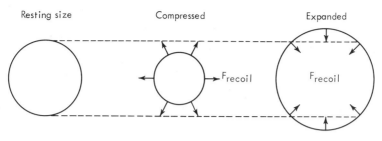

Resting size   Compressed   Expanded

F_{recoil} F_{recoil}

figure 5.11

A schematic illustration of the tendency for elastic recoil
forces to move a body toward its resting (equilibrium) size.
NOTE: When a structure is compressed, elastic recoil forces, pointing outward,
cause an expansion of the body toward its resting size. When a structure
is inflated, elastic recoil forces, pointing inward, cause a collapse
of the body toward its resting size.

thorax system by relaxing all your muscles while letting air escape as a sigh, keeping your larynx and mouth open. If thoracic volume is reduced below REL, the lung-thorax system recoils toward REL, developing a negative P_{lung} ($P_L < P_{atm}$) as it recoils. If lung volume is expanded above REL, the thorax recoils toward REL, shrinking in its size, developing a $P_L > P_{atm}$ as it recoils.

Examine Figure 5.12. Any increase or decrease of lung volume away from REL demands the use of muscle force to overcome the recoil of the lung-thorax system toward REL. Increasing lung volume above REL demands the use of muscles of inspiration. Thus, muscles of inspiration act to increase lung volume by overcoming the recoil of the thorax as one expands above REL. Any decrease of lung volume below REL demands the use of muscles of expiration to overcome recoil toward REL. If lung volume is above or below REL, the elastic recoil forces, *without* the use of muscle force, tug the thorax toward REL. You can test the recoil forces for yourself: Breathe deeply, then relax. You will recoil toward a smaller lung volume, toward REL, forcing air outward. Next, blow out all the air you can and relax. You will recoil toward a larger volume, toward REL, sucking air inward. Notice that at REL, there is no *net* recoil force, and hence no excess lung pressure developed by the elastic recoil force. To repeat: movement from REL toward lung volumes larger or smaller than REL *demands* the use of muscles of inhalation or exhalation to overcome the elastic recoil of the lung-thorax system.

Muscles of inhalation or exhalation can be used at any lung volume (see Figure 5.12). If the muscles of exhalation are active above REL, then the muscular force and elastic recoil force jointly combine to speed thoracic deflation toward REL. If muscles of inhalation are activated below REL, inflation toward REL is speeded up by the joint action of elastic recoil force and the force of muscles of inhalation force. Test this by inhaling fully and then blowing air out rapidly (this involves muscles of exhalation above REL). Note how much faster air flows outward compared with breathing deeply and merely letting elastic recoil force the air out relatively slowly. Conversely, exhale fully, then inhale rapidly; here muscles of inhalation are active *below* REL. The move-

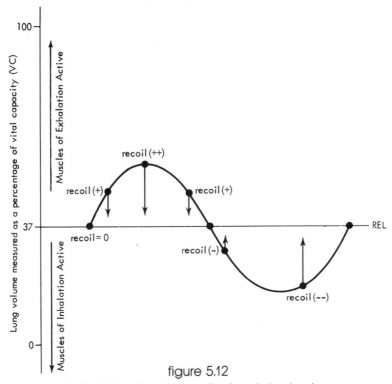

figure 5.12

An illustration of recoil forces developed at various lung
inflation volumes expressed as a % of vital capacity.
NOTE: All elastic recoil forces below REL develop negative (with reference to
atmospheric) lung pressures. All recoil above REL develop positive lung pressure. To
move above REL, muscles of inhalation must be active. Size of recoil force is equal
to length of arrow; direction of arrow indicates positive or negative lung pressure.

ment of the thorax above or below REL depends on the total force acting on
the thorax. Thus, at a given lung volume, total force = elastic recoil force + net
muscular force:

$$F_{net} = F_R + F_M$$

Muscles of exhalation generate a positive muscle force, and elastic recoil
forces above REL generate a positive force. Muscles of inhalation and elastic
recoil forces below REL generate negative force. Thus, if we assume that recoil toward REL from higher lung volumes yields a positive recoil force, then
the total force acting on the thorax is

$$F_{net} = F_M + F_R$$
$$F_{net} = (F_{MI} - F_{ME}) + F_R$$
$$since \ \ F_M = F_{MI} - F_{ME}$$

F_{MI} = force of muscles of inhalation F_R = elastic recoil force
F_{ME} = force of muscles of exhalation F_M = net muscular force

Above REL, $F_R = (+)$, below REL, $F_R = (-)$.

This equation implies that at any instant in time, three potential forces are act-ing: elastic recoil force F_R, which is positive above REL and negative below, muscles of inhalation force, F_{MI}, which is negative and muscles of exhalation force, F_{ME}, which is positive. Even normal speakers sometimes activate mus-cles of inhalation and exhalation simultaneously; as a result their muscular forces tend to cancel each other. The reader is reminded once again that if the thorax is inflated to any volume other than that at REL and all respiratory muscles are relaxed, the total force and pressure developed depend solely upon elastic recoil:

$$F_{net} = F_{recoil}$$

Elastic recoil forces acting on thorax walls produce a pressure in the lungs called *relaxation pressure,* P_{rel}. This pressure can be measured only if muscles are relaxed so that only the elastic recoil forces due to compression or expan-sion are acting on the thorax. When respiratory muscles are active, the result-ing lung pressure, P_L, is derived from the net total force, $F_{net} = F_M + F_R$, which is a combination of muscular and elastic recoil forces. The net force, acting upon the thoracic cavity, causes the walls to move inward if F_{net} total is posi-tive, generating a positive ($P_L > P_{atm}$) lung pressure. The exact size of the pres-sure developed by any given force is determined by a number of complex me-chanical factors, including the mechanical impedance of the thoracic walls and the mechanical advantage of the thoracic structures moving under the influence of those forces.

If you inhale and hold your breath, larynx open, the thorax does not de-flate because the muscles of inhalation continue to contract. A slow relaxation of the muscles of inhalation leads to a slow deflation of the thorax during ex-piration. The continuation of muscle of inhalation activity into the expiration phase is called *checking action.* It is one of the ways in which a speaker pre-vents the overrapid outflow of air during speech. Test checking action yourself by inhaling fully and *slowly relaxing* so that it takes at least 3 seconds to de-flate down to REL.

LUNG VOLUMES AND CAPACITIES   Just as gas tanks, bottles, and other containers are rated for their carrying capacity or volume, the thoracic cavity can be rated according to the total and partial volumes of air it contains. Figure 5.13 displays the volumes of air in the lung as a person inhales and exhales. The discussion of lung volume and capacities will center around REL, that point where the thorax is at rest. At REL, the respiratory system is typically between 35 to 40 percent full of air. The volume of air inhaled during quiet breathing is about 750 cm³ and is called *tidal volume.* Note that for quiet, tidal breathing, inhalation begins at REL and lung volume rises to a point called the end inspiratory level, whereupon expiration starts and the thorax deflates to REL. As breathing becomes deeper, the tidal volume of the breather may rise considerably above REL and descend considerably below it.

The maximum volume of air that can be inhaled and fully exhaled is called the *vital capacity, VC*. To illustrate this, breathe in as deeply as you can and

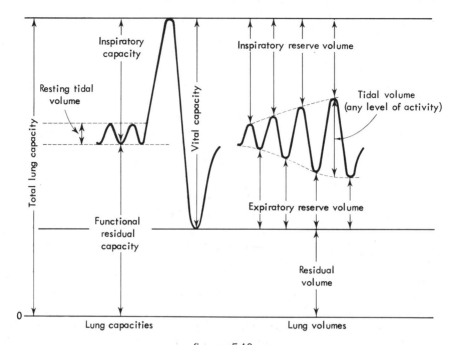

figure 5.13

A schematic illustration of lung volumes
and capacities during respiration

then exhale as deeply as you can. The total volume of air you have exhaled is
your vital capacity, about 3 liters for the average adult male. The maximum
volume of air you can inhale above REL is your inspiratory capacity, IC. As
you breathe tidally, the difference in lung volume between end inspiration level
and total lung volume is your inspiratory reserve volume, IRV. Note that as tidal volume increases in depth, IRV shrinks. A certain amount of air in the respiratory system cannot be forced out, since total collapse of the thorax, let
alone the respiratory airways and lung tissue, is impossible. This nonusable, or
at least nonexhalable, volume is called the *residual volume, RV,* and amounts
to about 2 liters of air for an adult. Total lung volume is the sum of VC and
RV. The volume of air that could be exhaled from the resting expiratory level
is the *expiratory reserve volume, ERV.* Note the following relationship:

$$IC = TV_{REST} + IRV$$
$$VC = TV + IRV + ERV$$
$$TLV = RV + VC$$

Tidal volume can be measured for each respiratory cycle, or it may be averaged over a number of respiratory cycles. Figure 5.14 shows the lung volumes
and capacities for a typical adult female.

LUNG VOLUME OR CAPACITY	MAGNITUDE (L)
Tidal Volume	0.5
Inspiratory Reserve Volume	2.5
Expiratory Reserve Volume	2.0
Residual Volume	2.0
Inspiratory Capacity	3.0
Vital Capacity	5.0
Functional Residual Capacity	4.0
Total Lung Capacity	7.0

figure 5.14

Typical values for various lung volumes
and capacities for a young adult female

As humans mature into adulthood, the thorax and its total capacity for air increases. With age and pulmonary illness, various lung volumes systematically decrease. To the respiratory physiologist, average values for these measures as a function of time, age, body weight, and so on are important diagnostic measures for the detection of respiratory pathology.

THE AERODYNAMICS
OF THE RESPIRATORY CYCLE   Breathing is a cyclical muscular behavior consisting of a period of inhalation with ingressive, inward flow of air into the respiratory system, and a period of outward, egressive flow during exhalation. Together, the inspiratory and expiratory phases of flow comprise a complete respiratory cycle. Inspiration is caused by increasing thoracic volume. The lungs expand in volume, lung pressure falls below atmospheric pressure, $P_L < P_{atm}$, and air rushes into the expanded lungs until $P_L = P_{atm}$. During expiration, thoracic volume is reduced, the lungs are compressed, P_{lung} rises above P_{atm}, and air is pushed outward until $P_{lung} = P_{atm}$ (see Figure 5.15). During inspiration above REL, muscles of inspiration must be active to increase thoracic volume above REL. However, during quiet (no exertion or speech) breathing, elastic recoil forces alone are generally enough to deflate the expanded thorax toward REL. Faster exhalation, or exhalation below REL, demands the use of expiratory muscle forces as well as elastic recoil forces.

Quiet or tidal breathing requires the expenditure of little energy. On the other hand, a worker or athlete may need oxygen badly enough to use nearly 100 percent of his or her vital capacity (total usable lung volume) many times a minute. In this case, the inspiration may start near 0 percent VC and terminate near 100 percent VC. Muscles of inhalation must be very strongly contracted to overcome increasing recoil forces as inspiration approaches 100 percent VC. Similarly, both recoil forces and muscles of exhalation are used to speed exhalation down to REL, beyond which muscles of expiration drive the thorax toward 0 percent VC. The more often we breathe and the more deeply we breathe, the more active our muscles of respiration must be.

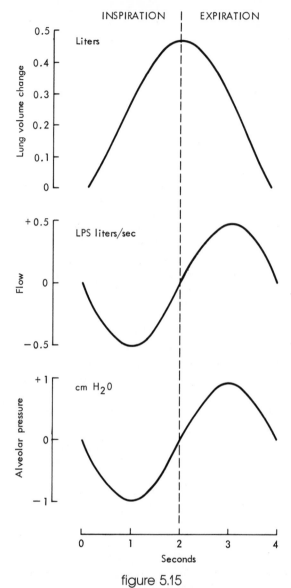

figure 5.15

A typical respiratory cycle pattern displayed in terms of lung volume changes, flow patterns, and lung (alveolar), pressures.

respiratory muscles: movements of the thoracic skeleton and diaphragm

As shown previously in Figure 5.10, the thorax increases and decreases its volume in three dimensions. Movement of the ribs upward and outward accounts for increased thoracic volume in a lateral (side to side) and antero-posterior (front to back) dimension. Downward movement of the diaphragm is accompanied by outward movement of the abdominal wall as the vertical dimension of the thorax increases.

THE RIBS AND DIAPHRAGM   Each of the first 10 ribs is connected at two pivotal points: one joint at the spinal vertebrae posteriorly and another at the costal cartilages, anteriorly. When appropriate muscles of inhalation contract, the ribs move in two ways: eversion and rocking. In eversion, each pair of ribs pivots on the four joints like the handles of a picnic basket (see Figure 5.16). As the rib pivots on its axis, the lateral width of the thorax increases as the rib rises, just as the basket handle does. The simultaneous upward and forward movement of the sternum and ribs as they pivot on the spinal column is a "pump-handle" motion, resulting in an antero-posterior expansion of the thorax. Vertical expansion of the thorax is attributable to contraction of the diaphragm, which moves downward, pushing the abdominal organs outward against the bulging abdominal wall, thus increasing the vertical size of the thorax.

figure 5.16

A schematic view of the two types of
rib movement used in thoracic expansion.

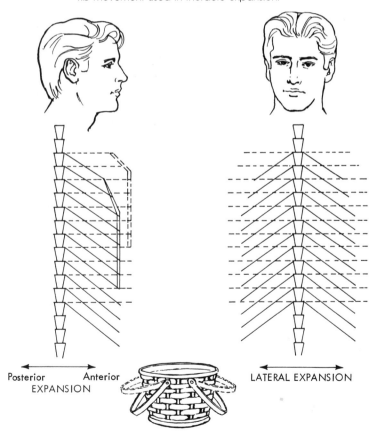

Posterior   Anterior   LATERAL EXPANSION
   EXPANSION

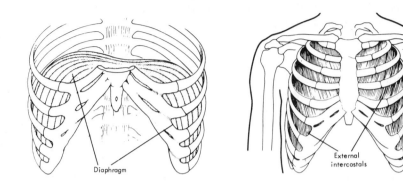

figure 5.17

The major muscles of inspiration. Reprinted by permission from
F. D. Minifie, T. J. Hixon, and F. Williams, eds., *Normal Aspects
of Speech, Hearing, and Language.* © 1973 by Prentice-Hall, Inc.

During expiration, the ribs are pulled down and inward in motions nearly opposite that for inhalation. The diaphragm relaxes, and the contraction of abdominal muscles compresses the abdomen, pushing the visceral organs up against the diaphragm and causing it to move upward, thus deflating the thorax.

THE MUSCLES OF INHALATION   The muscles of inhalation are grouped into thoracic muscles that contribute to the lifting of the rib cage and the diaphragm, which moves downward to increase the vertical dimensions of the thorax. The exact number of muscles which participate in inhalation depends upon (1) the speaker involved, and (2) the depth and strenuousness of the breathing. Zemlin (1968) has observed considerable anatomical variation in the respiratory and laryngeal musculature. This suggests that the degree to which certain muscles participate in respiration depends on their size, distribution, and presence in a particular speaker. The more rapidly and deeply we breathe, the greater the number of muscles called into play. The increased number of active muscles and their greater contraction are needed to (1) exert greater forces to overcome the increased recoil of the more drastically expanded or contracted thorax and (2) to speed up inflation and deflation of the thorax. During quiet respiration, only a few muscles of inhalation are active. Mechanically speaking, major muscles of inhalation and exhalation are those most efficiently positioned to create swift and substantial volume changes in the thorax. Physiologically speaking, the major respiratory muscles are those that are strongly active even during moderately loud speech. Based on these criteria, the diaphragm and external intercostals are the major muscles of inhalation (see Figure 5.17).

The External Intercostals   The eleven pairs of external intercostal muscles fill the spaces between the ribs. These thin sheets of muscle extend from the spine to a point somewhat short of the rib cartilages. Their muscle fibers run in superior-lateral direction between the upper margin of one rib and the lower margin of the rib immediately above. Contraction of the external intercostals causes the entire rib cage to lift upward and outward, thus increasing thoracic volume. Such an increase depends upon the upper ribs being fixed in position against the pull of the external intercostals as they lift the lower ribs.

The Diaphragm   The diaphragm is the other major muscle of inhalation. This large, dome-shaped structure has an outer ring of muscle fiber and a central tendon. When the muscle fibers contract, they pull the central tendon of the diaphragm downward toward the abdominal cavity, and at the same time tend to spread the lower few ribs. The muscle fibers of the diaphragm are attached to the lower ribs, the sternum and lumbar vertebrae, and the pericardium (the membraneous covering of the heart). Upon relaxation of the diaphragm, contraction of the abdominal muscles forces the viscera to push the diaphragm upward, the lower few ribs return to a precontracted position, and the volume of the thoracic cavity is reduced.

Secondary Muscles of Inhalation   During strenuous inhalation, numerous additional or "secondary" muscles of inhalation participate in thoracic expansion. These muscles assist in lifting the ribs or brace the upper ribs so that the lower ones may be lifted, primarily by the external intercostals (see Figure 5.18).

The pectoralis major originates from the humerus of the arm and fans out widely over the thorax, inserting broadly on the sternum, costal cartilages, and the clavicle. When the upper arm is held in a fixed position, contraction of this powerful muscle will lift ribs and sternum upward. The pectoralis minor is a relatively small muscle lying beneath the pectoralis major. It arises from the scapula and inserts upon the upper 7 or 8 ribs. If the scapula is fixed in position, contraction of this muscle will assist in lifting those ribs.

The costal levators are a set of 12 paired muscles (one for each rib on each side). The levators originate on vertebrae C_7 to T_{11} and course downward to insert on the superior rear surface of the rib immediately below. Contraction of these muscles assists in lifting the ribs.

The serratus anterior is a flat sheet of muscle arising from the anterior-lateral margin of each scapula. It courses around the angle of the ribs, where it fans out into fingers that insert into the upper 8 to 9 ribs. With the scapula fixed in position, contraction of the serratus anterior will tend to lift the ribs. The serratus posterior superior muscle originates as a band of fibers from vertebrae C_7 and T_{1-4}. The fibers course downward to insert on the upper edges of ribs 2 to 7. Contraction of the serratus posterior superior lifts these ribs.

The latissimus dorsi is a large, thin, fan-shaped sheet of muscle that originates on the humerus of the arm and fans out to attach to the lower ribs, 8 to 12, and lower vertebral column. With the humerus of the arm fixed in position, contraction of latissimus dorsi would tend to lift the lower ribs.

The scalenus muscle group, consisting of anterior, medial, and posterior bundles, arises from vertebrae C_{3-6} and courses downward to insert upon the superior surfaces of ribs 1 to 2, which they can lift or fixate when these muscles contract.

MUSCLES OF EXHALATION   If breathing is more rapid than during quiet breathing or exhalation deeper than REL, or if large expiratory air pres-

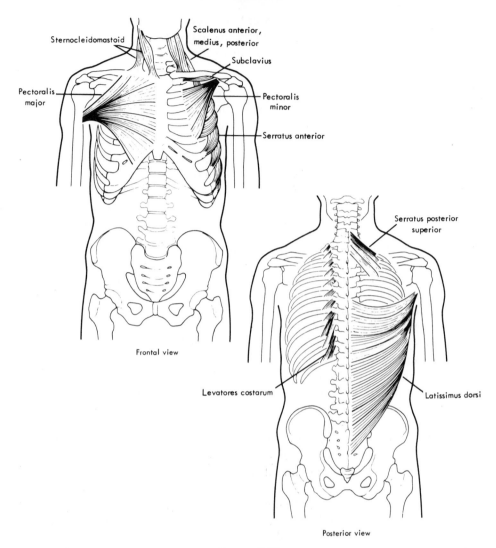

Frontal view

Posterior view

figure 5.18

The secondary (accessory) muscles of inspiration in frontal
and posterior views. Reprinted by permission from F. D. Minifie,
T. J. Hixon, and F. Williams, eds., *Normal Aspects of Speech,
Hearing, and Language.* © 1973 by Prentice-Hall, Inc.

sures are needed, the major muscles of exhalation are generally activated.
These include the internal intercostals and the abdominal muscles, taken as a
group (see Figure 5.19). Note that in *quiet* breathing, the major muscles of exhalation are not often called upon to cause thoracic deflation, since elastic recoil alone will deflate the thorax down to REL.

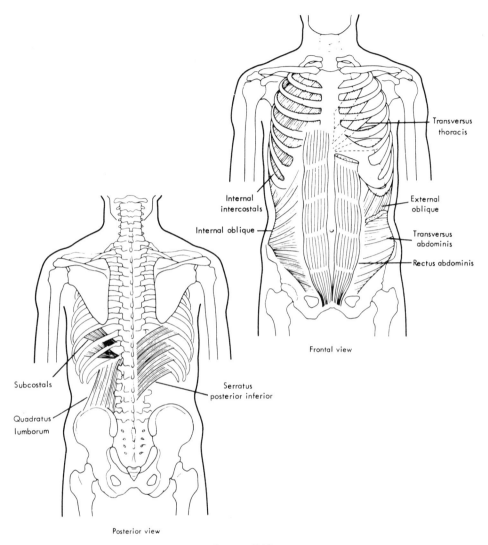

Transversus thoracis

Internal intercostals

Internal oblique

External oblique

Transversus abdominis

Rectus abdominis

Frontal view

Subcostals

Quadratus lumborum

Serratus posterior inferior

Posterior view

figure 5.19

The major and secondary muscles of exhalation as seen in frontal and posterior views. Reprinted by permission from F. D. Minifie, T. J. Hixon, and F. Williams, eds., *Normal Aspects of Speech, Hearing, and Language.* © 1973 by Prentice-Hall, Inc.

The Internal Intercostals   The internal intercostals are a set of 11 pairs of thin muscles that fill in the spaces between the ribs and extend from the sternum to a point short of the spine. They lie beneath the external intercostals, with fibers running inferiorly and medially at almost 90° to the external intercostal fibers. Upon contraction, each causes the rib above to be pulled toward the rib below. The internal intercostals deflate the thorax, reducing volume by pulling the ribs downward and inward.

The Abdominal Muscles   The abdominal muscles that are the other major muscles of exhalation are the rectus abdominis, the transversus abdominis, the external oblique, and the internal oblique muscles (see Figure 5.19).

The rectus abdominus is a large, long, twin-bellied belt of muscle, each belly of which is wrapped in a fascial sheath, with a thick layer of connective tissue, the abdominal aponeurosis, separating the two bellies. Rectus fibers extend from the pubis of the coxal bones upward to insert upon the lower sternum and the costal cartilages of ribs 3 to 7. Contraction of this muscle draws the ribs and sternum downward and compresses the abdomen, forcing the abdominal organs inward and upward.

The transversus abdominis is a large, flat muscle whose fibers course laterally from the upper surfaces of the coxal bones and from the cartilages of the lower ribs to insert into the abdominal aponeurosis. Contraction of this muscle flattens the abdominal wall, moving it inward.

The external oblique muscle fibers arise on the lower eight ribs; the fibers course downward laterally to insert into the abdominal aponeurosis and the pubis. When contracted, this muscle moves the abdominal wall inward.

The internal oblique, which lies beneath the external oblique, arises from the coxal bones and lumbodorsal fascia and fans out laterally, with fibers inserting into the lower few ribs and the abdominal aponeurosis. Contraction of this muscle also compresses and tenses the abdomen.

Secondary Muscles of Exhalation   The secondary muscles of exhalation are generally called into play when increased speed or depth of exhalation is necessary. They vary in number depending upon individual anatomy, habits, and strategies. Their primary function is either to lower the ribs or to fixate the lowest few ribs against the downward pull of the internal intercostals. These muscles are shown in Figure 5.19.

The serratus posterior inferior is a flat band of muscle arising from the lower few thoracic and upper few lumbar vertebrae. The fibers course upward laterally to insert on the lower margins of ribs 9 to 12. Contraction would, of course, result in lowering these ribs.

The quadratus lumborum is a powerful sheet of muscle that courses from the iliac crest of the coxal bone to insert into the inferior margin of rib 12. Upon contraction, it pulls rib 12 downward.

The subcostals are located on the interior of the posterior thoracic wall. They originate from the lumbar and thoracic vertebrae, coursing upward to attach to the lower margin of the ribs immediately above. Their contractions depress the ribs.

The latissimus dorsi can also function as a muscle of expiration, lowering the humerus and upper two or three ribs if the humerus is free to move.

Depending upon the experimental technique, the people studied, and the particular breathing task, there is wide variation in the number of secondary muscles of respiration used. If we breathe more deeply, more of them will be activated. However, the exact number activated depends upon the speaker and the task.

MUSCULAR MOVEMENTS
IN QUIET BREATHING

During quiet breathing (see Figure 5.13), we inhale about as fast as we exhale, and the tidal volume curve is nearly symmetrical. The muscles of inspiration are active in inflating the thorax above REL, with elastic recoil alone sufficing to deflate the thorax back to REL. As we begin to breathe more strenuously, respiration becomes faster and deeper. As a result, tidal volume increases at the expense of reductions in both inspiratory and expiratory reserve volumes. Stated simply, the more deeply we breathe, the more of our vital capacity we use. (Imagine what a person suffering from emphysema faces if his or her VC is reduced by 50 percent. Such a person finds it difficult to draw in sufficient air to satisfy oxygen demand.) The increased speed of exhalation is gained by adding the force of the muscles of exhalation to the elastic recoil forces. Increased speed of inhalation is gained by more forceful contraction of the muscles of inhalation. The magnitude and the sign (positive or negative) of the elastic recoil pressure depends only on lung volume. Above REL, recoil pressure is positive (above P_{atm}) as recoil force deflates the thorax toward REL. Below REL, recoil pressure is negative as recoil force inflates the thorax toward REL. Figure 5.20 shows the pressure that can be developed using the forces of elastic recoil alone.

figure 5.20

A graphic display of the recoil pressures developed at various degrees of lung inflation. The figure also displays possible lung pressures which may be developed at any lung volume if *muscle force* is added to the elastic recoil force acting on the thorax.

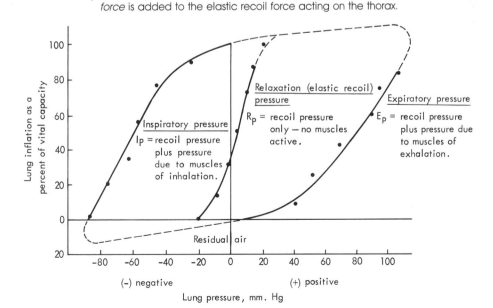

The relaxation pressure created by the forces of elastic recoil alone is measured in this way: A subject is asked to inhale sufficient air to achieve a particular lung volume, and then to hold his breath. He then places his mouth over a measuring device like the manometer shown in Figure 5.2 and relaxes all muscles, keeping the larynx open. As the thorax recoils toward REL, the relaxation pressure (there must be no air leaks!) builds up swiftly to a steady value and is attributable to elastic recoil forces alone. Notice in Figure 5.20 that as inflation increases above REL, the relaxation pressure is increasingly large and positive (airflow is egressive), $P_L > P_{atm}$. As one descends below REL, relaxation pressure is increasingly negative (airflow is ingressive, $P_L < P_{atm}$). Maximum recoil pressures are developed at or near 100% VC ($P_{relax} \cong 40$ cm H_2O), and 0% VC ($P_{relax} \cong -30$ cm H_2O).

The use of respiratory muscles permits a speaker to develop a wide range of positive or negative pressures at a given lung volume. For example, at a lung inflation of 60% VC, P_{relax} is +8 cm H_2O. To achieve +20 cm H_2O pressure, a speaker would activate the muscles of exhalation to develop the additional +12 cm H_2O pressure needed. Conversely, to develop -2 cm H_2O at 60% VC, he or she would have to activate the muscles of inhalation to develop the necessary $-P_L = -2$ cm, i.e.: (-10 cm$_{H_2O}$ +8 cm$_{H_2O}$) $= -2$ cm$_{H_2O}$. Any pressure to the right (increasing positive lung pressure) of the relaxation pressure curve is developed by adding appropriate force from the muscles of exhalation. Any pressure to the left of the P_{relax} curve demands addition of an appropriate negative force from the muscles of inhalation. Even if the lungs are nearly full, one can overcome the very large, positive P_{relax} and get a small negative lung pressure by strong activation of the muscles of inhalation. Test this for yourself by inhaling deeply. Then hold your breath a second, and inhale a bit more. You were able to inhale that bit more by adding a large, negative pressure developed by muscles of inhalation to the large, positive relaxation pressure.

breathing for speech

As we breathe during speech production, we are simultaneously (1) replenishing our oxygen supply and eliminating carbon dioxide and (2) using the compressed air to *phonate* (create speech sounds). Whether or not breathing during speech is fundamentally different from quiet breathing has long been a question. At the present time, the answer appears to be "No, they are not different." Functionally, we breathe in the same way during speech as for nonspeech. That is, we can talk quietly all day without experiencing oxygen starvation or CO_2 buildup. A soprano can sing Wagnerian opera for three hours at high sound-pressure levels without undue respiratory distress. Although patterns of muscle activity and airflow differ for speech and nonspeech, the differences are not so great as to contradict the fundamental need for maintenance of a steady oxygen supply.

For speech production, the respiratory system serves as a power supply that produces compressed air—air at pressures greater than atmospheric. The energy needed to compress the air is supplied by the muscles of respiration. Compressed air has the capacity to do work. The explosion of gasoline in the cylinder of an automobile creates a pocket of super-compressed gas that pushes the piston, spins a crankshaft, and causes wheels to turn. High explosives function by releasing huge volumes of compressed gas upon detonation.

During phonation, the potential energy of the compressed air is used to create acoustic vibrations, so-called speech sounds. Here we will examine the way in which the force of compressed air creates three general classes of speech sounds:

1. Explosive noises (pops)
2. Friction noises (fricatives)
3. Voiced sounds (buzzes)

Explosive or "plosive" sounds are created by building up compressed air behind a complete articulatory constriction of the vocal tract which is then rapidly opened. As the constriction opens, the compressed air escapes as an explosive transient that is heard acoustically as a "pop." Using your lips, make the sound [pʰ]. Listen to the explosion, and with the palm of your hand near your lips, feel the blast of air.

Fricative sounds are created when air is forced through a constriction under pressure. As the air flows through the constriction, its linear velocity of flow increases. All of us are familiar with the nozzle of a garden hose; as the nozzle is tightened, the water squirts out at higher velocities. As a high-speed jet of airflow escapes from a vocal tract constriction, the air begins to rotate and create eddies or vortices. The air turbulence created acts as a source of noisy acoustic vibration which we hear as fricative-type sounds. Sounds such as [s] in "sit," [f] in "free," or [θ] in "think," are examples of fricatives.

Voiced sounds are, technically speaking, buzzes. The buzz is created by forcing compressed air against the closed or nearly closed vocal folds. Since our lips vibrate much like the vocal folds do, let us use them to demonstrate buzzing. If you bring your lips together and build up oral pressure, your lips will begin to buzz. Each time the lips repetitively open and close, a burst of air escapes. The burst of compressed air creates an acoustic shock wave. If the air bursts escape in a periodic way (equal time between successive pulses), at a rate greater than about 20 pulses/sec, the resultant acoustic vibration is heard as a musical buzz. It is the rise in pressure above P_{atm} behind the lips that forces them to buzz. As long as there is sufficient difference in pressure between P_{atm} and P_{oral}, the lips will buzz. When the sound [u] is phonated, the larynx is buzzing rapidly, creating a train of air puffs that in turn create periodic acoustic vibrations, which escape out the appropriately shaped vocal tract to be heard as a [u] sound.

Speech production involves the creation of a smooth stream of explosions, frictions, buzzes, silences, and combinations thereof. The immediate source of power for the creation of the sounds is compressed air: The air is compressed by the respiratory muscle energy needed to expand the thorax, whereupon the resulting elastic recoil compresses the air. To repeat, much of the energy expended by the muscles of inhalation to inflate the thorax is stored as elastic recoil. The elastic recoil, in quiet speech, is enough to compress the thorax and thus to compress the air in the lung. In a number of languages, the lips, cheeks, tongue, and larynx are used to create the air compression (or decompression, if airflow is inward) for certain sounds. But the vast majority of sounds in all languages are created by the thoracic supply of compressed air.

PATTERNS OF AIRFLOW
AND PRESSURE FOR SPEECH
Although speech and quiet breathing are similar in that aeration of the blood is achieved, breathing for speech differs from quiet breathing in a number of ways. When we speak, we prolong our expiration. If we did not, speech, which depends upon expiratory flow of air, would last only a half second or so before we had to stop to breathe again. The typical duration of expiratory flow is 2.4 to 3.5 sec in soft speech (Figure 5.21 illustrates this difference graphically). Outward flow of air can be so well controlled that singers and orators can phonate loudly for more than 15 to 20 seconds without distress. The slow outflow of air during phonation can be attributed to two factors: (1) the impedance to air flow offered by glottal vibration or articulatory constriction, and (2) possible checking action by the muscles of respiration against the forces of elastic recoil. To see how glottal/articulatory constrictions limit the outflow of air, think of a balloon that has been blown up. Let it go, and the air rushes swiftly out the neck of the balloon. If the neck of the balloon is pinched, the air flows out very slowly, making noise as it does, because of the increased impedance to airflow offered by the constriction. To put it another way, the difference between a slow leak and a blowout in a tire is the size of the hole in the tire. So too for humans. If we

figure 5.21

The time pattern of lung volume change
during quiet and speech breathing.

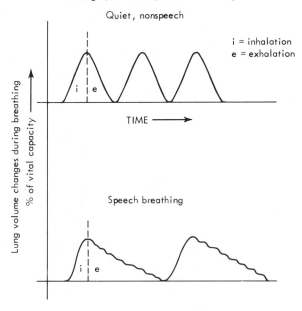

buzz our vocal folds, their opening and closing movements impede air flow. If we articulate stop or fricative consonants, these constrictions impede air flow, thus prolonging expiration. To prove this to yourself, produce the only sound with no glottal buzz and minimal articulatory constriction, the [h] sound. Breathe, and phonate [h] steadily. Your lungs will deflate rapidly. The absence of glottal or articulatory constrictions that would impede the flow of air during speech results in rapid exhalation. Now breathe in and phonate a prolonged [s]; you will phonate the [s] many times longer than [h] because of the greater impedance to airflow offered by the tongue constriction for [s]. Next phonate the vowel sound [a], and notice the increased duration of phonation because of the impedance to airflow offered by the vibrating vocal folds.

We use our muscles of inhalation to inflate the thorax, and then they are suddenly relaxed to permit elastic recoil to deflate the thorax. If instead we inhale and then very slowly relax the muscles of inhalation, they will check the recoil force. Pressure will be smaller, and deflation of the thorax prolonged. That is, if muscles of inspiration remain active during expiration, they reduce the expiratory air pressure and thus cut down expiratory flow. The delicate process of using glottal/articulatory impedance and checking action to smoothly prolong expiratory flow during speech is a vital part of breath control, a skill every singer and orator must master. To demonstrate a form of checking action, raise your arm in front of you to eye level. Then, let your arm fall rapidly under the force of gravity (elastic recoil). Lift the arm again to eye level, but this time let the arm fall very slowly. In this second case, you are "checking" the rapid fall of the arm (thoracic deflation) by slowly relaxing the contraction of the muscles that lifted the arm (muscles of inhalation), thus permitting a longer, slower, more precise fall (slower deflation) of the arm (thorax).

The relationship between driving pressure in the lung, impedance to airflow, and airflow (volume velocity) is as follows:

$$\frac{\text{driving pressure}}{\text{impedance}} = \text{flow}$$

$$\frac{P}{Z} = U$$

The ratio of driving pressure to combined glottal and vocal impedance is equal to the airflow volume velocity. According to this formula, airflow (U) will be decreased if either pressure (P) is reduced by checking or if impedance (Z) is increased.

THE ROLE OF LUNG PRESSURE
IN PHONATION
The more intense the voce is, the greater the P_{lung} needed. The more loudly we wish to speak, the greater must be the P_{lung} used during phonation. The reason for this is as follows: As air pressure builds up, the velocity of the air bursts which are released by the buzzing folds increases. The increased velocity of the air bursts results in a more energetic acoustic shock wave and a more intense acoustic vibration.

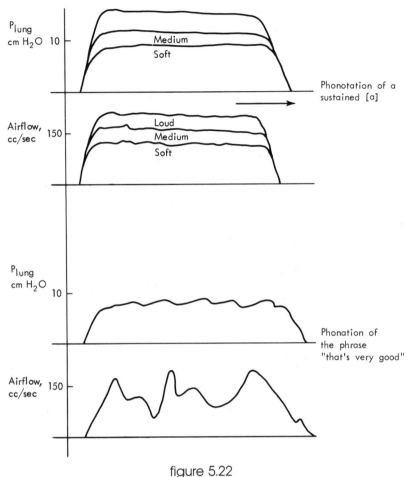

figure 5.22
Air pressure and airflow patterns for a speaker producing
speech and the sustained vowel [a] at three levels of loudness.

Demonstrate this relationship by buzzing your lips softly and then instantly increasing air pressure, taking care to notice the increased loudness of the buzz.

The size of P_{lung} needed for speech is quite small. As little as 2 to 3 cm H_2O pressure above atmospheric pressure will cause the vocal folds to buzz audibly. Typically, conversational speech demands 5 to 10 cm H_2O pressure. One of the loudest sounds we can make, according to Zemlin, is the "rebel yell"; it utilizes about 60 cm H_2O driving pressure. Thus, soft speech should not strain the body, since the pressures needed are so modest. The average airflow rates during speech are on the order of 150 to 200 cm³/sec, which is not a large volume flow, considering that the average inhalation for speech is in the vicinity of 500 to 800 cm³ air.

The air pressure and airflow patterns for continuous speech and for prolonged phonation of a single sound are shown in Figure 5.22. Notice that if we "sing" the [a] sound for a few seconds, both airflow and P_L are nearly constant. This means that impedance is nearly constant as well. For such sustained, steady phonation, the speaker finds it easy to deflate the thorax smoothly so that a constant P_{lung} is maintained. For connected speech, notice that there are ripples in the flow and pressure pattern. The ripples occur in part because impedance changes rapidly as the speaker shifts from the articulatory constriction and voicing pattern for one sound to that for each successive sound. The rapid variations in impedance that characterize connected speech make it more difficult for a speaker to control the deflation of the chest delicately enough to maintain a constant P_{lung}. Note also that as the loudness of the voice shifts from soft to medium to loud, air pressure and airflow increase. When greater lung pressure is used, air flows more rapidly through an impeding constriction. In general, during an utterance speakers appear to maintain a relatively constant P_{lung} and, despite fluctuations, a relatively constant average airflow. Increased intensity of the voice appears to demand increased P_{lung} and increased airflow. We may characterize respiration for speech by saying that we select an air pressure for the needed vocal intensity and attempt to maintain this constant pressure throughout the utterance. As a result, the average airflow is relatively constant, although it shows ripples because of the varying impedance of the vocal tract as speakers shift from sound to sound.

When speakers accentuate or emphasize a particular syllable or word, the air pressure and flow profiles will often show a rise for a strongly stressed syllable, and the listener will more often than not hear a greater loudness and higher pitch for that syllable. As the frequency of vocal vibration rises, the P_{lung} used also rises. Apparently, as the vocal folds are tensed for faster vibration greater P_{lung} is needed to overcome their increased stiffness (impedance) in order to set them into vibration. Thus, the frequency of vocal fold vibration is also dependent on pressure.

NEUROMUSCULAR CONTROL
OF P_{LUNG} DURING SPEECH
As a speaker talks he leaks air, and his thoracic volume is constantly decreasing. Because of the air leak, the speaker experiences a constantly decreasing relaxation pressure as his thoracic volume shrinks. How then does the speaker maintain a constant P_{lung} in the face of steadily falling elastic recoil pressure? As fast as relaxation pressure falls, muscle of exhalation pressure increases, so that total pressure can be maintained at a steady level. Figure 5.23 shows how a speaker might manipulate recoil force and muscle force to keep P_{lung} at a constant value. Suppose 10 cm H_2O are needed for a given loudness of speech. The speaker inflates sufficiently to generate 15 cm H_2O recoil pressure. To reduce the pressure to 10 cm H_2O, he or she exerts sufficient muscle of inspiration force to create a muscle-derived pressure of -5 cm H_2O, which reduces P_{lung} to $+10$ cm H_2O. As the speaker talks, he or she leaks air and relaxes the muscles of inhalation (checking action), until at some lung volume recoil pressure is equal to the desired lung pressure. As air continues to flow, relaxation pressure is increasingly insufficient and more and more muscle of exhalation force is added to keep

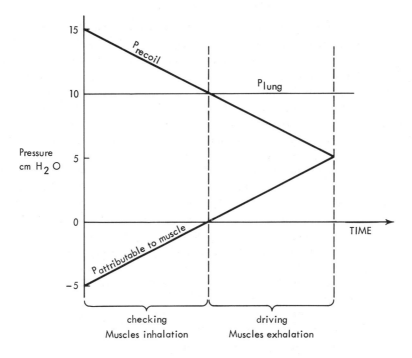

figure 5.23

A display of the changing patterns of elastic recoil
force and muscle force needed to maintain a constant
lung pressure. P_{lung} = 10 cm H_2O.

P_{lung} constant. This is shown in Figure 5.23. Notice that as air leaks out checking action by the muscles of inhalation ceases, and muscle of expiration activity slowly increases so that P_{lung} remains at a steady fixed level. To maintain a relatively constant lung pressure, the speaker adds appropriate, smoothly shifting amounts of muscle force to combine with the smoothly declining relaxation (elastic recoil) forces.

During normal speech, speakers usually inflate so that they rarely check recoil pressure (that is, P_{recoil} is not excessive). Rather, they use muscles of exhalation to supplement recoil pressure. It would appear that speakers more often prefer to squeeze a somewhat underinflated thorax to get the necessary lung pressure rather than checking the recoil of an overinflated thorax. Because of abnormalities of the neuromuscular system or unusual habits, some people simultaneously and strongly contract both muscles of inhalation and of exhalation. In this case, the more strongly contracting of the two muscle systems predominates, and along with elastic recoil determines whether the thorax moves to larger or smaller volumes. Such breathing is inefficient and very costly of muscular energy.

The muscles that contribute most to air intake and outflow probably vary from individual to individual and also depend on the degree of lung inflation desired. Generally speaking (Hixon et al., 1973), when the thorax is fully inflated, initial deflation toward REL results from movement inward of the thoracic walls; near or below REL, deflation results primarily from increasing abdominal muscle push upward against the diaphragm. Just before a speaker prepares to inhale for speech, the respiratory muscles contract slightly to set the thorax into an appropriate posture for phonation; that is, speakers adopt a "speech posture" with their respiratory systems. Presumably this posture optimizes the expenditure of energy and facilitates the muscular control needed to yield adequate P_{lung} for speech. All athletes know that proper stance or posture is crucial for successful movement, and the same appears to be the case for breathing. In fact, muscular activity in the respiratory system occurs $\frac{1}{3}$ to $\frac{1}{2}$ sec in advance of significant changes in lung volume.

BREATHING PATTERNS
FOR CONVERSATIONAL SPEECH   We can talk quietly all day with little respiratory or muscular distress, but a half-hour of loud, oratorical speech leaves us breathless, winded, short of oxygen, drained by the excess expenditure of muscular energy. To speak in this way demands breath control—the ability to optimize the expenditure of air and muscle contraction needed during breathing for speech.

Airflow patterns for quiet breathing and soft, conversational speech are relatively similar, except that exhalation is prolonged during speech so that phonation may have some continuity. The flow patterns observed during speech are bumpy (see Figure 5.22) because of variations in glottal and articulatory impedance as the speaker moves from sound to sound. The timing of respiratory cycles is more irregular during speech, and we tend to breathe a bit less often. As a speaker raises the level of the voice, he or she tends to breathe more deeply for several reasons. Greater thorax inflation gives more elastic recoil (relaxation) pressure, which is needed to provide the increased P_{lung} needed for increased vocal intensity. It also provides more lung inflation, which is useful since more intense speech often involves higher airflow rates. Quiet speech generally involves thorax movement between REL (37 percent VC) and about 50 to 60 percent VC; moderate intensity speech involves thoracic volume fluctuation up to about 55 to 65 percent VC; for very intense speech, lung inflation may be in the 60 to 80 percent VC range. As intensity increases, the speaker begins phonation at higher inflation levels, but ends at a lung inflation increasingly higher than REL.

In most cases, the speaker begins to phonate shortly after the start of egressive flow. If he or she pauses during speech, he or she may (1) continue to deflate, restarting phonation; or (2) release the remaining air quietly and reinflate for new phonation. The length of a single exhalation flow pattern is irregular because the length of the utterance a speaker may wish to produce on a single inflation of the thorax is variable. There is a tendency to breathe deeper if we know that we have a long utterance ahead of us, and to breathe less deeply if the oncoming utterance is short.

There is some question as to why speakers use the middle volume range of the thorax for speech breathing. A possible answer is both simple and complex. A general principle governing the movement of the body, *the economy of least effort,* suggests that we seek to minimize expenditure of energy to achieve any given physical movement. Since energy is defined as force times distance, we seek to reduce muscle force or distance traveled by the parts of the body. This applies to breathing as well. The thorax-lung system is stiffest at either extreme—when extremely inflated or extremely deflated. It is least stiff at REL. Think of a hollow rubber ball. As it is inflated, it becomes increasingly stiff; if it is increasingly compressed, it becomes increasingly stiff. Large quantities of muscular energy would be needed to overcome the forces of elastic recoil offered by the very stiff thorax-lung system at either extreme of inflation. If we wish to minimize the quantity of muscular energy needed to breathe, it is most advantageous to cause thoracic volume to fluctuate near REL in the mid-volume range 35 to 65 percent VC. Figure 5.24 shows the relative amount of energy which might be needed to produce a small change in lung volume at various degrees of lung inflation. Note that the least energy is needed in the mid-volume region, near REL. Because we are lazy (or is it smart?) in the sense that we expend as little energy as possible in performing a given task, we probably keep our fluctuations of thoracic volume in the mid-inflation level region in order to minimize energy expenditure. If we are forced out of the mid-volume region by having to breathe deeply, we end up struggling to breathe. This occurs as a result of the drain on the respiratory muscles, which have to strain against excess recoil forces at these lung volume extremes.

figure 5.24

A graph displaying the amount of muscle power needed to produce a small change in lung volume at various degrees of lung inflation.

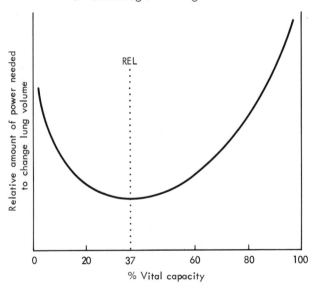

RESPIRATORY CONTROL
OF THE PARAMETERS OF SPEECH   Certain aspects of speech production are directly controlled by activity of the respiratory system. First, the intensity of speech (perceived as loudness) varies directly with P_L. The speaker is thus free to vary vocal intensity by varying lung pressure. At a given overall vocal intensity, speakers do not vary lung pressure for each different speech sound within a single utterance, but use roughly the same pressure for the entire stream of speech sounds produced on a single expiratory stream, or breath group as it is called. When a speaker strongly emphasizes or stresses a given syllable, he or she often utilizes a momentary increase or pulse of lung pressure. This temporary rise in lung pressure causes increased vocal intensity and vocal frequency for the heavily accentuated syllable. If the frequency of the voice is raised, the lung pressure used tends to increase. Presumably, as vocal fold stiffness is increased so that they will vibrate faster, more lung pressure is needed to overcome their increasing resistance to vibration. Finally, every utterance is characterized by a changing pattern of pitch and loudness collectively known as the intonation-stress contour. Since we know that frequency and vocal intensity increase as lung pressure increases, it seems to be clear that the pattern of variation of lung pressure contributes to the intonation patterns of our utterances. How then, should a beginning student characterize speech breathing? Let us look at it from the point of view of airflow and pressure patterns.

Air Pressure   The speaker appears to decide on how loudly he or she wishes to phonate and selects an appropriate depth of inhalation to produce the appropriate lung pressure. Then, he or she attempts to keep that lung pressure constant throughout the utterance. As the utterance goes on air escapes, and the recoil pressure of the lung diminishes. As it does, the speaker swiftly changes the size of the force of muscle contraction so that the sum of elastic recoil force and muscle forces yields the needed constant lung pressure (see Figure 5.23). At the end of the utterance, there is a universal tendency to drop both the intensity of voice and P_L. This drop in P_L marks the end of each utterance, breaking the flow of speech into separate breath groups. Physiologically, the pressure drop reflects preparation for the inhalation needed for the next utterance. If the speaker wishes to emphasize a given syllable, he or she may use a momentary pulse or rise in pressure during that syllable.

There has been much speculation concerning whether the lung provides a pulse of pressure for every syllable, whether a rise in P_L occurs only for heavily stressed syllables, or whether the lung is merely a wind chest that develops a steady pressure. At present, the data favor the latter interpretation, but differing speakers appear to control their respiratory systems in highly individual ways. At slow rates of speech, there appears to be a separate burst of pressure for each stressed syllable, but at faster rates of speech few if any separate pressure pulses are distinguishable. If one were to hazard a guess concerning how the respiratory system functions, it could be argued that it functions as a wind chest like that found on a pump organ or bagpipe. A large supply of air is put under pressure and leaked off slowly enough that the air loss does not cause a drop in pressure inside the air chest because we smoothly add sufficient muscle force to supplement the declining recoil force to keep pressure inside the air chest constant. Occasional demands for accentuation or rapid change in intonation of voice can be accommodated by varying the pressure in the chest, but a relatively constant pressure is the rule.

Airflow   What is the airflow pattern like for speech? Figure 5.25 shows that average airflow is relatively constant within an utterance. The fluctuations occur because the shift from sound to sound causes differing impedance to airflow, since each sound involves a changing vocal tract shape and/or laryngeal vibration. In continuous speech, the sounds are spoken quickly and the differences in airflow rate merge into a ripple. The flow pattern can be considered to consist of a steady flow outward coupled with a rippling flow associated with varying vocal tract impedance. The size of the steady flow depends mainly on vocal intensity. The more loudly we talk, the more air pressure we need and the greater the average airflow outward.

figure 5.25

A schematic display of the airflow patterns for connected speech
showing a division into a steady and a fluctuating airflow.

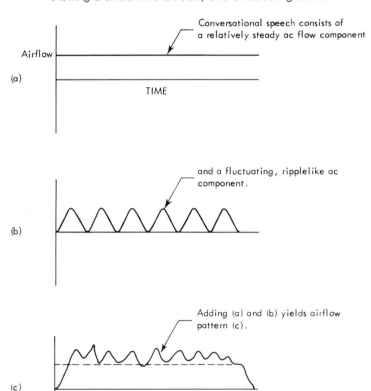

Which muscles are likely to be responsible for the pressure pulses that do occur? The likeliest candidates are the internal intercostals. They are fast acting and have good mechanical advantage for effecting such changes. Large shifts in expiratory lung pressure probably demand the cooperation of many expiratory muscles. Recent work has documented the presence of delicate stretch receptors in the respiratory muscles and pressure receptors in the laryngeal mucosa (Wyke, 1974). These sensory receptors permit a speaker to unconsciously monitor the size of the thorax and the resulting lung pressure so that as pressure and thorax size vary, feedback from these receptors can be used to increase or decrease muscle forces.

the relationship of respiratory pathology to speech

From what has been said thus far, we should be able to recognize certain possible consequences of pathological respiratory conditions. If, for instance, tidal volume is significantly reduced as a consequence of bronchial or pulmonary pathology, the increased breath rate needed to supply sufficient oxygen will cause certain changes in the characteristics of speech. Similarly, if the highly coordinated muscle contractions necessary for smooth, well-controlled inspiration and expiration are poorly timed, air pressure and flow will be inappropriate for laryngeal and articulatory gesturing. Finally, if certain nonorganic conditions, described as emotionally or cognitively based, result in aberrant thoracic posturing, diminished vital capacity, or poorly controlled respiratory initiation and subsequent airflow, speech will be negatively affected. Each of these three general areas is of particular interest and importance to the speech pathologist.

BRONCHIAL AND
PULMONARY PATHOLOGY   Most commonly, patients with certain bronchial or pulmonary pathologies describe their condition as "shortness of breath," "unable to get their breath," or "breathlessness." Medically, such conditions are referred to as *dyspnea* (difficult breathing). As such, dyspnea is a highly subjective description of behavior. In a sense, it is comparable to pain, which can be described as throbbing, burning, aching, stabbing, and so on and is a symptom rather than an abnormality. Typically, patients describe respiratory discomfort resulting from acute respiratory obstruction, emphysema, anemia, pulmonary (cystic) fibrosis, congestive heart failure, pulmonary embolism, neurocirculatory asthenia, acute neuromuscular paralysis, acidosis, or silicosis simply as "shortness of breath" or "difficulty in breathing."

As students of speech science and pathology, we are immediately aware of the possible influences of bronchial or pulmonary pathologies on vital capacity as related to breathing for speech. Consequences could range anywhere from mild intermittent shortness (at which time speech would be only moderately affected), to difficult, rapid, life-sustaining breathing (at which time speech is unimportant), to the cessation of breathing (at which time speech is impossible). As speech pathologists, it is imperative that we recognize symptoms that may be related to potentially severe pathological conditions. To treat a patient prior to medical referral is a form of professional insanity. To the speech pathologist, medical referral is the first and in many instances the only treatment for patients with suspected bronchial or pulmonary pathology.

SUGGESTED READINGS

BOUHUYS, A. *Breathing*. New York: Grune and Stratton, 1974. An excellent physiology text dealing with the process of respiration. Moderately difficult reading.

BOUHUYS, A. (ed.). "Sound Production in Man," *Annals of the New York Academy of Science,* 155 (1968). An extremely useful collection of articles dealing with the physiology of the larynx and respiratory system as they are involved in speech production. A useful reference for Chapter 6 as well.

DARLEY, F., A. E. ARONSON, and J. R. BROWN. *Motor Speech Disorders*. Philadelphia: W. B. Saunders, 1975. An introductory text focused on motor disorders of speech that includes a discussion of respiratory problems caused by neurological impairment.

DRAPER, M. H., P. LADEFOGED, and D. WHITTERIDGE. "Respiratory Muscles in Speech," *Journal of Speech and Hearing Research,* 2 (1959), 16–27. A classic electromyographic study of the function of the respiratory muscles during speech production.

FRY, D. B. "Duration and Intensity as Physical Correlates of Intrinsic Stress," *Journal of the Acoustical Society of America,* 35 (1955), 765–769. An investigation which linked intensity of phonation, and thus lung pressure, with stress production.

HIXON, T. J. "Respiratory Function in Speech." In. F. Minifie, T. J. Hixon, F. Williams (eds.), *Normal Aspects of Speech, Hearing and Language*. Englewood Cliffs, N.J.: Prentice-Hall, 1973. An introductory survey of the anatomy and physiology of the respiratory system.

HIXON, T. J., M. D. GOLDMAN, and J. MEAD. "Kinematics of the Chest Wall during Speech Production: Volume Displacements of the Ribcage, Abdomen, and Lung," *Journal of Speech and Hearing Research,* 16 (1973), 78–115. A difficult but important investigation of the movements of the abdomen and thoracic wall as they are engaged in lung volume changes for speech, singing, and quiet breathing.

HIXON, T. J., J. MEAD, and M. D. GOLDMAN. "Dynamics of the Chest Wall during Speech Production: Function of the Thorax, Ribcage, Diaphragm, and Abdomen," *Journal of Speech and Hearing Research,* 1976, 297–356. A complex but brilliant investigation of the forces active in the chest wall and abdomen during a wide variety of speech and nonspeech phonations. Also contains speculations on a model of speech breathing.

ISSHIKI, M. "Respiratory Mechanism of Vocal Intensity Variation," *Journal of Speech and Hearing Research,* 16 (1973), 78–115. A careful attempt to establish the relationship between vocal intensity, airflow, and subglottal air pressure. Useful, if controversial.

LADEFOGED, P. "Linguistic Aspects of Respiratory Phenomena." In A. Bouhuys (ed.), "Sound Production in Man," *Annals of the New York Academy of Science,* 155 (1968), 141–151. A well-written review of the contribution of the respiratory system to vocal intensity, stress, intonation, and segmental articulation, written from a linguistic point of view.

LADEFOGED, P., and N. P. McKINNEY. "Loudness, Sound Pressure, and Subglottal Pressure in Speech," *Journal of the Acoustical Society of America,* 35 (1963), 454–460. This investigation established the close relationship between lung pressure and vocal intensity. A bit difficult to read.

LIEBERMAN, P. C. *Intonation, Perception, and Language.* Cambridge, Mass.: MIT Press, 1967. An excellent survey of the phenomena of intonation, speech breathing, phonation, and their interrelationships. Although highly speculative in places, this is an excellent survey of the topic.

STETSON, R. H. *Motor Phonetics,* 2nd ed. Amsterdam: North-Holland, 1951. The collected work of a brilliant physiologist whose theory of speech breathing was based on the respiratory system producing pulses of pressure for each syllable of speech. Although his theory was disproved, it remains a cornerstone of respiratory research, historically and scientifically.

WARREN, D. W. "Aerodynamics of Speech Production." In N. Lass (ed.), *Contemporary Issues in Experimental Phonetics.* New York: Academic Press, 1976. A useful introduction to the aerodynamic aspects of breathing, phonation, and articulation for speech, as well as a survey of the instruments used in aerodynamic investigations.

WYKE, B. "Laryngeal Myotatic Reflexes," *Folia Phoniatrica,* 26 (1974), 249–264. A well-written review article that summarizes the evidence concerning how laryngeal vibration is controlled.

ZEMLIN, W. R. *Speech and Hearing Science, Anatomy and Physiology.* Englewood Cliffs, N.J.: Prentice-Hall, 1968. The best all-around text on the anatomy of the speech and hearing mechanism. The sections on the anatomy and physiology of phonation and respiration are quite fine.

6

THE PHONATION MECHANISM

The American composer Charles Ives once wrote that the "heroic ride to heaven would not be paved with pretty, little musical tones, but with strong, heroic sound." It is noteworthy that the heroic sounds of the human voice and the brass instruments are produced similarly. In both cases, the instrumentalists press a stream of compressed air against a pair of fleshy, muscular folds. The excess air pressure causes the folds to vibrate, releasing a train of recurring air puffs whose shock waves create an acoustic "buzz." For the singer, the two fleshy folds are within the larynx; for the trumpeter, the fleshy folds are the lips. The resulting vibrations travel down the tube of the trumpet or the tube of the vocal tract, emerging as a nobly resonated sound of notable quality. As will become evident in this chapter, the similarity of function between the human voice and wind-driven musical instruments is quite revealing of how the vocal tract works. Both as a musical instrument and as a speech production mechanism, the larynx is a highly individualistic mechanism of speech, revealing physical, emotional, and linguistic characteristics of the speaker. The composer Leos Janacek, who made lifelong studies of the intonation and prosody of human speech the basis for his music, commented: "When someone spoke to me, I did not always understand his words, but I did understand the melodic cadences of his speech. I knew at once whether that person lied or was inwardly agitated: sometimes during a most ordinary conversation, I felt and indeed heard, that my interlocutor was weeping."

A phonation mechanism is any vocal tract structure that operates to create sound by directly or indirectly modulating airflow (see Figure 6.1). The larynx is the primary mechanism. It participates directly or indirectly in the production of every human speech sound. When the larynx is buzzing it emits bursts of air, and the resulting sound is said to be "voiced." With your thumb and in-

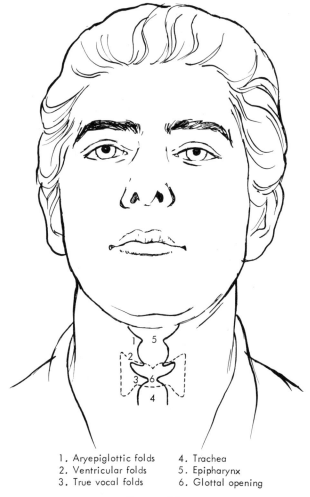

1. Aryepiglottic folds   4. Trachea
2. Ventricular folds   5. Epipharynx
3. True vocal folds   6. Glottal opening

figure 6.1

A frontal view of the neck showing the laryngeal folds.

dex finger, hold your laryngeal cartilage (Adam's apple) and feel the buzzing as you produce a loud, long [a-a-a] sound. If the vocal folds are held in an open position there is no buzzing, and the resulting speech sound is said to be voiceless. In both cases, the larynx to some degree modulates the flow of air through the vocal tract. In nontechnical terms, laryngeal vibrations are called "voice." This is inaccurate, because the acoustic vibrations created by the larynx are greatly modified during their passage through the vocal tract toward the open lips by the "resonance" characteristics of the vocal tract. It is more accurate to say that human voice is a resonated, acoustically altered, laryngeal "buzz."

vegetative "life-sustaining" laryngeal behaviors

All animals possessing lungs or air bladders have a sphincter muscle that closes or opens the airway to the air sacs. Sphincters are circularly arranged muscles which surround openings or tubes in the body; when contracted, they close the opening (lumen or meatus) of the tube. During the course of evolution, primitive muscular sphincters in the respiratory airways evolved into the complex musculocartilagenous larynxes seen in all mammalian species.

The larynx functions as an air valve. It regulates the flow of air from the lungs like a water faucet controlling the flow of water from a pipe or a choke controlling air intake to the carburetor of a gasoline engine. The laryngeal valve functions in three ways:

1. It prevents food, liquids, or other foreign substances from entering the trachea.

2. If such foreign matter does enter the laryngeal region, the cough reflex of the larynx-lung system evokes a blast of compressed air to expel it.

3. When closed, the larynx can trap sufficient air in the lungs to stiffen the thorax, providing support for lifting, excretion, childbirth, and other strenuous activities.

We are all familiar with stories of people choking to death on foreign objects. Unfortunately for us, air, food, liquids, and foreign objects share a common pathway, the pharyngeal tube, as they move toward the larynx or esophagus. Generally, the larynx is tightly closed when we swallow food and liquids. The various laryngeal folds prevent foreign objects from entering the airway of the laryngeal cavity. If an object does enter, its touch on the laryngeal walls triggers a cough reflex. During the cough the laryngeal folds close; the expiratory muscles rapidly build up a large lung pressure and the folds burst open, releasing an air blast that forces the object out. If we wish to exert great muscular force with our torso, the thorax must be mechanically rigid. Everyone knows that deflated balloons, air mattresses, and tires have no stiffness and little mechanical strength. Once inflated, they can and do support heavy loads. The same is true of humans. If we wish to lift, push, or pull heavy objects, we generally stiffen our thorax by inhaling air and trap it there by closing the laryngeal folds. To demonstrate this, blow out all the air from your lungs that you can. With your larynx open, try to lift something heavy. Be careful as you do it, and notice how difficult it is.

an overview of phonation

Phonation is the conversion of the potential energy of compressed air into the kinetic energy of acoustic vibration. This conversion is shown below:

potential energy→kinetic energy
(compressed air)→(egressive airflow *and* acoustic vibration)

By allowing the compressed air to escape as repetitive bursts or as a noisy, hissing air jet, the phonation mechanism converts the potential energy of compressed air into the kinetic energy of flowing air. The escaping air bursts in turn generate a repetitive series of air pressure fluctuations; the turbulently flowing air jet in the other case generates a noisy acoustic vibration. The process of controlling a compressed air supply so that it escapes as air bursts or as a noisy jet is called *airflow modulation*. Faucets, hose nozzles, and human larynxes are all examples of modulating devices.

Within the larynx, there are three sets of folds. Each set consists of a pair of muscular shelves that can be moved to open, constrict, or close the laryngeal airway (Figure 6.1 shows the aryepiglottic, ventricular, and true vocal folds). The folds are attached to the cartilages of the larynx. When these cartilages are moved by contraction of the laryngeal muscles, the folds will move to close or to open the laryngeal airway. During normal voice production, only the true vocal folds vibrate. Movement of the vocal folds toward closure at the midline is called *adduction;* movement away from midline that results in opening of the airway is called *abduction*. Perhaps these concepts will be clearer if you experiment with your lips in front of a mirror. The lips can be made to vibrate in a way which is quite like the vibration of the vocal folds. In fact, we could call the lips the oral folds, just as those of the larynx are called the laryngeal folds.

FORCING THE VOCAL
FOLDS TO OPEN   The first condition necessary for vocal fold vibration is a buildup of air pressure on one side of the folds. This is often called excess pressure, or a difference in air pressure or pressure drop across the folds. Recall from Chapter 5 that if two pressures are different, an accelerating force exists between the two different regions of pressure, since

$$P_1 > P_2$$

$$\frac{force_1}{area} > \frac{force_2}{area}$$

$$force_1 > force_2$$

$$\Delta F = F_1 - F_2 = F_{acceleration}$$

Figure 6.2 displays a set of fully adducted (closed) vocal folds. As subglottal pressure P_{sbg} rises above oropharyngeal pressure, $P_{sbg} > P_{oral}$, a force is developed that tends to push the folds open, accelerating them outward. When the net force outward caused by the pressure rise *exceeds* the elastic recoil force (which tends to keep the closed folds in place), the vocal folds pop open, releasing a burst of compressed air:

force of compressed air > force of elastic recoil of the closed folds

Once forced open, a burst of compressed air escapes through the glottal opening at high speed and collides with the much larger column of air inside in the

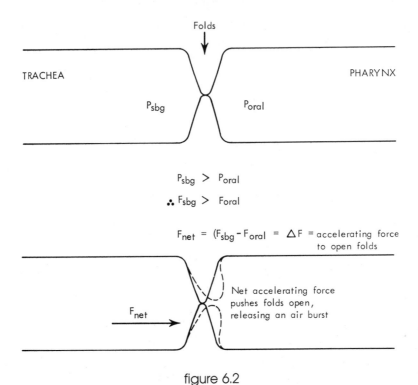

figure 6.2
An illustration of the accelerating force which forces
the vocal folds to open when there is a difference in pressure
between the two sides of the folds.

vocal tract. An acoustic shock wave created during the collision moves at the speed of sound up the vocal tract. After creating the acoustic shock wave, the air burst escapes the vocal tract as an outward (DC or egressive) flow of air. Examine the analogy shown in Figure 6.3. Drops of water accelerated by gravity fall and collide with the body of water in the bucket below. The force of collision creates waves which then speed across the surface of the bucket. As each droplet enters the bucket from above, a droplet spills over the edge of the bucket. That is, there is a slow, unidirectional (dc) flow of fluid out of the bucket to compensate for the amount entering it. Now, examine the vocal tract: an air burst (like a falling water droplet) slams into the column of air in the vocal tract (the bucket of water) and creates a fast-moving acoustic vibration (water waves); simultaneously, there is a slow dc leak of air from the lips to compensate for the incoming air bursts (flow of water drops out of the bucket). The efficiency of the conversion of the potential energy of the compressed air into acoustic vibration is very, very low. This is fortunate, however; for if we could convert most of the power of compressed air into acoustic vibration, the resulting sounds would be of sufficient intensity to damage our own or our listeners' hearing.

Demonstrate to yourself that compressed air has force. Dangle a sheet of paper in front of your lips and blow it aside. It is pushed aside by the force of the outwardly flowing compressed air. Now, puff out your cheeks; the force of compressed air is the agent responsible for stretching the cheeks. Next,

figure 6.3

An analogy between water droplets creating fluid vibrations in a pail of water and air bursts creating acoustic vibrations in the vocal tract.

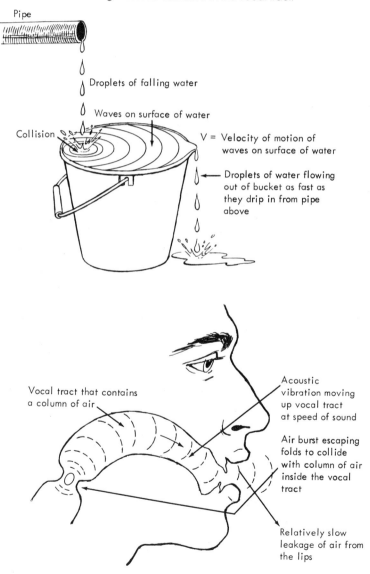

build up the pressure behind your lips, and then buzz them. As long as there is sufficient pressure behind the lips (oral folds), they will buzz, releasing air bursts. Feel the air bursts escaping from your lips with the palm of your hand. The sound you hear is not your lips striking each other, but the acoustic shock waves created by the escaping air bursts.

FORCING THE VOCAL FOLDS TO CLOSE

Two forces cause the opened folds to shut: (1) the force of elastic recoil of the folds and (2) the Bernoulli effect (drop in pressure).

Elastic Recoils

It was pointed out in Chapter 5 that all bodies have the property of elasticity. When a force acts upon a body (solid, liquid, or gas) causing a change of shape or volume, the body exerts an equal and opposite elastic recoil force. The greater the change from the original resting shape, the greater the opposing recoil force tending to restore the body to its original shape or position.

The laryngeal muscles move the vocal folds to a position of closure; when the force of air pressure blows the folds open, the folds are pushed away from rest position. An elastic recoil force arises that pushes the folds back toward their rest position of closure. Figure 6.4 illustrates this phenomenon, but you can test it for yourself. First, close your lips. Using your fingers, pluck your lower lip outward, and release it. It snaps back into place because of elastic recoil force.

figure 6.4

An illustration of the force of elastic recoil developed as the vocal folds are blown apart by air pressure.
NOTE: The tips of the vocal folds are blown upward a distance x from their rest position at closure and sideways at distance y from closure. The farther the folds are displaced (the greater x or y), the greater the elastic recoil force. Notice that the elastic recoil force pushes (accelerates) the folds back toward a rest position of closure. The recoil force pulls both downward and toward the middle of the larynx.

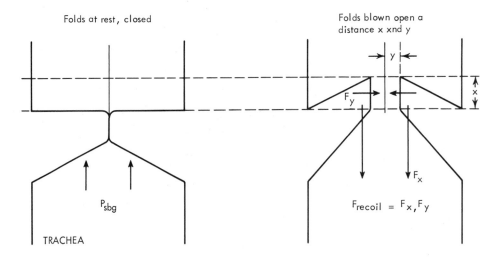

Folds at rest, closed

Folds blown open a distance x xnd y

The Bernoulli Effect   The second force responsible for vocal fold closure is a drop in air pressure at the glottal margin of the vocal folds caused by the Bernoulli effect. The high-speed airflow that occurs at a constriction in a tube causes the walls of the tube to be sucked together at the constriction. To illustrate this, dangle two sheets of paper below your lips. The sheets should be about an inch apart. Blow a vigorous stream of air through the constriction (passageway) between the sheets of paper. As you do, the pressure drop caused by the high-speed flow of air through the constriction will suck the two sheets of paper together, in much the same way that the jet of air in the larynx sucks the vocal folds together at the small opening called the *glottis*. To understand why this happens, we need to understand the Bernoulli effect.

If an ideal fluid (or gas) is made to flow through a tube, the fluid has a constant energy content at every point along the tube:

$$E = KE + PE$$

where E= total energy of fluid at every point
      KE= kinetic energy
      PE = potential energy

The total energy is the sum of the kinetic (energy of motion) and potential energy (energy of pressure) of the fluid. The energy content is constant at all points along the tube.

Everyone is familiar with the fact that if a tube is constricted, fluid will flow faster at the constriction. To get water to move faster, we tighten the nozzle of a garden hose. If we burn a finger, we cool it with high-speed air by pursing (constricting) our lips as we blow. We do not blow with a wide open mouth because the air speed would be too slow to cool the finger. Conversely, we do the opposite to warm our hands. Bernoulli's principle (see Figure 6.5) states that at any point, the total energy of a flowing ideal fluid is constant. Thus, in Figure 6.5, the energy of the fluid at points I, II, and III is equal $(E_I = E_{II} = E_{III})$. But we know that the gas is flowing faster at point II than at points I or III. The pressure sensor shows a lower pressure at II than at I or III. Why? Because as fast as the kinetic energy of motion increases, potential energy must decrease, so that total energy will remain constant.

$$E = KE + PE = K$$

$$KE = 1/2\rho V^2$$

$$PE = P$$

where ρ = density of fluid
      V = velocity of fluid
      P = pressure of fluid

Therefore

$$E = 1/2\rho V^2 + P$$

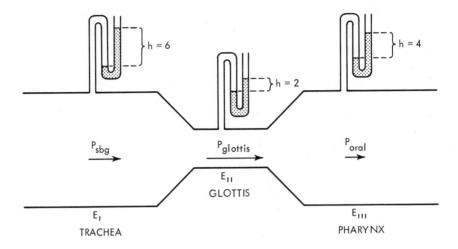

figure 6.5

An illustration of the Bernoulli effect in the larynx. Small
pressure–sensing manometers depict the air pressure. The size
of the arrow is proportional to the velocity of airflow; the height,
h, of the column of water in the manometer indicates air
pressure. Notice that the airflow is fastest at the glottal
constriction, but air pressure is lowest at that point.

figure 6.6

An illustration of the increased velocity of fluid flow
when the diameter of the pipe is constricted.

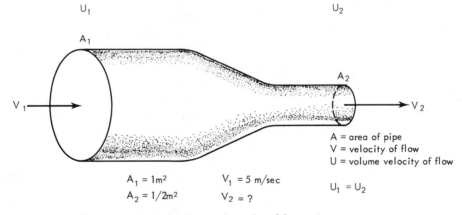

A = area of pipe
V = velocity of flow
U = volume velocity of flow

$A_1 = 1m^2$ $V_1 = 5 \text{ m/sec}$

$A_2 = 1/2m^2$ $V_2 = ?$ $U_1 = U_2$

At every point in the pipe, volume flow (U) must be

5 m³/sec. That is, as much air per second must flow
out of the pipe as flows in.

$U_1 = A_1 \times V_1$ $U_2 = A_2 \times V_2$

$5 = 1 \times 5$ $5 = 1/2 \times V_2$

$V_1 = 5\text{m/sec}$ $V_2 = 10 \text{ m/sec}$

As fluid velocity increases, *KE* increases; to compensate, *PE* decreases. The decrease in *PE* occurs as a drop in pressure. The phenomenon whereby the pressure of a fluid decreases as it flows ever faster through a tube is called the Bernoulli effect after the scientist who investigated the principles of fluid flow.

This effect can be illustrated in another way. Suppose that 5 m³ of fluid are flowing through a pipe each second. At one point we constrict the pipe to a cross-sectional area one-half that of the rest of the pipe (see Figure 6.6). Conservation of mass indicates that if 5 m³/sec of air enters the pipe, 5 m³/sec must also leave. Volume velocity, *U*, is measured as cubic units of fluid flow per unit of time (cm³/sec, m³/min, and so on). Notice that U m³/sec = area (cross-sectional) × linear velocity of flow (V):

$$U(m^3/sec) = A(m^2) \times V(m/sec) = m^3/sec$$

If the pipe has an area of 1 m², and fluid enters with a linear velocity of 5 m/sec, the volume flow is $U = 1 \times 5 = 5$ m³/sec. At the outlet of the pipe, volume flow must still be 5 m³/sec, but the area is cut in half:

$$U = A \times V$$
$$5 = \tfrac{1}{2} \cdot V \text{ outlet}$$
$$V_2 = 10 \text{ m/sec}$$

Notice that the linear flow rate (velocity) has doubled when the area of the pipe is decreased by half. But what does this all have to do with the closing of the vocal folds? Look at Figure 6.5. Notice that air pressure at the constriction is lower than P_{sbg}. When the airflow rate becomes fast enough, the pressure in the glottis becomes negative, and thus "sucks" the folds shut. Any difference in pressure means that an accelerating force exists. The accelerating force caused by the Bernoulli drop in pressure at the region of glottal constriction pulls the vocal folds shut. The very act of blowing open the folds creates a glottal constriction (opening), at which point the onrushing air burst achieves such a high linear rate of flow that the resulting drop in pressure literally causes the folds to be *pulled* together.

THE AERODYNAMIC–MYOELASTIC THEORY OF VOCAL FOLD VIBRATION

The vibration of the vocal folds is governed by a number of aerodynamic and myoelastic factors. First, the vocal folds can be blown apart to release an air burst if sufficient excess pressure is built up on one side of the folds. Second, the muscular tissue of the vocal folds is elastic; when the folds are blown apart, they resist by exerting an elastic recoil force that tends to close them. Third, the stream of air that escapes the larynx experiences a drop in pressure at the glottal constriction which tends to close the vocal folds by pulling them together. Taken together, these factors imply that if (1) the vocal folds are appropriately positioned (postured) in a closed or semi-closed position and (2) pressure is built up below the folds, then

(3) the vocal folds will repeatedly open and close automatically. Excess pressure opens the folds, and elastic recoil forces (myoelastic factors) and the Bernoulli drop in pressure (aerodynamic factors) close the folds.

The aerodynamic myoelastic theory is a simplification of the actual mechanics of fold movement, but it has a number of important implications:

1. The vocal folds do not open and close during phonation because there is a separate muscle contraction for each opening/closing movement.

2. The vocal folds open and close automatically as long as (a) the folds are in a position of closure or near closure, and (b) there is a sufficient buildup of pressure below them.

3. This means that the important factors governing vocal fold vibration are these:

a. Vocal fold *position;* that is, the degree to which the vocal folds are adducted/abducted.

b. Vocal fold *myoelasticity:* the degree of elasticity of the vocal folds, which depends on the position of the folds and the degree of tension in them as determined by muscle contraction.

c. The size of the *pressure drop* across the vocal folds.

These three factors are the major determinants of how fast, how vigorously, and in what way the vocal folds will or will not vibrate.

Figure 6.7 provides a graphic illustration of the principles of the aerodynamic-myoelastic (ADMET) theory of vocal fold vibration. In Figure 6.7 (2), the vocal folds are at rest, in an open position. As they close (2), subglottal pressure rises above oral pressure. Once the folds have closed (3) P_{sbg} rises to a peak and forces the folds apart (4). As the folds open, a burst of compressed air escapes (5) and strikes the column of air in the supralaryngeal vocal tract, creating an acoustic shock wave (6). The elastic recoil and the Bernoulli drop in pressure at the glottis (7) cause the folds to close, thus setting the stage (8) for another cycle of vibration.

PHONATION TYPE   Now that we understand the general principles governing how the vocal folds vibrate, let us look at the ways in which the folds operate to regulate airflow from the lungs. The vocal folds play a crucial role in the production of all speech sounds because of their ability to modulate the flow of air. For each class of speech sounds, the vocal folds adopt a peculiar position and/or pattern of vibration. They do this by moving in two distinct directions, each of which alters potential vibration: (1) their length may change, and (2) they may open or close. These movements are shown in Figure 6.8. It is the indirectional opening and closing movements of the vocal folds prior to or following phonation (not the extremely rapid open-shut motions which occur during phonation), which Ladefoged (1971) calls "spreading," that directly affect the degree and manner in which the larynx will modulate the flow of expiratory air. Ladefoged characterizes the different behaviors of the vocal folds during sound production as *phonation types*. Phonation type is the *average degree of vocal fold* opening during expiratory airflow. The closer the vocal

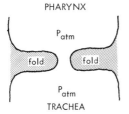

PHARYNX

P_{atm}

fold   fold

P_{atm}

TRACHEA

1. Folds at rest.

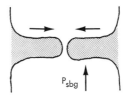

P_{sbg}

2. Folds move toward midline because of muscle contractions. Adduction occurs.

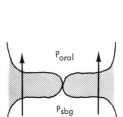

P_{oral}

P_{sbg}

$P_{sbg} > P_{oral}$

3. Pressure below the glottis ($P_{subglottal}$ or P_{sbg}) rises above oral pressure.

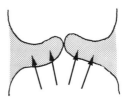

4. Excess pressure forcing folds apart.

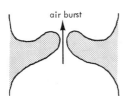

air burst

5. Folds explode open, releasing rapidly moving air burst.

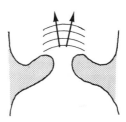

6. Air burst creates an overpressure which results in an acoustic shockwave that moves at the speed of sound up the vocal tract.

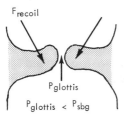

F_{recoil}

$P_{glottis}$

$P_{glottis} < P_{sbg}$

7. Folds rebound toward closure because of recoil and Bernoulli effect.

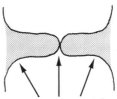

8. Folds closed, pressure below folds rises, pushing folds apart again!

figure 6.7

Successive stages in a cycle of glottal vibration.

(a) Increasing length

ANTERIOR

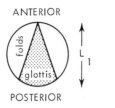

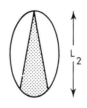

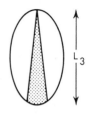

POSTERIOR

$$L_3 > L_2 > L_1$$

(b) Vocal fold spreading

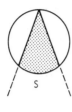

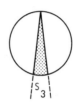

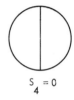

S_1 S_2 S_3 $S_4 = 0$

$$S_1 > S_2 > S_3 > S_4$$

figure 6.8

An illustration of the vocal folds showing the two movements
which cause the vocal folds to vibrate in certain ways:
(a) increasing length; superior view of the vocal folds. Note
the increasing length of the vocal folds. (b) Vocal fold
spreading. Note the decreasing spread (greater degree
of closure) of the vocal folds from left to right.

folds come toward complete closure, the more strongly they will modulate* the airflow from the lungs. Phonation type is a concept designed to give order and logical coherence to a wide variety of laryngeal behaviors. All these behaviors are points on a single physiological continuum (glottal opening or spreading), even though acoustically they yield very different results. In addition, the phonation type concept permits linguists to account for variations in human voicing within and between languages.

When a gas or fluid flows through a pipe, the pipe offers an impedance to the flow of air. If there is a constriction in the pipe, the impedance to air flow increases remarkably at that point. If the constriction is very tight, impedance is high and airflow is reduced to a trickle. If the constriction is not tight, impedance is lower and airflow increases. Recall from Chapter 5 that the relationship between driving pressure (P), volume airflow (U), and impedance (Z) is

$$P = ZU$$

*Modulation refers to a time-varying change in any parameter of interest. In this case, the parameter of interest is airflow (U). The time-varying impedance of the opening/closing folds, or the time-varying impedance of the turbulent eddies in the airstream, create modulations (changes) in the moment-to-moment airflow rate (U), which in turn result in the creation of acoustic vibration.

If driving pressure is constant, then any change in impedance will force a reciprocal change in flow U. The flow of air is *modulated* when there is a time-varying impedance to the flow in the tube. Thus, given constant driving pressure, if the rate of airflow rises or falls, it is being modulated by a varying impedance. The vocal folds act as a time-varying impedance to airflow. As the folds burst open, impedance falls and airflow increases; as the folds close, impedance increases and airflow decreases. Thus, the formation of the airburst that creates the buzz-vibration depends on the airflow modulation caused by the opening and closing of the vocal folds.

In a tube such as the vocal tract, if there is a constriction and air is flowing through it, one of two things will happen. If the walls of the constriction are compliant (floppy and stretchable), the Bernoulli drop in pressure will suck the folds shut, and air pressure will blow them open, releasing air bursts. If the walls are rigid and noncompliant, the drop in pressure at the constriction cannot suck the constriction/folds shut; as a result, a high-speed air jet occurs. Just beyond the constriction, the air jet begins to whirl and tumble turbulently. The disorderly, rotary, turbulent airflow acts as a time-varying impedance. The turbulence modulates airflow rapidly enough to create a noisy acoustic vibration. The difference between a buzz and a friction noise is small. If the walls of the constriction are compliant, the constriction will rhythmically open and close to regularly modulate airflow into a train of air bursts heard as a buzz. If the walls are stiff, they cannot be sucked shut, and a turbulent high-speed air jet arises just beyond the constriction. The turbulence of the air stream modulates its own flow rapidly enough to generate a noisy vibration. Thus, the physiological difference between buzzing the larynx or vocal tract and causing it to hiss depends on how "stiff" the walls of the tube are at the major constriction. Put this to the test yourself: hold your lips close together, keeping them stiff, and blow air through the constriction. They will not buzz, but instead will generate a turbulence noise. Now relax your lips, and holding them the same distance apart, blow air through them. They will begin to vibrate in a buzzlike fashion.

Vocal fold opening (phonation type) ranges from a fully open position (voiceless) to a fully closed, nonvibrating position (glottal stop). Let us examine each type shown in Figure 6.9 in turn. When we breathe quietly, the vocal folds are abducted (open); the glottal opening is about 40 percent of the tracheal width. During the phonation of voiceless sounds [s, f, and θ] the folds are spread open even more widely than for quiet breathing, so that they minimally impede the flow of air. (Readers can mimic the position for voiceless sounds with their lips by opening the lips fully and yawning.)

Whisper   During whispered phonation, the relatively motionless vocal folds present a glottal opening sufficiently narrow that airflow is impeded at the glottal slit, and the resulting turbulent air jet at the glottis generates noise. The turbulent eddies, or whorls, create a noisy acoustic vibration. This can be mimicked with the lips by pretending to blow out a

Phonation Type	Airflow	Vocal Fold Opening	Vocal Fold Position
Voiceless	Noiseless flow	Open	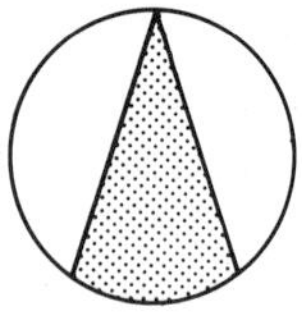
Whisper	Noisy friction type flow	Narrow vocal fold opening	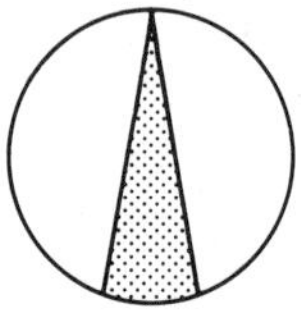
Breathy	Noise plus air burst	Vocal fold partly open, partly shut; closed portion vibrating	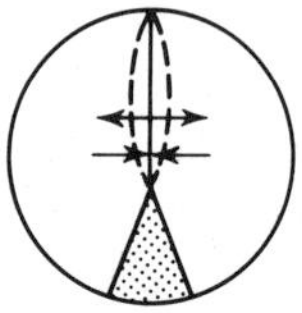
Voiced	Air bursts	Full opening and closing of vocal folds	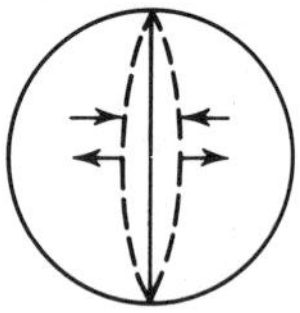
Creak	Low-frequency irregular air burst	Only a small portion of vocal fold margin opens and closes	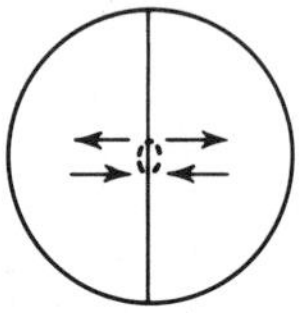
Glottal stop	No vibration at all	Folds fully shut, not vibrating	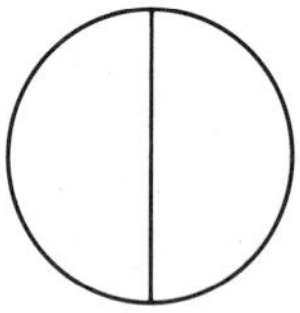

figure 6.9

Phonation types, ranging from least to greatest impedance to expiratory airflow.

match. The narrow lip opening produces a fast-flowing, turbulent air jet that yields a hissing vibration.

Breathy (Murmur) Phonation   During breathy phonation, the folds are partially closed. Generally, the anterior portions of the folds (membraneous glottis) are closed and vibrating, while the posterior portion between the arytenoid cartilages (cartilagenous glottis) remains open. The larynx emits both air bursts and a noisy air jet through the open portion of the vocal folds. The simultaneous emission of air bursts and friction noise is usually perceived as "breathy." Although some people find breathy voices sexy, extreme breathiness often reflects a functional or organic laryngeal pathology. To demonstrate breathy voice with your lips, hold your upper lip open at one corner of your mouth and buzz the lips. The open corner will leak air noisily while the closed portion of the lips buzzes.

Normal Voice   Because it is a mechanically complex organ, the larynx is capable of a wide range of vibratory behaviors. This is like saying that a pitcher can use wrist, arm, and shoulder to throw curves, sinkers, fastballs, screwballs, and sliders using an overhand, sidearm, or underhand delivery. This wide variety of muscular behaviors is possible using the finger-wrist-elbow-shoulder system. From the variety of possible laryngeal movements, a certain few behaviors are most commonly used, and these represent optimum laryngeal function. Observation of languages the worldwide and observation of people's daily speaking voices indicates that normal voicing is the most typical, habitual, and comfortable mode of phonation.

During normal voicing, the vocal folds generally open fully and close completely. The folds appear to be relatively relaxed, neither excessively stiff nor excessively soft. They are relatively compliant (they have a lot of "give" to them), so that as they open and close, ripples of compressed tissue appear to move over the surface of the relaxed folds as they slam shut. To demonstrate the complex open-closing pattern of lips in a normal voice, merely buzz your lips in front of a mirror and watch the relatively relaxed lip tissue bending and twisting. Normal voicing can be produced with the vocal folds in a very relaxed state (lax voice) and in a very tense condition (tense voice). Impedance to airflow in normal voice is relatively high, intermediate between that of breathy and creaky voice.

Creaky Voice   This next phonation type, which is not shown in Figure 6.9, reflects an even greater degree of laryngeal constriction. There is considerable tension in the vocal folds and the surrounding musculature. In addition, the epipharynx, the portion of the pharyngeal tube immediately above the larynx, may be tensed and constricted as well. The result is a choked, harsh, metallic voice characterized by an irregular buzz frequency, a reduced range of loudness, and a perceptible quality of strain. The best example of this is the voice of that language deviant character of "Sesame Street," the Cookie Monster, who encourages young children to say "me want cookie."

Creak (Pulse or Vocal Fry)   Creak (or pulse) is a pattern of vocal fold vibration in which short, thick, and relaxed folds are pressed together. The air escapes in a popping, irregular, and slow fashion, as if it were bubbling between the folds. This voice quality is unmistakable, as it is very low in frequency and to a listener's ear has an irregular pitch like the sound of popcorn popping. It can be mimicked easily with the lips. Bring them together and "bubble" the air out through the center of the lips in small bursts. There is evidence to suggest that during creak phonation, the ventricular folds may descend and make contact (see Figure 6.1) with the true vocal folds, thus causing their effective mass to be very high. As you mimic this phonation type with your lips, notice that only a small portion of the vocal folds (lips) actually moves. Creak frequently occurs in conversational speech when we hesitate at pauses and at the ends of sentences. It appears to occur at those points in time when we momentarily relax the laryngeal musculature.

Glottal Stop   The last phonation type, the glottal stop, can be considered either an articulation or phonation type. To demonstrate the glottal stop on the lips, buzz them and, in doing so, stop the buzz and start it again abruptly. The sudden cessation of buzzing (caused by a strong pressing of the folds together) is called the glottal stop, while the abrupt release into buzzing is called the glottal release (caused by rapidly relaxing the tight closure of the folds). The entire sequence of buzz-stop-release-buzz is called a *coup de glotte,* or *glottal blow.* This behavior is a convenient way to achieve rapid cessation/onset of glottal buzzing, and in certain languages the glottal stop functions as a stop consonant. For example, it commonly occurs in English when [t] precedes [h], as in the sentence "We got home at three o'clock" or in the colloquial term for "No," which is spoken as $[?_a?_a?]$ (uh-uh).

the anatomical framework
for phonation

THE LARYNGEAL CARTILAGES   Certain   anatomical   structures   are responsible for the laryngeal behaviors that generate the sounds of speech: the laryngeal cartilages, the laryngeal membranes and ligaments, and the laryngeal cavity.

The laryngeal cartilages, together with the hyoid bone, are the framework to which the three sets of laryngeal folds are attached. Movements of laryngeal cartilages cause the vocal folds to stretch or to shorten, to open or to close. The cartilages are bound together by a complex set of ligaments, and are sheathed in a number of strong, smooth membranes. Figure 6.10 presents a profile view of all the laryngeal cartilages. Movements of the laryngeal cartilages are caused by contraction of the intrinsic and extrinsic laryngeal muscles.

The Hyoid Bone The hyoid bone (Figure 6.11) is a horseshoe-shaped, free-floating bone of the neck. Attached to it are muscles of the jaw, tongue, larynx, and skull. It is held in place just below the mandible by a suspension system of muscles. The hyoid is positioned superior to the thyroid cartilage (Figure 6.13), at about the level of cervical vertebra C_3. It consists of a central body or corpus and two posteriorly directed projections, or horns. The larynx is attached to the trachea inferiorly, and to the hyoid bone superiorly.

The Cricoid Cartilage This cartilage is the foundation of the larynx, since the other important laryngeal cartilages are attached to it from above. The cricoid resembles a signet ring (see Figure 6.12), having a large, flattened lamina or plate at the back and a smaller arch anteriorly. The anterior arch and posterior laminae are connected by upswelling lateral walls, and the central opening of the cricoid is the laryngeal airway. The cricoid sits atop the first tracheal ring, with the arch facing anteriorly and the laminar plates facing posteriorly. On the exterior of either lateral wall of the cricoid are two pairs of complex, oval indentations, the superior and inferior articular facets, which are the points of contact for the arytenoid and thyroid cartilages, respectively.

The Thyroid Cartilage The thyroid cartilage is large, butterfly-shaped cartilage, consisting of two wings or plates. At the posterior margin of each plate arises a pair of superior and inferior horns (projections) which are attached via ligaments, respectively, to the hyoid bone and the cricoid cartilage (Figure 6.13). The plates join anteriorly at the angle of the thyroid, which is marked superiorly by a deep V-shaped notch. This notch projects against the skin of the neck and can be seen moving up and down as the thyroid cartilage rocks on its horns (the Adam's apple). The angle of juncture of the thyroid lamina is about 90° in males and 120° in females, thus resulting in a greater anterior-posterior length of the vocal folds for the male larynx. Each thyroid lamina is marked by an indentation called the oblique line, which extends from the inferior laryngeal tubercle upward and laterally to the superior tubercle. The thyroid lamina form the frontal and lateral walls of the larynx. The true vocal folds attach to either thyroid lamina near the thyroid angle, just below the notch.

The Arytenoid Cartilages The two arytenoid cartilages are four-sided, and each, like a pyramid, has a base surface, an apex, and three lateral surfaces (Figures 6.10, 6.14). The medial surface forms a portion of the glottal margin (Figure 6.20), and is relatively smooth; the angles at the base of the arytenoid serve as points of attachment for various muscles. The muscular process is the angle between the posterior and lateral surfaces, and serves as a point of attachment for the lateral cricoarytenoid and posterior cricoarytenoid

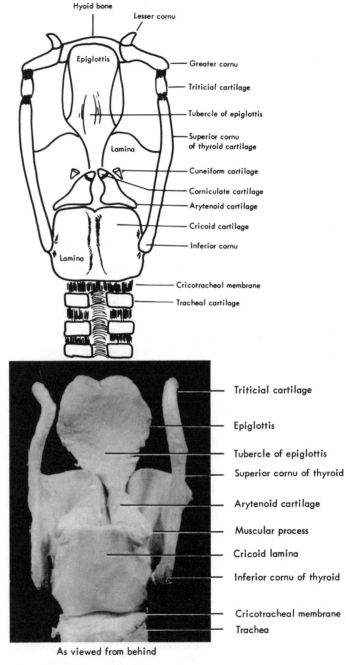

As viewed from behind

figure 6.10

The laryngeal cartilages as seen in frontal, lateral, posterior, and superior views. Reprinted by permission from W. R. Zemlin, *Speech and Hearing Science: Anatomy and Physiology.* © 1968 by Prentice-Hall, Inc.

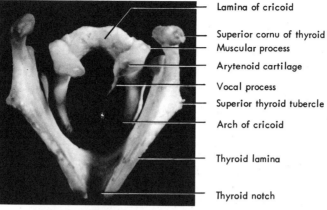

Lamina of cricoid

Superior cornu of thyroid

Muscular process

Arytenoid cartilage

Vocal process

Superior thyroid tubercle

Arch of cricoid

Thyroid lamina

Thyroid notch

As viewed from above

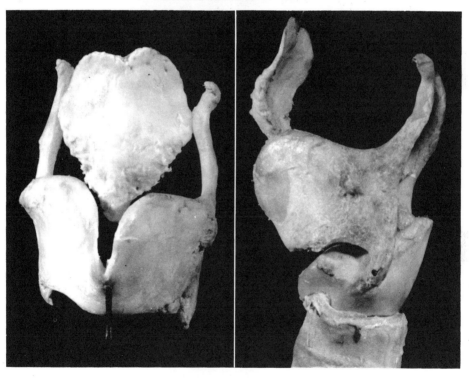

figure 6.10
(cont.)

muscles. The vocal process is the point of attachment for the vocal ligament. The apex of each arytenoid is capped by the tiny, beadlike corniculate cartilages (Figure 6.10).

The Epiglottal Cartilage   The epiglottal cartilage, shown in Figure 6.10, is shaped like a leaf. It rises from a long, narrow stalk attached to the angle of the thyroid immediately below the thyroid notch. The stalk flares upward and backward into a large, gently rounded leaf-shaped portion that juts into the epipharynx. It is thought that when the aryepiglottic muscles contract or the tongue is retracted, the body of the epiglottis moves posteriorly to cover the laryngeal *aditus,* or opening into the laryngeal cavity, to assist in preventing food from entering the larynx.

figure 6.11

The hyoid bone seen from various angles. Reprinted by permission from W. R. Zemlin, *Speech and Hearing Science: Anatomy and Physiology.* © 1968 by Prentice-Hall, Inc.

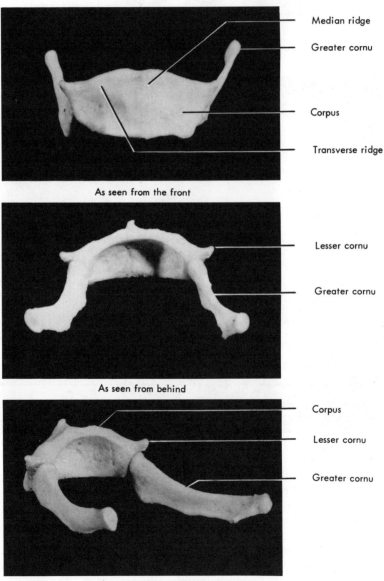

Median ridge

Greater cornu

Corpus

Transverse ridge

As seen from the front

Lesser cornu

Greater cornu

As seen from behind

Corpus

Lesser cornu

Greater cornu

As seen in perspective

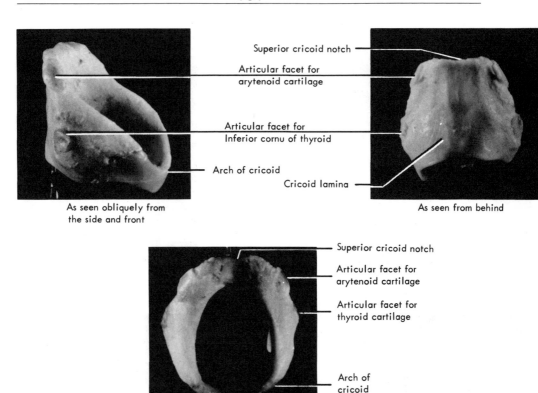

figure 6.12

Selected views of the cricoid cartilage. Reprinted by permission from W. R. Zemlin, *Speech and Hearing Science: Anatomy and Physiology*. © 1968 by Prentice-Hall, Inc.

LARYNGEAL MEMBRANES   Figure 6.15 presents various views of the laryngeal membranes and ligaments. Let us look first at the ligaments.

The cricotracheal ligament connects the base of the cricoid cartilage with the upper margin of the first tracheal ring. The hyothyroid membrane, a large, curtainlike sheet of fibroelastic tissue, runs from the superior margin of the thyroid lamina upward, inserting, ringlike, on or near the entire undersurface of the hyoid bone. It connects the thyroid cartilage firmly to the hyoid bone. The medial fibers of this membrane are somewhat thickened and often are referred to as the middle hyothyroid ligament. The lateral hyothyroid ligament is a strong, thick, cablelike elastic ligament that fastens the superior horns of the thyroid cartilage to the posterior tip of the major horns of the hyoid bone. The hyoepiglottic ligament is a sheet that at the midline extends from the anterior surface of the epiglottis to the body of the hyoid bone, connecting the two.

The interior surface of the larynx, from the trachea to the glottal margin, is lined with a smooth sheet of elastic tissue called the conus elasticus that drapes

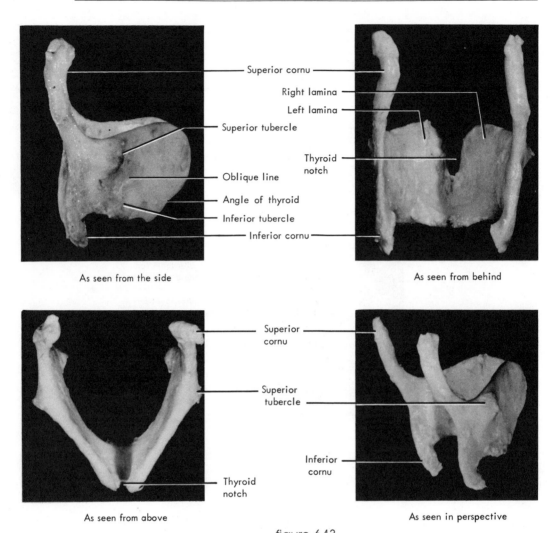

Superior cornu

Right lamina

Left lamina

Superior tubercle

Thyroid notch

Oblique line

Angle of thyroid

Inferior tubercle

Inferior cornu

As seen from the side

As seen from behind

Superior cornu

Superior tubercle

Inferior cornu

Thyroid notch

As seen from above

As seen in perspective

figure 6.13

Selected views of the thyroid cartilage. Reprinted by permission from W. R. Zemlin, *Speech and Hearing Science: Anatomy and Physiology.*© 1968 by Prentice-Hall, Inc.

the interior airway. It connects the thyroid, cricoid, and arytenoid cartilages with each other (see Figure 6.15). The anterior portion of this ligament is called the cricothyroid ligament. It connects the inferior margin of the thyroid with the upper lip of the anterior arch of the cricoid at the midline. The lateral portions of the conus are called the cricothyroid membranes. They arise from the superior border of the cricoid and extend upward and medially, where they end in the free margins of the vocal folds, extending from the angle of the thyroid to the arytenoid cartilages at the vocal processes. The cricothyroid membranes are thickened at the free margin of the true vocal folds and are often called the vocal ligaments.

The laryngeal cavity, above the medial margin of the ventricular folds, is sheathed by the quadrangular membrane. This membrane arises from the lateral margins of the epiglottis and thyroid cartilage, coursing downward to the free margins of the ventricular folds where they terminate as thickened bands called the ventricular ligaments. The ventricular ligaments attach to the arytenoids posteriorly, and anteriorly to the thyroid cartilage, near the notch. The aryepiglottic folds consist of a surface covering of quadrangular membrane and an inner layer of aryepiglottic muscle. They extend from the sides of the epiglottis posteriorly to an attachment on the apex of the arytenoid cartilages. The arytenoid cartilages are attached to the superior articular facets of the cricoid by a pair of complex (lateral and posterior) cricoarytenoid ligaments that limit the forward and backward motion of the arytenoids.

figure 6.14

The arytenoid cartilages seen at various angles. Reprinted by permission from W. R. Zemlin, *Speech and Hearing Science: Anatomy and Physiology.* © 1968 by Prentice-Hall, Inc.

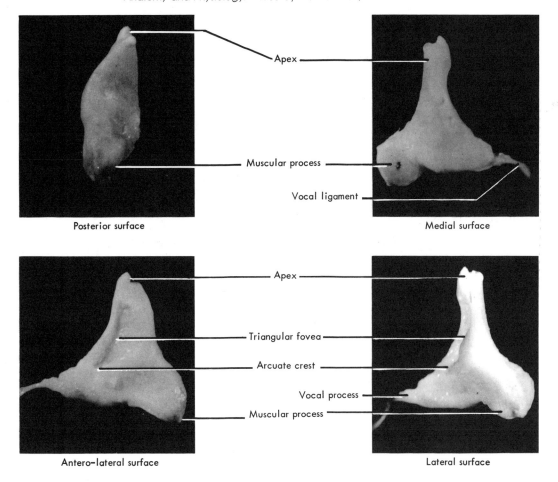

Apex

Muscular process

Vocal ligament

Posterior surface

Medial surface

Apex

Triangular fovea

Arcuate crest

Vocal process

Muscular process

Antero-lateral surface

Lateral surface

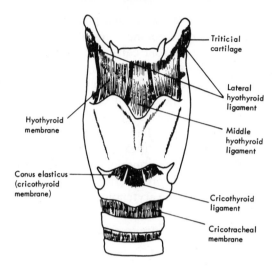

Ligaments and membranes of the larynx as seen from the front.

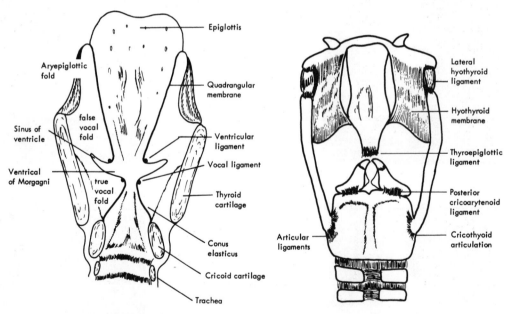

Frontal section of larynx illustrating the relationship of quadrangular membrane with conus elasticus.

Ligaments and membranes of the larynx as seen from behind.

figure 6.15

Anterior, posterior, and cross-sectional views of the laryngeal ligaments and membranes. Reprinted by permission from W. R. Zemlin, *Speech and Hearing Science: Anatomy and Physiology.* © 1968 by Prentice-Hall, Inc.

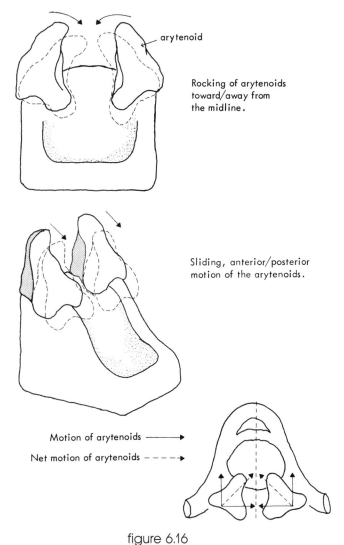

arytenoid

Rocking of arytenoids
toward/away from
the midline.

Sliding, anterior/posterior
motion of the arytenoids.

Motion of arytenoids ⟶

Net motion of arytenoids ⇢

figure 6.16
A schematic view of the rocking/sliding motion
of the arytenoid cartilages.
NOTE: rocking of arytenoid in toward midline, effecting closure of laryngeal airway.

The Cricoarytenoid Joint   Because of the importance of the cricoarytenoid joint to stretching of the vocal folds and the opening and closing of
the vocal folds, it will be discussed in some detail. The vocal folds (as well as
the ventricular and aryepiglottic folds) attach posteriorly to the arytenoid cartilages. Movements of the arytenoid cartilages shift the vocal folds toward closure at the midline or pull them away from the midline, thus opening the laryngeal airway. The mechanical motion of the arytenoids is a complex
combination of sliding and rocking (see Figure 6.16). Each arytenoid can rock
inward toward the midline of the laryngeal airway. This motion carries the vo-

cal folds toward a condition of adduction (closure). The arytenoids will also slide forward along the lateral wall of the cricoid: the combination of the arytenoids rocking inward and sliding forward closes the vocal folds; sliding backward and rocking outward opens the laryngeal airway.

The thyroid and cricoid cartilages attach on the inferior articular facets of the cricoid cartilage. When the cricothyroid muscle contracts, the thyroid cartilage tilts forward and downward. At the same time the cricoid, which is attached to the flexible trachea, tends to be pulled upward and forward. This combination of motions (see Figure 6.17) has been likened to that of a visored helmet. As a result of this rotation, the distance between the arytenoids (which have been tilted back) and the angle of the thyroid (which has tilted forward) has increased. The increased distance between the two points of attachment of the vocal folds increases vocal fold length because of stretching. This is a principal way in which the vocal folds are elongated and tensed.

THE LARYNGEAL CAVITY   The laryngeal cavity extends from the epipharynx to the trachea, and can be divided into two sections: the portion above the glottis and the portion below. The glottis is the opening between the medial, free margins of the true vocal folds. This opening is roughly 14 to 16 mm long in males and 12 to 14 mm long in females. When the folds are

figure 6.17

An illustration of the general nature of cricoid-thyroid movement which results in a lengthening (or shortening) of the vocal folds.

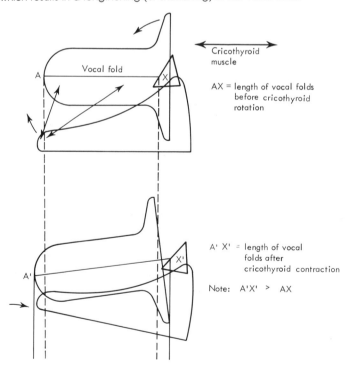

Vocal fold

A

X

Cricothyroid muscle

AX = length of vocal folds before cricothyroid rotation

A' X' = length of vocal folds after cricothyroid contraction

Note: A'X' > AX

A'

X'

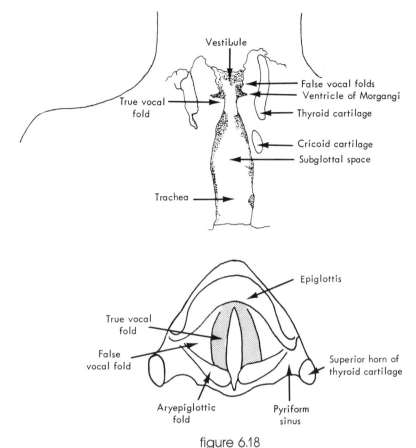

Vestibule

False vocal folds
Ventricle of Morgangi
True vocal fold
Thyroid cartilage
Cricoid cartilage
Subglottal space
Trachea

Epiglottis
True vocal fold
False vocal fold
Superior horn of thyroid cartilage
Aryepiglottic fold
Pyriform sinus

figure 6.18
The laryngeal cavities in cross-sectional view, and as
seen from above, a superior view of the vocal folds.

closed, there is no glottal opening, so it makes more sense to refer to the margins of the opening than to its presence or absence. Glottal margins can be divided into two sections. The anterior three-fifths of the margins are called the membranous glottis because they are composed of the vocal ligaments of the true, fleshy vocal folds. The posterior one-third are called the cartilagenous margins because the lateral surfaces of the arytenoid cartilage surfaces comprise that portion of the margins (see Figure 6.18).

The Vestibule   The portion of the laryngeal cavity above the glottis is called the vestibule. It extends from the aditus laryngeus, the triangular opening of the vestibule at the base of the epipharynx, to the glottis. As the vestibule extends downward, it narrows toward the true vocal folds. Immediately above the vocal folds, the vestibule walls are marked by two deep clefts, the so-called ventricles of Morgangi, which contain many mucous secreting cells used for lubrication of the vocal folds. This ventricle separates the false (ventricular) folds above from the true folds below.

The True Vocal Folds   The true vocal folds form the boundary between the vestibule and the inferior portion of the laryngeal cavity. These muscular folds arise anteriorly from the thyroid lamina near the angle, at a point below the thyroid notch. Their posterior attachment is to the anterolateral surface of the arytenoid cartilage. Each vocal fold projects, wedgelike, into the laryngeal airway. Each is wrapped in mucosal tissue which, at the free margin, thickens into a distinct, highly elastic white band called the vocal ligament. The exact shape of the vocal folds depends on the degree to which they have been stretched or tensed by muscle contraction.

The Inferior Laryngeal Cavity   The inferior portion of the laryngeal cavity is a smooth tube that tapers sharply from the nearly circular trachea to the wedgelike slit of the glottis. Its walls are covered with the smooth crico-thyroid membranes of the conus elasticus.

the physiology and anatomy of the laryngeal muscles

The laryngeal muscles can be separated into two groups: extrinsic and intrinsic. The intrinsic laryngeal muscles have both points of attachment on the laryngeal cartilages or tissues, whereas the extrinsic laryngeal muscles have at least one attachment outside the larynx. Physiologically, the intrinsic muscles determine vocal fold tension, glottal opening, and vocal fold compression — in other words, the mechanical operating characteristics of the larynx. The extrinsic muscles play a prime role in the position and posture of the larynx, which is a flexible array of cartilages placed atop the highly elastic tracheal tube. When the extrinsic muscles contract, they may elevate or depress the entire larynx one centimeter or more. As the larynx is being positioned by these elevations or depressions, the size and shape of the epipharynx and the vestibule are also altered. In addition, movements of the entire larynx caused by the extrinsic muscles may affect the tension and stiffness of the tissue between the ventricular and the true vocal folds. Thus, both sets of muscles affect the vibratory characteristics of the vocal folds. When these muscles contract, they cause changes in a number of the physiological parameters of glottal vibration, the most important of which are (1) vocal fold tension and length, (2) vocal fold position, and (3) medial compression, or tightness of closure.

FUNCTIONS

Vocal Fold Tension   Vocal fold tension is a prime determiner of vibratory frequency. As the vocal folds are stretched, they become thinner (less mass per unit length) and their stiffness increases. As a result, it takes greater air pressure to blow them open, and the greater air pressure causes them to open at higher speed. The increased tension causes increased elastic recoil, which with reduced mass per unit length results in a faster closing movement of the folds. As higher air pressures are used, the speed of airflow through the glottis increases and the Bernoulli drop in pressure also increases, further enhancing speed of closure.

Vocal fold tension may be increased in two general ways: (1) The folds may be passively stretched if the thyroid cartilage is tipped or rotated forward upon the cricothyroid joint, thus increasing tension; or (2) the muscles internal to the vocal folds (thyroarytenoid muscle) can contract, increasing the tension in an active manner. Vocal fold length itself is not critical, but as the folds are stretched, there is greater fold tension and decreasing thickness of the folds (less mass per unit length).

Vocal Fold Position   The muscles responsible for opening the vocal folds are the laryngeal abductors. Their antagonists, the adductors, close the folds. The abductor-adductor system controls phonation type. At various points along the dimension of the glottal opening, the vocal folds vibrate in differing ways, modulating the airflow differently. Full abduction results in voiceless sound production. Partial opening results in whisper. Vocal folds which are closed and vibrating along part of the glottis and open at another part result in breathy voice. Full closure with relaxed folds pressed together results in creak (pulse) phonation. Fully closed vocal folds pressed tightly together result in glottal stoppage and no phonation.

Medial Compression   The more tightly closed the folds are, the more strongly they will press against each other at the midline (glottal margin). The degree of medial compression is important for two reasons. First, the more tightly closed the folds are, the less fully open they swing when they are blown apart. More important, the larynx is an airvalve. To increase the intensity of phonation, the air burst must move at a higher speed so that the acoustic shock is more intense. The speed of the air burst increases as subglottal driving pressure increases. The thorax is like a pressure cooker. When pressure rises to a certain point, the valve blows open to release the excess. If subglottal pressure is increased, the laryngeal valve must be capable of resisting the pressure rise until the appropriate pressure is achieved. If the larynx failed to resist the pressure rise, any attempt to increase the intensity of phonation would result in useless escape of air pressure each time we attempted to increase P_{lung}.

As the folds are compressed medially (adducted ever more strongly), they can impound more pressure before blowing open, thus generating greater intensity of phonation. With each rise in subglottal pressure, there must be increased medial compression so that the laryngeal valve does not release or blow off prematurely. Experiment with your lips. Press them together gently, and notice how easily they can be blown open. Now, compress them tightly. Notice how much more pressure they will withstand before opening. In addition, the vocal folds tend to vibrate faster as air pressure increases. We have all observed that as we grow excited, both intensity and frequency of the voice tend to rise. It is a particularly interesting experiment to control both pitch and loudness at some point during a heated argument. More often than not, it has a cooling effect.

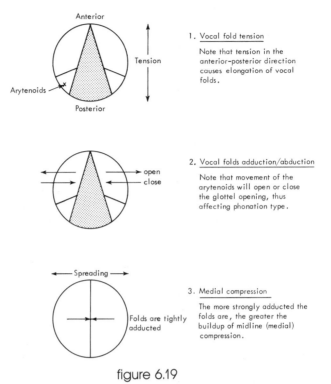

figure 6.19

The major physiological parameters of glottal behavior
and their corresponding vocal fold movements.

Figure 6.19 illustrates the three functions of the laryngeal muscles. Note that they are responsible for movements in both front to back (tension) and lateral spreading (adduction or abduction) directions.

THE INTRINSIC LARYNGEAL MUSCLES

The Glottal Tensors   The cricothyroid (Figure 6.20) is a large, two-bellied sheet of muscle that arises from the anterolateral arch of the cricoid and runs superiorly and posteriorly where it attaches to the thyroid cartilage. The more superiorly directed bundle, the pars recta, attaches to the inferior rim of the thyroid laminae. Contraction of this bundle rotates the thyroid forward and pulls the anterior arch of the cricoid upward. The pars oblique courses superiorly and posteriorly, inserting on the inferior horn of the thyroid. Contraction of this bundle tends to slide the thyroid forward and rotate it as well. Contraction of the entire cricothyroid muscle tilts the arytenoids backward and rotates the thyroid cartilage forward (Figure 6.17), thus increasing the distance between the two points of insertion of the vocal folds. In most cases, contraction of this muscle increases vocal fold length and tension. Increases in the

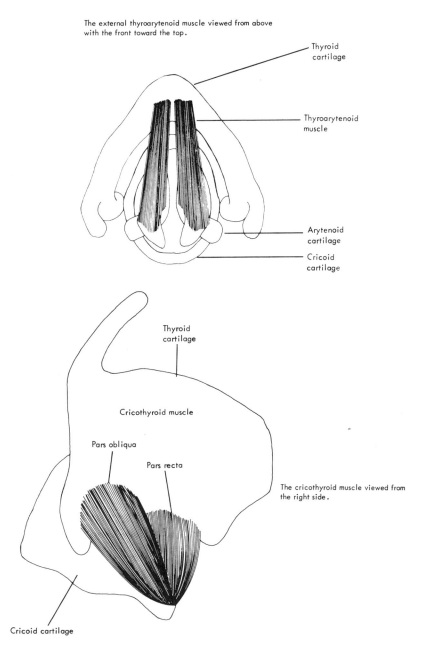

The external thyroarytenoid muscle viewed from above with the front toward the top.

Thyroid cartilage

Thyroarytenoid muscle

Arytenoid cartilage

Cricoid cartilage

Thyroid cartilage

Cricothyroid muscle

Pars obliqua

Pars recta

The cricothyroid muscle viewed from the right side.

Cricoid cartilage

figure 6.20

The cricothyroid and thyroarytenoid muscles, two major glottal tensors. Reprinted by permission from F. D. Minifie, T. J. Hixon, and F. Williams, eds., *Normal Aspects of Speech, Hearing, and Language.* © 1973 by Prentice-Hall, Inc.

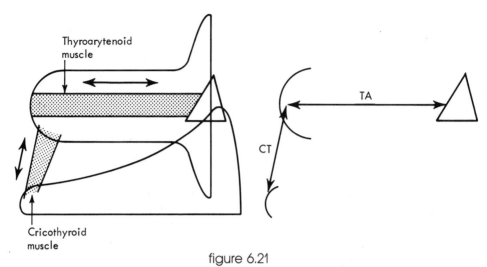

figure 6.21

An illustration of the antagonistic functioning of the cricothyroid
and thyroarytenoid muscles in terms of vocal fold tension.
NOTE: The cricothyroid and thyroarytenoid are antagonistic in that each pulls the
vocal fold in opposite directions. The cricothyroid lengthens and the thyroarytenoideus
shortens the vocal folds. However, if cricothyroid and thyroarytenoids are
simultaneously active, folds do not shorten and relax, but instead internal
tension builds up, effectively stiffening vocal folds.

frequency of glottal pulsation correlate strongly with increases in cricothyroid
contraction. Clearly this muscle causes a passive tension (passive because the
vocal fold muscle remains inactive as it is stretched by the cricothyroid) in the
vocal folds that contributes to control of the frequency of glottal pulsation. To
mimic this stretch of the vocal folds, put two fingers in the corners of your lips
and stretch the relaxed lips so that the tension in them rises. Contraction of the
cricothyroid muscle very probably increases vocal fold tension in a similar
manner.

The second glottal tensor muscle (Figures 6.20, 6.21), the thyroarytenoideus, can also function as a glottal relaxor. The thyroarytenoid consists of
two bundles, the thyromuscularis and the thyrovocalis. The muscularis, or
more external part of the thyroarytenoid, arises from the lower portion of the
angle of the thyroid and muscular process of each arytenoid. Laterally, this
muscle is attached to the wall of the thyroid lamina. When it contracts, it tends
to pull either the thyroid cartilage backward, the arytenoids forward, or both.
As a result, it opposes the action of the cricothyroid by shortening and thus relaxing the vocal folds. If the cricothyroid is simultaneously active, then contraction of the thyroarytenoid causes the tension of the vocal fold to increase
because the two muscles are contracting in opposite directions in an isometric
maneuver.

The vocalis portion of the thyroarytenoid lies nearer the glottal margin than
does the muscularis. It arises from the angle of the thyroid medial to the muscularis and courses posteriorly to attach to the vocal process and anterolateral
surface of the arytenoids. The vocalis muscle is adjacent to the vocal ligament. In

most cases, careful inspection reveals that the portion of the vocal fold which vibrates contains the vocalis, vocal ligament, and mucosa, but is only a portion of the muscularis. This suggests that because it is a portion of the folds which actually moves, the vocalis is crucial to vocal fold vibration. Contraction of the vocalis would also appear to be antagonistic to cricothyroid contraction (see Figure 6.21) because the vocalis would tend to shorten and relax the folds. If both cricothyroid and vocalis were active, the vocalis would then be effectively tensing the folds. Both functions are possible; in fact, since the vocal folds have multiple layers of tissue with differing elasticity, it is possible that strong vocalis contraction would effectively damp out vibration of nearly all the vocal fold except the mucosa and vocal ligaments at the free margins. This would reduce the vibrating mass of the vocal fold and raise the frequency of vibration. The vocalis is richly innervated, indicating that its contraction and tension can be delicately and finely controlled for rapid and precise contractions. Small shifts in frequency of the voice and changes in vocal "register" may be a function of differential contraction of the vocalis.

The Glottal Abductor   The major glottal abductor is the posterior cricoarytenoid, a broad, paired muscle that arises from the posterior surface of the cricoid lamina and courses superiorly and laterally to insert upon the muscular process of the arytenoid cartilage (Figure 6.22). Upon contraction, this muscle produces a vocal fold opening by causing the arytenoids to rotate and slide outward or laterally. That is, as the posterior cricoarytenoid pulls down, back, and out on the muscular process, the vocal process follows, pulling the vocal folds away from the midline. The posterior cricoarytenoid

figure 6.22

Major adductor/abductor intrinsic laryngeal muscles: posterior
cricoarytenoid, interarytenoid, and lateral cricoarytenoid.

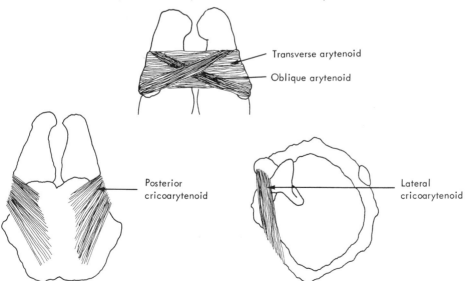

Transverse arytenoid

Oblique arytenoid

Posterior
cricoarytenoid

Lateral
cricoarytenoid

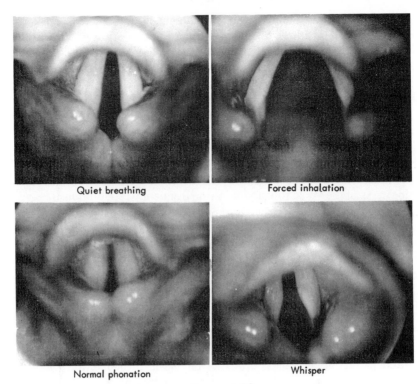

Quiet breathing

Forced inhalation

Normal phonation

Whisper

figure 6.23

Photographs of various degrees of laryngeal dilation
attributable to differential contraction of the posterior
cricoarytenoid muscle. Vocal folds observed from above
with a laryngeal mirror. Reprinted by permission from
W. R. Zemlin, *Speech and Hearing Science:
Anatomy and Physiology.* © 1968 by Prentice-Hall, Inc.

has been called the *laryngeal dilator*. This muscle is constantly active during quiet breathing, keeping the vocal folds out of the midline as air flows inward. Forced inhalation produces a very strong adduction (opening) known as the laryngeal dilation maneuver (Figure 6.23). In most cases when a speaker moves from a voiced to a voiceless sound, this muscle is responsible for devoicing by abducting the folds for the voiceless sound.

The Glottal Adductors   The lateral cricoarytenoideus, a glottal adductor, arises from the upper rim of the lateral wall of the cricoid. It extends upward and backward upon the rim to attach to the muscular process of the arytenoid. Figure 6.23 shows that it is a direct antagonist of the posterior cricoarytenoid; it tends to tilt and rotate the arytenoid inward, downward, and forward, closing the glottis. As it closes the folds, they would tend to shorten and relax as well. This muscle also probably functions as a medial compressor for the membranous portion of the glottis.

The Interarytenoid Muscle   The interarytenoid fills the space between the two arytenoids, extending from the posterior surface and lateral margin of one arytenoid to the other. This muscle can be divided into two functional parts: Transverse and oblique.

The fibers of the transverse interarytenoid arise on one arytenoid cartilage and course horizontally to insert on the margin and posterior surface of the other. Contraction of this muscle would cause the arytenoids to slide toward each other. The oblique interarytenoid consists of two bellies of fibers, each coursing at an angle from the muscular process of one arytenoid toward the apex of the other. The muscle bellies cross in an X pattern, and the fibers continue beyond the apex of the arytenoid to become the muscles of the aryepiglottic folds. Contraction of this muscle tips and slides each arytenoid toward the other.

During phonation the intrinsic muscles oftentimes function in such a way that reciprocal inhibition appears to occur: when the glottal adductors are active the activity of glottal abductors is suppressed, and vice versa. Muscle contraction patterns in which either but not both are active yield very high speeds of movement. Indeed, the structures of the larynx move rapidly, going from opening to closure and vice versa in as little as 20 to 30 milliseconds. The speed and timing of laryngeal movements for opening, closing, tensing, and so on are about as fine and delicate as those found anywhere in the vocal tract.

THE EXTRINSIC
LARYNGEAL MUSCLES   The extrinsic laryngeal muscles function to support, stabilize, and maintain laryngeal cartilage position. They do so by strapping in the larynx, either to bony structures above or below the hyoid bone. In the course of raising and lowering the larynx, they may also affect laryngeal tension or closure and thus the physiological parameters of phonation as well.

Laryngeal Elevators: Figure 6.24 shows a frontal view of
The Suprahyoid Muscles   the extrinsic laryngeal muscles: the stylohyoid, the digastric, the mylohyoid, the hyoglossus. The stylohyoid muscle runs from the styloid process of the temporal bone at the base of the skull downward and forward to attach to the body of the hyoid. Contraction of this muscle pulls the hyoid up and back. The digrastic is a two-bellied muscle with an intermediate tendon between the two bellies that attaches to the corpus and horns of the hyoid bone. The anterior belly is attached to the lower border of the mandible. The posterior belly is attached to the mastoid process of the temporal bone. If contracted, this muscle will raise the hyoid if the mandible is fixed in position, or lower the mandible, if the hyoid is fixed in position. The mylohyoid is a sheet of muscle fiber that forms the floor of the mouth. Fibers arising from the entire rim of the inner surface of the mandible course backward to insert upon a central tendon attached to the hyoid. Contraction of this muscle will either raise the hyoid or lower the mandible, depending on which is more

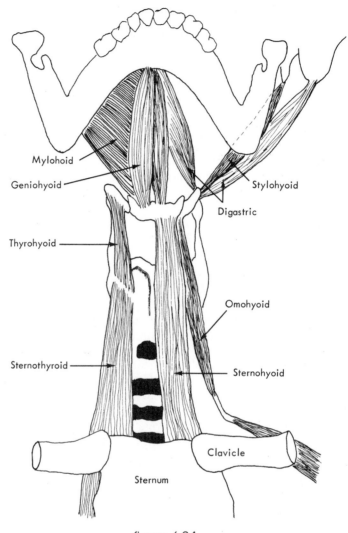

figure 6.24
The extrinsic laryngeal muscles.

fixed in position. The hyoglossus muscle (see Figure 7.13) arises from the upper rim of the corpus of the hyoid and fans out upward into the tongue. Thus, elevation of the tongue would tend to raise the hyoid. The genioglossus originates along the interior surface of the angle of the mandible, and certain of its fibers course posteriorly to insert into the hyoid. Its activity would be similar to that of the mylohyoid.

Laryngeal Depressors:
The Infrahyoid Muscles

The infrahyoid muscles are the sternohyoid, the thyrohyoid, and the omohyoid. The sternohyoid is a flat, straplike, paired muscle, whose large, strong belt of fibers courses upward from an attachment on the posterior surface of the manubrium of the sternum to insert on the lower rim of the corpus of the hyoid. Depending on which bone is better braced, contraction of the sternohyoid will lower the hyoid or raise the sternum. The sternothyroid, a flat, thin belt of muscle, lies deep to the sternohyoid, and runs vertically from an attachment on the manubrium and first few costal cartilages to insert on the oblique line of the thyroid lamina. Contraction of this muscle draws the thyroid down and forward. The thyrohyoid arises from the oblique line of the thyroid and runs vertically to an insertion on the lower rim of the greater horn of the hyoid. Contraction of this muscle depresses the hyoid or elevates the thyroid, depending on which is less firmly fixed in place. The omohyoid, a two-bellied strap muscle, winds a long course from the upper border of the scapula under the skin of the shoulder to an intermediate tendon at the base of the neck, where the second belly rises vertically to an attachment on the lower border of the greater horn of the hyoid. Contraction of this muscle depresses the hyoid bone.

phonation: current theories and hypotheses

Having threaded our way through a maze of anatomy, we can now look at some interesting aspects of phonation. The human voice can be described physiologically, acoustically, and perceptually, and each level of description can be interrelated with the others. The following discussion is speculative, and reflects current physiological theory. Because the human body is so complex, because we cannot get inside the brain, and because we cannot perform destructive experiments on human subjects, we have limited information and few laws and models concerning the process of speech production. As a result, hypotheses change rapidly, and even the experts seem to disagree. But this is not chaos; it means that the study of human communication is still in its infancy, and simply inexact and limited.

THE GLOTTAL VIBRATORY CYCLE

Figure 6.25 shows a series of frontal and superior views of the vocal folds as they move through a cycle of vibration. If you examine these pictures, you will see that the folds open and close first along the bottom edge. Nor do they appear to open and close simultaneously in an anterior-posterior direction. These differences in times of opening and closing of the upper and lower edges of the vocal folds are called *vertical phase lags* or *phase effects*. Phase (see Chapter 4) refers to the relative starting time of a waveform. If we were to plot the movement patterns of the upper and lower edges of the vocal folds, the movement of the upper edge would be seen to lag behind (start later than) the movement of the lower edge. These vertical phase effects shed light on the process by which the vocal folds extract energy from the air stream in order to vibrate. They are also a key to understanding how the folds vibrate in normal voice phonation.

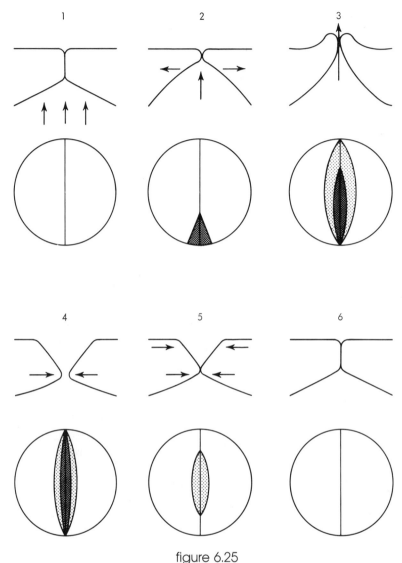

figure 6.25

A representative illustration of a cycle of glottal vibration
showing the phase difference in the opening
time of the upper and lower edges of the vocal folds.

The lower edges of the vocal folds are more compliant than the upper edges. As a result, air pressure rising below the vocal folds first pushes aside the lower edges. As the lower edges move aside, they drag the upper edges with them toward glottal opening. Once the folds open, air begins to flow through the slit. Due to an aerodynamic coupling effect, as the upper fold edges move apart the airflow and the Bernoulli drop in air pressure become very large in the region of the lower edges. Because of their greater compliance and the fact that the Bernoulli pressure drop is greatest at the bottom edge of the glottis, the lower vocal fold edges begin to move toward closure, once again, in advance of the stiffer upper edges, which they pull along with them. This sequence is shown in Figure 6.25: (1) As air pressure increases, (2) the lower edges of the folds are the first to be pushed apart. The lower edges, with the assistance of air pressure, pull/push the upper edges apart, resulting in an air burst (3). The Bernoulli effect of the air burst and elastic recoil (4) cause the lower edges of the fold to move toward closure (5), where they, along with the drop in pressure, cause the upper edges of the folds to shut, preparing the folds (6) for another cycle of glottal vibration.

Glottal vibration generally does not begin with the vocal folds completely closed. Instead, the folds are brought toward the midline, but not fully closed. As air pressure rises, air flows through the small glottal opening. The Bernoulli drop in pressure causes the folds to move toward the midline. As the folds are pulled toward midline closure, elastic recoil increases and airflow is reduced. The folds recoil outward, airflow rises, and the Bernoulli effect increases, once again drawing the folds toward the midline. As momentum increases with each successive cycle of vibration, the vocal folds move nearer and nearer until they finally achieve closure, and the result is a full cycle of opening and closing. Thus, the normal onset of phonation is slightly breathy because closure is incomplete during the first few cycles of glottal oscillation. You can demonstrate normal voice onset with your lips. Hold them very slightly open and blow air through them swiftly. They will start to tremble and then burst into a full opening-closing pattern of vibration.

As a speaker prepares to phonate, he or she goes through prephonatory positioning of the vocal folds, and then an attack phase. During the prephonatory phase, the folds move from an open, abducted position (see Figure 6.26) toward closure, even if the first sound is voiceless. During the attack phase, the folds continue toward closure if the sound is to be voiced; if the sound is to be voiceless, the folds also begin to move toward closure, only to be reversed

figure 6.26

An illustration of the prephonatory positioning of the
larynx, illustrating the width of the glottis
during the prephonatory and attack phases of phonation.

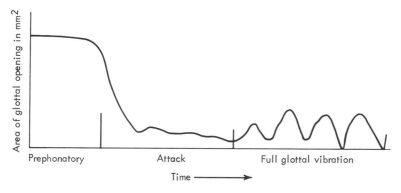

in direction by a command to move toward a more open "voiceless" position. (The entire episode lasts only between $\frac{1}{10}$ and $\frac{1}{5}$ of a second.) Some people never achieve full vocal fold closure because there is an opening between their arytenoids, along the cartilaginous glottis, throughout a full glottal vibratory cycle. This may result in a "breathy" voice. Of course, at the same time that the vocal folds prepare for vibration, there must be coordinated activity in the respiratory system to provide the needed air pressure. If the pressure rises too soon, before the folds are closed, there will be a loss of air through the folds that is heard as an aspirative hiss. (You can demonstrate this by saying "ha.") In this case, the hiss is associated with the [h] sound. If air pressure rise lags behind glottal closure, there will be a glottal stop closure in advance of normal voicing. If both vocal fold closure and the rise in air pressure are well coordinated, the normal or "soft" glottal attack described above is heard.

THE PARAMETERS OF THE HUMAN VOICE

As we have said, the human voice can be described on the physiological, acoustic, and perceptual levels. Each of the parameters of the voice has its correlates at the other levels of description, as the listing below shows. For example, the acoustic parameter of vocal frequency is correlated strongly with the physiological parameter of vocal fold tension and with the psychological-perceptual parameter of vocal pitch.

PHYSIOLOGICAL	ACOUSTIC	PERCEPTUAL
Vocal fold tension	Frequency of vibration	Pitch of voice
Medial compression and air pressure	Intensity of phonation	Loudness of voice
Vocal fold adduction/abduction	Spectral differences	Quality of voice

Vocal fold tension is the major determinant of the frequency of glottal pulsation. As the folds become more tense, they vibrate faster because of increased elastic recoil forces and because tense folds are usually thinner, so that there is less vibrating mass/unit length. Acoustically, tensed folds vibrate faster so that one observes a higher frequency of glottal pulsation. Psychologically, the listener perceives increasing frequency of glottal pulsation as a rise in "pitch," a psychological sensation closely related to frequency of vibration.

Vocal fold medial compression is an important determinant of vocal intensity. If we wish to increase the intensity of the voice, the air bursts must move with greater velocity. Greater driving pressure from the lungs is needed. To sustain this increased pressure, the laryngeal valve must be more tightly closed in order to contain the rise in air pressure. When the folds do burst open, the greater pressure produces a faster moving air burst which in turn causes a stronger, more intense acoustic vibration because of the greater impact of the collision of the air burst with the column of air in the vocal tract. Perceptually, the listener experiences greater acoustic intensity as an increase in loudness.

Physiologically, adduction/abduction refers to the degree to which the vocal folds are opened or closed. As the arytenoids abduct by rotating and sliding open, the airflow is less impeded; as they adduct, sliding inward, the airflow is more impeded. Acoustically, each phonation type describes a differing degree of airflow modulation (see Figure 5.9). If airflow is not modulated, there will be no sound production.

PHONATION TYPE	AIRFLOW MODULATION
VOICELESS	Folds are wide open; they minimally impede flow, and the resulting airflow is noiseless. No sound.
WHISPER	Folds are closer together: air moves through glottal constriction, picks up speed, and begins to rotate in turbulent eddies. These provide the modulation of flow that gives noisy vibration. Random distribution of energy across frequency.
VOICE	Folds obstruct the airway. Air pressure gives rise to periodic opening-closing movements. The resulting air puffs give rise to a rhythmic series of acoustic shock waves heard as a laryngeal buzz. Harmonically related frequencies present in signal.
GLOTTAL STOP	Folds are totally and abruptly closed. Modulation is total, and there is no airflow. The ear interprets the sudden cessation of buzzing plus silence, or silence followed by rapid onset of buzzing, as a glottal stop.

Psychologically, the acoustic differences in spectrum caused by differing airflow modulations are perceived as changes in the "quality" of the voice. If the modulation results in periodic air burst, we hear a pleasing, "musical" quality in the voice. If the modulation results in noise plus buzzing, the perceived quality is "breathy." If we hear only noise modulation (friction), the perceived quality is noisy. If the modulation results in irregularly spaced, low-frequency air bursts, the quality of the perceived voice is "creaky," and so on.

All three levels of description are useful and valid. Which level is chosen depends on the needs of the particular investigator. Speech pathologists are generally concerned with the physiological aspects of voice; engineers worry about the acoustic parameters of voice; phoneticians and teachers of singing react most strongly to perceptual qualities of voice.

THE USE OF VOCAL
PARAMETERS FOR SPEECH   In this section, we will examine briefly what is known about the ways in which speakers control their voices for speech. The critical aspects of voice control are the parameters that govern how the vocal folds vibrate: tension, medial compression, and phonation type.

Generally speaking, the human voice can be compared to a musical instrument. But pitch, melody, and expressiveness, although revealing aspects of voice, are unfortunately difficult to study scientifically. It would be useful to consider the kinds of information that the human voice conveys to a listener. As speech pathologists and scientists, we have generally focused on the linguistic aspects of voice: phonation type, prosody-intonation cues, and so on. Yet, we should be aware that people generally react most strongly to the idiolectal, aesthetic, or sex-bearing cues of voice. Indeed, vocal pathology is generally first noticed as changes in the aesthetic, idiolectal, or paralinguistic aspects of voice. If vocal pathology is so severe that the speaker loses control of phonation type and intonational parameters, he or she will experience extreme difficulty in communicating.

Before describing how speakers physiologically control the parameters of voice, a word of caution is in order. The larynx is a complex mechanism. A change in vocal fold tension will indeed affect vocal frequency, but it may well cause changes in intensity and quality as well. When strong emotion causes the contraction of laryngeal as well as other muscles, all the parameters of voice—pitch, loudness, quality—change simultaneously. Indeed, it is the hallmark of the untrained singing or speaking voice that the vocal parameters tend to change simultaneously. That is, the speaker finds it difficult to change one parameter independently of the others.

Regulation and Role of Vocal Intensity The intensity of the human voice depends upon two physiological parameters: subglottal pressure and medial compression. Acoustically speaking, intensity is related to the degree to which the particles of the medium (in this case, air) are disturbed (pushed away from their rest position). The faster-moving the glottal air burst, the greater the momentum of its impact on the larger column of air in the vocal tract, and the more intense the resulting acoustic vibration. Therefore, to increase the velocity of the escaping air burst, the speaker needs a greater subglottal driving pressure. In order to contain this greater pressure so that it does not blow off uselessly, the glottal air valve must be tightened—that is, glottal impedance must be increased by increasing medial compression.

Electromyographic research has shown that as vocal intensity increases, so does the strength of contraction of the laryngeal adductor muscles, especially the interarytenoids and, to a lesser degree, the lateral cricoarytenoids. In addition, there may also be some increase of glottal tension. Many investigators have confirmed the fact that the relationship between subglottal pressure and acoustic intensity of voicing is a strong and direct one. That is,

$$\text{vocal intensity} \propto \sqrt[3]{P_L}$$

Each doubling of lung pressure produces about an 8 to 12 dB increase in the intensity level of the voice. For very soft speech, as little as 2 to 3 cm H_2O pressure will suffice for a soft glottal buzz. For loud speech, 15 to 20 cm H_2O will suffice, and for a loud shout, 40 to 60 cm H_2O pressure may be used. Conversational speech is typically produced at a sound pressure level of 60 dB, whereas the limits of shouting may carry the level to 108 dB (at a distance of about 1 meter from the mouth).

Intensity variations are crucial to the production of the so-called prosodic factors of stress and intonation. When we wish to emphasize or accentuate a syllable, we tend to produce it with higher frequency, greater intensity, or longer duration than is found in surrounding syllables.

Regulation and Role
of Vocal Frequency
The typical adult speaker can produce glottal buzzing that extends over a range of frequencies in excess of two octaves. An octave interval is a range of frequencies such that the highest frequency of vibration is double that of the lowest. For example,

$$2F_{low} = F_{high}$$

Given the lowest sustainable glottal buzz rate, most of us can double that frequency at least twice, if not more. Test this for yourself. Sing "do" (dough) at the lowest pitch you can, and then sing a scale, do-re-mi-fa-so-la-ti-do. Providing the scale is sung properly, it represents an octave jump. How many times can you sing "do" to "do"? Practice this. Average adults can sing a 2 to $2\frac{1}{2}$ octave frequency range. That is, their highest glottal buzz frequency $F_h = 2.5$ F_{lowest}. The average speaker usually phonates at the most comfortable frequency. This is called the *modal* or most frequently occurring glottal buzz rate. We can phonate above or below that frequency. We can also define an *average* or *median* frequency. The modal frequency for males (Figure 6.27) is about 128 Hz, and about an octave higher at 260 Hz for females. The average range (highest to lowest frequency of phonation) for either males or females is about 2 octaves. The modal frequency for speech is located at about the lower one-fourth to one-third of a speaker's vocal range. That is, we tend to habitually phonate toward the lower end of our range of sustainable vocal frequencies.

What factors determine modal frequency? We get some clues if we examine male-female differences. Female larynxes are smaller than male larynxes. Their vocal folds are shorter in length, thinner in cross-section, less massive in size. As a result of reduced length and mass, they vibrate faster at any given P_L than do male larynxes. Such data lead one to speculate that an individual's modal frequency is governed in large part by the physical size, shape, and mass of vocal folds and larynx. Also in part, our vocal habits and training accustom us to select a frequency range that is comfortable, so that modal frequency is

figure 6.27

The distribution of modal vocal frequencies for a large population of adult males and females.

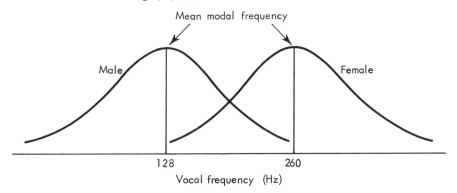

the result of a compromise between personal habit and optimum mechanical buzz frequency.

Numerous investigations concerning the way in which the frequency of glottal pulsation is increased have shown that as f_0 increases, there is a strong correlation between cricothyroid and thyroartenoideus activity and vocal frequency, indicating that both muscles acting together function as cooperative glottal tensors. There is also a tendency to increase P_{lung}, as f_0 rises, presumably because the ever-increasing tension of the folds demands greater air pressure to blow them open. As the cricothyroid contracts, the vocal folds grow longer and thinner. Such elongation, thinning, and tensing not only make the folds less massive in cross-section, but tend to decouple both the muscularis and even a portion of the vocalis from the vibrating portion of the folds. At the very highest frequencies, only the very edge, the vocal ligaments and associated mucosa, are seen to vibrate during glottal opening. Figure 6.28 demonstrates the relationship between vocal fold length and glottal pulse rate, and the vocal fold thickness. Notice that as frequency of glottal buzz increases, the increasing stretch and length of the folds results in a reduced thickness of vocal fold tissue. This results in less mass per unit length, M/l, of the vocal folds. Less massive bodies accelerate faster when a force is acting, $F/M = a$, as Newton's law shows.

Thus, vocal fold stretching not only increases tension and thus elastic recoil force, but decreases the vibrating mass of the folds. That is, F increases and M decreases, resulting in increased acceleration, a. The folds are accelerated open and shut faster and faster as the folds are stretched. In summary, large, relaxed, massive folds vibrate more slowly than do tense, less massive folds. Vocal folds tend to be shortest in length, least stiff, and thickest at the lowest sustainable vocal pitch (except for creak). As we sing upward to about the 75 to 80 percent point of the frequency range, the folds may increase in length by as much as 40 to 60 percent. The fact that the vocal folds are shortest not when they are at rest but at low vocal pitches suggests that muscle contraction is needed to shorten the vocal folds for pitch lowering.

Because in some cases lowering of vocal frequency is faster than raising of f_0, we can assume that merely relaxing the glottal tensor muscles and reducing P_L is insufficient to lower f_0. Presumably, several glottal relaxor muscles must be active in lowering vocal frequency. If its contractions are unopposed by cricothyroid activity, contraction of the thyroarytenoid will shorten the vocal folds and relax them by pulling the thyroid and arytenoid cartilages closer together. In addition, the sternohyoid muscle is active during rapid pitch lowering. Presumably, such contraction lowers the hyoid bone, relieving strain on the thyrohyoid ligament and allowing the thyroid cartilage to be pulled back, relaxing the folds. The thyroepiglottic muscles (folds) may contract and lower f_0 by relieving vertical tension on the true folds, and by constricting the laryngeal airway, thus damping the glottal buzz.

Another factor affecting vocal frequency is the degree of vocal tract constriction during speech articulation. With each consonantal constriction of the vocal

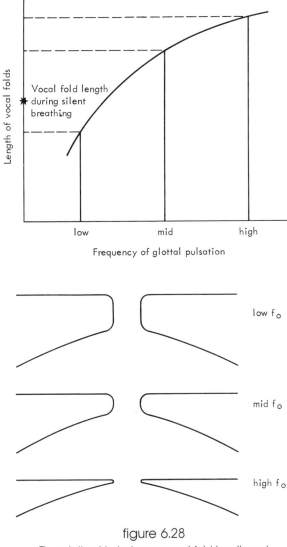

figure 6.28
The relationship between vocal fold length and
glottal pulse rate (frequency). Also shown are
vocal fold thickness at three vocal frequencies.

tract above the larynx, there is an impedance to airflow at that point and a rise in
air pressure behind the constriction. As a result, the pressure drop across the
larynx is reduced, the vocal folds are not forced apart so vigorously, and the
frequency of glottal buzzing decreases. If the vocal tract is fully closed, after
only a few glottal pulses the pressure above and below the folds is equalized and
buzzing ceases. Test this yourself by holding your nose shut tightly and saying
"m". Your folds stop buzzing very quickly because the air in the vocal tract

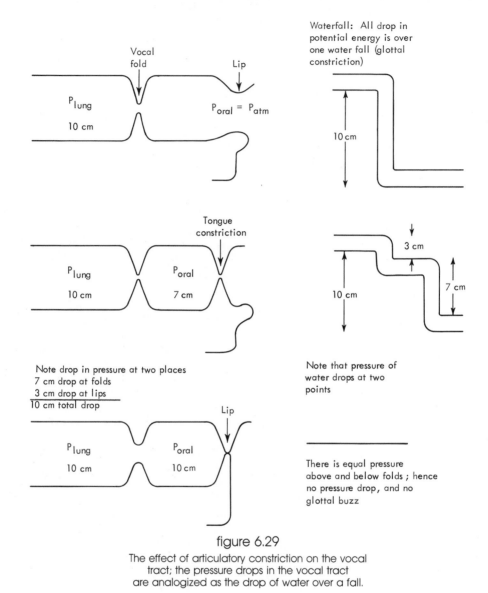

figure 6.29
The effect of articulatory constriction on the vocal
tract; the pressure drops in the vocal tract
are analogized as the drop of water over a fall.

cannot escape, and pressure above and below the folds becomes equal. At that
point, there is no accelerating force to open the folds, and pulsation ceases.
Figure 6.29 shows what happens as vocal tract constriction increases. Less and
less of the pressure drop from lungs to atmosphere occurs across the larynx, and
more and more occurs across the articulatory constriction. The smaller transglottal pressure difference results in slower, less intense vibration. In the extreme
case, complete stoppage of vibration occurs when the vocal tract constriction is
complete and pressure is equalized above and below the vocal folds. This can be

summarized by saying that the impedance of the vocal tract is

$$Z_{\text{vocal tract}} = Z_{\text{glottis}} + Z_{\text{articulation}}$$

since P/U_{flow} equals $Z_{\text{impedance}}$ and since U is generally the same (same total volume flow) at every point in the vocal tract:

$$\frac{P_{\text{total}}}{U} = \frac{P_{\text{glottis}}}{U} + \frac{P_{\text{artic}}}{U}$$

$$P_{\text{total}} = P_{\text{glottis}} + P_{\text{artic}}$$

Thus, as more of the total pressure drop appears across the articulatory constriction, less is available across the vocal folds, so that they vibrate more slowly, or cease to vibrate. When the vocal folds vibrate during articulatory constriction, there is sometimes a tendency on the speaker's part to relax them (reduce tension), since relaxed folds can be blown open (buzzed) with less pressure.

THE PRODUCTION OF SUPRASEGMENTAL ASPECTS OF SPEECH

The suprasegmental aspects of speech are those features that extend over more than a single sound segment. Suprasegmental cues include sentence intonation and syllable stress, and some investigators argue that the two are inseparable. Intonation is the perceived pitch pattern of an utterance which conveys syntactic and semantic cues. Acoustically, the perceived pitch pattern is best estimated by determining the vocal frequency contour. For example, take the utterance, "He'll obey me immediately." If the utterance is spoken as a question, the frequency pattern will show a sharp rise at the end. If it is spoken as a simple statement in a declarative fashion, the frequency is relatively constant until the end of the utterance, when it falls rapidly. If it is spoken as a command, the frequency contour will be relatively flat throughout. Vocal loudness tends to vary with frequency in a correlated fashion throughout most of the utterance. In general, the larynx appears to be the primary determiner of frequency except at the end of an utterance, when there is a natural tendency for both lung pressure as well as laryngeal tension to decrease as the speaker prepares to inhale. For the question pattern, the terminal rise in frequency occurs despite a drop in lung pressure, which indicates that increasing laryngeal tension must cause the pitch rise. Nevertheless, lung pressure also contributes to the intonation contour of sentences.

With respect to stress, which will be discussed in Chapter 8, it appears that when a speaker wishes to add prominence to a syllable, he or she *may* use more muscular energy in its production. This would, of course, mean greater lung pressure, greater laryngeal tension, and stronger, faster, longer articulatory gestures. Ideally, such a strongly stressed syllable would be longer, louder, higher-pitched, and more crisply articulated. Unfortunately, in many cases the stressed syllable displays none or only a few of the expected physiological or acoustic cues. Perhaps the fact that stress is predictable from the word structure and syntactic function of the words in an utterance permits listeners to predict the expected syllable stress levels even when the cues are missing. The larynx, more than the lungs, may show enhanced activity for stressed syllables, but very often such cues are not observable physiologically or acoustically. It is difficult to demonstrate either physiologically or acoustically that there are 3 to 4 linguistically distinct levels of stress, since very often even the most heavily stressed syllables reveal no consistent change in acoustic characteristics.

VOICE ONSET TIME   In intravocalic (VCV) or prevocalic (CV) position, the voicing contrast (±voice) for stop consonants is conveyed most strongly by the acoustic cue called *voice-onset time (VOT)*. Voice onset time can be measured as the period of time between the release of the stop consonant (usually observed as an explosive burst of noise) and the beginning of vocal fold vibration. That is, the voicing contrast is conveyed by manipulating the timing between onset of glottal vibration and the moment of stop release. Figure 6.30 shows the VOT measurement for glottal vibration beginning before, at, and after articulatory release. In English, most voiced stops are produced with a VOT that ranges from a negative value to a small positive value. That is, voiced stops are produced with prevoicing (voicing before release) or with a short voicing lag of up to 20 msec. Voiceless stops are generally produced with VOTs of 30 to 120 msec. There is some overlap between voiced and voiceless stops along the VOT dimension, so that VOT cannot be the only cue for voicing in stops. Indeed, the VOT that is produced shows systematic variation with place of articulation, with VOT values increasing as one moves from labial to alveolar to velar place of articulation (see Chapter 7). VOT also varies with speaker and phonetic context.

Perceptual studies have shown that at some point along the continuum of VOT values, a listener will rather swiftly shift perception of the stop consonant from voiced to voiceless. This crossover is relatively abrupt; that is, between 100 percent perception of [d] at +20 msec VOT and 100 percent perception of [t] at 50 msec and beyond, there is a 30 msec region where one hears a proportion of voiced and voiceless stops. The crossover region and width is language-dependent. In any case, the larynx participates crucially in the voiced-voiceless distinction.

VOCAL REGISTERS   As a person sings from his lowest sustainable pitch to his highest, not only does glottal pulse rate increase, but the voice undergoes *register* shifts. That is, the range of vocal frequencies of the human voice is separated into overlapping vocal registers. The literature on vocal registers is vast and conflicting, but claims have been made that there are as many as five to seven registers. We will maintain at this point that there are *three* vocal registers: a low-frequency or *pulse* register; a mid-frequency or *modal* register, and a high-frequency or *loft* (falsetto) register (Hollien, 1974). It would appear that at each change from one register to the next, the vocal folds change over, shift, or switch into a different, mechanical mode of vibration. According to Hollien, a vocal register is a "series or range of con-

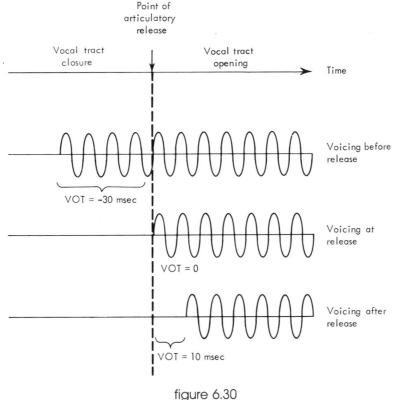

Point of
articulatory
release

Vocal tract
closure

Vocal tract
opening

Time

Voicing before
release

VOT = -30 msec

Voicing at
release

VOT = 0

Voicing after
release

VOT = 10 msec

figure 6.30

A schematic illustration of the relationship between
articulatory release and glottal vibration in stop consonants.

secutively phonated frequencies which can be produced with nearly identical
vocal quality and . . . ordinarily there should be little overlap in fundamental
frequency (f_0) between adjacent registers. Furthermore . . . a vocal register is a
totally *laryngeal* event, and . . . it can be operationally defined: (1) perceptually,
(2) acoustically, and (3) physiologically." The complex physiological structure
of the larynx can vibrate in three (or more) relatively different ways, giving rise
to airflow modulation that yields acoustically and perceptually distinct vocal
quality.

One object of vocal training for singers is to enable them to shift from register to register in a smooth manner. We are all familiar with the adolescent boy
whose voice undergoes pitch breaks as he struggles to control a larynx that
has rapidly increased in size.

The pulse register includes the lowest frequency range of vocal fold vibration. The vibratory pattern consists of low-frequency irregularly occurring
bursts of air. The vocal folds are short, thick, and relatively compliant, and
there is evidence that they are pressed together rather tightly. X rays reveal

that during pulse phonation, the ventricular folds may descend and ride atop the surface of the true folds. As a result, when air pressure is applied to the compliant short, thick, compressed, mass-loaded folds, the air escapes along the glottal margins in a "bubbling" fashion. The folds move little, if at all; instead, the compliant glottal margins, which are relatively "floppy," allow air to escape in irregularly timed, low-frequency bursts. The range of vocal intensity in pulse register is limited, as is the range of frequencies, 3 to 50 Hz.

Aerodynamically, pulse phonation represents a strong modulation of airflow, since the vocal fold opening is tiny and occurs so infrequently. Hence glottal impedance is probably higher in pulse than in the other registers. The sensation aroused by phonation in this register is that of a harsh, popping vocal quality. Although the glottal pulse emitted during pulse phonation is rich in harmonics, they are closely spaced in frequency and do not excite the higher resonances of the vocal tract very strongly. You can demonstrate such vibration by pressing your lips together and bubbling air through the medial lip margins. Notice that although the lips are pressed together along both upper and lower margins, only the center or medial margins of the lips vibrate as air compressed in the oral cavity is forced through them. The broad expanse of the upper and lower lip is relatively stationary except for the vibrating mass of the medial portions, which produce repetitive, bubbling, flatulentlike noise.

In modal register, the vocal folds present an upper and a lower edge (see Figure 6.26) at the glottal margin and are relatively compliant. When they burst open, almost the entire vocal fold moves, including the vocal ligament, mucosa, and body of the fold. Motion pictures reveal that the opening motion has a complex, phase-dependent quality (Figure 6.26). The lower edge of the glottal margin opens first and then the top edge, and in general the glottis opens first posteriorly, with the opening spreading anteriorly. At the lower end of modal register, the folds are sufficiently compliant that little surface waves or bulges are seen to move across the surface of the folds in a rippling fashion at the instant of vocal fold collision. As pitch rises in the modal register, the folds are stretched increasingly and fold length increases as fold thickness decreases. The folds lose their extreme compliance, and at the highest modal pitches the glottal margin presents only a single edge in shape and has minimal phase differences in opening and closing, either vertically or anterior-posteriorly. The range of sustainable frequencies is very wide in modal phonation, approximately $1\frac{1}{2}$ octaves or more, and a wide dynamic range of intensities (40 to 110 dB) is possible, particularly at mid-frequencies. Modal phonation vocal quality is rich, pleasing, and mellow. The modal air bursts yield a pressure pulse rich in harmonics that span a 4- to 6-octave range of frequencies. Generally, vocal pitch in modal register is relatively steady, with small variations of f_0 which listeners find pleasing.

Aerodynamically, modal phonation offers an impedance to airflow comparable to that of fricative consonant constrictions. Airflow is moderate at 100 to 250 cc/sec, as is glottal impedance. The characteristic fold vibration pattern involves an opening of the glottis followed by a complete (airtight) closure. As vocal intensity rises, the vocal fold opening occurs more swiftly, while the closed phase becomes longer in duration. In certain people, however, modal vocal fold closure is never complete because of a small glottal opening between the arytenoid cartilages. Modal phonation is very probably an optimum way to phonate, since it is the phonation type used by most people throughout their speaking day. Certainly, vocal agility involving swift changes in pitch or loudness is most easily accomplished in this register. You can mimic modal phonation with your lips by holding them gently together and applying oral pressure by blowing outward. Observe the complexity of the lip motion in a mirror. Both lips move in almost their entirety; the lips open along their full margin and bulge and wobble strongly as they open and close, showing phasal opening-closing effects.

At some point in the upper portion of the modal register, phonation shifts from modal to loft glottal pulsing. Presumably, as tension increases, the folds become so stiff that only the portion near the glottal margins is free to vibrate. There is not an upper and lower lip to each vocal fold, but only a single, tense edge (see Figure 6–28). In addition, the heightened tension prevents the folds at the most anterior and posterior portions of the glottis from vibrating. The restraint of the anterior and posterior glottal margins in loft register effectively reduces the length of the vibrating margins of the folds, thus raising frequency. Try this with your lips. Buzz your lips; as they buzz, put a finger over the lips on one side of your mouth. As you stop them, the buzz rate of the lips on the other side will increase — that is, frequency of vibration will rise. You can mimic loft phonation on the lips by tensing them strongly and bearing down on them while applying oral air driving pressure. The result is a high-pitched vibration marked by movement not of the entire lip, but only of the fleshy margin at the border. Notice that the vibration is limited to central (but not lateral) portions of the lip margins.

Loft vibration involves simple open-closing movements of the folds with little, if any, phase effects. It is possible that in loft register the thyroarytenoid muscle is so tense that it is partially decoupled and is no longer a part of the vibrating portion of the folds. The resulting air bursts in loft register are relatively simple in nature, with relatively fewer harmonies than occur for air bursts in other registers. The impoverished harmonic spectrum may account in part for the thin, unattractive quality of loft phonation. A wider range of intensities is possible in the modal than in the loft register, with least intensity variation occurring in the pulse register. Because of a tendency in loft register for the folds not to close completely, a "breathy" quality is often perceived and airflow is relatively high. The increased airflow may be the result of higher driving pressures sometimes used at such high pitches, or it may result from the incomplete vocal fold closure typical of loft phonation.

With the assistance of the instructor, the student should sing easily and smoothly in all registers so that he becomes familiar with the perceptual quality of each mode of phonation.

some pathological vocal qualities

Each of the many phonation types yields a different voice quality. Depending on the language, many of these phonation types convey phonemic distinctions. In English, the [s] and [z] sounds are distinguished by the presence or absence of voicing, just as in another language, two sounds may be distinguished by breathy or normal phonation. The overall quality of the voice depends on both the phonation source and the resonance properties of the vocal tract. We are concerned here with those voice quality changes attributable to the phonation source—that is, the larynx.

If the vocal folds do not close fully during glottal pulsation, there will be a turbulence noise associated with the air leak mixed with the glottal buzz. Paralysis of or injury to one or both folds may prevent full closure, as may the presence of a space-filling growth or a swelling on the vocal folds. Such an air leak, if it persists, will definitely result in an abnormal voice quality, even if it is not pathological. It appears to be normal in many people to have a small opening between the arytenoids throughout a complete glottal cycle, but apparently the noise produced by the air leak is sufficiently weak so as not to be obtrusive. Zemlin (1968) also correctly points out that even if vocal fold closure is complete, an excessively wide laryngeal opening when the folds do open can lead to perception of a breathy voice quality. Students should practice breathy phonation so that they become familiar with both the perceptual quality and physiological posture necessary for this phonation.

The normal vocal folds are almost "twins" in the sense that their mechanical properties are similar—similar mass, length, thickness, tension, and so on. If for any reason, such as swelling, irritation, tumor, muscular weakness, the two folds have sufficiently differing mechanical properties, they may not vibrate in unison. The resulting glottal buzz has a peculiar, objectionable quality. If the difference in the two rates of vibration is small, the voice sounds harsh. If it is great, the listener will hear what sounds like "two voices"—that is, the vocal tract is being excited at two fundamental frequencies. Excessive, prolonged laryngeal tension is associated with irregularity of the glottal buzz rate—that is, successive air bursts are not released in unison, but each succeeding one occurs a bit earlier or later. This too yields a harsh vocal quality.

Excess laryngeal tension may also result in abnormally high vocal pitch, harsh quality, and other pathologies. The combination of harshness and breathiness is often called "hoarseness," a voice quality characteristic of people suffering from laryngitis. Inflammation, swelling, and pain distort the normal mechanical operation and sensory feedback from the inflamed larynx. As a result, abnormalities of glottal frequency and completeness of closure result in a noticeably different vocal quality.

THE RELATIONSHIP OF LARYNGEAL
PATHOLOGY TO SPEECH   Disorders associated with laryngeal functioning and phonation are presented by pathologies that range from major surgical removal of the larynx to laryngitis resulting from minor upper respiratory infection. Because the larynx serves as a valving mechanism and generator

of sound, laryngeal pathologies cause certain vocal characteristics to occur. In this sense, *dysphonia* (disorders of phonation) refers to a broad class of rather specific categories of pathology. Dysphonia should not, however, be confused with the highly subjective and abstract descriptions of voice, such as breathiness, harshness, hoarseness, huskiness, and stridency. The "quality" of voice is never the problem. The problem or disorder, as such, lies in the structure and function of the quality-producing source.

DYSPHONIAS RESULTING
FROM VOCAL FOLD ASYMMETRY   The more frequently occurring voice disorders involve a disturbance of normal voice fold closure and opening during phonation. Certain disorders of phonation are primarily related to changes in vocal fold symmetry as a result of differences in *mass*. Changes in vocal fold mass may affect compliance, length, and tension. Other disorders may affect compliance, length, and/or tension. Again, it is important to realize that while we may assign the primary relationship for vocal disorder to any one of the physical parameters, malfunction along any one parameter always affects function in the others.

Carcinoma   A carcinoma or cancer of the larynx is typically accompanied by persistent periods of hoarseness. Later symptoms include minor pain in the laryngeal area, difficulty in swallowing (dysphagia), shortness of breath (dyspnea), and small nodal masses in the neck. Although cancer of the larynx may occur at any age, it is most frequently among males in their fifties or sixties. As with many cancers, causal factors have been only vaguely defined. It has, however, been unquestionably determined that a significant relationship exists between smoking and laryngeal cancer.

Fortunately, cancer of the larynx, comprising from 3 to 5 percent of human cancer, is one of the relatively more curable. Unfortunately, removal of the cancer generally involves removal of the larynx. In a laryngectomy, the entire laryngeal mechanism, including the hyoid bone, is removed. Figure 6.31 illustrates the relative pre and postoperative configurations of the laryngeal region. Postoperatively, the trachea is no longer continuous with the pharynx and oral cavity; it opens through the surface of the skin slightly above the suprasternal notch as a trachealstoma. Speech as a product of laryngeal sound generation is no longer possible.

Contact Ulcers   Contact ulcers, appearing as erosions of the mucosal lining, may be observed via laryngoscopy. Occasionally larger ulcerations surrounded by granulations may require surgery. The presence of a contact ulcer on either or both folds results in an inability to achieve complete fold adduction. As a result of the erosion, an air leak during the closed phase of the phonatory cycle causes a pressure imbalance resulting in a lower pitch and noticeable glottal effort. Obviously, the presence of a contact ulcer would be most directly related to vocal fold compliance and mass. Patients typically notice undue vocal fatigue and occasional pain in the laryngeal area. Voice therapy is recommended for most cases involving disorder resulting from contact ulcers.

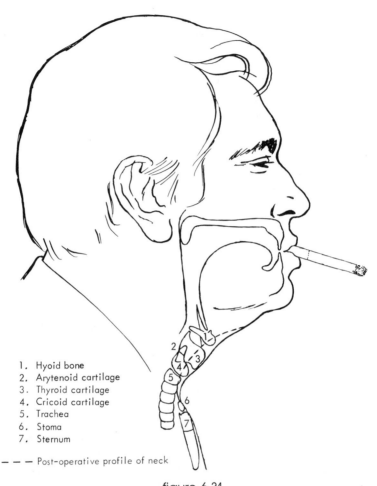

1. Hyoid bone
2. Arytenoid cartilage
3. Thyroid cartilage
4. Cricoid cartilage
5. Trachea
6. Stoma
7. Sternum

− − − Post-operative profile of neck

figure 6.31

The potential laryngectomee. Dotted lines
represent structures surgically removed.

Cord Thickening   The presence of cord thickening is
most frequently associated with allergy, smoking, and various forms of cheer-
leading (vocal abuse). As a result of either functional or infectious causes, the
glottal edges become swollen (edematous). If phonation is continued during this
edematous stage, increased blood flow may result in minor hemorrhages. Further swelling of the vocal folds may result in fibrotic formations. Such conditions frequently lead to either nodules or polyps. Speakers diagnosed as having
cord thickening will demonstrate a change in voice quality. The increase of vocal fold mass typically results in dysphonia characterized by lowering of optimal fundamental frequency and air escape during phonation. As such, intervention strategies are designed to assist the patient in reducing vocal abuse or
misuse.

Laryngitis   Laryngitis is usually defined as an inflammation of the vocal folds and/or mucosal lining of the larynx. Inflammation can be caused by allergy, infection, or abuse. Frequently, it results from prolonged shouting or vocal abuse. Other excesses that often result in laryngitis include excessive smoking and consumption of alcohol.

Nodules   Vocal nodules are one of the more frequent laryngeal disorders. Their cause is related to prolonged hyperfunctional misuse of the laryngeal mechanism. If the vibrating folds make contact with excessive force, their inner margins become irritated at the midpoint (the anterior middle one-third). During such prolonged irritation, callouslike layers of epithelium form over the site of irritation. The formation of these layers is called a nodule and may occur on one or both folds.

Nodules interfere with adequate contact of the folds during the vibratory cycle, restricting achievement of complete closure. Thus, during the closed phase, an air leak occurs that results in a noise component added to glottal source. Nodules occur in children and adults. Speaking behavior is typified by abnormal vocal fatigue and a constant minor cough, as if clearing the throat.

Papilloma   Papilloma occurs most frequently among children as benign wartlike tumors on the vocal folds. Their cause is unknown and they frequently disappear as quickly as they appear. When papilloma appears on the vocal folds their additive mass interferes with normal phonatory function. The real danger of papilloma is that its rapid growth may seriously interfere with respiration. For this reason, treatment of papilloma must be the responsibility of a laryngologist.

Polyps   Polyps tend to be the result of vocal abuse and are similar in many ways to vocal nodules. They occur at the same location as nodules (the anterior middle one-third of the fold). They are, however, more likely to be unilateral than bilateral. And unlike nodules, the lesion begins with an irritation that results in hemorrhage. As the hemorrhage is absorbed, its surrounding tissue becomes somewhat swollen and distended. Thus, in comparison to the nodule, the polyp has a vascular origin that results in a blisterlike structure over a small blood vessel.

Any resultant dysphonia depends upon the polyp mass. Since its location lies generally in the anterior middle one-third of the fold, interference causes an air leak during the closure phase of the vibratory cycle.

Pubertal Change   One of the more dramatic physiological changes to occur during a person's life involves laryngeal growth during puberty. In the relatively short period of several years or even several months, the overall mass and length of the folds, along with laryngeal size, increases swiftly. In many instances, accompanying dysphonias and voice changes are directly related to pubertal growth. During this period, boys experience changes that result in an approximate one-octave lowering in optimal fundamental frequency. Girls experience an approximate lowering of two to three notes. Consequently, frequent pitch breaks and hoarseness are typical during this period.

Cordectomy   In the event that a malignancy is small, focal, and involves only one of the vocal folds, a surgical cordectomy is performed. During this procedure one fold (and occasionally an arytenoid) is removed. Postoperatively, the voice is weak and breathy. Remaining scar tissue, in addition to possible injections of Teflon in glycerin, may enable the patient to achieve a stronger voice. At best, subsequent control of loudness and pitch variation is seriously limited. Such patients, as a result, are treated in an effort to determine optimal use of their impaired laryngeal mechanism.

Functional Aphonia   Functional aphonia is characterized by underadduction of what appears to be normal folds. Laryngoscopic examination reveals that when the patient attempts to phonate, the folds hyperabduct. As a result, laryngeal function produces whispered phonation. Functional aphonia is frequently the result of some form of trauma and is thus considered to be psychogenically based. The prognosis for such problems is positive and involves conditioning or behavior modification strategies.

Functional Dysphonia   Functional dysphonia is characterized by inability to achieve optimum vocal fold approximation. Resultant vocal fold approximations may be either too tight or too loose. From our earlier discussion of physiology we would predict a general harshness and extreme pitch and loudness variation during excessively tight vocal fold approximation. Similarly, breathiness and restricted pitch and loudness variation would occur during loose or underadducted vocal fold approximation. Such is indeed the case with functionally dysphonic patients. Unlike functional aphonia, functional dysphonia is not generally associated with trauma. Most often, people have learned and accepted "their voice" as something unique to them. Nonetheless, providing they are motivated to change, the prognosis is good.

Spastic Dysphonia   Spastic dysphonia is characterized by extreme hyperadduction of the vocal folds. As a result, the egressive air stream flow necessary for vocal fold vibration is severely limited. The extreme tension of the laryngeal mechanism produces an explosive, creaky voice full of silent pauses caused by prolonged glottal stoppages. The origin of the problem may be psychogenic in nature but evidence also points to a potential neurophysiological source as well. Frequently, when alone the patient has little difficulty talking aloud, singing, or laughing. Vocal dysfunction occurs when attempting to talk with others. As reported by Boone (1971), the prognosis for patients diagnosed as spastic aphonics is guarded. According to Boone, "the patient's persistent use of the primitive valving action of the larynx when attempting to speak to someone is highly resistant to voice therapy modification." Recent treatment includes surgical destruction of the recurrent laryngeal nerve to one of the vocal folds, leading to paralysis of that vocal fold, which retracts from the midline, and thus relieves the tightness of glottal closure.

Vocal Fold Paralysis   Vocal fold paralysis occurs as a result of damage to the peripheral motor nerve fibers of the larynx. These nerves, the superior laryngeal nerve and the recurrent laryngeal nerve, innervate the intrinsic and extrinsic muscle fibers of the laryngeal mechanism. Bilateral damage to the superior laryngeal nerve results in paralysis of both cricothyroid muscles, and pitch variation is affected. Unilateral damage results in paralysis of the cricothyroid on one side only, thus lengthening only one fold and not the other. A lesion of the recurrent laryngeal nerve, whether uni- or bilateral, affects the abductor or adductor muscles of the folds. Thus, depending on the type of nerve damage, the person's voice may be either aphonic or breathy, with restricted pitch and loudness variation.

Vocal fold paralysis occurs most frequently as a result of thyroid operation, removal of parathyroid tumors, nerve compression by tumors or enlarged glands, and traumatic damage. Prognoses for patients with vocal fold paralysis vary according to the degree of damage and possibility for operative management. At best, the results from corrective surgery and subsequent voice therapy are limited by a less than adequate laryngeal mechanism.

SUGGESTED READINGS

BOONE, D. R. *The Voice and Voice Therapy*. Englewood Cliffs, N.J.: Prentice-Hall, 1971. A standard text detailing the physiological, acoustic, and perceptual aspects of abnormal voice and laryngeal pathology.

COLLIER, R. "Physiological Correlates of Intonation Patterns," *Journal of the Acoustical Society of America*, 58 (1978), 249–255. A recent experimental article detailing the complex interaction between P_{lung} and contraction of the laryngeal muscles as they cooperate to produce intonation.

HIROSE, H., and T. GAY. "The Activity of the Intrinsic Muscles in Voicing Control: An Electromyographic Study," *Phonetica*, 25 (1972), 140–164. An electromyographic investigation of the function of the intrinsic laryngeal muscles as they operate to control voicing in speech. Difficult but rewarding.

HOLLIEN, H. "On Vocal Registers," *Journal of Phonetics*, 2 (1974), 25–43. A controversial article in which Hollien puts forth his three-register theory of vocal fold vibration. The review of the literature on the parameters of vocal fold vibration is extensive and quite valuable.

LADEFOGED, P. *Preliminaries to Linguistic Phonetics*. Chicago: University of Chicago Press, 1971. An outstanding text that outlines Ladefoged's concept of "phonation type" as it relates to laryngeal function. This book is a standard reference for all aspects of physiological phonetics.

LADEFOGED, P. "The Features of the Larynx," *Journal of Phonetics*, 1 (1973), 73–83. A short and readable analysis of the linguistic functioning of the larynx in terms of segmental, suprasegmental, and paralinguistic features of speech. It clearly establishes the distinctly linguistic role of the larynx in speech.

"The Larynx and Language." *Phonetica*, 34 (1977) (whole issue). An up to date survey of laryngeal research, with a great deal of speculation concerning the theory of vocal fold vibration and the linguistic role of the larynx. See especially the articles by Stevens and Fuijmura.

LISKER, L., and A. S. ABRAHAMSON. "A Cross-Language Study of Voicing in Initial Stops: Acoustic Measurements," *Word*, 20 (1964), 384–422. The classic article in which the authors define and investigate the role of voice onset time in distinguishing voicing in stop consonants.

NEGUS, V. E. *The Comparative Anatomy and Physiology of the Larynx.* New York: Grune and Stratton, 1949. A classic survey of the anatomy and physiology of the larynx.

SAWASHIMA, M. "Laryngeal Research in Experimental Phonetics." In T. Sebeok (ed), *Current Trends in Linguistics,* Vol. 12. The Hague: Mouton, 1974. A useful survey of modern laryngeal research that covers both research findings and the experimental techniques used to provide such data.

SHIPP, T., and R. E. McGLONE. "Laryngeal Dynamics Associated with Vocal Frequency Change," *Journal of Speech and Hearing Research,* 14 (1971), 761–768. An excellent research article that clearly presents the relationship between vocal frequency, vocal fold tension, and subglottal pressure.

TIMCKE, R., H. VON LEDEN, and G. P. MOORE. "Laryngeal Vibrations: Measurements of the Glottic Wave," *Archives of Otolaryngology*, 10 (1958), 205–238. An early and well-written study concerning high-speed motion pictures of the larynx that details the opening-closing movements of the vocal folds.

VAN DEN BERG, J. W. "Myoelastic-Aerodynamic Theory of Voice Production," *Journal of Speech and Hearing Research,* 1 (1958), 227–244. An early and excellent presentation of the aerodynamic myoelastic theory of vocal fold vibration.

VAN DEN BERG, J. W. "Mechanism of the Larynx and the Laryngeal Vibrations." In B. Malmberg (ed.), *Manual of Phonetics.* Amsterdam: North Holland, 1968. A fine survey of the instrumentation used in laryngeal research, the history of laryngeal research, the theory of vocal fold vibration, and the physiology of the larynx.

WYKE, B. "Laryngeal Myotatic Reflexes," *Folia Phoniatrica*, 26 (1974), 249–264. A well-written review article that summarizes the evidence concerning how laryngeal vibration is controlled.

ARTICULATION: STATICS

7

describing the articulatory mechanism / the vocal tract and its cavities
the articulators / speech sounds: problems of classification
acoustic characteristics of speech sounds / conclusion / suggested readings

On a typical day, the average person might be awake for 16 hours. If he or she talked for 10 minutes of each hour at a rate of 150 words per minute, and if each word contained 4 sounds, then our speaker would produce about 96,000 sounds per day. Or, as Fletcher (1953) states, "When the sentence 'Joe took father's shoe-bench out,' is spoken by a typical voice, the potential and kinetic energy in the resultant sound wave is about 300 or 400 ergs. If this is compared to the billion ergs per second passing through an ordinary incandescent lamp, it is seen to be a very small amount of energy. Indeed, it would take 500 people talking continuously for a year to produce enough energy to heat a cup of tea." Further calculations reveal that the power emitted by more than 4 billion speakers talking an average of 10 minutes during each of 12 hours in a waking day (as opposed to a sleeping day), at an average speech power of 36 microwatts, would produce enough energy to lift a battleship whose mass was 100 million kilograms, one meter. That is, the average daily power output of the world's talkers could lift a battleship approximately three feet. It would appear that an enormous amount of talking is necessary before any significant amount of work is done. Talking is either of great importance or very easy. In most cases the former is an assumption of the talker; the latter, of the listener.

One of the first steps in achieving an understanding of any complex behavior is to break it down to its component parts. Very often, such a reduction is inaccurate or misleading, but it does enable us to better organize our knowledge. Speech is just such a complex, synergistic behavior, and we break the complex articulatory motions of speaking down into simple, segmental subunits called "speech sounds." Although the essence of speech articulation is movement, the complex, dynamic articulatory movements will be split into *static* subunits for purposes of description. Such a static description of speech is convenient as a starting point for learning about articulation.

220

As Figure 1.5 shows, the final step of speech encoding is articulation. The articulatory movements produce the changes of vocal tract shape needed to generate the differing sounds of speech. The air stream mechanism serves as a power supply; the phonation mechanism excites the vocal tract by converting the energy of compressed air into acoustic vibration via modulation of air flow; and the articulation mechanism alters the resonance properties of the vocal tract by modifying its shape. As the vibrations created by airflow modulation travel through the vocal tract, they are selectively attenuated so that certain frequencies are transmitted more strongly than others.

describing the articulatory mechanism

The articulation mechanism serves a dual function in speech production:

> 1. Selective alteration of vocal tract shape: Any change in vocal tract shape results in a changing pattern of vocal tract resonances. The changing resonance pattern in turn selectively alters the frequency content of the speech sounds produced by the vocal tract.
>
> 2. Constriction of the vocal tract: this results directly or indirectly in selective airflow modulation, and such modulation creates the explosive or frictionlike noises characteristic of most consonant sounds.

Changes in vocal tract shape are caused by tongue, lip, and jaw movements. Seat yourself before a mirror and produce the vowels [i, u, æ, a]. Notice the high (closed) jaw position for [i and u], and the low (open) jaw position for [æ and a]. Notice also that the tongue is high and tightly constricted for [i and u] and seemingly low and less constricted for [æ and a]. Constriction of the vocal tract also causes airflow modulations that generate explosive or friction noise. Such noisy sounds include the voiceless [p, t, k, s, ʃ, tʃ, f], and the voiced [b, d, g, z, ʒ, dʒ, v]. Thus, the articulatory mechanism also serves as a secondary sound-generating system in addition to the larynx.

TERMS   In every science, there are fundamental units of description. As students of human verbal behavior, we seek to identify the fundamental units or bits of mental reality that are organized in the brain and implemented by the muscles to yield speech. Speech can be separated into hierarchical levels, each with a differing function. The basic linguistic unit of meaning is the morpheme. The morpheme may be a word such as "cat" [kaet], or it may be a single sound segment such as the plural morpheme [z] or [s] as in dog*s* or cat*s*, or the past tense morpheme, such as "-ed" in "kill + ed". Morphemes may in turn be divided into smaller units called abstract or underlying segments, [k + æ + t], or morphophonemes. We will not use the terms phoneme or morphophoneme; rather, we will use segment, underlying segment, or abstract segment. When referring to actual sounds, we will use the term sound segment.

The underlying segments serve to differentiate morphemes from each other by contrasting with each other. Consider the words "pin, tin, kin, sin, thin, fin, gin, bin, win." Each differs from the others by a single segment in the word-initial position. The underlying segment can be further subdivided into smaller descriptive units called distinctive features. Each segment can be described as a set of distinctive features. For example, the abstract segment /s/ is characterized by the following distinctive features:

+coronal
−voice
+continuant
−nasal
−lateral
+sonorant
+anterior
+strident

In a given language, two segments are said to be distinctively different if they differ by one or more distinctive features. The segments /s/ and /š/ differ in that one is [+anterior] and the other is [−anterior]. Thus, the units of linguistic description of speech stand in the following relationship:

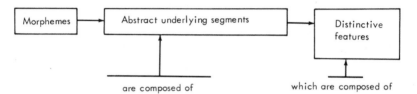

Each morpheme consists of one or more segments and each segment consists of a set or bundle of distinctive features. Figure 7.1 displays the matrix of distinctive features that characterize the morpheme /kæt/. The columns are morphophonemes and the rows are features. Notice that the segmental units are redundant in the sense that each unique column of features defines that underlying segment as unique from other underlying segments in the word.

Morphemes, segments, and distinctive features are units of linguistic *description*. These units exist as abstractions on paper, or perhaps as mental realities in the mind of any speaker. Phoneticians and speech scientists analyze speech in their search for the physiological and acoustic correlates of each of these units. Decades have been spent in the search for physiological or behavioral evidence to support or deny the existence of the various units of speech. The assumption behind such research is that if physiological-perceptual correlates for the various units can be identified, there is good reason to assume that these linguistic units exist as mental realities as well. The search for these units has been difficult. To illustrate this, consider the verb "can." It can be spoken in three different ways:

SEGMENTS

FEATURE	/k/	/æ/	/t/
Consonantal	+	−	+
Vocalic	−	+	−
Anterior	−	−	+
Coronal	−	−	+
Continuant	−		−
Strident	−		−
Voice	−		−
Lateral	−		−
Nasal	−		−
High	+	−	
Low	−	+	
Back	+	−	
Round	−	−	

figure 7.1

A matrix of the distinctive features for the morpheme "cat."

proper speech	"Can I?"	[k æ n + aᴵ]
rapid (allegro) speech	"C'n I?"	[K n + aᴵ]
dialectal variant	"Kin I?"	[KIn + aᴵ]

In all three cases, speakers intend to articulate the morpheme "can." And yet, [k æ n] is articulated in three differing ways. The ideal, invariant morpheme "can" may exist mentally, but it is highly variable across speakers at the articulatory level.

A similar situation holds for the segment. The ideal, invariant segment may exist mentally, but at the articulatory level, the segment varies. Let's assume that the sound segment [æ] is representative of the abstract, underlying segment /æ/. In the word "pap" [p æ p], the sound segment [æ] is considerably shorter in duration than in the word "bab" [b æ b]. In the word "ban" the [æ] is nasalized. Thus, the articulatory sound segment [æ], a representative of the ideal, invariant underlying segmental class /æ/, varies. It is long or short in duration, nasalized or nonnasalized, depending on the phonetic context in which it occurs. The articulatory features that represent the distinctive features at the mental level also vary. For example, /t/ and /d/ differ by a single feature,

[±voice] at an abstract level. At an acoustic level, they may differ by as many as six or seven acoustic features. A given abstract distinctive feature may be produced in such a way that any one of a number of articulatory-acoustic features conveys the distinction intended.

Among the problems in describing articulation meaningfully and usefully are the following:

1. We cannot enter a speaker's brain and observe the nature and/or reality of the linguistic units we suspect the speaker is using.

2. In the process of encoding, the conversion of the abstract, mental units of speech is a one-to-many mapping system. That is, each more abstract unit may be converted into several differing forms at the articulatory-acoustic level.

3. If we rely on listeners' perception of speech to determine what has been articulated, we must contend with the fact that listeners use more than the physical-acoustic cues present in the speech signal. They also use everything they unconsciously or consciously "know" about the language to assist in their interpretation of the signal. Thus, we cannot easily discover what the acoustic cues of speech signals are.

But the reader should not be misled into thinking there is so much variability in the articulation process that it is hopeless to determine either the basic units of speech or the regularities which occur during their production. It is astonishing that we come as close as we do to producing the features, sounds, and syllables of speech in an invariant fashion. We are so successful that we are understood quite well despite the wide range of variation present in the speech of any speaker. The reader may well ask why invariance is so important to any discussion of articulation. Invariance is crucial because encoding systems fail if the symbols used vary unsystematically. Think of the chaos in telegraphy if the dot and dash system of encoding changed from moment to moment so that we did not know what pattern of dots and dashes signified each letter of the alphabet.

the vocal tract and its cavities

The articulation of speech occurs within the vocal tract. Figure 7.2 displays an outline of a vocal tract superimposed on the profile of a speaker's face. The vocal tract is a set of interconnecting tubular passageways that extend from the vocal folds to the lips and nares. The walls of the vocal tract are formed by muscular and bony tissues; when the vocal tract is fully open, a column of air extends from the glottal margins of the vocal folds to the lips. When the velum is lowered, the air column extends to the nareal openings of the nose. Test this for yourself: First puff air out of your mouth; then shut your mouth and blow air out of your nose.

Figure 7.3 shows an outline of the vocal tract cavities (pharyngeal, oral, and nasal) superimposed on a speaker's profile. The pharyngeal cavity is further subdivided into three subcavities: oropharynx, nasopharynx, and laryngopharynx. Airflow and acoustic vibrations pass from the glottis into the laryngopharynx. The laryngopharynx (sometimes called the epipharynx) extends

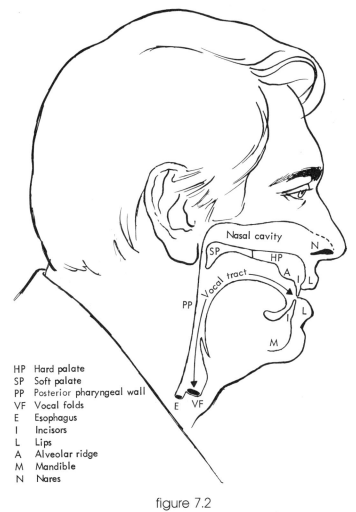

figure 7.2
A view of the vocal tract superimposed upon a speaker's profile.

HP Hard palate
SP Soft palate
PP Posterior pharyngeal wall
VF Vocal folds
E   Esophagus
I   Incisors
L   Lips
A   Alveolar ridge
M   Mandible
N   Nares

from the glottis to the level of the hyoid bone; the posterior and lateral pharyngeal walls and tongue root form its walls. The laryngopharynx connects directly with the oropharynx, and the oropharynx in turn connects with the other two cavities: the oral cavity anteriorly, and the nasopharynx superiorly. The oropharynx extends from the level of the hyoid inferiorly to the undersurface of the soft palate superiorly. The pharyngeal walls and the tongue dorsum form its walls. The anterior boundary of the oropharynx is marked by the posterior faucial pillars (palatopharyngeus muscle), which is the landmark indicating where the oropharynx joins the oral cavity.

The oropharynx and the nasopharynx connect via the velopharyngeal port, which is opened when the soft palate relaxes. The walls of the nasopharynx are formed by the superior surface of the soft palate inferiorly, and by the posterior

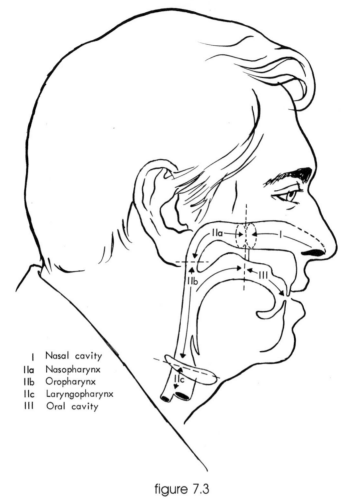

I   Nasal cavity
IIa   Nasopharynx
IIb   Oropharynx
IIc   Laryngopharynx
III   Oral cavity

figure 7.3
The cavities of the vocal tract and their boundaries.

and superior pharyngeal walls superiorly. Anteriorly the nasopharynx connects with the nasal cavity, the boundary being the openings (choanae) into the nasal cavity. The nasal cavity extends from the nasopharynx to the nareal openings of the nose: it is characterized by a labyrinthine set of passageways lined with mucosal tissue that warms, humidifies, and cleans incoming air. The oral cavity extends from the oropharynx to the opening of the lips; it terminates posteriorly at the anterior faucial pillars (palatoglossus muscles). The superior surface of the oral cavity is the hard palate, the inferior surface is the tongue blade and dorsum, and the lateral surfaces are formed by the cheeks.

The nasal cavity is nearly fixed in size because it contains few, if any, muscles and movable structures along its length that could contract and work to change its shape (only the inflammation of a cold or allergy can do that). The cavity has a large interior surface area compared to its volume, and acts as a highly damped (energy-absorbing) resonator. When sound is emitted from the nose, the great damping and unusually complex shape of the cavity contribute to the unmistakeable, characteristic quality of a nasal sound. The nasopharynx also varies only slightly in size as the velum rises or lowers, to couple (or decouple) the nasal cavity with the oropharynx. The laryngopharynx is both small and relatively invariant in shape because the tongue root moves only slightly during articulation. However, the vertical movements of the larynx observed during speech could cause the laryngopharynx to increase and decrease in length as the larynx rises or descends.

The oropharynx and oral cavity are extremely important to articulation because these two cavities undergo the greatest change in shape when the speech articulators move, and thus most strongly determine the resonance pattern of the vocal tract.

the articulators

The articulators are the vocal tract structures involved in the movements used to produce speech sounds. By definition, the word "articulate" implies movement. However, the speech articulators are of two types: *fixed* and *movable*. Among the movable articulators are the lips, mandible, soft palate, tongue, pharyngeal walls, and larynx. Among the fixed articulators are the upper incisors, alveolar ridge, and hard palate.

The articulatory mechanism functions so that the movable articulators constrict and in doing so simultaneously alter the shape of the vocal tract. The constrictions (1) modulate airflow, thus creating acoustic vibration, and (2) alter the resonance frequencies of the vocal tract. If the constriction is not very tight, airflow is not strongly impeded and the constriction primarily affects shape, which in turn determines vocal tract resonance frequencies. Before discussing the acoustics of speech production, we shall describe the important articulators in some detail.

Figure 7.4 presents a schematic view of the important articulators and places of articulation. Place of articulation refers to the location in the vocal tract of the greatest constriction; manner of articulation refers to the extent (tightness) of the constriction.

THE LIPS   At the periphery of the vocal tract, the lips are a pair of muscular folds that form the oral sphincter. The lips are capable of dozens of different movements, each expressive of differing emotions. For the articulation of speech, there are only a few important kinds of lip movement. Both lips may be maneuvered for opening or closing movements, although the lower lip is the more mobile of the two. The lips also perform protrusion (rounding) and spreading (retraction) movements during speech. When the lips are protruded outward and away from the teeth, the vocal tract is lengthened and the size of the lip opening is reduced. This results in a lowering

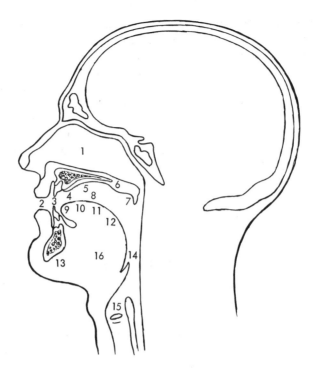

1. Nasal cavity	7. Uvula	12. Tongue dorsum
2. Lips	8. Oral cavity	13. Mandible
3. Incisors	9. Tongue tip	14. Pharyngeal cavity
4. Alveolar ridge	10. Tongue blade	15. Vocal folds
5. Hard palate	11. Tongue front	16. Tongue root
6. Velum		

figure 7.4 (a)

A sagittal view of the head and neck displaying
(a) major articulators and (b) places of articulation.

of vocal tract resonance frequencies and a reduction of the intensity of the sound being generated. Test this by phonating an [i] and slowly rounding your lips. Note the fall in the timbre and loudness of the vowel as the lips are rounded. Lip retraction (or spreading) is the opposite of lip rounding. During spreading, the lips are pulled toward the teeth, and the corners of the lips are spread. The net result is a shortening of vocal tract length and an increase in lip opening. Practice spreading and rounding of the lips in front of a mirror and observe the process in fine detail. Practice the movements silently, and then observe that the vowel [u] is rounded, while the vowel [i] displays spreading.

The muscles of facial expression, which are also responsible for lip protrusion/retraction and opening/closing, are shown in Figure 7.5. The muscle most responsible for lip protrusion is the orbicularis oris, the largest of the lip muscles. This large sphincteric ring of muscle fibers encircles the oral opening, and

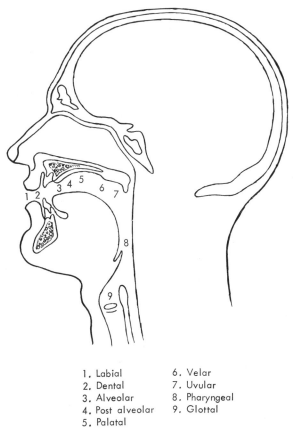

1. Labial   6. Velar
2. Dental   7. Uvular
3. Alveolar   8. Pharyngeal
4. Post alveolar   9. Glottal
5. Palatal

figure 7.4 (b)

upon contraction it simultaneously puckers (rounds) and tends to close the lips. The majority of the extrinsic facial muscles that move the lips insert into the orbicularis oris.

THE FACIAL MUSCLES   The muscles inserting into the lip may be divided into three functional groups, which can be seen in Figure 7.5. The vertical muscles insert vertically into the orbicularis oris and thus serve to open the lips when they contract. The angular muscles enter the lips at an angle, from below or above. They are responsible for frowning/smiling gestures. The transverse muscles enter the lips horizontally at the corners of the mouth. Their contractions retract the lips, pulling them against the teeth and spreading the mouth open at the corners.

The Vertical Muscles   Among the vertical muscles, the mentalis consists of a small paired bundle of fibers that extend vertically from the incisive fossa of the mandible upward, where they insert into both the skin near the

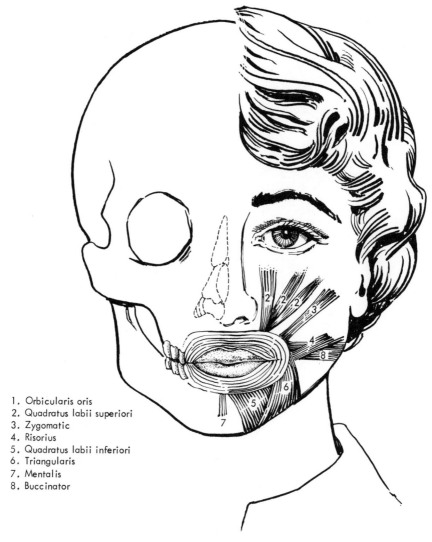

1. Orbicularis oris
2. Quadratus labii superiori
3. Zygomatic
4. Risorius
5. Quadratus labii inferiori
6. Triangularis
7. Mentalis
8. Buccinator

figure 7.5
Facial muscles important for lip articulations.

orbicularis oris and into the ring of orbicularis oris fibers. Contraction of this muscle wrinkles the chin and everts (pouts) the lower lip, pulling it downward. The triangularis muscle arises from the oblique line of the mandible, coursing upward to insert into the orbicularis oris at the angle of the mouth. Contraction of this muscle depresses the lower lips, especially at the corners of the mouth. The canine originates superiorly on the canine fossa of the infraorbital foramen of the maxilla. Its fibers course downward into the upper lip near the corner; contraction of this muscle draws the upper lip and corner of the mouth upward.

The Transverse Muscles   Among the transverse muscles, the buccinator, the major cheek muscle, arises from a complex origin on the ptery-gomandibular raphe as well as the outside surfaces of the posterior alveolar processes of the maxilla and mandible. Contraction of this muscle compresses the cheeks and pulls the corners of the mouth laterally. The risorius muscle arises from the fascial sheath that covers the masseter muscle. The fibers course horizontally to insert into the corner of the mouth, where its contractions retract the corners of the lips.

The Angular Muscles   The quadratus labii inferiori originates on the mandible near the oblique line; its fibers course upward and medially to insert into the lower lip. Contraction draws the lower lip downward. The quadratus labii superiori, also known as the levator labii superiori, arises from a complex three-headed insertion from the infraorbital margin of the maxilla, from the malar surface of the zygomatic bone and from the infraorbital margin. The fibers course downward, inserting into the upper lip near the midline. Contraction of this muscle elevates the lip. The zygomatic muscle originates on the zygomatic bone, lateral to the quadratus muscle. The fibers course downward and medially to insert into the upper lip, where contraction of this muscle draws the upper lip and corners of the mouth upward.

THE INCISORS   The four upper and the four lower incisors are flat, chisel-shaped teeth set on either side of the midline of the mouth, resting in sockets located in the alveolar process of the premaxilla superiorly, and in the alveolar process of the mandible inferiorly. The lower lip and tongue may make contact with the upper incisors (or the lower) for dental articulations. The upper incisors are crucial for the production of strident (sibilant) sounds such as [s, z, ʃ, ʒ]. During production of these sounds, the air stream strikes the incisors and lips, creating a turbulence that emits a high-pitched noise. The reader can demonstrate such turbulence by blowing air past the edge of a 3 × 5 card placed perpendicular to the air stream emerging from the lips.

THE PALATE

The Hard Palate   The hard palate, the roof of the oral cavity, is dome shaped and is composed of four bones. Anteriorly, the palatine processes of the maxillary bones join at the midline to form the anterior two-thirds of the hard palate; posteriorly, the palatine bones form the remainder of the hard palate (see Figure 7.6). The majority of speech sounds in most languages are formed by contact or constriction between the hard palate and the tongue. In particular, the tongue tip and the adjacent alveolar ridge of the hard palate are utilized for many speech sound articulations in English: [t, d, s, z, n, l] each have an alveolar or postalveolar constriction or contact. Acoustically, the dome shape of the hard palate provides a generous oral cavity depth, permitting the tongue to form a wide variety of oral cavity shapes as it moves about in the vocal tract.

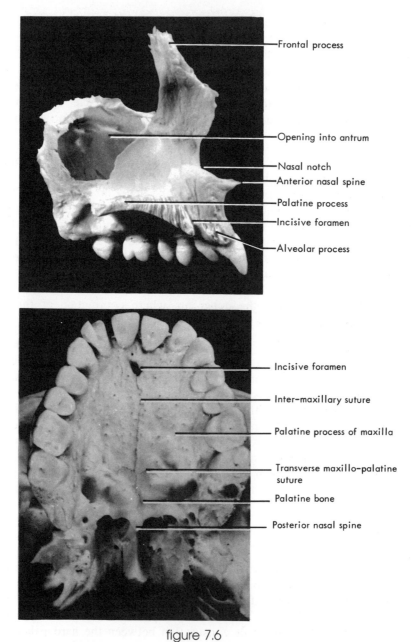

Frontal process

Opening into antrum

Nasal notch

Anterior nasal spine

Palatine process

Incisive foramen

Alveolar process

Incisive foramen

Inter-maxillary suture

Palatine process of maxilla

Transverse maxillo-palatine suture

Palatine bone

Posterior nasal spine

figure 7.6

Selected views from the bony palate. Reprinted by permission from W. R. Zemlin, *Speech and Hearing Science: Anatomy and Physiology.* © 1968 by Prentice-Hall, Inc.

The Soft Palate   The soft palate (velum) is a flexible muscular flap of tissue that extends from the hard palate toward the posterior pharyngeal wall. When the levator palatini muscles of the palate relax, the soft palate hangs down into the oropharynx, permitting direct flow of air and vibration from the oropharynx into the nasopharynx via the velopharyngeal port, as the opening between the soft palate and the posterior pharyngeal wall is called. Figure 7.7 displays the soft palate in cross-section so that the action of the palatal muscles can be visualized.

The palatal levator muscle extends from the midline of the soft palate (palatal aponeurosis) upward and backward to insert upon the temporal bone and cartilage of the eustachian tube. When contracted, the twin bellies of the levator lift the palate upward and backward toward the posterior pharyngeal wall. The levator is the major adductor (closer) of the velopharyngeal port in the majority of speakers. For a small percentage of people, the pharyngeal walls may serve as a secondary adductory mechanism: The pharyngeal mus-

figure 7.7

The muscles of the soft palate. Reprinted by permission from W. R. Zemlin, *Speech and Hearing Science: Anatomy and Physiology.* © 1968 by Prentice-Hall, Inc.

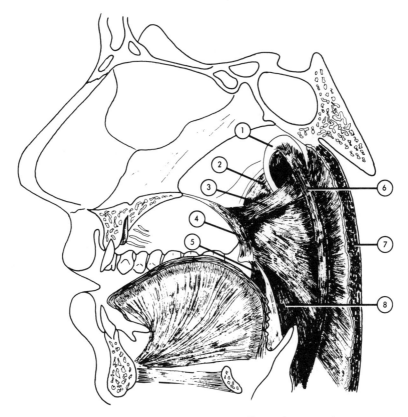

1. Orifice of Eustachian tube
2. Tensor palatine muscle
3. Levator palatine muscle
4. Uvular muscle
5. Glossopalatine muscle
6. Salpingopharyngeus muscle
7. Superior constrictor muscle
8. Palatoglossal muscle

cles, especially the superior constrictor muscle, may contract during velopharyngeal closure, causing the pharyngeal walls to move inward toward the velum at the same time that the palatal levator moves the velum upward.

The palatoglossus muscle extends from an insertion on the sides of the tongue upward along the wall of the oral cavity, where it forms a visible muscle bundle called the anterior faucial pillar. The palatoglossus then inserts into the palatal aponeurosis. Contraction of this muscle either lowers the velum or raises the tongue, depending on which structure is more firmly braced. The palatopharyngeus muscle fibers extend from the palatal midline posteriorly and inferiorly, where they insert into the base of the pharynx and along the upper margin of the thyroid cartilage near the superior horns. As they pass along the walls of the oropharynx, the palatopharyngeus muscles form the posterior faucial pillars. Upon contraction, these muscles will draw the palate downward, constrict the pharyngeal opening, or elevate the larynx and pharynx. The uvular muscle consists of a twin-bellied set of fibers on either side of the midline aponeurosis of the palate. Fibers run from the posterior nasal spine of the hard palate posteriorly to the tip of the uvula, the small, tablike tip of the velum. Contraction of the uvular muscles may tense the velum.

Velar Articulation   During speech production, the velum controls the air stream path. If it is elevated, all acoustic vibration and airflow are directed out of the mouth and the sound is nonnasal. If the velum is lowered and the oral cavity is open, sound and airflow escape both orally and nasally, and the sound is said to be nasalized. If the oral cavity is closed and the velum is open, all vibration and airflow escape through the nose, and the sound is said to be a nasal. In English, we appear to use either oral or nasal air paths to convey distinction between sounds. We rarely use nasalization, combined oral and nasal opening, to create a distinction between words, although nasalization does convey distinctions in other languages.

The position of the tongue and velum are relatively well correlated in speech, so that low tongue and low velum positions seem to co-occur, as do high tongue, high velum positioning. The palatoglossus muscle appears to be the mechanical restraint that forces the concordant movement between tongue and velum. Failure of the velum to close tightly seriously affects the production of "obstruent" consonants, including stops, fricatives, and affricates. Obstruent consonant articulation involves the use of elevated air pressure trapped behind an oral constriction. The impounded air pressure is used to create the explosion of stops and the noisy air jet of fricatives. A velar opening causes a leakage of air into the nose, preventing proper air pressure buildup, thus severely disturbing adequate sound generation for these consonants. Once again, practice producing various combinations of obstruent sounds with the velum elevated or lowered. For instance, if the velum is lowered, the sentence "Bobby ate an apple pie" is produced as [mɔmi + ẽn + æ̃n + æ mɫ + maˈ. Similarly, when the velum is elevated, sounds which are normally nasalized are changed. For example, the sentence "Mommy sings nicely" sounds like [babi + sɪgz + daˈsli].

THE PHARYNX   The pharyngeal cavity serves an articulatory function, since movements of the velum and the tongue change the
shape of the pharynx and thus alter its resonance properties. In addition, the
muscular pharyngeal walls may contract to assist in the closure of the velopharyngeal port or dilate the pharyngeal airway.

The pharynx is a trumpet-shaped, almost conical muscular tube that arises
from a small circular orifice above the larynx (epipharynx) and widens into an
elliptical shape superiorly. Superiorly, the pharyngeal tube opens into the nasal
cavity and anteriorly, into the oral cavity via the oropharyngeal and naso-
pharyngeal cavities (see Figures 7.7 and 7.8). The pharyngeal walls consist of
layers of horizontal muscle fiber that encircle the circumference of the tube.
Several muscles also insert into the pharyngeal walls vertically from above.
The pharynx is sheathed in a fibrous coat called the pharyngeal aponeurosis.

The Pharyngeal Muscles   Among the pharyngeal muscles are the
superior, medial, and inferior constrictors; the stylopharyngeus; salpingo-
pharyngeus; palatopharyngeus; and cricopharyngeus muscles. The superior
constrictor [see Figure 7.8(a,b)] arises from a complex origin on the pterygoid
plate and hamular process of the sphenoid bone as well as the pterygomandibular
raphe and tongue. The fibers course backward and insert into the posterior
midline raphe of the pharyngeal tube at the level of the soft palate. The middle
constrictor is a fan-shaped muscle that arises from the upper border of the
greater horn of the hyoid bone, the lesser horn, and the stylohyoid ligament.
Its fibers course horizontally rearward and insert around the pharyngeal tube
at the posterior median raphe of the pharynx. When contracted, this muscle,
as well as the superior and inferior constrictors, constricts the pharyngeal airway, assisting in the act of swallowing by constricting and pushing the bolus of
food being swallowed downward toward the esophagus.

The inferior constrictor is the largest of the three constrictor muscles. It
originates on the cricoid cartilage near the cricothyroid joint as well as from the
thyroid cartilage along the oblique line. The muscle fibers fan out and backward, both upward and downward, encircling the pharyngeal tube, interconnecting with fellow fibers from the other side, forming the midline raphe of
the pharyngeal tube. The inferior constrictor muscle fibers overlap those of the
middle constrictor, and those of the middle constrictor overlap the fibers of the
superior constrictor. The lowermost fibers of the inferior constrictor encircle
the esophagus and cricoid cartilage; these fibers are known as the cricopharyngeus muscle. The constrictor muscles play a crucial role in swallowing:
When swallowing, the tongue sweeps the food back to the faucial pillars, where
a wave of constriction of the pharynx begins. In conjunction with tongue movement, the wave moves down the pharynx toward the esophagus, pushing the food
ahead of it in a peristaltic fashion.

The stylopharyngeal muscle arises from the styloid process of the temporal
bone. This long band of muscle fiber courses downward along the sides of the
pharynx, blending with the constrictors and palatopharyngeus muscles, inserting upon the superior horn of the thyroid. Contraction of this muscle might

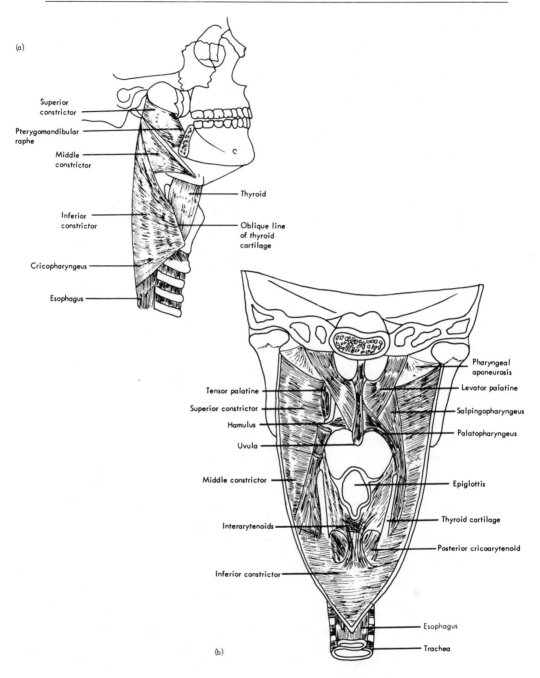

(a)

Superior
constrictor

Pterygomandibular
raphe

Middle
constrictor

Thyroid

Inferior
constrictor

Oblique line
of thyroid
cartilage

Cricopharyngeus

Esophagus

Tensor palatine

Superior constrictor

Hamulus

Uvula

Middle constrictor

Interarytenoids

Inferior constrictor

Pharyngeal
aponeurosis

Levator palatine

Salpingopharyngeus

Palatopharyngeus

Epiglottis

Thyroid cartilage

Posterior cricoarytenoid

Esophagus

Trachea

(b)

figure 7.8

The pharynx and its associated muscles as seen in (a) lateral
and (b) posterior views. Reprinted by permission from
W. R. Zemlin, *Speech and Hearing Science: Anatomy
and Physiology.* © 1968 by Prentice-Hall, Inc.

dilate the pharyngeal lumen and perhaps elevate the larynx. The salpingo-pharyngeus muscle arises from the lower edge of the eustachean tube cartilage and courses downward to blend with the palatopharyngeus muscle fibers. Contraction of this muscle may constrict the pharyngeal lumen or elevate the pharynx. It is assumed to be especially active during swallowing.

Pharyngeal Articulation   For speech, several important pharyngeal behaviors have been identified. In a small percentage of speakers the pharyngeal walls move inward to assist in velopharyngeal closure. The contraction of the superior constrictor muscle fibers raises a bulge or pad on the posterior pharyngeal wall that moves toward the midline of the pharynx to meet the rising velum. In a few other speakers, the lateral walls move inward during closure. But in the majority of speakers, there is little or no pharyngeal wall contribution to velar closure. Investigators have also observed a systematic and differential pharyngeal expansion and contraction for certain classes of vowels and consonants. In particular, there appears to be active expansion of the pharynx during production of voiced stop consonants. Presumably, the pharyngeal expansion yields an increased vocal tract volume that can absorb the air bursts emitted from the buzzing larynx. Thus, despite the vocal tract closure for stop consonant sounds, glottal pulsing can continue for a short time because pharyngeal expansion absorbs glottal air flow, slowing down the very rapid oral pressure rise that would prevent glottal vibration. Practice buzzing the larynx with the vocal tract closed at the lips and velum to demonstrate for yourself that you are utilizing vocal tract expansion to absorb glottal airflow. As the larynx is buzzed, let your cheeks bulge outward to absorb the glottal airflow and thus extend the duration of voicing.

THE MANDIBLE (JAW)   The mandible, shown in Figure 7.9, is an important speech articulator. Because the tongue nestles inside the arch of the mandible, mandibular movement is crucial for tongue positioning for speech. In addition, the lower lip rides on the mandible, so that lip gestures also depend on mandibular positioning. Finally, a number of muscles connect the mandible with the hyoid bone, so that the mandible can affect laryngeal position and vice-versa.

The body of the mandible consists of a horseshoe-shaped corpus; from the extreme ends of the corpus there arise the ramii, two vertically directed bony struts, one on either side. Each ramus ascends to form an articulation with the temporal bone at the temporomandibular joint. At its top, the ramus displays two jutting bony processes: the coronoid process, the more anterior of the two, is a point of attachment for the temporalis and masseter muscles. The condyloid process makes contact with the articular disc of the temporomandibular joint. The external pterygoid muscle in turn attaches to the condyloid process. Inferiorly, the ramus joins the corpus of the mandible at the angle of the mandible. The two halves of the corpus of the mandible join at the midline, at the mental symphysis (see Figure 7.9). The surface of the mandible reveals two lines: the oblique line courses along the external surface from a low anterior to

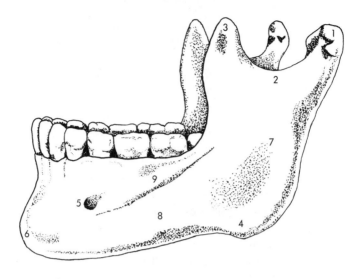

1. Condyloid process
2. Semilunar notch
3. Coronoid process
4. Angle of the mandible
5. Mental foramen

6. Mental protuberance
7. Ramus of the mandible
8. Corpus of the mandible
9. Oblique line

figure 7.9
A lateral view of the mandible.

a high anterior position. The mylohyoid line extends on the inner surface in an upward-backward direction toward the ramus.

Figure 7.10 displays some mandibular muscles; they are jointly responsible for opening-closing movements of the mandible as well as the side-to-side movements characteristic of chewing. Mandibular opening-closing is a complex motion at the temporomandibular joint, a combination of rotation and sliding.

Mandibular Elevators   The temporalis is a broad, fan-shaped muscle arising from a wide insertion on the temporal fossa of the temporal bone. The fibers converge inferiorly into a tendon that inserts upon the ramus of the mandible. Contraction would, of course, elevate the mandible. The masseter muscle, which is quite powerful, consists of a thick band of muscle that arises from the zygomatic arch and courses inferiorly to insert upon the mandible. The superficial fibers attach at the angle and lateral surface of the ramus. The deep fibers attach to the lateral surface of the coronoid process and the lateral surface of the ramus. Contraction of this muscle raises the mandible. The internal pterygoid muscle originates on the lateral pterygoid plate and on the palatine bone. The fibers course posteriorly and inferiorly to insert upon the ramus and angle of the mandible where their contraction would tend to elevate the mandible.

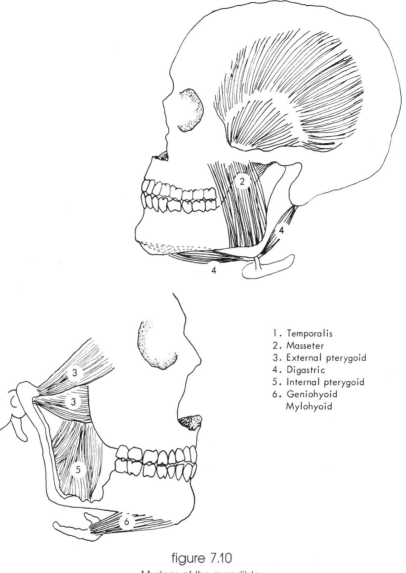

1. Temporalis
2. Masseter
3. External pterygoid
4. Digastric
5. Internal pterygoid
6. Geniohyoid
   Mylohyoid

figure 7.10
Muslces of the mandible.

Mandibular Depressors   The external pterygoid is a two-headed muscle with fibers arising from the infratemporal fossa of the greater wing of the sphenoid bone and from the lateral surface of the lateral pterygoid plate. The fibers run horizontally, inserting upon the neck of the condyle of the mandible and into the articular capsule of the temporomandibular joint. Contraction of this muscle depresses (opens) the mandible. If only one of the two external pterygoids is activated, it causes the jaw to move to one side.

As we noted above, three muscles that attach to the hyoid play a role in opening the jaw. The digastric muscle consists of two bellies. The posterior belly arises from the mastoid process of the temporal bone and courses down and forward to insert into an intermediate tendon attached to the corpus of the hyoid bone. The anterior belly runs from the intermediate tendon upward and forward to attach to the inner surface of the lower border of the mandibular symphysis. Provided that the hyoid is fixed, contraction of the anterior belly of the digastric depresses the mandible. The mylohyoid muscle fills the base of the body of the corpus of the mandible, forming the floor of the mouth. The fibers arise from the inner walls of the corpus of the mandible along the mylohyoid line and course medially and downward to attach to a midline raphe or to the hyoid. The geniohyoid, which is exterior to the mylohyoid, arises from the inferior mental spine of the posterior surface of the mental symphysis of the mandible and courses inferiorly and rearward to insert on the anterior surface of the corpus of the hyoid bone. Contraction of these two muscles may open the mandible, raise the hyoid, or cause the tongue dorsum to bulge upward toward the palate, depending upon which structures are fixed.

Mandibular Articulations   As the mandible opens or closes, the lips open and close and the tongue is carried up toward the palate or down away from the palate, altering the shape of the oral cavity. Sit in front of a mirror and open and close your jaw, watching how lips and tongue are carried along. Notice that it is difficult to round the lips when the mandible is fully lowered. It is a well-established phonetic fact that for the majority of speakers, the mandible moves in a systematic fashion for the production of speech sounds. It is opened slightly for "close" sounds, more open for "mid" sounds, and even more open for "open" sounds. Sit facing a mirror and practice; note that the sounds [i, ɪ, u, ʊ, s, z, ʃ, ʒ] are all produced with a barely opened mandible. The sounds [k, g, r, ɛ, o] are produced with a somewhat more lowered mandible, while [æ, a, ɔ, ʌ] are produced with a wide (or open) mandibular opening.

Investigators have claimed that the tongue and mandible function synergistically. That is, the tongue adopts a particular shape, and then various degrees of mandibular movement provide the additional fine positioning needed to achieve the vocal tract shapes for the vowel sounds. However, the existence of speakers who use exaggerated tongue movements with little or no jaw movement, and others who use exaggerated mandibular movements with little tongue movement suggest that the tongue-jaw synergy for speech must be relatively individualistic in nature. The fact that people can suck on cigars or puff on pipes, and speak quite intelligibly with their jaws clenched on their nicotine flavored pacifiers suggests that speakers can compensate swiftly with the jaw-mandible system in order to provide satisfactory sound production. Practice speaking with your jaws clenched on a pencil to experience "articulatory compensation." Be aware also of the fact that jaw-tongue movements affect the function of the larynx, since both structures are attached to the hyoid bone by numerous muscles. Try singing the lower notes of your vocal range and notice the tendency for your jaw to lower for the very lowest notes. As the jaw lowers, the vocal tract opens up. An open vocal tract offers less impedance to airflow and to the transmission of acoustic vibration. Thus, at a given level of respiratory effort, a vowel phonated with an elevated mandibular position will be 4 to 5 dB less intense than a vowel phonated with a lowered mandible.

THE TONGUE   The tongue (or lingual articulator) is perhaps the most important speech articulator. Biologically, the tongue is crucial to mastication of food; it sweeps food onto the grinding surfaces of the teeth, pushes pieces of food back toward the pharynx for swallowing, and clears the oral cavity after eating. Also, most of the sensory organs of taste are embedded on the surface of the tongue.

Look at Figures 7.2 and 7.3. The tongue can be divided into four functional subdivisions: tip, blade, dorsum, and root (body). The apex or tip of the tongue is thin, narrow, and agile, and rests against the lingual surface of the teeth. The blade of the tongue is actually the anterior-most portion of the dorsum, that part of the dorsum just below the alveolar ridge when the tongue is at rest. The remainder of the dorsum may be divided into a front or oral dorsum, lying in front of the faucial pillars, and a back or pharyngeal dorsum, lying behind the faucial pillars. The main mass of the body of the tongue, the so-called tongue root, constitutes the fourth division of the tongue.

The tongue is crucial to speech production because it is the prime determinant of vocal tract shape. The tongue forms a movable wall of both the oral and pharyngeal cavities, so it literally alters the entire vocal tract shape when it moves. As an articulator, the tongue's major functions are to (1) modulate airflow (to create noisy vibrations); and (2) alter vocal tract shape and thus control resonance frequencies. Vocal tract shape is the overall length and the cross-sectional area of the vocal tract at every point, from the glottis to the lips. Students have remarked that if people can still "speak" after surgical removal of the tongue, how can the tongue be so important an articulator? The only sounds producible without the tongue are the single "nasal" sound [m], the labial sounds [p, b], the dental sounds [f, v], and the pharyngeal sounds [h, ʔ]. Without the tongue, the slight modification of vocal tract shape caused by mandibular opening will probably permit production of a few vowel-like sounds, which if the speaker were lucky might sound vaguely like normal vowel sounds. The sounds [t, d, s, z, g, ʃ, ʒ, t, d, k, l, r, j, i, ɪ, e, ɛ, æ, a, ɔ, o, ʊ, u, ʌ, aᶦ, ɔᶦ, aᵁ, eᶦ, y, n] would probably be missing or severely distorted.

Careful inspection of tongue movements during speech (see Chapter 8) suggests that the various parts of the tongue can function semi-independently, so it is possible to consider the tongue as consisting of three semi-independent articulators: the tip, the dorsum, and the root (or body). To illustrate what is meant by semi-independence, consider the following example. Hold your arm in front of you, rigid to the fingertip, and slowly lift the arm. Note that the arm-wrist-finger system moves as a single unit. Now, again hold your arm in front of you, and as you lift it, wag your fingers. Notice that as the arm lifts, the fingertip can move up, down, and around independently of the arm. The semi-in-

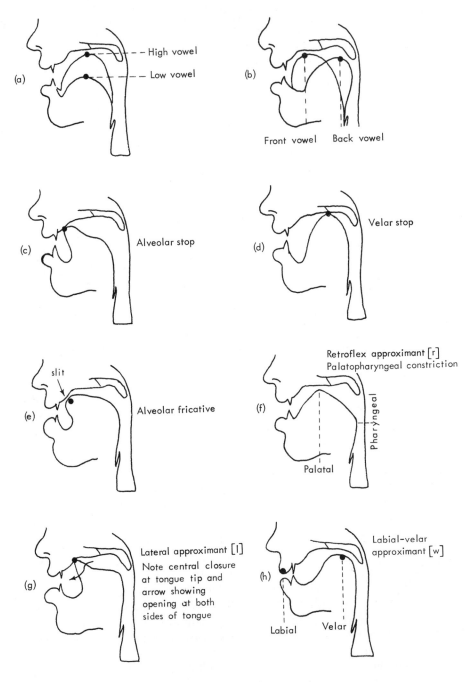

figure 7.11

Typical articulatory positions of the tongue for
vowels, stops, fricatives, and approximants.

dependence comes from the fact that as the arm rises, the fingertip, even as it moves up or down, is carried along by the arm. The tongue moves in a similar manner, insofar as when the tongue root moves, it carries the dorsum and tip along with it, even while they are performing other movements.

The movement patterns and tongue shapes typical of lingual articulations are shown in Figure 7.11(a–h). The tongue can be moved up and down in the vocal tract, from a low (open) to a high (closed) position (7.11a). The tongue may also advance from front to back (7.11b). In the front-back, high-low movements, the root and dorsum are involved. The tip and dorsum can completely close the vocal tract at any point from the lips to the uvula, cutting off airflow and allowing air pressure to rise behind the constriction (7.11c,d). The tip, dorsum, and root may also form narrow, slitlike constrictions for the production of fricative sounds anywhere from the lips to the pharynx (7.11e). Air pressure will also rise behind these slitlike constrictions. The tongue can form one or even two simultaneous constrictions anywhere in the vocal tract (7.11g,h). If the constrictions are not so tight that air pressure rises behind them, the sound produced is called an approximant. Note the raised tongue tip for the [r] sound (7.11f). Note also that for the [l] sound (7.11g), the tip closes the vocal tract at the midline, but openings along the sides of the tongue permit air and vibrations to escape the lips.

In fact, the tongue is capable of a very, very wide range of shapes, positions, and movements. It can easily move between one constriction or position and the next in as little as $\frac{1}{20}$ of a second (50 msec) or less. The tip can move between opening and closure as many as nine times per second, the dorsum somewhat more slowly, and the tongue root (body) even more slowly. Test this for yourself by saying "ta-ta-ta-ta-ta" or the word "indubitably" as fast as you can. The word contains *eight* different tongue positions, which can be completed in less than $\frac{1}{2}$ second. Let us look now at the musculature that makes these movements possible.

TONGUE MUSCULATURE

The Intrinsic Tongue Muscles   The intrinsic muscles of the tongue have their point of origin and attachment entirely within the tongue proper. Their primary role is to change the shape of the tongue mass, and to a lesser degree, to alter tongue position (high-low, front-back). They are the muscles responsible for lifting or curling the tip or edges, and for the bowing or flattening of the body. The muscles are named according to the direction in which their fibers pass through the tongue body: (1) superior longitudinal, (2) inferior longitudinal, (3) transverse, and (4) vertical (see Figure 7.12). Their locations are shown in Figure 7.14.

The vertical muscle fibers originate from the upper surface of the tongue dorsum and run vertically downward to insert into the inferior-lateral surface of the anterior portion of the tongue. Contraction of the vertical muscle fibers depresses and flattens the tongue. The superior longitudinal fibers originate at the base of

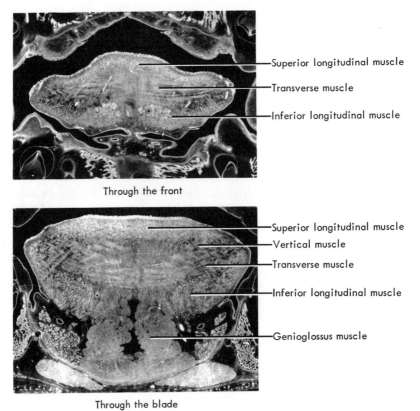

Through the front

Through the blade

figure 7.12

Views of the intrinsic tongue muscles. Reprinted by
permission from W. R. Zemlin, *Speech and Hearing Science:
Anatomy and Physiology.* © 1968 by Prentice-Hall, Inc.

the tongue and course forward toward the tip, just beneath the mucosal surface
of the dorsum. Contraction of these fibers curls the tip and/or lateral margins of
the tongue upward, and shortens the tongue. Observe these movements and
shapes before a well-lighted mirror. The inferior longitudinal muscle fibers run
from the base of the apex of the tongue along its undersurface. Contraction of
these fibers tends to shorten the tongue and depress the tip. The transverse
muscle fibers run laterally from one side of the tongue to the other, between
the two longitudinal muscles. This muscle inserts into the mucosa of the sides
of the tongue and into the lingual septum, a layer of connective tissue that runs
down the midline of the tongue. Contraction of these muscle fibers tends to
narrow and elongate the tongue. If, as seems likely, there are muscle spindle
stretch receptors present in the fibers of the four intrinsic tongue muscles, the
sensory information from them would provide the speaker's nervous system
with information concerning the three-dimensional position and velocity of the
tongue body as she or he articulated a stream of speech sounds.

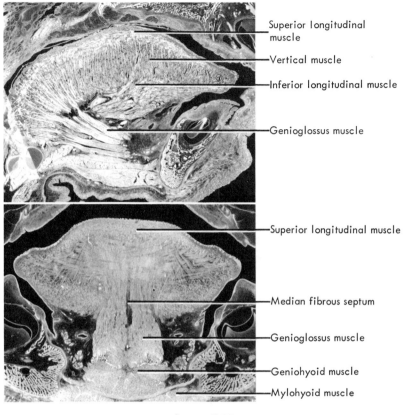

Superior longitudinal muscle

Vertical muscle

Inferior longitudinal muscle

Genioglossus muscle

Superior longitudinal muscle

Median fibrous septum

Genioglossus muscle

Geniohyoid muscle

Mylohyoid muscle

figure 7.12
(cont.)

The Extrinsic Tongue Muscles   The extrinsic tongue muscles have one point of attachment within and another outside the tongue. The major function of these muscles is to move the tongue about in the vocal tract in front-to-back and up-and-down directions. Their contractions also alter tongue shape to some degree. Keep in mind the fact that the tongue is strapped to the mandible, soft palate, hyoid bone, and skull by the extrinsic muscles.

The genioglossus is the largest muscle of the tongue, its fibers forming the bulk of the mass of the tongue. It originates near the midline of the lingual surface of the mandible in the region of the superior (mental) spines. The fibers fan outward, horizontally and vertically, along either side of the median, fibrous septum. One bundle of fibers courses upward to insert into the tongue tip. A medial bundle passes rearward and upward to insert along the dorsum. An inferior bundle penetrates rearward and downward to attach to the root of the tongue and to the body of the hyoid bone. Contraction of any or all of these genioglossus fibers may produce the following movements: the vertical fibers

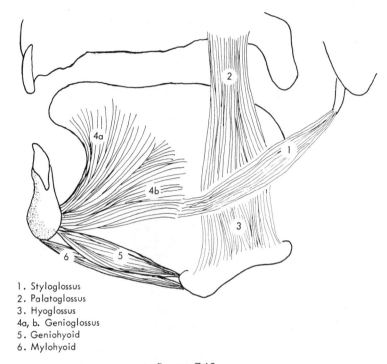

1. Styloglossus
2. Palatoglossus
3. Hyoglossus
4a, b. Genioglossus
5. Geniohyoid
6. Mylohyoid

figure 7.13
A lateral view of extrinsic tongue muscles.

pull the tongue tip down and back into the oral cavity; the middle layer of fibers flattens the dorsum and pulls it slightly forward, while the inferior bundle will pull the entire tongue body forward, causing the tip to protrude between the teeth.

The styloglossus muscle arises from the styloid process of the temporal bone and courses down and forward, entering the sides of the tongue and blending with inferior longitudinal and hyoglossus muscles. Contraction of this muscle raises and retracts (pulls backward) the tongue body, causing the dorsum to bulge upward as well. The palatoglossus muscle that connects the side of the tongue with the soft palate has been described before. Contraction of this muscle elevates the tongue and humps the dorsum, provided that the soft palate is relatively fixed in position. The hyoglossus muscle is a thin sheet of muscle that arises from the upper edges of the greater horn of the hyoid bone. The fibers run vertically and anteriorly, inserting into the body of the tongue and the medial fibrous septum. Contraction of this muscle retracts and lowers the tongue body or elevates the hyoid, depending on which structure is the more securely fixed in position when it contracts. The geniohyoid and mylohyoid muscles may be considered to be both extrinsic laryngeal and extrinsic tongue muscles. When the fibers of the mylohyoid contract, they may not only

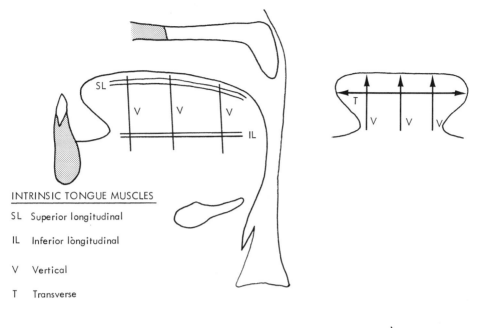

INTRINSIC TONGUE MUSCLES

SL   Superior longitudinal

IL   Inferior longitudinal

V   Vertical

T   Transverse

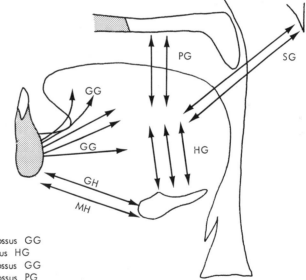

EXTRINSIC TONGUE MUSCLES

Forward movement:	Genioglossus GG
Downward movement:	Hyoglossus HG
Tongue tip downward:	Genioglossus GG
Upward movement:	Palatoglossus PG
	Geniohyoid GH
	Mylohyoid MH
Backward movement:	Styloglossus SG

figure 7.14

Schematic view of the direction in which extrinsic and
intrinsic muscle fibers run through the tongue.

lower the mandible or raise the hyoid, but also cause the floor of the tongue to bulge upward, pushing the dorsum upward toward the palatal region. Now that we have considered the anatomical structures of the vocal tract in some detail, we can discuss, on firm footing, the way in which the sounds of speech are produced. Before doing that, we shall have to consider some ways of classifying speech sounds into related classes.

speech sounds: problems of classification

At one time doctors labored under the impression that health was best explained by claiming that the healthy human body displayed a balance of elements. The four elements, earth, air, fire, and water, were exemplified in each of four "biles"—yellow, black, red, and white. Explanations were then dictated by the units of description. For example, if a patient was infected, and his temperature rose and his limbs or body became *red* and swollen, an excess of red bile had accumulated. The treatment then was to bleed the patient with knife or leech to reduce the excess red bile. Today, given our biochemical and genetic frameworks of description and a germ-virus theory of infectious disease, such illnesses are described and treated differently. The framework and units of phonetic description also dictate in large part how successful we are in capturing the essence of the act of speaking.

If we assume that the smallest controllable unit of speech utterance is the sound or sound segment, then the descriptive framework is built around the so-called segmental speech sound or phone. Originally, and even today, the act of articulation is most easily observed by describing the positions and shapes of the organs of speech. An acoustic description of sounds is nearly impossible without skillful use of delicate electronic equipment. An auditory description in which a listener identifies and interprets the speech sound according to past articulatory and language experience is highly subjective and prone to error, even though it is convenient and easy. Most systems of phonetic description therefore use an articulatory-physiological framework. Such systems should provide a distinctive description of each segmental sound so that it can be differentiated from every other sound in the sound pattern of that language.

But there are limitations inherent in a description based on segmental speech sounds. First, it is often impossible to cut up the stream of speech into separate segments. The stream of speech is an overlapping set of sounds. Any piece of speech cut, let us say, from a magnetic tape recording will contain information concerning *several* sounds. In rapid speech, sounds are articulated so swiftly and in such an overlapping way that we may not always be able to identify the separate segments. The claim that each speech sound can be produced in isolation so that its properties can be studied at leisure is a mistaken one. Take, for example, the stop sounds [p, t, k, b, d, g]. If we produce them in isolation, the vocal tract is first closed and then dynamically opened. But the minute the vocal tract opens, the rush of the air burst excites the vocal tract into production of an accompanying vowel, so that each stop is produced in a syllabic (consonant + vowel) fashion. Another example of the failure of the notion that a single invariant speech sound can be extracted from the stream of speech is the fact that the same sound is produced differently in differing contexts. In utterance-initial position, such as [p] occupies in the phrase "put it down," stop consonants are articulated with a closure and a release accompanied by a burst of air. Feel the air burst in the word "put" with the palm of your hand. In utterance-final position, stops are generally articulated with a closure but without a release—for example, "Come to a stop." In fact, it is a primary task of phonetic science to document and to account for the overlap and variability that "sounds" display in a conversational context. Contextual factors such as rate of speech, stress, intonation, juncture, phonetic context, syntactic structure, and so on have a powerful effect on the articulation of speech sounds.

But despite the difficulties we have in identifying, segmenting, and specifying speech sounds, there are good reasons for using the speech sound as the basic unit of description. First, our system of written symbols more or less corresponds to a speech sound system of one sound for each symbol, and our early experience with writing carries over into adulthood in terms of a preference for speech sounds as basic units of description. Second, the meaning of words ("sat" vs. bat") appears to change with each shift in the *sound* pattern of the word. Third, the error patterns in speech known as spoonerisms, in which sounds are switched ("dot hog" for "hot dog" or "modka vartini" for "vodka martini") suggest that at some level of speech production, speech-sound-sized units that we will call *segments* are utilized, and errors are made in the way in which they are serially ordered. Finally, when the vocal tract is activated for speech production, the minimum unit of output is the "sound" or sound segment, or in certain cases, the syllable. For each change in vocal tract shape, phonation mechanism, or air stream, a new sound results. The temptation is to suggest a sound-vocal tract shape correspondence such that for each vocal tract shape, a unique "sound" results. Remember, however, that even though the sound segment may be the basic unit of description, each sound can also be described in terms of its phonetic features. As a useful analogy, the basic unit of human life is the person—the whole, living person. But for purposes of description, we can characterize each person (speech sound) by a number of physiological features (phonetic features) such as height, weight, sex, age, eye color, scars, hair color, fingerprints, blood type, and so on. Given enough descriptive features, any person (or sound) can in theory be distinguished from every other on the basis of these features.

ARTICULATORY CLASSIFICATION   An articulatory description of the sounds of speech should specify the important air stream, phonatory, and articulatory characteristics of speech. A truly universal phonetic description should be capable of describing the essential features of sound production in all languages of the world. Why, you may ask? Because human vocal tracts and the physiological responses observed during speech should be the same the world over. As a physical system, vocal tracts are very much alike; hence, description of sounds in purely articulatory (physiological) terms should, in theory, be the same the world over. The only flaw in this is that the semantic and grammatical structures of language differ widely. Each speech utterance we produce is a product of our entire language-generating process, which includes the syntactic, semantic, and phonological components as well as physiological-phonetic factors. A purely physiological description would be inadequate, since physiological activity is not the only contributor to the shape of the speech sounds and how they are interpreted. At any rate, a physiologically realistic system of features for the classification of segments is vital, and in the authors' opinion, the physiological feature system of Ladefoged (1971) is as satisfactory as any other. In his system, each speech sound can be described in terms of a number of articulatory features:

1. Place of articulation
2. Manner of articulation
   a. Airpath
   b. Articulatory stricture
3. Phonation type features
4. Cover (abstract) features

We have previously discussed 3 phonation type features in Chapter 5. Cover (abstract) features are for the moment beyond the scope of our discussion, so we will not consider them at this point in any detail. The cover or abstract features refer to certain combinations of the other four features that have unique linguistic or physiological implications and thus deserve to be assigned feature values of their own. Feature descriptions of speech production and speech sounds were initially and still are primarily devised by linguists and phoneticians to describe linguistically interesting facts and generalizations concerning the structure of language. As such, their descriptions may not be at all satisfactory for a more physiological or acoustic description that might be of interest to the speech pathologist.

PLACE OF ARTICULATION   Place of articulation is the location of the primary constriction in the vocal tract during production of a given sound. In Figure 7.4, examine the eleven places of articulation, ranging from labial to glottal. Articulatory places are best interpreted as points along a physiological continuum, distance from the glottis. The number of separate places of articulation identified along this continuum varies, depending upon the phonetician. Ladefoged argues that in any given language, no more than six differing places of articulation are used. Most languages, for example, use an alveolar place of articulation. However, exactly where in the vicinity of the alveolar ridge the constriction with the tongue is formed may depend on the language in question.

But for purposes of description, the term "alveolar" is sufficient. The places of articulation are these:

1. Labial. Major constriction is at the lip; if both lips form the constriction, it is called bilabial. Sounds such as [p] in "pot" and [m] in "more" involve labial constrictions.

2. Labiodental. Major constriction generally formed between upper incisor and lower lip, such as [f] in "fan" or [v] as in "violet."

3. Dental (lingua-dental). Major constriction is made between the tongue tip or blade and the edge or lingual surface of the upper incisors, such as [θ] in "think." If the tongue protrudes between the upper and lower incisors, it may be called an interdental place of articulation.

4. Alveolar. Constriction is made between tongue tip (or blade) and the alveolar ridge, such as [t] as in "tin," [n] as in "no," [s] as in "sit," [z] as in "zoom," [l] as in "lie."

5. Retroflex. In the retroflex articulation, the tongue tip is lifted up toward the hard palate, as in the [r] sound of the word "read."

6. Prepalatal (palato-alveolar). The tongue blade is raised to a constriction behind the alveolar ridge. Examples are the sound [ʃ] in "shoe" or [ʒ] in "leisure."

7. Palatal. The tongue dorsum rises to form a constriction against the hard palate, such as the [ç] in "garçon".

8. Velar. Typically, the dorsum of the tongue is raised to form a constriction with the soft palate. Examples are [k] as in "coat," [g] as in "goo," or [ŋ] as in "sung."

9. Uvular. Constriction is made between the dorsum and the uvula.

10. Pharyngeal. The pharyngeal dorsum of the tongue forms a constriction against the posterior pharyngeal wall.

11. Glottal. The rapid cessation of voicing caused by strong glottal adduction, and/or the rapid release of the closed, motionless vocal folds into vibration, is both an articulation place and a phonation type (see Chapter 6).

Acoustically, the place of greatest constriction is a critical determinant of the resonance-frequency pattern of the vocal tract. As the articulatory constriction is moved from the glottis toward the lips, resonance frequencies shift in a systematic fashion. Only rarely do constrictions at different, well separated, places give relatively similar patterns of frequencies for the vocal tract. Perceptually, the ear is sensitive to the changes in resonance frequency patterns as the place of articulation changes, although place of articulation is one of the more easily misperceived phonetic features.

Occasionally, more than one tight articulatory constriction is formed in the vocal tract. For example, during articulation of the [w] sound, there are two constrictions, one at the lips, and a constriction between the tongue dorsum and the velum (Figure 7.11h). The constriction which is tightest (greatest) and/or nearest to the glottis is considered to be the primary constriction, and that which is more open or farther from the glottis is the secondary constriction. Places of articulation commonly used as points for secondary articulation are the lips, hard palate, soft palate, and pharynx. Sounds produced with a secondary constriction at any of these points are called, respectively, labialized, palatalized, velarized, or pharyngealized sounds. Practice a secondary constriction yourself by articulating an [s] sound and then rounding your lips as you phonate [sʷ]. Note the change in sound quality. Now, practice your knowledge of place of articulation by producing stop consonants, fricatives, and nasals at every one of the places listed above. At which places are you unable to produce sound? Can you account for this?

MANNER OF ARTICULATION   Manner of articulation is a complex articulatory feature. It concerns the ways in which air flows out of the vocal tract. We generally examine three aspects of manner of articulation: (1) direction of air stream (oral or nasal air path), (2) type of air stream path (central or lateral tube pathway for airflow), and (3) articulatory stricture (size and length of the constriction).

Oral vs. Nasal Air Path   Sounds made with the velum elevated result in airflow and vibration escaping from the lips, and such sounds are called oral sounds. Sounds such as [p, t, s, w] are oral sounds. When the oral cavity is closed and the velum is lowered, the air stream and acoustic vibrations escape through the nose, and the sound is said to be nasal in manner of production. If both the oral cavity and the nasal cavity are simultaneously open for the passage of airflow and vibration, the sound is said to be nasalized.

Central vs. Lateral Air Path   If the vocal tract is constricted so that the sides are closed, with a single opening down the center of the tract, the sound is classified as having a central manner of articulation. The majority of English speech sounds are produced with a single central opening at the place of greatest articulatory constriction. If, however, the center of the vocal tract is obstructed by the tongue but there is incomplete closure of either side of the tongue, air and vibration will escape around the constriction. Such sounds are called laterals. The [l] in "lip" involves a central alveolar constriction, with the sides of the tongue on either side of the constriction relaxed and opened, permitting air flow bilaterally. The vocal tract tube shape for [l] reveals a splitting into a two-tube system at the constriction (see Figure 7.11 g).

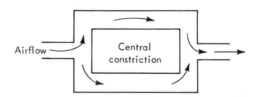

Articulatory Stricture (Constriction)   During speech, there is simultaneously an outward flow of air and acoustic vibration through the vocal tract. If the vocal tract is constricted at any point, the impedance to both airflow and acoustic vibration increase at that point. Given a constant driving pressure from the lungs, P_L, then as Z_{dc} increases or decreases, airflow must reciprocally decrease or increase, since

$$P = Z_{dc}U$$

If the vocal tract tube is sufficiently constricted, linear velocity of airflow increases to the point of turbulence whereupon fluctuating eddies in the jet stream cause instantaneous, rapid fluctuations in airflow rate, which in turn generate noisy, acoustic vibration. When the larynx rhythmically opens and closes, the airflow rises rapidly from zero to a peak and back again, yielding a variable airflow rate because of the varying impedance of the opening-closing vocal folds. The varying airflow (air burst) yields a concomitant air-pressure pulse that moves down the vocal tract. In both cases, a time-varying impedance, the vocal folds for voiced sounds, and turbulent eddies of air flow for fricatives cause rapid variations in airflow which in turn cause rapid variations in air pressure that travel down the vocal tract as acoustic vibrations. We can picture the relationships in this way:

For voiced sounds

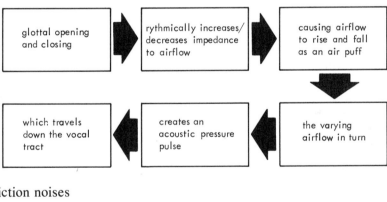

For friction noises

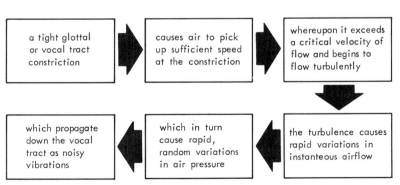

At any point where there is a constriction of sufficient tightness to strongly modulate airflow, there will generally be a pressure rise behind the constriction. Test this yourself. Open your mouth widely and breathe out rapidly. There is little or no pressure buildup in your mouth. Now, close your mouth, except for a small opening at the lips, and exhale rapidly. Notice the bulging of your lips as the labial constriction causes the pressure to rise in the mouth behind the constriction.

Those sounds articulated with sufficient constriction to cause pressure to rise above atmospheric pressure in the oral and pharyngeal cavities are called *obstruent* consonants, and they include the stops, fricatives, and affricates.

stop consonants Stop consonants are produced with a rapid, complete vocal tract closure that offers infinite impedance to the flow of air during the closure phase. The closure is held sufficiently long (25 msec or more) for a rise in oral pressure to occur. If the level of oropharyngeal pressure is sufficiently high when the closure is swiftly released, the sudden outflow of air, like the snap of a balloon being pricked by a needle, causes an acoustic burst transient (explosion). If pressure is high enough, after the burst there will be a noisy outrush of air which is called aspiration noise. If air pressure rise is insufficient because of low P_L or because of a short duration of closure, the burst and aspiration may be weakened or missing. The only portion of the stop consonant that must be articulated is the *closure*. In word-initial position—for example, [p] in "pit"—articulation begins with closure and ends in a burst and aspiration leading into the vowel. In word-final position as in [p] in "stop," there is a movement toward closure (the implosion phase) and closure, but very often no release.

The closure phase of stop sounds (and even fricatives) creates difficulty in maintaining voicing. When the vocal tract is closed, air bursts from the vibrating larynx cannot escape from the lips or nose. Thus, oral pressure rises until $P_{oral} = P_{lung}$, at which point the vocal folds *must* stop vibrating since there is no pressure drop to force them to open. Because vocal intensity and frequency of vibration depend on the size of the pressure drop across the vocal folds, there is a predictable reduction in frequency and intensity and often a cessation of vocal fold vibration as we articulate voiced stop consonants. It has been suggested that voicing can be maintained during the closure phase of stops and other obstruents by allowing air to escape through the opened velopharyngeal port, by active or passive expansion of the compliant pharyngeal walls, or by a lowering of the larynx to increase vocal tract volume vertically. Also, a relaxation of the vocal fold tension can serve to prolong phonation by allowing a smaller pressure drop to create vibration. In any case, the nasal air leak or the expanding cavity volume can absorb the airflow for a while, slowing the rise of oral pressure or the vocal folds may be relaxed. As a result, the folds can continue to vibrate during the closure phase.

fricative consonants Fricative articulation involves constricting the vocal tract to create a small slit through which air will flow fast enough to achieve turbulence just beyond the constriction. The smallness of the slit is crucial: It must be small enough to cause a pressure rise behind it. Given the pressure rise, the smallness and shape of the slit determine how fast the air stream will flow as it is pushed through the slit by air pressure. The faster it flows, the more intense and higher-frequency the turbulence noise will be.

As you already know from Chapter 6, the Bernoulli effect indicates that as air flows through a constriction in a tube, the velocity of airflow increases while the air pressure within the flowing air jet decreases. If tube size is sufficiently small and driving pressure high enough, there comes a point, depending upon the viscosity (internal friction) and density of the air, where the rapidly moving air jet escaping the constriction will begin to rotate randomly. As they mix with the air beyond the constriction, these rotations or turbulent eddies modulate the air pressure sufficiently rapidly to yield a noisy vibration called *turbulence noise*. In plain terms, given enough pressure and a tight enough constriction, the jet of escaping air will begin to spin randomly, yielding a friction-turbulence noise. This is the essence of fricative production. In certain cases, the high-speed air jet strikes an object (such as tooth or lip) in its path and generates additional high-pitched noise. Such sounds are called *sibilant* or *strident* fricatives. Examples of sibilant fricatives are [s] in "sit" and [ʃ] in "shoe." The fricative [f] in "frank" is nonstrident.

Because obstruents such as stops, affricates, and fricatives generally need a high oral air pressure, any air leak through an open or partially opened velopharyngeal port is a serious problem for sound production. Try to sustain an [s] sound while your velum is open. Practice until you succeed. Notice that friction noise is made in the nose, and not in the mouth, and that the resulting nasalized fricative is grossly distorted.

affricate consonants Affricate sounds are articulated so that a complete vocal tract closure is abruptly released into a fricative slit which yields a strong, fricativelike noise. The combination of stop-like, abrupt release and friction noise constitutes an affricate sound. Phoneticians have suggested that the affricate be viewed as a combination of stop and fricative manners of production. The affricate sound [tʃ] as in "church" would then consist of a [t]-like stop release and an [ʃ]-like fricative. Along with stops and fricatives, affricates are classified as obstruent consonants. The tight constriction results in an increase of intra-oral pressure and modulates the airflow sufficiently strongly to produce a burst release and friction noise.

Approximant Sounds   The approximant sounds are representatives of a manner of production that is intermediate between the obstruent sounds and the open, vocalic (vowel-like) sounds. Nasals, liquids, and glides (semi-vowels) comprise the approximant sounds. It has also been suggested that the close-high vowels [i] and [u] qualify as approximants, but this may only be a superficial resemblance.

The approximant sounds do indeed display constriction of the vocal tract when they are articulated. However, the constriction is not so tight that turbulence noise is produced; the jet of airflow at the constriction is not ordinarily "audibly" turbulent. The key to this statement is "not ordinarily." Under "normal" speech conditions (which involves lung pressures of 5 to 15 cm H_2O, and transglottal flows of 150 to 200 cc/sec through the buzzing larynx) the velocity of airflow is not sufficiently high through the constriction to create turbulence noise. If greater than average P_L is used, or if airflow rate is increased, then any approximant will yield "audible" turbulence noise generated near the major constriction. Demonstrate this to yourself. First phonate a sustained [m], as in "mother." Then remove the impedance offered to the air stream by the buzzing glottis by devoicing, holding the glottis open. The unimpeded air stream now rushes turbulently through the rather constricted nasal passageways as you phonate the voiceless [m̥]. The quality of the turbulence of the [m̥] is rather like that of a person blowing the nose or sniffing in disbelief. Now, produce voiceless [n̥, y̥, r̥, l̥, j̥, w̥], and listen to the turbulence noise of these approximants. The approximants can also be made noisily if elevated lung pressure is used to push sufficient air past the impedance of the buzzing glottis to cause friction at the approximant constriction. Try it. First make a soft, sustained [m] as in "m-m-m-m-m." Now, phonate [m] as loudly as you can, and you will hear nasal turbulence noise mixed in with the nasal buzz.

In English, the approximants are characterized as being nonnoisy, relatively intense voiced sounds whose resonance frequency patterns are well defined. The approximants generally function as consonants, although many approximants, especially [r] sounds, can function vocalically, such as [ɝ] in "bird."

nasal consonants In English, nasal sounds are produced with a closed oral passageway and an open nasal airway extending from the nares through the open velopharyngeal port down to the larynx. Nasals are like stops insofar as the oral constriction for them may be rapidly released. The articulation of a nasal such as the [m] in "mice" involves an oral closure phase during which the velum is open, releasing a nasal buzz or nasal murmur. The oral closure is then rapidly released, almost as swiftly as in stop consonants, while the velum simultaneously closes. The nasal murmur is characterized by strong low-frequency energy. The presence of an oral cavity closed on one end but open and coupled to the nasopharynx at the open velopharyngeal port causes antiresonances to appear in the frequency spectrum of the sound. Very little if any vibratory energy is present at these antiresonance frequencies. The differing nasal sounds of English are articulated by closing the oral cavity at the lips [m], alveolar ridge [n], and soft palate [ŋ].

liquid consonants For English, the liquid approximants consist of the lateral sound [l] and the retroflex sound [r]. In the case of [l], the air path is occluded by a tongue tip constriction at the alveolar ridge. However, the sides of the tongue behind the constriction are open. The air stream divides into *two,* one flowing over either side of the tongue, which rejoin beyond the alveolar ridge. Occasionally the [l] constriction is released so rapidly that an air burst is noted. The [l] is characterized by a peculiar resonance pattern that yields a highly distinctive perceptual quality.

The retroflex liquid sound [r] is characterized by a raising of the tongue tip or blade toward the palatal region of the hard palate with a secondary constriction between the tongue dorsum and the posterior pharyngeal wall. Cineradiography reveals that the articulation of [r] is highly variable; a variety of lingual shapes yield sounds with a satisfactory [r] quality. The /r/ segment can function as a consonant, such as [r] in "red," as a stressed vowel [ɝ], as in "burn," as an unstressed vowel [ɚ] as in "brother," or as an element of a complex diphthongal sound, as in "bear," "buyer," "boar." Acoustically, [r] is characterized by a well-defined, intense frequency spectrum in which resonances 2 and 3 are quite close and relatively low in frequency.

glides The glide manner of articulation is also called the semi-vowel manner of articulation. These consonants are closely related to corresponding vowel sounds. The semi-vowel [w] as in "wow" is closely related to the vowel [u] as in "new," while the glide [j] as in "yes" is closely related to the vowel [i] as in "beat." If [u] is constricted by more lip protrusion and velar constriction than is ordinary, a [w] sound will result. Practice saying [wu] repeatedly. Notice that there is only a small change in lip and tongue position in shifting from [w] to [u]. In the case of [j], practice saying [ji] as in "ye." Notice that only a small increase of palatal constriction changes [i] to [j]. Thus, articulation of the glides [j] and [w] involves slightly more constriction of the vocal tract than for [i] and [u]. The acoustic and physiological characteristics of glides are quite vowel-like. The glides tend to be articulated with a deliberate opening or closing movement preceding or following a brief constriction phase. Practice saying "wow" and "yeah," paying attention to the "gliding" open and close of the lips in "wow," and the opening and closing (gliding) movements of the tongue in "yeah" [jæ].

PHONATION TYPE   In English, the phonological voiced-voiceless contrast between sounds can be considered a phonation feature. Phonetically speaking, voiced sounds are articulated with glottal pulsing throughout the sound in question, whereas voiceless sounds are produced with an open, nonvibrating glottis achieved by an abductory (devoicing) gesture of the laryngeal muscles. Thus, the [s-z, ʃ-ʒ, t-d, f-v] sound pairs contrast primarily on the basis of presence or absence of voicing. In conversational speech, however, the picture is not so simple. The voiced sounds may show periods of voicelessness, and the voiceless sounds show some voicing. The glottal pulsing may also be highly irregular. Demonstrate this to yourself by saying "aha" very slowly. Note the voiceless [h]. Now say it very swiftly. Observe the voicing of the [h] segment. Repeat this with [aza]. Once again, at slow speed, notice the tendency of [z] to be "devoiced." In rapid speech, the voicing contrast for the consonant sounds is conveyed in part by cues present in sounds adjacent to the consonants. For example, vowel sounds preceding voiced consonants have greater length than those preceding voiceless consonants. Speak the words "piece" and "peas," [pis] and [piz]. Note that [i] is longer in "peas" than in "piece."

Measurements made of oral air pressures for voiced and voiceless consonants reveal that the pressure for voiced consonants is slightly more than half that for the voiceless ones. In large part, the difference occurs because the buzzing larynx impedes the flow of air for the voiced consonants, so that the full pressure in the lungs does not appear in the oral cavity. Thus, there is a pressure drop across both the glottis and the articulatory constriction. The glottis does not impede airflow in the voiceless obstruent consonant, and full P_L occurs behind the articulatory constriction.

Voice Onset Time   Voice onset time (VOT), discussed in Chapter 6, may be considered a major voicing cue for stop consonants. Voice onset time is operationally defined as the period of time between the articulatory burst-release of the stop consonant and the point at which glottal pulsing begins. In English, voiced stop consonants generally exhibit a VOT of 30 to 40 msec or less, or even negative VOTs (voicing begins before release). Voiceless stops generally have VOTs 40 msec or greater. The two categories overlap somewhat in their distribution. Voiceless stops, because they are produced with a higher intra-oral air pressure, have sharper, longer, more intense air bursts, a longer period of noisy airflow after the burst (aspiration), and noise-excited transitions. In addition, variations in fundamental frequency of glottal pulsation, and the duration and intensity of surrounding vowels, furnish further cues for the distinction between voiced and voiceless stops. The reader should practice producing stops with varying VOT. Practice making stops with voicing before the release, voicing that starts at the release, and voicing that starts considerably after the release. Listen to the loudness of the burst and aspiration noise in such voiced and voiceless stops. Figure 7.15 shows a voiced and a voiceless stop for which VOT has been measured. Observe that VOT for the voiceless stop is +108 msec, while that for the voiced stop is +14 msec.

VOWEL ARTICULATION

Classificatory Features   Vowel sounds are articulated with a vocal tract that is relatively open. Nevertheless, for each vowel sound a point between glottis and lips may be found where vocal tract constriction, however slight, is greatest (Figure 7.16). In addition to the location of the point of greatest constriction, we may also identify the highest point on the tongue—that is, the place on the dorsum where the distance between tongue and palate is least. For front vowels, the high point of the tongue and the point of greatest constriction generally coincide, but for back vowels, the two points are not the same. Still another classificatory feature of vowels is lip rounding or spreading.

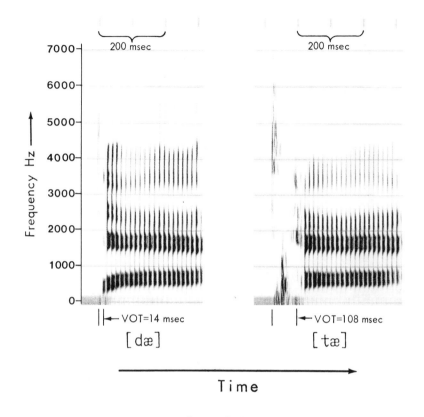

figure 7.15

VOT (voice onset time) as measured on the syllables "da-ta."
VOT is the time interval between the burst release and the
onset of glottal pulsing (voice) as indicated by the appearance
of vertical voice striations on the spectrogram.

If the lips are protruded out and away from the incisors during vowel production, the vowel is said to be rounded. If it is produced with the lips retracted, pulled against the teeth, the vowel is said to be spread or retracted. The effect of protrusion/retraction is to alter vocal tract length and size of lip opening, as can be seen in the bottom two profiles of Figure 7.16. Lip rounding tends to lengthen the vocal tract at the lips and produces a smaller lip opening. Lip retraction or spreading shortens vocal tract length and tends to increase the labial opening. A third feature of vowel sounds is jaw lowering. Vowels made with the mandible raised are called close or high vowels. This is because the mandible carries the dorsum to a position near the palate. When the mandible is lowered, the dorsum is carried down and away from the palate, so that the vocal tract is relatively open. Thus, vowels may be classified according to three features: tongue height (closely correlated with mandibular position), tongue

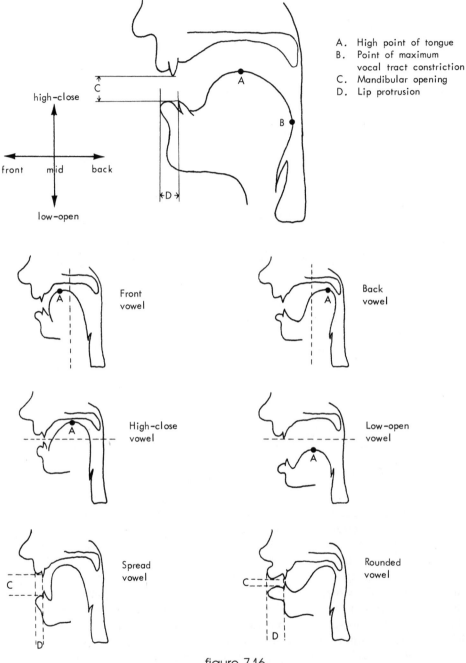

A. High point of tongue
B. Point of maximum vocal tract constriction
C. Mandibular opening
D. Lip protrusion

high-close

front   mid   back

low-open

Front vowel

Back vowel

High-close vowel

Low-open vowel

Spread vowel

Rounded vowel

figure 7.16

A view of the vocal tract showing how vowels are classified
according to the high point of the tongue, the point of
greatest constriction, lip rounding, and mandibular opening.

table 7.1

representative words containing vowels and diphthongs
of general American speech

[i]	feet	[u]	boot	[ʌ]	but
[ɪ]	sit	[ʊ]	hood	[ɜ-]	bird
[e]	bay	[o]	boat	[ɚ]	brother
[ɛ]	fed	[ɔ]	caw		
[æ]	cat	[a]	father		
		[eɪ]	hay		
		[aʊ]	how		
		[ɔɪ]	boy		
		[oʊ]	coat		

advancement (front or back), and lip rounding or spreading. Sample words containing the various vowel sounds are shown in Table 7.1.

Figure 7.16 displays profiles of the vocal tract made during production of vowels exhibiting the various features described. Each vowel is classified according to the position it occupies in the three-feature space shown in Figure 7.22. Figure 7.23 represents an "articulatory space" that differentiates the vowels from one another on the basis of articulatory features. Note, for example, that [i] is a high, front, spread vowel, whereas [ɔ] is a mid-low, back, partially rounded vowel.

Acoustic Features   Vowels are unique because of the acoustic properties of the open vocal tract. In English, all vowels are voiced. When a relatively unconstricted acoustic tube such as the vocal tract is excited by recurrent air bursts, it radiates a complex acoustic wave, the *vowel sound*. Vowel sounds are characterized by being long in duration, intense in energy, and having a well-defined pattern of resonance frequencies (see Figure 1.7). Relatively open acoustic tubes (columns of air inside the walls of a tube or container) are characterized by having, in theory, infinitely many resonance frequencies. Figure 1.7 shows that if the acoustic tube is symmetrical, having *no* constrictions along its length, the resonance frequencies will occur at $f_n = nc$ $4L$, where n = the number of the resonance frequency, and L = length of the tube (see Chapter 4). The resonance frequencies increase as the length of the tube decreases. When a slight constriction is introduced into the tube, the resonance frequencies are no longer equally spaced; they are perturbed, moving to higher or lower positions. Acoustic theory (Fant, 1960) indicates that if the shape of the vocal tract at every point is known, then the resonance frequencies of the vocal tract are predictable. *Thus, articulatory shape determines the location of the resonance frequencies.*

Figure 7.17 gives spectrographic examples of the resonance frequencies of English vowels. The variations in location of the resonance frequencies seen in

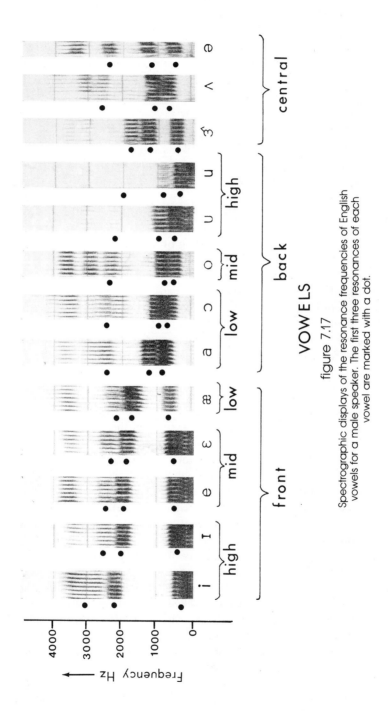

VOWELS

figure 7.17

Spectrographic displays of the resonance frequencies of English vowels for a male speaker. The first three resonances of each vowel are marked with a dot.

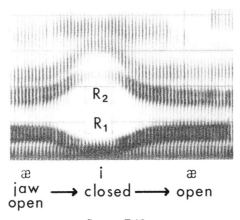

æ   i   æ
jaw ⟶ closed ⟶ open
open

figure 7.18

A spectrographic example of the dependence of resonance
frequency 1 on mandibular opening (tongue height). As the
mandible opens, the tongue moves to a lower position in the
oropharynx, and resonance 1 increases in frequency. As the jaw
closes and the tongue moves higher, resonance 1 falls in frequency.

the figure are caused by variations in each of the three articulatory features
that characterize vowels. As the mandible lowers, and vowel height changes
from high to low (or close to open), resonance 1 increases in frequency (see
Figure 7.18). As lip rounding increases, resonances 1 and 2 are increasingly
lowered in frequency (see Figure 7.19). Try this for yourself. Make the vowel

figure 7.19

A spectrographic example of a vowel for which the lips are
first rounded and then spread. As the lips spread, R_1 and R_2
rise; as the lips are rounded, R_1 and R_2 fall in frequency.

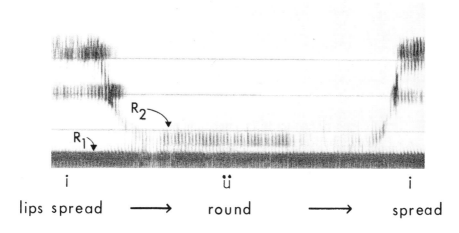

i   ü   i

lips spread ⟶ round ⟶ spread

[i] with spread lips, and as you phonate [i] begin to round your lips. Pay attention to the fall in timbre of the vowel as it is more and more "rounded." As the major constriction for the vowel moves forward from the pharyngeal to the palatal region, from [u] to [i], there is a tendency for resonance frequency 2 to rise (see Figure 7.17). If there is a retroflexion of the tongue tip, such as for the vowel [ɝ] (Figure 7.17), resonances 2 and 3 are very close together and relatively low in frequency.

Open vowels such as [a, ɔ, æ] are acoustically more intense than the close vowels [i, ɪ, ʊ] and especially [u] by about 3 to 5 dB. The open vocal tract for low vowels offers less acoustic impedance to vibration than does the more closed vocal tract of high vowels. The vowel [u], which is especially weak (see Figure 7.17), offers both a labial and velar constriction to impede the transmission of acoustic energy. One of the difficulties in describing vowels is that we cannot see or easily feel the tongue as it moves from place to place, because it forms few, if any, contacts or sharp constrictions. In addition, vowel articulation is continuous. That is, between any two vowels, the tongue can adopt an intermediate position and thus create a vowel that is intermediate in value. For example, given a front and back vowel, we can move the tongue to create a large number of vowels which are intermediate in position between the two extreme vowels. The possibility of articulating vowels at many different points leads some phoneticians to differentiate vowels from consonants by saying that consonants can be made only at a few places of articulation, with few if any intermediate places or manners of articulation, but there are no distinct boundaries between vowels. Experiment with moving your tongue smoothly from one vowel to another. For example, try saying "baa" and prolonging the [æ], and as you do, move slowly toward [i]. Notice the steady change in vowel quality as you move from [æ] to [i].

Diphthongs   The diphthongs are a special class of vocalic sounds. If a vowel sound is articulated with a fixed, unchanging vocal tract shape, a "monophthong" vowel sound emerges. This can be seen in Figure 7.20, where the resonance pattern for the vowel [ɔ] is very steady, indicating that the vowel was spoken monophthongally. By contrast, for the diphthongs [ɔ¹, a¹, aᵁ] notice that after an initial steady state, vocal tract shape changes steadily and smoothly, producing a transition during which the resonances shift, and a final shorter steady state where the resonances are once again nearly steady. The diphthong may be considered to be a *dynamic* vowel in which there is a movement from one vocal tract shape to another. The transition is the most crucial element of the diphthong. Notice that although the diphthong [ɔ¹] is transcribed as though it starts with an [ɔ]-shaped vocal tract, inspection of the monophthong vowel [ɔ] in Figure 7.20 reveals that the [ɔ] and the [ɔ] portion of [ɔ¹] are not the same. Rather, the diphthong starts near the resonance frequencies of the [ɔ] shape, but not exactly there. In English, most diphthongs start in an open—or relatively open—vowel position and end with a closer, more constricted target.

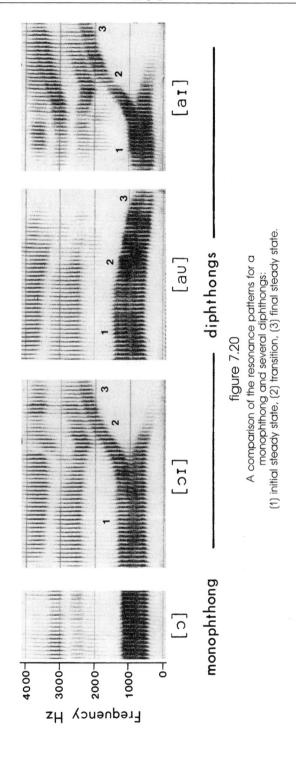

figure 7.20

A comparison of the resonance patterns for a
monophthong and several diphthongs:
(1) initial steady state, (2) transition, (3) final steady state.

A final distinction to be made concerning vowels is the fact that they may be divided into long (tense) and short (lax) groups. The tense vowels are [i, e, ɔ, o, u]. The lax vowels are [ɪ, ɛ, æ, ʊ, ʌ]. The tense or long vowels are longer in duration, acoustically more intense, more resistant to coarticulatory variations caused by surrounding phonetic context than are corresponding lax vowels. In addition, long vowels can appear in open syllables, whereas short vowels must always appear in closed syllables ("hid, head, mud"). The tense vowels often have lax counterparts produced with a similar lip and jaw position. Examples of such pairs of long/short vowels are [i-ɪ, e-ɛ, u-ʊ].

CONSONANT AND VOWEL CHARTS Now that we have discussed vowels and consonants and feature systems in detail, we are ready to consider consonant and vowel charts, which are a convenient, shorthand way of compressing a great deal of information into a compact, and informative form. Given a collection of things, we can classify them according to their distinguishing features. For example, the inhabitants of Chicago can be subdivided into groups by using age, sex, and height as distinguishing features. Note that these three factors serve to divide the population into natural classes. One natural class, for example, might be old or young. In general, a natural class is a collection of things characterized by a set of features such that the members of a class share a small subset of the total number of possible features. If we use place and manner of articulation as features for description of consonant sounds, then the result is shown as a table or chart of the consonants (Figure 7.21). Place of articulation is divided into eight places and manner of articulation into six types. The natural classes, for example, include stops, fricatives, and nasals, or velars, labials, and dental sounds. The chart provides a natural and convenient means for separating and classifying consonants. In addition, the physiological-phonetic features of place and manner correlate nicely with most of the abstract linguistic features linguists use to describe abstract sound segments.

Vowels may also be arranged in a chart according to the tongue height, tongue advancement, and lip rounding or spreading features (see Figure 7.22). Unfortunately, tongue height is perhaps not in satisfactory agreement with the articulatory facts, since it is the place and amount of constriction that is acoustically most important for vowels. For back vowels, tongue height and place of greatest constriction do not coincide; for this reason, Ladefoged advocates that instead of tongue height, the term height be used to refer to resonance frequency 1 (R_1) for vowels. When the vowel is high, R_1 is low; when the vowel is low, R_1 is high in frequency (see Figure 7.17).

acoustic characteristics
of speech sounds

Speech sounds are characterized by their temporal, intensity, and spectral properties. The problem is being able to identify the acoustic features that are crucial for the identification of a particular sound. Ideally, one would like to

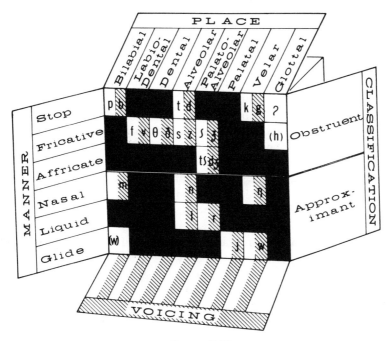

figure 7.21
A chart of the English consonants classified
according to place and manner of production.

figure 7.22
A vowel quadrilateral that shows the vowels classified
according to the articulatory criteria:
tongue height, tongue fronting, and lip rounding.

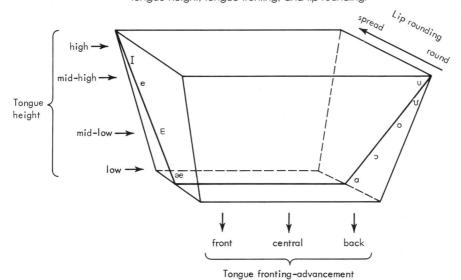

know exactly how the listener analyzes speech sounds. We could then use the acoustic features the auditory system uses to classify the sounds. Physicists initially speculated that the ear performed a spectral analysis of the sound. That is, the ear represented the continuously varying speech pressure wave in terms of its spectral (amplitude × frequency) representation. Figure 7.23 shows an actual vowel spectrum, the harmonically related frequencies that compose the vowel wave. An envelope can be drawn over the harmonic structure to reveal the presumed resonance frequencies of the vocal tract for that vowel. The assumption that the ear is a spectrum analyzer (see Chapter 9) contributed to the use of spectrum analyzers for the study of speech. The most widely used speech spectrum analyzer, the spectrograph, produces a display by burning a wax paper sheet with a spark emitted from a moving wire stylus. Figure 7.24 shows a spectrographic display of the sentence "We play ball on summer days."

The interpretation of spectrograms is a matter of experience, knowledge of acoustics and physiology, and practice. Vowels and most approximant consonants (except nasals) generally reveal at least 3 to 4 resonance frequency bars below 4000 Hz on a spectrogram. It has been demonstrated that the listener is acutely sensitive to the frequency location of these resonances; as the resonances shift, the sound we perceive generally changes. These obvious resonance patterns are marked *R*. Silences, which occur as pauses in the flow of speech, during the closure phase of stops, or during transition from fricatives to stop consonants, are indicated with an *S*. Bursts may occur when a rapid opening of the vocal tract releases air pressure as an acoustic transient. Such bursts are of short duration, but have a rich high-frequency energy content and often extend across the whole spectrographic pattern display width of 8000 Hz. They are marked with a *B*. Friction noises occur during production of fricatives, affricates, or stop consonant aspiration. The friction noise generally has a strong high-frequency content, over the frequency range of 3000 to 8000 Hz and often beyond, which shows up on the spectrogram as an irregular blur and occasionally reveals broadly defined resonances. The friction noises are marked with an *N*. If the speech sound is excited by glottal pulsing (voicing), the pulsing is evident as regularly spaced vertical stripes. The presence of these stripes reveals that glottal pulsing is occurring, and is a convenient way of distinguishing voiceless consonants from vowels and most approximants. The time between any two stripes is a measure of the frequency of glottal pulsing. In Figure 7.24, all portions of the utterance that reveal the vertical stripes typical of glottal pulsing are underlined.

Finally, the resonance pattern reveals regions such as [ɔ] in "ball," where the resonances and hence vocal tract shapes are changing very little. These are called *quasi-steady states,* or *targets.* In other places, the resonances are changing swiftly. These regions of rapid resonance shift are called *transitions,* and are marked on the spectrogram with a *T*. Transitions occur when the vocal tract swiftly opens or closes, rapidly changing shape. If we presume that every distinctive speech sound has a distinctive vocal tract shape and/or phonation

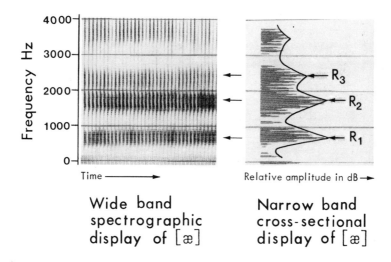

Wide band
spectrographic
display of [æ]

Narrow band
cross-sectional
display of [æ]

figure 7.23

The spectrum of the vowel [æ] taken from a spectrographic
section. A hypothetical transfer function is drawn over the
harmonic pattern to reveal the resonance peaks of the vowel
spectrum. Each line seen in the cross-sectional spectrum is one of
the harmonically related frequencies present in the vowel wave.

type, then transitions will generally, but not always, be observable as articulators move from one sound segment to the next. Not surprisingly, the listener interprets these transitions when identifying the consonant or vowel involved. Consonant to vowel transitions are rapid, generally 40 msec or less, whereas the transitions associated with diphthongs such as the [eᶦ] in "play" are usually longer. What can a spectrogram tell us? It will reveal the duration of sounds, the resonance patterns, transitions, noises, voicing, intensity, and many other important acoustic parameters. But it does not necessarily tell us how the listener perceives these sounds.

ACOUSTIC EXAMPLES
OF VOWEL SOUNDS   Figure 1.6 illustrates the fundamental
process of speech sound production. The vocal tract is an acoustic tube, a column of air enclosed by muscular walls. This column of air may be excited at any point along the tube from glottis to lip. The source of excitation may be a (1) periodic glottal buzz, (2) a friction noise, (3) an explosive-transient burst, or (4) a combination of the above. In all cases, the acoustic excitation is *complex*. As you will recall from Chapter 4, a complex acoustic excitation is characterized by the presence of vibratory energy at many frequencies. The glottal buzz is very nearly a complex periodic acoustic vibration, characterized by many co-occurring harmonically related simple harmonic vibrations, whereas friction noises and explosive bursts are complex aperiodic vibrations.

If the vocal tract is excited only at the glottis, the velum is closed; and if the air stream is central (not lateral), the resulting sound is characterized by a

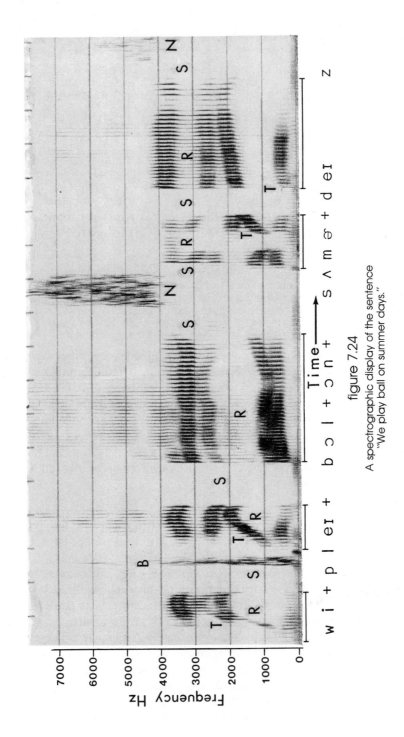

figure 7.24
A spectrographic display of the sentence
"We play ball on summer days."

frequency spectrum that displays numerous resonance frequencies. The majority of vowels and oral approximants are just such sounds. They are acoustically
powerful; they are periodic since, ideally, all vowels and approximants in
English are voiced; and their spectrum shows the strong, well-marked resonance frequency bars seen in the spectrograms of Figures 7.18, 7.19, 7.20, and
7.24. When the sound is an obstruent consonant, nasal, or lateral, an antiresonance may occur when (1) the velum is open at the same time the mouth
is; (2) when the mouth is closed and the velum is open; (3) when the air stream
is bilateral; or (4) when there is a supraglottal constriction sufficient to generate
friction noise or complete stoppage. The frequency spectrum of obstruents and
nasals is therefore marked by gaps or regions of low energy due to the presence of antiresonances. Observe in Figure 7.24 that the [s] in "summer" has
little or no energy below 3500 Hz, and that the spectrum for [m] in "summer"
also shows reduced mid- and high-frequency energy. This can be attributed in
part to the presence of antiresonances in the consonants' spectrum.

As we indicated in Chapters 1 and 4, acoustic theory states that the resonance
pattern of a tube is characterized by infinitely many resonances. If the tube is perfectly symmetrical along its length, as shown in Figure 7.25, the resonances are

figure 7.25
A three-parameter model of the vocal tract for vowel production.

(a)

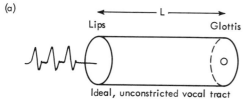

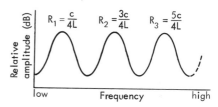

Ideal, unconstricted vocal tract

For unconstricted vocal tract

$$Fn = \frac{NC}{4L}$$

C = velocity of sound
L = length of tube
N = odd integers

Resonances are equally spaced

Vocal tract shape and
resonance frequency pattern
for unconstricted vocal tract

(b)

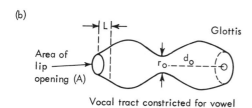

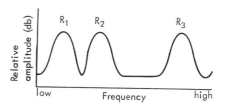

Vocal tract constricted for vowel

A three parameter model of the vocal
tract for vowel production. The three
parameters can be used to predict
R_1, R_2, R_3, etc. for the constricted
(perturbed) vocal tract

d_o = distance from glottis to major constriction
r_o = radius of major constriction
A/L = area off lip opening divided by length
of lip opening

equally spaced in frequency; the longer the tube, the more closely spaced the resonances. When the symmetrical tube is constricted, the resonances shift position. The shape of the vocal tract at every point contributes to the position of the resonance frequencies. Stevens and House (1955) demonstrated that the crucial aspects of vocal tract shape for vowels are these: (1) the distance *(d)* from the glottis to the major constriction (r_0), (2) the size of the major constriction (r_0), and (3) the area of the lip opening *(A)* and length of the lip tube *(l)*. These phonetic-shape parameters are shown in Figure 7.25. They can be used to predict the cross-sectional area of the vocal tract. Once the area function is known, we can predict the resonance frequencies for the vowels with good accuracy. As a constriction (r_0) becomes ever tighter, resonance 1 (R_1) decreases in frequency, as can be seen in Figures 7.17 and 7.18. As a constriction moves from the pharyngeal region out toward the lips, there is a tendency for resonance 2 (R_2) to rise; see Figures 7.17 and 7.19. To demonstrate this, make a fricative sound as far back on your palate as you can and then move the constriction forward as far toward the teeth as you can. As the constriction is moved forward, resonance 2 and then resonance 3 rise in frequency, giving the noise an ever-higher pitch. A spectrogram taken of such a noise (Figure 7.26) shows the steadily rising resonance frequency. The effect of increasing lip rounding is shown in the spectrogram of Figure 7.19. As the lips

figure 7.26

A spectrogram taken of a fricative noise made while the constriction is smoothly moved forward from the soft palate toward the teeth. Notice the steady rise in resonance frequency from 1500 to about 3200 Hz. The graph illustrates the fact that d_0, which may be interpreted as "place of vowel articulation" and place of consonant articulation, has a profound effect upon resonance frequency location, as well as airflow modulation.

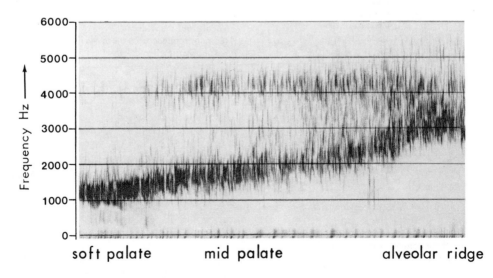

are rounded, the resonance frequencies fall; as they are unrounded or spread, they rise.

THE PARAMETERS
OF VOWEL PERCEPTION

Given that vowel sounds are characterized by a relatively long, intense acoustic wave that displays a strong resonance pattern, what are the cues for vowel perception? Examination of the spectrographic patterns for the vowels, Figure 7.17, will be useful at this point. Some of the following acoustic factors appear to be important for the perception of vowels:

1. Resonances 1 and 2 are the two most distinguishing acoustic parameters for the separation of vowels into different phonemic classes.

2. For a single speaker, over many productions of each vowel, there is little overlap between vowel categories when they are plotted in a resonance$_1$, resonance$_2$ space.

3. When the vowels of many speakers are plotted together, the same resonance frequencies may represent different vowels in the speech of different speakers.

4. There are systematic differences in vowel intensity and fundamental frequency: high vowels are 3 to 5 dB less intense and higher in f_0 than low vowels.

5. The long, tense vowels [i, e, a, o, u] are longer in duration, more intense acoustically, and more stable than the short, lax vowels [ɪ, ɛ, æ, ʊ].

6. Males have longer vocal tracts than females, and females in general have longer vocal tracts than children. As a result, male vowels have the lowest resonances on the average and children, the highest resonance frequencies. However, listeners are rarely confused by sex- or age-related differences in vowel resonance patterns; they learn to normalize these variations.

Figure 7.27 and Table 7.2, taken from the pioneering study of Peterson and Barney, display the resonance$_1$ vs. resonance$_2$ plot of American vowels spoken by men and children. The vowels of female speakers are omitted to make the differences in frequency between men and children as clear as possible. (The resonance frequency values for women are intermediate, between those for men and children.)

In an attempt to classify vowels acoustically, phoneticians have devised an acoustic feature description of vowels based on their spectral properties. Vowels such as [u], in which most of the energy is concentrated in the low frequencies (below 1000 Hz), are called *grave* vowels. *Compact* vowels are acoustically intense and show a tight concentration of acoustic energy in the mid-frequency region of 800 to 1800 Hz. *Acute* vowels show a high-frequency concentration of energy in the R_2-R_3-R_4 region above 2000 Hz. Not surprisingly, the quantal vowels [i, u, a] are the prime examples of acute, grave, and compact vowels. The neutral, reduced, unstressed vowel [ə] is neither acute nor grave nor compact, but rather diffuse, insofar as its formants are equally spaced (see Figure 7.17), and its spectral energy is quite well spread. The quantal vowels, because they are easily identified, rarely confused, and stable articulatorily, are the anchor points for any description of vowel sounds.

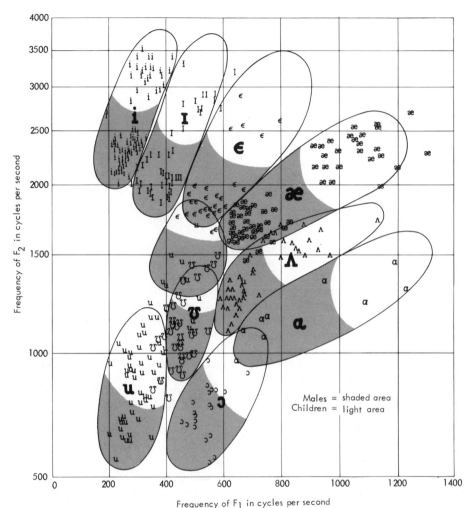

figure 7.27

A display of American English vowels plotted according
to their resonance 1 and resonance 2 values.
The data are for adult males and children.

ACOUSTIC EXAMPLES
OF CONSONANT SOUNDS   Consonants, whether obstruent or approximant, are produced with a strong supraglottal constriction in the vocal
tract. Obstruents are tightly constricted, display elevated oral air pressure, and
modulate airflow strongly enough to yield explosions or turbulence noises. Ap-

table 7.2
averages of fundamental and formant frequencies and
formant amplitudes of vowels spoken by 76 speakers

		i	ɪ	ε	æ	a	ɔ	ʊ	u	ʌ	ɝ
FUNDAMENTAL FREQUENCIES (cps)	M	136	135	130	127	124	129	137	141	130	133
	W	235	232	223	210	212	216	232	231	221	218
	Ch	272	269	260	251	256	263	276	274	261	261
FORMANT FREQUENCIES (cps) F_1	M	270	390	530	660	730	570	440	300	640	490
	W	310	430	610	860	850	590	470	370	760	500
	Ch	370	530	690	1010	1030	680	560	430	850	560
F_2	M	2290	1990	1840	1720	1090	840	1020	870	1190	1350
	W	2790	2480	2330	2050	1220	920	1160	950	1400	1640
	Ch	3200	2730	2610	2320	1370	1060	1410	1170	1590	1820
F_3	M	3010	2550	2480	2410	2440	2410	2240	2240	2390	1690
	W	3310	3070	2990	2850	2810	2710	2680	2670	2780	1960
	Ch	3730	3600	3570	3320	3170	3180	3310	3260	3360	2160
	L_1	-4	-3	-2	-1	-1	0	-1	-3	-1	-5
	L_2	-24	-23	-17	-12	-5	-7	-12	-19	-10	-15
	L_3	-28	-27	-24	-22	-28	-34	-34	-43	-27	-20

Source: Peterson and Barney, "Control Methods for a Study of the Vowels," Journal of the Accoustical Society of America 24 (1952), 175-184. Reprinted by permission.

proximants are constricted, but not so tightly that oral air pressure rises, and noisy modulation of airflow does not occur under "ordinary" conditions. A constriction sufficient to modulate flow strongly enough to generate noise (stops, fricatives, affricates) generally results in an antiresonance in the frequency spectrum of the consonant that cancels one or more resonances of the vocal tract, generally R_1, R_2, or R_3. Nasals and lateral air-path consonants also have antiresonances in their frequency spectrum.

Stops   Stop consonants are articulated with a complete closure of the vocal tract (for at least 25 msec or more), during which time airflow through the glottis causes air pressure to rise behind the constriction in the oral cavity so that P_{oral} is slightly less than or equal to P_{lung}. If the glottis is pulsing, the airflow modulation at the glottis prevents the oral pressure from rising as fast for voiced stops as it does for voiceless stops. In prevocalic position, the stop is released with a swift opening movement assisted by the air pressure behind the constriction. The sudden release of pressure, if swift enough, generates an acoustic transient, a burst, similar to that encountered when a balloon is punctured. Practice making the explosion for the stop. If air pressure is sufficiently high, as the constriction opens up air will rush out noisily from the open glottis or from the oral constriction for some time after the burst. This is called the aspiration phase. As soon as oral pressure has fallen sufficiently so that the pressure drop across the glottis is sufficient to cause voicing, the glottis will resume pulsing. In voiceless stops, the closure is somewhat longer and the oral air pressure higher, so that bursts are stronger, aspiration longer, and delay in voicing onset greater than for voiced stops. Perceptual studies reveal that burst and aspiration are sufficient to give good perception of the stop consonant.

While the vocal tract is moving toward or away from a stop closure, resonances are shifting because of the changing constriction. This period of rapid resonance movement is called the *transition region,* or *formant transition.* The R_2 and to a lesser degree R_3 and R_1 transitions are crucial to the correct perception of the stops involved. Figure 7.28 shows a group of stops with the burst, aspiration, and transition regions marked for observation. The burst and aspiration are clearly seen for the voiceless [tʰ] and [kʰ], but the burst is weak and aspiration absent for the voiced [b]. Notice that the position of resonance 2 at the point of burst release, which is called the *locus,* shifts upward in frequency from about 1250 Hz for [b] to about 2750 Hz for [k]. The locus frequency is a distinguishing feature for stops, since it varies systematically with place of production.

Fricatives   For fricative consonants, the elevated oral pressure drives a high-speed jet of air through the constriction, whereupon the air jet begins to spin turbulently beyond the constriction. If the air jet strikes the teeth or lip, additional high-frequency turbulence noise will be generated. Fricatives may be separated in strident [s, z, ʃ, ʒ] and nonstrident [f, v, θ, ð] groups on the basis of the extra-high-frequency turbulence generated upon

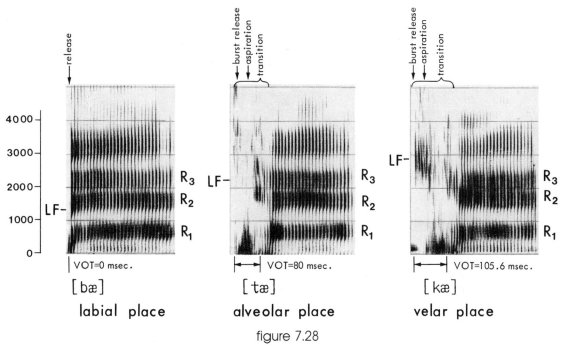

figure 7.28
Spectrograms of stop consonant, CV, syllables. Illustrated are the
burst, aspiration, and transition phases of the stop consonant,
as well as VOT and locus frequency for each consonant.

striking a tooth or lip obstruction. Figure 7.29 shows the strident fricatives. The alveolar [s, z] have a low-frequency cutoff of 3500 to 4000 Hz, whereas [ʃ, ʒ] have energy down to about 2000 Hz. The [s, z] noise is higher pitched, "hissier," than [ʃ] and [ʒ]. The fricatives are of long duration, and the noise is quite intense. Small transitions can be seen between the noise and the steady state vowel in these syllables. Observe further that the [ʃ] and [ʒ] noises show a broad resonance (heavily damped) in the noise spectrum at about 2500 Hz, whereas [s] shows a broad resonance at about 4800 Hz. By comparison, the nonstrident fricatives shown in Figure 7.30 reveal weak intensity and short duration noises, with very clear transitions into the vowel. The noise for these fricatives is so weak and often nondistinguishing that listeners rely upon the transitions to differentiate between [f] and [θ]. The affricates seen in Figure 7.30 show a sharp, burstlike release into a short but intense fricative noise, demonstrating clearly why Ladefoged classifies them as having a +fricative, +stop manner of production.

Nasals   The nasal consonants may be classified as approximants or as stops. If the oral closure during nasal sounds is released rapidly, the resulting sharp shift in resonance frequency during the transition is quite stoplike. During the production of nasal sounds, the air path to the nares

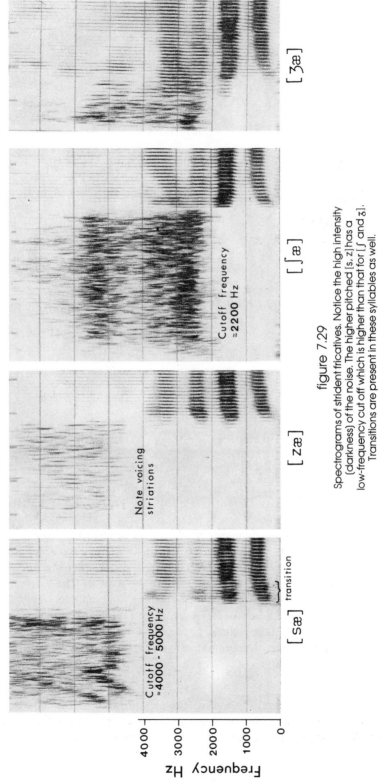

figure 7.29

Spectrograms of strident fricatives. Notice the high intensity (darkness) of the noise. The higher pitched [s, z] has a low-frequency cut off which is higher than that for [ʃ and ʒ]. Transitions are present in these syllables as well.

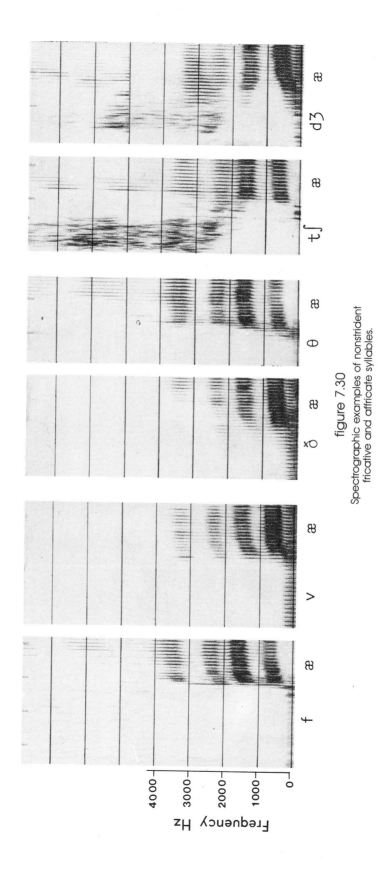

figure 7.30

Spectrographic examples of nonstrident
fricative and affricate syllables.

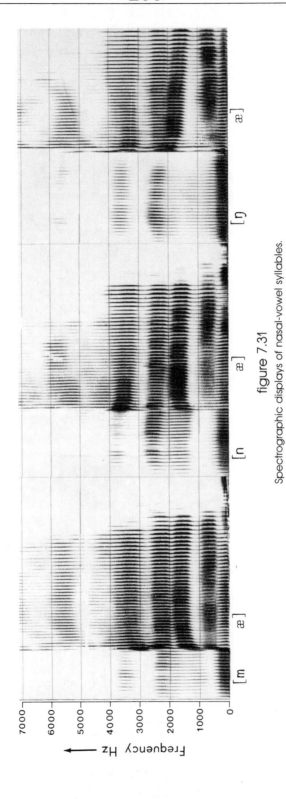

figure 7.31

Spectrographic displays of nasal-vowel syllables.

is longer than for an oral air path; the nasal cavities also have an enormous surface area as well as many side branches (sinuses). The soft mucosal lining of the large nasal surfaces acts as an acoustic damper because it absorbs acoustic energy, especially at higher frequencies. In addition, the closed oral cavity acts as a side-branch resonator that introduces an antiresonance into the nasal spectrum. The combination of low resonance frequencies because of a long vocal tract tube, strong high-frequency damping, and antiresonances in the mid-frequency region yield a distinctive "nasal" sound. The so-called nasal murmur is characterized by a strong, very low-frequency component in the region of 0 to 300 Hz, an antiresonance between 500 and 1000 Hz, and little high-frequency energy (see Figure 7.31).

The nasal consonants have a strong effect upon surrounding vowels through the process of coarticulation of nasality. Because of the presence of the nasal consonant, velopharyngeal opening occurs for surrounding vowels. The open velopharyngeal port introduces resonances, antiresonances, and strong high-frequency damping into the vowel spectrum. Nasalized vowels reveal an upward shift in resonances, a reduction of high-frequency energy, increased resonance bandwidths, and antiresonances. Only when consonants suffer nasalization, or when vowels not adjacent to nasals are nasalized, are there serious problems with the quality of speech.

Liquids and Glides

Figure 7.32 shows spectrograms of the liquid and glide approximant consonants. All four approximant consonants are characterized by strong, clear resonances. Only [l] reveals the suggestion of a "burst" release at the moment the central constriction is opened. The [r] sound

figure 7.32

Spectrographic displays of liquid and glide approximant consonants.

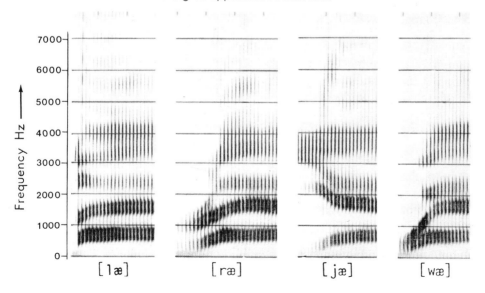

[læ] [ræ] [jæ] [wæ]

is characterized by a retroflexive raising of the tongue tip toward the palatal region, as well as a dorsal constriction near the pharyngeal wall and a moderate degree of lip rounding. The net result is that the vocal tract appears to be constricted into three tubes. The unique resonance pattern for [r] includes R_2 and R_3 being very close together and very low in frequency. This can be seen in Figure 7.32, where R_2 and R_3 are no more than 600 Hz apart in frequency and occupy the frequency region of 1000 to 1600 Hz. Acoustically equivalent [r] sounds can be made with a variety of tongue postures, so that it is difficult to specify an "ideal" articulation. In American English dialect, [r] can function consonantally, such as [r] in "red"; vocally, such as [ɝ] in "bird" or [ɚ] in "butter"; or in a diphthongal fashion, as in "bear" or "buyer." Hence, it is difficult to argue that there is a single, simple /r/ phoneme. Rather, the syllabic function dictates which [r] sound will appear.

The [l] sound is characterized by an apical alveolar closure, with the sides of the tongue down and open so that the oral passageway splits bilaterally into two tubes before rejoining as a single central airway beyond the constriction. In word-final position, [l] is articulated with an additional constriction between the dorsum and the soft palate, such as [ɫ] in "pill." Acoustically, the [l] sound has R_1 and R_2 close together in the region 350 to 900 Hz, with lesser energy in the upper portion of the spectrum; the splitting of the airway into two tubes causes an antiresonance. Figure 7.32 shows that [l] and [r] differ most significantly in that R_3 moves very little for [l], but glides upward rapidly for [r] during the transition toward the vowel.

The glides, the labiovelar [w] and palatal [j], are characterized by formant frequency patterns similar to the vowels [u] and [i]. Compare the resonances for [u] and [w], and for [j] and [i], by comparing Figures 7.17 and 7.32. The [w] resembles [u] closely, whereas the resonance pattern of [j] resembles [i] closely. Both glides are characterized by a short, quasi-steady-state resonance period followed by a relatively long gliding of resonances toward the values for the oncoming vowel.

conclusion

We have completed a survey of the articulatory and acoustic characteristics of the speech sounds of English. The survey is far from complete. Worse yet, human beings speak in *streams* of overlapping, interconnected sound. Even children who are mastering a new speech sound do not first produce it in isolation as a single sound. Rather, they produce it as part of a word or syllable. Dynamic speech differs strongly from static productions. In the next chapter, we will first discuss how dynamic differs from static speech, both in terms of how the static segments change, and in terms of the new articulatory and suprasegmental parameters which dynamic, flowing speech introduces. Following that, we will discuss various aspects of dynamic speech which must be taken into account by any proposed model of dynamic speech behavior. We will conclude with a discussion of several models of dynamic speech production.

SUGGESTED READINGS

FANT, G. *Acoustic Theory of Speech Production.* The Hague: Mouton, 1960. Undoubtedly, the most renowned book in all of acoustic phonetics. In it the author presents the acoustic theory that accounts for the nature of speech sounds. Very technical in nature.

FANT, G. *Speech Sounds and Features.* Cambridge, Mass.: MIT Press, 1973. Advanced reading. The collected research and writings of an eminent phonetician, and a formidable analysis of the acoustic characteristics of sounds and their features.

FLANAGAN, J. L. *Speech Analysis, Synthesis and Perception,* Vol. 2. Berlin: Springer Verlag, 1975. A highly technical view of the acoustic nature of speech by a telephone engineer.

FLETCHER, H. *Speech and Hearing in Communication.* New York: Van Nostrand, 1953. A collection of early research into the acoustics and perception of speech. Parts are easy to read and still highly informative concerning the acoustic characteristics of vowels and consonants.

JACOBSON, R., G. FANT, and M. HALLE. *Preliminaries to Speech Analysis.* Cambridge, Mass.: MIT Press, 1963. A classic monograph in which the authors set forth an acoustically based theory of distinctive features.

LADEFOGED, P. *Preliminaries to Linguistic Phonetics.* Chicago: University of Chicago Press, 1971. An invaluable linguistic evaluation and presentation of consonant and vowel feature systems, classificatory systems, and the nature of phonetic theory.

LADEFOGED, P. *A Course in Phonetics.* New York: Harcourt Brace Jovanovich, 1975. A highly readable text incorporating spectrograms, pronunciation and transcription exercises, and clear, precise descriptions of the articulation of the sounds of English.

LASS, M. J., ed. *Contemporary Issues in Experimental Phonetics.* New York: Academic Press, 1976. A fine survey of the state of the art of experimental phonetics, with excellent chapters on the acoustics and physiology of speech sound articulation.

LEHISTE, I. *Readings in Acoustic Phonetics.* Cambridge, Mass.: MIT Press, 1967. The classic compilation of original research articles that define the acoustic characteristics of speech.

LIBERMAN, A. M. "Some Results of Research on Speech Perception," *Journal of the Acoustical Society of America,* 29 (1957), 117–123. A fine survey of the perceptually important acoustic cues used in the perception of consonant sounds.

LIEBERMAN, P. C. *Speech Physiology and Acoustic Phonetics.* New York: Macmillan, 1977. A new and readable survey of speech production, perception, and acoustics that can serve as an alternate to this text for readers wishing alternative points of view with a linguistic bias; also contains a valuable description of spectographic analysis.

PETERSON, G. E., and H. L. BARNEY. "Control Methods Used in a Study of Vowels," *Journal of the Acoustical Society of America,* 24 (1952), 175–184. A most famous acoustic-phonetic article; classic description of the acoustic characteristics of vowel sounds.

PETERSON, G. E., and J. E. SHOUP. "A Physiological Theory of Phonetics: The Elements of an Acoustic Phonetic Theory," *Journal of Speech and Hearing Research,* 9 (1966), 5–99. For students interested in the principles behind the classification of vowels, consonants, features, and so on, this integrated theory of phonetics will be valuable reading.

POTTER, R. K., G. A. KEOPP, and H. GREEN. *Visible Speech*. New York: Dover Books, 1947. A useful spectrographic survey of all of the sounds and many of the syllables of English. A reference for anyone interested in the spectrography of speech.

SHOUP, J. E., and L. PFEIFFER. "Acoustic Characteristics of Speech Sounds." In N. J. Lass (ed.), *Contemporary Issues of Experimental Phonetics*. New York: Academic Press, 1976. A comprehensive survey of the acoustic characteristics of speech sounds.

STEVENS, K. N., and A. S. HOUSE. "Development of a Quantitative Description of Vowel Articulation," *Journal of the Acoustical Society of America*, 27 (1955), 484–493. The article in which the authors present a three-parameter model of vowel articulation.

ARTICULATION: DYNAMICS

8

Dynamics is a branch of physics that describes how forces cause the movements of mechanical structures. The human body is a complex biomechanical system that moves under the influence of muscular forces. The study of body motions caused by applied forces, especially muscular forces, is called biomechanics. The production of continuous speech involves the skillful coordination of a serially ordered* stream of steadily changing articulatory, laryngeal, and respiratory movements. In the opinion of Karl Lashley, the gestalt (overall pattern) of muscular movements for speech is the most complex and skillful neural and physical activity that human beings display. This is a sweeping claim with which we hope you may sympathize after reading this chapter.

Humans act upon themselves and their surroundings with their muscles. When muscles contract, they exert forces on the body that cause it to move and in turn to exert force on the environment. Most machines are extensions of our bodies and muscles. When we move our bodies through space, we rely heavily on feedback from our senses of sight, hearing, and balance to guide us. These senses are *exteroceptory*—that is, they provide information about the world outside the body. Speech is rather unique as a muscular behavior because it involves motion of the articulators through the "inner space" of the vocal tract, which is entirely inside the body. This motion is guided by both exteroceptory and somesthetic sensory feedback. Somesthetic feedback involves such senses as touch, limb position, and pain. The somesthetic receptors provide sensory feedback about the interior of the body.

Both sensory systems provide "conscious" feedback—that is, we are consciously aware of them. Certain types of sensory feedback do not ascend to the level of consciousness in the brain. For example, we are not aware of the CO_2

*Serial order refers to a process in which one object, event, or action follows another in time.

level of our blood, although there are chemo-receptors which monitor it and provide precise feedback to the neural centers that control breathing. One important source of somesthetic feedback of which we are not ordinarily conscious arises from the muscle spindle stretch receptors, which monitor the length, tension, and velocity of stretch of muscle fibers and relay it to the central nervous system. Recent work (Matthews, 1977) appears to show that muscle spindles contribute to kinesthesia; that is, feedback from muscle spindles concerning the tension on them signals to the person information concerning the position of the limbs and joints. As such, spindle sensation is a part of the "conscious" system of somesthetic sensory feedback.

Movements within the inner space of the vocal tract are also guided by the auditory feedback derived from hearing ourselves talk. Vocal tract movements and resulting vocal tract shapes create predictable and perceptibly different speech sounds. Speakers monitor the success or failure of articulatory movements by listening to the quality of the resulting sounds. As a result, we both *hear* and *feel* our articulatory movements.

Some of the reasons why we are so immensely skillful at producing the stream of movements for speech include the following: (1) *The articulatory space is within our body;* (2) *the space is small in size;* (3) *there are a limited number of possible articulatory motions within that space;* and (4) *speakers practice each movement pattern an enormous number of times.* When a skilled muscular movement like speech is practiced many thousands of times, it becomes a habit, and we lose awareness of the complexity of the behavior. Such well-practiced, overlearned behavior is typical of speech. It is important to keep in mind that articulatory movement is linguistically motivated. As we emphasized in Chapter 3, the intent to communicate by speaking is guided by a linguistic system which we have acquired by daily contact with our language community.

If we treat speech a bit more abstractly, we can say that the output of the speech production system is a *stream* of speech sounds. Each different speech sound represents a different vocal tract output. It has become common to call each unit of vocal tract output a *target sound* or "target." In this chapter we wish to discuss how targets are achieved in continuous speech. To begin the discussion of continuous articulation, it is useful to examine the source of all movement — muscle tissue.

muscle tissue: structure and function

Some simple definitions and facts concerning the structure of muscle tissue and muscle contraction are needed to understand articulatory movements (see also Chapter 2). The process of contraction causes movement of the body. Muscles are composed of tiny fibers, ranging from 1 to 120 mm in length and .01 to .1 mm in diameter. Each fiber is composed of bundles of even smaller myofibrillae en-

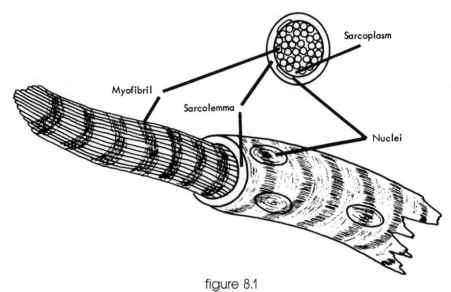

figure 8.1

A schematic view of the structure of muscle fiber within a muscle
body. Reprinted by permission from W. R. Zemlin,
Speech and Hearing Science: Anatomy and Physiology.
© 1968 by Prentice-Hall, Inc.

cased in a matrix of sarcoplasm (Figure 8.1). The sarcoplasm is enclosed by a delicate membrane called the sarcolemma. The individual muscle fibers are bundled
into functional groups, or fasiculi, by a connective tissue called endomysium. At
either end, muscle fibers are attached to tendons, to the periosteal covering of
bones, or to the perichondral covering of cartilage. When muscle fibers are excited
into a state of contraction, they can force the movable structures to which they are
attached into motion. The motion of the body part is limited by (1) the force of
muscle contraction, (2) the mass of the moving parts, (3) the mechanical structure
of the moving part, and (4) the viscoelastic properties of the moving parts, including the muscles, tendons, and joints.

Each muscle body extends from an origin (initial point of attachment) to an
insertion (final point of attachment). During contraction, a muscle fiber shortens, *decreasing* the distance between its points of origin and insertion, generally by causing rotation of structures at a joint. Demonstrate this by contracting the muscles of your arm slowly so that your arm bends at the elbow.
As you can see, muscle fibers attached to jointed bones or cartilages cause
movement of these structures at the joints. If the muscle fibers are attached to
fibrous tissue or to other muscles, as is the case for certain muscles of the lips
and tongue, contraction of muscle fibers causes the soft tissue to move. Test
this by puckering your lips and then by smiling. As the muscles contract, they
grow stiffer and their mechanical properties change. Because muscles often pull
against or upon other muscles, the mechanical load against which the contracting muscle pulls (and the resulting movement) depends on the state of contraction of the muscles against which it is tugging.

Muscles as Lever Systems   Human skeletal muscles force the movable bones of the body to act as levers. The bones are the lever arms, and the joint between the two bones is the fulcrum. As Zemlin notes, two classes of lever systems are of interest to the student of speech science. Certain levers obtain amplification of force (mechanical advantage) by sacrificing speed, whereas others obtain amplification of speed at the price of loss of force (mechanical disadvantage). Muscles display an architectural arrangement of their fibers; certain muscles are designed for speedy contraction through long distances, whereas other muscles are more suited for power. Most of the bones and cartilages of the body are attached to more than one muscle. Because of this, the result of a single muscle's contraction (the speed, direction of motion, and distance traveled by the moving body part) depends on what all the other muscles attached to that structure are doing. As an analogy, picture six or seven ropes (muscles) attached to a car (bone). If people tug on all seven ropes, the direction and speed with which the car moves depends on the number of ropes pulled, the direction in which they are pulled, and the force with which each is pulled. During speech production, when dozens of muscle groups may be active within seconds, it is often difficult to determine accurately what the mechanical load of a given muscle is, since the load depends on the potential contribution of so many other muscles. This is particularly the case for the muscles of the tongue and larynx.

Muscles exert force by contracting in only one direction. Thus, if a bone is to move upon its joint in more than one direction, pairs of opposing muscles must be attached to that bone. One muscle causes movement in one direction, while the other member of the pair tugs in the opposite direction. Demonstrate this by swiftly opening your lips with one set of muscles and closing them with another set. Then rapidly flex and extend your index finger, observing that one set of muscles open and another closes it. One of the opposing pair or set of muscles is called the *agonist;* the other which opposes it is called the *antagonist.* Figure 8.2 shows such a pair: the masseter and the anterior belly of the digastric. The masseter elevates the mandible, while contraction of the anterior belly of the digastric lowers it. During swift to and fro movements of a structure, the nervous system appears to suppress activity in one member of the pair for motion in one direction, and in the other for the opposite motion.

Rapid movement of body structures occurs when either agonist or antagonist alone, but not both, contract strongly. The moving structure accelerates swiftly and stops only when it strikes another structure or when it reaches the elastic limits of the moving joint or surrounding soft tissue. These rapid, relatively less-precise but swift motions have been called *ballistic* motion. A ballistically moving structure follows a *trajectory,* as the path of motion is called, characterized by swift acceleration, high velocity, and sharp deceleration. The very swiftness can reduce the precision with which the person can guide that movement. Try this yourself by flicking your finger outward as if you were flicking off a troublesome insect or a lint ball. A swift motion indeed, but not a most precisely controlled one. Many articulatory movements are relatively ballistic, with speed, but not precision, being at a premium.

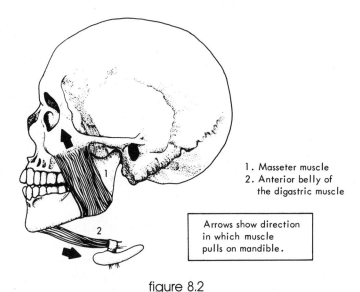

1. Masseter muscle
2. Anterior belly of
   the digastric muscle

Arrows show direction
in which muscle
pulls on mandible.

figure 8.2

An agonist-antagonist pair of mandibular muscles. The
masseter raises the mandible while the anterior
belly of the digastric muscle lowers it.

If a precise motion of the structure is needed, speed is traded for accuracy. Slower and more precise motions occur when both agonist and antagonist contract simultaneously against each other but with unequal strength. The motion that results is slower, since the two muscles oppose each other so that only a small net force causes the movement. Such accurate motion occurs in articulation when the tongue forms a precise fricative slit for production of [s] noise. Lack of precision can result in distorted [s] production. A lesser price is paid during a swift stop-consonant closure if the trajectory of closure is somewhat imprecise, since speed is of the essence.

Because there are often many muscles attached to a structure such as the mandible or tongue, the muscle most responsible for causing the desired movement is called the *prime mover*. Those muscles that act to stabilize the structure as it moves, and after it achieves its final position, are called *fixation muscles*. Muscles that cooperate directly in achieving a desired motion are said to be *synergists*.

The Motor Unit   The smallest individually controllable group of muscle fibers is the motor unit (see Figure 8.3). The motor unit consists of a motor nerve cell (neuron) connected to a group of muscle fibers. The axon of the motor neuron approaches the muscle fibers, then divides into a number of fibrils, each of which terminates at a muscle endplate. The endplates are in close but not direct physical contact with the muscle fibers of the motor unit. A given motor neuron may supply as few as several or as many as several hundred muscle fibers. When the motor nerve is excited, a wave of electrical depolarization sweeps down the axon, reaching the motor endplates. At the endplate, an enzyme is released and swiftly arouses the muscle to contraction. All the muscle fibers in the motor unit contract simultaneously, with one contraction occurring per neural impulse arriving from the neuron. A smooth, steady contraction of an entire muscle is caused by the summation in time of many individual motor unit contractions. When muscle fibers contract, their electrical potential becomes negative relative to surrounding tissue. This change in electrical potential, which can be recorded by an electrode located near or within the muscle, is called the *electromyographic (EMG) potential.* The strength with which a muscle body

figure 8.3

A schematic display of a complete muscle motor unit including the efferent motor neuron and its associated motor endplates. Reprinted by permission from W. R. Zemlin, *Speech and Hearing Science: Anatomy and Physiology.* © 1968 by Prentice-Hall, inc.

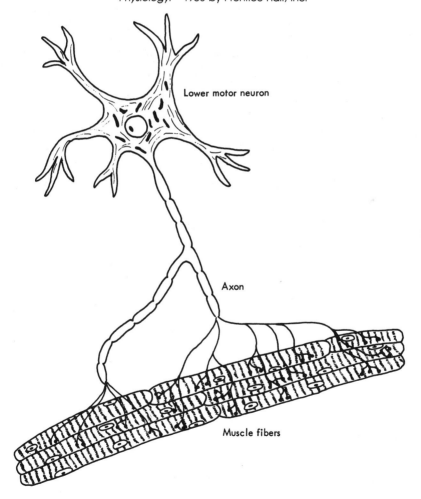

Lower motor neuron

Axon

Muscle fibers

contracts depends upon how many motor units are active and how fast the neurons are discharging. The faster (more frequently) motor nerve impulses arrive at the muscle endplates, the greater is the overall force of the contraction. If more muscle force is needed, more motor units are activated and an increasing rate of motor nerve impulsation is used.

The number of muscle fibers in a motor unit, the so-called innervation ratio, can be used in a general way to predict the precision of muscle contraction. When a muscle with a high innervation ratio such as the leg muscle is stimulated, each motor neuron activates many muscle fibers, and the resulting contraction results in large, relatively imprecise movements. For muscles whose innervation ratio is low, such as those of the eye or tongue tip, the smaller motor units allow smaller, finer movements, since fewer muscle fibers are activated by a single neuron. Most of the musculature in the vocal tract has a relatively low innervation ratio, which indicates that these muscles are capable of rapid *and* precise movements.

serial ordering of behavior and the control of speech: Lashley's contribution

In 1951, Karl Lashley brilliantly summarized possible control patterns involved when a speaker produces a serially ordered stream of complex, articulatory movements. Speech is a superb example of serially ordered neuromotor behavior. The production of each speech sound involves a gestalt of neural activity in the brain, which in turn causes a complex pattern of muscle contractions to occur within the vocal tract. Suppose the sounds are to be spoken not separately, but as a single word, "Pat." The speaker serially orders the sounds by producing [p] first, [æ] second, and [t] last; he or she does so not in a jerky or clumsy way but in a smooth, temporally integrated, coarticulated fashion. How do they do it, and how can this complex behavior be explained?

Speaking involves the "orderly arrangement of *thought* and *muscle action*," said Lashley, and "Speech consists of predetermined, orderly sequences of action which are unique for each language." In other words, each differing language has a unique grammar that governs the orderly relationship of phrases, constituents, morphemes, phonemes, and features. In fact, he claimed that "grammar is the most direct approach to the physiology of the cortex," and quotes Fournie to the effect that "Speech is the only window through which the physiologist can view the cerebral life." Any explanation of serially ordered behavior must account for how behaviors are *placed* in temporal order — that is, why one word follows another, why one sound follows another, and so on. Such temporally integrated actions appear in great complexity only if the animal has a cerebral cortex.

Stimulus-response (SR) theorists argued that successive, serially ordered behaviors are temporally ordered via a chain of reflexes in which the performance of each element of the series causes excitation in the next unit. So, for example, in saying the name "Paul," production of [p] yields feedback that stimulates release of [ɔ], which in turn triggers the release of movement for [ɫ]. Thus, Lashley (1951) says, speech is a "succession of vocal acts in which kinesthetic impulses (feedback) from each movement (sound) serve as a unique stimulus for the next in the series," and "verbal thought is a simple chain process in which each element serves to arouse the next." An example of this stimulus response process of serial ordering of units is shown in Figure 8.4.

The SR model is unsatisfactory for a number of reasons. For example, take the pronunciation of the word "pit." First, the lips are closed and oral air pressure rises. As the lips open with an explosion of air, the tongue is raised to a position near the palate simultaneously with the onset of glottal buzzing for the vowel [ɪ], after which the tongue tip is raised to make contact on the alveolar ridge, and the vocal folds open for the voiceless [t]. These motor movements need not follow each other in the order given in the word "pit"; articulation of the word "tip" involves production of the same movements in reverse order. Thus, the order in which the movements occur must be imposed upon the motor movements, by some organizing factor other than the direct SR associative connections between them:

> So, too, for the individual movements in writing or typing the word, finger strokes occur in all combinations. No single letter invariably follows g, and whether gh, ga, or gu is written depends upon a set for a larger unit of action, the word.

figure 8.4

A diagram illustrating how each sound, as it is produced, generates kinesthetic feedback which triggers production of the next sound.

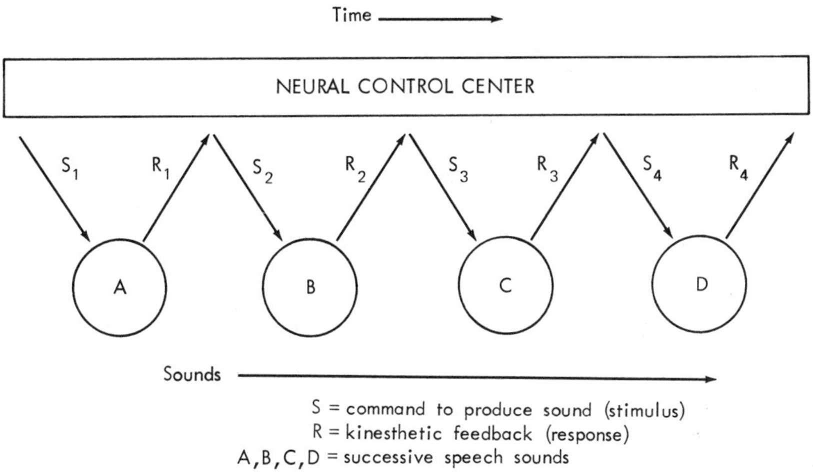

Time ──────▶

NEURAL CONTROL CENTER

S₁ R₁ S₂ R₂ S₃ R₃ S₄ R₄

A   B   C   D

Sounds ──────────────────────────▶

S = command to produce sound (stimulus)
R = kinesthetic feedback (response)
A,B,C,D = successive speech sounds

Lashley then examined the serial ordering of words in speech and made the following observations:

> Words stand in relation to the sentence as letters do to the word; the words themselves have no intrinsic temporal "valence." The word "right," for example, is noun, adjective, adverb, and verb, and has four spellings and at least ten meanings. In such a sentence as "The mill-wright on my right thinks it right that some conventional rite should symbolize the right of every man to write as he pleases," word arrangement is obviously not due to any direct associations of the word "right" itself with other words, but to meanings which are determined by some broader relations.
>
> It has been found in studies of memorization of nonsense syllables that each syllable in the series has associations, not only with adjacent words in the series, but also with more remote words. The words in the sentence have, of course, associations with more remote words. However, the combination of such direct associations will not account for grammatical structure. The different positions of the word "right" in the illustrative sentence are determined by the meanings which the positions in relation to other words denote, but those meanings are given by other associations than those with the words in the spoken sentence. The word can take its position only when the particular one of its ten meanings becomes dominant. This dominance is not inherent in the words themselves. (Lashley, 1951)

To emphasize his point, Lashley offered the famous example, "Rapid $\begin{Bmatrix} \text{writing} \\ \text{righting} \end{Bmatrix}$ with his uninjured left hand was the only thing which saved the contents of the canoe from capsizing." Notice that the word "righting," which could have been interpreted as "writing," stands in strong and intimate association with the noun "canoe," even though 15 words separate them. It is highly unlikely that a given word serves to trigger the appearance of the word next to it in serial ordering via a feedback loop. If this were so, "canoe" would be most strongly associated with the word "the." As Lashley (1951) concluded:

> From such considerations, it is certain that any theory of grammatical form which ascribes it to direct associative linkage of words of the sentence overlooks the essential structure of speech. The individual items of the temporal series do not in themselves have a temporal "valence" in their associative connections with other elements. This order is imposed by some other agent.
>
> This is true not only of language but of all skilled movements or successions of movement. In the gaits of a horse, trotting, pacing, and single footing involve essentially the same pattern of muscular contraction in the individual legs. The gait is imposed by some mechanism in addition to the direct relations of reciprocal innervation among the sensory-motor centers of the legs.

Lashley then argued that the ordering of any unit of behavior is governed by a *hierarchical structure* (or set of rules) similar to those found for the grammar of a language:

> I have devoted so much time to discussion of the problem of syntax, not only because language is one of the most important products of human cerebral action, but also because the problems raised by the organization of language seem to me to be characteristic of almost all other cerebral activity. There is a series of movements in pronouncing the word, the order of words in the sentence, the order of sentences in the paragraph, the rational order of paragraphs in a discourse. Not only speech, but all skilled acts seem to involve the same problems of serial ordering even ... the mechanism which determines the serial activation of the motor units is relatively independent, both of the motor units and of the thought structure.

The grammar of a language provides the ordering of speech units; when the time comes for a sentence to be translated into a sequence of movements, a large chunk of the sentence is held in storage and run off in serial order in a single sweep. Said Lashley:

> There are indications that, prior to the internal or overt enunciation of the sentence, an aggregate of word units is partially activated or readied. Evidence for this comes also from "contaminations" of speech and writing. The most frequent typing errors are those of anticipation; the inclusion in the word being typed of some part of a word or word structure which should properly occur later in the sentence. It may only be a letter. Thus I wrote *wrapid* writing, carrying the *w* from the second word to the first. Not infrequently words are introduced which should occur much later in the sentence, often five or six words in advance.
>
> In oral speech, Spoonerisms illustrate the same kind of contamination. The Spoonerism is most frequently an inversion of subject and object: "Let us always remember that waste makes haste." But it may be only a transposition of parts of the words: "Our queer old dean" for "our dear old queen." The frequency with which such contaminations occur is increased by haste, by distraction, by emotional tension, or by uncertainty and conflict as to the best form of expression. In these contaminations, it is as if the aggregate of words were in a state of partial excitation, held in check by the requirements of grammatical structure, but ready to activate the final common path, if the effectiveness of this check is in any way interfered with.

Lashley then noticed that a timing mechanism was required to control temporally ordered sequences of movement, so that units of speech followed in a correct *tempo* and rhythm. He used music as a way of demonstrating how rhythm provides a timing mechanism, even for speech:

> *The simplest timing mechanisms are those controlling rhythmic activity.* Musical rhythms seem to be an elaboration of the same sort of thing. The time or beat is started and maintained at some definite rate, say 160 per minute. This rate is then imposed upon various activities. The fingers of the musician fall in multiples of the basic rate. If the leader of a quartet speeds up the time or retards, all the movements of the players change in rate accordingly. Not only the time of initiation but also the rate of movement is affected.
>
> There are, in addition, still less regular rhythms of phrasing and emphasis. Parallels to these can be found in speech. The skilled extemporaneous speaker rounds his phrases and speaks with a definite though not regular rhythm.
>
> The rhythms tend to spread to almost every other concurrent activity. One falls in step with a band, tends to breathe, and even to speak in time with the rhythm. The all-pervasiveness of the rhythmic discharge is shown by the great difficulty of learning to maintain two rhythms at once, as in three against four with the two hands. The points to be emphasized here are the widespread effects of a rhythmic discharge indicating the involvement of almost the entire effector system, the concurrent action of different rhythmic systems, and the imposition of the rate upon both the initiation and speed of movement. Consideration of rhythmic activity ... forces the conclusion, I believe, that there exist in the nervous organization, elaborate systems of interrelated neurons capable of imposing certain types of integration upon a large number of widely spaced effector elements.

Lashley's insight is further evidenced in his argument that movement patterns could be organized in terms of spatial targets:

> ... work has shown that the *tonic discharge to every muscle in the postural system is influenced by afferent impulses from every other muscle toward increased or decreased activity, according to its synergic or antergic action.* To these influences are

added vestibular and cerebellar effects. Diagrammatically these mutual influences of the muscular system may be represented by separate reflex circuits from each receptor to every muscle, as Sherrington (21, p. 148) has done.

This postural system is based on excitations from proprioceptors. The distance receptors impose an additional set of space coordinates upon the postural system, which in turn continually modifies the coordinates of the distance receptors. The dropped cat rights itself, if either the eyes or the vestibular senses are intact, but not in the absence of both. The direction of movement on the retina imposes a directional orientation on the postural system. Conversely, the gravitational system imposes an orientation on the visual field. Upright objects such as trees or the corners of a room appear upright, at no matter what angle the head is inclined. Derangement of the vestibular system can disturb the distance orientation or the orientation of the receptors, as in the apparent swaying of the vertical as a result of the after-images of motion following hours of rocking in a small boat.

Finally, there is a still more plastic system in which the concepts of spatial relations can be voluntarily reversed, as when one plays blindfold chess alternately from either side of the board. ... I wish to emphasize only the existence of these systems of space coordinates. *Their influences pervade the motor system so that every gross movement of limbs or body is made with reference to the space system. The perceptions from the distance receptors, vision, hearing and touch are also constantly modified and referred to the same space coordinates.* The stimulus is there, in a definite place; it has definite relation to the position of the body, and it shifts with respect to the sense organ but not with respect to the general orientation, with changes in body posture.

Lashley, then, perhaps incorrectly, reasoned that the complex movements involved in serially ordered movement could be controlled without the use of feedback:

This independence of sensory controls is true not only of intensity and duration of contraction of a synergic muscle group but is true also of the initiation and timing of contraction of the different muscles in a complex movement. The hand may describe a circular movement involving coordinated contractions of the muscles of the shoulder, elbow, and wrist in about 1/10 second, and the stopping of movement at a given position, of course, is only a small fraction of that time. The finger strokes of a musician may reach sixteen per second in passages which call for a definite and changing order of successive finger movements. The succession of movements is too quick even for visual reaction time. In rapid sight reading it is impossible to read the individual notes of an arpeggio. The notes must be seen in groups, and it is actually easier to read chords seen simultaneously and to translate them into temporal sequence than to read successive notes in the arpeggio as usually written.

Sensory control of movement seems to be ruled out in such acts. They require the postulation of some central nervous mechanism which fires with predetermined intensity and duration or activates different muscles in predetermined order.

Lashley's thinking concerning the problem of the serial ordering of complex movements can be summarized as follows:

1. Simple associative stimulus-response linkages between one complex unit (feature, sound, word) and another will not automatically trigger the next movement or unit.

2. All serially ordered skilled movements or behaviors (speech, typing, playing an instrument, playing tennis) appear to demand the existence of a hierarchically organized motor control network, which in the case of language is grammar. Thus, grammar provides the serial order of speech, at least to the point where the sentence, consisting of a fully specified set of words and segments, is placed, chunk by chunk, into the motor-production system.

3. Speech movements stand in hierarchical order to sounds, sounds stand in hierarchical order to words, words in hierarchical order to clauses, clauses in hierarchical order to sentences, sentences in hierarchical order to meaning (thought).

4. The movements of the body in serially ordered motion are based on spatial targets (position in space). Thus, each speech sound, as the unit of movement, may have a spatial target. We will see later that we may organize the sound pattern of a language in terms of auditory images. Depending on context, each auditory image of an underlying segment can be translated into a series of motor commands needed to achieve this image.

5. The serial ordering of speech, at the neuromotor level, demands that a rhythm generator produce timing pulses which sequentially trigger the release of smooth chunks of speech movement.

6. The movements of speech are as complex or more complex than those for most other kinds of skilled motor behavior.

Lashley's conceptualization of the problems of serial ordering of movement is masterful. The issues of hierarchical order, organization based on large chunks of behavior, and the necessity for a complicated timing system are all *central* to any model of speech production, and we will discuss them in detail in the remainder of this chapter. Lashley erred in his notion that skilled serial order did not rely heavily on feedback because feedback is not fast enough to provide the information needed to modify control signals in rapid sequences of movement. But he worked in the 1930s and 1940s, when experimental phonetics, speech physiology, and linguistics were less developed and equipment and research techniques were far less sophisticated than they are today.

the output of the speech production mechanism*: continuous articulation

For most people, speech is a voluntary muscular activity — that is, we must consciously will to speak; the muscle activity does not occur in an automatic fashion as it does for breathing or for blinking of the eyes. Voluntary movements are purposeful. In order to understand speech movements, we must understand the results or "output" of these voluntary articulatory movements.

The purpose of vocal tract movement is to control airflow simultaneously with changing the shape of the vocal tract so that a stream of sound is created. The control of airflow is an aerodynamic purpose; the control of shape is an acoustic purpose. This is a very important point, since it means that the intent to speak implies *making sounds,* and the positions and movements of articulators are not ends in themselves but the *means* of making sounds. Sim-

---

*The speech production mechanism (SPM) consists of the muscles, tissues, and organs of the vocal tract, larynx and respiratory system, along with the associated portions of the central and peripheral nervous systems needed to control and direct their movements.

ilarly, the function of the respiratory mechanism is to provide compressed air as a source of power for speech production, while the phonation mechanism converts the potential energy of compressed air into the kinetic energy of acoustic vibration. When he or she talks, a speaker is using vocal tract musculature to achieve aerodynamic and acoustic variations that result in a steady flow of target speech sounds. Ordinarily, speakers are aware of the resulting sounds, but not of the physiological patterns of muscle contraction that alter the aerodynamic and resonance properties of the vocal tract.

ARTICULATORY TARGETS   Muscle contraction may cause the body to adopt a fixed or static position, or it may result in dynamic movement which involves a steady change of position. Demonstrate this for yourself in several ways. First, lift your arm and hold it straight in front of you. Although the arm is still and unmoving, the muscles of the arm maintain a steady, active contraction to overcome the force of gravity. Notice that the arm had to be moved from a "resting" position in order to achieve a "static target" position out in front of your body. For the articulators, a *static target* is a fixed position in three-dimensional space. Next, move your arm up and down as though waving goodbye. In this case, the target is not a fixed position, but a trajectory, a track through space, that defines a continuum of successive positions. A *dynamic target,* therefore, is a set of movements through three-dimensional space. Each phonation type is a potential phonational target, and each subglottal pressure or airflow may be a respirational target. In the case of the speech production mechanism (SPM), the targets are intended segments of sound. For the larynx, each target is the "voicing" for a segment. For the respiratory mechanism, the target is probably not a sound segment, but perhaps a phrase or whole sentence, and thus the target is suprasegmental.

It is our opinion that the targets a speaker seeks to achieve in speech are *speech sounds.* Suppose the word "seat" is spoken. Three successive targets must be attained in serial order: [s], then [i], then [t]. Once the tongue muscles have moved to create the steady slit constriction for [s], no further movement of the tongue is required for [s] production. Thus, [s] is a quasi-static target sound, as is [i], since both can be held indefinitely by keeping the tongue and lips in position. However, [t] is articulated with a swift closing movement of the tongue tip. The [t] target is a dynamic one because of the necessary movement toward closing and opening of the vocal tract. Examine the spectrograms for the diphthongs in Figure 7.20; notice there that the most important portion of the diphthong is not a fixed target position, but rather a smooth movement of the tongue and lips that results in a steadily shifting pattern of resonance frequencies, which is a dynamic acoustic target.

In continuous speech, a speaker can articulate 10 to 15 sounds per second, and still come very close to achieving every target sound. When someone fires a rifle at a bullseye, the distance between the bullseye and the bullet hole is the degree to which the target is missed (undershooting or overshooting). Accuracy is measured as the distance between the bullet hole and bullseye. For speech, there may be spatial, aerodynamic, and acoustic "target" values for each sound at which the speaker "aims" articulators. There are two ways of defining target sounds. If a speech sound is articulated by itself, in an isolated, sustained fashion, there are no contaminating contextual or coarticulatory influences of surrounding sounds in context, and there is plenty of time to move to the target. The assumption here is that at the input to the speech production mechanism, each target sound has an underlying ideal or "iconic" mental representation.

We may assume that the ideal underlying representation of each target sound is an *extrinsic allophone,* a phonetic segment in which each distinctive feature has been specified so that exact variations in each feature needed for linguistically correct production are present. For example, if the underlying extrinsic allophone is a voiced stop consonant, the feature (+voice) may well be specified very exactly as a neural command sufficient to produce a voice-onset time of +30 msec. Each of the distinctive features of the sound segment is sufficiently spelled out to represent what the speaker knows to be the linguistically appropriate way to produce the target sound. The accuracy with which a speaker achieves a target depends on several factors: *First,* accuracy depends on the size of the target. If the target is small, say a $\frac{1}{2}$ inch bullseye at 50 yards, extreme accuracy of aim is needed. If the target is a bullseye 10 yards square, then even a novice can hit it since a wide range of aims of the rifle will still result in hitting the target. This holds for speech as well. *Second,* the number of targets crowded into a given physical space is crucial. If a given language uses three places of palatal articulation for three distinctively differing underlying segments, the speaker will generally have to be quite careful in placing the tongue for the palatal constrictions, since only a narrow range of articulatory places and resulting resonance frequencies distinguishes the three target sounds. On the other hand, if there is only *one* palatal consonant, then the speaker need not be so precise, since the nearest neighboring sound is quite far away, and considerable variability in the position of palatal constriction is possible before the resonance frequency pattern could possibly overlap and cause confusion to the listener. Thus, the "accuracy" of target-seeking depends in a large part on how close or far away, articulatorily and hence acoustically, the other targets are in the speaker's sound pattern.

Third, acoustic theory predicts that there are many ways in which a single speech sound can be produced. For example, given a vocal tract length of 17 cm, if we wish to produce a vowel with a vocal tract length of 19 cm, we will have to lengthen the resting length of the vocal tract by 2 cm. We can do this by rounding the lip to increase the length of the lip orifice, or we can lower our larynx by a centimeter or two. Differing speakers could thus use lip or larynx or some differing combination of both on different occasions to get the vocal tract length needed to produce the desired vowel resonance frequencies.

With the three sources of variability associated with achieving a sequential target in mind, let us return to the ways in which experimenters have sought to minimize the variability in a target sound production. It seems likely that by removing phonetic context, and by speaking slowly, the resulting isolated sound is the best (target) representative of the mental image of the "phoneme" in the speaker's mind. Knowing the "target," we then can measure the effects of continuous speech as deviations from target. However, such a "target" is unnatural—we do not speak isolated, sustained sounds. Also, sounds such as stop consonants cannot be produced alone, without an accompanying vowel, since the minute that the stop closure is released, the speaker has opened the vocal tract for a vowel. Another way of defining a target is to take a statistical average of the articulator positions, airflow, air pressure, and so on. When the sound is produced in many differing phonetic and rate contexts. The effects of producing a sound with many differing neighboring sounds and at differing rates of speech can be averaged, and the mean or median value of articulator positions and acoustic and aerodynamic features can be calculated and used as the target values. Both the isolated sound production and the statistical average value are useful ways of describing targets.

TARGET PARAMETERS   Each target can be defined as a set of ideal articulatory and acoustic parameters. What these parameters are depends on the interests of the investigator. Below are some target parameters that have been measured and tabulated for target sounds.

1. *Articulatory parameters.* Positional data: The position and placement of lips, tongue, jaw, velum, pharynx in space either in static position or in terms of a dynamic trajectory if the articulation is a dynamic one. These measurements establish the place and manner of the target. Musculomechanical data: Electromyographic data on the timing and size of EMG discharge of the muscles, as well as measurement of the actual force of muscle contraction and measurements of the area of articulator contact over time.

2. *Phonational parameters.* Laryngeal vibration depends on the conditions under which speech occurs. The most common speaking conditions are conversational conditions, which are typified by a modest effort level and vocal loudness. Under these conditions, the intensity, frequency, and duration of laryngeal vibration (or any other noise source) may be measured for the target sound.

3. *Aerodynamic parameters.* Because the vocal tract is an air-driven device, pulmonic and intra-oral air pressure and flow can be measured for each target articulation to serve as aerodynamic targets.

4. *Acoustic parameters.* For each target sound, an acoustic analysis will reveal the duration, formant frequencies, noise bandwidths and resonance frequencies, intensity, and f_0 that characterize the acoustic pattern of the target sound.

As you can see, when a target value is established for a sound segment, it can be any one of many target measurements, each suitable for a different experimental purpose. When the speech pathologist listens to a speaker's speech, he or she compares the speaker's attempts at achieving speech sound targets to the "ideal" image of the sound stored in his or her memory. For reasons previously discussed, it appears that the targets speakers *aim* to achieve are best represented by the acoustic pattern of the speech sounds, and not the physiological-articulatory movements which create the sound.

TRANSITIONS   As speech sounds are produced in serial order, the speaker must move the articulators from target to target. To illustrate, examine the motion of the hands. Suppose that the two target positions of the hand are (1) fingers fully extended and with the hand totally open, palms up, and (2) the hand clenched in a fist. Examine each target position. Then swiftly move from open fingers to clenched fist. The entire swift movement between the two target positions is the transition. Transitions between speech sounds can be completed in a fraction of a second. If the two targets are very different in vocal tract shape or position, the transition movement may take a bit more time. Figure 8.5 presents the transition phenomena graphically. A string of speech sounds is shown as separate targets. When the sounds are articulated together in the stream of speech, a transitional movement must occur between one target and the next. Now demonstrate this behavior with your lips. Take the word "steel," and make each target sound independently, using no transitions. It should sound like [s] + [t] + [i] + [ɫ], four disconnected, choppy, separate sounds. They can be seen in Figure 8.6. Now produce the sounds together, smoothly, with transitions between them by speaking the word "steel." As you can see, the sounds are shorter, rapid transitions, indicated by the onset and bending of the vowel formants, are visible in the coarticulated word. No choppiness or long silences are heard as the articulators move smoothly from target to target during their transitions. Instead, the movement patterns for speech production involve a smooth and steady movement from target to target with transitional movements between one target and the next. The transition movements in speech are generally swift. For example, the transition between [p] and [i] in the word "Pete" may take as little as $\frac{1}{20}$ second.

See how many syllables per second you can produce by saying "ta-ta-ta" as fast as you can. If you can articulate 6 to 8 ta-ta-ta's per second, you have

figure 8.5

An illustration of the presence and function of transitions between serially ordered target sounds.

ISOLATED TARGET SOUNDS: NO TRANSITION

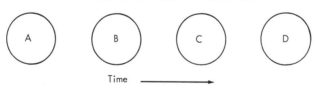

Time ⟶

CONTINUOUSLY ARTICULATED SOUND WITH TRANSITIONS

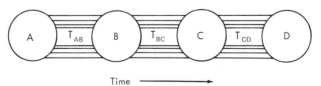

Time ⟶

A, B, C, D = target sounds

T_{AB}, T_{BC}, T_{CD} = transitions between sounds

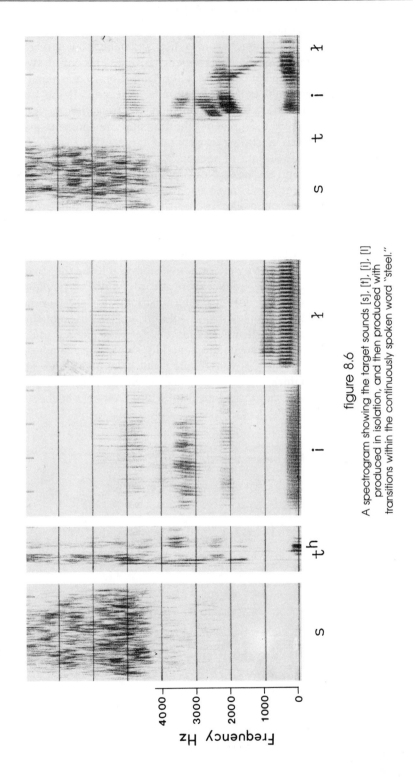

figure 8.6

A spectrogram showing the target sounds [s], [t], [i], [l]
produced in isolation, and then produced with
transitions within the continuously spoken word "steel."

produced a stream of about fourteen targets and thirteen transitions in less than a second. This is an amazing rapidity of motion, and yet it is quite ordinary for most people to articulate that swiftly on occasion. Depending on the size and strength of the articulators and their muscles, and depending on the age and health of the speaker, maximum speeds of movement have been established which reveal that an exceptional speaker can produce upwards of 25–30 target sounds per second. If you speak the word "indubitably" as fast as you can, in about $\frac{1}{2}$ second, you will have been speaking at a rate of 22 sounds per second, since the word contains 11 successive target sounds. Such rapidity represents phenomenal physical performance; we cannot strike typewriter or piano keys as fast as we can produce sounds in continuous speech.

In Chapter 7 we pointed out that transitions, rather than being a nuisance, carry much of the phonetic information in the speech signal. Stop consonants, glides, liquids, nasals, and even fricative consonants will often show transitions when adjacent to other consonants, although most phonetic information occurs in consonant-vowel transitions. Transitions serve as cues for the place of consonant production (the direction and rate of bending of the formants in the transition), voicing of stop consonants (voice onset time), and manner of production ([b, m, w] are distinguished by the rate at which the transition occurs).

Transitions appear to be relatively precisely timed. The speaker appears to make every effort to keep the duration of transitions relatively constant despite changes of rate of speech or changes in the surrounding phonetic context of a given sound. Thus, we may assume that transition movements, although not sounds in their own right, are crucial elements in the production of smooth, high-quality, intelligible speech. As such, the SPM appears to exercise great control over the guidance and timing of these movements.

SUPRASEGMENTAL ASPECTS OF CONTINUOUS SPEECH

Each speech sound is characterized by its set of segmental features. When a group of sounds is articulated in continuous speech the continuous stream of speech reveals new features, called suprasegmental features, which apply to units of speech larger than or different from the individual sound segment. The suprasegmental features and their associated physiological-acoustic features are listed in Table 8.1.

THE SYLLABLE

After the speech sound or segment, the next higher unit of phonological and physiological integration of speech is the syllable. Most suprasegmental features of speech apply to syllables or to streams of syllables. Most people have an intuitive "feel" for what a syllable is, but it is notoriously difficult to unambiguously define this unit. In general, the following properties of syllables, for English, are listed. First, each syllable generally consists of a vowel or vocalic nucleus. Each syllable nucleus has an onset and an offset formed by consonants or consonant clusters. The offset/onset regions, functionally, are points of greater vocal tract constriction than the vowel. Although a single vowel / V / can be a syllable, even a single vowel is

table 8.1
suprasegmental features

LINGUISTIC FEATURE	PHYSIOLOGICAL/ACOUSTIC CUE
Stress (emphasis or prominence of syllables)	Variations in duration, f_o, I_o, and target positions for a syllable
Intonation of sentence	Variations in f_o occurring as a pattern over an entire utterance
Rhythm	The pattern of stress accents placed on the stream of syllables in speech, along with variations in syllable duration
Juncture	Variations in f_o, I_o, and allophonic variations of sounds used to mark boundaries between syllables, words, and larger units
Tempo	The rate at which syllables are produced in the stream of speech

generally articulated with a glottal release and glottal offset—for example, [ʔaʔ] or [ʔaʔa], a sound which often is taken to mean "No, no!" The simplest syllable structure is the "open" syllable shape, with a consonantal onset and a glottal stop or breathy offset. A list of syllable shapes (structures) includes CCV, CCCV, CVC, CCVC, CCVCC, CVCC, CVCCC, CCCVC, CCCVCC, and so on. Syllables are interesting because the segment-ordering (phonotactic) rules on possible sound combination operate within them. For example, the [t s] consonant cluster is permitted only in final, postvocalic position ("pets"), whereas [sl] is permitted only initially, prevocalically, as in "slip." The cluster [st] may occur in both positions, as in "stop" and "post."

Syllables also appear to be the smallest speech unit that can be stressed. For example, if you say "sister" and stress the first syllable, you emphasize the entire syllable; you do not emphasize the consonant [s + ɪstɚ] or vowel [sɪstɚ] alone. Syllables are separated from each other by potential boundary signals called *junctures*. Since every utterance can be broken into a stream of syllables, all higher-level juncture boundaries between words, phrases, clauses, and sentences occur at syllable junctures. These boundaries are often, but not always, marked by pauses, variations in vocal pitch and intensity, and other signals. The tempo (rate) at which continuous speech is produced is commonly measured by measuring the number of syllables spoken per second. Thus, syllables appear to be a natural unit for the estimation of speech tempo. If we examine the distribution of stresses applied to a string of syllables in continuous speech, we also have the data needed to establish the rhythmic pattern of the speech.

It should be clear that the syllable, which combines important stress, rhythm, tempo, junctural, and phonotactic cues, is a key unit for the motor organization of speech. For that reason, we will discuss the role of syllabic units in the stream of speech in detail, since we will claim that syllables are a basic unit of articulation. Let us look first at an early attempt to conceptualize continuous speech as a modulated carrier signal similar to that used in TV and radio broadcasting.

THE CARRIER NATURE
OF CONTINUOUS SPEECH

To facilitate the beginning student's grasp of what is happening in dynamic, continuous speech production, it is useful to consider speech from an engineering point of view. The following conceptualization, proposed in 1939 by Homer Dudley, an engineer at Bell Telephone Laboratories, is still useful.

Radio and TV stations broadcast a modulated carrier signal. This powerful, high-frequency electromagnetic signal travels hundreds of miles through the atmosphere from the transmitter. At the radio station, the speech or music that constitutes the information signal and the carrier signal are passed through a modulating device. The information signal can be used either to *frequency* (FM) or *amplitude* (AM) modulate the carrier signal. During amplitude modulation, the amplitude of the carrier signal is forced to fluctuate with a waveform identical to that of the information signal (Figure 8.7). The amplitude-modulated carrier signal is transmitted to a receiver, where a demodulation circuit splits the signal back into the carrier signal and the information signal. The speech signal, as it were, rides piggyback on the carrier signal. In frequency modulating circuits, the instantaneous frequency of the carrier signal is caused to fluctuate at a rate proportional to the waveform of the information signal. The FM receiver demodulates the signal, separating the information signal from the carrier wave (Figure 8.7).

How does this apply to speech? We know that in continuous speech consonants carry more information than vowels. Consonants can therefore be compared to the information signal used to modulate a carrier signal. The vowels are acoustically powerful speech signals, made with an open, unconstricted vocal tract and buzzing larynx. Vowels can be compared to the carrier signal. Notice that every speech utterance can be broken into a string of con-

figure 8.7

An illustration of the process of amplitude modulation (AM) and frequency modulation (FM). Both the carrier and information signal, and the resulting modulated carrier signal, are shown.

INFORMATION SIGNAL   INFORMATION SIGNAL

Carrier signal   Amplitude modulated   Frequency modulated
                  carrier signal   carrier signal

sonans and vowels. For example, the sentence "She saw you" [ʃi + sɔ + ju] consists of $C_1V_1 + C_2V_2 + C_3V_3$. If vowels and consonants are separated, the utterance consists of a stream of vowels

$$\begin{bmatrix} i & \to & ɔ & \to & u \\ V_1 & & V_2 & & V_3 \end{bmatrix}$$

and consonants

$$\begin{bmatrix} ʃ & \to & s & \to & j \\ C_1 & & C_2 & & C_3 \end{bmatrix}$$

If this sentence is compared with a modulated carrier signal, then the utterance consists of a more slowly varying (because vowel duration is usually longer than that of consonants) powerful vowel carrier [i → ɔ → u] signal which is rapidly amplitude- and frequency-modulated by the consonants [ʃ → s → j]. Consonants are best described phonetically by the place and manner of their greatest articulatory *constriction*. When the open vocal tract for the vowel is suddenly closed for a consonant, two things happen. First, as the vocal tract tube becomes constricted, it increasingly impedes the transmission of vibratory energy; every constriction (except those near the base of the pharynx) tends to lower the intensity of the speech signal. Second, each consonantal constriction shifts the vocal tract resonance frequencies. Each consonant simultaneously modulates the amplitude and resonance frequencies of the vowel carrier signal.

A continuous speech utterance can be compared to a slowly varying, powerful vowel wave that is periodically amplitude- and resonance-frequency-modulated by the rapid closures of consonants. Thus, speech can be pictured as a simple, rhythmic, open-closed modulation of the vocal tract. The stream of intense vowel sound that is slowly varying from vowel to vowel is punctuated by periodic consonantal modulations (closures). The modulations naturally divide continuous speech into syllables, each syllable being a vowel and adjacent consonantal modulations. Thus, the carrier signal conceptualization of speech defines the syllable as an open-close modulation episode. Tempo of speech corresponds to the modulation rate. Consonants are the information-bearing signal, representative of a more closed vocal tract; vowels represent the more open tract. Juncture between syllables occurs at the modulation between two vowels. The importance of transitions, which occur during the onset and offset of consonantal modulation, is self-evident, since it is the modulation that carries the major share of speech information.

Figure 8.8 pictures the phrase "she saw you" as a modulated carrier signal. As the carrier vowel wave slowly shifts from [i → ɔ → u] it is modulated by three successive consonant constrictions, [ʃ → s → j]. During the modulations, the amplitude and resonance frequencies of speech signal shift, and noise may occur. Consonant clusters such as the [str] in "strike" are treated as single,

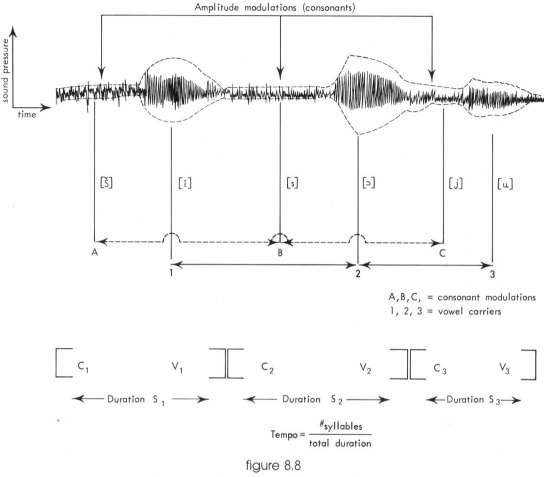

sound pressure

time

Amplitude modulations (consonants)

[š]   [i]   [s]   [ɔ]   [j]   [u]

A   B   C

1   2   3

A, B, C, = consonant modulations
1, 2, 3 = vowel carriers

C_1 V_1 C_2 V_2 C_3 V_3

← Duration S_1 →   ← Duration S_2 →   ← Duration S_3 →

$$\text{Tempo} = \frac{{}^\#\text{syllables}}{\text{total duration}}$$

figure 8.8

An analysis of the utterance "She saw you" in terms
of Dudley's conceptualized "carrier nature of speech."

complex modulations. The modulated vowel wave is split into naturally occurring syllabic units. Each syllable displays a vowel-nucleus peak intensity
marked by strong quasi-steady resonance frequencies, and consonantal on-
sets/offsets marked by formant frequency transitions, a rise or fall in intensity,
and noise vibration (see Figure 8.8).

The "carrier" conceptualization of speech exemplifies nicely the dynamic
nature of articulation. The vocal tract moves slowly but continuously from
vowel to vowel, with periodic interruptions caused by brisk consonantal modulations. In this scheme, any two vowels separated by a consonant overlap with
each other because the tongue moves or drifts slowly from one vowel carrier
wave to the next. Consonants and vowels overlap because consonant articulations are superimposed on a continuous, steadily shifting vowel articulation pattern. As a result, *coarticulation,* the label for the overlap properties of speech

sounds, is built into the very nature of the articulation process. The time pattern of speech can be seen as a *flow* of successive syllable units. At a given rate of speech, each syllable has a specified duration; overall speech rate can be computed as the number of syllables articulated per second.

PROPERTIES OF SYLLABLES
WITHIN AN UTTERANCE

Rate, Rhythm, Stress, Juncture   The stream of syllables has both a rate and a rhythm. Rhythm is the pattern of accentuation applied to the stream of syllables. When a syllable is accentuated, a number of things may happen. Accentuated syllables may be made with greater duration, intensity, f_o, and more extreme articulator positions. It has been suggested that when a syllable is chosen for heavy accentuation, the speaker delivers a more vigorous muscular impulse to the entire speech production system—thorax, larynx, and vocal tract. Thus, for the stressed syllable, there may be greater than usual lung pressure, greater tension and adduction of the vocal folds, and a brisker, more extreme set of articulatory movements for the articulators. Rhythm is the distribution of stress across the syllable train. This can be illustrated as follows: the numbers 1 to 6 represent syllables. If stressed, they are uppercase; if not, lowercase. Read the numbers, raising your voice to emphasize each uppercase example, and lowering your voice for each lowercase (unstressed):

1	**2**	3	**4**	5	**6**	Every other syllable is stressed
1	2	**3**	4	5	**6**	Every third syllable is stressed
1	2	3	4	5	6	Every syllable receives equal stress

As the carrier vowels are modulated by the closure of consonantal constrictions, not only can the resulting syllables be differentially stressed, but they also receive differing juncture boundaries. That is, a string of speech sounds can be divided into syllables, words, and phrases in many different ways. Juncturing is the process whereby a speaker inserts acoustic cues into the stream of speech, separating syllables, words, and phrases. For example, take the utterance consisting of the following segments: [gɪvhɪmðenaˈtreˈt]. If syllable juncture boundaries (+) are inserted where shown below, we get [gɪv + hɪm + ðə + naˈtreˈt], or "Give him the nitrate." If, instead, the last juncture is shifted to the right by one phoneme [gɪv + hɪm + ðə + naˈtʔ + reˈt], we get "Give him the night rate." The meaning of the string of sounds [naˈtreˈt] changes from [naˈ + tre ˈt] = nitrate (a chemical), to [naˈtʔ + reˈt] = night rate, the cost of using something at night. Both the meaning of the word and the utterance depend on the placement of the juncture boundary signal. Typical examples of junctures and the differences they make are these:

1. plum + pie vs. plump + eye
   [plʌm + pʰaˈ]   [plʌmp= + ʔaˈ]

2. I scream   ice cream
[aⁱ + skrim]   [aⁱs + krim]

3. great ape   grey tape
[greⁱt + ʔeⁱp]   [greⁱ + tʰeⁱp]

Listeners detect the boundaries of words and syllables both by using their linguistic competence and by detecting boundary signals. Knowledge of grammar, syntax, and semantics allows listeners to predict where a juncture should occur, even if the boundary signals are absent. For example:

A gorilla is a   A₁ great ape.
             A₂ grey tape.

A₁ I screamed
           bloody murder.
A₂ Ice creamed

Clearly, a listener will predict that the appropriate juncture in both cases is variant A₁ without even having heard a juncture boundary.

If juncture boundary signals are used, they may be one of several diverse cues. For example, boundaries *may* be marked with silent pauses, with a lowered vocal frequency or vocal fry (glottal pulsing), or by the use of different allophones for the sounds adjacent to the juncture. In the phrases "I scream"– "ice cream," the [aⁱ] is longer in "I" than in "ice," and the [k] in "ice cream" has an aspiration [kʰ] not present in the [k] of "scream." The process of adding boundary signals to mark the juncture, in conjunction with a listener's knowledge of where junctures should occur, permits us to hear rapid speech with rarely a mixup concerning the words that were intended.

Pitch and Loudness

           The stream of syllables produced by the rhythmical modulation of vocal tract shape also convey a pitch and loudness pattern to the listener's ear. Except for voiceless sounds and silent pauses, the larynx buzzes continuously through the stream of syllables within an utterance. Each sentence displays a fundamental frequency pattern or *contour* which the ear detects as a pitch pattern. For example, given the declarative sentence, "Phonetics is easy," vocal frequency falls toward the end of the utterance, on the word "easy." If the sentence is spoken as a question, "Phonetics is easy?" the vocal frequency rises on the final word, "easy." Both sentences have the same phonetic form, but the meaning is entirely different as a result of the differing intonation contours. In continuous speech in English, the use of vocal frequency patterns across a sentence to convey semantic and grammatical cues is called intonation (see Chapter 6). In languages other than English, vocal frequency varies over individual words or syllables in such a way that different patterns change the meaning of the word. For example, in Chinese, the word [ma] can be spoken with a rising vocal frequency [m̌a] or falling vocal frequency [m̂a]. The same word has different meanings, depending on the tone of the syllable.

In such tone languages, the vocal frequency pattern for each word or syllable throughout the utterance is crucial to meaning.

Because males, females, and children have vocal frequencies ranging from low to high values, it is obvious that the distinguishing feature of such pitch and intonation patterns must be *relative* frequency. For example, a child saying "No!" may have a vocal frequency falling from 350 to 200 Hz, whereas in males, "No!" falls from 125 to 50 Hz. What is crucial about the frequency pattern is that it falls from high to low. The absolute frequencies are relatively unimportant, and a listener quickly learns to normalize the speech he or she hears; that is, the listener extracts the pitch pattern without paying attention to the exact frequency, intensity, or time cues present in the pattern.

In addition to being marked by a pitch contour, the sentence also has a co-occurring loudness contour. The intensity of the sound arouses a sensation of loudness in the listener. We assume that once a speaker chooses a particular loudness level for speech, the lungs provide a steady driving pressure for all the sounds in that utterance. The difference in intensity from one sound to another depends on the degree of vocal tract constriction and the phonation mechanism. Other things being equal, a high-constricted vowel like [i] or [u] will be 4 to 5 dB less intense than an open vowel like [a], despite the use of the same lung pressure for both. This occurs because the more tightly constricted vocal tract for [i-u] impedes the flow of acoustic vibrations, whereas the more open [a] offers less impedance to the passage of vibration. In addition, the efficiency of conversion of compressed air into acoustic vibration is generally less for a turbulence sound source than for a buzz source. Thus, fricative stop consonants are of lower intensity than a corresponding vowel sound, even if vowel and consonant are articulated with the same driving pressure. The human auditory system is remarkable in that it normalizes these phonetically caused inequalities in intensity for differing sounds. Thus, an [a] vowel that is 5 dB more intense than [i] or [u] sounds as loud as the other two. The intensity variations accounted for by phonation source and constriction are not linguistically interesting. Rather, as listeners we must detect the variations in vocal intensity that are linguistically motivated.

There is a natural tendency for perceived pitch and loudness to fall at the end of the utterance, as the speaker prepares for an inhalation. Preparation for inhalation demands that the larynx relax and open up, and that lung pressure change from positive to negative in relation to atmospheric pressure. Both factors, relaxation of laryngeal adductors and tensor muscles and relaxation of expiratory muscles, contribute to the fall in vocal f_0 and intensity. Lieberman (1977) claims that the *breath group,* defined as a single sustained speech utterance, produced on one speech exhalation characterized by the terminal fall in f_0 and I_0 is a natural phonological unit vital to the orderly demarcation of sentence-sized utterances in speech production and perception. Heavily stressed syllables generally reveal patterns of increased lung pressure. The use of elevated lung pressure to mark heavily stressed syllables serves a linguistic function; it also causes greater vocal intensity and elevated vocal frequency. Underlying the greater lung pressure is the use of greater muscle force for heavily stressed syllable production.

When greater muscle force is used in respiratory, laryngeal, and articulatory muscles, the syllable produced tends to be louder, higher pitched, longer, and more sharply articulated, with articulator positions nearer to target values. On a given syllable, stress may be conveyed by any one or a combination of these four patterns. Such differential stress on words, which can change function or meaning, is called *lexical stress*. Notice the difference in the meaning of the words:

NOUN	VERB
imports	imports
insight	incite
August (month)	august (dignified)
redcoat (soldier)	red coat (a red-colored coat)

These variations in pitch, loudness, duration, and sharpness can also be used to focus attention on the semantically most important elements of a sentence (emphatic stress). For example, notice the shift in emphasis on what is important in the following sentences: "The *student* drank a bottle of beer" emphasizes that the student, and not a bartender, professor, or coal miner, drank the beer. "The student drank a *bottle* of beer" emphasizes that one *bottle,* not a stein, tankard, or case, was drunk. "The student drank a bottle of *beer*" emphasizes that beer, and not wine, water, or whiskey was drunk. Just as with juncture, the acoustic cues needed to signal stress may not be present, but our linguistic competence permits us to predict where lexical stress should occur, so that only rarely is there confusion concerning perceived stress.

Let us review the argument to this point. The conceptualization of continuous speech as a steady and continuous modulation of an open-vowel-shaped vocal tract by periodic consonantal constrictions suggests that speech consists of a stream of syllables. Each syllable, consisting of a vowel nucleus, is separated from the others in the stream by an amplitude, vocal frequency, or resonance frequency modulation (shift) at the consonantal onsets and offsets that mark the juncture boundaries between syllables. The syllable stream not only has a rate (tempo) of syllable production, but each sentence-sized stream of syllables displays frequency and intensity contour patterns that affect the meaning of the sentence (intonation type) as well as the meaning of words or prominence (stress) of syllables. The syllable is therefore crucial as a fundamental unit of speech production and organization. It has been argued that the syllable is the basic unit of speech neuromotor organization. Although we speak sounds, they are clumped into syllables by the rhythmic modulation of the vocal tract opening. The syllables and syllable trains in turn carry the stress, juncture, rhythm, rate, and intonation cues that convey word meaning, sentence type, semantic focus, rate of speech, and rhythm of speech. We will return to the syllable and its special properties in the section entitled "Models of Speech Production."

allophonic variation in continuous speech

Life would be simple for linguists and most phoneticians would be out of jobs if each of the 35 or so distinctive, underlying phonemic segments of English (or any language, for that matter) was produced in continuous speech in only one way. In other words, the underlying phoneme segments at the mental level would stand in a one-to-one relationship with their physical manifestation, the target sound. Fortunately, such a simplistic relation between phonetics and phonology does not occur. The sounds of speech are not produced in an unvarying, constant way; variability of sound production is the norm. For various reasons, each underlying abstract segment is produced as follows:

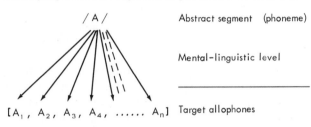

/ A /   Abstract segment   (phoneme)

Mental-linguistic level

[A₁ , A₂ , A₃ , A₄ , ... Aₙ]   Target allophones

Physiological-phonetic level

We can observe each allophone as it is produced, but we do not know directly what the exact "shape" of the underlying phoneme segment is. At the phonetic level, allophones are classes of equivalent sounds whose differences are not distinctive. As a group, a set of allophones is representative of an underlying abstract segment (or phoneme segment). For example, take the phoneme segment /i/. It can be produced, phonetically, as the allophones:

[iː]	[i]	[i.]	[i̥]	[ĩ]	[ï]
long	normal	short	voiceless	nasal	rounded

The question is, why do these allophonic variations occur? Can the appearance of a particular allophone be predicted? The vast majority of interesting allophonic variations occur in continuous speech; therefore, processes unique to continuous speech production must be sought when explaining these variations.

SOURCES OF ALLOPHONIC VARIATION

Among the sources of allophonic variation are interspeaker differences and intraspeaker differences.

Interspeaker Differences

Some sound segment variations are due to age-linked, sex-linked, and idiosyncratic physical differences in the vocal tract anatomy and physiology of differing speakers. For example, adult males generally have larger, longer vocal tracts than do adult females, and females have longer vocal tracts than children. As vocal tract length changes, resonance frequencies shift markedly. The same vowel produced by men and children (see Figure 7.27) differs widely in resonance frequency. As children mature, their vocal tracts increase in size, so that over time their speech sounds slowly approach the adult resonance frequency pattern. Idiosyncratic differences between speakers are easily visualized: some people may have larger or smaller or more oddly shaped oral, pharyngeal, or nasal cavities than other speakers, and their speech sounds will have acoustic characteristics unique to them. For example, speakers who have lost their teeth, especially the incisors, generally produce strident fricatives which are different from those of people with normal dentition. Every human face is different, in some way, from every other. The same holds for our vocal tracts; every vocal tract differs from every other in physical construction. Thus, there will be smaller or larger differences between the same target sounds produced by different speakers depending on the extent of the physical differences.

Another aspect of idiosyncratic differences contributes to interspeaker variation in allophones. Some people articulate crisply and clearly; others speak in slurred fashion. Indeed, human speech ranges on a continuum of allophonic variation from very crisp to heavily slurred articulation. In certain cases, such differences may be caused by vocal tract pathology—cleft palate, stroke, multiple sclerosis—but generally they represent individual styles of articulation. In addition to idiosyncratic and physiological differences, dialect differences also cause allophonic variation. Each major language is divided into a number of subgroups or dialects. Each dialect is distinguished in part by the particular allophones it uses. Who is not familiar with the New England broad [a], or the substitution of [ɚ] for [ə] in words such as Cuba [kjubə] → [kjubɚ] or Worcester [wʊstɚ] → [wʊstə]. The allophones a person learns and uses are a part of his or her linguistic competence and reflect a long process of language learning. We can account for these allophones on the basis of the listener's dialect-specific acquisition of certain allophones.

Intraspeaker Differences   All human acts are impossible to repeat exactly. We change from moment to moment, and our changing body and memory prevent us from *exactly* duplicating any behavior. Changes in attention, distraction, fatigue, task, etc., all tend to cause differences in successive productions of the same sound. If we could exactly repeat a movement or behavior, we would be machines. Thus, if a person were to speak the same sound ten times in a row, all ten productions would differ in some way. Such variability of human performance is a fact of life, and allophonic variations caused by idiosyncratic performance factors can be expected to occur constantly.

EXTRINSIC AND
INTRINSIC ALLOPHONES   At this point we wish to discuss two kinds of allophones that can be observed in the speech of any speaker. Extrin-

sic allophones are those that appear to be a part of the sound pattern of the language. They are voluntarily produced and fully under the speaker's conscious control. A good example of an extrinsic allophone is the velar/alveolar alternation: word-initial [l] is spoken as an alveolar [l] as in "low"; word-final [l] is spoken as the velar-form [ł] as in "fill." However, we can easily produce [ł] or [l] in word-initial or final position *if we please,* and thus we voluntarily select to produce these allophones to fit our sound pattern. Many extrinsic allophones serve to mark word position, juncture boundaries, and so on. The intrinsic allophones reflect the limitations and preferred patterns of functioning of the SPM itself. These limitations are of two kinds: (1) neuromuscular and mechanical limitations, and (2) preferred patterns of neuromuscular functioning.

The neuromuscular limitations reflect the mechanical limitations of the vocal tract. For example, articulators can move only so far and so fast. Movements of the soft palate are affected by tongue movement because of muscular interconnections. The vocal folds cannot buzz unless there is a pressure differential above and below them. The preferred patterns of neuromuscular functioning of the SPM reflect the fact that there are preferred, most natural, modes of behavior in all systems. For example, consider human locomotion. The most natural, preferred mode of motion is walking, smoothly swinging the legs forward in a steady stride or run. On the other hand, the human can choose to hop, skip, or jump forward. However, these less preferred modes of locomotion rarely occur unless there is compelling reason to use them. On the other hand, we might choose to move by flying, but in this case, the surface area of our arms, the strength of the muscles needed, and body weight are too great even to permit us to use our arms as an alternative means of locomotion. So too for speech production. Certain preferred modes of operation can be inhibited and alternative strategies adopted, while still other modes of operation cannot be altered. For example, it is often observed that when a stop consonant is produced adjacent to a rounded vowel such as [u] in "coo" [ku], the allophone of the velar stop consonant which is articulated is rounded, [Kʷ]. However, with a bit of practice, a speaker can produce the word [ku] without rounding the [k]. Thus, this intrinsic allophonic variation, representing a preferred mode of operation of the SPM, can be inhibited if the sound pattern calls for it. On the other hand, to our knowledge it is a universal phenomenon that when producing a stop consonant + vowel syllable, speakers anticipate the vowel by moving part or all of the tongue into position for the vowel even before the stop is released. Thus, each stop consonant becomes a different intrinsic allophone depending upon the adjacent vowel. As far as can be determined, this physiological process cannot be resisted, and this set of intrinsic allophones will always occur. Thus, extrinsic allophonic variations are part of the sound pattern of the language and present at the input to the SPM. Intrinsic allophonic variations occur because of the limitations and preferred patterns of functioning of the SPM, and can only be resisted or prevented in certain cases.

sources of intrinsic variation

Intrinsic allophonic variations are those predictable, regularly occurring allophonic variations of a sound that occur within a given phonetic or speech tempo context. They are caused by phonetic and rate *context* and reflect the neuromuscular, mechano-inertial limitations and preferred physiological operating strategies of the SPM. Explanations of the occurrence of intrinsic allophones focus on context as the source of variation. Temporal context is the tempo of speech production—fast, normal, or slow. Speakers are capable of varying their speaking rate from about 40 to over 300 words per minute. Speech can be speeded up or slowed down over a relative rate of about seven to one, and each change in speed causes differing intrinsic allophones to occur.

Perhaps the most important source of intrinsic allophonic variation is that caused by phonetic context. In continuous speech, the speech sounds are produced in a stream, each sound following the next in serial order. Targets are missed, and the sounds overlap and otherwise affect one another. Phonetic context is specified as follows: Suppose the segment [æ] occurs in the words [bæd], [sæs], and [ræg]. In each case, the sounds preceding and immediately following [æ] are called the *near* phonetic context for that sound. Thus, the near phonetic contexts for [æ] are [b-d], [s-s], and [r-g]. The sounds that are two segments away or more from the sound in question are called the *far* phonetic contexts. For example, in the word "scandals" [skændəlz], the near context is [kæn] and the far context is [s___dəlz]. Total phonetic context for [æ] is [sk__ndəlz]. Each change in the near, and less often the far, phonetic context of a sound causes an allophonic variation of that sound. Continuous speech is characterized by much intrinsic allophonic variation; expected, ideal target values are often "missed."

NEUROMUSCULAR MECHANO-
INERTIAL LIMITATIONS OF THE SPM   The vocal tract is a biochemical structure consisting of muscle, connective tissue, cartilage, ligament, tendon, bone, and mucosa. Each part of the vocal tract has mechanical properties that determine how a structure will move when muscles contract. The greater the inertia, the more a body resists being accelerated or decelerated. In addition, the various articulators are mechanically interconnected in unique ways. For example, lip and tongue are connected to the jaw; when the jaw moves, the lower lip moves as well. The tongue and soft palate are interconnected by the palatoglossus muscle; the mandible and hyoid bone are interconnected; and so on. The vocal tract is therefore a complex biomechanical machine and like every machine has a limited range of functions dictated by its structure. A machine can move only so far, so fast. So can the vocal tract.

Newton's first law of motion says that in an isolated system, bodies at rest will remain at rest, and bodies in uniform motion will remain in motion unless acted upon by an outside force. That is, momentum is conserved. Momentum is the product of mass (M) times velocity (V). Momentum = mass × velocity. If a force acts upon that body,

$$F = \frac{d(MV)}{dt}$$

Since mass is essentially constant for speeds not near velocity of light, then

$$F = M \frac{dV}{dt} = Ma$$

This familiar equation states that if we wish to increase or decrease the velocity of motion of a body of mass *(M)*, it must be accelerated by a force *(F/M = a)*. If the mass of a moving articulator is large, its inertia is large and the muscular force must be large. If the mass is small, its inertia is small and a proportionally smaller force will achieve the same acceleration. Since our muscles have a finite, fixed strength and neurons can fire only so fast, there is an upper limit to the maximum speed of movement the structures of the vocal tract can achieve. Because the articulators have mass, they have inertial limitations; they can be accelerated or decelerated only so fast. Mechanical interconnections also limit speed and range of motion; if, for example, the tongue is low in the oral cavity, the palatoglossal connection with the soft palate tends to lower the position of the velum during velar closure for the low vowels.

If neurons can fire only so fast, and muscles can exert only limited force; if vocal tract structures have mechanical properties of inertia, elasticity, and resistance; and if the structures are mechanically interconnected, it can be deduced that neuromuscular, mechano-inertial limitations cause allophonic variation. Consider the following example. Suppose we have two cities 200 km apart (about the distance between New York and Philadelphia) and we are driving a car capable of 50 km/hr top speed.

Philadelphia ←————————————→ New York

distance = 200 km

Target A ● ←————————————→ ● Target B

At this top speed, a driver can travel from target A to B, Philadelphia to New York, in 4 hours. A round trip would be 8 hours. If the driver is given only 2 hours to make the outward trip from Philadelphia, he will get only halfway (100 km) before he has to turn back. In other words, because his top speed is limited, the driver *undershoots* his target, New York, by a distance of 100 km. If the car were faster moving, 200 km/hr top speed, he could make the round trip and thus achieve target. Thus, target sounds will be missed if the tempo of speech production is very fast, since the articulators have a fixed top speed that prevents targets being achieved if they follow each other too closely in time. For example, the distance from the upper incisors to the soft palate of an individual may be 4 cm. Suppose that person's tongue tip had to move from incisors to soft palate during continuous speech. If the tongue tip had a maximum speed of 10 cm/sec, it would take at least 400 msec to accomplish the tongue tip movement between targets. If the tempo of speech were sufficiently high and commands for moving from teeth to soft palate occurred in serial order, within less than 400 msec, the person would undershoot the palatal target. If the tongue muscles were stronger or offered less impedance, or the tongue tip were less massive, less than 400 msec would suffice to achieve the palatal target.

To further illustrate the fact that if target commands are issued in close succession undershoot will occur, suppose the speaker says the word "ABC," consisting of three phonemic segments, [A, B, C]. If the speaker talks at a fast rate, then a command to move toward target B will occur before target A is achieved, and the articulators undershoot target A. As the tongue moves toward target B, a command arrives to start movement toward target C, causing undershooting of target B. The faster one talks, the more likely that there will be insufficient time to achieve target articulatory positions. The oncoming sounds occur so quickly in serial order that before an articulator can achieve target, a command for the next phoneme interrupts movement toward target, starting movement toward the next target, which may also be missed. Picture, if you will, a string of targets (A, B, C, D, E) in space. At a sufficiently high rate of speech, the articulator does not have enough time, even at top speed, to achieve these targets; it undershoots them all (Figure 8.9). As we talk faster, less time is spent on "target"; at a sufficiently high rate of speech, target is un-

figure 8.9

A schematic illustration of mechano-inertial
timing undershoot of target positions.

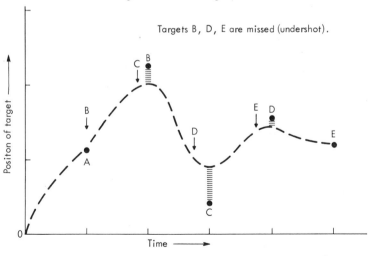

A, B, C, D, E = successive, serially ordered targets

↓ = arrival of motor command for the next target in serial order

≡ = amount by which target missed; notice that greatest
undershooting occurred for targets furthest apart (B–C)

dershot unless we are capable of exerting more force, reducing moving mass, or somehow reducing distance between targets.

In addition to inertial limitations on speed, there are mechanical limitations to achieving target. For example, as we open our mandible, it stretches the skin of the lips and cheeks; when the mouth is fully open, it prevents lip protrusion from occurring to any great extent. Try it yourself: open your mandible very widely and try to round your lips. You will see that you can do so only very slightly. Imagine now that you are going to make a syllable such as "tap" at high speed. The mandible must open for [æ], and as it does it carries the lower lip away from the upper. Notice that [p], which follows [æ], involves lip closure. At a fast rate of speech, the speaker will be forced either to limit mandibular opening or to use greater muscle force of lip closure if he or she is going to achieve closure for [p] following [æ].

The undershooting of vowel target shape because of mechano-inertial limitations of the vocal tract can generally be seen in the speech signal. Figure 8.10 shows a spectrogram of the word "indubitably" spoken at a moderate speed, and then spoken much faster. In the spectrogram, resonance 2 has been marked for your inspection. Notice the resonance 2 values in the rapidly spoken word. At high speeds, extreme vowel tongue/lip positions are undershot: high vowels are not as high, low vowels not as low, front vowels not as fronted, back vowels not as back. The net result is that vowels are "neutralized" and occupy a more central position. Picture, if you will, tongue position for the vowels [i, ɔ, u] in the sentence "he saw you" (Figure 8.11). At a fast tempo of speaking*, the tongue undershoots the high/front target for [i], it undershoots the low/back target for [ɔ], and it undershoots the high, back rounded target for [u]. In Figure 8.11, you will see that tongue position for [i] in the fast production is lower in height than that of the slow version. Notice that tongue position for [u] in the fast version is lower in height and the lips are less rounded than for the slow production. As a result, at high speed the vowels are neutralized; vowel tongue positions regress toward a neutral position, neither high nor low, neither front or back, neither rounded or spread, which is characteristic of the [ə] neutral vowel.

THE TARGET LOCUS DESCRIPTION OF SPEECH SOUNDS

In order to provide a basis for the discussion of coarticulation, it is worth examining the target locus description of speech sounds and syllables proposed by Potter, Koepp, and Green (1941). In the course of attempting to teach deaf people to "read" speech by visually scanning spectrograms, Potter and his co-workers made a careful spectrographic analysis of all the distinctive sounds of English speech, both in isolation and when embedded in syllables. They observed that isolated sounds could generally be characterized by their steady-state resonance frequency pattern if the sound was a vowel (see Figure 7.23), by the dynamically changing resonance pattern if the sound was a diphthong or glide (Figures 7.20 and 7.32) or

*Sometimes called "allegro" speech.

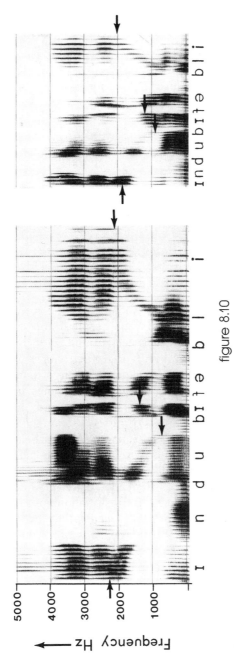

figure 8.10

Spectrograms of the word "indubitably" spoken at a moderate
and a fast tempo. Vowel formant frequencies are marked on both
samples. Notice that formant frequencies, in the fast version
differ (undershoot) from those of the slower version of the word.

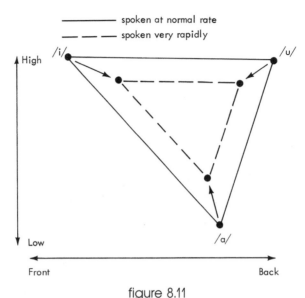

figure 8.11

An illustration of the neutralization of the
vowel triangle that occurs in rapid speech.

by the starting point and duration of the transition of the resonance frequencies if the sound was a dynamic articulation such as the stop consonants (Figure 7.15). Acoustic theory predicts that a speech sound with a unique resonance frequency pattern can be produced by a vocal tract with a unique articulatory shape. That is, each unique vocal tract shape results in a unique resonance frequency pattern. Potter et al. called the resonance frequency pattern for the isolated sound its "hub" value. (For our purposes, "hub" and "target" are equivalent.) When speech sounds are combined into syllables, the "locus" or "hub" resonance frequencies of each individual sound *shift* upon being combined with other sounds; the neighboring sounds within a syllable mutually affect each other's resonance frequency patterns. The sounds in near phonetic context strongly affect each other's resonance frequency pattern, which is equivalent to saying that phonetic context causes intrinsic allophonic variation. Physiologically, the shifting of the resonance hubs means that the shape of the vocal tract for each sound changes when it is combined with other sounds.

The changes in hub frequencies are quite predictable. For example, if a sound with a high second resonance frequency is combined with a sound with a low second resonance frequency, the high resonance frequency is lowered a bit for the first sound, and the low resonance frequency raised for the second sounds. *The hub frequencies for adjacent sounds move toward each other.* In terms of vocal tract shapes, if sounds A and B are adjacent in continuous speech, the vocal tract (VT) shape for A shifts toward that for B, and the shape of the vocal tract for B shifts a bit toward the shape for A. Thus, when articulated in a syllable, VT shape A + VT shape B = VT A_BB_A. The subscripts indicate that the tract shape for A has become a little like that for B, and the tract shape for B, a little like that for A. Isolated sounds joined in continuous speech or even in syllables tend to shift toward each other, to overlap and share their articulatory and acoustic features. This overlap property is a major difference between continuous speech and isolated sound production.

PREFERRED PHYSIOLOGICAL
OPERATING STRATEGIES OF THE SPM

Variations due to Coarticulation   A second and quite interesting cause of intrinsic allophonic variation is the *coarticulation* process. Within the stream of continuous speech, serially ordered sounds are produced in an overlapping, or shingled, fashion. Rather than being articulated separately and independently, like beads on a string, the successive targets are coarticulated in a smooth and overlapping fashion (Figure 8.12). The coarticulatory overlap is greatest in near phonetic context—that is, between directly adjacent sounds—but it can spread over as many as three or four adjacent sounds. Sounds overlap only partially, not completely. Picture this homely analogy: a foolish fellow puts a white shirt

figure 8.12
An illustration of the fact that within continuous speech, sounds are not produced separately, but with overlap and smooth transitions between them.

1. Isolated Sounds in Serial Order

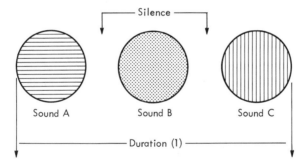

2. Non-overlapping Sounds with Transitions

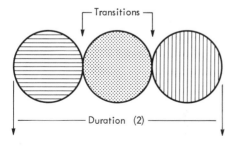

3. Coarticulated, Overlapping Sounds with Transitions

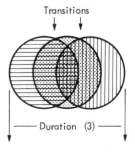

Duration = 3 < 2 < 1

and a pair of new blue jeans together in the washing machine. The blue dye runs in the first wash and stains the white shirt so that it has a bluish tint. Imagine that speech sounds are colored objects; when articulated in the stream of speech, their colors "run" and overlap each other, so that each sound is "stained" with the colors of the surrounding sound. It is physically impossible to articulate two *differing* sounds simultaneously, since different sounds must differ by at least one feature. When coarticulatory overlap occurs, what happens is that one or more, but not all, of the articulatory features of one sound overlap with those of an adjacent sound. If two sounds could be completely coarticulated or totally overlapped, a listener could not detect which sound came first or second. But listeners have no problem determining serial order of sounds in continuous speech. Although sounds overlap, they do not overlap so completely that serial ordering is violated.

Other Causes of Variation   Many intrinsic allophonic variations attributable to the preferred mode of physiological functioning of the SPM do not reflect coarticulation processes. For example, the length (duration) of speech sounds varies systematically depending on phonetic and junctional context. Vowels that occur before voiced obstruent consonants [b, d, g, z, dʒ] are generally longer than the same vowels occurring before the voiceless obstruents [s, ʃ, tʃ, p, t, k]. Speak the words "beat" [bi t] and "bead" [bid], and notice that the vowel in "bead" is the longer of the two. Consonants that occur in utterance-final or in a prepausal position (just before a long pause) are generally much longer than the same consonants found in other positions. Still another example of such allophonic variation is the fact that voiceless stop consonants embedded in [st, sk, sp] clusters are produced without a large air burst, and with short VOTs. In these clusters, the vocal folds move toward closure on the stops much earlier than when the stops are produced alone. These intrinsic allophonic variations reflect the involuntary operation of preferred modes of physiological operation of the SPM, or as yet undetermined neuromuscular mechano-inertial limitations.

coarticulation: direction and extent

TYPES OF COARTICULATION   The two basic types of coarticulatory overlap are right-to-left (RL) or "anticipatory" and left-to-right (LR) or "carryover" coarticulations. In order to illustrate each, we will use an imaginary phonetic context consisting of the sounds [A B C D E], which are spoken in continous speech. Suppose that the speaker, at the instant in time that we photograph his or her vocal tract with an X-ray camera, has just made the constriction for sound [B]. If an articulatory feature of sound [A], which has already been articulated, is observed during the production of [B], then a left to right or carryover coarticulation has occurred: The sound on the left has influenced the sound on the right, which is currently being articulated. If during production of [B] we observe a feature of sound [C] or [D] neither of which has yet been articulated, then we say that right to left or anticipatory coarticulation has occurred. The sounds on the right, [C, D], which have yet to be spoken, have influenced the sound on the left [B], which is currently being articulated. Both LR and RL coarticulations are numerous in continuous speech, and *they occur because of different physiological processes.*

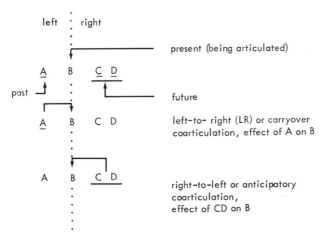

LR Coarticulation   It has been suggested that LR coarticulation represents a process of phonetic accommodation which promotes the swift and effortless transition of the articulators from one sound to the next. In other words, in a string of sounds, the coarticulatory influence of [A] on [B] promotes the smoothness of the [A to B] transition. Suppose the sound [s] occurs as in the words below. Listed to the right are the near phonetic contexts. Notice that the movement of the articulators toward target position for [s] must start from three differing points: [i], high/front; [æ], low/front; [ɔ], mid-back. And the path from [s] leads in three differing directions: [t], alveolar position; [p], labial position; [k], velar position. The solution for how to move toward and away from a given sound, such as [s], is different for each different phonetic context.

WORD	PHONETIC CONTEXT
east [ist]	[i_t]
asp [æsp]	[æ_p]
mosque [mɔsk]	[ɔ_k]

The LR coarticulatory influence of [i, æ, or ɔ] on [s] reflects the fact that the tongue, mandible and lips move from the preceding sounds toward [s] along three differing paths; because the transition from [i, æ, ɔ] to [s] is a part of [s], the [s] is coarticulated with the preceding sounds. As Potter, Koepp, and Green noted, the speaker may deliberately cause [s] to vary so that the target for [s] is shifted, or moved toward that for [i, æ, or ɔ]. If the target position for [s] is shifted toward that of the previously occurring sound, the two sounds [is, æs, ɔs] will mesh more smoothly, since the articulators will not have to move so far or so fast if these targets are shifted (coarticulated) toward each other. Thus, a sound may experience LR coarticulation with the previous sound so that the transition from the previous sound to the oncoming target is rendered as short, smooth, and simple as possible.

RL Coarticulation   The RL or anticipatory coarticulation process is clearly the result of different physiological processes than for the LR coarticulation. Anticipatory coarticulation can occur *only* if the speaker can "look ahead" in time and anticipate oncoming sounds. RL coarticulation must reflect a high-level, central type of phonological-phonetic processing, since an entire utterance must be scanned in order for anticipation to be deliberately programmed. Consider the following example. The word "spoon" consists of these sounds: [s + p + u + n]. In isolation, the sounds [s, p, n] are made without protrusion of the lip, whereas [u] in isolation is produced with lip protrusion. When the sounds are coarticulated in the continuously articulated word "spoon," the sounds show lip rounding: [s^w p^w u n^w]. If we indicate the presence of rounding by (+) and its absence by (−), then

$$
\begin{array}{lcccc}
\textit{in isolation} & [\,s\; + & p\; + & u\; + & n\,] \\
\text{rounding} & - & - & + & - \\
\textit{in continuous speech} & [\,s & p & u & n\,] \\
\text{rounding} & + & + & + & + \\
\end{array}
$$

Notice that the rounding of [u] has spread in an RL fashion over to [sp] and has carried over in the LR fashion to [n]. The entire word is rounded. Unless the speaker knew in advance that the [u] sound would occur in the word "spoon," he or she could not anticipate the [u] by coarticulating it with [sp]. For the LR carryover of rounding from [u] to [n], the speaker has allowed the feature [+ round] to continue past the [u] into the time slot for [n].

The coarticulatory spread of a given feature is usually facilitated if neighboring sounds are not "specified" or are neutral with respect to the potentially coarticulated feature. In the word "spoon," you can produce [s, p, n] with any amount of lip rounding or lip spreading — try it yourself. Such rounding or spreading may change the quality of the sound a bit, but all three sounds are recognizable and do not lose their identity. Thus, we may say that [s, p, n] are neutral or nonspecified with regard to the feature lip rounding, whereas [u] is specified (must be articulated) with lip rounding. When the sounds are combined in "spoon," the coarticulation process spreads the specified feature over all three adjacent sounds, since they are neutral with regard to rounding and can be made with or without it. If the [sp__n] phonetic context is combined with a spread vowel, then lip spreading will be coarticulated over the whole word, as in the word "span."

$$
\begin{array}{lcccc}
[\,s + p + æ + n\,] & \rightarrow & [\,s\; p\; æ\; n\,] \\
+ \text{spread} \,[0 \quad 0 \quad + \quad 0] & & [+ + + +] \\
\end{array}
$$

Blockage of Coarticulation   The coarticulatory spread of a feature is usually blocked if the opposite (contradictory) value of that feature occurs in adjacent sounds. For example, the larynx can either buzz [+ voice] or not buzz [− voice], but it cannot simultaneously produce both values of the feature voice [± voice]. Thus, if [æ] is voiced and [s] is voiceless, in articulation of [sæ] as in the word "Sam," the spread of [− voice] feature from [s] to [æ] is blocked by the occurrence of its contradictory value, [+ voice], in [æ]. If we examine the articulatory gesture [± mandibular lowering], we notice that the mandible is elevated for [s] and lowered for [æ]. During articulation of "Sam" there is no RL spread of mandibular lowering from [æ] to [s] because [s] and [æ] have contradictory values of [±] mandible lowering. On the other hand, [m] is neutral with regard to mandible lowering, and an LR spread of mandibular lowering is possible from [æ] to [m].

$$[s + æ + m] \rightarrow [s \; æ \; m]$$
$$\text{mandibular lowering } [- \quad + \quad 0] \quad [- \; + \, +]$$

There is evidence to suggest that if two contradictory features occur in adjacent sounds, each "weakens" the other, so that neither is as extreme as it might otherwise be. Such a featural weakening may be in part due to neuromotor, mechano-inertial factors, since it seems unlikely that the speaker would consciously wish to remove the distinctiveness of the underlying segments within a word. Distinctiveness is probably lost because of the limitations of the SPM.

THE ROLE OF CONSONANT, VOWEL, AND JUNCTURE BOUNDARIES

Continuous speech consists of a stream of consonants and vowels. There is evidence to suggest that the coarticulatory effect of the vowel on the consonant is generally greater than that of the consonant on the vowel. The coarticulatory influence of one consonant on another in many cases is as strong as the influence of vowels on the consonant. For example, a back vowel such as [u] may cause the place of contact for [k] as in "coo" to shift backward, but the velar [ɬ] as in the word "article" [artɪkɬ] causes an equally large coarticulatory rearward shift of [k]. In V_1CV_2 words, such as the name "Abby," the medial intravocalic consonant [b] coarticulates a bit more strongly with V_1 than with V_2, in most cases.

Studies of coarticulation have revealed that the spread of features often crosses juncture boundaries between syllables and words. A juncture boundary generally does not appear to inhibit coarticulation unless the juncture is of high rank, such as the juncture between clauses, and only if the juncture is marked by a silent pause. For example, in the sentence "Can Sue bake lasagna?" the spreading of the rounding feature for [u] crosses the juncture boundary between the words [kæn + su] so that the [n] is also rounded.

$$[+ kæn^w + s^wu + be^lk + \ldots.]$$

This indicates that the motor-programming processes of the SPM operate on chunks of sound which may not correspond with the syllables and words produced by the speaker's phonological component.

ENCODING AND COARTICULATION   The question of why LR/RL coarticulation occurs is bound up with the process of speech encoding. Before attempting to answer, let us examine the concept of encoding. Recall, from Chapter 1, that the process of converting ideas into speech sound was a form of encoding. The essence of encoding is the conversion of information from one form into another. For example, language can be encoded as speech, as writing, or as Morse code. In Morse code, dots, dashes, and silences are used to encode writing. Each dot and dash is separated by silence from the next. Each dot and dash must be of a fixed length, and there are only two distinctive elements of the code, dot or dash. In the more complex speech code, there are 35 or more distinctive code units—underlying, abstract phonemic segments. In the simpler Morse code, the dot or dash elements are separated by silence and may not be overlapped, but in speech the sounds overlap each other in a complex way. Demonstrate this to yourself. Say the word "pea." At the instant that your lips are closing for the [p] sound, your tongue is already in position for the [i] vowel. At the moment the lips open for the explosion of [p], the vocal tract is emitting a noise burst that contains information about both [p] and [i]. Listeners can predict the identity of the vowel that follows [p] with considerable accuracy on the basis of hearing the noise burst alone.

This overlapping of adjacent speech sounds during the production of continuous speech has been called *encoding* by psychologists, *coarticulation* by phoneticians, and *assimilation* by linguists. At least three reasons for this overlapping have been offered:

1. Coarticulation enchances the speed and efficiency of articulation by telescoping sounds.
2. Coarticulation prevents the intrusion of unwanted sounds into the stream of speech.
3. Coarticulation "eases" or overcomes the mechano-inertial, neuromotor difficulties of articulation—the principle of the economy of least effort.

Let us examine each in turn and consider their implications for dynamic speech production.

Speech is produced swiftly. At our fastest rate of speaking, the vocal tract is capable of making nearly 20 to 30 sounds per second. If speech were articulated in a non-overlapping fashion, two things would happen: First, at a rate of 20 sounds/sec, each sound would have to be spoken in about 50 msec or less, and the articulators would have to be swiftly jerked toward oncoming targets twenty times/second. This would result in a "choppy," almost buzzlike, perceptibly interrupted stream of speech. But instead, what we hear is a smooth, uninterrupted stream of coarticulated sound with few perceptible discontinuities, because coarticulation permits smooth transitions. If the sounds of speech overlap, as shown in Figure 8.12, this telescoping effect shortens the amount of time needed to articulate words and syllables and permits an increase in the *speed* of articulation. Thus, coarticulation may enhance both speed and smoothness of articulation.

A second possible reason for coarticulation is the prevention of intrusive sounds. If two sounds, [A] and [B], are not coarticulated, then the transition between them can be rather unusually prolonged and may often be heard by listeners as a third sound occurring between them. Take, for example, the syllable [bu]. The coarticulation between [b] and [u] is very strong; at the instant the lips close for [b], the tongue is already in position for the oncoming [u] sound. Try to articulate [bu] without coarticulation. Do not round your lips for [b]. Keep them normally positioned. Do not move your tongue back into the [u] position during [b], but hold it in a neutral or slightly fronted position. Then, as you articulate [b + u], the resulting syllable should sound like this:

$$/b + u/ \rightarrow \text{[bju] or [bəu]}$$

The prolonged transition acquires a distinctiveness of its own, appearing as a third segment intruder between [b] and [u]. Thus, failure to coarticulate would tend to cause the appearance of intrusive sounds that would disrupt the expected sound shape of words and syllables.

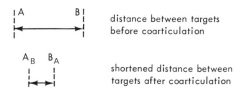

A third reason for the occurrence of coarticulation involves the principle of the economy of least effort. When musicians, dancers, or athletes rehearse a particular set of physical movements for a long period of time, the movements become skillful and precise. They exhibit little or no wasted motion; movements are accomplished with a minimum of effort, a minimum of motion, and a maximum of grace. Considered from a physical point of view, the motion of a skilled performer reveals a minimum expenditure of effort. Skilled motions appear to involve a minimum expenditure of energy; hence the term *economy of least effort*. Human beings are "naturally lazy"; they generally seek to perform a task with minimum expenditure of effort and energy. (Who on campus has not seen how students and staff will walk across the diagonal of a lawn rather than take the longer rectangular route of a sidewalk?) We may suppose that the physical task of speaking is no exception to such a phenomenon. Given two target sounds that must be articulated in succession, how might effort to articulate them be minimized? If the two targets were coarticulated with one another, then they would move toward each other within the vocal tract space and the transition movements would be smaller, reducing the muscular effort to be expended. Potter, Koepp, and Green's work on target loci appears to support this interpretation. As the distance between coarticulated targets shrinks, not only is distance to be moved minimized, but lesser force and a slower velocity of movement is needed to traverse the lesser distance. By facilitating smaller, smoother, less effortful transitions between sounds, coarticulation may significantly enhance the ease of articulation of continuous speech.

SAMPLE COARTICULATIONS   Coarticulation has been described as feature spreading. If this is accurate, which articulatory features can be spread from one sound to its neighbors in the serial stream of speech? The answer is all, or nearly all, of the articulatory features listed in Chapter 7 can be coarticulated given the proper phonetic environment. Thus, the primary articulatory features of place, manner, voicing, and nasality can be coarticulated as well as the secondary features of labialization, palatalization, velarization, and pharyngealization. Of all the articulatory features, the one most resistant to coarticulation appears to be manner. If manner of articulation changes, the phonemic identity of sound is sure to change, whereas this is not generally the case if the other features are coarticulated. The infrequent occurrence of coarticulation of manner features probably reflects our desire not to "lose" the phonetic shape of words.

Coarticulation of Place   If the [k] sound is articulated in a front vowel context, such as [i] in "leak" [lik], the place of [k] contact is on the hard palate. When articulated in a back vowel environment, such as "Luke" [luk], the place of contact moves back a centimeter or more toward the soft palate. Spectrograms of [ki] and [ku] (Figure 8.13) show that the starting frequency of resonance 2 is at about 1300 Hz for [ku] and at 2250 Hz for [ki]. This difference is caused by the coarticulation of place of [k] production attributable to the adjacent vowel. Another example involves the place of articulation of [n]. Ordin-

figure 8.13

Spectrograms of the stop-vowel CV syllables, [ki] and [ku]
The coarticulatory influence of the vowel upon the [k],
causes the locus resonance frequency value for
reasonance 2 to shift as the vowel environment changes.

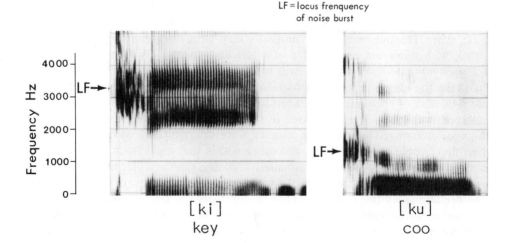

LF = locus frenquency
of noise burst

[ki]
key

[ku]
coo

arily, [n] contact is made on the alveolar ridge. However, when [n] is adjacent to the dental fricative [θ], the dental place of [θ] spreads to the nasal segment. For example, in the word "month" [mʌnθ], the place of nasal articulation shifts from the alveolar ridge to the upper incisors—that is, /n/ → [n̪]. Feel the difference in place by noticing the shift in tongue position for both coarticulations. Still another example of place coarticulation occurs in the word "question" [kwɛs + tʃən]. Spoken slowly (see Figure 8.14), the [s] is normally articulated with a noise cutoff frequency of 4000 Hz. Spoken rapidly and casually, the place of [s] articulation shifts from an alveolar to a postalveolar position characteristic of [ʃ]. Thus, the postalveolar place of [tʃ] has spread to the [s], causing it to shift from [s] to [ʃ]—that is, /s/ → [ʃ]. The [ʃ] with a 2000 Hz cutoff is clearly seen in the more casually spoken [kwɛʃ + tʃɛn].

Coarticulation of Nasality

When a vowel occurs in a prenasal position, such as in the word "pan" [pæn], the velopharyngeal port opens during the preceding vowel, causing it to be nasalized. If the vowel occurs after the nasal. as in "nap" [næp], as the velum moves toward closure the port is open for a brief portion of the postnasal vowel, although to a lesser extent than for vowels in a prenasal position. Figure 8.15 shows a spectrogram of the word "dame" [deˈm]. The arrow indicates the approximate point in the vowel where the velopharyngeal port opens. As the port opens, resonance 1 appears to fall in frequency, and resonances 2 and 3 weaken as the opened cavity begins to damp out vibratory energy at higher frequencies. Notice the almost complete lack of high-frequency energy for the nasal [m]. Such nasality may spread over as many as two vowels preceding [n], as in the name "Leon" [lian], or even four or five sounds if the speaker is French.

Coarticulation of Voicing

When words such as "slide" [slaˈd] or "strike" [straˈk] are spoken rapidly, the initial portions of [I] and [r] are voiceless—that is, the [−voice] feature of [s] or [st] spreads to the adjacent liquid consonants [l̥] and [r̥]. Equally interesting, consider the exclamation "Aha!" [a + ha]. If spoken slowly (see Figure 8.16), the [h] is voiceless—there are no voicing striations visible in the spectrogram. If spoken rapidly, the [h] is very nearly voiced throughout, presumably because of the coarticulatory spread of voicing from the vowels. Try producing "aha" slowly, and then rapidly. Can you feel (fingers on thyroid cartilage) and hear the difference?

Coarticulation of Manner

Coarticulation of manner is very rare. However, some instances of historic (diachronic) sound change that are plausible examples of manner coarticulation occur. For example, consider the town name of "Depford," spoken as [Dɛ + fɚd]. Historically it was "Deep Ford" [dip + ford]. If the fricative manner of [f] were coarticulated to the [p], the [p] would become the labial fricative [ɸ], which would easily merge with [f] to become /dɛɸ + fɚd/ → [dɛ + fɚd]. That is, /ɸf/ → [f].*

---

*We are indebted to Dr. Dale Woolley for this example.

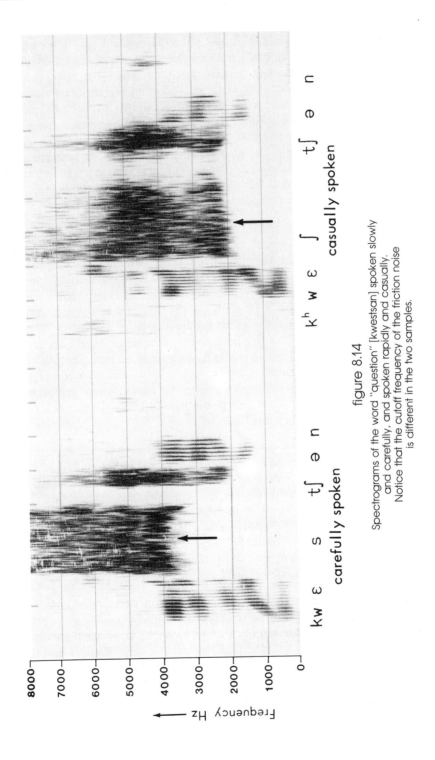

figure 8.14

Spectrograms of the word "question" [kwestsan] spoken slowly
and carefully, and spoken rapidly and casually.
Notice that the cutoff frequency of the friction noise
is different in the two samples.

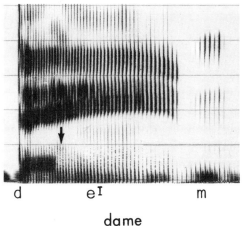

d e^I m

dame

figure 8.15
A spectrogram of the word "dame" [deɪm]. The arrow indicates
the approximate point where the velum opens during the
[eɪ] diphthong, causing coarticulation of nasality.

figure 8.16
A spectrogram of the exclamation "aha!" spoken slowly, then
rapidly. Notice the continuous voicing throughout the rapid
version and the voiceless [h] of the slower version.

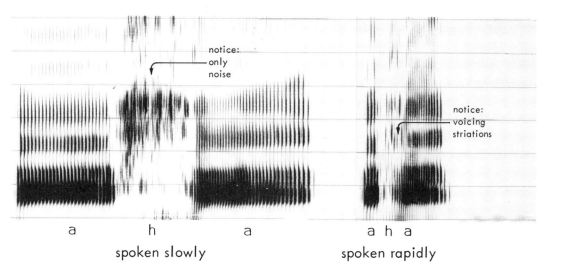

notice:
only
noise

notice:
voicing
striations

a   h   a   a h a
spoken slowly   spoken rapidly

Coarticulation of
Secondary Features   It is worth noting that the secondary articulations (labialization, palatalization,
velarization, and pharyngealization), which generally do not convey a phonemic
contrast in English, do so in other languages. These secondary features are readily
coarticulated in English. For example, Figure 8.17 shows a spectrogram of the
fricative [s] spoken in the words "sue" [su] and "see" [si]. In this case, the spread
labial position for [i] coarticulates with [s], causing the "spread" [s] to have a
noise cutoff frequency of at least 4400 Hz. In the rounded [u] vowel context of
"sue," the protruded lip position of [u] coarticulates with [s], causing a rounded
[s] with a low-frequency cutoff of about 2900 Hz.

Lingual Coarticulation   Because vowels do not involve an actual place or manner of production as do the consonants, in certain cases the
coarticulatory effect of the vowel on the adjacent consonant cannot easily be
specified as the coarticulation of a particular articulatory feature. For this reason, the coarticulatory overlap of the vowel with adjacent stop consonants is
called *lingual* coarticulation. Even before closure is achieved for a stop consonant, the tongue has begun movement toward a position appropriate for the
following vowel. If the stop is an alveolar or a velar, then both stop and vowel
compete for the use of the tongue. Since the stops precede the vowel in serial
order, the tongue tip and dorsum closure are first achieved; at the same time,
the tongue body, insofar as it is independent of tip and dorsum, will advance or
retract, raise or lower, in anticipation of the vowel, even as the stop consonant
closure is made. For the labial stop, there is little impediment to full lingual
coarticulation, and tongue position for the vowel is completely coarticulated.
This means that at the moment of stop consonant release and during the transition, the vocal tract shape reflects the influence of the vowel. As a result, the
transitions for the *same* stop consonant start and bend in differing directions,
depending on the vowel. Figure 8.18 shows spectrograms of the labial consonant [b] combined with front and back vowels. Notice that the starting frequency for resonance 2 is at about 2200 Hz for [bi], 1850 Hz for [be], 1250
Hz for [ba], 900 Hz for [bo], and 800 Hz for [bu]. Such extreme coarticulation is characteristic of the stop consonants, and for this reason, they have
been called the most highly encoded speech sounds.

OTHER SOUND CHANGES:
SHIFTS AND DELETIONS   In addition to coarticulation, the rapidity of continuous speech brings forth a complex pattern of sound shifts, and
syllable deletion or alteration. Martinet (1955) suggests that sound may change
because we are "lazy"; we tend to slur, to simplify, and to render easy most
"difficult" articulations. However, such simplification often results in sounds
that are acoustically less distinct. Indeed, the sounds of speech are not separate
entities, free to be changed at will. Individual sounds occur within a sound pattern for a given language. The sound pattern is like a fishnet. Each sound
within the net stands connected to and in opposition to all other sounds in the
pattern. Change of one sound tends to release compensatory shifts for many of

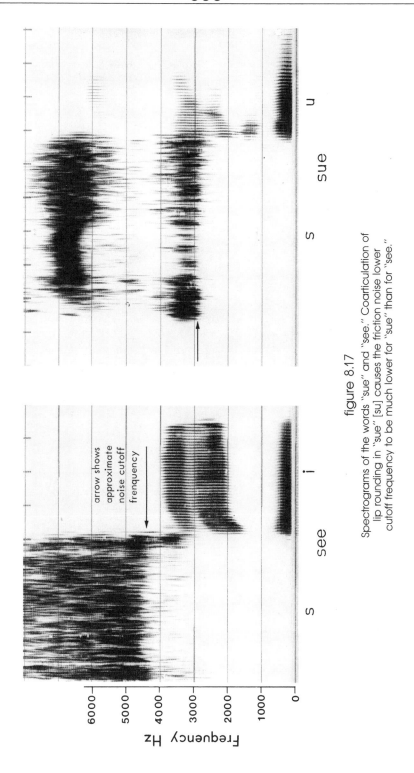

figure 8.17

Spectrograms of the words "sue" and "see." Coarticulation of
lip rounding in "sue" [su] causes the friction noise lower
cutoff frequency to be much lower for "sue" than for "see."

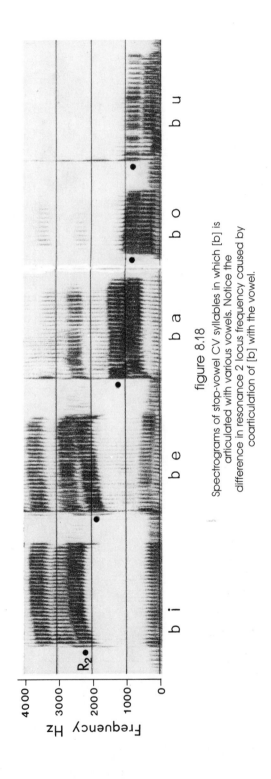

figure 8.18

Spectrograms of stop-vowel CV syllables in which [b] is
articulated with various vowels. Notice the
difference in resonance 2 locus frequency caused by
coarticulation of [b] with the vowel.

the other sounds in the pattern. Listeners presumably like to hear crisp, distinct sounds because it makes the task of listening easier. It would appear that ear and mouth are in a state of dynamic tension, the physiological tendency to simplify articulation contradicting the perceptual need for distinctiveness.

Let us assume that in rapid, colloquial speech, speakers, being naturally lazy and prone to simplify what is complex, tend to make things "easy" for themselves by rearranging or deleting sounds and/or syllables. *Metathesis* is a rearrangement of the order of sounds, especially consonants within a cluster. For example, the word "ask" [æsk] may be colloquially pronounced as "axe" [æks], with [k] and [s] having shifted position. Or a child may say "Fisk it daddy" [fɪsk], rather than "Fix it daddy" [fɪks], with [s] and [k] switched in position. *Epenthesis* is segment deletion, usually of a consonant. For example, the words "last time" [læst + taˈm], if spoken casually and rapidly, will be pronounced "las time" [læs + taˈm] with a deletion of [t]. Another example is the deletion of [v] in the phrase "cup of coffee" [kʌp + əv + kɔfi] → [kʌp + ə + kɔfi]. *Syncope* is even more drastic deletion of whole syllables and words. For example, the phrase "did you eat yet?" [dɪd + ju + it + jɛt] becomes "djeet yet?" [djit + jɛt]. Or, "It's another one" [ɪts + ənʌðɚ + wʌn] becomes "snother wʌn" [snʌðɚ + wʌn]. An example of the epenthetic loss of a vowel occurs for the word "below" [bəloᵁ]; when spoken colloquially, it easily suffers the loss of the vowel [ə], [bloᵁ], and occurs as a monosyllabic word. Figure 8.19 shows the syncope of "did you eat?" These and many other interesting, but as yet unexplained shifts, losses, and changes of sound are characteristic of casual, colloquial, conversational speech. They are not often seen in the laboratory because people tend to speak carefully when they know that they are being recorded or used as subjects for the study of their speech.

Coarticulation has some interesting consequences for speech perception. If three segments, [ABC], are coarticulated, they overlap so that certain of the features of each segment spread(s) to a neighbor. Let us indicate this overlap

figure 8.19

A spectrogram of the phrase "did you eat" spoken carefully,
and then spoken colloquially with the loss of two syllables.

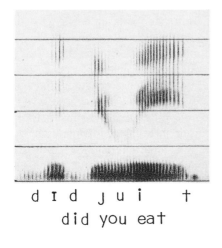
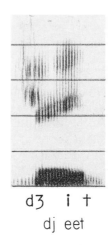

d ɪ d ɟ u i   t   dʒ i t

did you eat   dj eet

with a subscript. After coarticulation, the word "ABC" becomes $A_B \, {}_A B_C \, {}_B C$. If the overlap is very nearly complete, such as for stop-vowel syllables, a listener must *hear* a complete syllable, since the necessary acoustic cues for detection of the stop are spread over a large part of the syllable. When a listener hears the coarticulated allophone $[A_B]$, he hears not only $[A]$, but certain acoustic cues for $[B]$. When he hears $[{}_A B_C]$, he hears not only $[B]$ but cues for $[A]$ and $[C]$. When he hears $[{}_B C]$, he hears $[C]$ as well as cues for $[B]$. In other words, coarticulation spreads, or smears, the acoustic cues to neighboring sounds. This often allows the listener to predict that $[B]$ is present on the basis of hearing $[A_B]$, to predict that $[C]$ is present having heard only $[{}_A B_C]$, and so on. This might enable a listener to predict the missing or obscured sound in the case of noise masking certain speech sounds. Furthermore, if the acoustic cue for a segment is spread over several adjacent sounds, a listener has more time to process acoustic cues before making a decision as to what sounds were heard. Failure to coarticulate speech sounds in a natural way causes speech to sound artificial and unnatural, which is one of the reasons that computer-generated speech sounds strange — the appropriate coarticulations are missing.

COARTICULATION IN OTHER LANGUAGES

To our knowledge speakers of all languages display coarticulation processes, although only a small fraction of the thousands of languages currently in existence have been studied for coarticulation. What is both troublesome and exciting is this: certain coarticulations present in one language are not found in another language. According to Tatham (1971), some intrinsic allophonic coarticulations are probably a physiological necessity; they occur because of the neuromuscular operating characteristics of the SPM. However, some of these intrinsic allophonic variations reflected as coarticulations can voluntarily be modified or prevented, whereas others cannot. It is the phonetician's task to determine the entire set of coarticulations, and to determine which reflect the automatic operation of the SPM and are intrinsic allophones, and which are linguistic whims determined by the sound pattern.

The speaker of a given language must learn those extrinsic coarticulations that do not arise naturally from the SPM as a child by hearing and mastering production of those coarticulations which his or her language group deliberately uses. Thus, many extrinsic coarticulation allophones are a part of learned linguistic competence. Other intrinsic coarticulation allophones seem to be *universal;* they appear in every language studied and presumably need not be learned. For example, as far as is known, when a stop consonant and a vowel are produced in syllable, the tongue shape for the vowel is coarticulated with the consonant articulation. If all languages were studied and certain coarticulations were found to be truly universal, there would be good reason to believe that they constitute a set of involuntary, noncontrollable, intrinsic coarticulation allophones that reflect the natural operating characteristics of the SPM. Knowledge of which coarticulation allophones are intrinsic and which are extrinsic would be a valuable means for sorting and classifying developmental and functional disorders of articulation.

PROCESSES ANALOGOUS
TO COARTICULATION IN OTHER
SKILLED MOTOR BEHAVIORS   If we extend the concept of coarticulation to another skilled motor activity, playing musical instruments, we find that
there exist skilled anticipatory behaviors which appear to "chunk" motion into
overlapping wholes.* In speech, coarticulation is important in the production of
syllabic units; in music, it plays a vital role in the expression of the musical
motif (a motif is the briefest melodic or rhythmic unit, consisting of two or
more notes). Since music, like speech, takes place over time, we hear a succession of notes in some defined order. Different notes occurring before or after a
given note will often cause predictable variations in how that note is mechanically produced (articulated) by the performer. For example, were a string
player given two motifs (see Figure 8.20) to be played on the same string
(D string), he or she would perform them in a different manner. That is, since
motif A involves a leap between E and B, it would necessitate shifting the entire hand (and arm) from first to fourth position. In motif B, the notes A + B +
C are "neighboring pitches" and could all be played within the same hand posi-

figure 8.20

(a) Two musical motifs to be played on the same string;
(b) the same motifs shown on a piano keyboard, illustrating
the difference in space between keys for the two motifs.

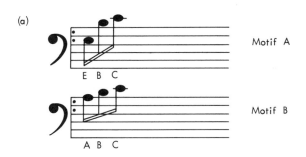

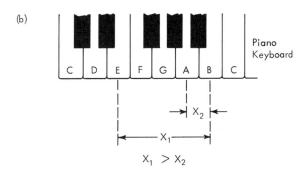

*We are indebted to Elizabeth Osterle, cellist, for these examples.

tion. It is this physical difference in the performance of motifs A and B that demands the use of a coarticulationlike strategy.

Because motif A contains a larger interval leap than motif B, the hand and arm have to travel a greater distance. Perhaps it is easier to understand this by looking at the piano keyboard (Figure 8.20b). Here, one can readily observe that the distance from E to B is greater than the distance from A to B. The same principle holds for the string instrument. As a result, the hand must move a greater distance in motif A than in motif B. It is this greater distance, combined with a second important factor, the difference in mass, that results in a longer transition period between notes 1 and 2 in motif A than in motif B. Motif A involves the change of the hand, arm, and finger locations, but motif B requires only the lifting of the individual fingers. Since the mass of the hand, arm, and finger is far greater than the mass of the fingers alone, it is a much clumsier unit and cannot be handled as rapidly as the single finger.

When played at a very rapid speed, all these factors combined would serve to lengthen motif A in relation to motif B. Were rhythm not such an important musical factor, the performer would not worry about this elongation. But, because rhythm is an indispensable musical parameter, the performer will "overlap" the various positions. That is, either consciously or unconsciously, he or she will attempt to shorten the total time and minimize the distance traveled between the pitches (targets). In this particular example, the performer would accomplish this in the following manner: (1) Raise the arm level for the E so that it was higher up than the normal arm position used to produce an isolated E on the D string. (2) Position the arm so that the elbow was pointed closer toward the bridge than it would be for the normal arm position used to produce an isolated E. Thus, he or she would be shortening the actual distance to be traveled along two dimensions, vertical and horizontal. This, in turn, serves to decrease the transition time between E and B and allows him or her to adhere to the beat.

Yet another musical factor, that of clarity, demands the use of overlap. Ideally, in a rapid passage the performer strives for as much clarity and clearness of articulation as possible. Once again, referring back to our motif A, we see that it involves shifting of hand and arm positions and thus entails a "sliding sound" as the hand moves up the string. This sliding sound only serves to muddle a rapid passage by providing an intrusive mixture of sounds. For this reason, the performer attempts to eliminate the sliding or shifting sound by altering position for the E, as discussed earlier, in order to prepare or anticipate the upcoming B, thereby shortening the transition period between the two. Releasing some of the pressure of the traveling finger itself would further serve to eliminate the shifting sound.

Coarticulation-type processes, then, play a role in both music and speech production and appear to occur for the same reasons. That is, overlap serves to minimize the distance between targets or notes, to reduce travel time, enhance rapidity, and eliminate or prevent intrusive sounds.

problems in constructing models of articulation

In this discussion of models, we will treat the terms articulation, articulation processes, phonetic component, and sound production mechanism (SPM) as equivalents. A model is an abstraction which permits "predictions." When a system or structure is modeled, the unnecessary detail is stripped away to reveal the vital framework of structures, arranged in some order and bearing working interrelationships. Before examining the phenomena a model of articulation must explain, we should consider one of the major reasons for the difficulties people have had in modeling the production of speech. In the physical sciences, when an experiment is performed the physicist or chemist knows quite exactly what chemicals, materials, forces, fields, and so on are present before the interaction occurs. The scientist then measures the results of the interaction, and by comparing the antecendent conditions (causes) and results (effects), he or she can explain or model the processes involved. Conversely, knowing the causes and the system (model), he can predict the effects (outputs). Conceptually, the processes are shown in Figure 8.21. When studying a human behavior such as speech, we are handicapped because we do not directly know what the input or antecedent conditions of speech are. We do not directly know what units of speech are input to the speech production mechanism. We do not know whether words, phrases, syllables, phonemes, or features are the basic input units. We do not know how timing, stress, juncture, and rate signals are represented and inserted into the system. Each linguistic theory offers a choice of differing speech units which might be input for the model. As a result, the majority of physical measurements and observations made of speech have been

figure 8.21

A block diagram illustrating the nature of cause
and effect viewed in terms of a system whose operation
is explained by comparing cause with effect.

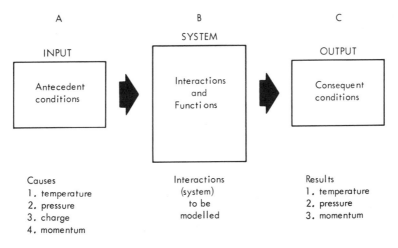

made at the output of the system (physiological or acoustic data). Thus, models of articulation are based on speculation about what goes into the system. You might say that the speech scientist has one equation with two unknowns, which if you are mathematically sophisticated, means that no *single* solution is possible. Until we get inside a human being's head and in a sophisticated way understand how the brain works, our models of speech production will be, at best, educated speculations.

Most authorities, beginning with Lashley, agree that a model of articulation must bridge the gap between the phonological level of language representation and the *biomechanical* level of articulator movement, as shown in Figure 8.22. When a speaker talks, his or her encoding process involves communication of an idea (semantic level) which is organized into a string of morphemes with proper order, shape, and relationships (grammatical level). The phonemic segments within the morphemes at the grammatical level are then rearranged, deleted, and allophonically varied systematically at the phonological level. The output of the phonological component consists of a systematic phonetic representation in which all allophones are fully interpreted, including many of the subtle coarticulations attributable to phonetic context. Following this, the string of fully specified allophones is sent to the production mechanism, where a series of motor commands are assigned, one set for each sound at the neuromotor level. The motor commands for successive sounds are carefully blended within the articulation mechanism so that the stream of speech will be smoothly and rhythmically executed. Finally, the neuromotor commands arrive at the muscles of the vocal tract to initiate speech at the myomotor (muscular) level. The biomechanics of the vocal tract system result in vocal tract movements, which in turn produce the sounds of speech.

We will assume that the output of the phonological component of the grammar serves as input to the SPM. At the systematic phonetic level of description, the phonological output consists of a sentence composed of words, each consisting of a string of fully specified extrinsic allophones. Fully specified means that an allophone is sufficiently described so that each extrinsic allophone contains enough information to serve as an adequate input for the SPM. At the input to the SPM, we would also suppose that the input sentence is marked for intonation type, stress levels, junctures, and so on. Tempo of speech must be generated elsewhere, perhaps in the SPM itself, since rate is not part of the linguistic code. Within the SPM, each extrinsic allophone is converted into a set of neuromotor commands. The neuromotor commands for

figure 8.22

A schematic illustration of where a model
of articulation fits into the encoding process.

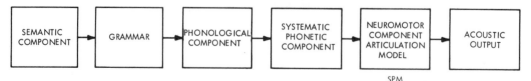

SPM

each segment are subtly mixed or adjusted with those of neighboring segments so that the resulting speech output will be smoothly continuous. These commands in turn arrive at the muscle motor units to initiate speech at the *myomotor* (muscular) level. Here the biomechanics of the vocal tract system result in vocal tract movements which in turn cause the production of speech sound. If we wish to further elaborate and speculate on the operation of the SPM, we may assume that the SPM encodes each extrinsic allophonic segment in terms of its distinctive features. Each "abstract" distinctive feature is converted into a set of physiological-articulatory features during the encoding process. Thus, the SPM model must accept a whole phrase or sentence as in *input,* and at the output of the model, there must emerge a steadily changing stream of muscle contractions and contingent articulator movements.

Any SPM model must account for the following aspects of production:

1. It must specify a basic unit or units of speech production, the actual unit of speech which as a whole is directly converted into a unitary, integrated gestalt of muscle contraction.

2. It must specify the target(s) as: (a) auditory, (sounds of a particular quality); or (b) a set of particular positions of the articulators within vocal tract inner space; or (c) a set of muscle contractions: either the strength of muscle contraction of the length of the contracted muscle is fixed for all articulatory muscles for each target.

3. It must provide for a timing mechanism that can set an overall tempo of utterance; once tempo is set, assign consonants and vowels their proportionate durations within a syllable; and determine a rhythmic pattern when a pattern of stresses is applied to the train of speech syllables.

4. It must account for how feedback is used to control both target seeking *and* timing behavior.

5. It must provide a natural, realistic, and economical set of mechanisms to account for LR and RL coarticulatory overlap. That is, the model must have some type of look-ahead device for RL coarticulations and look-behind mechanism for LR coarticulations.

6. It must provide a complete neuromotor myomechanical description of the structure and dynamic function of the SPM that will reflect both the neuromotor and myomechanical constraints of the system, as well as the natural physiological operating characteristics that jointly give rise to intrinsic allophonic variations.

Most models of speech production account for some but not all the points listed above, and the points themselves are far from being a complete list of the aspects of continuous articulation for which we must account. Let us look now at the evidence we have about the SPM.

THE NATURE OF THE SPM

Articulator Controllability   The evidence is firm that the smallest controllable vocal tract structures are the articulators. This suggests that any description of the SPM should be based on articulator movements. Since each articulator moves in one or several distinctive ways, we can consider the independent, speech-related articulator movements as articulatory features. For example, as the velum lowers, the [+ nasal] articulatory feature occurs; as the velum elevates, the opposite [− nasal] feature occurs. So too for [+ voicing, ± lip rounding, ± mandible lowering, ± tongue advancement]. These and more articulatory features can be treated as binary, plus-minus (present-absent) movements or features. If needed, each feature can be specified more continuously, as any one of a range of values, rather than just present-absent or plus-minus. Such articulatory features can specify the position in space of the lip, mandible, tongue tip, tongue blade, tongue dorsum, velum, pharyngeal walls, and larynx. Every unique speech sound can thus be specified in terms of a unique set of articulatory features. One trouble with this notion is that in some instances, there is more than one acceptable way of articulating a target segment such as [r]. For different people, somewhat different articulatory feature descriptions would be necessary.

It appears likely that the output of the articulation mechanism consists of motor commands issued to the relatively independent but coordinately controllable articulator muscles. The results of the motor commands are binarily described positions or movements in inner, articulatory vocal tract space.

Serial Ordering Errors (Spoonerisms)

It is a relatively common occurrence, when we speak, for the serial order of phonemes, consonant clusters, or even syllables to be switched. For example, the phrase "give me a cup of tea" can be spoken as "give me a tup of kea." In this case, there is a switch of word-initial consonant phonemes:

$$/k\Lambda p + \partial v + ti/ \rightarrow [t\Lambda p + \partial v + ki].$$

The most frequent switches of phonemes involve consonants rather than vowels; occasionally, entire consonant clusters are switched:

> "It's a pretty cloudy day outside"
> "It's a klitty proudy day outside"
> /prɪti + klaᵁdi/→ [klɪti + praᵁdi]

Such switches in the serial order of sounds and clusters can occur over a distance of up to three to four words. Generally, the switches do not occur if they cause sounds to occur in an impossible order—that is, if they violate the morpheme structure rules of language:

   1. "Schlitz beer"   [blɪts + ʃɪɚ] Blitz Sheer
   2. "Schlitz beer"   [ʃbɪts + lɪɚ] Shbitz leer

Alternative 2 is rather unlikely, since the consonant sequence [ʃb] in [shbɪts + lɪɚ] is not permissible in English, whereas [bl] in [blɪts + lɪr] is a permissible consonant cluster.

These errors in the serial ordering of sound are called *Spoonerisms* and have profound implications for models of speech production. For example, the fact that serial ordering is interrupted by switches of sounds argues that the segment may well be the smallest, independently manipulable element of linguistic behavior. Second, the fact that Spoonerism switches can span up to three or even occasionally four words implies that at some point in time a large chunk of speech is held in storage prior to articulation; otherwise, such switching could not occur. The fact that the switches are primarily consonants suggests that consonants, as releasing and arresting elements in syllables, may be uniquely difficult to order serially. The fact that the sound switches only rarely violate rules of sound ordering (phonotactic rules) suggests that the switching error process is not a complete breakdown, but rather an orderly, predictable error in serial ordering at a relatively high level in the grammar.

Coarticulation

Examination of continuous speech reveals that coarticulation processes occur everywhere; as many as three to four sounds on either side of the sound exerting the influence may be coarticulated. The existence of such coarticulation has implications for models of production. For example, the RL anticipatory coarticulation may spread three or four phonemes in advance of the sound that is the source of the coarticulated feature, and the coarticulation is not often hindered by the presence of word or syllable junctures in its path:

$$\text{"this too"} \rightarrow [\theta\text{ɪ}s^w + t^wu]$$

Notice that lip rounding spreads across the word juncture to the [s] segment. This implies that at the level at which long-range anticipatory coarticulation occurs, the speaker must be holding as many as several words in storage as he or she systematically introduces the appropriate degree of coarticulation into the motor commands to the speech musculature. LR or carryover coarticulation generally does not spread over as many sounds as the RL effect, but it has been reported to be a "stronger" effect: the coarticulatory shifts of the articulatory features are more pronounced for LR than for RL effects. It has been shown that LR coarticulation is not simply a result of mechano-inertial limitations; the speaker must retain, as was suggested, a several-word chunk of speech in storage until all the sounds and syllables within are issued as commands. Such LR effects probably reflect the speaker's deliberate strategy of adjusting two sounds to make the transition between them as smooth and short as possible.

In general, the coarticulation data indicate that coarticulation is not a solely peripheral, mechanical process. Rather, much of it is a deliberate, preferred physiological operating characteristic of the SPM that causes speech sounds to overlap. As a result, any model of articulation must explain coarticulation as a vital part of the articulation process.

Language Differences in Coarticulation

If coarticulation represented uncontrollable natural physiological operating characteristics of the SPM, then speakers of all languages would display roughly the same kinds and amounts of coarticulation. Coarticulation, as a physiological necessity, would be a phonetically universal, source of intrinsic allophonic variation. This is not the case. Certain nasal coarticulations characteristic of French or Hindi speakers are not found in English; certain place and manner coarticulations characteristic of Swedish and English do not occur in Russian, and so on. In fact, of the thousands of languages spoken worldwide, only speakers of a few of these languages have been subjected to thorough investigation for even a few types of coarticulation. It would appear that many coarticulations are language specific. This means that certain universal coarticulations can be voluntarily prevented by the speaker, or that certain coarticulations must be learned as part of linguistic competence. Such learned or manipulable coarticulations would serve as a source of extrinsic allophones.

A model of the SPM must eventually be able to specify (1) why coarticulation occurs, (2) which coarticulations are learned and language-specific, and (3) which are physiologically universal, whether or not they can be voluntarily suppressed or altered.

The Representation of Targets

Investigators such as Lashley who have studied the nature of complex motor programming for skilled movements such as speech, dance, sports, and music have argued that the performer stores neural commands for subunits of movement. When called upon to produce a serially ordered stream of movement, he or she calls forth each subunit and skillfully joins the subunits into a stream by means of transition movements.

In what form are these subunits stored in the brain? Lashley, and somewhat later, MacNeilage, noticed that a given target sound can occur in thousands of differing contexts: sound [A] can occur in contexts [BAC, CAB, XAY], and so on. This implies that the transition movement pattern from [A] to the next sound changes with each change in phonetic context. Thus, a single set of motor commands that specify a single, fixed set of muscle tensions or lengths is impossible since a different physical path through articulatory inner space is needed for [A] in each new context. MacNeilage used tennis to illustrate this problem. A single set of motor commands to the muscles of the body for an overhead smash of the tennis ball over the net is impossible. Each time the player prepares such a shot, he or she is at a differing spot on the court, moving at a different speed, with his or her body in a different posture. Thus, the invariant aspect of an overhead shot is that it must get the ball over the net. The target aimed for is a spatial one — ball over the net. The tennis player uses a variety of different muscular movements (means) to achieve a constant spatial target (end).

It appears likely that speakers, who "know" or have a precise mental representation of their inner vocal tract space, aim for a "spatial" target when making speech sounds. For example, since lip opening depends on both lip and mandible position, the same or differing speakers can achieve a given lip opening using a wide variety of muscular commands because many combinations of lip and mandible movement can give rise to a given lip opening. Indeed, the size and shape of the oral and pharyngeal cavities depend on tongue position. Tongue position and shape depend on the contraction of tongue muscles and position of the mandible. This implies that, within limits, a speaker can produce a given vocal tract shape with a wide variety of combined tongue and mandibular movements, and this appears to be the case. For example, a smoker who clamps a jaw shut on a pipe or cigar restrains the normal mandibular movements for speech, but can compensate by using the tongue alone to produce the needed shapes for speech. All of us are unconsciously aware that some people speak with little or no lip and mandible movement (like Humphrey Bogart) and rely mainly on tongue movement, whereas others use less tongue movement and more lip/jaw movement to achieve the desired vocal tract shape. Thus, we can compensate swiftly and unconsciously in the face of restraint of articulator movement, or when the phonetic context changes, and still achieve targets accurately. This implies that targets for speech consist of *positions* of the articulators in the three-dimensional inner space of the vocal tract, rather than a particular set of muscle contractions. In MacNeilage's words, ". . . the essence of the speech production process is not an inefficient response to invariant central signals, but an elegantly controlled variability of response to the demand for a relatively constant end (spatial target)."

We can extend MacNeilage's idea that target sounds are best represented as mental images of the "spatial position" of the articulators needed to produce the sound. It may be simpler and more economical to suppose that the speaker stores the perceptual image of the sound as the target. In the process of acquiring language, children perform millions of experiments in which they produce a vocal tract shape and then listen to its acoustic result, the sound. Since we know that many alternative vocal tract shapes can produce the desired sound, one may assume that the speaker has stored the mental image of all the sounds in the sound pattern of his or her language within a "perceptual space." When he or she wishes to produce the sound, the speaker makes a note of where the articulators are and then issues the commands needed to produce the acoustic target. Every speaker "knows" intuitively the rules governing conversion of vocal tract shape to acoustic patterns. That is what learning to speak is all about. We may hypothesize, then, that the speaker stores "acoustic target sounds" in perceptual space. When called upon to use them, he or she naturally uses knowledge of acoustic theory, the rules for conversion of vocal tract shape to speech sound, to issue appropriate target commands. The rules, presumably, reflect the flexibility of the articulatory system in that a wide variety of shapes can be, and often are, used to create a single acoustic target.

The Problem of Phonemic Invariance

As you may have noticed, an underlying (abstract) phonemic-segment-sized unit of speech is crucial to any model of the SPM. If the phonemic segments are mental realities, they must exist in the speaker's mind as ideal, invariant units. At the input to the SPM each phonemic segment is one of a class of extrinsic allophones the speaker has selected to fit the junctural, stress, or word-position context. Beyond this point, the normal physiological operating characteristics and constraints of the SPM, among which is coarticulation, produce intrinsic allophonic variations of the extrinsic allophones. At the speech output, there are no observable invariant segments. The long and frustrating search for invariant motor commands, invariant muscle contractions, and invariant vocal tract shapes has been unsuccessful. Much of this frustration probably results from the fact that in a changing phonetic context, differing muscle commands are used to move toward and away from the target sound. The muscle contractions and associated vocal tract shapes are variable for at least two physiological reasons: (1) There is a deliberate RL–LR overlap that causes intrinsic allophonic variations to occur, and (2) articulatory compensation is possible – a speaker can produce the same acoustic target sound with variety of muscle contraction patterns. When these factors are coupled with variability attributable to mechano-inertial timing limitations, age-sex factors, and performance limitation factors, the surprising thing is not that continuous speech is variable, but that it is as nearly invariant and intelligible as it is.

Feedback Control of Continuous Speech

During the process of continuous speech, a swiftly changing stream of vocal tract movement occurs. The central nervous system must be kept informed about velocity of motion, articulator positions, and the magnitude of air pressure and flow at the larynx and in the oropharyngeal cavity. The articulation control system can be compared with a servosystem. The servomechanism (Figure 8.22) samples its own output, compares it to the input, and if the two are not in agreement, uses the error signal (the difference between the input signal and feedback from the output signal) to correct the input so that the output matches target. Typical servomechanisms include such things as thermostats, autopilots, and cruise controls on automobiles. All servomechanisms are characterized by a feedback delay time; the time between sampling the output, comparing it with input, and generating an error signal that will cause the error in the output to be corrected.

A speaker can consciously sample his or her articulation by hearing it (auditory feedback), by feeling it (tactile sensation) or by sensing the position of the body in space (kinesthesia). If the auditory feedback signal is reduced by masking or altered by a time delay, rate, duration, vocal intensity, vocal frequency, and fluency will be disrupted. If an anesthetic is applied to the oral cavity or vocal folds, there is a loss of tactile and muscle spindle feedback. The resulting speech shows a loss of articulatory precision, misarticulation of fricatives, slowing of transitions, and loss of secondary articulations such as labialization and retroflexion. Although speech is still fairly intelligible, there are enough errors and allophonic variations caused by anesthesia to indicate that the speaker depends upon feedback systems to monitor and to control speech production.

Other investigators have observed that articulator movement depends on the position, direction, and speed of movement at the instant when the articulators begin the transitional movement toward an oncoming sound. For example, consider the mandibular movement needed for lip closure for [p] in words like [p₁æp₂] or [p₁ip₂]. At the instant that the mandible is lowered for [æ] or elevated for [i], a motor command arrives that causes the mandible to move toward closure for [p₂]. In the case of the [i-p₂] transition, the distance to be moved is slight, whereas the [æ-p₂] transition involves a considerably larger distance. In the [æ-p₂] transition, the mandible moves forcefully and swiftly to effect closure, whereas in the [i-p₂] case, it moves more slowly. If closed-loop feedback were being used to control this differential speed of closure, we might suppose that sensory feedback from muscle stretch receptors or tendon receptors at the temporomandibular joint of the mandible would signal the brain concerning the degree of mandible lowering, and in the [æ-p₂] transition, cause the brain to emit a stronger motor command to get closure because of the larger distance to be traveled. Movement toward target may vary widely because of the differing articulator positions caused by differing preceding sounds, so swift feedback is probably necessary. Such feedback must include not only positional information (where the articulator is) but velocity information (how fast and in what direction). In order that the articulator arrive at target in a certain time, some knowledge of how fast the articulator is moving is needed. If the speaker could not closely control the speed and duration of consonant-vowel transitions by using such feedback, the encoding of stop consonants would be changed, since too slow or fast a transition would cause a shift in consonantal identity.

Abbs (see Lass, 1976) claimed to be able to disrupt feedback from the muscle spindles (γ-affect receptors) of the mandibular muscles. When this source of feedback was disrupted, jaw movements were characterized by reduced acceleration, alteration of the timing of movement, and a loss of fine positional control. In other words, the transitions were slowed and clumsy, and jaw targets took longer to achieve and were more often undershot. In another study, Folkins and Abbs (see Lass, 1976) demonstrated that when the jaw was restrained (prevented from achieving target) suddenly during an articulation of [p], the lips were able to compensate and achieve closure within 20 to 30 msec, indicating that feedback from the muscles of the suddenly restrained jaw caused the brain to emit a swift corrective, compensatory command to the lip to achieve closure.

The Sensory Receptor System
of the Muscles

The muscles of the tongue, both extrinsic and intrinsic, the lips, the mandible, the intrinsic muscles of the larynx, and certain of the muscles of respiration (especially the inter-costal muscles), have been shown to contain muscle spindles that could relay feedback to the central nervous system concerning the length, tension, and rate of change of tension in these muscles. Recently, Matthews (1977) has shown that such muscle spindle receptors contribute strongly to the sense of position (kinesthesia) of the limbs and other body parts in space. Thus, the spindles contribute to both conscious and unconscious levels of sensation. Within the oral cavity, the lips, tongue tip, and blade are richly endowed with tactile receptors. The mucosa covering the vocal folds have been shown

(Wyke, 1974) to contain sensory receptors sensitive to variations in air pressure below the folds. Feedback from these sensory systems, especially the muscle spindle sensors, can provide the brain with information concerning when a movement is started, when a target is achieved, and when the target ends and transition starts toward the next target.

For feedback to be useful, it must be swift. Otherwise, the speech movement a speaker sought to control would be completed before the feedback reached the brain to correct an error in the ongoing sound. The muscle spindles can apparently cause afferent impulsation in the nervous system which can travel from a muscle to the cortex of the brain in as little as 20 msec. The swift conduction speeds for such muscle spindle feedback leads us to believe that the muscle spindle feedback loop are used to control the rapid motor acts of speech.

THE ROLE OF FEEDBACK IN MODELS
OF SPEECH PRODUCTION

In most models of speech production, the invariant extrinsic-allophone-segment-sized target can be represented in two different ways. The target segment, as Cooper (1966) suggests, may consist of an invariant ensemble of neuromotor commands to the articulators. Coarticulation arises because of mechano-inertial limitations and deliberate overlap, both of which become increasingly prominent as the speaker increases tempo. Or, as MacNeilage asserts, each target consists of the neural engram of a set of positions in the three-dimensional inner space of the vocal tract. It seems unlikely that a segmental target consists of invariant motor commands for several reasons. First, speakers can compensate by using different amounts of contraction in different muscles to achieve the same sound (the cigar or pipe smoker are good examples as they speak with their nicotine flavored pacifiers clenched between their teeth). Second, there is in fact more than one way to articulate many sounds. And, third, the transition toward a given sound (and the muscle contractions moving it there) depends on the past position (what the previous sound was) of the articulators.

Rather, either a spatial (positional) or even more likely an acoustic target is to be preferred. Thus, it appears that the speaker must monitor, via sensory feedback, the position in space and the velocity of articulator movement if he or she is to achieve the appropriate position within inner space for each segmental target. The intricate muscle spindle systems of the tongue, lips, jaw, thoracic wall, and larynx can provide the swift feedback needed to keep the motor control system "aware" of muscle length, velocity, and spatial position. Such a delicate and swift feedback system undoubtedly assists us achieving targets despite changes in tempo, stress, juncture, and phonetic context. These factors might ordinarily cause us to miss the target if the motor control system could not rely on feedback, but had to issue central commands without "knowing" what was going on in the mouth.

some models of speech production

COOPER'S PARALLEL-PROCESS,
PHONEME-BASED MODEL   Figure 8.23 is a by now famous diagram of a simplified conceptual model of the process of articulation. This
model, first described by F. A. Cooper (1966), indicates that the syntax of the
language provides a sentence output which is then subject to phonological pro-

figure 8.23

A simplified conceptual model of articulation
proposed by Cooper, 1966.

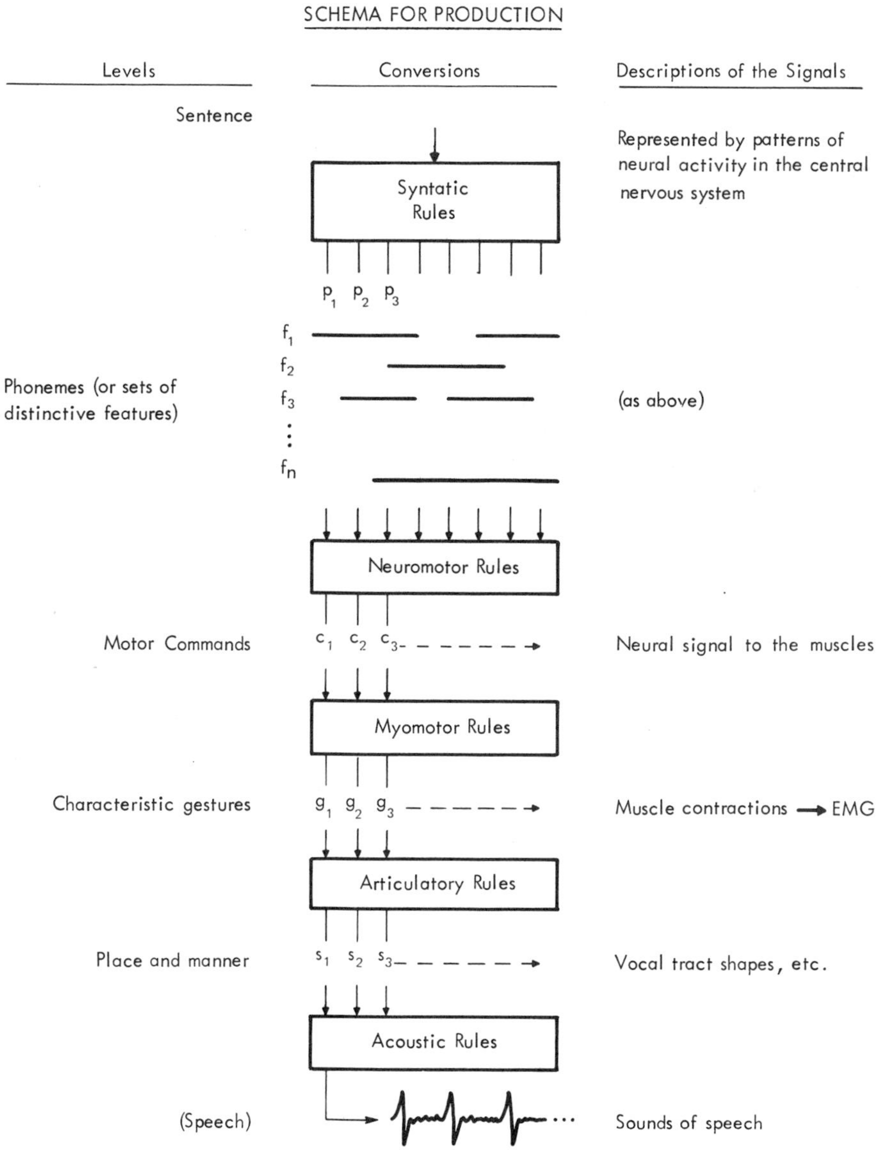

SCHEMA FOR PRODUCTION

Levels	Conversions	Descriptions of the Signals

cesses. They in turn give rise to a "phonetically interpreted" sentence, a sentence with all the proper allophones in place. The neat, invariant, non-overlapping string of allophones are then input to the production system, and at the output, the sounds emerge as an overlapping stream of coarticulated speech. Cooper argues that the coarticulatory overlap of phonemes is a deliberate strategy for speeding up articulation and smoothing transitions. Such speed is possible because the articulators are separately controllable muscular structures. A movement from one phoneme to the next does not generally involve a shift in all the articulatory structures, but only a few. According to Cooper, "Dividing the load among the articulators allows each to operate at a reasonable pace." Such independence of articulator movement is called *parallel processing* and is one of the requirements for high-speed speech.

Cooper argues that phonemes are represented as sets of binary distinctive features, each binary feature being represented in the central nervous system as an "on-off" control command to an articulator(s). The neural signals resulting from the features cause the contraction of the muscles of articulation. However, the simple, invariant on-off muscle motor commands are probably modified by the complex biomechanical and mechano-inertial constraints of the SPM. Cooper recognizes that there must be a central control mechanism which takes into account the tempo of speech and adjusts the duration of the muscle contractions accordingly. The overlapping of adjacent phonemes is a deliberate SPM strategy, but overlapping cannot be so great that the temporal order and phonemic identity of the phonemes is lost. The theoretical model of articulation offered by Cooper is important because it emphasizes that the basic unit is probably the phoneme, with motor commands being issued to each separately controllable articulator to cause the production of a distinctive feature of the phoneme. The coarticulatory overlap primarily results from the need for smooth high-speed production of sounds, and because of mechano-inertial timing limitations that cause allophonic undershoot of targets.

THE KOZHEVNIKOV AND CHISTOVICH MODEL

At certain times, it is useful to study what is incorrect in order to understand what led to the correct solution to a problem. For example, astronomy students learn about the ancient geocentric theory of planetary motion in which the sun and moon and planets circled the earth in spherical paths. This was later modified to a heliocentric theory, in which the planets, including earth, move around the sun at the center of the solar system in elliptical orbits. The students then learn how research data that conflicted with the geocentric theory eventually led to the more satisfactory heliocentric model. In speech production, Kozhevnikov and Chistovich (1965) for convenience, we will abbreviate their names as KC) provided one of the earliest and most complete models of articulation, and that model has sparked much creative research and discussion. KC argued that the fundamental unit of speech production is the syllable, for two reasons. First, it is the minimal *timing unit*. Second, it is the basic *unit of coarticulation*. Thus, a single unit of speech, the syllable, combines both spatio-temporal (coarticulatory) and temporal (tempo, duration) properties needed to describe continuous speech. Everything we know about poetry, rhythm, and music suggests that something like the syllable is the minimal unit of timing. Second, KC argue that articulation in the stream of speech is not the successive articulation of independent phonemic-segmental targets, but the coarticulation of all the phonemic segments within a syllable. Continuous speech consists of the ordering of coarticulated syllables. Coarticulation is greatest within a syllable and smallest between syllables. Thus, the syllable is the fundamental temporo-spatial unit of continuous speech.

The syllable KC propose is unusual; it consists of CV units where C may be a single consonant or a cluster. This "Russian" syllable does not coincide with word boundaries. For example, in the sentence, "Give Tom some paper" [gɪv + tɔm + sʌm + peˈpɚ], you will notice the word junctures. However, KC syllabify the sentence in this way:

$$\frac{gɪ}{S1} + \frac{v \ Tɔ}{S2} + \frac{m \ sʌ}{S3} + \frac{m \ p \ eɪ}{S4} + \frac{pɚ}{S5}$$

The syllables gɪ, vtɔ, msʌ, mpeˈ, and pɚ, do not seem sensible in shape or structure. However, it is on such syllables that KC based their articulation model.

Timing Invariance

KC reasoned that if there was a basic unit of timing in speech, that unit should show some sort of invariance no matter what the tempo of speech. They held that the speaker stored a large chunk of speech, preparatory to speaking, within a "buffer" or short-term memory. This chunk of speech had to be meaningful, since speech consists of meaningful utterance. They suspected that the meaningful clause or *syntagma,* as they called it, was the largest unit of articulation production. The syntagma (clause) consisted of a string of up to seven CV-type syllables marked by a *pause* at either end. Thus, a clause such as "Tonya topila Banyu" was marked by a pause at either end. This syntagma had a total duration, D_{synt}. Each word had a duration, D_{word}, and each syllable had a duration, D_{syll}, and each consonant and vowel had a duration, D_{con} and D_{vow}. Thus, the time pattern of a syntagma consisted of the following measured durations arranged in a hierarchy:

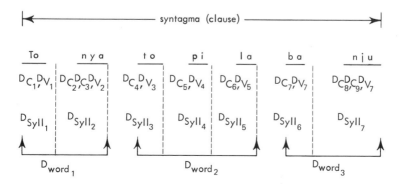

They computed the relative duration of each vowel and consonant relative to their carrier syllable, the duration of each syllable relative to its carrier word, and the duration of each word relative to its carrier clause (syntagma), as shown below:

$$\text{Relative duration:} \quad \begin{aligned} \text{segment} &= D_{con_1}/D_{syll_1}, \; D_{vow_1}/D_{syll_1} \\ \text{syllable} &= D_{syll_3}/D_{word_2} \\ \text{word} &= D_{word_2}/D_{syntag} \end{aligned}$$

They proposed that every syntagma had a particular tempo of utterance, but that changes in tempo did not change the relative time relationship between units of speech. They therefore used a sophisticated battery of articulatory measurements to measure the duration of each word, syllable, and phoneme within a syntagma as it was spoken at a wide range of tempos, from very fast to very slow. They then computed the relative duration of the words to that of the syntagma, the relative duration of syllables to that of their carrier word, and the duration of each phoneme relative to the duration of its carrier syllable.

Within the accuracy with which they could measure the duration of the sounds, syllables, and words, they found that the relative duration of syllables and words was invariant (fixed) even when rate of speech varied, as shown in Figure 8.24. If at a slow rate of speech the syntagma's duration was 6 seconds,

figure 8.24

A graph adapted from Kozhevnikov and Chistovich (1965) which
shows that syllables and words preserve an invariant relative duration
as a speaker changes tempo, but that consonants
and vowels change relative duration as a function of tempo.

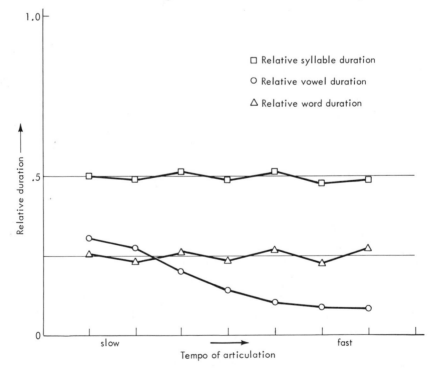

and if the duration of a word within the syntagma was 2 seconds, the relative word duration was $D_{word}/D_{synt} = \frac{2}{6} = .33$. When the rate of speed increased, the duration of the syntagma might shrink to 3 seconds, that of a word one to 1 second, and $D_{word}/D_{synt} = \frac{1}{3} = .33$. Thus, as one slowed down or sped up the rate of speech, the relative proportion of time that each word and syllable occupied in the utterance was unchanging. However, the relative duration of consonants and vowels was not invariant as tempo of speech changed. As one spoke faster and faster, the relative duration of the vowel within a carrier syllable tended to shrink, and shrink faster than the accompanying consonant. Thus, KC argued that the syllable was the smallest time-invariant unit of speech, and as such might be the basic unit of motor programming.

Coarticulation in Syllables   KC then examined coarticulation within and between syllables. Each syllable had a CCV type construction. They presumed that if the unit of speech production was the syllable, coarticulation should be at a maximum within such a basic unit of production, and much less between syllables. This meant that the vowel overlapped strongly with the preceding consonant, and not the following consonant:

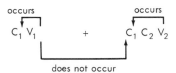

KC investigated numerous coarticulations ranging from lip protrusion to place of consonantal constriction. What they observed was that coarticulation occurred within such CV syllables, but not between them. Within a syllable, they observed that articulatory gestures for the consonants and vowel began nearly simultaneously with the onset of the initial consonant within a syllable:

$$C_1\ C_2\ C_3\ V$$

Thus, given a word such as "postu," lip rounding associated with [u] was observed to start simultaneously with the formation of a friction slit for [s], which is, of course, the first consonant in the CCV syllable [stu]. KC also performed statistical analyses of the variability of the duration of each of the syllables, words, and phrases their subjects spoke. From their data, they concluded that motor commands for the syllables were emitted centrally without the need for feedback from the vocal tract to signal when and how to release commands for the oncoming syllable.

An Outline of the KC Model   A simplified outline of the KC articulation model is shown in Figure 8.25. KC proposed that the timing for speech was controlled by a clocklike generator located within the central nervous system. The "clock" emitted a steady stream of equally timed pulses. KC assumed that the intent to articulate speech begins with an idea, at a cognitive level. The idea is inserted into the grammar, where the output is a sentence in the form of words,

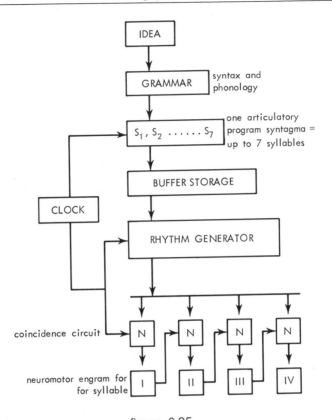

figure 8.25
A simplified illustration of the Kozhevnikov
and Chistovich model of speech production.

each word consisting of one or more syllables. The output of the grammar is a string of up to seven words in a meaningful clause, the syntagma. The syntagma is placed in temporary storage (buffer), where each word is called forth by the rhythm generator. When each word is prepared for activation, a signal corresponding to each syllable within the word is placed in a coincidence detector. When the command to produce the word is issued, a command from the rhythm generator excites all the syllable engrams simultaneously. However, the neural circuitry is arranged so that the command to start the first syllable is the strongest. When the command for syllable 1 is issued, a central feedback circuit excites the coincidence detector for syllable 2, which is already partially excited, and causes it to fire, triggering feedback to syllable 3's coincidence detector, and so on, until all syllables in the word are emitted in serial order. The next word is then prepared for articulation, and so on.

KC maintain that each syllable consists of an open CC-V type structure. Each phoneme consists of an ordered list of articulatory features. Each articulatory feature (place, manner, nasality, voicing, secondary articulatory constrictions, and so on) can be produced by activating a group of muscles. Thus, each syllable is a *feature matrix*. If a particular feature is not specified (is zero) for a given sound, then the next specified (+ or −) value of that feature will be *spread* (coarticulated) from the following sound.* When the command to articulate the syllable occurs, every articulatory feature is activated. However, since the first consonant is produced first, only the noncontradictory features of C_2 and V will be simultaneously articulated at the start of C_1. Notice in Table 8.1 that for feature D, coarticulation has spread the (+) D feature from the vowel to C_2 and C_1. Thus, at the start of articulation, the plus value of feature D is already present. As a result, C_1, C_2, and V are fully coarticulated with respect to feature D. On the other hand, for feature C, consonant 1 is plus and consonant 2 is specified minus. Since these two values are contradictory, the minus is not spread to the plus value, and upon production of C_1, production of the plus value for feature C is completed. All neutral values of an articulatory feature are replaced with the next nonneutral value of that feature via deliberate coarticulatory overlap.

When the command to produce the syllable arrives, as many features of C_2V and so on that do not contradict the articulation of C_1 are actuated and produced simultaneously with the start of the features of C_1. All the movements of the vowel not contradictory to the articulation of the consonant(s) begin simultaneously with the start of the syllable. In other words, all articulatory movements for a CV syllable are accomplished simultaneously except for those movements that are antagonistic.

Articulation of the consonant cluster seems to occur as follows: The first consonant, C_1, is started. The command to start C_1 is fed back to the effector for C_2. C_2, which is already in a state of subliminal excitation, and is raised to the threshold of excitation on receipt of the C_1 feedback signal, whereupon the C_2 command is released. Figure 8.26 shows a schematic diagram of the system needed to produce a CCV syllable. Let us suppose that element$_1$ controls opening and closing of the lips, and element$_2$, the opening and closing of the tongue. When the command to produce the syllable arrives, both system 1 and 2 are excited. However, the signal to 1 is strong enough to cause it to "fire," whereas the signal to 2 is not strong enough to cause 2 to discharge. The signal emitted by 1 is sent to both B_1 and 2. The signal to B_1 causes the lips to open for C_1 and excites 2 to emit a signal that causes the tongue to form a constriction for C_2 somewhat later than the opening movement for C_1. Feedback, the dotted line from 2 to 1 prevents 1 from issuing a second command to close the lips while the tongue constriction is being made. Following the onset of C_2, the command for the vowel is released, causing both system 1 and 2 to open both lips and tongue for the vowel.

Problems of the KC Model

First, the KC model of articulation was only sketchily outlined and difficult to test. Investigators have claimed that articulator movements and the duration of consonants, vowels, and syllables cannot be measured accurately enough to permit a test of the invariance of the

---

*This implies that RL anticipatory coarticulation is the only type provided for in the KC model.

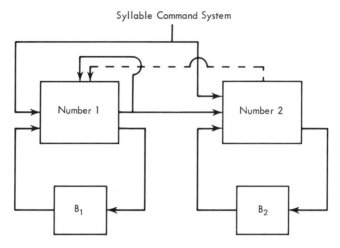

Syllable Command System

Number 1

Number 2

B_1

B_2

Number 1 = system which opens/closes lips
Number 2 = system which opens/closes tongue
B = neuromotor effectors

figure 8.26

A diagram of the neural circuitry needed to produce a
syllable, according to Kozhevnikov and Chistovich.

relative syllable and word durations. Second, in English and many other languages, there is coarticulation in VC and VVC type syllables. For example, in the word "Freon," [frian], the nasalization spreads from the nasal consonant to the preceding vowels: [frian] → [frĩɔ̃n]. Thus, a syllable of VVC construction shows coarticulation, a contradiction to KC's CCV type of coarticulatory syllable. Also, KC focused on RL or anticipatory coarticulation of the vowel on the consonants preceding it, $C_1 C_2 V$, or the effect of C_2 on C_1, $C_1 C_2 V$. However, the overlap of the features of C_1 on C_2 or $C_1 C_2$ on V, $C_1 C_2 V$ in an LR direction are ignored. In Arabic, the pharyngealization of the [k] segment, written as [ḵ], is observed to spread over the following vowel in an LR direction. Such LR coarticulations are not very well accounted for by KC. To put it plainly, there

$$[ḵ \; a \; s] \rightarrow [ḵ \; ạ \; s]$$

is no strong evidence to show that coarticulation is strongest within a CCV syllable. In languages other than Russian many syllable types appear to exist and many types of coarticulation can cross syllable boundaries.

What then is the value of the KC model of articulation? First, KC emphasize that a model of articulation must accommodate both timing and coarticulation as central phenomena. Second, they emphasize that the syllable is probably the major unit of both timing and articulatory integration. However, we still have no hard and fast rules concerning the structure of the syllable. The KC model suggests that the speaker will coarticulate as much as possible; but he or she cannot or will not attempt fully to coarticulate contradictory articulatory gestures, for that would tend to destroy serial order and phonemic identity. Most important, KC's speculations suggest that coarticulation reflects the efficiency and naturalness of overlapping successive skilled motions; the resulting stream of overlapped motions occur swiftly and smoothly, with a minimum of energy expended.

OTHER MODELS OF THE SPM   Because there are so many phenomena to be explained by a model of speech production, there are few models of the SPM, and they are usually incomplete. They are, however, worth examining briefly.

Wickelgren's Model   Wickelgren (1969) proposed a simple but cumbersome model of the SPM using the extrinsic allophone as the basic unit of speech. The allophones depend upon phonetic context; that is, given the phonemic string [A, B C D E F] in a word, then [AB__DEF] is the neighboring phonetic context for [C]. Thus, the allophonic variations in [C] caused by [B] to the left and [D] to the right are indicated as $[_B C_D]$. If we assume that sounds two phonemes away can cause allophonic variations in [C], then we must specify the allophone $[_{AB} C_{DE}]$. If we assume that there are 44 phonemes in English and we compute how many possible combinations of two phonemes may precede and follow each of the 44 in such a context, there are hundreds of thousands of such contextual allophones. If we add stress, juncture, and word position as factors causing allophonic variation, there are even more allophones. And since rate of speech causes allophonic variation, we might have to multiply the phonetic-context/rate/juncture allophones many times over to accommodate all the rate allophones of speech. As you can see, this demands that a *huge* number of allophones be stored in the speaker's memory.

When Wickelgren's speaker prepares to speak, he or she merely orders the proper allophones to be assembled for the selected words and produces them in serial order. They "fit" each other very nearly perfectly. Thus, there is no coarticulation per se, but instead, a clever chaining of the appropriate differing allophones. The speaker would be burdened by having to learn each of several hundred thousand allophones and storing each until needed. This is a brute-force method of producing speech and does not appear to fit the elegant, hierarchical schemes utilized by the central nervous system to control complex movement.

Henke's Model   Henke (1966) proposed a phonemic-segment model of the SPM. The input to the model is a string of phonemic segments. Each segment is a matrix of articulatory targets. The target features change abruptly as one moves from segment to segment. RL coarticulation occurs because a "look ahead" mechanism allows scanning and anticipation of future targets if they are not contradictory to ongoing articulation. LR coarticulation occurs because the articulators move along different paths toward a given target, depending upon where (the past target) they have been. Thus, the past history (position) of the articulator coupled with mechano-inertial and neuromotor constraints provides for the LR coarticulation. The Henke model of the SPM was implemented as a gross computer simulation of speech movement. The model is useful for the notion that phonemic segments are implemented, as Cooper suggested, as articulatory commands to the speech organs. Also useful is the notion that the articulation mechanism can look ahead and anticipate oncoming sounds, causing RL coarticulation to occur.

Ohman's Model   In still another SPM model, Ohman used Dudley's carrier nature of speech production model. Ohman speculated that speech is produced in such a way that there is a slow but steady movement of tongue and lips and mandible from vowel to vowel

$$\begin{array}{cc} C_1 & C_2 \\ \downarrow & \downarrow \\ V_1 \rightarrow V_2 \rightarrow V_3 \end{array}$$

Upon this steadily shifting vowel movement are superimposed the sharp consonantal modulations, V_1 C_1 V_2 C_2 V_3, that interrupt the vowel movement, causing more or less coarticulation, depending on how extensively each consonant must use the tongue and lips and thus interrupt or overlap with vowel-directed tongue movements. The coarticulation between vowels occurs because of steady movement from vowel to vowel. Consonant-vowel coarticulation arises from the superimposition of a consonantal movement on the never-ceasing vowel to vowel movements of the tongue. Ohman's model is interesting but excessively simple.

MacNeilage's Model   MacNeilage (1970), using Lashley's guidelines, also offered a model of the SPM. MacNeilage supposes that the abstract phonemic segment is the minimal unit of speech production. Each segment (extrinsic allophone) is stored in the brain as a mental map of articulator positions within the vocal tract space. The SPM translates allophonic segments into a series of spatial target specifications. The neuromotor system then generates commands that cause the articulators to move toward each successive spatial target in serial order. The command patterns that propel articulators toward target are open-loop: the command system does not await the arrival of feedback information associated with reaching the previous sound before it issues a command for the oncoming sound. The articulation control mechanism stores a large chunk of speech (perhaps a whole phrase) and generates phoneme commands that reflect deliberate, preplanned coarticulation. For example, given the word [ABC], the phoneme [B] is coarticulated with [A] and [C] so that the resulting central phoneme commands [A_B, $_AB_C$, $_BC$] will smoothly and swiftly carry the articulators from target A to B to C without severe interruption, undershooting, or jerky transitions. However, in MacNeilage's words,

> When one considers that any phoneme can be preceded by any one of 20 phonemes, each making unique mechanical demands on any articulator involved in the phoneme-phoneme transition, it becomes obvious that an openloop (feedback independent) control of this system would require the storage and availability to the motor system of an enormous amount of a priori information.

MacNeilage then speculates that an open-loop portion of the command system delivers a context-free command for an articulator to go to a certain ideal or target position. Then a closed-loop feedback circuit samples the velocity and position of the articulator at each point in time and adjusts the muscle driving force so that the target is not over- or undershot. As MacNeilage says, "The most likely possibility for closed loop control of speech is that a muscle may be made to attain an invariant length by the action of a feedback loop controlled by the gamma motor system."

articulation development

The pattern of language development tells us much about the way in which adults use language. The first thing to be noted about articulation development is that it is variable: a few children have mastered the production of all single and clustered phonemes in the language by age 3, and some as late as ages 6 to 7. This implies that neuromuscular maturation and cognitive development play a role in learning to articulate continuous speech. Just as with other complex motor behaviors, a mature sensory-motor system is a vital prerequisite.

Second, the sounds are not learned in a random fashion; certain classes of sounds are acquired early and others late. For example, the labial stops [p] and [m] are acquired early, the labial fricatives [f, v, θ] and velar stops [k, g] are acquired midway in the course of development, and the lingual fricatives [s, z, ʃ, ʒ] and lingual liquid sounds [r, l] are acquired late. This ordering is the average trend for most children, but of course individuals differ. The implication of this sequence is that the motorically easy and natural, feedback-rich, and easily heard sounds should be the first developed by the child. Since most vowels are acquired very early, before most consonants, vowels must be easier tasks than consonants. Since single consonants are acquired earlier than consonant clusters, clustered consonants such as [str, sl, spr, ts] must be a more difficult task than either single consonants or CV combinations. In the course of development, voiced and labial and stop consonants are among the earliest consonants acquired; they may well be less taxing than voiceless, lingual, fricative, and liquid consonants.

Misarticulation is also revealing. For example, children who misarticulate often take CVC syllables like "book" and simplify the closed CVC syllable by deleting the final consonant, making it an open CV syllable: [bʊk] → [bʊ]. Perhaps syllable-final consonants are a more skilled motor task than syllable-initial ones. Children who misarticulate consonants tend to substitute, as an error response, a consonant further forward in the mouth. For example, if [k] in "cake" is misarticulated, a common error is a [t] substitution: /keᶦk/ → [teᶦt] or [teᶦ]. Perhaps anterior consonants are more easily produced, or perhaps children move the consonants anteriorly in order to utilize the richer tactile and visual feedback with which such anterior consonants are endowed.

Perhaps most important, certain consonants are frequently misarticulated: [z], [s], [r], [l] are perhaps the most frequently misarticulated. These are lingual consonants and are among the last sounds to be acquired normally. Perhaps they are acquired last and misarticulated most because they represent a substantial sensory-motor challenge to the young child. Is it an accident that when adults are anesthetized and thus deprived of much of their orosensory feedback, they frequently misarticulate or distort [s], [z], [l], [r], [f], and [θ], the very fricative and liquid and lingual consonants children find to be a sensory motor challenge?

One of the most intriguing findings in the misarticulation literature is that children often misarticulate inconsistently. That is, a particular allophone of a sound is more often correctly produced than another. For example, given the [r] allophones, [r, ɝ, ɚ], the consonantal, prevocalic [r] as in "red" is least frequently misarticulated, whereas unstressed, syllabic [ɚ] is most often misarticulated. This implies that certain allophones caused by stress, syllabic, junctural, or word-position context make the sensory motor task more or less difficult. Even more interesting is the fact that in certain phonetic contexts, some sounds are more often correctly produced than others. Since phonetic contexts cause coarticulation of a given sound, it may be that certain coarticulatory contexts are easier sensory-motor tasks than others. Such misarticulation data from children, data from sensory deprivation studies, and data from other populations suffering from sensory-motor disorders may in the future shed more light on the process of articulation than the work done on normal subjects.

Still other interesting data concerning articulation can be derived from phonetics and phonology. For example, certain sounds like [m] and [s] are very nearly universal, occurring in almost every language worldwide, whereas sounds like [θ] or [ð] are relatively rare. What does it mean, in sensory-motor terms, that such a worldwide preference for certain sounds and not others exists? Is it because certain sounds are easier? Or because certain sounds are acoustically distinctive, and therefore highly contrasting, which is a useful property for speech sounds to have? Equally important are the patterns of sound change, those that have occurred historically (diachronically) or are happening now (synchronically). There is little doubt that the close and patient study of sound change — the patterns, the direction, the types, and the hypothesized reasons — may explain many of the processes of dynamic articulation.

disorders of articulation

Disordered articulation has many causes: anatomical deficits, deficits resulting from disordered sensory feedback, deficits related to neuromotor and sensory-motor immaturity or disorders, and deficits for which there are no obvious anatomical-physiological causes. The cause of any particular disordered articulation may very well be a combination of many such factors. Therefore, it is crucial that we understand the relationships involved in the physiological bases of speech as we attempt to describe and assess disorders.

As speech pathologists, we know that the dynamic processes involved in the act of speaking must be practiced to the point of automaticity — in other words, overlearned. Speakers cannot afford to think about what they are doing. By the time children are talking, they have spent so much time rehearsing or automatizing that clinicians cannot simply *talk* them out of what they're doing. In the following descriptions of articulatory disorders, keep in mind that the disordered speech is, in most instances, automatized. In order to establish the sensory-motor synergy essential for speech rehabilitation, new patterns must also be rehearsed and overlearned to the point of automaticity.

MISARTICULATION   The largest single category of articulation defects includes those problems for which there is no known cause. Those who typify this category include children and adults who release air laterally around the sides of the tongue when approximating [s] and frequently [t, d, tʃ and ʃ]; who approximate [r] and its allophones with [w, l, ʒ, ə]; who approximate [l] and its allophones with [w, j]; or who approximate [s, z] with [θ, ð]. The speaker's sensory-neuromotor systems and intellect appear to be intact or *normal*. By default, we conclude that the speaker is learning or has learned an aberrant phonological pattern not in correspondence with the standard adult phonology. The most important point here is that these misarticulations are *automatized*. As indicated earlier, speech is overlearned to the point of automaticity. Thus, if variant phonological patterns are not identified by the child as such during the period of acquisition, the variant forms become the norm for that speaker. Because the subsystems of language are hierarchically structured, misarticulation must never be regarded as simply a phonetic problem; it has phonological and even syntactic manifestations. Just as there is a sound pattern underlying adult standard articulation, there is a differing or disordered sound pattern underlying nonstandard misarticulation.

During the process of automatization, the phonetic gestalt (shape) of a word supersedes the serial order of its constituent sounds. If during the learning-automatizing process speakers satisfactorily produce the sound segments of their language, then they are subsequently able to distinguish or identify inappropriate sound patterns. When a misarticulating speaker automatizes phonetic patterns inappropriate for his or her language, he or she generalizes the inappropriate sound to all newly learned words. The truth of this can be demonstrated by asking a child or friend with normal articulation to say [θɪŋ + ə + θɔŋ]. Although they may regard it as an odd request, they should be successful. Conversely, if you ask a child or friend who already misarticulates [θ/s] to say [sɪŋ + ə + sɔŋ], he or she will say [θɪŋ + ə + θɔŋ] and swear on a stack of preprimers it is correct. We can make similar observations by asking certain natives of Minnesota to articulate [part] and [pɔrt], those of Pennsylvania's Monogahela Valley to produce [sɪŋɡɚ] and [sɪŋɚ] or [stɪl + mɪl] and [stilmɪl], and those of southern Indiana to produce [paᵘɚ + sɔ] and [par + sɔ]. The difference between the groups demonstrating dialect characteristics and an individual who misarticulates is that the former acquired the phonological distinctions of their linguistic environment, while the latter, for some reason, did not.

Analysis of articulatory performance typically includes a survey of sound production. Sound segments are evaluated according to their position in a word (initial, medial, final, clustered) and according to production adequacy (omission, substitution, distortion, correct form). Modern terminology for this suggests that every attempt to produce a sound segment is an approximation. Some approximations are nearer to the target segment than others, but all of them, however defective, are approximations of the target. The resulting production profile indicates, in part, those segments that were correctly or incorrectly produced in specified word positions. Certain assumptions underlying traditional articulation testing are questionable for a number of reasons. Unfortunately, recent attempts to analyze segmental productions by using a distinctive feature analysis are also questionable. To date, normal and abnormal phonological and phonetic development and articulation testing/analysis are two exciting areas in which continued investigation is necessary.

CLEFT PALATE   The occurrence of a palatal cleft is most often regarded as being related to trauma or insult during the first trimester of pregnancy. During this developmental period, the orofacial complex undergoes rapid and massive change; if the palatal shelves fail to join at midline, then a cleft (opening) of the palate is generally obvious at birth. Palatal clefts may involve the soft palate alone or the soft and hard palate. In addition, clefts of the soft and hard palate may extend unilaterally or bilaterally through the upper lip and/or alveolar ridge. The most difficult cleft to diagnose is a submucous cleft. Whereas other clefts are obvious due to their lack of palatal tissue, the submucous cleft generally occurs as the result of an uneven jointure between the hard and soft palate and lack of muscle integrity covered by a normal-looking mucosal lining. Confirmation is usually provided with cinefluorographic evaluation.

Several factors regarding the early management of the child with a cleft palate are important to the rehabilitation team. Among them are early surgical repair, health care, parent counseling, speech therapy, dental care, and cosmetic repair. Although our viewpoint may seem biased, adequate speech is the most crucial determinant of a successful program. Surgeons, pediatricians, social workers, dentists, and parents may be satisfied with the cosmetic appearance resulting from surgical repair. However, the speech pathologist knows that nasally emitted speech will cause ridicule, embarrassment, and shame. Most important, it will result in inadequate inter- and intrapersonal communication.

Unlike other members of the cleft palate team, the speech pathologist is aware of certain relatively predictable characteristics in the speech patterns of children either diagnosed or suspected of having velar insufficiency. The child who is physically incapable of achieving or sustaining velopharyngeal closure may appear to successfully produce and sustain high intra-oral pressure sounds (fricatives and stops) as segments or within single words. However, within syllable trains or continuous speech, velopharyngeal closure is impossible to maintain and the nasal cavities are inappropriately coupled to the oral cavity. The speech pathologist's most important responsibility is to determine whether or not the client can achieve the velopharyngeal closure necessary for speech. Once such a determination has been made, a treatment program must proceed on an intensive basis.

Frequently, the child with an adequately repaired velopharyngeal port retains earlier overlearned, disordered sound patterns. Because of earlier physical limitations, such a feature set includes [+ nasality] as a feature of many consonants. Glottals are frequently approximated for other stops, in addition to inordinate release of nasally emitted sound. Simply telling the child it is no longer appropriate to nasalize or glottalize is not helpful, because he or she may have learned that *our* nonnasalized productions and *his* or *her* nasalized productions are equivalent. As a result, it is often better to begin automatization (practice) of correct sound production in the absence of semantic and syntactic constraints. In other words, rehearsal should first focus on various nonmeaningful vowel-consonant-vowel (VCV) combinations and then on more linguistically constrained units such as real words, phrases, or sentences.

As a further complication, children who are developing or who have developed speech during surgical or prosthetic restoration tend to minimize overall articulator movement. That is, they tend to minimize jaw movement, tongue elevation, and lip rounding and spreading. They are aware of their articulatory inadequacies and attempt to minimize them through minimal movement. Such behavior should come as no surprise. It can be directly compared to college students who frequently sit in back rows, avoid eye contact with the instructor when questions are asked, mumble when in doubt, and minimize study so that in the event of failure they can blame it on anything but effort and brains.

APRAXIA   *Apraxia* is a generalized disorder that has existed under several different labels, such as aphemie, motor aphasia, phonetic disintegration, dyspraxia, cortical dysarthria, and apraxie dysarthria. Such a collage of labels has tended to obscure the clinical picture of the patient whose speech is distinguished by several recognizable characteristics. Patients diagnosed as apraxic generally do not demonstrate problems in auditory comprehension or written expression. The problem appears to stem from lesions to certain motor control centers of the anterior region of the left hemisphere of the brain. Although patients are able to choose appropriate phonetic sequences and words and employ appropriate syntactic structure, articulatory performance is disordered in a number of ways. According to Johns and Darley:

> Initial consonant production in speech apraxia is characterized by a high degree of inconsistency of articulation errors; predominance of substitution, repetition, and addition errors as opposed to distortion errors of dysarthria; marked prosodic disturbances without phonatory and resonance changes; increase of difficulty from spontaneous to oral reading to imitative speech conditions; facilitation of correct articulation by visual monitoring in the auditory-visual stimulus mode in contrast to the auditory (repeating tape-recorded stimuli) or visual (reading words) modes; deterioration of articulation with increase in length of word; and improvement when the patient is allowed to make several consecutive attempts to produce a desired response. (1970)

DYSARTHRIA   In contrast to apraxia, dysarthria is characterized by paresis, generalized weakness, and articulatory incoordination. Neural lesions may have occurred anywhere from the cerebellum to lower motor neurons. As a result, hyperkinesia (excessive motor function) or hypokinesia (reduced motor function) may occur during respiration, phonation, and articulation. Darley and his associates at the Mayo Clinic have classified five major types of dysarthria identified according to certain characteristic speech and voice parameters:

1. Spastic dysarthria (spasm): hypernasality, imprecise consonants, monotony, harshness
2. Flaccid dysarthria (flaccid): hypernasality, imprecise consonants, breathiness, monopitch
3. Ataxic dysarthria (uncoordinated): excess and equal stress, harshness, irregular articulatory breakdown
4. Hypokinetic dysarthria (reduced): imprecise consonants, reduced stress, monopitch, monoloudness
5. Hyperkinetic dysarthria (excessive): distorted vowels, harshness, monopitch, irregular articulatory breakdown

Persons with either dysarthria or apraxia tend to be aware of their articulatory errors, lack of intelligibility, and rhythm imbalance. They are generally hypersensitive to their lack of communicative ability and are easily discouraged. This is especially true of older children and adults whose articulatory approximations elicit impatience, bewilderment, and inattention from listeners. Unlike typical "all-American" children with misarticulations or children with repaired clefts, treatment programs designed for the apraxic or dysarthric are simultaneously more intensive and more extensive.

HEARING DEFICIT   Disorders of articulation are frequently the result of reduced hearing sensitivity or acuity. Hearing, as a feedback mechanism, is the prime channel for speech decoding. Depending upon the degree of hearing impairment, certain frequencies or frequency regions of the sound spectrum are not adequately transmitted. As a result, the speaker is deprived of information that alerts him as to how he is doing and what minor vocal and articulatory adjustments must be made in order to sound better. Reduced intelligibility of speech in the deaf and hearing-impaired is characterized by several factors: Pitch and loudness tend to be monotonous, and speech phrasing is slow, labored, and simplistically rhythmical. The primary deterrent to adequate intelligibility, however, involves articulation. Lack of correct timing in articulatory movements results in somewhat stylized articulatory approximations. Sounds requiring greater articulatory precision over time, especially those containing higher-frequency information (fricatives and affricates) are frequently omitted or substituted. There is also a tendency for the hearing-impaired and deaf to reduce vowels to more neutral positions. Hence, vowels such as [ʌ, ə] are used most frequently or substituted for other vowels. Not surprisingly, degree of visibility plays an important role in their speech. Those sounds which are more visible or contain visible features [p, b, t, d, f, v, θ, ð, i, u, o] tend to be approximated with greater articulatory accuracy than less visible sounds.

The confusions and problems of the hearing-impaired and deaf are extremely complex and interesting and will increasingly be the focus of the research and clinical efforts of speech pathologists and speech scientists. Finally, the significance of the relationship between sound production and auditory processing will become apparent in the following chapter on audition.

SUGGESTED READINGS

Abbs, J. H. "The Influence of the Gamma Motor System on Jaw Movements during Speech: A Theoretical Framework and Some Preliminary Observations." *Journal of Speech and Hearing Research,* 16, (1973), 175–200. An excellent review of the role of feedback in the regulation of speech production as well as data bearing on the question of how the γ-system may regulate articulation.

Cooper, F. S. "Describing the Speech Process in Motor Command Terms." *Status Reports on Speech Research,* Haskins Laboratories, SR 515, (1966), 2.1–2.7. A brief, clear, and concise model of the speech production mechanism based on the phonetic segment, distinctive features, and strong encoding processes.

Daniloff, R. G., and R. Hammarberg. "On Defining Coarticulation." *Journal of Phonetics,* 1, (1973), 185–194. A review of the coarticulation literature and an analysis of the meaning of the idea of *coarticulation.*

Daniloff, R. G., and K. L. Moll. "Coarticulation of Lip Rounding." *Journal of Speech and Hearing Research,* 11, (1968), 707–721. An early study of coarticulation that will reveal how coarticulation effects are measured and interpreted.

Fairbanks, G. "Systematic Research in Experimental Phonetics, I: A Theory of the Speech Mechanism as a Servosystem." *Journal of Speech and Hearing Disorders,* 19, (1954), 133–139. An early, easily read, discussion of the role of feedback in the regulation of speech.

Folkins, J. W., and J. H. Abbs. "Lip and Jaw Motor Control during Speech: Responses to Resistive Loading of the Jaw." *Journal of Speech and Hearing Research,* 18, (1975), 27–52. A report on an ingenious experiment that demonstrates the swiftness with which the afferent feedback systems of speech can compensate for errors in articulator movements.

Henke, W. L. "Dynamic Articulatory Model of Speech Production using Computer Simulation." Unpublished doctoral dissertation, MIT, 1966. A description of a speech production model based on phonemes in which LR and RL coarticulation are built-in processes.

Kent, R. D., and F. Minifie. "Coarticulation in Recent Speech Production Models." *Journal of Phonetics,* 5, (1977), 115–133. An excellent survey of the coarticulation literature in which the authors demonstrate that coarticulation data, while important, do not constrain the nature of articulation models sufficiently to be of critical importance.

Kozhevnikov, L., and L. A. Chistovich. *Speech: Articulation and Perception.* Moscow. Translation by Joint Publications Research Service, Washington, D.C., U.S. Department of Commerce, JPRS 30543, 1965. A work of genius, but poorly translated. The articulation model offered here is based on a wealth of data; even though much of the data is disputed, this is a classic.

Lashley, K. S. "The Problem of Serial Order in Behavior." In L. A. Jeffress (ed.), *Cerebral Mechanisms in Behavior: The Hixon Symposium.* New York: Wiley, 1951. An early but still outstanding conceptualization of the problems of serial ordering of behavior.

Liberman, A. M. "The Grammars of Speech and Language." *Cognitive Psychology,* 1, (1970), 301–323. A very well-written, coherent, and sensible account of the encoding and decoding process.

Liberman, A. M., F. S. Cooper, D. P. Shankweiler, and M. Studdert-Kennedy. "Perception of the Speech Code." *Psychological Review,* 74, (1967), 431–459. A brilliant review. A well-known research team presents their ideas concerning the encoding and decoding of speech and how intimately the two are related.

MacNeilage, P. F. "Motor Control of Serial Ordering of Speech." *Psychological Review,* 77, (1970), 182–196. A superb review of the problem of serial ordering in speech; a review of the literature and suggestions for a speech production model. Difficult but well-written.

Matthews, P. C. B. "Muscle Efferents and Kinesthesia." *British Medical Bulletin,* 33, (1977), 137–142. A discussion of the role of muscle efferent feedback in the control of movement and the possibility that such sensation can signal the position of the limbs and joints.

Ohman, S. E. G. "Coarticulation in VCV Utterances: Spectrographic Measurements." *Journal of the Acoustical Society of America,* 39, (1966), 151–168. An excellent study of the coarticulation in VCV units that led the author to propose a model of coarticulation–articulation based on the carrier nature of speech.

Stevens, K. N., A. S. House, and A. P. Paul. "Acoustic Description of Syllable Nucleii: An Interpretation in Terms of a Dynamic Model of Articulation." *Journal of the Acoustical Society of America,* 40, (1966), 173–182. An excellent research article which convincingly demonstrates the very large coarticulatory overlapping that occurs between consonants and vowels within syllables.

Sussman, H. "What the Tongue Tells the Brain." *Psychological Bulletin,* 77, (1972), 262–272. A fine review of feedback systems in the tongue and other speech organs along with speculation concerning the role of feedback in the control of speech.

Tatham, M. A. A. "Classifying Allophones." *Language and Speech,* 14, (1971), 140–145. A short but pithy discussion of allophonic variation that clearly separates the linguistic factors from the phonetic-physiological ones responsible for allophonic variation. Easy reading.

Wickelgren, W. A. "Context-sensitive Coding, Associative Memory, and Serial Order in (Speech) Behavior." *Psychological Review,* 76, (1969), 1–15. A simplistic (but not simple) model of serial ordering of speech based on the storage of a large number of allophones which can be directly assembled in linear order to give an appropriate speech output.

Wyke, B. "Larnygeal Myotatic Reflexes," *Folia Phoniatrics,* 26 (1974), 249–264. A well-written review article that summarizes the evidence concerning how laryngeal vibration is controlled via feedback loops.

AUDITION
THE SENSE OF HEARING

9

the flow of sound energy in the periphery / the outer ear / the middle ear
the inner ear / the mechanical response of the inner ear
cochlear electrophysiology / the auditory nerve
the central auditory system / suggested readings

The division of the nervous system specialized for the processing of sound is called the *auditory system,* or often simply the ear. The only parts of this complex sensory system visible to the casual observer are the pinnae located on either side of the head. We may divide the auditory system into peripheral and central portions, just as we did for the nervous system as a whole. The decision as to which parts fall into the periphery and which belong in the central system is somewhat arbitrary. We will base our decision on anatomical consideration alone. Those structures outside the brain or brainstem will be classified as part of the periphery. (Figure 9.1 shows the structures that make up the peripheral auditory system.) The peripheral system is usually further subdivided into the outer, middle, and inner ear.

The central auditory system is shown in Figure 9.2. It consists of an ascending pathway, a descending pathway, and multiple interconnections between them. The more central portions of the auditory system are less well understood than the peripheral portions. Our understanding of the auditory system has progressed from the periphery toward the cortex since we first became interested in understanding the workings of the human mind. Wever (1949), in tracing the various theories of hearing, shows how increasing knowledge of the details of successively more central components of the auditory system has led scientists to assign the perceptual functions to higher and higher centers. Thus, auditory perception was once thought to take place in the ear canal, and then in the middle ear until more plausible explanations of the functions of the ear canal and middle ear were advanced. We may still be susceptible to this phenomenon, for even now perceptual processes once thought to be cochlear functions are being ascribed to "higher neural centers."

In our discussion of the ear, we will usually write as though people had only one. Most of the sound processing required of humans can be done by either ear alone, usually equally well. The second ear is not simply a natural

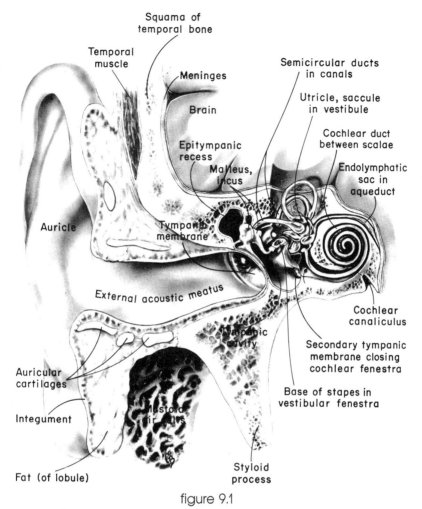

figure 9.1

The peripheral auditory system. Reprinted by permission from
B. J. Anson and J. A. Donaldson, *The Anatomy of the
Temporal Bone and Ear.* © 1967, W. B. Saunders Company.

backup system in case something should happen to one, however. Full auditory
function requires that both ears be intact and fully functional if the listener is to
be able to locate sound sources in space or listen selectively to one source to
the exclusion of other background sounds. Your mother was misinformed when
she told you, some years ago, that you had two ears and one mouth so that you
could listen twice as much as you talked.

In our discussion, we will follow the flow of information through the auditory
system. Beginning at the most distal portion, the outer ear, we will discuss the
structure and function of the peripheral portions of the ear. We will then document the influence of the outer and middle ear structures on the sound energy
that arrives at the cochlea. Within the cochlea, we will describe the early stages

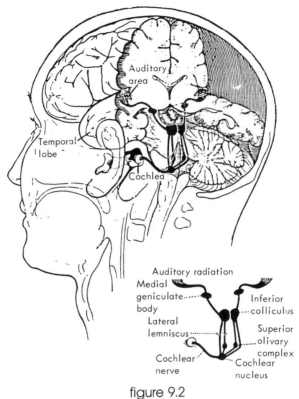

figure 9.2

The central auditory system. Major nuclei of the ascending auditory pathway. Reprinted by permission from S. Grollman, *The Human Body.* © 1964, The Macmillan Company.

of analysis that take place and discuss the theories that attempt to explain the way information encoded in a sound waveform is translated into complex patterns of nerve fiber firings. Finally, we will present what we know about the more central portions of the auditory system.

the flow of sound energy in the periphery

The structures that make up the peripheral auditory system extend from the pinna to the cochlea. The cochlea, or inner ear, is a system of three fluid-filled ducts, one of which contains the sensory receptor cells for hearing. Many years of research were required before we had an understanding of the way in which sound energy is conducted from the air surrounding the listener's head to the sensory receptor cells within the cochlea. Before examining each portion of the periphery in detail, let us follow the flow of sound energy through the peripheral structures. Figure 9.3 shows the auditory periphery in schematic form. The three boxes represent the outer, middle, and inner ear, respectively. Sound traveling in the air surrounding the listener's head enters through the outer ear. The ear canal provides a transmission pathway for airborne sound energy, delivering it to the tympanic membrane (eardrum). The energy continues through the middle ear structures, eventually reaching the hair cells of the cochlea, where it is converted into patterns of neural activity which the central nervous system can process. We have called this last process *sensory transduction,* because energy is changed from mechanical to electrochemical form.

The path followed by the sound energy is by no means a simple one, and we might ask why such a complex sound transmission system should have evolved. It would seem much simpler to have sound receptor cells at, or just inside, the surface of the head and to dispense with the intervening structures. In fact, some species of fish do have a sound reception system on the surface of their bodies. These sensory organs are not "ears" in the usual sense of the word, but they do have pressure-sensitive hair cells arranged in straight-line segments along the fish's body. This type of receptor is called a lateral line organ. Some of our knowledge of hair-cell function has come from studies of hair cells in the lateral line.

The fact that sound receptor organs are found at the body's surface only in fish gives us an important clue to the function of the outer and middle ear structures. The cochlea is filled with fluid of higher density than air. If a sound-wave traveling in air were to impinge directly upon the fluid within the cochlea, most of the sound energy would be reflected from the surface of the cochlear fluid. This reflection would occur because of the difference in acoustic impedance between the air and the fluid. It has been estimated that 99.9 percent of the sound energy would be reflected, if we consider the cochlear fluid to be physically like water. Expressed in decibels, this would be a 30 dB potential loss of hearing sensitivity. That is, a listener would be expected to have a hearing threshold level 30 dB less sensitive if soundwaves were to impinge directly upon the surface of the cochlear fluid.

The function of the middle ear structures is one of *impedance matching.* That is, the tympanic membrane (eardrum) presents an acoustic impedance to the soundwaves traveling in the ear canal that is not appreciably different from

figure 9.3
Functions of the major divisions of the peripheral auditory system.

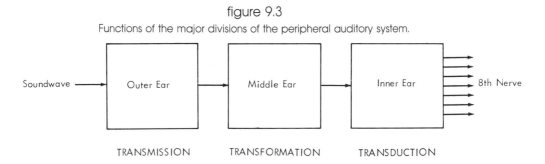

TRANSMISSION   TRANSFORMATION   TRANSDUCTION

that of the air inside the canal. In turn, the stapes footplate, which delivers the sound to the cochlea, is able to work efficiently into the higher acoustic impedance presented by the cochlear fluid. Impedance matching is accomplished by increasing the sound pressure while reducing volume velocity proportionally. This action is like that of an electrical transformer used to step up or step down the voltage required to run electric motors, radios, and appliances. Thus, we often say that the middle ear acts as a sound pressure transformer.

We have summarized the functions of the outer, middle, and inner ear as those of transmission, transformation, and transduction—the "three Ts" of peripheral auditory function. We now will examine the structure and action of each in more detail to gain an understanding of how these functions are accomplished in the ear.

the outer ear

ANATOMY   The outer ear is composed of the pinna, also called the auricle, and the external auditory meatus, or ear canal, which extends from the surface of the head to the tympanic membrane. These structures are illustrated in cross-section in Figure 9.1. The pinna is roughly oval in shape and marked by a series of cavities and ridges. The deepest of these cavities, called the cavum conchae, is located somewhat inferior and anterior to the center of the pinna. This cavity leads to the external auditory meatus, the canal which connects the pinna with the middle ear.

The external auditory meatus, rather than being the straight, cylindrical tube often illustrated, is approximately S-shaped. The lateral portion of the canal is cartilage; the more medial portion is bony. Because the cartilage is elastic, small objects can be inserted part way into the canal. However, the bony portion of the canal does not stretch, which probably aids in protecting the delicate tympanic membrane from damage. The skin over the cartilagenous portion of the external auditory meatus contains hair follicles, sebaceous glands, and ceruminous glands, which secrete cerumen (commonly called ear wax).

FUNCTIONS   Unlike the more central portions of the auditory system, in humans the outer ear plays no active role in hearing. The pinna and external canal do affect the soundwaves that eventually reach the eardrum, but humans have no control over that influence. In some nonhuman species, such as dogs, cats, and horses, the pinnae are mobile and play an active part in helping to locate a sound source in space. The few humans who have some muscular control over their pinnae find it useful only for social occasions. It is often said that the irregular shape of the pinna helps to direct very high frequency sounds into the external auditory meatus. It is also thought that the pinnae aid in eliminating front-to-back confusions in sound-source localization because of the sound shadows they cast for high-frequency sounds delivered from behind the head of the listener.

The external canal affects the soundwave that reaches the eardrum because it acts as an acoustical resonator. At low and middle frequencies, its influence can be predicted quite accurately by assuming that it is a simple right-circular acoustic tube closed at one end. Recall from Chapter 4 that such a tube acts as a resonator, with peaks and valleys in its transfer function which are determined only by the length of the tube. For the average adult male, the effective length of the external canal is approximately 25 mm, leading to a predicted first resonance peak at a frequency of about 3.5 kHz. The resonance peak due to the ear canal is broad and not very prominent because of the damping introduced by the tissues lining the canal.

It is possible to illustrate the acoustical effects of the external ear by determining the so-called field-to-drum characteristics. In this procedure, a uniform sound field is established in a controlled, usually echo-free space. The sound-pressure level at a point in the sound field is measured over the range of frequencies of interest. Then an "average" listener is placed in the sound field in a way that the point at which the previous measurements were taken is now occupied by the center of the listener's head. A small probe microphone is placed very close to the eardrum of the listener, and the sound-pressure-level measurements are repeated. Differences between the two sets of measurements are reported as sound field-to-drum characteristics. Figure 9.4 illustrates just such carefully completed measurements. The curve plotted in Figure 9.4 shows not only the influence of the pinna and ear canal, but also the acoustical effects of the whole head and body of the listener. Depending on the location of the sound source, two acoustical effects are possible when the listener is introduced into the sound field: *sound baffle* and *sound shadow* effects.

The shadow effect is like the shadow cast by an opaque object in a beam of light. Whenever a traveling soundwave encounters an object of dimensions greater than the wavelength of the sound, there will be a region of reduced sound pressure just beyond the object. Farther on, the influence of the large object will be minimal because the soundwaves bend slightly around it. This phenomenon is known as refraction. For an object of a given size, such as a human head, the strength of the sound shadow will vary with the wavelength of the incident sound. Thus, the human head casts a better sound shadow at 10,000 Hz than at 1000 Hz. The second influence of the listener on the sound field is the baffle effect. At the side of an object, such as the human head, which faces the sound source, there is a slight elevation in sound pressure. The elevation is due to the reflection of soundwaves from the object back to the measuring microphone. The reflected soundwave may combine with the incident or oncoming wave to result in a sound pressure slightly higher than that which would be found in the same location without the object.

In summary, then, the influence of the external ear may be described as a complex acoustical filtering action that depends upon both the frequency of the incident soundwave and the direction of the source from the ear. In most auditory testing, this effect is either ignored completely or circumvented by presenting test signals through headphones. Of course, signal presentation through

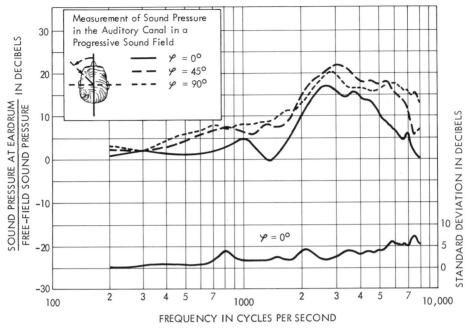

figure 9.4

Field-to-drum transfer characteristics. The ratio in decibels of the sound pressure of the eardrum to the sound pressure in the free field at the point occupied by the center of the listener's head (averaged over 6 to 12 male ears). Reprinted by permission from F. M. Wiener and D. A. Ross, "The Pressure Distribution in the Auditory Canal in a Progressive Round Field," *Journal of the Acoustical Society of America*, 18 (1946), 401–408.

headphones leads to a new set of acoustical problems. Covering the ear with a headphone creates an unnatural occlusion (closure) of the ear canal. That is, the occluded external auditory meatus no longer behaves acoustically as a tube open at one end and closed at the other. Instead, depending upon the type of headphone used, the outer ear may resemble a tube closed at both ends or a tube connected to a volume of enclosed air. The former condition occurs both for headphones inserted into the meatus and for many of the earmolds used to couple a hearing aid to a listener's ear. Headphones that enclose the entire pinna are better represented as a volume of entrapped air coupled to the ear canal.

The frequent use of headphones in auditory testing has led to two ways of specifying the sound-pressure levels considered to represent normal hearing thresholds. If the measurements are made using standard calibrated head-phones, the sound pressure at the listener's eardrum can be specified for each test frequency. This measurement is typically called the *minimum audible pressure* (MAP). Typical values of MAP for the average adult population are shown in Figure 9.5. Another way of specifying the normal hearing threshold

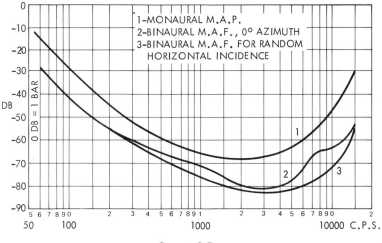

figure 9.5

Comparison of minimum audible field with minimum audible pressure determination of auditory threshold. Reprinted by permission from L. J. Sivian and S. D. White, "On Minimum Audible Fields," *Journal of the Acoustical Society of America*, 4 (1933), 288–321.

uses the sound field presentation method. As we discussed above, the sound pressure in a controlled acoustical environment is measured very carefully. The listener is then introduced into the sound field in a position such that the center of the head occupies the point at which the previous measurements were made. The sound-pressure level that can just be detected by the listener in this situation is called the *minimum audible field* (MAF). Figure 9.5 also shows typical averaged MAF values across the frequencies of interest. Notice that the differences between the MAF and MAP definitions of normal hearing thresholds reach approximately 6 dB. This so-called missing 6 dB has given impetus to a long series of research projects and scholarly discussion.

the middle ear

ANATOMY   In our consideration of the path of sound energy into the ear, it is important to recognize that a major contributor to middle ear action is a complex air-filled space. The major chambers of this space are the tympanic cavity proper, the epitympanic recess, the antrum, and a short acoustic tube, the aditus. The antrum is connected to numerous small, air-filled chambers within the mastoid bone. Because of the honeycomb nature of these mastoid cells, it is difficult to determine the true volume of air enclosed by the middle ear cavities. Although the tympanic membrane seals the cavities from the air in the external canal, they are connected to the nasopharynx by the Eustachian tube. The Eustachian tube, also called the auditory tube, provides a pressure equalization between the middle ear chambers and the atmosphere. Under normal conditions, the tube is closed except for a brief time during yawning or swallowing. When the Eustachian tube is swollen due to infection, allergic reaction, or other pathological conditions, we experience a feeling of fullness in our ears. If we undergo a rapid change in atmospheric pressure, such as in an elevator or in a descending airplane, that same sensation is apparent until we are able to "clear our ears."

The tympanic membrane, or eardrum, serves as the partition between the ear canal and the middle ear cavities. The drum is a shallow, circular cone approximately 9 mm in diameter at its base. The "tip" of the cone is known as the umbo. The eardrum is a thin, semi-transparent membrane made up of four layers of tissue. On the lateral (outside) surface, there is a layer of skin that is continuous with the skin lining the ear canal. On the medial (inside) surface of the drum, there is a layer of the same mucous membrane that lines the middle ear cavities. The two internal layers of tissue in the drum are fibrous. One layer has fibers that course radially, like spokes in a bicycle wheel. The fibers in the other layer run in concentric circles. This structure apparently allows the very thin membrane to vibrate in much the same manner as the vibrations of the cone of a loudspeaker.

The sound energy delivered to the tympanic membrane is transferred to the cochlea primarily by the action of the *ossicular chain*. The ossicular chain, shown in Figure 9.6, is a series of three small bones named for the implements their shapes suggest. The lateral bone in the chain has a long process suggestive of a handle and a large ball-shaped head that gives it the appearance of a hammer. Thus its name, the *malleus.* The *manubrium* (handle) of the malleus is attached to the medial surface of the tympanic membrane from the umbo to the superior-posterior margin.

The *incus,* the second bone in the chain, articulates with the malleus. The incus was given its name because its shape suggests that of an anvil. However, since anvils have become as rare as horseshoes and blacksmiths, it might be more enlightening to think of the incus as being tooth-shaped, with two roots of unequal length. The longer "root," or process, is approximately parallel with the manubrium of the malleus. The incus and malleus are bound tightly together at their joint, so that there is little or no relative movement between them. The short process of the incus has, in turn, a projection called the *lenticular process,* which forms the body's smallest synovial joint, the *incudostapedial joint,* with the head of the stapes. The *stapes* is the third and smallest of the ossicles. It is shaped like the stirrup on a saddle, hence its name. The head of the stapes connects with the arches of the stapes, called the crura, by a slender neck. The arches are attached to the *footplate,* which fits into the opening in the vestibule known as the *oval window.*

At high frequencies, the vibrating pattern of the tympanic membrane is complex because it apparently does not move as one unit. At middle and low frequencies, however, the entire membrane moves as a unit, much like the one in a loudspeaker. The longitudinal waves of compression and rarefaction at the drum are transformed into the motion of the manubrium, shown by the arrows

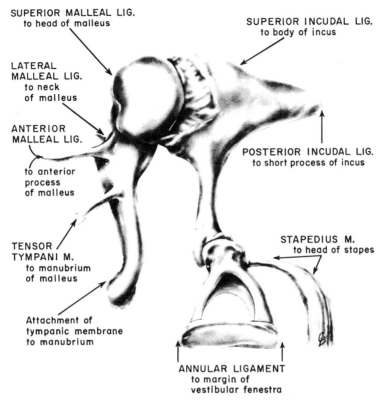

SUPERIOR MALLEAL LIG.
to head of malleus

SUPERIOR INCUDAL LIG.
to body of incus

LATERAL
MALLEAL LIG.
to neck
of malleus

ANTERIOR
MALLEAL LIG.

to anterior
process
of malleus

POSTERIOR INCUDAL LIG.
to short process of incus

TENSOR
TYMPANI M.
to manubrium
of malleus

STAPEDIUS M.
to head of stapes

Attachment of
tympanic membrane
to manubrium

ANNULAR LIGAMENT
to margin of
vestibular fenestra

figure 9.6

The ossicular chain with the attachments of middle ear muscles
and ligaments. Reprinted by permission from B. J. Anson
and J. A. Donaldson, *The Surgical Anatomy of the Temporal Bone
and the Ear.* 2nd ed. © 1973, W. B. Saunders Company.

in Figures 9.7 and 9.8. This translational motion is in turn delivered to the
stapes footplate. For many years, it was thought that the action of the stapes
footplate was similar to that of a door opening and closing. Bekesy (1960) reported that when the middle ear action was observed under stroboscopic illumi-
nation, the footplate appeared to be hinged at its posterior margin. More recent
observations by Guinan and Peake (1967) have failed to demonstrate the hinged-
door action suggested by Bekesy. Instead, they observed a simple pistonlike
action of the stapes footplate.

The ossicular chain is held in place by a system of ligaments and muscles.
An understanding of the placement of these attachments is important because
the suspension of the ossicular chain helps to determine its mode of vibration.
These attachments are shown in Figures 9.6, 9.7, and 9.8. Two ligaments are
illustrated in Figure 9.7, the superior ligament and the lateral ligament. The superior ligament is attached to the roof of the epitympanic recess and to the
head of the malleus. The lateral ligament is attached to the lateral wall of

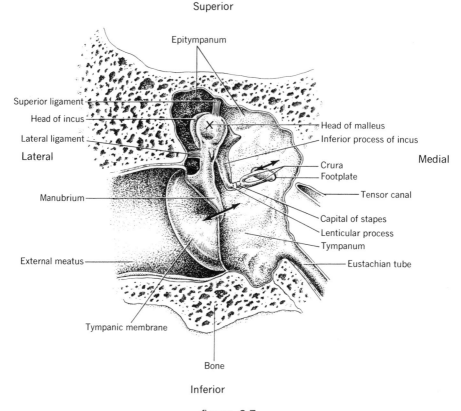

Superior

Epitympanum

Superior ligament

Head of incus

Lateral ligament

Lateral

Head of malleus

Inferior process of incus

Medial

Crura

Footplate

Tensor canal

Manubrium

Capital of stapes

Lenticular process

Tympanum

External meatus

Eustachian tube

Tympanic membrane

Bone

Inferior

figure 9.7

A section through the middle ear approximately parallel
with the frontal plane. Reprinted by permission from W. L.
Gulick, *Hearing: Physiology and Psychophysics.*
© 1971, Oxford University Press.

the middle ear cavity, just above the tympanic membrane and to the neck of
the malleus. In Figure 9.8, the middle ear is seen in a horizontal section. Two
more ligaments are visible, the anterior and posterior ligaments. The anterior
ligament is attached to the neck of the malleus and the posterior ligament is attached to the incus in such a way that they are aligned with the axis of rotation
of the whole ossicular chain.

Also shown in Figure 9.8 are the tendons of the two middle ear muscles,
the tensor tympani and the stapedius. The tendon of the tensor tympani
emerges from a bony canal that parallels the Eustachian tube and bends laterally to attach to the neck of the malleus. The tendon of the stapedius emerges
from the pyramidal eminence on the posterior wall of the tympanic cavity to attach to the neck of the stapes. We will have much more to say about these
middle ear muscles when we discuss the acoustic reflex later in the chapter.

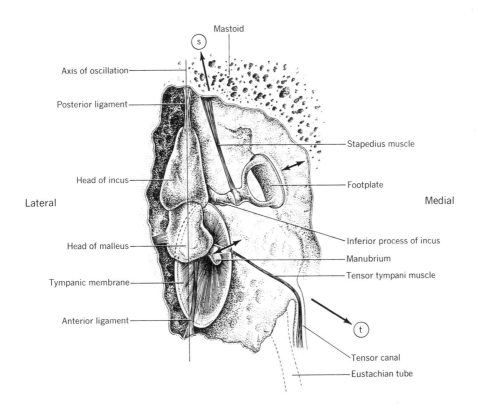

Posterior

Mastoid

Axis of oscillation

Posterior ligament

Stapedius muscle

Head of incus

Footplate

Lateral

Medial

Inferior process of incus

Head of malleus

Manubrium

Tensor tympani muscle

Tympanic membrane

Anterior ligament

Tensor canal

Eustachian tube

Anterior

figure 9.8

Horizontal section through the middle ear. Reprinted by permission from W. L. Gulick, *Hearing: Physiology and Psychophysics.* © 1971, Oxford University Press.

FUNCTION The major function of the middle ear is one of matching the acoustical impedance of air to the acoustical impedance of the fluid within the cochlea. This function is accomplished by a sound pressure transformation. Before we describe how the impedance match is effected, let us review briefly the need for such impedance matching.

The fluid within the cochlea is physically very similar to water [although somewhat similar to cerebrospinal fluid (CSF) in chemical composition]. For the purposes of describing sound transmission into the cochlea, we may think of it as being similar in response to water. Recall from Chapter 4 that the acoustical impedance of water is 1000 times higher than that of air. If a soundwave traveling in air were to encounter a new medium, say a body of water, then the impedance mismatch between the air and the water would lead to the reflection of most of the sound energy from the surface of the water. Very little sound would penetrate the surface and continue to travel in the water. A similar situation would be true if sound traveling in air were to encounter the surface of the oval window of the cochlea directly. Most of the sound energy would be reflected, and very little would enter the cochlear fluid to be available for stimulating the sensory cells within. A good estimate is that 99.9 percent of the incident sound energy would be reflected and only 0.1 percent would be transmitted into the cochlea. If this loss of sound energy due to reflection is expressed in decibels, it amounts to about a 30 dB loss. That is, if we had no middle ear to perform the requisite impedance matching function, then our hearing would be about 30 dB less sensitive than it is. Very quiet sounds, at threshold, would have to be 30 dB more intense to be heard.

The acoustical impedance match between the air in the ear canal and the fluid within the cochlea is effected by sound pressure transformation. That is, the action of the middle ear results in increased sound pressure delivered to the oval window. At the same time, the volume velocity at the oval window is reduced proportionally. The reduction in volume velocity is required because the sound intensity (power/area) must remain unchanged. Recall from Chapter 4 that the equation for sound intensity was given as

$$I \text{ (watts/cm}^2) = p \text{ (dyne/cm}^2) \times U \text{ (cm}^3\text{/sec)}$$

Thus, for a given sound intensity, causing the pressure (p) to be increased requires the volume velocity (U) to be reduced proportionally. Perhaps a simple numerical example will help. Suppose that the sound pressure at the input to an acoustical transformer (Figure 9.9) is 2 dyne/cm^2 and that the volume velocity is $\frac{1}{2}$ cm^3/sec. Then $I = p \times U$ gives $I = 2 \times \frac{1}{2} = 1$ watt/cm^2. Now assume that the acoustical transformer acts to increase the sound pressure by a factor of 4, so that the sound pressure out of the transformer is $4 \times 2 = 8$ dyne/cm^2. Because intensity, I, must remain equal to 1 watt/cm^2, the volume velocity at the transformer output will be reduced to $\frac{1}{8}$ cm^3/sec. Then $I = 8 \times (\frac{1}{8}) = 1$ watt/cm^2. The requirement that the sound intensity cannot increase in an acoustical transformer is imposed by the law of conservation of energy from classical physics. Since intensity represents rate of energy flow, any increase would imply that the acoustical transformer was able to add energy to the signal. In reality, the opposite is true. Somewhat less sound energy flows out of the acoustical transformer than flowed into it because some is converted into other energy forms. If the loss of sound energy is not great, we often ignore it and assume no loss in the transformation process.

Examination of another equation from Chapter 4 will further illustrate the impedance matching concept. Recall that acoustical impedance was defined as the sound pressure applied divided by the volume velocity flowing into a system. In

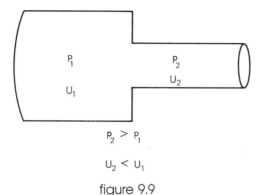

$$P_2 > P_1$$

$$U_2 < U_1$$

figure 9.9

A schematic representation of an acoustical transformer.

an equation, $Z = p/U$. At the input to our hypothetical acoustical transformer, the impedance would be $Z_{input} = 2/(\frac{1}{2}) = 4$ acoustical ohms. At the output of the transformer, after increasing sound pressure and decreasing volume velocity in proportion, the equation yields $Z_{output} = 8/(\frac{1}{8}) = 64$ acoustical ohms. Thus, the acoustical impedance at the transformer output is greater than at the input. Further, notice that while sound pressure was multiplied by a factor of 4, acoustical impedance was increased by a factor of 16. Thus, the amount by which the impedance is multiplied is the square of the multiplier of sound pressure. A 10 to 1 increase in sound pressure gives a 100 to 1 increase in impedance.

Now let us return to the middle ear transformer. Its impedance matching function is accomplished by increasing the sound pressure delivered to the oval window above the pressure presented to the tympanic membrane. This sound pressure increase is effected by two simple mechanical mechanisms. The first, and larger of the two, is due to the reduced area of the stapes footplate in comparison with the area of the tympanic membrane. Recall that sound pressure is defined as force per unit of area. The sound pressure at the tympanic membrane can be represented by a *sound force*. If the tympanic membrane were flat, then the calculation would be straightforward. Sound force would be sound pressure times the area. However, the conical shape of the drum makes it less effective in the transformer action. Stated more simply, a flat, circular membrane of somewhat smaller area than that of the tympanic membrane would be just as efficient in the transformation process. This equivalent surface has an area known as the effective area of the tympanic membrane. To summarize, then, the sound force applied to the ossicular chain is the sound pressure delivered to the tympanic membrane multiplied by its effective area.

If we assume, for the moment, that the sound force applied at the malleus is transferred without change to the stapes, then distributing that force over a smaller area gives a sound pressure increase. Accepting the usual ratio of 17 to 1 for the effective area of the tympanic membrane to the area of the stapes footplate, we find that due to the area transformation, sound pressure is in-

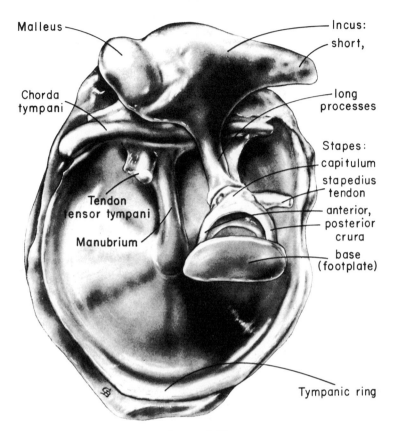

Malleus

Incus: short,

Chorda tympani

long processes

Stapes: capitulum

stapedius tendon

Tendon tensor tympani

anterior, posterior crura

Manubrium

base (footplate)

Tympanic ring

figure 9.10

A view from the cochlea showing the approximate ratio of effective area of the tympanic membrane to the area of the stapes footplate. Reprinted by permission from B. J. Anson and J. A. Donaldson, *The Surgical Anatomy of the Temporal Bone and the Ear.* © 1967, W. B. Saunders Company.

creased by 17 to 1 at the stapes footplate relative to the tympanic membrane. Figure 9.10 illustrates the relative areas of the tympanic membrane and the stapes footplate. If the 17 to 1 sound pressure increase is expressed in decibels, we find a 24.6 dB increase in sound pressure level. Thus, the area transformation accounts for the recovery of much of the potential 30 dB loss of sensitivity that would have resulted if the oval window were directly stimulated by airborne soundwaves.

The second factor in the sound pressure increase results from a simple lever action in the ossicular chain. Notice in Figure 9.7 that the distance from the axis of rotation of the ossicular chain (the fulcrum) to the umbo is slightly longer than the distance from the axis to the lenticular process of the incus. Because the ossicular chain rotates about this axis, its action is like that of a simple lever. The best-known example of a simple lever system is the child's teeter-totter (Figure 9.11). A small child can lift a heavier one by moving along the board farther from the center. That gives the lightweight child a mechanical advantage that multiplies his weight by the ratio of the lengths of the two arms of the teeter-totter. We may think of the ossicular chain as a badly bent teeter-totter, which effects a multiplication of the force applied to it by a factor equal to the ratio of the lengths of the two arms. On the average, the malleolar arm is 1.3 times longer than the incudal arm. Thus, the force delivered to the stapes is 1.3 times greater than that delivered to the malleus.

The two factors, the area transformation and the lever arm advantage, are multiplied to give the final ratio of sound pressure at the stapes footplate to sound pressure at the tympanic membrane. The ratio is 17×1.3 or 22.1 to 1. In decibels the increase in sound pressure level is approximately 27 dB. Consideration of area transformation and lever arm advantage has demonstrated that most of the potential loss of sensitivity due to mismatched impedance is eliminated by the middle ear action. We may conclude that the middle ear transformer does a credible, if not ideal, job of matching the impedance of air to that in the fluid-filled cochlea.

The Transfer Function   The impedance matching process in the middle ear which we have just described is not, unfortunately, performed with equal efficiency at all frequencies. At extreme frequencies, sound energy is not

figure 9.11

A child's teeter-totter bent to illustrate the lever ratio model of the ossicles of the middle ear.

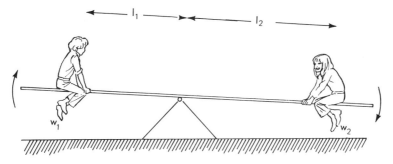

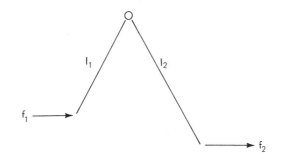

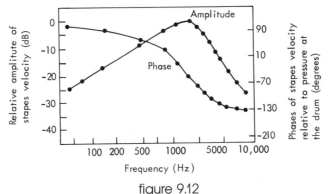

figure 9.12

Transfer characteristics (magnitude and phase) of the human
middle ear. Reprinted by permission from J. L. Flanagan,
"Models for Approximating Basilar Membrane Displacement,
Part II," *Bell System Technical Journal*, 41 (1962), 959–1009.

conducted into the cochlea as readily as it is in the middle range. At the lower frequencies, energy is diverted from the ossicular chain pathway into the compression and expansion of elastic structures such as the tympanic membrane and the air in the middle ear cavities. At the higher frequencies, the mass of the ossicular chain becomes dominant and again the efficiency of sound transmission suffers.

Combined, these observations on the transmission of sound through the middle ear form a transfer function. Recall that we discussed transfer functions for filters in Chapter 4. Similarly, we may summarize the sound transmission characteristics of the middle ear by knowing its transfer function. To be complete, the transfer function must have both amplitude and phase characteristics, as shown in Figure 9.12. Consider, for the moment, only the amplitude function shown in Figure 9.12. The behavior of the middle ear structures is best described as that of a broadly tuned bandpass filter. The frequencies most efficiently transmitted are those for which the normal-hearing listener is most sensitive. There is considerable evidence to support the observation that the middle ear transfer function determines the shape of the normal audibility curve. Note that when the amplitude transfer characteristic is inverted, its shape is strikingly similar to the audibility curve displayed in Figure 9.5.

Input Impedance   In our discussion of the transmission of sound in air, we stated that the impedance of a sound-conducting medium was an indicator of the ease with which sound energy would flow through it. The middle ear structures may be considered as an elastic sound-conducting medium. An application of such impedance concepts to the middle ear has led to new diagnostic procedures in audiology. The tympanic membrane is the only portion of the middle ear that is accessible without surgical intervention. Thus, we must specify the acoustical impedance of the middle ear at its input, the tympanic membrane. A number of instruments have been designed to determine the input impedance of the middle ear, but we will confine our discussion to the basic concepts of impedance measurement. We wish to indicate the use to which such information can be put. Although it is theoretically possible to measure the input impedance of the middle ear over a range of frequencies, practical considerations have led to standardized measurements at only two frequencies, 220 and 660 Hz. Impedance measurements at higher frequencies are more difficult to make and variability renders them difficult to interpret.

At a low frequency (220 Hz), the normal middle ear input impedance shows a small resistive component of about 550 acoustical ohms and a reactive component of about −3000 acoustical ohms. This means that the structures exhibiting acoustical compliance are dominant at these low frequencies. If we were to make input impedance measurements at higher frequencies, the influence of the compliant structures would be decreased and the influence of the ossicular chain (mass reaction) would increase. Thus, the reactive part of the input impedance would eventually change from a compliant reactance into a mass reactance.

The determination of the acoustical impedance of the middle ear at the tympanic membrane condenses the behavior of the whole system into two components, resistance and reactance. The value of impedance measurements is found in the fact that many pathological conditions within the middle ear affect the sound conduction pathway in such a way that they are readily apparent from determinations of middle ear input impedance. For example, the compliant reactance observed at low frequencies is primarily due to the volume of air contained within the middle ear. A pathological condition which reduces that volume substantially can be detected, because a smaller volume of air will lead to a smaller than normal compliant reactance measurement. It has been determined that the cochlear input at the oval window contributes most to the resistive component of the input impedance. If the cochlea is uncoupled from the ossicular chain, as it would be in a disarticulation of the incudostapedial joint, then the resistive component of input impedance will be reduced. Other pathological conditions lead to still other alterations in the normal input impedance of the middle ear. Zwislocki (1962) has developed an electrical model of the middle ear structures that is of great value in illustrating the contribution of the major anatomical structures of the middle ear to the total input impedance as measured at the tympanic membrane. But the clinical audiologist does not have to refer back to mechanical or electrical models of the middle ear for each determination of middle ear impedance. Test procedures have been developed and standardized to some degree, so that impedance determinations can be performed routinely. It is, however, often beneficial to appreciate the scientific bases of such tests, especially in cases where you may have to depart from the established routine.

THE ACOUSTIC REFLEX   The two tiny muscles (tensor tympani and stapedius) attached to the ossicular chain may be activated by moderately intense sounds. When this action occurs, the efficiency of sound transmission through the middle ear is altered. Middle ear muscle contractions cause a stiffening of the ossicular chain. In addition, the stapes footplate is slightly retracted from the oval window so that its mode of vibration is altered. Rather than the simple pistonlike action observed by Guinan and Peake, the stapes footplate undergoes a rocking action in response to sound input. This rocking action is about an axis that passes through the long diameter of the oval-shaped footplate. The result is a much less efficient transfer of sound energy into the cochlear fluid than can be found with the middle ear muscles at rest.

Generally, the action of the reflex causes low-frequency sounds to be attenuated by perhaps 10 to 20 dB. Progressively less attenuation is produced for higher frequencies, so that the contraction of the middle ear muscles has little effect on the transmission of sound at frequencies above about 2 kHz. Contractions of the middle ear muscles are not coincident with the onset of even the most intense sounds. Their activation exhibits a *latency,* the period of time between the onset of the sound stimulation and the contraction of the muscles. For very intense sounds, the latency may be as brief as 10 msec; for moderate sounds, the latency may extend beyond 100 msec. In general, latency decreases as stimulating intensity increases.

Because the acoustic reflex is mediated by muscle contractions, it is subject to muscle fatigue. You would find that it becomes difficult to hold this textbook at arm's length for an extended period of time, if you were to attempt it. The middle ear muscles are subject to a similar form of fatigue, and after prolonged periods of contraction they will relax regardless of the intensity of stimulation.

There is still some uncertainty about the evolutionary purpose of the acoustic reflex. One popular notion is that it evolved to protect the delicate sensory cells within the cochlea from overstimulation. Although the reflex does afford some protection to the cochlea from damage due to intense sound exposure, its protection is limited and many potentially damaging stimuli are unaffected. The attenuation offered by contraction of the middle ear muscles is negligible for frequencies above 2 kHz. Thus, high-frequency sounds may still be transmitted into the cochlea at levels sufficient to damage or destroy sensory cells. Even more critical is the latency of response to any sound. Impulsive noises such as those due to explosions or gunfire are so brief that the entire blast will have traversed the middle ear before the reflex occurs. (A case of closing the door to the china shop after the bull has done his damage, if we are permitted to mix our metaphors.) Protection from industrial noise sources is also limited when the exposure is continuous for the normal eight-hour work shift because of the onset of muscle fatigue.

Perhaps the most damaging evidence against the noise protection explanation of acoustic reflex action is Simmons' (1964) assertion that no intense noises exist in nature to evoke this reflex action. Most sounds that are capable of causing damage to the sensory cells within the cochlea are the result of human effort and of very recent origin when we consider the time required for natural selection. Simmons points out that the only function of middle ear muscle contraction that consistently has survival value is the attenuation of self-generated noise. In some species—perhaps the bat is the best example—the self-generated noise is the animal's own cry. The attenuation due to the acoustic reflex would not prevent damage where there was no danger of injury, but it would serve to reduce the effect of the cry in masking the faint echo which the bat must hear. Simmons further indicates that low-frequency physiological noises due to head movements, chewing, and swallowing might interfere with a grazing animal's ability to detect and localize the sounds made by a predator. Given the absence of natural loud sounds and the limited protection from sounds generated by humans afforded by the middle ear reflex, Simmons' arguments are quite convincing.

the inner ear

ANATOMY

A Macroscopic View   The sensory receptor cells (hair cells) for hearing are located within the cochlea, part of the structure known anatomically as the *labyrinth.* In Greek mythology, the Minotaur, a beast that was half human and half bull, was confined in the labyrinth, a prison made up of tunnels and passages in a randomly arranged maze. The labyrinth is composed of two major systems of canals hollowed out in the temporal bone, the *cochlea* and the *semi-circular canals.* The cochlea and the semi-circular canals are connected to a central structure known as the *vestibule.* The vestibule and semi-circular canals contain the receptor cells for the sense of balance. These structures are often called simply the vestibular system. Figure 9.13 shows the relationship of the semi-circular canals and cochlea to the vestibule. In mammals, the cochlea is wound in a spiral so that it has the appearance of a snail shell. The number of turns in the spiral and the length of the cochlear duct varies from species to species. In humans, there are nearly three ($2\frac{3}{4}$) turns of the cochlea. In an adult, the unwound cochlea would measure about 35 mm in length. Because the shape is similar to a spiral pyramid, we often refer to the base (first turn) or the apex (third turn, in humans) of the cochlea. The basal turn connects with the vestibule.

In humans and other primates, the labyrinth is almost inaccessible because it is embedded within the petrous portion of the temporal bone of the skull. In lower mammals, such as the guinea pig, chinchilla, or cat, these structures are found within an air-filled space called the bulla. This difference in gross anatomy has led to much confusion, because the cochlea that often appears in textbook illustrations shows a diagram or photograph using nonprimate specimens. In the human labyrinth, there are really two labyrinthine structures. The osseous (bony) labyrinth is the complex set of tunnels in the temporal bone that course off from the vestibule. The osseous labyrinth has no external structure apart from the temporal bone in which it is found. In humans and other primates, the osseous labyrinth is a space within the temporal bone filled with

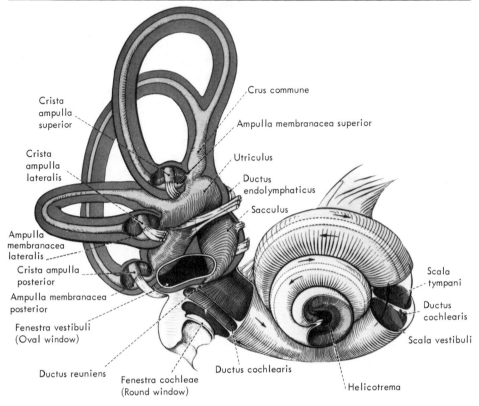

Crus commune

Crista ampulla superior

Ampulla membranacea superior

Crista ampulla lateralis

Utriculus

Ductus endolymphaticus

Sacculus

Ampulla membranacea lateralis

Crista ampulla posterior

Ampulla membranacea posterior

Fenestra vestibuli (Oval window)

Scala tympani

Ductus cochlearis

Scala vestibuli

Ductus reuniens

Fenestra cochleae (Round window)

Ductus cochlearis

Helicotrema

figure 9.13

The central labyrinth including the cochlea, vestibule, and
semi-circular canals. Reprinted by permission from
Abbott Laboratories. *Some Pathological Conditions of the Eye, Ear
and Throat: An Atlas.* © 1957, Abbott Laboratories, Chicago.

fluid and other structures. Approximately the center one-third of the osseous
tube is taken up by the membranous labyrinth, the *scala media*. Figure 9.14 illustrates this relationship in a cross-section of the cochlea. The fluid that fills
the space between the osseous walls of the labyrinth and the membranous labyrinth is called *perilymph*. It is this fluid which we have said has the physical
properties of ordinary water, although its chemical composition is more like
that of CSF.

The perilymphatic spaces within the cochlea form two ducts or canals that
course through the length of the cochlea. One canal, connected directly to the
vestibule, is known as the *scala vestibuli*. We often think of sound entering
the cochlea through the scala vestibuli because the oval window is found in the
area where the scala vestibuli joins the vestibule proper. The *scala tympani* is
found on the opposite side of the scala media. At the basal end, the scala tympani terminates in a bony wall, except for the round window membrane. It, too,
is filled with perilymph. The scala vestibuli and scala tympani are connected

through a very small hole at the apical end of the cochlea called the *helicotrema*.

The membranous duct that lies between the scala vestibuli and scala tympani is known as the *scala media*. *Reissner's membrane* divides the scala vestibuli from the scala media. Reissner's membrane is a very thin membrane that acts as a chemical but not a physical barrier between the canals. That is, sound energy encounters very little loss in traveling from the scala vestibuli into the scala media.

The boundary between the scala media and the scala tympani is made up of three structures. Toward the inner margin (edge) of the spiral, there is a bony ridge called the *spiral lamina*. The spiral lamina is wound around a hollow center portion of the cochlea known as the *modiolus*. If all other structures are removed, the spiral lamina wound around the modiolus would have the appearance of a large wood screw. On the outside margin of the cochlear duct is a ligament known as the *spiral ligament*. Between the spiral lamina (bone) and the spiral ligament, we find the *basilar membrane*. We will see later that the physical properties of the basilar membrane play a major part in determining mechanical response in the cochlea. This mechanical response constitutes the

figure 9.14

The three ducts of the cochlea. From A. T. Rasmussen, *Outlines of Neuroanatomy* (Dubuque, Iowa; Brown, 1943).

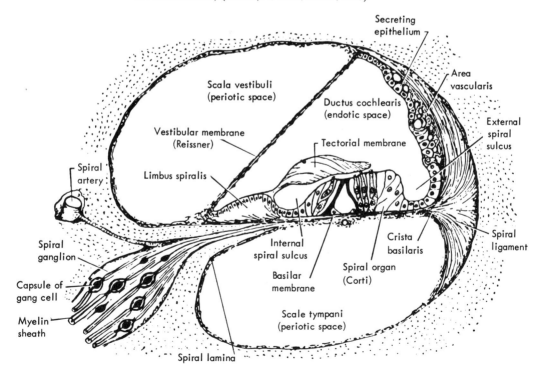

first stage of analysis of the incoming soundwave. The basilar membrane extends from the basal turn to the helicotrema in the apical turn. It is tapered in shape so that it is narrow at the basal end and wider at the apex. Although early anatomists thought that the basilar membrane was stretched between the spiral lamina and spiral ligament, Bekesy showed that it exhibited no evidence of transverse tension. Within the scala media, the complex structure known as the *Organ of Corti* rests on the basilar membrane. The Organ of Corti contains the sensory receptor cells (hair cells) and their supporting structures. We will take a much closer look at this organ after describing the remaining structures found within the scala media.

Lying just above the Organ of Corti is the *tectorial membrane,* which is attached to the spiral limbus at its inner margin, but free at its outer margin. It is thought to be essentially structureless, an "amorphous blob" in unscientific terms. Running along the outer wall of the scala media for its entire length is a region rich in blood vessels known as the *stria vascularis.* The spaces between these major structures within the scala media are filled with a watery substance known as *endolymph.* Endolymph is chemically different from perilymph. The interior of the membranous labyrinth is filled with endolymph. Because the composition of endolymph is similar to the cytoplasm of the hair cells, it is difficult to explain how hair cells bathed in endolymph could maintain a difference of potential across their cell membranes. For that reason, Engstrom (1960) suggested that a different fluid, cortilymph, may fill the tunnel spaces beneath the reticular lamina. Figure 9.15 shows the structures of the membranous labyrinth and the small ducts that interconnect them. A complete anatomical description

figure 9.15

A schematic representation of the membranous labyrinth.
Reprinted by permission from D. D. DeWeese
and W. H. Saunders, *Textbook of Otolaryngology,*
3rd ed. © 1968, The C. V. Mosby Company.

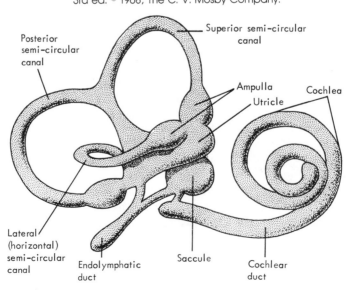

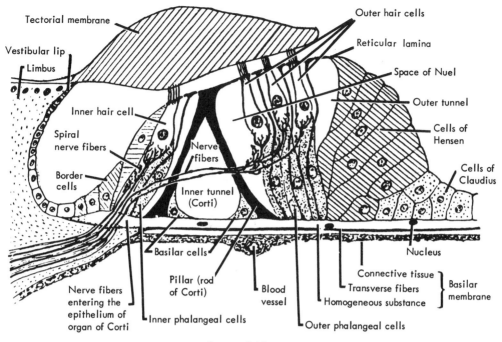

figure 9.16

Schematic representation of the structures that comprise
the Organ of Corti. Reprinted by permission from A. T. Rasmussen,
Outlines of Neuroanatomy (Dubuque, Iowa: Brown, 1943).

of these structures is beyond the scope of this text; the reader is directed to the
references at the end of this chapter for more detailed treatments.

A Microscopic View   Figure 9.16 shows a diagram of the
typical cross-section of the Organ of Corti. Notice that there are three rows of
outer hair cells and one row of inner hair cells. The innermost row of outer
hair cells is separated from the inner hair cells by the *tunnel of Corti*. The tunnel is framed by supporting cells, the inner and outer pillar cells, collectively
called the *rods of Corti*. Most of the cells in the Organ of Corti serve to hold
the inner or outer hair cells in place. Hensen's cells and Deiters' cells support
the outer hair cells; the inner phalangeal cells support the inner hair cells. The
most striking supportive cells are the Deiters' cells, which support individual
outer hair cells. Figure 9.17 shows a typical outer hair cell—Deiters' cell arrangement. Each Deiters' cell has a cup-shaped base and a long phalangeal process that extends to the region surrounding the tops of the hair cells. Viewed
from above, as in Figure 9.18, the hair cells appear to be held in place like pav-
ing stones in a sidewalk. The cement in this arrangement is the *reticular lamina,* which serves to hold the hair cells in place. The arrangement of the cilia
(hairs) on the tops of individual hair cells is also found to be very orderly. The
cilia on the outer hair cells are formed into a sort of W-shaped pattern, with the

open end of the W always oriented toward the modiolus. There are usually several rows of cilia, with the longer ones found in the row most distant from the modiolus. An orderly arrangement of cilia on inner hair cells is not so apparent.

The position of the tectorial membrane is illustrated in Figure 9.16. Its attachment on the modiolar side is evident. The relationship of the tectorial membrane to the hair cells has been a matter of controversy in the literature. Some authors have stated that the cilia are merely in contact with the tectorial membrane; others suggest that the hairs are actually embedded in the tectorial membrane. Since most tissue-fixing procedures produce damage to these structures, it has been difficult to determine that relationship. However, recent studies of the cochlea, using the scanning electron microscope, show clear evidence of indentations in the tectorial membrane that correspond with the cilia of the outer hair cells (Lim, 1972; Hunter-Duvar, 1977). Indentations corresponding with cilia of the inner hair cells were not found in these studies.

figure 9.17

Schematic representation of a Deiters' cell supporting an outer hair cell. Reprinted by permission from W. R. Zemlin, *Speech and Hearing Science: Anatomy and Physiology.* © 1968 by Prentice-Hall, Inc.

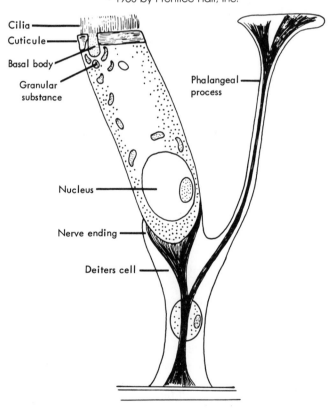

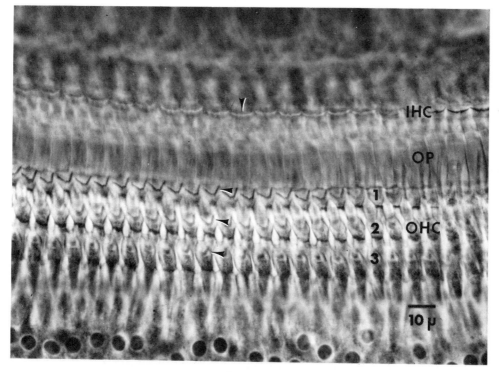

figure 9.18

Phase contrast photomicrograph of surface of the Organ of Corti.
Stereocilia (arrows) can be seen projecting from surface
of inner hair cells (IHC) and outer hair cells (OHC$_{1,2,3}$).
OP = heads of outer pillar cells. Courtesy of B. A. Bohne,
Ph.D., Department of Otolaryngology,
Washington University School of Medicine.

The anatomical description of the cochlea is really incomplete without a description of the pattern of innervation of the hair cells by the dendritic endings of the VIIIth nerve. However, we will delay a discussion of the innervation pattern until after we have covered the mechanical and electrophysiological responses of the cochlear structures.

the mechanical response of the inner ear

Much of our current knowledge of the mechanical response of the cochlea was first reported by Bekesy, and most of his work was published as a book entitled *Experiments in Hearing* (1960). One can appreciate the contributions of this man to our understanding of the auditory system only by reading his first-hand accounts of a series of experiments and observations that spanned over thirty years. Our description here, of course, must omit most of these details.

Sound energy is usually delivered to the inner ear through the vibratory action of the stapes footplate in the oval window. We must qualify this statement, because it is possible to deliver sound energy to the cochlea by other means. If the whole skull is set into vibration by an intense airborne sound or through contact with a vibrating body, sound energy can be delivered to the cochlea without traveling the normal middle ear pathway. This means of sound stimulation is generally called *bone conduction*. There are disagreements among audiologists about the exact mechanism by which this bone-conducted sound energy excites the cochlear fluids. Some suggest that, in effect, the cochlea moves while the stapes remains stationary. (A case of the tail wagging the dog?) Others suggest that direct compression of the bony labyrinth is possible because of pressure relief provided by the round window, oval window, and the cochlear ducts. Whatever the mechanism, bone conduction stimulation is of interest in clinical audiology because it gives the audiologist an opportunity to assess the status of the inner ear in the presence of middle ear disorders. Because direct stimulation of the skull is called bone conduction, the normal sound pathway to the cochlea has been called *air conduction*. Therefore, anytime one sees a reference to air conduction testing, it is safe to assume that the sound was delivered to the ear canal via a headphone or loudspeaker.

We have thus far presented experimental evidence on the mechanical behavior of the ear that is widely accepted at this time. Perhaps in the future more evidence will be found to support these observations, but it is also possible that contradictory evidence so overwhelming will appear that we will have to abandon these explanations and seek better ones.

In mammals, the cochlea is wound in a spiral. You may have better understanding of the structure if you picture a soft ice cream cone. The ice cream comes from the machine as a thin circular tube and is wound in a circular spiral on the cone. The hollow space on the inside of the ice cream spiral corresponds to the modiolus in the cochlea. It is easier to illustrate the mechanical action within the cochlea if we unwind the spiral and represent it as a straight tube. We do this for the ease of illustrating the traveling wave. Figure 9.19 presents our schematic representation of the cochlea. The scala vestibuli is at the top, the scala tympani below, and the scala media is represented by the single thick horizontal line. The oval window and round windows are at the basal end; the helicotrema is at the apical end.

THE TRANSIENT RESPONSE   If the stapes footplate were pushed into the oval window very slowly, then the perilymph in the scala vestibuli would be displaced toward the apex. Some perilymph would probably stream through the helicotrema into the scala tympani. The overload of perilymph in the scala tympani would be relieved by an outward bulging of the round window. We have chosen this extreme example to point out the pressure relief function of the round window membrane. At very low stapes velocity, the flow of perilymph may provide the means for offsetting a pressure increase or decrease introduced into the oval window. At the stapes velocities required for the frequencies within our audible range, the streaming of perilymph cannot act

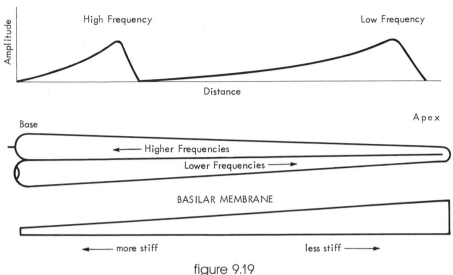

figure 9.19

A schematic diagram of the cochlea "unrolled" into a straight
tube. Reprinted by permission from J. D. Durrant and J. H. Lovrinic,
Bases of Hearing Science. © 1977, Williams and Wilkins.

quickly enough to provide the necessary pressure relief. Since perilymph behaves physically like ordinary water, it is not surprising to find that perilymph
is nearly incompressible. Since the perilymph cannot yield to compressional
forces and also cannot flow to relieve the overpressure (or underpressure) introduced by the stapes footplate, something must yield. That something is the
membranous scala media.

If we follow a half-cycle of stapes displacement in slow motion, perhaps
the illustration will become clearer. Assume that the stapes begins at its rest
position. Then, due to a compressional wave conducted along the ossicular
chain, it begins to move into the cochlea. A pressure wave is set up in the perilymph fluid of the scala vestibuli which quickly travels the length of the cochlea. (Sound travels faster in media of higher density.) As the wave travels the
scala vestibuli, sound energy is delivered to the scala tympani through the scala
media. To do this, the scala media is displaced from its rest position. If a compression were introduced into the scala vestibuli, then the scala media would
bulge slightly toward the scala tympani. In this process, the sound energy delivered by the stapes is delivered to the structures of the scala media.

Once the scala media has been distorted toward the scala tympani, the
overpressure delivered to the oval window can be relieved in part by an outward bulging of the round window membrane. Only partial relief would be
needed, because some of the sound energy has been delivered to the structures
of the scala media. These structures, the basilar membrane in particular, are
elastic. Thus, the temporary bulge is opposed by elastic restoring forces and
the structures return to their rest position. The return to rest position takes on

a unique characteristic, however, because of the physical properties of the basilar membrane. If only one compressional pulse were delivered to the cochlea by the stapes, then the response of the basilar membrane (and therefore the entire scala media) would best be characterized as a traveling wave that begins at the basal end and moves toward the apical end of the cochlea. The estimated travel time of this wave is about 5 msec, a value much slower than the time required for the sound pulse to travel from the stapes to the helicotrema in the perilymph. The speed of sound in perilymph is much greater than the time it takes for the traveling wave response to move from base to apex. Thus, it is often said that the sound energy introduced into the cochlea is delivered to the entire length of the basilar membrane at the same instant. After the sound energy has been delivered to the basilar membrane, the traveling wave response begins at the base and moves to the apex.

THE STEADY-STATE RESPONSE   We have described briefly the transient response (that is, the response to a very brief, pulselike stimulus) of the scala media. The transient response is a traveling displacement waveform that begins at the basal end and moves toward the apex. Our appreciation of cochlear mechanics will be improved if we next consider the response to a continuous sinusoidal sound wave.

We oversimplify a bit, but it may be instructive to think of the continuous sinusoidal soundwave as an alternating series of compressions and rarefactions. Each compression or rarefaction will, in turn, produce a response on the basilar membrane. After a brief time at the beginning of the soundwave, the basilar membrane will fall into a steady-state response. That is, since the stimulus (an alternating sequence of compressions and rarefactions) is periodic, the responses are periodic. The basilar membrane vibrates at the stimulus frequency along its entire length. However, the relative amplitude of the displacement at a given place on the membrane depends upon the frequency of the soundwave. Of course, the amplitude of the displacement waveform depends on the strength of the sound stimulus. The more intense the soundwave, the greater the amplitude of basilar membrane vibration everywhere along its length. What we are saying is that for a given soundwave intensity, the amplitude of basilar membrane displacement will vary as we look along its length from base to apex. An example is shown in Figure 9.20. At some place along the basilar membrane, the displacement waveform will have a maximum. If we are able to watch the displacement waveform, we would see that the amplitude of the response is small at the basal end of the cochlea. The amplitude grows as we progress toward the apex, until at some point there is a maximum in the response. Beyond the maximum, the amplitude falls off very sharply. For many sound input frequencies, there may be no detectable mechanical response near the helicotrema.

If we connect the peaks of the basilar membrane displacement waveform with a smooth curve, we obtain the envelope of the basilar membrane displacement wave. Figure 9.20 shows such an envelope as a dotted line. Be-

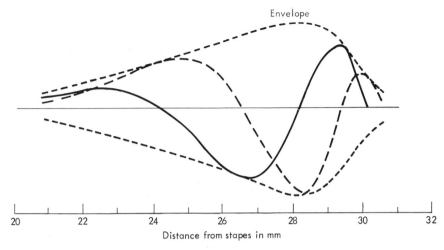

figure 9.20

Illustration of the displacement of the basilar membrane in a
cochlear model. Displacements for two instants in time are
shown as a solid line and heavy dashed line. Also shown is the
envelope of the traveling wave (thin dashed line). Reprinted
by permission from G. von Bekesy, *Experiments in Hearing*.
© 1960, McGraw-Hill Book Company.

kesy's observations showed that the place at which the traveling wave envelope maximum occurs depends upon the frequency of the soundwaves. The
maximum in the traveling wave envelope occurs near the basal end of the
cochlea for high-frequency sounds. As the frequency of the stimulus is lowered, the place of maximum displacement migrates toward the helicotrema (the
apical region). There is an orderly relationship between the place of maximum
displacement and the stimulus frequency. This relationship is called *tonotopic
organization*. In general, whenever we find a relationship between stimulus frequency and place in the nervous system, we will say that the structure exhibits
tonotopic organization.

From the discussion above it may seem that the steady-state response of
the basilar membrane is stationary—that is, vibration "in place" as in a standing wave. However, that is not the case. The timing of the response to a given
part of the input waveform varies with distance along the cochlea. Thus, the response "lags" (falls behind in time) the driving waveform to a greater degree as
distance from the stapes increases. Recall that the response to a single pulse
was seen to travel from the basal end toward the apex. The response to a given
point on the driving waveform is also seen to "travel" from base to apex, but
the response to one point on the input waveform is added to those just preceding it, so that the motion is difficult to display without moving pictures.
(Several excellent motion pictures are available that illustrate both transient
and steady-state responses in the cochlea. Ideally, one of these films should be
available to every reader.)

THE UNIQUENESS OF COCHLEAR
TRAVELING WAVES Let us briefly summarize our observations to this point. First, the sound energy delivered into the cochlea by the stapes is carried to the scala media almost instantly by a rapid pressure wave in the perilymph. Next, the energy in the perilymphatic wave is coupled into the basilar membrane, which responds with a unique traveling wave response. We have not yet told you why this traveling wave is unique, but be patient; we will. The response to a brief pressure pulse delivered to the oval window is a wave of basilar membrane displacement that begins at the basal end and moves toward the apex. In response to a single sinusoid, the displacement envelope is found to have a maximum at a place along the basilar membrane determined by the stimulus frequency. This relationship between stimulus frequency and anatomical location is called tonotopic organization.

Bekesy found the cochlear traveling wave to be unique in two ways. First, most "ordinary" traveling waves (the ripples on a still pond, for example) have a maximum amplitude at their source and decay as they move away. However, the traveling wave response of the basilar membrane actually grows in amplitude as it moves from the base of the cochlea toward the apex. If we think of the oval window as the "source" of the traveling wave, it would appear that the cochlear response grows in amplitude as it moves away from its source. Of course, after reaching a maximum at a place determined by the frequency of the signal, the basilar membrane traveling wave does decay rapidly in amplitude as it continues toward the apex.

Bekesy made another observation that makes the cochlear response seem unique, even "paradoxical," as he put it. In order to conduct this experiment, he developed special techniques for observing the traveling wave. First, he made a small "window" in the bony shell of the cochlea so that he could observe the mechanical response. Then, he put very small reflective particles along the patch of basilar membrane visible through his window and illuminated the area with a stroboscopic light. The light was synchronized to the signal, so that the motion of the silver particles was "frozen" in time. Bekesy could thus see the envelope of the traveling wave. By changing the frequency of the signal slightly or by altering the synchronization of the light flashes, he could observe the movement of the traveling wave response in slow motion. With this experimental setup, Bekesy carefully observed the traveling wave response to sounds delivered to the cochlea through the oval window. Then he carefully drilled a new oval window in the apical turn of the cochlea. An artificial stapes footplate attached to a mechanical vibrator was inserted into the new window. Thus, sound energy was delivered to the cochlea from the end opposite the oval window. The response that Bekesy observed in the basilar membrane traveling wave was unchanged by the relocation of the source. The displacement waveform still began at the basal end and traveled toward the apex, toward its source! Bekesy at first found this puzzling, and called the response a *paradoxical* wave because it apparently traveled toward its source.

His explanation for the paradoxical nature of the basilar membrane response lies in the fact that the oval window is not the true "source" of excitation for the basilar membrane. The basilar membrane is excited by the soundwave in the perilymph. Recall that the speed of that wave is so fast that it is often said to excite the entire basilar membrane at once. Thus, Bekesy found that the source of the perilymphatic wave had no influence on basilar membrane response. This finding helps to explain bone-conducted excitation of the cochlea as well. If the response of the basilar membrane varied with the location of the vibrating source, then bone-conducted sounds, which enter the cochlea directly through the bony walls, might sound entirely different from their air-conducted counterparts.

Bekesy found that the traveling wave response in the cochlea depends almost entirely upon the physical properties of the basilar membrane. These properties are (1) the tapered shape of the membrane, and (2) the gradual change in the stiffness of the membrane along its length. The basilar membrane is narrow at the basal end, where the cochlear tube itself is at its widest. As it extends toward the apex, the basilar membrane width increases until it is about ten times as wide at its apical end as it is at the basal end. Even more striking is the variation in stiffness that Bekesy found along the basilar membrane. The basal end of the basilar membrane exhibits 100 to 200 times the stiffness found at the apical end. Further, the variation in stiffness changes gradually over the length of the cochlea. Using a number of scale models of the cochlea, Bekesy showed that the response of the basilar membrane changed only when the shape, or—more important—the graded stiffness, was altered. In his models, he could alter the length of the membrane, its overall size, and the size of the fluid-filled ducts adjacent to the membrane without changing the essential nature of the waveform.

THE COCHLEAR RESPONSE
AND AUDITORY ANALYSIS   The mechanical response of the basilar membrane is the most peripheral stage of the analysis of auditory signals. The cochlea is said to perform a filtering action because the place at which the maximum in the basilar membrane displacement envelope occurs depends upon the stimulus frequency. A complex signal made up of several frequencies would produce several envelope maxima of basilar membrane displacement. We shall see later in this chapter that the dendritic endings of the VIIIth nerve are distributed in a complex but orderly fashion along the length of the basilar membrane. It thus appears logical to assume that if the hair cells could respond only to maxima in the envelope of the displacement waveform, then the mechanical response would be similar to that of a bandpass filter (Chapter 4).

If we take Bekesy's observed basilar-membrane envelope functions to represent the filtering characteristics of a given place along the cochlea, we see that the frequency-resolving power of the ear should be very gross indeed. Frequency-resolving power is indicated by the ability of the listener to distinguish

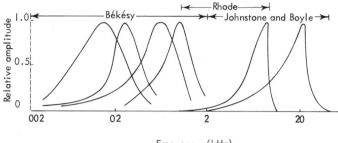

figure 9.21

The mechanical response of the basilar membrane as reported
by three different investigators. Notice that the three sets of
figures cover much of the audible frequency range. Reprinted
by permission from B. M. Johnstone and P. M. Sellick, "The
Peripheral Auditory Apparatus," *Quarterly Review of
Biophysics*, (part 1), 5 (1972), 1–57. © Cambridge University Press.

a tone at one frequency from another tone identical to the first except for a small difference in frequency. If we made the usual assumptions about the auditory peripheral filter, then the tones would have to be separated by an amount equal to the −3 dB bandwidth of the supposed filter. Bekesy's observations would indicate the separation would have to reach about 40 percent of the center frequency before the tones could be resolved. We know from a number of experiments that the well-practiced listener can distinguish between successive tones that differ by as little as 0.3 percent in frequency. Therefore, either we don't use this peripheral filter alone in performing frequency analysis of a complex signal, or Bekesy's observations were in gross error.

Some critics of Bekesy have indicated that the mechanical response he observed was limited to the apical end of the cochlea. Further, they have pointed to the very high signal intensities (perhaps 130 dB or more) that were required to generate displacements large enough to be seen even through a microscope. Those high intensities may have driven the basilar membrane into a nonlinear region of response, broadening the apparent bandwidth of the filter. Recent investigations of the mechanical response of the basilar membrane have used much more sensitive nonvisual techniques to sense the displacement waveform. These methods, which use the Mössbauer technique or a capacitive probe (similar to a condenser microphone), have two advantages. First, the response can be detected at much lower stimulus levels than those used by Bekesy. Second, the measure of displacement can be made on an objective basis. But although there are some subtle differences between these more modern observations and those of Bekesy, his basic hypotheses are still supported. Figure 9.21 shows a composite of Bekesy's data and those of two later studies. One could say that there seems to be an orderly progression of bandwidths of the traveling wave envelope as the place along the basilar membrane is varied from apex (low frequency) to base (high frequency).

If Bekesy's observations are essentially correct, there must be more signal processing in the auditory system than the simple gross filtering exhibited by the traveling wave response. Of course, many other aspects of auditory perception have led to this conclusion, but it is still surprising that a number of writers assume that the function of the auditory system can be described as a simple spectrum analysis by means of a bandpass filter bank. This peripheral filtering is simply the first of a number of stages necessary for the analysis of auditory signals.

We have still not indicated the mechanism by which the hair cells are stimulated. Most current evidence points to a shearing force as the mechanical stimulus for the hair cells. Figure 9.22 illustrates the way in which displacement of the basilar membrane is transformed into shearing forces. Shearing forces are those forces acting when two surfaces slide past one another. Thus, shearing forces act to cut a sheet of paper held between the blades of a pair of scissors. In Figure 9.22, notice that the basilar membrane is attached at both edges to the spiral lamina on the modiolar side and to the spiral ligament on the strial edge. The tectorial membrane is attached only on the modiolar side; its outer edge (toward the stria) is free to move up and down along a line between the scala vestibuli and the scala tympani. Given that the tectorial membrane is hinged at only one margin, it is thought to slide over the tops of the hair cells whenever the basilar membrane is displaced. Bekesy supported the suggestion that shearing forces act to stimulate the hair cells by another clever experiment. He developed a vibrating needle that moved in a linear fashion. Using the electrical response of the hair cells (the cochlear microphonic, which we will discuss below), he demonstrated that the outer rows of hair cells respond maximally when a radial shearing force is applied to the tectorial membrane over them. Radial shearing forces would move along a line perpendicular to the direction of travel of the response. They would be parallel to a radial spoke extending from the modiolus to the stria. Bekesy showed further that the inner row of hair cells seemed to respond best to shearing forces applied in the longitudinal direction.

Calculations and computer-generated models of the traveling wave response have shown support for this "directional sensitivity" of the hair cells to the shearing forces applied. Further, it seems that the radially directed shear is at a maximum at the displacement maximum, but the magnitude of shearing force is distributed over a much narrower region of the basilar membrane. The longitudinal shear over the inner row of hair cells is at a maximum on the apical side of the displacement envelope. It is difficult to visualize longitudinal shear from the simple one-dimensional diagram of the basilar membrane response. Figure 9.23 shows Tonndorf's illustration of the traveling wave envelope, which takes into account the attachment of the basilar membrane at both the modiolar and strial margins.

So far, we have followed the sound energy from the air surrounding the head of the listener, through the outer ear and middle ear, to the traveling wave response of the cochlea. We have seen that the traveling wave response repre-

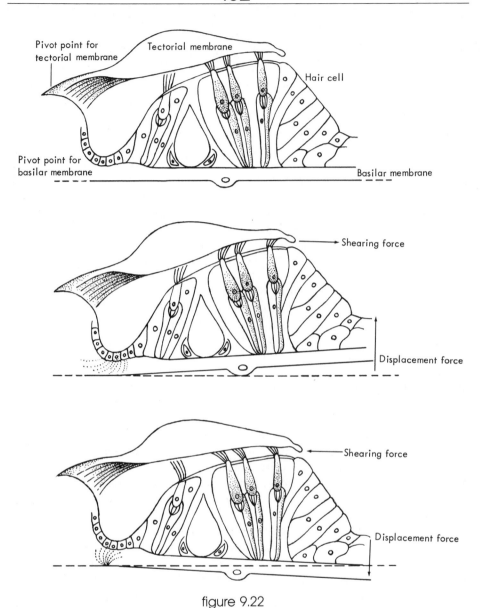

figure 9.22

An illustration of the transformation of basilar membrane displacement into shearing force at the tops of the hair cells.

sents the most peripheral, and probably the least frequency-selective, portion of auditory analysis. The displacement of the basilar membrane was seen to generate shearing forces at the tops of the hair cells, which are apparently the mechanical stimuli for these cells. We must now confess almost total ignorance of the means by which the hair cell converts mechanical force at its top into an

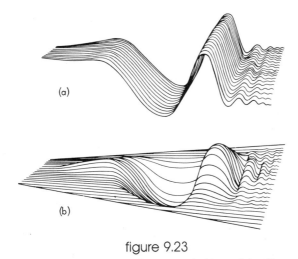

figure 9.23

(a) A traveling wave pattern executed by a ribbonlike approximation of the cochlear partition. (b) A closer approximation to actual basilar membrane motion. The edges of the membrane are attached at the spiral ligament of the osseous spiral lamina. Reprinted by permission from J. Tonndorf, "Shearing Motion in Scala Media of Cochlear Models," *Journal of the Acoustical Society of America,* 32 (1960), 238–244.

effective stimulus for the dendritic endings of the VIIIth nerve fibers. Hair cell function is presently the subject of active research, perhaps exceeded only by the active speculation concerning the possible mechanisms that lead from shearing force to nerve fiber stimulation.

While there are gaps in our knowledge at this most crucial level, there are some important findings in cochlear physiology which we shall discuss next. They are important for two reasons. First, these observations must be explained by any mechanism proposed to explain hair cell function. Perhaps of more immediate importance is the fact that some clinical test procedures have been based on these findings.

cochlear electrophysiology

The presence of electrical signals within the cochlea has been known since 1930, when Wever and Bray made their discovery of the *cochlear microphonic (CM)*. They found that a fine wire placed on the VIIIth nerve of a cat picked up an electrical signal which reproduced the acoustical input to the ear with reasonable fidelity. Because the inner ear seemed to be acting like a simple microphone, they called their signal the cochlear microphonic, although some writers call it the Wever-Bray effect. Nearly twenty years passed before techniques were developed to permit recording from within the cochlea itself. Microelectrodes made of very thin glass pipettes filled with an electrically con-

table 9.1

COCHLEAR POTENTIAL	ELECTRICAL NATURE	STIMULUS DEPENDENT?
1. Cochlear microphonic (CM)	ac	yes
2. Summating potential (SP)	dc	yes
3. Endocochlear potential (EP)	dc	no
4. Intracellular (Organ of Corti) potential (IP)	dc	no
5. Whole nerve action potential (AP)	ac	yes

ducting solution were first inserted into the cochlea by Bekesy, and by Davis and his collaborators. Today a number of laboratories use refined versions of those early techniques to study the electrical potentials generated within the cochlea.

There are several ways in which to classify the electrical potentials recorded from within the cochlea. Four potentials generated from within, plus one generated by the VIIIth nerve fibers in the modiolus, can be recorded by an electrode inserted into the cochlea. These five potentials can be classified simply as either *ac* (the voltage varies over a brief time period) or *dc* (a constant voltage over a brief time period) electrical signals. Alternatively, they can be classified as being dependent upon stimulation of the cochlea, or independent of stimulation. Stimulus-dependent potentials are often called *receptor potentials*. Receptor potentials are generated by specialized sensory cells in response to outside (stimulus) energy. Electrophysiologists (Davis, 1961; Dallos, 1973) distinguish between this type of receptor potential and the graded electrical activity that must occur in the dendritic endings of the VIIIth nerve fibers. The latter signal is called a *generator potential*. The generator potential in the dendritic ending of a sensory nerve fiber is in many ways analogous to the postsynaptic potentials discussed in Chapter 2. The generator potential must reach the initial segment of the nerve fiber with sufficient strength to trigger a nerve impulse. We must presume that the initial segments for VIIIth nerve fibers lie within the modiolus, although their location has never been established. Neither have any of the electrical potentials recorded from the cochlea been identified as the generator potential for VIIIth nerve fibers.

The electrical potentials found within the cochlea that do not depend on the occurrence of a stimulus are often called *resting potentials* because they are found even when the cochlea is resting (not stimulated). As we discuss each of the potentials recorded from the cochlea, keep in mind the simple classification schemes shown in Table 9.1.

THE COCHLEAR
MICROPHONIC (CM) Perhaps because it has been known for the longest period of time or is easiest to record, there probably have been more reports of research studying the cochlear microphonic (CM) than all the other cochlear potentials. The CM is a stimulus-dependent ac signal that is thought to be the receptor potential for the hair cells. Although the CM has been subjected to study in numerous animals, by a considerable number of researchers, and with several different experimental techniques, we still are uncertain of its role in the hearing process. We do know that the CM is generated by the hair cells, because when the hair cells are either congenitally absent or damaged by exposure to ototoxic drugs or intense noise, the CM cannot be recorded. Thus, the CM depends upon the existence of healthy, intact hair cells. It was the CM potential that Bekesy used to demonstrate the directional sensitivity of the hair cells.

Round window recordings of the CM exhibit waveforms that mirror the acoustical input to the animal's ear. Presumably, the electrode on the round window records the CM generated by all active hair cells, although some may contribute more directly than others. CM magnitude depends, in part, on electrode placement. That is to say, the potential generated in the apical turn of the cochlea may be attenuated somewhat as it is conducted to the round window electrode. Generally, the CM potential has no known threshold. As the sensitivity of electronic equipment has improved, the CM has been found at still lower stimulus intensities. The magnitude of the CM voltage is proportional to the stimulus strength from the lower limits of recording over a range of perhaps 60 dB. Beyond that level, the CM magnitude fails to grow in proportion to the stimulus, eventually reaching saturation. At saturation there is no further increase in CM magnitude for increased stimulus levels. If the stimulus level is increased beyond the saturation level, the magnitude of CM voltage may even decrease. These regions are shown in Figure 9.24. It is surprising that even in the saturation region and beyond, the CM waveform appears to mirror the stimulus waveform without obvious signs of distortion.

Tasaki et al. (1954) devised a recording technique that greatly improved our understanding of the CM. In this method, two electrodes are inserted into the cochlea, one on either side of the scala media (one in the scala tympani and one in the scala vestibuli). The recording equipment is set to reject signals that are common to both electrodes, reproducing only the difference in potential between them. As a result, this differential pair of electrodes delivers the CM generated by those hair cells that lie within a millimeter or so of the point on the basilar membrane that falls just between the electrodes. Using this technique, Tasaki and many others have demonstrated that the CM potential is related to local basilar membrane movements. Bekesy had demonstrated that the CM was proportional to the displacement of the basilar membrane. Many of Bekesy's observations of cochlear mechanics have been confirmed from studies using multiple pairs of differential electrodes.

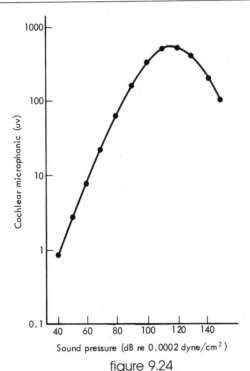

figure 9.24

An input-output function for the CM recorded from the basal
turn of the cochlea. Reprinted by permission from P. Dallos,
The Auditory Periphery. © 1973, Academic Press.

Although much useful information has been gleaned from studies of the
CM, there remains the question about the nature of its role in the chain of
events leading from hair bending to nerve fiber action potential. Some authors
have speculated that the CM from a single hair cell is necessary for the stimulation of the VIIIth nerve endings at its base. Critics of this theory regard the
CM as an interesting epiphenomenon, an event that parallels the critical sequence of events, but is not part of the chain. They argue that the CM potential is too widely spread to be able to stimulate only one (or a few) nerve fiber
endings. The critical sequence of events from the mechanical shearing force applied to the cilia of the hair cells to the generation of an electrical potential in
the dendritic ending of an VIIIth nerve fiber might require an intermediate
electrical step. Electron micrographs of hair cells show evidence for a chemical
transmitter substance in the hair cell base. The CM potential might be required
to trigger the release of transmitter substance, just as the neural spike triggers
the release in the terminal endings of the neuron. Newer, more refined research
techniques, such as the recording of electrical potentials from single hair cells
in vivo, will help to answer these puzzling questions.

Cochlear microphonic potentials have been of great value in the study of
hearing, regardless of whether or not they are epiphenomena. CM recordings
have confirmed our knowledge of the mechanical action of the basilar membrane

and given impetus to the studies of cochlear electrophysiology that will eventually lead to a more complete understanding of hair cell functions.

THE SUMMATING POTENTIAL (SP)   The summating potential (SP) is a stimulus-dependent dc voltage that is recorded in conjunction with microelectrode recordings of the CM. The SP was first observed as a baseline shift in the CM waveform. The magnitude of the SP is often said to mimic the envelope of the acoustical stimulus. (Recently Dallos, 1978, has suggested that CM follows the instantaneous displacement pattern of the basilar membrane while the SP is related to a rectified and smoothed version of the displacement pattern.) Early reports of SP recordings have produced an unclear picture of the influence of stimulus variables on the SP. The magnitude and even the polarity of the SP depend in a complex way on stimulus frequency and intensity, as well as the location of the recording electrode. As with the CM, the SP seems to have no threshold. In contrast with the CM, however, there is apparently no stimulus level beyond which the SP saturates. The source of the SP is still a matter of lively discussion among physiologists. At one time, it was assumed that the SP represented the receptor potential of hair cells having high thresholds and generally those located near the basal (high-frequency) end of the cochlea.

There are some who speculate that the Organ of Corti contains two sensory systems for hearing—the inner hair cells and the outer hair cells. Such dual systems are not unknown in nature. Humans, for example, have dual visual systems represented by the rods and cones in the retina of the eye. The rods mediate black-white vision in very dim light. The cones are much less sensitive than rods, but they mediate color vision. There is evidence to support a dual auditory system, one much more sensitive than the other, but not enough to convince everyone who is actively pursuing the study of cochlear electrophysiology. We cannot, in this text, pursue these very interesting arguments. For by the time the reader has read this section, new evidence either for or against the dual system will surely have been presented. Suffice it to say that some of those who favor a dual sensory system would suggest that the SP is the receptor potential for the inner hair cells, and the CM is the response of the outer hair cells. Others (e.g., Dallos et al., 1972) suggest that the contribution of inner hair cells to the CM is proportional to basilar membrane velocity and only one-tenth the magnitude of the outer hair cell contribution.

Aside from the dual sensory system controversy, there is another plausible explanation for the SP. Since the SP is stimulus-dependent and dc, it has been suggested that the SP represents the nonlinear portion of hair cell response to acoustical stimulation. By its very nature, the SP seems to be a product of some nonlinearity, although the locus of the nonlinear action is still unknown. Some evidence indicates that the nonlinearity is in the mechanical action of the basilar membrane displacement. Other evidence points to nonlinearities in the hair cell transduction process. Again, this area of study is one that has attracted much attention lately, and more definitive answers should be forthcoming.

THE ENDOCOCHLEAR POTENTIAL
(EP) AND THE INTRACELLULAR
POTENTIAL (IP)   A dc voltage can be recorded from an
electrode placed inside the scala media even when the cochlea is unstimulated.
Thus, it is one of the cochlear resting potentials and is called *endocochlear potential*. Since this voltage (about +80 mv) can be recorded whenever the electrode is immersed in endolymph in the scala media, it is also called the *endolymphatic potential*. In either case, the standard abbreviation is EP. The
source of EP has been identified as the stria vascularis. EP can be recorded
from the surface of the stria even in the absence of endolymph. EP magnitude
does not depend upon the level of stimulation or even the presence of a stimulus,
but is affected by the physiological state of the animal. Shutting off the cochlear
blood supply deprives it of oxygen and slowly reduces the EP magnitude in
a reversible manner if the blood supply is not removed for too long.

Another dc resting potential found within the cochlea is recorded when a
microelectrode is passed through the Organ of Corti. It is assumed that this
voltage represents the normal electrical negativity found inside all living cells.
Thus, this voltage is called the *intracellular potential* (IP), although some prefer the designation *Organ of Corti potential* (OCP).

These two dc resting potentials are of interest because it is thought that the
CM and SP are generated by resistance modulation of a current flow through
the hair cells. The dc resting potentials (EP and IP) would serve as the "battery" to provide the electrical potential needed to establish such a flow. The resistance modulation theory was first proposed by Davis in 1956 and has undergone some modifications since then. Basically, the explanation says that the
mechanical shearing at the hair cell tops alters the resistance of the hair cells.
In turn, the current flowing through the hair cells meets resistance proportional
to basilar membrane displacement. For a higher resistance, there would be a
higher voltage drop across the hair cell, and that voltage drop would be recorded as the CM. A number of investigators have reported results that support the resistance modulation theory for the generation of the CM. Dallos
(1973) has shown that a complex network of linear resistances such as we may
assume exists in the Organ of Corti can even produce nonlinear potentials such
as the SP.

Although the resistance modulation theory remains a theory, there is strong
evidence that the source of the CM is at the tops of the hair cells. Figure 9.25
shows a result first reported by Tasaki. As the electrode passes through the reticular lamina (at the hair cell tops) the polarity of the CM waveform is reversed. The most plausible explanation for the waveform inversion is that the
electrode has gone from one side of the CM source to the other. The mechanism for the generation of CM and SP may be coming clearer, but we still have
no direct evidence to support their roles in the sequence of events leading from
mechanical stimulation at the hair cell tops to the generation of neural spikes in
single VIIIth nerve fibers.

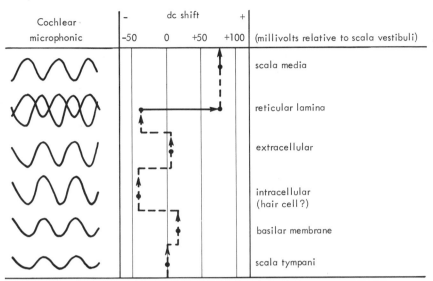

Penetration of organ of Corti by a microelectrode
with phase reversal of CM at the reticular lamina

figure 9.25

Penetration of the Organ of Corti by a microelectrode.
Reprinted by permission from W. A. Yost and D. W. Nielsen,
Fundamentals of Hearing: An Introduction © 1977 by
Holt Rhinehart and Winston; and I. Tasaki, H. Davis,
and D. H. Eldredge, "Exploration of Cochlear Potentials
with a Microelectrode," *Journal of the Acoustical
Society of America*, 26 (1954), 765–773.

THE WHOLE-NERVE
ACTION POTENTIAL (AP)

Since we have covered the electrical signals that can be recorded from within the cochlea, we must mention the VIIIth nerve action potential (AP). Although not generated within the cochlea itself, it is easily recorded in conjunction with the previously mentioned potentials. In fact, some signal processing is required to separate the AP from the CM and SP signals. The AP is the electrical sum of all the neural spike responses in the whole VIIIth nerve. The properties of the AP are well known. The AP response is maximum when the cochlear input is a brief transient signal. An acoustical click or high-frequency tone burst are most often used to elicit the AP. The AP response to longer signals or to tone bursts of low frequencies is not strong. A long-standing explanation for this observation is that the high-frequency units contribute disproportionately to the whole-nerve AP. Most likely this is because units near the basal end of the cochlea are more apt to fire in synchrony at stimulus onset. Single units that respond to middle or low frequencies must await the arrival of the mechanical traveling wave, and thus the synchrony is lost. Dallos presents convincing evidence to show that the AP waveform is the result of the wave of spike potentials emerging from the internal auditory meatus, that hole in the skull through which the VIIIth nerve passes on its way to the brainstem.

Recently, instrumentation and recording techniques have been developed to permit the recording of whole-nerve AP in humans. Electrodes may be placed in the external canal or on the surface of the promontory of the temporal bone to receive the cochlear potentials. Both CM and AP potentials may be recorded in this way; a technique called electrocochleography (ECoG). These potentials provide gross electrophysiological information on the status of the inner ear and primary auditory nerve fibers. As the behavior of ECoG potentials from human ears becomes better documented, these techniques promise to be of value as indicators of cochlear dysfunction.

the auditory nerve

In Chapter 2, we indicated that the VIIIth cranial nerve represented both auditory and vestibular sensory input to the central nervous system. In this chapter, we have so far referred to units of the VIIIth nerve, when we should have said "units of the cochlear division of the VIIIth nerve," but like many authors who are not anatomists, we have been somewhat sloppy in our terminology. The cell bodies of the neurons that make up the cochlear division of the VIIIth nerve make up the *spiral ganglion,* which lies within the modiolus. In humans, it is estimated that there are about 30,000 single neurons in each VIIIth nerve. The number varies from species to species. For example, in the cat the number of VIIIth nerve neurons is closer to 50,000. Quoting these numbers without keeping the species in mind has led to some misinformation in earlier texts.

The neurons of the cochlear nerve are centrally directed, as with any sensory system. That is, the flow of information goes from the periphery to the central nervous system (CNS). With respect to the CNS, then, we would say that these fibers are afferent. The dendritic endings of the VIIIth nerve fibers are distributed to the hair cells within the cochlea in a rather complex fashion. We will discuss this innervation pattern in more detail below after presenting the overall picture of the VIIIth nerve structure. The dendritic endings reach the hair cells via small holes in the bony spiral lamina surrounding the modiolus. These openings are called the *habenula perforata*. Apparently, each opening accommodates about twenty fibers. Between the hair cells and the habenula, the dendritic endings of VIIIth nerve fibers are unmyelinated. It is thought that their electrical activity must be graded rather than pulsatile (neural spikes).

The fibers of the cochlear division of the VIIIth nerve are wound in a ropelike fashion as they pass through the internal auditory meatus, the opening in the cranium that passes the nerve to the brainstem. The ropelike twisting preserves the spiral nature of the cochlea. The reader should imagine the at-

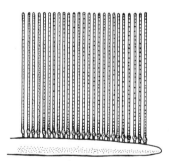

figure 9.26

Schematic illustration of the winding of a "straight tube"
cochlea into a spiral shape. Notice in particular the twisting
of the VIIIth nerve fibers into a ropelike form.

tachment of single fibers along the length of a straight-tube cochlea. If these fibers remain attached when the straight tube is wound into a spiral, then the ropelike twisting would result. The arrangement is illustrated in Figure 9.26. The fibers from the apical end of the cochlea end up on the inside of the "rope," with the basal-turn fibers on the surface.

From the spiral ganglion to the brainstem, the cochlear fibers are myelinated, and their electrical activity is the typical axonal spike. Within the brainstem, the VIIIth nerve fibers make synaptic connections with the cells of the *dorsal* and *ventral cochlear nuclei*. Before we follow the auditory pathway through the brainstem, let us look first at the complex innervation pattern within the cochlea and then review some basic findings on the electrical response of VIIIth nerve units.

THE INNERVATION PATTERN
OF THE COCHLEA   Spoendlin (1971) distinguishes three components of the innervation supplied to the cochlea: (1) the afferent fibers that conduct information from the cochlea to the brainstem, (2) the efferent fibers that arise within the brainstem and presumably exert central control over the centripetal (toward the CNS) flow of information, and (3) the autonomic nerve supply. The autonomic supply probably does not enter the Organ of Corti, but has a more indirect influence on the flow of nerve impulses from the cochlea to the cortex. The afferent sensory supply is, of course, the bundle of fibers that make up the cochlear division of the VIIIth nerve.

We have not discussed the pathway followed by the efferent supply because we have yet to discuss the brainstem. With this lack of information in mind, we will briefly consider the origins of the efferent supply to the cochlea. The actual number of efferent fibers entering the cochlea is surprisingly small;

it is estimated that only 500 efferent fibers enter each cochlea. Of that number, about three-fourths originate from cells in the contralateral (opposite side) superior olivary complex (SOC) of the brainstem. These fibers are often called the crossed olivocochlear bundle (COCB). The remaining one-fourth of the efferent fibers arise from cells of the homolateral (same side) and are called the homolateral olivocochlear bundle (HOCB). Within the cochlea, these few fibers branch extensively to deliver an estimated 40,000 vessiculated nerve endings to the inner and outer hair cell regions. The efferent endings delivered to inner versus outer hair cells differ in size, distribution pattern, and synaptic connections.

Spoendlin (1971, 1974) has studied the innervation pattern of the cochlea in the cat. By sectioning (cutting) the COCB or the HOCB fiber tracts, or both, Spoendlin has been able to identify which fibers in the Organ of Corti are afferent and which are efferent. Further, he has identified which efferents arise from the COCB tract and which originate in the homolateral tract. Our brief discussion is based on a series of articles by Spoendlin; the reader is directed to the original works for details of the rationale and the anatomical techniques.

After sectioning the OCB tracts, Spoendlin maintained his research animals for several weeks to allow the efferent fibers within the cochlea to degenerate. The result is an animal with only afferent fibers. In these animals, Spoendlin found that most of the remaining fibers (perhaps 95 percent) were delivered to the inner hair cells. Only about 5 percent of the afferent supply innervates the outer hair cells, although the outer hair cells outnumber the inner by more than 3 to 1. The fibers that innervate the inner hair cells travel from the modiolus in a *radial* direction, like the spokes of a bicycle wheel. They innervate *inner* hair cells, and thus we call these fibers the *inner radial fibers*. In general, Spoendlin reports that each inner radial fiber is supplied to only *one* inner hair cell. A given inner hair cell receives as many as 20 inner radial fibers. Thus, we would say that the innervation density of inner radial fibers is *many* fibers to *one* hair cell. The various fibers within the Organ of Corti are classified in Table 9.2.

The afferent fibers supplied to the outer hair cells cross the tunnel of Corti then turn toward the apex to run in a spiral or "longitudinal" direction. These are called the *outer spiral fibers*. The innervation of outer hair cells is not a simple one-to-one relationship. The course of a single outer spiral fiber is shown in Figure 9.27. The fiber is seen to travel along the inner row of outer hair cells for a short distance, sending terminal branches to a few hair cells along the way. After a short run through the first row of outer hair cells, the fiber steps to the next row, again sending endings to a few hair cells along its path. Finally, another outward step brings the fiber to the outer row of outer hair cells, where again a few hair cells are innervated. The total distance covered by one outer spiral fiber is estimated to be 0.6 to 0.7 mm. In its "stair-step" pathway, one outer spiral fiber supplies endings to perhaps ten outer hair cells. Thus, the innervation density would be characterized as *one* fiber to *many* hair cells.

table 9.2
innervation pattern of the cochlea

HAIR CELLS INNERVATED	DIRECTION OF TRAVEL WITHIN THE COCHLEA	FLOW OF INFORMATION	INNERVATION RATIO
Inner	radial	afferent	many (fibers) to one (cell)
Outer	spiral	afferent	one (fiber) to many (cells)
Outer	radial	efferent	one (fiber) to few (cells)
Inner	spiral	efferent	one (fiber) to many (fibers) *

*Inner spiral fibers apparently synapse with afferent fibers rather than with hair cells.

figure 9.27

Illustration of the innervation pattern of the Organ of Corti.
Reprinted by permission from H. Spoendlin, "Structural Basis of
Peripheral Frequency Analysis," in R. Plomp and
G. Smoorenburg, eds., *Frequency Analysis and Periodicity
Detection in Hearing.* © 1971, A. W. Sitjhoff; Leiden.

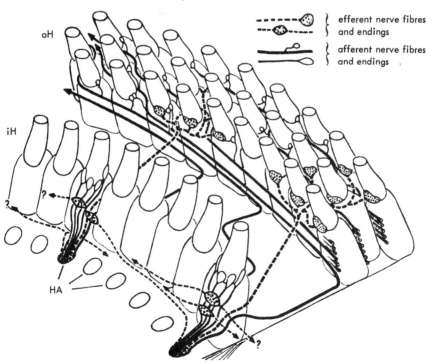

Spoendlin has found that the afferent fibers in the cochlea differ not only in the innervation pattern just described, but also structurally, metabolically, and in terms of their degeneration from one another depending on whether they innervate inner or outer hair cells. These differences have led Spoendlin and many others to argue that, in effect, the Organ of Corti contains two sensory systems. One system, the inner hair cells, should be very sensitive to the place of excitation, since there is a redundant point-to-point innervation of a given inner hair cell. This system should be good for fine discriminations of frequency. The innervation pattern of the afferent fibers to the outer hair cells lends itself to the summation of very low-level activity over an appreciable length of the cochlea, because one fiber contacts many hair cells. This action is sometimes called *spatial summation.* Fibers attached to a number of hair cells, as the outer spiral fibers are, should have better (lower) thresholds than those innervating only one hair cell. Thus, it is often said that the outer hair cell system is the highly sensitive one, while the inner hair cell system operates at levels well above threshold.

It is likely that no part of the nervous system functions without central control. Certainly, the existence of efferent fibers in the Organ of Corti indicates that some form of central control is active right at the sensory receptor cells. The efferent supply to the Organ of Corti differs between the inner hair cells and the outer hair cells. As indicated in Figure 9.27, most of the efferent supply (80 percent) is delivered to the outer hair cells. These fibers cross the tunnel of Corti to innervate a number of outer hair cells in all three rows. There is very little spiral extension in these fibers, and they are called *outer radial fibers* (Table 9.2). These fibers have large vessiculated terminal endings that make synaptic connections with the outer hair cells. It is presumed that these fibers, when activated, have some inhibitory influence on the outer hair cells.

The efferent supply to the inner hair cells is distributed as the *inner spiral bundle* (Table 9.2). These fibers are thought to rise predominantly from the HOCB, whereas the outer radials originate from COCB neurons. The inner spiral fibers apparently do not make direct synaptic contact with the inner hair cells. Rather, their synaptic connections are thought to be with the afferent inner radial fibers.

The anatomical evidence for a dual inner hair cell–outer hair cell sensory system presented by Spoendlin and others is compelling, but physiological evidence has been less one-sided. Although several investigators have reported systematic differences in single neuron behavior that would support the dual system, others have mounted arguments and experimental evidence against this theory. The issue remains one of intense interest that is likely to spur useful research work no matter which side finally "wins" the debate.

SINGLE UNIT ACTIVITY
IN THE VIIIth NERVE

Although recordings from intact single hair cells have only recently been successfully made (Russell and Sellick, 1977), techniques for recording electrical responses from single axonal fibers in the

VIIIth nerve were first reported in the 1940s. The best source of information concerning the preparation of the animal, the instrumentation for processing the responses, and the basic types of data displays can be found in a research monograph by Kiang, Watanabe, Thomas, and Clark (1965). The reader interested in following this area of auditory research is directed to that publication (now out of print) for many of the details we must omit here.

The axons of the individual neurons that comprise the cochlear division of the VIIIth nerve respond with the typical all-or-none spike response discussed in Chapter 2. Thus, stimulus parameters cannot be encoded by changes in the size or shape of the neural impulses that travel from the cochlea to the brainstem; the information must be encoded in the *temporal patterning* of the responses in each fiber and in terms of the *distribution of neural activity* across the 30,000 or so fibers.

Most experimental results have been obtained by electrophysiologists who insert a microelectrode into the VIIIth nerve to study one neuron at a time. Thus, we have an abundance of information concerning the responses of individual VIIIth nerve fibers to a wide variety of stimulus configurations. Most of our discussion of the distribution of responses over the entire cochlear nerve has been derived from these single unit studies. The results of these studies are displayed in several ways that may be new to the beginning student. We will describe briefly some of the more widely used displays before attempting to discuss the interpretation of these studies.

DISPLAY TECHNIQUES

The Rate-Intensity Curve   The most straightforward display of single unit response data is the *rate-intensity curve*. Figure 9.28 illustrates a typical rate-intensity function. Here the independent variable, plotted on the horizontal axis, is the stimulus intensity. The dependent variable, on the vertical axis, is the firing rate of the fiber—that is, the number of neural spikes that occur each second. Generally, we may notice three features of the rate-intensity curve shown in Figure 9.28. First, within limits, the rate of firing increases as stimulus intensity is increased. However, the increase in firing rate does not continue without end. The second feature is the upper limit to the firing rate. Beyond a given intensity, the fiber will fire no faster. At this point, the fiber is said to have reached saturation. The third feature is seen at the opposite end of the rate-intensity curve. Notice that the firing rate is not zero even for a nonstimulus condition. This fiber, as apparently is true of most VIIIth nerve fibers, has a "spontaneous" firing rate. We will later take note of the fact that the range of stimulus intensities, from the first change in the spontaneous rate to the saturation level, is limited to perhaps 30 dB. We say, then, that the *dynamic range* of the fiber is 30 dB.

The Tuning Curve   A second widely used method for displaying single neuron activity is the *tuning curve* shown in Figure 9.29. Kiang et al. (1965) referred to this curve as an "isospike rate contour." In this sense, the tuning curve *is* analogous to the isotherms and isobars shown on weather

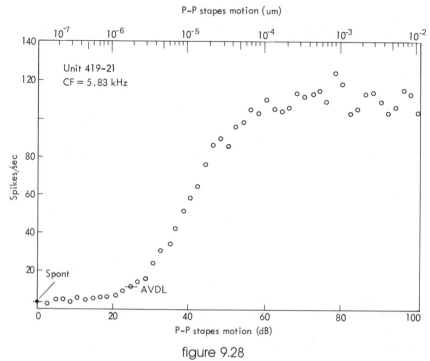

P-P stapes motion (um)

Unit 419–21
CF = 5.83 kHz

Spikes/sec

Spont

AVDL

P-P stapes motion (dB)

figure 9.28
Rate-intensity function for a single neuron in the VIIIth nerve
of a cat. Reprinted by permission from N. Y-S. Kiang, "A Survey
of Recent Developments in the Study of Auditory Physiology,"
Annals of Oto-Rhino-Laryngology, 77 (1968), 656–675.

maps, or to elevation contours on topographical maps. To generate an VIIIth nerve neuron tuning curve, the physiologist must prepare the animal surgically and insert the microelectrode into the VIIIth nerve. The tip of the electrode must be just inside one single axon. This is ensured by observation of the spontaneous discharge recorded as the electrode enters the fiber. Once the physiologist is certain that the electrode is inside a single axon, the determination of a tuning curve may begin. A given neuron spike rate is selected as the "criterion rate." That is, based upon knowledge of the animal being tested and past experience, the physiologist will choose a given target firing rate. The tuning curve is generated by plotting the combinations of stimulus frequency and stimulus level for a pure tone that produces neural firings in the fiber at the criterion rate.

Let us illustrate this method by a hypothetical example. Suppose that the criterion firing rate we choose is 100 spikes per second. Then, if we were making the adjustments by hand, we might set the oscillator producing the stimulus to 125 Hz. We would then adjust the stimulus level until our unit responded at 100 spikes/sec. Next, we might increase the frequency to 250 Hz and again determine the level required to produce 100 spikes/sec. We would proceed in this fashion to determine a large set of pairs of numbers, a frequency, and the stimulus level at that frequency which produces 100 spikes/sec from the single neuron we have selected for study. If we plot stimulus frequency along the horizontal axis and stimulus level along the vertical axis, then we can plot each pair of numbers as a point on the chart. If we connect each of the points by straight lines, then we have an isospike rate contour, or more simply, a tuning curve.

The tuning curves illustrated in Figure 9.29 are typical of those for most VIIIth nerve units in a number of ways. Notice first that not all frequencies are equally effective in producing spikes at the criterion rate. In particular, one frequency seems to be more efficient than any other because it requires the minimum stimulus level to reach the criterion. That frequency is called the fiber's *characteristic frequency* (CF). Because the neuron responds best to a given frequency, we say it is tuned to that frequency — hence the description of Figure 9.29 as a tuning curve. We use the word "tune" in the same sense you would if you were to think of closing this text and tuning in your favorite radio station.

The VIIIth nerve tuning curve is said to be very sharply tuned in comparison with the traveling wave envelope for the same stimulus frequency. Notice that the curves shown in Figure 9.29 have very steep sides. The slope of the

figure 9.29

Examples of tuning curves from a single neuron in the VIIIth nerve of a cat. Reprinted by permission from N. Y-S. Kiang, T. Watanabe, E. C. Thomas, and L. F. Clark, *Discharge Patterns of Single Fibers in the Cat's Auditory Nerve.* © 1965, MIT Press.

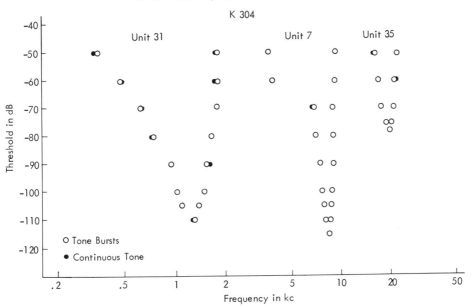

high-frequency sides (above the CF) is typically 200 dB/octave. That is, the unit is so unresponsive to a frequency an octave higher than its CF that an increase in stimulus level of 200 dB would be needed to reach criterion. Of course, that stimulus level would be impossible to attain. The mechanical response to such an intensity would destroy the middle ear and cochlea. Returning to the point then, we may say that, in general, VIIIth nerve fibers are very unresponsive to stimulus frequencies which lie above their CF. On the lower side of the tuning curve, the unit is not quite so unresponsive. The initial portion of the curve may have a slope of perhaps 60 dB/octave. Generally, high CF units exhibit "tails" in the tuning curve that extend over much of the audible range below the CF of the unit. Thus, a given unit will respond to stimulus frequencies below its CF if stimulus intensity is made great enough.

After sampling a large number of VIIIth nerve neurons, physiologists found that the fibers exhibit tuning curves with characteristic frequencies distributed over the test animal's full audibility range. Keeping in mind the distribution of dendritic endings within the Organ of Corti, we should not be surprised by this finding. The innervation pattern of 95 percent of the afferent fibers, those to the inner hair cells, preserves the tonotopic organization found in the mechanical response of the cochlea. Tonotopic organization is then carried to the brainstem by the VIIIth nerve.

Tuning curves are often generated by automated means with a small computer monitoring the response, varying the stimulus frequency and level, and producing a plot of the isospike rate contours. By selecting different criterion rates, whole families of curves can be generated. Often, if a second tone is combined with the stimulus tone, it will have an effect on the behavior of the single neuron under test. At appropriate combinations of frequency and intensity for the second tone, the response of the unit may be reduced. Some investigators attribute this decrement in response to a neural interaction between adjacent neurons. Others have suggested that the cause of the decrement could be found in the nonlinear movement of the basilar membrane. It would be inappropriate to label this decrement in the response as *inhibition* without further evidence that neural interactions mediate the result. Thus, the behavior may be called a *two-tone interaction,* or *suppression.* Figure 9.30 shows a tuning curve and the "islands" of suppression that surround it. It should be evident that the neural response area even at this most peripheral point in the auditory system is not a simple one.

The Histogram   Neither the rate-intensity curve nor the tuning curve reveal the temporal characteristics of single VIIIth nerve unit responses. Several specialized displays have been developed to emphasize the temporal response features. These displays are generated by using minicomputers designed for use in the physiology laboratory. Although we cannot go into the details of the generation of these special temporal displays, the brief discussion is necessary to understand the results of recent VIIIth nerve electrophysiological studies.

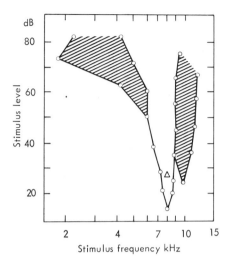

figure 9.30

An example of inhibitory areas adjacent to an excitatory
tuning curve for a single neuron in the VIIIth nerve of a cat.
Reprinted by permission from R. M. Arthur, R. R. Pfeiffer, and
N. Suga, "Properties of 'Two-Tone Inhibition' in Primary
Auditory Neurons," *Journal of Physiology,* 212 (1971), 593–609.

Basically, the data displays are bar graphs known as *histograms.* In the histograms used to display the temporal characteristics of single units of the VIIIth nerve, the ordinate (vertical axis) indicates the number of times an event has occurred. The abscissa (horizontal axis) for these histograms is divided into discrete intervals of time usually called *bins.* The width of the bin is designated by the experimenter, thus the bin width must be specified with the display.

Histograms used to display the temporal characteristics of VIIIth nerve responses represent the distribution of the times between two events. The choice of these events determines the nature of the histogram. An example will better illustrate this point. The poststimulus time (PST) histogram displays the distribution of time intervals between a specific point on the stimulus waveform and the occurrence of an impulse in the single fiber. Every stimulus marker resets a timer to zero. When a neural impulse is recorded, a tally is entered into the bin which marks the interval of time elapsed since the specified point on the stimulus waveform. After delivering a number of stimuli to the animal's ear, the tallies in the bins are found to fall into preferred orderly time intervals.

Figure 9.31 shows a typical PST histogram for a low CF VIIIth nerve fiber in response to a brief acoustical click. In this figure, the bins are so small that they may seem to blend together. Three major peaks are evident in this histogram. The time from click occurrence to the first peak is called the *latency (L)* of the unit. The latency for all VIIIth nerve fibers includes the time re-

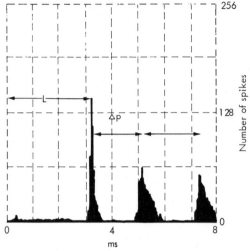

figure 9.31

An example of a PST histogram for a single neuron in the VIIIth nerve of a cat. Reprinted by permission from N. Y-S. Kiang, T. Watanabe, E. C. Thomas, and L. F. Clark, *Discharge Patterns of Single Fibers in the Cat's Auditory Nerve.* © 1965, MIT Press.

quired for the stimulus to travel from the headphone to the cochlea. In addition, a variable part of the latency reflects the time required for the traveling wave response to reach the point of innervation for the fiber under test. Finally, a small fixed time reflects the time required for the nerve impulse to travel to the electrode from the spiral ganglion. If we plot the latency versus CF for a number of fibers, then the relationship between the two is evident. Fibers with lower CF have longer latencies, reflecting the time required for the traveling wave to reach the point in the apical region of the basilar membrane innervated by the fiber.

Also indicated in Figure 9.31 is the time interval, ΔP, which separates subsequent peaks in the histogram. For most fibers in the VIIIth nerve, there is good agreement between the value of ΔP and the characteristic period ($1/CF$) of the fiber producing the histogram. This relationship seems to indicate that the mechanical response to a brief click causes the nerve to fire several times for each stimulus. The mechanical tuning of the basilar membrane is such that the frequency for which the traveling wave is a maximum determines the CF found for the fiber. Further, since the responses seem to be synchronized, it is likely that the nerve is always triggered at the same phase point on the basilar membrane displacement waveform.

Further work using both rarefaction clicks and condensation clicks as stimuli have strengthened this notion. A rarefaction click is one that causes the stapes footplate to move rapidly outward; a condensation click moves the footplate inward. At high stimulus levels, the earliest peak always occurs with shorter latency for a rarefaction click than for an equivalent condensation click. The small numbers of neural responses in the bins between the peaks, and in those spanned by the latency, are thought to reflect the spontaneous firings of the fiber. Kiang et al. (1965) reported that there seemed to be not only increased responsiveness to rarefaction clicks, but also a suppression of responses by condensation clicks. When rarefaction and condensation clicks were presented in successive alternation, spontaneous responses seemed to be reduced after the condensation click.

A variation on the poststimulus time histogram is used to study responses to tonal stimuli. In this technique, a phase point on the stimulus waveform is chosen. At every occurrence of that point (zero crossing or peak, for example) the timer is reset. Thus, responses for successive periods of the tone accumulate on top of one another. This display is called a *period histogram*. It too shows phase locking of the VIIIth nerve fiber to the stimulus tone. For some studies, an *interstimulus interval* (ISI) histogram is generated. Here, time between successive neural spikes is tallied in the histogram without reference to the occurrence of the stimulus. The time between successive spikes is plotted on the abscissa; the ordinate shows the number of interspike intervals falling into a given bin. ISI histograms are shown in Figure 9.32. The multiple peaks are spaced regularly and show that the fiber responds at the same phase point on the waveform, if it responds at all. That is, the fiber may not respond on every cycle of a tonal stimulus, but when it does, it is at a favored point on the waveform. Thus, we say that the nerve firings are synchronized with the stimulus waveform—that is, the time between peaks in the ISI histogram depends on the stimulus frequency, *not* on the fiber's CF.

Studies of single neurons in the VIIIth nerve of laboratory animals have added greatly to our knowledge of the auditory system. Determination of the tuning curves of these neurons has confirmed the tonotopic organization of the cochlea. Further, some controversy over the apparent sharpening of the neural tuning curves over the mechanical response of the basilar membrane has stimulated still more work on cochlear electrophysiology. The tuning curves for neurons with high characteristic frequencies indicate that these units will respond to a wide range of stimulus frequencies. Apparently, these higher CF units will respond to a moderately intense stimulus as the traveling wave motion passes through their region on its way to the apical turn. The temporal characteristics of VIIIth nerve fiber responses indicate a phase locking of the unit to the stimulus waveform. This is clear from the ISI histograms for low- and moderately high-frequency stimuli. For very high frequencies the evidence is less compelling, but it may be that these units are partly synchronized.

There is still much that is not known about the processes which transform the mechanical shearing action of the hair cells into the patterns of neural firings that represent auditory input to the central nervous system. We have very little information on the interactions of adjacent nerve fibers, if these interactions occur. We know even less about the influence of the CNS through the efferent connections within the cochlea. Although this lack of information may

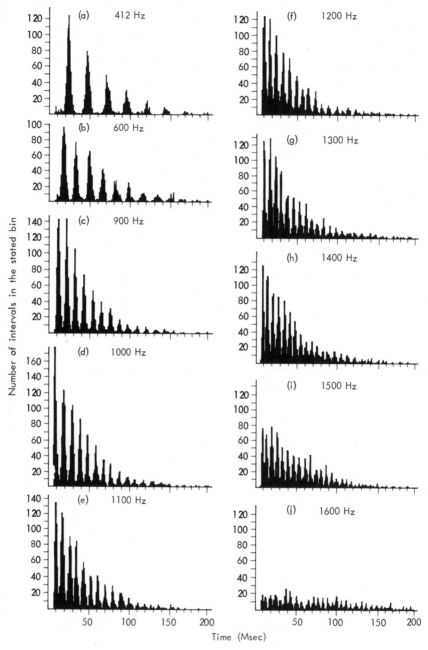

figure 9.32

Interval histograms for a single neuron at ten different
frequencies. Notice that the peaks in the histograms occur at
integer mutliples of the period of the stimulating tone.
Reprinted by permission from J. E. Rose, J. F. Brugge, D. J.
Anderson, and J. E. Hind, "Phase-Locked Response to Low
Frequency Tones in Single Auditory Nerve Fibers of the
Squirrel Monkey", *Journal of Neurophysiology*, 30 (1967), 769–793.

discourage the student who wants "facts," not theories or models, it does serve as the impetus for further research work and thinking concerning the auditory system.

FREQUENCY
AND INTENSITY CODING

The information carried by a sound-wave arrives at the cochlea of the listener encoded in the complex time variations of the pressure waveform. More peripheral portions of the auditory system may alter the sound pressure wave, but decoding begins at the cochlea. We have seen that the complex sound pressure wave introduced into the cochlea is subjected to an imperfect spectrum analysis. Sound energy at diverse frequencies in the pressure waveform is mapped into mechanical action at different places along the basilar membrane. In many ways the mechanical response of the cochlea acts as a low-pass filter system, with frequency-selective characteristics distributed along the length of the basilar membrane. Such mapping of stimulus frequency into place in the sensory system is called tonotopic organization. The patterns of mechanical activity distributed along the basilar membrane must be transformed into patterns of neural activity by the cochlear hair cells and the units of the VIIIth nerve. Each succeeding level of the central portion of the auditory system presents the opportunity for further transformation of the neural activity pattern. Needless to say, we have just begun to understand these transformations of the sensory code.

From the way in which most of the afferent fibers are supplied to the hair cells, one might assume that the tonotopic organization of the cochlea is preserved in the VIIIth nerve. Electrophysiological studies of single units (axons) in the VIIIth nerve have confirmed its tonotopic organization. Further, single unit studies have shown that the probability of a given fiber responding to a stimulus increases with stimulus intensity. The range of intensities over which the probability of response grows is much more restricted (<30 dB) than the range of intensities over which listeners hear (perhaps 120 dB or more).

To account for the encoding of stimulus magnitudes that extend over a much greater range of intensities than a single neuron can cover, we use the *recruitment phenomenon*. At very low intensities, only a small number of fibers supplied to the place of maximum basilar membrane displacement respond to the stimulus. As intensity is increased, these fibers reach saturation and are unable to respond more frequently. However, at higher intensity the mechanical displacement pattern spreads along the cochlea, and fibers are activated which are not supplied to the place of maximum response. These fibers are said to be *recruited* into the pool of active units by the more intense stimulus. As stimulus intensity is raised further, units supplied to places that respond best to frequencies far below (or above) the stimulus frequency will respond. The shape of the traveling wave envelope and that of the VIIIth nerve single unit tuning curve indicate an asymmetry in this physiological recruitment process. A fiber supplied to a given place along the basilar membrane will be much more responsive to tones at frequencies below the fiber's characteristic frequency than to stimuli at frequencies above its CF.

figure 9.33

Discharge pattern of the auditory nerve fiber array. Each
vertical line represents 50 to 100 fibers; and its height the
mean discharge rate in those fibers. Adjacent lines represent
fibers arising from adjacent points on the basilar membrane.
The heavy lines represent the response to a weak stimulus, the
lighter lines that to a stronger stimulus. Reprinted by permission
from I. C. Whitfield, *The Auditory Pathway.*
© 1967, The Williams & Wilkins Company.

For simple pure-tone stimuli, Whitfield (1967) has derived the excitation patterns shown in Figure 9.33. The height of each line represents the level of activity (excitation) in individual fibers. The horizontal scale shows distance along the cochlea. As stimulus intensity grows, the pattern expands to recruit "new" fibers into the pool of active units. Those units near the center of a pattern may not be conveying useful information to the CNS. It may be that stimulus magnitude is conveyed to higher neural centers by the size of the excitation pattern. Thus, the CNS may make use of the location of the pattern edges but not the neural activity from units in the interior of the pattern.

Support for this notion can be gathered from the behavior of listeners with hearing losses due to hair cell damage. Low-intensity signals with mechanical response maxima in the region suffering hair cell losses are not heard by these listeners. The intensity of the signal must be increased by 40 to 60 dB before the listener can just detect its presence. We say that the listener has an elevated threshold in the region sustaining the loss. Often, when the intensity of a tone is increased beyond the elevated threshold level, the listener hears it at nearly the same loudness as a normal-hearing listener would. An early explanation for this abnormal growth of loudness in the ear with hair cell damage invoked the recruitment phenomenon. That explanation was so widely accepted that the ear exhibiting abnormal loudness growth is often said to exhibit recruitment.

One approach to the general problem of determining the neural code for a given sensory modality has been outlined by Uttal (1973). He says that careful distinction must be made between stimulus dimensions and the perceptual attributes of those stimuli. We may attempt to relate attributes to stimulus dimensions, as in various psychophysical experiments. Alternatively, we may seek a relationship between stimulus dimensions and the response of a portion of the nervous system, as in experimental neurophysiology. But we are still left with the problem of relating psychological attributes to the neural activity engendered by the stimuli, an area Uttal calls psychobiology. We still have much to learn about the psychobiology of hearing.

Neural activity patterns must convey information to the CNS concerning the quality and quantity of the stimulus. In hearing, the quantity of sound is perceived as loudness. There are several qualitative attributes of sound; *pitch* and *timbre* are the more obvious ones. Uttal also suggests that neural activity patterns must carry information concerning temporal variations in the stimulus, and must convey information concerning its spatial parameters. In hearing, we know that spatial information is derived from a central comparison of neural activity from the two ears.

In the study of auditory neurophysiology, the stimulus is often a pure tone, noise burst or click. Such simple stimuli are easily generated and controlled. Often, it is *assumed* that the neurophysiological responses to natural stimuli such as speech, music, or environmental sounds can be predicted from the responses to tones, noises, and clicks. Certainly, the stimulus waveform can be analyzed into a properly sequenced collection of tonal, random, or transient components.

In auditory psychophysics (psychoacoustics), we attempt to relate the psychological dimensions of a sound to the physical characteristics of the pressure waveform. Thus, we know that loudness is related primarily to the intensity of a soundwave, but that the frequency content and temporal pattern of a sound may influence that relationship significantly. The psychophysics of pitch perception is even more complex. If the listener heard nothing but pure (single-frequency) tones, we would certainly conclude that pitch depends primarily on the frequency of the pure tone. Secondary effects would be noted for intensity and duration of the tone. Because the pitch of a pure tone is directly related to the frequency of that tone, and because the mechanical response in the cochlea transforms stimulus frequency into a place of maximum displacement, many early researchers concluded that the pitch of a sound is encoded in the place of maximum excitation. Studies of pitch perception conducted since the 1940s have shown that a simple place theory of pitch perception is untenable. For most naturally occurring sounds, the preliminary spectral analysis due to the mechanical action in the cochlea would lead to displacement maxima at several places along the basilar membrane. Yet, the pitch perceived for such spectrally complex sounds often matches a pure tone of a frequency for which there is little or no basilar membrane response.

The response of single fibers in the VIIIth nerve is synchronized to the stimulus waveform. When a unit responds to a pure tone, it is most likely to "fire" at the same phase point on the stimulus waveform. We often say that the unit exhibits phaselocking to the stimulus waveform. Keep in mind that the place along the basilar membrane to which a neuron is supplied determines the characteristic frequency for the unit. However, given sufficient stimulus intensity, a neuron may respond to a broad range of stimulus frequencies. In particular, those fibers supplied to the basal end of the cochlea will respond to low and middle frequencies if the intensity is sufficiently high.

When a single unit responds to a pure tone, it fires in synchrony with the frequency of basilar membrane motion not at the characteristic frequency. We might assume that stimulus frequency could be carried to the CNS in the temporal firing patterns of the primary neurons. However, a single neuron does not exhibit a range of responses sufficient to encode the range of frequencies normal listeners can hear. At 20 to 30 dB above threshold, the single unit will be so well synchronized with the stimulus tone that a spike will almost certainly occur on every cycle. However, the neural spike requires a millisecond or more of recovery time before another spike can be generated. Thus, single units cannot "follow" a stimulus tone, cycle for cycle, at frequencies above 1 kHz. Wever (1949) invoked the *volley principle* to explain how neurons limited to firing rates below 1 kHz might follow stimulus tones ten or twenty times higher in frequency. Since each place along the basilar membrane is supplied with several nerve fibers, a given fiber would not have to fire for each cycle of the tone. Instead, an array of fibers supplied to a given location may be synchronized so that each fiber fires on every third, or tenth, or twentieth cycle. Neural centers higher up in the CNS may then decode this synchronized pattern of neural spikes (volley) from the several fibers supplied to a place on the basilar membrane.

the central auditory system

The patterns of neural activity generated within the cochlea are delivered to the central nervous system via the cochlear division of the VIIIth cranial nerve. The detail with which we have followed the path of auditory stimulation through the periphery is impossible to maintain in the CNS. The peripheral auditory systems of most mammals are so similar that there is little danger of gross error in making comparisons across species, but this cannot be said for their central nervous systems. The brainstem structures in lower mammals, such as rodents or the cat, may differ substantially from those found in primates. Obviously, the closer one moves to the cortex, the more differences one is likely to encounter among the various species. We are therefore in a quandry. Anatomical descriptions of the central auditory system of humans are available in various texts. No physiological work of the type possible on lower species can be carried out on humans. The electrophysiological results on lower animals, although of interest in their own right, may not be valid for the human system. Major differences are sometimes even found between two "lower" species. Thus, we can present the reader interested primarily in the human auditory system only with the anatomical diagrams shown in Figure 9.34. We will then discuss the physiological results from animal studies that seem robust enough to carry into the human auditory system.

BRAINSTEM PATHWAYS The cochlear division of the VIIIth nerve enters the brainstem at the cochlear nucleus (CN). Each fiber *bifurcates* (splits into two branches) upon entry, sending one branch to the dorsal coch-

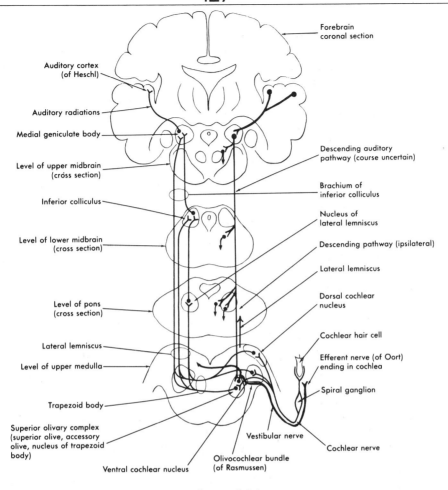

Forebrain
coronal section

Auditory cortex
(of Heschl)

Auditory radiations

Medial geniculate body

Level of upper midbrain
(cross section)

Inferior colliculus

Level of lower midbrain
(cross section)

Level of pons
(cross section)

Lateral lemniscus

Level of upper medulla

Trapezoid body

Superior olivary complex
(superior olive, accessory
olive, nucleus of trapezoid
body)

Ventral cochlear nucleus

Descending auditory
pathway (course uncertain)

Brachium of
inferior colliculus

Nucleus of
lateral lemniscus

Descending pathway (ipsilateral)

Lateral lemniscus

Dorsal cochlear
nucleus

Cochlear hair cell

Efferent nerve (of Oort)
ending in cochlea

Spiral ganglion

Vestibular nerve

Cochlear nerve

Olivocochlear bundle
(of Rasmussen)

figure 9.34

A schematic diagram of the central auditory pathway. The
ascending fibers are shown on both sides, the efferent
connections are indicated on the right side only. Reprinted
by permission from J. Minckler, *Introduction to
Neuroscience.* © 1972, The C. V. Mosby Company.

lear nucleus (DCN) and one into the ventral cochlear nucleus (VCN). The
branch to the ventral division of the cochlear nucleus divides again, sending
endings both into the posteroventral cochlear nucleus (PVCN) and the antero-
ventral cochlear nucleus (AVCN). Early studies of the cochlear nucleus revealed that it was not one homogeneous center. Lorente de No and Harris (1933)
established that there were at least 13 histologically distinct regions. Rose,
Galambos, and Hughes (1959) demonstrated that the three major subdivisions,
DCN, AVCN, and PVCN, each contain a complete tonotopic representation
of the cochlea. More recently, Osen (1969) established tonotopic organization
in three of nine distinct cell groups. It has been estimated that each VIIIth

nerve fiber entering the cochlear nucleus sends terminal endings to about 400 different cells. Likewise, each cell in the CN probably receives terminal endings from about 400 different VIIIth nerve fibers. Further, many of the CN cells are interneurons that make connections wholly within the nucleus. This arrangement, the divergence of VIIIth nerve input to the CN, the large number of possible interconnections, and the possible convergence of activity on each CN cell, provides many opportunities for recoding of the stimulus patterns developed in the periphery. The CN has many features in common with the outer layers of the retina in the eye, where there is stronger evidence for stimulus recoding (contrast enhancements, and so on).

Fiber pathways from the CN subdivisions have not been fully documented in humans. In animals, the cat in particular, the major tracts are as follows: The DCN sends fibers across the midline to the contralateral lateral lemniscus, where they ascend to the inferior colliculus. The AVCN and PVCN send fibers to the lateral superior olivary nucleus on the same side of the brainstem, and to the medial superior olivary nuclei on both sides of the brainstem.

Rate-intensity functions, tuning curves, and temporal histograms have been obtained for cell bodies within the cochlear nucleus since the middle 1940s. The tuning curves are used to establish the tonotopic organization of the subdivisions. Inhibitory regions surrounding the tuning curves are apparent in the CN as in single units of the VIIIth nerve. Rate-intensity functions and temporal histogram displays show greater variety across CN cells than is evident for VIIIth nerve fibers. Nonmonotonic rate-intensity functions are often seen — that is, a unit will begin to fire at a low stimulus level, and the rate of firing will increase with stimulus level until a maximum is found. Unlike VIIIth nerve units, the response does not remain at the maximum rate as intensity is increased further, but may fall back to the rate found for very low stimulus levels.

PST histograms similarly show a greater variety of behaviors for CN units than are seen at the periphery. Units may respond only to the beginning and/or termination of a stimulus; they may respond after a brief pause; they may switch on and off throughout the stimulus; or they may show a reduction in ongoing activity whenever the stimulus is introduced. The variety of response patterns seen here at the CN and farther along the ascending auditory pathway seems to be a clear indication of the recoding of peripheral neural patterns.

THE SUPERIOR OLIVARY COMPLEX   Clusters of auditory nuclei in the brainstem just above the cochlear nuclei are known collectively as the *superior olivary complex (SOC)*. The complex contains two major nuclei, the *medial superior olivary nucleus (MSO)* and the *lateral superior olivary nucleus,* also known as the S segment because of its shape in lower mammals. The MSO is sometimes called the *accessory nucleus*. A third major nucleus in the SOC is the *nucleus of the trapezoid body*. Variations between humans and lower species are greater at the SOC than at the CN, as expected.

The SOC has been studied extensively in animals. It is the first point in the

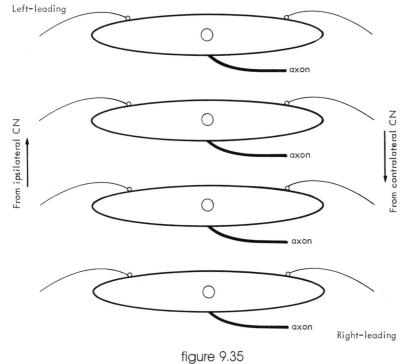

figure 9.35

A schematic diagram showing the ipsilateral and contralateral
connections to the bipolar cells in the medial superior olivary
nucleus. Below is a delay-line model suggesting the means by
which this nucleus might decode interaural time information.

ascending auditory pathway at which input from the two ears is processed. Of
particular interest here is the medial superior olivary nucleus because its
unique bipolar neurons seem especially well suited for the decoding of binaural
interactions. The large bipolar neurons of the MSO have two dendritic projections. The neurons are arranged in a line with one dendrite pointed roughly toward the midline and the other toward the lateral surface. The medial dendrite
receives fibers from the region of the contralateral AVCN tonotopically organized for low- to middle-frequency tones. The lateral dendrite of each bipolar
cell receives similarly tonotopically organized input from the homolateral
AVCN. The bipolar cells of the MSO apparently respond only when there is a
coincidence of inputs at both medial and lateral dendrites.

It is thought that the MSO may be arranged so that inputs from the two
ears start at opposite ends of the line of bipolar cells. The nucleus could then
act as a decoder of interaural time delays, as shown in Figure 9.35. If the signal arrives at the two ears simultaneously, then the "middle" bipolar cell will
be the only one to receive coincidental inputs from both ears. If the left ear receives a sound just microseconds before the right ear, then the stimulation from
the left will have traveled past midline, and the coincidence of input will occur

on the side labeled left-leading. Of course, a similar response would obtain if the signal were delivered to the right ear first. If the time of arrival at the two ears differs by more time than it takes for neural pulses to travel the length of the delay line, then no coincidence can be decoded. In fact, when we experience an artificially long delay in the time of arrival of a sound at the two ears, we hear two separate events.

The SOC is also of interest because it gives rise to the efferent fibers found within the cochlea, the olivocochlear bundle (OCB). Although the origins of HOCB and COCB fibers are documented in lower species, details are lacking in humans. Physiological studies of OCB action have had little success in showing an activation of these fibers due to acoustical input to the ear. Most results are obtained by direct *electrical* stimulation of the HOCB or COCB fibers. A number of studies have documented changes in the CM (increased) and AP (decreased) recorded in a cochlea after electrical stimulation of the OCB tracts. After sectioning of some, or all, of the OCB fibers, the changes in CM and AP are similar to those obtained by electrical stimulation. A great deal of work will be needed before our knowledge of the OCB is clear.

MIDBRAIN, THALAMUS,
AND CORTEX   Above the SOC, species-specific differences across laboratory animals become even more of a problem for the student who wishes to gain an understanding of the human auditory system. Fibers from the SOC join those from the DCN in ascending to the inferior colliculus (IC). SOC output is thought to be about equally distributed to both the contralateral and homolateral lateral lemniscus (LL). The lateral lemniscus is a fiber tract, but it does have a nucleus of cell bodies (nucleus of the lateral lemniscus) associated with it. Thus, some fibers from the DCN or SOC may synapse in the nucleus of the lateral lemniscus, while others may continue to the inferior colliculus. The reader is probably thoroughly confused by now; the pathway above the SOC *is* confusing. Anatomical details for different species are divergent and physiological results are scarce at these centers above the SOC, compared with the information available for lower centers. There seems to be no alternative except to wait patiently until neuroanatomists have untangled this puzzle. There is some speculation that the quadrigeminal body, of which the inferior colliculus and superior colliculus are a part, coordinates sound localization with eye movements. Many animals do look reflexively toward the source of a sound. Perhaps studies that involve both sound localization and eye movement would help to elucidate the function of the IC.

The thalamus receives all sensory input bound for the cerebral cortex. Every sensory area of the cortex has an associated area in the thalamus. For the auditory system, this area is the *medial geniculate body (MGB)*. We can only speculate about the role of the thalamic centers in the processing of sensory input to the cortex. It may be a simple gating of important versus unimportant inputs. It is more likely, though, that the thalamus performs some processing functions for which the cortex need not be involved. Anatomists have used ab-lation studies to confirm the corticothalamic connections. Cell bodies in the thalamus degenerate (die) whenever their axons are cut in the cortex. Such behavior is called *retrograde degeneration*. Thus, if sections of cortex are removed from an animal's brain and the animal is maintained for a time to allow retrograde degeneration to occur, the thalamus can be studied histologically. Where the thalamic cells send only one fiber to the cortex, removing one small cortical area will lead to degeneration of the region of the thalamus that supplies the fibers. These connections are often called essential projections. Areas within the temporal lobes may be identified as primary auditory cortex in terms of the essential projections from the MGB. Sometimes an MGB cell will send a collateral (branches from the axon) to different cortical areas. Retrograde degeneration may not occur for these cells unless both branches of the axon are cut. Additional supplies to the cortex from the MGB have been identified by removing two or more patches of cortex. Branching fibers so identified are said to supply sustaining projections to the cortex.

Tonotopic organization for neural centers up to the inferior colliculus has been well documented. It is fairly certain that the IC, too, is tonotopically organized. But evidence for tonotopic organization of the MGB and auditory cortex is, at best, equivocal. Early studies showed a tonotopic organization for the auditory cortex, but those results depended not only on the species under study but also on the type and level of anesthesia used. Generally, awake or lightly anesthetized animals have not revealed tonotopic organization at the cortex. Since heavily anesthetized animals do show tonotopic organization in cortical areas, it is perhaps indicative of fiber connections more directly tied to these areas.

In mammals, such as the cat or guinea pig, several areas of auditory cortex have been identified, each with its own tonotopic organization. In the literature, reference to cortical auditory areas AI, AII, and the posterior ectosylvian region (EP) is applied to nonprimate species. In primates, including humans, the auditory cortex is found within the Sylvian fissure of the temporal lobe. Recent studies (cited by Yost and Nielsen, 1977) have demonstrated well-defined tonotopic organization within the auditory cortex of the monkey at several levels of anesthesia. Apparently, one problem with earlier studies was the inconsistency of organization for different individual animals. Previously, a small number of data points from each of a number of animals was combined to produce the map of best frequencies in the cortex. The recent studies were able to show tonotopic organization in the cortex of one monkey by collecting a larger sample of responses from that individual. The frequency map for one animal did not necessarily agree with that for another. Because of the decussations (branching to both left and right sides) of the ascending auditory pathway, the auditory cortex in each cerebral hemisphere receives input from both left and right ears.

The electrophysiological techniques used in the study of VIIIth nerve fibers and units of the brainstem have also been applied to the study of the auditory cortex. Cortical units yield tuning curves that are similar to those of lower centers. PST and ISI histograms may be generated to study the temporal properties of the cortical units. In general, there is a wider variety in the nature of responses for cortical units than for the units of the brainstem.

The cells of the cortex are found in as many as six layers of different cells. Auditory cortex is arranged in columns. The cells in any layer of cortex tend to have the same characteristic frequency as the cells just above or below them.

Cortical units are generally unresponsive to steady-state sounds. Whitfield and Evans (1962) has shown that many cortical units respond to stimuli that are frequency-modulated (that is, stimulus frequency varies with time). These units remain unresponsive to stimuli of fixed frequency, and may respond differently to stimuli that differ in the direction of their frequency change. This discovery has led some to speculate that such cells might act as "feature detectors" for the ultimate decoding of speech. If feature detectors exist in the cortex, they are more likely to be whole neural networks than single cells. Thus, these cells might supply information to feature detectors, but they are unlikely to be feature detectors in themselves.

Electrophysiological studies of the central auditory system in humans have, of necessity, been confined to those dealing with the components of the electroencephalogram (EEG) that can be shown to be synchronized with the stimulus. These components are generally called the *auditory evoked response (AER)*. An electrode is placed on the surface of the scalp, often at the very top (or vertex) of the head. The cortical response to a sound is added to all the other electrical activity generated by the cortex. To identify and display the auditory evoked response, the electrical signal from the scalp electrode is recorded for a brief period following the sound stimulus. Each recording is added to the sum of previous recordings. In this way, events in the EEG that are synchronized with the auditory stimulus will be reinforced by the summation process. Randomly occurring events, those not synchronized to the stimulus, will sum to zero over a large number of presentations. Using the signal-averaging technique, AER waveforms characterized by alternating positive and negative peaks have been identified. The AER response extends for more than 300 msec after the stimulus onset. A surprising amount of information concerning the status of the auditory system has been learned from this very crude method of investigation.

Recent studies of the time-locked events in the ongoing EEG waveform have concentrated on the period very early in the response. Peaks in these AER components have been attributed to electrical activity at subcortical centers. These responses are often called *brainstem evoked responses (BSER)*. A closer coordination of single unit activities with the evoked response recordings promises to reveal more of the working of this most complex decoding system.

Our discussion of the auditory system has been, of necessity, incomplete. Much remains to be discovered about the function of this sensory system. We found that the application of basic concepts from acoustics was often sufficient to explain the workings of the more peripheral portions of the ear. However, the brainstem and cortex are relatively inaccessible, and our knowledge of neuroscience is still insufficient to allow an equally detailed discussion of the central auditory system.

SUGGESTED READINGS

BEKESY, G. VON *Experiments in Hearing*. New York: McGraw-Hill, 1969. Required reading for the serious student of auditory physiology. This text details Bekesy's years of diligent work in understanding the mechanical action of the cochlea.

DALLOS, P. *The Auditory Periphery: Biophysics and Physiology*. New York: Academic Press, 1973. Required reading for the serious student of auditory physiology. This text presents a thorough and vigorous discussion of middle ear, cochlea, and VIIIth nerve functions.

DURRANT, J. D., and J. H. LOVRINIC. *Bases of Hearing Science*. Baltimore: Williams and Wilkins, 1977. An introductory text that is very readable. Less detailed than Yost and Nielsen, 1977.

EVANS, E. F., and J. P. WILSON (eds). *Psychophysics and Physiology of Hearing*. New York: Academic Press, 1977. Proceedings of a 1976 conference that presents state-of-the-art ideas not yet found in standard text books.

GERBER, S. E. *Introductory Hearing Science: Physical and Psychological Concepts*. Philadelphia: Saunders, 1974. A collection of chapters by different authors, several chapters give excellent coverage of various areas of psychoacoustics.

GREEN, D. M. *An Introduction to Hearing*. New York: Lawrence Erlbaum Associates—Wiley, 1976. Aimed at the more advanced student, there is excellent coverage of most areas of psychoacoustics and a good discussion of auditory physiology of the cochlea.

KIANG, N. Y-S, T. WATANABE, E. C. THOMAS, and L. F. CLARK. *Discharge Patterns of Single Fibers in the Cat's Auditory Nerve*. Cambridge: MIT Press, 1965. Required reading for the serious student of auditory physiology. This monograph documents the early experiments on single cell recordings in the auditory nerve and could serve as a guide to setting up a laboratory for the study.

PLOMP, R., and G. F. SMOORENBURG (eds). *Frequency Analysis and Periodicity Detection in Hearing*. Lieden, Netherlands: Sijthoff, 1970. Proceedings of a 1969 conference on hearing. Several excellent papers are presented. The work of Spoendlin is of special interest to the readers of this chapter.

TOBIAS, J. V. *Foundations of Modern Auditory Theory*, Vol. I and II. New York: Academic Press, 1970, 1972. These two volumes contain chapters contributed by those working at the state-of-the-art in auditory research. Although some material is now dated, the reviews are well worth the effort.

UTTAL, W. R. *The Psychobiology of Sensory Coding*. New York: Harper & Row, 1973. A novel approach to the study of sensory systems, including the auditory system.

WEVER, E. G. *Theory of Hearing*. New York: Dover, 1970. A paperback reprint of Wever's 1949 monograph. The historical summary on theories of hearing is of interest to the serious student.

WEVER, E. G., and M. LAWRENCE. *Physiological Acoustics*. Princeton, N.J.: Princeton University Press, 1954. A classical treatment of auditory physiology, now somewhat dated but of interest to the serious student.

WHITFIELD, I. C. *The Auditory Pathway*. London: Arnold, 1967. An excellent summary of our knowledge of the physiology of the central auditory pathway.

YOST, W. A., and D. W. NIELSEN. *Fundamentals of Hearing: An Introduction*. New York: Holt, Rinehart and Winston, 1977. This is an excellent introductory text for the study of auditory physiology and psychoacoustics. The scanning electron micrographs of the cochlea bring a perspective never before available to the beginning student.

ZWICKER, E., and E. TERHARDT. *Facts and Models in Hearing*. New York: Springer-Verlag, 1974. A collection of papers presented at a 1974 conference on psychophysical models and physiological facts in hearing. Many of these papers discuss ideas not yet found in standard text books.

REFERENCES

BEKESY, G. (1960). *Experiments in Hearing.* New York: McGraw-Hill.

BONTRAGER, O. R. (1962). *General Semantics and Psychotherapy.* Paper presented to V.A. Hospital (Psychiatric), Pittsburgh.

BOONE, D. R. (1971). *The Voice and Voice Therapy.* Englewood Cliffs, N.J.: Prentice-Hall.

COOPER, F. A. (1966). Describing the speech process in motor command terms. *Status Reports on Speech Research,* Haskins Laboratories, SR 515, 2.1–2.7.

DALLOS, P. (1973). *The Auditory Periphery: Biophysics and Physiology.* New York: Academic Press.

DALLOS, P. (1978). Cochlear receptor potentials. In R. J. Rubin, C. Elberling, and G. Salomon (eds.), *Electrocochleography.* Baltimore: University Park Press.

DALLOS, P., M. BILLONE, J. D. DURRANT, C.-Y WANG, and F. RAYNOR (1972). Cochlear inner and outer hair cells: Functional differences. *Science, 177,* 356–358.

DAVIS, H. (1956). Initiation of nerve impulses in the cochlea and other mechano-receptors. In T. H. Bullock (ed.), *Physiological Triggers and Discontinuous Rate Processes.* Washington, D.C.: American Physiological Society.

DAVIS, H. (1961). Some principles of sensory receptor action. *Physiological Reviews, 41,* 391–416.

ENGSTROM, H. (1960). The cortilymph, the third lymph of the inner ear. *Acta Morphologica Neer. Scand., 3,* 192–204.

FANT, G. (1960). *Acoustic Theory of Speech Production.* The Hague: Mouton.

GUINAN, J., and W. T. PEAKE (1967). Middle ear characteristics of anesthetized cats. *Journal of the Acoustical Society of America, 41,* 1237–1261.

HENKE, W. L. (1966). Dynamic articulatory model of speech production using computer simulation. Unpublished doctoral dissertation, MIT.

HIXON, T. J., M. D. GOLDMAN, and J. MEAD (1973). Kinematics of the chest wall during speech production: Volume displacements of the ribcage, abdomen, and lung. *Journal of Speech and Hearing Research, 16,* 78–115.

HOLLIEN, H. (1974). On vocal registers. *Journal of Phonetics, 2,* 25–43.

HUNTER-DUVAR, I. (1977). Figure 5.10. In W. A. Yost and D. W. Nielsen, *Fundamentals of Hearing: An Introduction.* New York: Holt, Rinehart and Winston.

JOHNS, D. F., and F. L. DARLEY (1970). Phonemic variability in aprazia of speech. *Journal of Speech and Hearing Research, 13,* 556–583.

KELLY, GEORGE A. (1955). *The Psychology of Personal Constructs.* New York: Norton.

KIANG, N. Y-S, T. WATANABE, E. C. THOMAS, and L. F. CLARK (1965). *Discharge Patterns of Single Fibers in the Cat's Auditory Nerve.* Cambridge, Mass.: MIT Press.

KOESTLER, A. (1968). *A Ghost in the Machine.* New York: Macmillan.

KORZYBSKI, A. E. (1950). *The Manhood of Humanity.* New York: E. P. Dutton.

KOZHEVNIKOV, L., and L. A. CHISTOVICH (1965). *Speech: Articulation and Perception.* Moscow. Translation by Joint Publications Research Service. Washington, D.C.: U.S. Department of Commerce, JPRS 30543.

LADEFOGED, P. (1971). *Preliminaries to Linguistic Phonetics.* Chicago: University of Chicago Press.

LASHLEY, K. S. (1951). The problem of serial order in behavior. In L. A. Jeffress (ed.), *Cerebral Mechanisms in Behavior: The Hixon Symposium.* New York: Wiley.

LASS, M. J. (ed.) (1976). *Contemporary Issues in Experimental Phonetics.* New York: Academic Press.

LIEBERMAN, P. C. (1975). *On the Origins of Language: An Introduction to the Evolution of Human Speech.* New York: Macmillan.

LIEBERMAN, P. C. (1977). *Speech Physiology and Acoustic Phonetics.* New York: Macmillan.

LIM, D. J. (1972). Fine morphology of the tectorial membrane: Its relationship to the organ of Corti. *Archives of Otolaryngology, 96,* 199–215.

LORENTE DE NO, R., and A. S. HARRIS (1933). Experimental studies in hearing. *Laryngoscope, 43,* 315–326.

MACNEILAGE, P. F. (1970). Motor control of serial ordering of speech. *Physiological Review, 77,* 182–196.

MATTHEWS, P. C. B. (1977). Muscle efferents and kinesthesia. *British Medical Bulletin, 33,* 137–142.

OSEN, K. K. (1969). The intrinsic organization of the cochlear nuclei in the cat. *Acta Otolaryngologica, 67,* 352–359.

OHMAN, S. E. G. (1966). Coarticulation in VCV utterances: Spectrographic measurements. *Journal of the Acoustical Society of America, 39,* 151–168.

POTTER, R. K., G. A. KOEPP, and H. GREEN (1947). *Visible Speech.* New York: Dover Publications.

ROSE, J. E., R. GALAMBOS, and J. R. HUGHES (1977). Microelectrode studies of the cochlear nuclei of the cat. *Bulletin of Johns Hopkins Hospital, 103,* 211–251.

RUSSELL, I. J., and P. M. SELLICK (1977). The tuning properties of cochlear hair cells. In E. F. Evans and J. P. Wilson (eds.), *Psychophysics and Physiology of Hearing.* London: Academic Press.

SIMMONS, F. B. (1964). Perceptual theories of middle ear muscle function. *Annals of Otology, Rhinology and Laryngology, 73,* 724–740.

SPOENDLIN, H. (1971). Structural basis of peripheral frequency analysis. In R. Plomp and G. F. Smoorenburgh (eds.), *Frequency Analysis and Periodicity Detection in Hearing.* Leiden, Holland: A. W. Sythoff.

SPOENDLIN, H. (1974). Neuroanatomy of the cochlea. In E. Zwicker and E. Terhardt (eds.), *Facts and Models in Hearing.* New York: Springer.

STEVENS, K. N. (1972). Quantal nature of speech. In E. E. David, Jr., and P. B. Denes (eds.), *Human Communication: A Unified View.* New York: McGraw-Hill.

STEVENS, K. N., and A. S. HOUSE, Development of a quantitative description of vowel articulation. *Journal of the Acoustical Society of America, 27,* 484–493.

TASAKI, I., H. DAVIS, and D. G. ELDREDGE (1954). Exploration of cochlear potentials with a microelectrode. *Journal of the Acoustical Society of America, 26,* 765–773.

TATHAM, M. A. A. (1971). Classifying allophones. *Language and Speech, 14,* 140–145.

UTTAL, W. R. (1973). *The Psychobiology of Sensory Coding.* New York: Harper & Row.

WEVER, E. G. (1949). *Theory of Hearing.* New York: Dover Publications.

WHITFIELD, I. C. (1967). *The Auditory Pathway.* Baltimore: Williams and Wilkins.

WHITFIELD, I. C., and E. F. EVANS (1965). Response of auditory cortical neurons to stimuli of changing frequency. *Journal of Neurophysiology, 28,* 655–672.

WICKELGREN, W. A. (1969). Context-sensitive coding, associative memory, and serial order in (speech) behavior. *Psychological Review, 76,* 1–15.

References

WYKE, B. (1974). Laryngeal myotatic reflexes. *Folia Phoniatrica, 26,* 249–264.

YOST, W. A., and D. W. NIELSEN (1977). *Fundamentals of Hearing: An Introduction.* New York: Holt, Rinehart and Winston.

ZEMLIN, W. R. (1968). *Speech and Hearing Science: Anatomy and Physiology.* Englewood Cliffs, N.J.: Prentice-Hall.

ZWISLOCKI, J. (1962). Analysis of the middle-ear function, part I: Input impedance. *Journal of the Acoustical Society of America, 34,* 1514–1523.

INDEX

P

W

Z